Service Management

Operations, Strategy, Information Technology

Ninth Edition

Sanjeev Bordoloi

Associate Professor of Operations Management
University of St. Thomas, Minnesota

James A. Fitzsimmons

Seay Professor of Business Emeritus
University of Texas at Austin

Mona J. Fitzsimmons

SERVICE MANAGEMENT: OPERATIONS, STRATEGY, INFORMATION TECHNOLOGY, NINTH EDITION

Published by McGraw-Hill Education, 2 Penn Plaza, New York, NY 10121.

This book is printed on acid-free paper.

1 2 3 4 5 6 7 8 9 LWI 21 20 19 18

ISBN 978-1-259-78463-7
MHID 1-259-78463-0

Portfolio Manager: *Noelle Bathurst*
Product Developer: *Ryan McAndrews*
Marketing Manager: *Harper Christopher*
Content Project Managers: *Pat Frederickson* and *Angela Norris*
Buyer: *Laura Fuller*
Designer: *Matt Diamond*
Content Licensing Specialist: *Lori Slattery*
Cover Image: *©Shutterstock/Monkey Business Images, ©wavebreakmediamicro/123RF, ©geopaul/Getty Images, ©KidStock/Blend Images LLC*
Compositor: *SPi Global*

All credits appearing on page or at the end of the book are considered to be an extension of the copyright page.

Library of Congress Cataloging-in-Publication Data

Names: Bordoloi, Sanjeev, author. | Fitzsimmons, James A., author. | Fitzsimmons, Mona J., author.
Title: Service management : operations, strategy, information technology / Sanjeev Bordoloi, Associate Professor of Operations Management, University of St. Thomas, Minnesota, James A. Fitzsimmons, Seay Professor of Business Emeritus, University of Texas at Austin, Mona J. Fitzsimmons, University of Texas at Austin.
Description: 9 Edition. | Dubuque : McGraw-Hill Education, [2018] | Revised edition of the authors' Service management, 2014.
Identifiers: LCCN 2017048452 | ISBN 9781259784637 (alk. paper)
Subjects: LCSH: Service industries–Management.
Classification: LCC HD9980.5 .F549 2018 | DDC 658–dc23 LC record available at https://lccn.loc.gov/2017048452

mheducation.com/highered

The McGraw-Hill/Irwin Series in Operations and Decision Sciences

SUPPLY CHAIN MANAGEMENT

Benton
Purchasing and Supply Chain Management
Second Edition

Burt, Petcavage, and Pinkerton
Supply Management
Eighth Edition

Bowersox, Closs, Cooper, and Bowersox
Supply Chain Logistics Management
Fourth Edition

Johnson and Flynn
Purchasing and Supply Management
Fifteenth Edition

Simchi-Levi, Kaminsky, and Simchi-Levi
Designing and Managing the Supply Chain: Concepts, Strategies, Case Studies
Third Edition

PROJECT MANAGEMENT

Brown and Hyer
Managing Projects: A Team-Based Approach
First Edition

Larson and Gray
Project Management: The Managerial Process
Seventh Edition

SERVICE OPERATIONS MANAGEMENT

Bordoloi, Fitzsimmons, and Fitzsimmons
Service Management: Operations, Strategy, Information Technology
Ninth Edition

MANAGEMENT SCIENCE

Hillier and Hillier
Introduction to Management Science: A Modeling and Case Studies Approach with Spreadsheets
Sixth Edition

Stevenson and Ozgur
Introduction to Management Science with Spreadsheets
First Edition

MANUFACTURING CONTROL SYSTEMS

Jacobs, Berry, Whybark, and Vollmann
Manufacturing Planning & Control for Supply Chain Management
Sixth Edition

BUSINESS RESEARCH METHODS

Cooper and Schindler
Business Research Methods
Twelfth Edition

BUSINESS FORECASTING

Keating and Wilson
Business Forecasting
Seventh Edition

LINEAR STATISTICS AND REGRESSION

Kutner, Nachtsheim, and Neter
Applied Linear Regression Models
Fourth Edition

BUSINESS SYSTEMS DYNAMICS

Sterman
Business Dynamics: Systems Thinking and Modeling for a Complex World
First Edition

OPERATIONS MANAGEMENT

Cachon and Terwiesch
Operations Management
First Edition

Cachon and Terwiesch
Matching Supply with Demand: An Introduction to Operations Management
Third Edition

Finch
Interactive Models for Operations and Supply Chain Management
First Edition

Jacobs and Chase
Operations and Supply Chain Management
Fifteenth Edition

Jacobs and Chase
Operations and Supply Chain Management: The Core
Fourth Edition

Jacobs and Whybark
Why ERP? A Primer on SAP Implementation
First Edition

Schroeder and Goldstein
Operations Management in the Supply Chain: Decisions and Cases
Seventh Edition

Stevenson
Operations Management
Twelfth Edition

Swink, Melnyk, Hartley, and Cooper
Managing Operations Across the Supply Chain
Third Edition

PRODUCT DESIGN

Ulrich and Eppinger
Product Design and Development
Sixth Edition

BUSINESS MATH

Slater and Wittry
Practical Business Math Procedure
Twelfth Edition

Slater and Wittry
Math for Business and Finance: An Algebraic Approach
Second Edition

BUSINESS STATISTICS

Bowerman, O'Connell, and Murphree
Business Statistics in Practice
Eighth Edition

Bowerman, O'Connell, Murphree, and Orris
Essentials of Business Statistics
Fifth Edition

Doane and Seward
Applied Statistics in Business and Economics
Sixth Edition

Doane and Seward
Essential Statistics in Business and Economics
Second Edition

Lind, Marchal, and Wathen
Basic Statistics for Business and Economics
Ninth Edition

Lind, Marchal, and Wathen
Statistical Techniques in Business and Economics
Seventeenth Edition

Jaggia and Kelly
Business Statistics: Communicating with Numbers
Third Edition

Jaggia and Kelly
Essentials of Business Statistics: Communicating with Numbers
First Edition

McGuckian
Connect Master: Business Statistics

To Our Families:
Basanti and Chandra Dhar Bordoloi
Mandira, Indira, Ranjeeta, Rajeev, and Trideev
Michael, Kate, and Colleen
Gary
Samantha and Jordan
In memory of Melba Jett

About the Authors

Sanjeev K. Bordoloi, Associate Professor of Operations and Supply Chain Management in the Opus College of Business at the University of St. Thomas, Minnesota, received his B.Tech. in electrical engineering from the Indian Institute of Technology, Varanasi; an MBA from Xavier Labour Relations Institute (XLRI); and a Ph.D. from The University of Texas at Austin. His prior full-time teaching experience includes the University of Illinois at Urbana-Champaign, the College of William and Mary, and the University of Alaska Fairbanks. He won the Alfred Page Graduate Teaching Award at the College of William and Mary and was featured in the "List of Teachers Ranked by Students as Excellent" at the University of Illinois at Urbana-Champaign. His research interests include operations management, process analysis and design, lean management, and theory of constraints. He has worked full-time in the service industry at the executive level, primarily in project management and technology management. He has consulted for several firms, including Sentara Healthcare, TRIA Orthopaedic Center, Archer Daniels Midland, Accenture India, Northwestern University medical unit, Fairbanks Memorial Hospital, ServiceWare (knowledge management), Humanics Incorporated, and Intandem Incorporated (event management).

James A. Fitzsimmons, Seay Professor of Business Emeritus, McCombs School of Business, The University of Texas at Austin, received a B.S.E. from the University of Michigan, an MBA from Western Michigan University, and a Ph.D. with distinction from the University of California at Los Angeles. His research in the area of emergency ambulance location won the Stan Hardy Award in 1983 for the best paper published in the field of operations management. Consulting assignments include the RAND Corporation; the U.S. Air Force; the cities of Los Angeles, Denver, Austin, Melbourne, and Auckland; the Texas comptroller; General Motors; La Quinta Motor Inns; Greyhound; TRICON Restaurants International; and McDonald's. Teaching experience includes faculty appointments at the University of California at Los Angeles, California State University at Northridge, the University of New Mexico, Boston University Overseas Graduate Program, California Polytechnic State University at San Luis Obispo, Seoul National University, and the Helsinki School of Economics and Business. He is a registered professional engineer in the state of Michigan and has held industrial engineering positions at Corning Glass Works and Hughes Aircraft Company. He served in the U.S. Air Force as an officer in charge of base construction projects. During his tenure at The University of Texas, he was Ph.D. graduate advisor, chair of the undergraduate programs committee, and nominated for six teaching awards. He is a Franz Edelman Laureat in the class of 1973. In 2004 he received an IBM Faculty Award in recognition for his contributions to the field of service operations management.

Mona J. Fitzsimmons, a graduate of the University of Michigan, received her undergraduate degree in journalism with major supporting work in chemistry and psychology. Her graduate work was in geology and she has taught in public and private schools and at the university level. She has done writing and editing for the Encyclopaedia Britannica Education Corporation and for various professional journals and organizations. With James Fitzsimmons she edited *New Service Development: Creating Memorable Experiences* published in 2000 by Sage Publications. Her nonprofessional activities have included volunteer work for the Red Cross aquatics program and in wildlife rehabilitation. She has particular interests in the areas of environmental issues and the responsibilities of patients and physicians in health care.

Preface

Services touch the lives of every person in this country every day: food services, communication services, and emergency services, to name only a few. Our welfare and the welfare of our economy now are based on services. The activities of manufacturing and agriculture always will be necessary, but we can eat only so much food and we can use only so many goods. Services, however, are largely experiential, and we always will have a limitless appetite for them.

Service operations management is established firmly as a field of study that embraces all service industries. The discipline was first recognized as an academic field by the Decision Sciences Institute (DSI) at its 1987 Boston meeting. In 1989 the *International Journal of Service Industry Management* was inaugurated. The First International Research Seminar in Service Management was held in France in 1990.

The *Journal of Service Research* was first published in August 1998 and quickly became the leading journal of the field. At the 2004 Boston meeting of the Production and Operations Management Society (POMS), a College on Service Operations was established. In 2005 the IBM Almaden Research Center launched an initiative to establish a new discipline called Service Science, Management, and Engineering (SSME). Visit the Academic Initiative SSME website at https://developer.ibm.com/academic/ to find articles, case studies, and lecture materials. The first issue of *Service Research* was published by INFORMS in September 2011.

This edition continues to acknowledge and emphasize the essential uniqueness of service management. These are some key features:

- The book is written in an engaging literary style, makes extensive use of examples, and is based on the research and consulting experience of the authors.
- The theme of managing services for competitive advantage is emphasized in each chapter and provides a focus for each management topic.
- The integration of technology, operations, and human behavior is recognized as central to effective service management.
- Emphasis is placed on the need for continuous improvement in quality and productivity in order to compete effectively in a global environment.
- To motivate the reader, a vignette of a well-known company starts each chapter, illustrating the strategic nature of the topic to be covered.
- Each chapter has a preview, a closing summary, key terms and definitions, a service benchmark, topics for discussion, an interactive exercise, solved problems and exercises when appropriate, and one or more cases.
- Available on the text's Online Learning Center at www.mhhe.com/bordoloi9e, is access to the Mortgage Service Game, a facility location Excel spreadsheet, chapter quizzes, and websites.
- The instructor's side of the text website contains an instructor's manual, case analyses, exercise solutions, sample syllabi, a yield management game, and lists of supplementary materials.

Key Updates in the Ninth Edition

This edition has benefited greatly from thoughtful suggestions from students, colleagues, and reviewers. In particular, we have incorporated emerging technologies throughout the book. We note several changes and additions to this new edition:

- A new Service Benchmark in Chapter 1, The Service Economy, features the pioneers of the emerging sharing economy Uber and Airbnb.

- Chapter 2, Service Strategy, introduces two new topics: recent advances in the mathematical analysis of big data or data analytics and the Internet of Things (IoT), an extension of the Internet into our everyday lives.
- The disruptive technology called blockchain based upon the internet currency Bitcoin is explored in Chapter 3, New Service Development, with illustrations of its impact on financial services. The stages of building a service blueprint are illustrated by taking us to a San Francisco Giants baseball game.
- In Chapter 7, Process Improvement, the topic of Lean Service is extended to include value-stream mapping using an example of a loan approval process.
- The emerging idea of using multiple sources and distribution methods is captured in the concept of omnichannel supply chain found in Chapter 9, Service Supply Relationships.
- In Chapter 11, Managing Capacity and Demand, the daily workshift scheduling problem is illustrated with a new example, Marin County 911 Response.
- The interactive exercise found in Chapter 14, Forecasting Demand for Services, now engages students in a Delphi exercise to forecast the date that a human colony on Mars will be established.

Special thanks and acknowledgment go to the following people for their valuable reviews of the first edition: Mohammad Ala, California State University, Los Angeles; Joanna R. Baker, Virginia Polytechnic Institute and State University; Mark Davis, Bentley College; Maling Ebrahimpour, University of Rhode Island; Michael Gleeson, Indiana University; Ray Haynes, California Polytechnic State University at San Luis Obispo; Art Hill, the University of Minnesota; Sheryl Kimes, Cornell University; and Richard Reid, the University of New Mexico.

The second edition benefited from the constructive comments of the following reviewers: Kimberly Bates, New York University; Avi Dechter, California State University, Northridge; Scott Dellana, East Carolina University; Sheryl Kimes, Cornell University; Larry J. LeBlanc, Vanderbilt University; Robert Lucas, Metropolitan State College of Denver; Barbara Osyk, University of Akron; Michael Showalter, Florida State University; and V. Sridharan, Clemson University.

The following reviewers contributed their experience and wisdom to the third edition: Sidhartha Das, George Mason University; Avi Dechter, California State University at Northridge; Byron Finch, Miami University of Ohio; Edward M. Hufft, Jr., Metropolitan State College of Denver; Ken Klassen, California State University at Northridge; Richard Reid, University of New Mexico, Albuquerque; Ishpal Rekki, California State University at San Marcos; and Ronald Satterfield, University of South Florida.

The fourth edition reflected the insights and suggestions of the following reviewers: Sanjeev Bordoloi, College of William and Mary; Sid Das, George Mason University; John Goodale, Ball State University; Ken Klassen, California State University, Northridge; Peggy Lee, Penn State University; Matthew Meuter, California State University, Northridge; Jaideep Motwani, Grand Valley State University; Elzbieta Trybus, California State University, Northridge; Rohit Verma, University of Utah; and Janet Sayers, Massey University, New Zealand. A special thanks to colleagues Ed Anderson and Doug Morrice for permission to include their Mortgage Service Game and to Mark Linford, an MBA student at the University of Texas at Austin, for preparing the computer software.

The fifth edition benefited from insights gathered at a focus group session in Washington, DC, at the 2003 Decision Sciences Institute annual meeting. We are grateful for the many suggestions provided by the following participants: Uday Apte, Southern Methodist University; Sanjeev Bordoloi, College of William and Mary; Joe Felan, University of Arkansas at Little Rock; Richard Franze, Kennesaw State University; Craig Froehle, University of Cincinnati; Yung Jae Lee, St. Mary's College of California; Katherine McFadden, Northern Illinois University; Mary Meixell, George Mason University; Elliott (Chip) Minor, Virginia Commonwealth University; and Jake Simons, Georgia Southern University. We are also indebted to Mrs. Margaret Seay who continues her generous support.

The sixth edition benefited greatly from the thoughtful suggestions of an outstanding group of reviewers: Sanjeev Bordoloi, University of Illinois-Urbana; Robert Burgess, Georgia Institute of Technology; Maureen Culleeney, Lewis University; Dick Fentriss, University of Tampa; Craig Froehle, University of Cincinnati; Susan Meyer Goldstein, University of Minnesota; Jaideep Motwani, Grand Valley State University; Rodney Runyan, University of South Carolina; and Rajesh Tyagi, DePaul University. We give special thanks to Ravi Behara, Florida Atlantic University, for his comprehensive revision plan.

The seventh edition benefited from the constructive suggestions of the following reviewers: Michael Bendixen, Nova Southeastern University; Dan Berg, Rensselaer Polytechnic Institute; Elif Kongar, Bridgeport University; Stephen Kwan, San Jose State University; Mary McWilliams, LeTourneau University; Kenneth Shaw, Oregon State University; and Donna Stewart, University of Wisconsin-Stout. We appreciate the contributions for improvements from Jeanne Zilmer, Copenhagen Business School.

The following reviewers contributed their generous time and expertise to the eighth edition: Laura Forker, University of Massachusetts-Dartmouth; Mike Galbreth, University of South Carolina; David Geigle, Texas A&M University; Lowell Lay, Texas Tech University; Mark Leung, University of Texas at San Antonio; Mark McComb, Mississippi College; Jaideep Motwani, Grand Valley State University; Rene Reitsma, Oregon State University; Jeff Smith, Florida State University; G. Peter Zhang, Georgia State University; and Shu Zhou, San Jose State University.

We thank the following reviewers for their thoughtful comments on our preparation of the ninth edition: Ajay Das, Baruch College; Adelina Gnanlet, California State University Fullerton; Diana Merenda, Baruch College; Jose Santiago, Baruch College; and Sheneeta White, University of St. Thomas.

We wish to acknowledge two students who assisted us. Fang Wu, Ph.D. student at The University of Texas at Austin, assisted in the development of some exercises and preparation of the PowerPoint lecture presentations for the second edition. Edmond Gonzales, an MBA student at Texas, prepared the chapter quizzes for the third edition CD-ROM. A special thanks is extended to Christine Bunker of the ProModel Corporation for allowing us the use of Process Simulator to illustrate applications of computer simulation to process analysis.

We express special appreciation to all of our friends who encouraged us and tolerated our social lapses while we produced this book. In particular, James and Mona Fitzsimmons are indebted for the support of Richard and Janice Reid, who have provided lively and stimulating conversations and activities over many years, and who generously allowed us the use of their mountain retreat. The beginning of the first edition was written in the splendid isolation of their part of the Jemez Mountains of New Mexico. No authors could want for better inspiration.

Sanjeev K. Bordoloi

James A. Fitzsimmons

Mona J. Fitzsimmons

Overview of the Book

Part One begins with a discussion of the role of services in an economy. We first look at the historical evolution of societies based on economic activity and conclude with a discussion of the emerging experience economy. Next, we consider the distinctive characteristics of service operations, concluding with an open-systems view of service operations management. The strategic service vision begins the final chapter in this section. The concept of sustainability and triple bottom line in services is introduced. The impact of data analytics and the Internet of Things (IoT) on services is explored. Competitive service strategies are discussed with an emphasis on the role of information as illustrated by the virtual value chain.

Designing the service enterprise to support the competitive strategy is the topic of Part Two. New services are developed using techniques such as a service blueprint that diagrams the flow of activity occurring onstage above a line of visibility and backstage functions that are not seen by the customer. The notion of a service encounter describes the interaction between service provider and customer in the context of a service organization. The importance of the supporting facility is captured by how the servicescape affects customer and employee behavior. Process analysis is treated in depth by identifying the bottleneck and calculating performance metrics such as throughput time. The challenge of delivering exceptional service quality is addressed by comparing customers' perceptions and expectations. The process improvement chapter describes tools and programs for continuous improvement, and a supplement measures service productivity using data envelopment analysis. The strategic importance of service facility location is explored with analytical models in the conclusion of this part.

Management of service operations is addressed in Part Three. The topic of service supply relationships includes a discussion of professional services and the disruptive impact of the blockchain technology. The next chapter is devoted to the topic of service-firm growth and the importance of globalization in services. Strategies to manage capacity and demand follow including the concept of yield management. We address the question of managing waiting lines from a psychological viewpoint. Capacity planning using queuing models with a supplement on computer simulation featuring a Visio plug-in Process Simulator concludes this part.

Part Four is devoted to quantitative models for service management. The first chapter addresses the topic of forecasting service demand using exponential smoothing models. The next chapter explores models for managing service inventory and discusses the uses of RFID. The topic of project management using Microsoft® Project software as the foundation concludes the final part.

Supplemental Features

INSTRUCTOR LIBRARY

A wealth of information is available online through McGraw-Hill's *Connect.* In the *Connect* Instructor Library, you will have access to supplementary materials specifically created for this text, such as:

- Instructor Solutions Manual
- PowerPoint Presentations
- Instructor Video List
- Digital Image Library
- Test Bank

ASSURANCE OF LEARNING

Many educational institutions today are focused on the notion of assurance of learning, an important element of some accreditation standards. *Service Management: Operations, Strategy, Information Technology* is designed specifically to support your assurance of learning initiatives with a simple, yet powerful, solution.

Each test bank and end-of-chapter question for *Service Management: Operations, Strategy, Information Technnology* maps to a specific chapter learning goal listed in the text. You can use the test bank software to easily query for learning goals that directly relate to the learning objectives for your course. You then can use the reporting features of the software to aggregate student results in similar fashion, making the collection and presentation of assurance of learning data simple and easy.

MCGRAW-HILL CUSTOMER CARE CONTACT INFORMATION

At McGraw-Hill, we understand that getting the most from new technology can be challenging. That's why our services don't stop after you purchase our products. You can e-mail our Product Specialists 24 hours a day to get product training online. Or you can search our knowledge bank of Frequently Asked Questions on our support website.

For Customer Support, call **800-331-5094** or visit www.mhhe.com/support. One of our Technical Support Analysts will be able to assist you in a timely fashion.

McGraw-Hill Connect® is a highly reliable, easy-to-use homework and learning management solution that utilizes learning science and award-winning adaptive tools to improve student results.

Homework and Adaptive Learning

- Connect's assignments help students contextualize what they've learned through application, so they can better understand the material and think critically.
- Connect will create a personalized study path customized to individual student needs through SmartBook®.
- SmartBook helps students study more efficiently by delivering an interactive reading experience through adaptive highlighting and review.

Over **7 billion questions** have been answered, making McGraw-Hill Education products more intelligent, reliable, and precise.

Connect's Impact on Retention Rates, Pass Rates, and Average Exam Scores

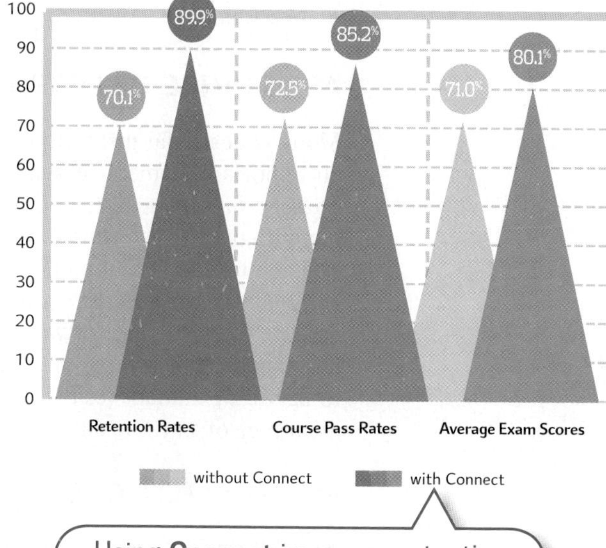

Using **Connect** improves retention rates by **19.8%,** passing rates by **12.7%, and** exam scores by **9.1%.**

73% of instructors who use **Connect** require it; instructor satisfaction **increases** by 28% when **Connect** is required.

Quality Content and Learning Resources

- Connect content is authored by the world's best subject matter experts, and is available to your class through a simple and intuitive interface.
- The Connect eBook makes it easy for students to access their reading material on smartphones and tablets. They can study on the go and don't need internet access to use the eBook as a reference, with full functionality.
- Multimedia content such as videos, simulations, and games drive student engagement and critical thinking skills.

Robust Analytics and Reporting

©Hero Images/Getty Images

- Connect Insight® generates easy-to-read reports on individual students, the class as a whole, and on specific assignments.
- The Connect Insight dashboard delivers data on performance, study behavior, and effort. Instructors can quickly identify students who struggle and focus on material that the class has yet to master.
- Connect automatically grades assignments and quizzes, providing easy-to-read reports on individual and class performance.

TO DO
LATE Acounting week 1 quiz — PRACTICE
LATE CH 02 - Quiz Intermediate — QUIZ
PRE LATE Chapter 4 — HOMEWORK
Ch 05. En casa: Vocabulario — LS
CH 05 States of Consciousness — HOMEWORK
Quiz - Extra Credit — QUIZ
RECHARGE Ch 02. En la universidad: Vocabulario — LS
connect

Impact on Final Course Grade Distribution

without Connect		with Connect
22.9%	A	31.0%
27.4%	B	34.3%
22.9%	C	18.7%
11.5%	D	6.1%
15.4%	F	9.9%

More students earn **As** and **Bs** when they use **Connect**.

Trusted Service and Support

- Connect integrates with your LMS to provide single sign-on and automatic syncing of grades. Integration with Blackboard®, D2L®, and Canvas also provides automatic syncing of the course calendar and assignment-level linking.
- Connect offers comprehensive service, support, and training throughout every phase of your implementation.
- If you're looking for some guidance on how to use Connect, or want to learn tips and tricks from super users, you can find tutorials as you work. Our Digital Faculty Consultants and Student Ambassadors offer insight into how to achieve the results you want with Connect.

www.mheducation.com/connect

Brief Contents

Table of Contents

PART TWO
DESIGNING THE SERVICE ENTERPRISE 61

Chapter 3
New Service Development 63

Chapter 4
The Service Encounter 95

Chapter 5
Supporting Facility and Process Flows 119

Part 1

Understanding Services

We begin our study of service management in Chapter 1, The Service Economy, with an appreciation of the central role that services play in the economies of nations and in world commerce. No economy can function without the infrastructure that services provide in the form of transportation and communications and without government services such as education and health care. As an economy develops, however, services become even more important, and soon the vast majority of the population is employed in service activities.

However, services have distinctive features that present unique challenges for management. Perhaps the most important characteristic of service operations is the presence of the customer in the service delivery system. Focusing on the customer and serving his or her needs is the basis for a service-dominant logic that is an alternative to the traditional goods-centered paradigm.

An effective competitive strategy is particularly important for service firms because they compete in an environment that has relatively low barriers to entry. We begin Chapter 2, Service Strategy, with a discussion of the strategic service vision, a framework in the form of questions about the purpose and place of a service firm in its market. The well-known generic competitive strategies–overall cost leadership, differentiation, and focus–are applied to services. Porter's five forces and SWOT analysis are applied to service firms. The topics of sustainability and economics of scalability are discussed in the context of growing a service firm. The competitive role of information in services is highlighted throughout.

Chapter 1

The Service Economy

Learning Objectives

After completing this chapter, you should be able to:

1. Describe the central role of services in an economy.
2. Identify and differentiate the five stages of economic activity.
3. Describe the features of preindustrial, industrial, and postindustrial societies.
4. Describe the features of the experience economy contrasting the consumer (B2C) with the business (B2B) service experience.
5. Explain the essential features of the service-dominant logic.
6. Identify and critique the six distinctive characteristics of a service operation, and explain the implications for managers.
7. Describe a service using the five dimensions of the service package.
8. Use the service process matrix to classify a service.

We are witnessing the greatest labor migration since the industrial revolution. This migration from agriculture and manufacturing to services is both invisible and largely global in scope. The migration is driven by global communications, business and technology growth, urbanization, and low-cost labor. Service industries are leaders in every industrialized nation, they create new jobs that dominate national economies, and have the potential to enhance the quality of life of everyone. Many of these jobs are for high-skilled knowledge-workers in professional and business services, health care, and education. As shown in Table 1.1, the extent of this movement to services is significant in the industrialized nations (European Union, United States, and Japan) but also represents a proportion of the labor force larger than that employed in goods production for the developing BRIC economies (Brazil, Russia, India, and China).

TABLE 1.1
Sector Employment in Top Ten Nations by 2015 Labor Force Size

Source: https://www.cia.gov/library/publications/resources/the-world-factbook/rankorder/2095rank.html

Nation	% of World Labor	% Agri	% Goods	% Services
China	21.2	33.6	30.3	36.1
India	13.9	49.0	20.0	31.0
European Union	6.4	5.0	21.9	73.1
United States	4.3	0.7	20.3	79.0
Indonesia	3.4	38.9	13.2	47.9
Brazil	3.0	15.7	13.3	71.0
Bangladesh	2.3	47.0	13.0	40.0
Russia	2.1	9.4	27.6	63.0
Japan	1.8	2.9	26.2	70.9
Pakistan	1.7	43.7	22.4	33.9

Chapter Preview

In a discussion of economic development, we learn that modern industrialized economies are dominated by employment in the service sector industries. This represents a natural evolution of economies from preindustrial to industrial and finally to postindustrial societies. The nature of the service economy is explored in terms of employment opportunities and the transition to experienced-based relationships for both consumers and businesses.

The distinctive characteristics of service operations suggest that the service environment is sufficiently unique to question the direct application of traditional manufacturing-based management techniques. In particular, the service manager operates in a system in which the customer is present and a co-creator of value. The concept of a service package to describe a service from an operations point of view is the foundation for an open-systems view of service management challenges. We begin with a selection of service definitions.

Service Definitions

Many definitions of service are available but all contain a common theme of intangibility and simultaneous consumption. The following represent a sample of service definitions:

> Services are deeds, processes, and performances. (Source: Valarie A. Zeithaml, Mary Jo Bitner, and Dwayne D. Gremler, *Services Marketing,* 4th ed., New York: McGraw-Hill, 2006, p. 4.)
>
> Services are economic activities offered by one party to another, most commonly employing time-based performances to bring about desired results in recipients themselves or in objects or other assets for which purchasers have responsibility. In exchange for their money, time, and effort, service customers expect to obtain value from access to goods, labor, professional skills, facilities, networks, and systems; but they do not normally take ownership of any of the physical elements involved. (Source: Christopher Lovelock and Lauren Wright, *Services Marketing: People, Technology, Strategy,* 6th ed., Upper Saddle River, NJ: Prentice-Hall, 2007, p. 6.)
>
> A service system is a value-coproduction configuration of people, technology, other internal and external service systems, and shared information (such as language, processes, metrics, prices, policies, and laws). (Source: Jim Spohrer, Paul Maglio, John Bailey, and Daniel Gruhl, *Computer,* January 2007, p. 72.)

Facilitating Role of Services in an Economy

As shown in Figure 1.1, services are central to the economic activity in any society. Infrastructure services, such as transportation and communications, are the essential foundation of an economy. Both infrastructure and distribution services function as economic intermediaries and as the channel of distribution to the final consumer. Infrastructure and distribution services are a prerequisite for an economy to become industrialized; therefore, no advanced society can be without these services.

In an industrialized economy, specialized firms can supply business services to manufacturing firms more cheaply and efficiently than manufacturing firms can supply these services for themselves. Thus, we find advertising, consulting, and other business services being provided for the manufacturing sector by service firms.

Except for basic subsistence living, where individual households are self-sufficient, service activities are absolutely necessary for the economy to function and to enhance the quality of life. Consider, for example, the importance of a banking industry to transfer funds and a transportation industry to move food products to areas that cannot produce them. Moreover, a wide variety of personal services, such as restaurants, lodging, and child care, have been created to move former household functions into the economy. In fact, the consumer performing self-service activities is a service contributor often using technology (e.g., boarding kiosk) to eliminate non-value-adding tasks or affording personalization and control (e.g., online brokerage).

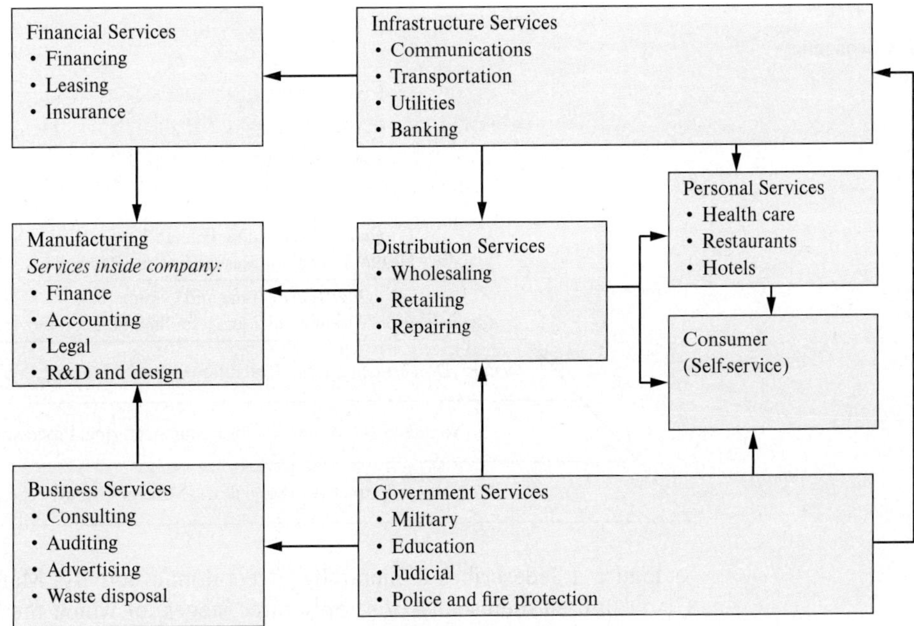

FIGURE 1.1
Role of Services in an Economy

Source: Bruce R. Guile and James Brian Quinn, eds., *Technology in Services: Policies for Growth, Trade, and Employment,* Washington, D.C.: National Academy Press, 1988, p. 214.

Government services play a critical role in providing a stable environment for investment and economic growth. Services such as public education, health care, well-maintained roads, safe drinking water, clean air, and public safety are necessary for any nation's economy to survive and people to prosper.

Increasingly, the profitability of manufacturers depends on exploiting value-added services. For example, automobile manufacturers have discovered that financing and/or leasing automobiles can achieve significant profits. Otis Elevator long ago found that revenues from after-sales maintenance contracts far exceed the profits from elevator equipment sales. This revenue enhancement strategy by manufacturers of deliberately coupling a service with their product is referred to as *servitization*. Almost every product today has a service component.

Thus, it is imperative to recognize that services are not peripheral activities but rather integral parts of society. They are central to a functioning and healthy economy and lie at the heart of that economy. Finally, the service sector not only facilitates but also makes possible the goods-producing activities of the manufacturing sectors. Services are the crucial ingredient for today's global economy.

Economic Evolution

In the early 1900s, only 3 of every 10 workers in the United States were employed in the services sector. The remaining workers were active in agriculture and industry. By 1950, employment in services accounted for 50 percent of the workforce. Today, services employ about 8 out of every 10 workers. Since WWII, we have witnessed a major evolution in sector employment from being predominantly manufacturing and agriculture to being predominantly services. This change in employment opportunities has made a significant impact on culture, demographics, and education.

Economists studying economic growth are not surprised by these events. Colin Clark argues that as nations become industrialized, there is an inevitable shift of employment from one sector of the economy to another.[1] As productivity (output/labor-hour) increases in one sector, the labor force moves into another. This observation, known as the *Clark-Fisher hypothesis,* leads to a classification of economies by noting the activity of the majority of the workforce.

FIGURE 1.2
Stages of Economic Activity

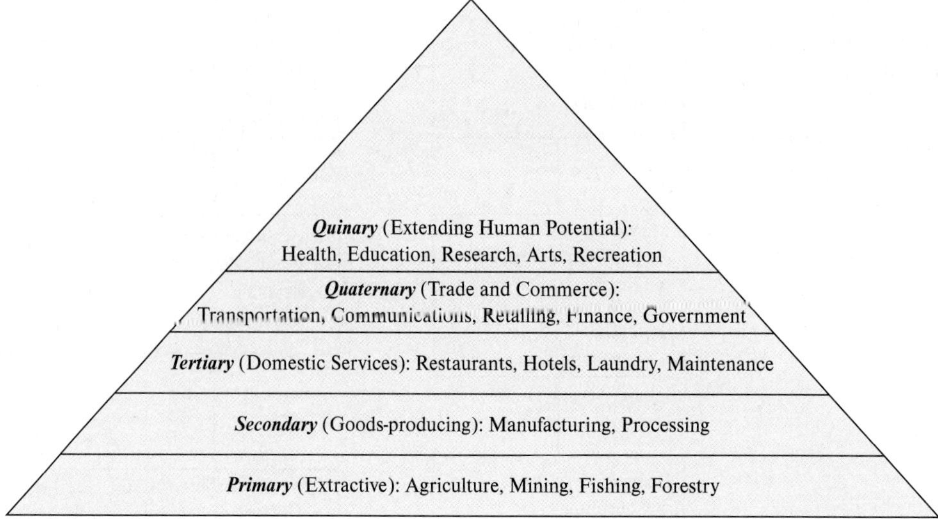

Figure 1.2 describes a hierarchy of economic activity. Many economists, including Clark, limited their analyses to only three stages, of which the tertiary stage was simply services. We have subdivided the service stage to create a total of five stages.

Today, an overwhelming number of countries still are in a primary stage of development. These economies are based on extracting natural resources from the land. Their productivity is low, and income is subject to fluctuations based on the prices of commodities such as sugar and copper. In much of Africa and parts of Asia, more than 70 percent of the labor force is engaged in extractive activities.

Figure 1.3 shows the rapid increase in service employment in the United States and illustrates the almost mirror image decline in agriculture employment. This sector employment trajectory is repeated for all of the nations represented in Table 1.1. We can observe that migration to services is a predictable evolution in the workforce of all nations, and successful industrial economies are built on a strong service sector. Furthermore, competition in services is global. Consider the growth of Indian call centers and British financial services. Trade in services remains a challenge, however, because many countries erect barriers to protect domestic firms. India and Mexico, for example, prohibit the sale of insurance by foreign companies.

Stages of Economic Development

Describing where our society has been, its current condition, and its most likely future is the task of social historians. Daniel Bell, a professor of sociology at Harvard University, has written extensively on this topic, and the material that follows is based on his work.[2] To place the concept of a postindustrial society in perspective, we must compare its features with those of preindustrial and industrial societies.

Preindustrial Society

The condition of most of the world's population today is one of subsistence, or a *preindustrial society*. Life is characterized as a game against nature. Working with muscle power and tradition, the labor force is engaged in agriculture, mining, and fishing. Life is conditioned by the elements, such as the weather, the quality of the soil, and the availability of water. The rhythm of life is shaped by nature, and the pace of work varies with the seasons. Productivity is low and bears little evidence of technology. Social life revolves around the extended household, and this combination of low productivity and large population results in high rates of underemployment (workers not fully utilized). Many seek positions in services, but of the personal or household variety. Preindustrial societies are agrarian and structured around tradition, routine, and authority.

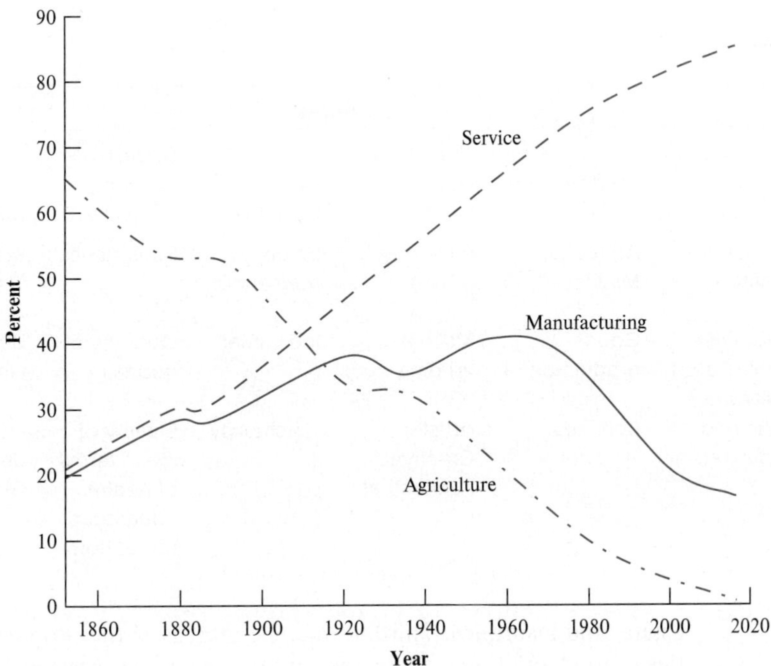

FIGURE 1.3
Trends in U.S. Employment by Sector, 1850–2015

Source: http://www.census.gov/library/publications/1975/compendia/hist_stats_colonial-1970.html; http://www.census.gov/library/publications/2011/compendia/statab/131ed.html; http://www.bls.gov/emp/ep_table_101.htm.

Industrial Society

The predominant activity in an *industrial society* is the production of goods. Energy and machines multiply the output per labor-hour and structure the nature of work. Division of labor is the operational "law" that creates routine tasks and the notion of the semiskilled worker. Work is accomplished in the artificial environment of the factory, and people tend the machines. Life becomes a game that is played against a fabricated nature—a world of cities, factories, and tenements. The rhythm of life is machine-paced and dominated by rigid working hours and time clocks. Of course, the unrelenting pressure of industrial life is ameliorated by the countervailing force of labor unions.

An industrial society is a world of schedules and acute awareness of the value of time. The standard of living becomes measured by the quantity of goods, but note that the complexity of coordinating the production and distribution of goods results in the creation of large bureaucratic and hierarchic organizations. These organizations are designed with certain roles for their members, and their operation tends to be impersonal, with persons treated as interchangeable. The individual is the unit of social life in a society that is considered to be the sum total of all the individual decisions being made in the marketplace.

Postindustrial Society

While an industrial society defines the standard of living by the quantity of goods, the *postindustrial society* is concerned with the quality of life, as measured by services such as health, education, and recreation. The central figure is the professional person, because rather than energy or physical strength, information is the key resource. Life now is a game played among persons. Social life becomes more difficult because political claims and social rights multiply. Society becomes aware that the independent actions of individuals and organizations can combine to create havoc for everyone, as evidenced by environmental pollution and traffic congestion. The community rather than the individual becomes the social unit.

Bell suggests that the transformation from an industrial to a postindustrial society occurs in many ways. First, there is a natural development of services, such as transportation and utilities, to support industrial development. As laborsaving devices are introduced into the production process, more workers engage in nonmanufacturing activities, such as maintenance and repair. Second, growth of the population and mass consumption of goods increase wholesale and retail trade, along with banking, real

TABLE 1.2
Comparison of Societies

	Features						
Society	Game	Predominant Activity	Use of Human Labor	Unit of Social Life	Standard of Living Measure	Structure	Technology
Preindustrial	Against nature	Agriculture Mining	Raw muscle power	Extended household	Subsistence	Routine Traditional Authoritative	Simple hand tools
Industrial	Against fabricated nature	Goods-production	Machine-tending	Individual	Quantity of goods	Bureaucratic Hierarchical	Machines
Postindustrial	Among persons	Services	Artistic Creative Intellectual	Community	Quality of life in terms of health, education, recreation	Inter-dependent Global	Information

estate, and insurance. Third, as income increases, the proportion spent on the necessities of food and home decreases, and the remainder creates a demand for durables and then for services.

Ernst Engel, a Prussian statistician of the 19th century, observed that as family incomes increase, the percentage spent on food and durables drops while consumption of services that reflect a desire for a more enriched life increases correspondingly. This phenomenon is analogous to the Maslow hierarchy of needs, which says that once the basic requirements of food and shelter are satisfied, people seek physical goods and, finally, personal development. However, a necessary condition for the "good life" is health and education. In our attempts to eliminate disease and increase the span of life, health services become a critical feature of modern society.

Higher education becomes the condition for entry into a postindustrial society, which requires professional and technical skills of its population. Also, claims for more services and social justice lead to a growth in government. Concerns for environmental protection require government intervention and illustrate the interdependent and even global character of postindustrial problems. Table 1.2 summarizes the features that characterize the preindustrial, industrial, and postindustrial stages of economic development.

Nature of the Service Sector

For many people, *service* is synonymous with *servitude* and brings to mind workers flipping hamburgers and waiting on tables. However, the service sector that has grown significantly over the past century cannot be described accurately as composed only of low-wage or low-skill jobs in hotels and fast-food restaurants. Instead, as Figure 1.4 shows, approximately 27 percent of the total employment in 2014 occurred in high-skill service categories such as professional and business services, health care and social assistance, and educational services.

Changes in the pattern of employment will have implications on where and how people live, on educational requirements, and, consequently, on the kinds of organizations that will be important to that society. Industrialization created the need for the semiskilled worker who could be trained in a few days to perform the routine machine-tending tasks. The subsequent growth in the service sector has caused a shift to white-collar occupations. In the United States, the year 1956 was a turning point. For the first time in the history of industrial society, the number of white-collar workers exceeded the number of blue-collar workers, and the gap has been widening since then. The most interesting growth has been in the managerial and professional-technical fields, which are jobs that require a college education.

FIGURE 1.4
Distribution of U.S. Employment by Industry, 2014.

Source: http://www.bls.gov/emp/ep_table_201.htm.

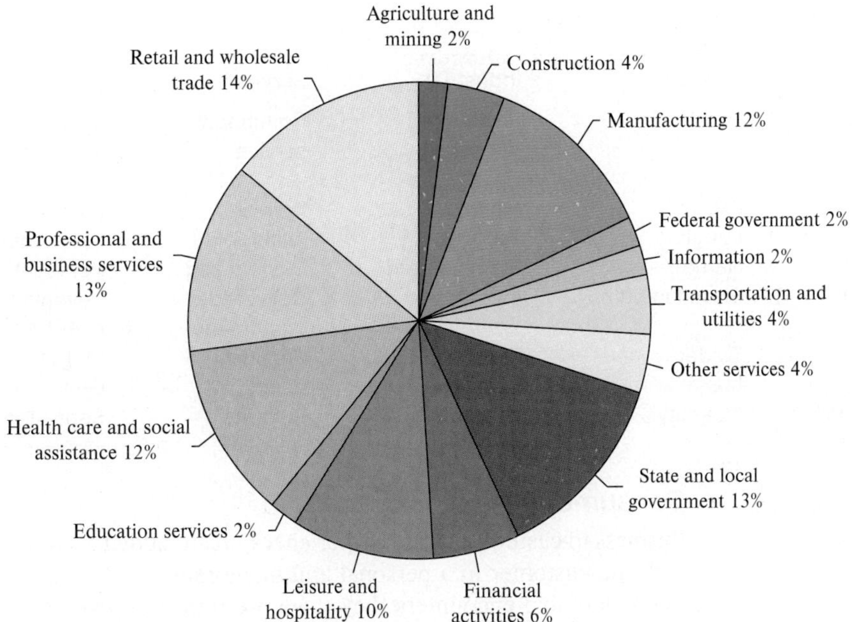

Today, service industries are the source of economic leadership. During the past 30 years, more than 44 million new jobs have been created in the service sector to absorb the influx of women into the workforce and to provide an alternative to the lack of job opportunities in manufacturing. The service industries now account for approximately 70 percent of the national income in the United States. Given that there is a limit to how many cars a consumer can use and how much one can eat and drink, this should not be surprising. The appetite for services, however, especially innovative ones, is insatiable. Among the services presently in demand are those that reflect an aging population, such as geriatric health care, and others that reflect a two-income family, such as day care.

During the past four recessions in the United States (the exception being the 2008 bank crash), employment by service industries fell much less than the loss of jobs in manufacturing. This suggests that consumers are willing to postpone the purchase of products but will not sacrifice essential services like education, telephone, banking, health care, and public services such as fire and police protection.

Several reasons can explain the recession-resistant nature of services. First, by their nature, services cannot be inventoried, as is the case for products. Because consumption and production occur simultaneously for services, the demand for them is more stable than that for manufactured goods. When the economy falters, many services continue to survive. Hospitals keep busy as usual, and, while commissions may drop in real estate and insurance, employees often need not be laid off.

Second, during a recession, both consumers and business firms defer capital expenditures and instead fix up and make do with existing equipment. Thus, service jobs in maintenance and repair are created.

The Experience Economy

The nature of the service economy has moved past the transactional nature of services to one of experience-based relationships. Consider how Starbucks and Disney World have defined their respective services as an experience. Table 1.3 describes the features of different economies in the historical evolution from agrarian to experience. To appreciate the subtle differences, pay particular attention to the words used to describe each economy. Note that the *experience economy* is further divided into consumer services and business services.

TABLE 1.3 Language of Economic Evolution

Economy	Agrarian	Industrial	Service	Experience	
Economic Offering	Food	Packaged goods	Commodity service	Consumer services (B2C)	Business services (B2B)
Function	Extract	Make	Deliver	Stage	Co-create
Nature	Fungible	Tangible	Intangible	Memorable	Effectual
Attribute	Natural	Standardized	Customized	Personal	Growth
Method of Supply	Stored in bulk	Inventoried	Delivered on demand	Revealed over time	Sustained over time
Seller	Trader	Producer	Provider	Stager	Collaborator
Buyer	Market	Customer	Client	Guest	Collaborator
Expectation	Quantity	Features	Benefits	Sensations	Capability

Consumer Service Experience

Business-to-customer (B2C) experiences create added value by engaging and connecting with the customer in a personal and memorable way. As businesses explicitly charge for the memorable encounters they stage, we transition from a service economy to the new experience economy. Figure 1.5 displays four types of consumer experiences characterized by the level of customer participation and level of interaction with the environment. Entertainment (e.g., watching a movie) is the least involved level of experience and escapist (e.g., scuba diving) requires the most commitment from the customer.

Consumer service experience design is based on five principles. *Theme the experience* is illustrated by the Forum Shops in Las Vegas that are decorated with Roman columns and where salespeople wear togas. An example of *harmonize impressions with positive cues* is found at the O'Hare Airport Parking Garage where each floor is painted with a distinctive color and unique music is played to help returning travelers find their parked automobiles (e.g., hard rock on the first floor and classical on the second). *Eliminate negative cues* is illustrated creatively by the use of talking trash containers (i.e., the container says "thank you" when an item is discarded) at a Cinemark Theater in Austin, Texas. An example of *mix in memorabilia* is providing group pictures of vacationers at Club Med. *Engage all five senses* is found at the Rainforest Café in Las Vegas (e.g., jungle sounds and mist in the air).

Business Service Experience

For business-to-business (B2B) services, value is derived from the coproduction or collaborative nature of the relationship such as we see in a consultancy engagement. The B2B service experience has three dimensions:

Co-creation of value

- The customer is a coproducer of the value extracted from the relationship.
- The customer is an input to the service process.

Relationships

- The relationship with the customer is of paramount importance because it is a source of innovation and differentiation.
- Long-term relationships facilitate the ability to tailor the service offerings to customers' needs.

FIGURE 1.5
The Four Realms of an Experience

Adapted from James A. Fitzsimmons, Mona J. Fitzsimmons, Sanjeev Bordoloi, Service Management Operations, Strategy, Information Technology, 8th edition, (2014), p 11.

		Environmental Relationship: Absorption	Environmental Relationship: Immersion
Customer Participation	Passive	Entertainment (movie)	Estheticism (tourist)
	Active	Education (language)	Escapism (scuba diving)

Scuba divers escape to an underwater world that requires special equipment for survival.
©Georgette Douwma/Getty Images RF

Service capability

- Provide service capacity to meet fluctuations in demands while retaining quality of service.
- Quality of service is measured primarily from the perspective of the customer.

The core experience of B2B service is one of creating, enabling, problem solving, and innovative use of information that is not consumed in the exchange, but is enhanced and remains available for further use by others.

Table 1.4 presents a complete listing of both consumer and business service experiences to be found in the 21st century, all of which rely heavily on a skilled knowledge-based workforce.

Service-Dominant Logic[3]

The service environment is sufficiently unique for us to question the direct application of traditional manufacturing-based techniques to services without some modification, although many approaches are analogous. Ignoring the differences between manufacturing and service requirements will lead to failure, but more importantly, recognition of the special features of services provides insights for enlightened and innovative management.

TABLE 1.4
Typology of Services in the 21st Century

Source: Adapted from J. R. Bryson, P. W. Daniels, and B. Warf, *Service Worlds: People, Organizations, Technologies,* New York: Routledge, 2004, p. 33.

Core Experience	Essential Feature	Examples
Creative	Present ideas	Advertising, theater
Enabling	Act as intermediary	Transportation, communications
Experiential	Presence of customer	Massage, theme park
Extending	Extend and maintain	Warranty, health check
Entrusted	Contractual agreement	Service/repair, portfolio mgt.
Information	Access to information	Internet search engine
Innovation	Facilitate new concepts	R&D services, product testing
Problem solving	Access to specialists	Consultants, counseling
Quality of life	Improve well-being	Health care, recreation, tourism
Regulation	Establish rules and regulations	Environment, legal, patents

TABLE 1.5
Foundational Premises (FPs) of Service-Dominant Logic

Source: Stephen L. Vargo and Melissa Archpru Akaka, "Service-Dominant Logic as a Foundation for Service Science: Clarifications," Service Science 1, no. 1 (2009), p. 35.

FP	Premise	Explanation/Justification
1	Service is the fundamental basis of exchange.	The application of operant resources (knowledge and skills), "service," is the basis for all exchange. Service is exchanged for service.
2	Indirect exchange masks the fundamental basis of exchange.	Goods, money, and institutions mask the service-for-service nature of exchange.
3	Goods are distribution mechanisms for service provision.	Goods (both durable and nondurable) derive their value through use (i.e., the service they provide).
4	Operant resources are the fundamental source of competitive advantage.	The comparative ability to cause desired change drives competition.
5	All economies are service economies.	Service (singular) is only now becoming more apparent with increased specialization and outsourcing.
6	The customer always is a co-creator of value.	This premise implies that value creation is interactional.
7	The enterprise cannot deliver value, but only offer value propositions.	The firm can offer its applied resources and create value collaboratively (interactively) following acceptance, but cannot create/deliver value alone.
8	A service-centered view is inherently customer-oriented and relational.	Service is customer-determined and co-created; thus, it is inherently customer-oriented and relational.
9	All economic and social actors are resource integrators.	The context of value creation is networks of networks (resource-integrators).
10	Value is always uniquely and phenomenologically determined by the beneficiary.	Value is idiosyncratic, experiential, contextual, and meaning-laden.

Advances in service management cannot occur without an appreciation of the service delivery process that creates the experience for the customer.

We begin our discussion of the nature of services and implications for operations management with a discussion of the service-dominant logic paradigm. *Service-dominant logic* is a service-centered alternative to the traditional goods-centered paradigm for describing economic exchange and value creation. The central idea is that service is the fundamental basis of value creation when defined as the application of competencies for the benefit of another through exchange. As a component of the service, goods might be involved in the exchange, but value-in-use (value as realized and determined by the customer) is the important feature.

Table 1.5 contains the 10 foundational premises (FPs) of service-dominant logic and a brief explanation/justification of each. We will look at each of the premises in more detail.

FP1: Service is regarded as an activity or process (singular), rather than an intangible unit of output (plural in the goods analogy). The service is derived from applying competencies (knowledge and skills) for the benefit of another party.

FP2: The process of value creation in a postindustrial society is complex and has many intermediary systems (e.g., Internet) that facilitate the process of exchange.

FP3: Although goods are a store of energy, material, and labor costs, they realize a value only upon use (e.g., a car providing the service of transportation).

FP4: Competitive advantage is captured in a service firm's intellectual capital, skills, and knowledge that can be applied to creating value for the customer.

FP5: If service is the application of competencies for the benefit of others, then all economic activity is essentially service, no matter if the economy is considered agrarian, industrial, or postindustrial.

FP6: If value is co-created with the customer, then by definition, the service activity involves the customer in some capacity (e.g., mind, body, belongings, information) in an interactive relationship.

FP7: Just as a product has no intrinsic value until used, a service is only a capacity to create value upon customer activation (e.g., a seat on an airplane has no value if empty upon takeoff).

FP8: Because a service is co-created with the customer, the service exchange necessarily must become customer-focused.

FP9: Value is created when the customer integrates and applies the resources of the service provider along with other resource-integrators (e.g., using PayPal to make a purchase on eBay) to achieve the exchange.

FP10: Each customer determines the value or quality of the service experience based on personal needs at the specific time (e.g., quick lunch or dinner party) and in the particular context (e.g., alone or in a group).

Service-dominant logic is the foundation of a new field of study called service science, management, and engineering (SSME), championed by the IBM Almaden Research Center in San Jose, California. SSME is the application of scientific, management, and engineering disciplines to tasks that one organization beneficially performs for and with another organization or individual. The objective is to make productivity, quality, performance, compliance, growth, and learning improvements more predictable in work-sharing and risk-sharing (coproduction) relationships. The heart of *service science* is the transfer and sharing of resources within and among service systems. The normative function of service systems is to connect people, technology, and information through value propositions with the aim of co-creating value for the service systems participating in the exchange of resources within and across systems.

Distinctive Characteristics of Service Operations

In services, a distinction must be made between *inputs* and *resources.* For services, inputs are the customers themselves, and resources are the facilitating goods, employee labor, and capital at the command of the service manager. Thus, to function, the service system must interact with the customers as participants in the service process. Because customers typically arrive at their own discretion and with unique demands on the service system, matching service capacity with demand is a challenge.

For some services, such as banking, however, the focus of activity is on processing information instead of people. In these situations, information technology, such as electronic funds transfer, can be substituted for physically depositing a payroll check; thus, the presence of the customer at the bank is unnecessary. Such exceptions will be noted as we discuss the distinctive characteristics of service operations. Note here that many of the unique characteristics of services, such as customer participation and perishability, are interrelated.

Customer Participation

The presence of the customer as a participant in the service process requires an attention to facility design that is not found in traditional manufacturing operations. That automobiles are made in a hot and noisy factory is of no concern to the eventual buyers because they first see the product in the pleasant surroundings of a dealer's showroom. The presence of the customer on-site requires attention to the physical surroundings of the service facility that is not necessary for the factory. For the customer, service is an experience occurring in the *front office* of the service facility, and the quality of service is enhanced if the service facility is designed from the customer's perspective. Attention to interior decorating, furnishings, layout, noise, and even color can influence the customer's perception of the service. Compare the feelings invoked by picturing yourself in a stereotypical bus station with those produced by imagining yourself in an airline terminal. Of course, passengers are not allowed in the terminal's *back office* (e.g., the luggage-handling area), which is operated in a factory-like environment. However, some innovative services have opened the back office to public scrutiny to promote confidence in the service (e.g., some restaurants provide a view into the kitchen, some auto repair bays can be observed through windows in the waiting area).

An important consideration in providing a service is the realization that the customer can play an active part in the process. A few examples will illustrate that the knowledge, experience, motivation, and even honesty of the customer all directly affect the performance of the service system:

1. The popularity of supermarkets and discount stores is predicated on the idea that customers are willing to assume an active role in the retailing process.
2. The accuracy of a patient's medical record can influence the effectiveness of the attending physician greatly.
3. The education of a student is determined largely by the student's own effort and initiative.

Fast-food restaurants best illustrate the value of customer participation. The customer not only places the order directly from a limited menu but also is expected to clear the table after the meal. Naturally, the customer expects faster service and less expensive meals to compensate for these inputs, but the service provider benefits in many subtle ways. First, there are fewer personnel who require supervision and such things as fringe benefits. Second, and more importantly, the customer provides the labor just at the moment it is required; thus, service capacity varies more directly with demand rather than being fixed by the size of the employed staff. The customer acts like a temporary employee, arriving just when needed to perform duties to augment the work of the service staff.

Taking the customer out of the process, however, is becoming a common practice. Consider retail banking, in which customers are encouraged to use online transactions, direct deposit, and automatic-debit bill paying instead of actually traveling to the bank. Moreover, the advent of Internet commerce gives new meaning to the phrase "window shopping."

Simultaneity

The fact that services are created and consumed simultaneously and, thus, cannot be stored is a critical feature in the management of services. This inability to inventory services precludes using the traditional manufacturing strategy of relying on inventory as a buffer to absorb fluctuations in demand. An inventory of finished goods serves as a convenient system boundary for a manufacturer, separating the internal operations of planning and control from the external environment. Thus, the manufacturing facility can be operated at a constant level of output that is most efficient. The factory is operated as a *closed system,* with inventory decoupling the productive system from customer demand. Services, however, operate as *open systems,* with the full impact of demand variations being transmitted to the system.

Inventory also can be used to decouple the stages in a manufacturing process. For services, the decoupling is achieved through customer waiting. Inventory control is a major issue in manufacturing operations, whereas in services, the corresponding problem is customer waiting, or "queuing." The problems of selecting service capacity, facility utilization, and use of idle time all are balanced against customer waiting time.

The simultaneous production and consumption in services also eliminates many opportunities for quality-control intervention. A product can be inspected before delivery, but services must rely on other measures to ensure the quality of services delivered.

Perishability

A service is a perishable commodity. Consider an empty airline seat, an unoccupied hospital or hotel room, or an hour without a patient in the day of a dentist. In each case, a lost opportunity has occurred. Because a service cannot be stored, it is lost forever when not used. The full utilization of service capacity becomes a management challenge, because customer demand exhibits considerable variation and building inventory to absorb these fluctuations is not an option.

Consumer demand for services typically exhibits very cyclic behavior over short periods of time, with considerable variation between the peaks and valleys. For example, the custom of eating lunch between noon and 1 PM places a burden on restaurants to accommodate the noon rush. Many examples can be found in the public sector; for example, the demand for emergency ambulance service normally peaks around the 6 PM rush hour and has a lull around 3 AM while the city sleeps.

For recreational and transportation services, seasonal variation in demand creates surges in activity. As many students know, flights home often are booked months in advance of spring break and the year-end holiday.

Faced with variable demand and a *time-perishable capacity* to provide the service, the manager has three basic options:

1. Smooth demand by:
   a. Using reservations or appointments.
   b. Using price incentives (e.g., matinee discounts at movie theaters).
   c. Demarketing peak times (e.g., advertising to shop early and avoid the Christmas rush).
2. Adjust service capacity by:
   a. Using part-time help during peak hours.
   b. Scheduling work shifts to vary workforce needs according to demand (e.g., call centers staff their operators to match call demand).
   c. Increasing the customer self-service content of the service.
3. Allow customers to wait.

The last option can be viewed as a passive contribution to the service process that carries the risk of losing a dissatisfied customer to a competitor. By waiting, the customer permits greater utilization of service capacity. The airlines explicitly recognize this by offering standby passengers an unsold seat on the departing flight.

Intangibility

Services are ideas and concepts; products are things. Therefore, it follows that service innovations are not patentable. To secure the benefits of a novel service concept, the firm must expand extremely rapidly and preempt any competitors. Franchising has been the vehicle to secure market areas and establish a brand name. Franchising allows the parent firm to sell its idea to a local entrepreneur, thus preserving capital while retaining control and reducing risk.

The intangible nature of services also presents a problem for customers. When buying a product, the customer is able to see it, feel it, and test its performance before purchase. For a service, however, the customer must rely on the reputation of the service firm. In many service areas, the government has intervened to guarantee acceptable service performances. Through the use of registration, licensing, and regulation, the government can assure consumers that the training and test performance of some service providers meet certain standards. Thus, we find that public construction plans must be approved by a registered professional engineer, a doctor must be licensed to practice medicine, and the power company is a regulated utility. In its efforts to "protect" the consumer, however, the government may be stifling innovation, raising barriers to entry, and generally reducing competition.

Heterogeneity

The combination of the intangible nature of services and the customer as a participant in the service delivery system results in variation of service from customer to customer. The interaction between customer and employee in services, however, creates the possibility of a more satisfying human work experience. In services, work activity generally is oriented toward people rather than toward things. There are exceptions, however, for services that process information (e.g., communications) or customers' property (e.g., brokerage services). In the limited customer-contact service industries, we now see a dramatic reduction in the level of labor intensiveness through the introduction of self-service technology.

Even the introduction of automation may strengthen personalization by eliminating the relatively routine impersonal tasks, thereby permitting increased personal attention to the remaining work. At the same time, personal attention creates opportunities for variability in the service that is provided. This is not inherently bad, however, unless customers perceive a significant variation in quality. A customer expects to be treated fairly and to be given the same service that others receive. The development of standards and of employee training in proper procedures is the key to ensuring consistency in the service provided. Monitoring the output of each employee often is rather impractical, so customers play a role in quality control through their feedback.

The direct customer–employee contact has implications for service (industrial) relations as well. Autoworkers with grievances against the firm have been known to sabotage the product on the assembly line. Presumably, the final inspection will ensure that any such cars are corrected before delivery. A disgruntled service employee, however, can do irreparable harm to the organization because the employee is the firm's sole contact with customers. Therefore, the service manager must be concerned about the employees' attitudes as well as their performance. At a resort hotel, for example, it is difficult to have happy guests with unhappy employees. Through training and genuine concern for employee welfare, the organizational goals can be internalized.

Nontransferrable Ownership[4]

From a marketing perspective, services, unlike goods, do not involve transfer of ownership. If customers do not receive ownership when they purchase a service, then what are they buying? One view is that customers gain access or rental of resources for a period of time such as a hotel room for the night or a seat in an airplane. Service industries share their resources among customers by allocating the use of them. Customers do not purchase an asset but, instead, have use of the asset for a specific time, whether it is the use of human labor (e.g., dentist), technology (e.g., cellular network), or a physical asset (e.g., theme park). Notice that in each example, customers often share the service provider's asset concurrently with other customers. Table 1.6 lists the five classes of nonownership services with examples.

Sharing resources among customers presents management challenges. In the case of goods rental, convenience of a rental office location for pickup and drop-off is essential. Car rentals, for example, are found at airports. However, Enterprise is an exception, because it began delivering vehicles to the local population instead of catering primarily to travelers.

TABLE 1.6
Nonownership Classification of Services

Type of Service	Customer Value	Examples	Management Challenge
Goods rental	Obtain temporary right to exclusive use	Vehicles, tools, furniture, equipment	Site selection and maintenance
Place and space rental	Obtain exclusive use of defined portion of a larger space	Hotel room, seat on airplane, storage unit	Housekeeping and achieving economies of scale
Labor and expertise	Hire other people to do a job	Car repair, surgery, management consulting	Expertise is a renewable resource, but time is perishable
Physical facility usage	Gain admission to a facility for a period of time	Theme park, campground, physical fitness gym	Queuing and crowd control
Network usage	Gain access to participate	Electric utility, cell phone, Internet	Availability and pricing decisions

Maintenance of the rental good and returning the good to acceptable condition between customer rentals is a necessary and ongoing activity. In the case of place and space rental, customers are able to participate in the economies of scale derived from sharing a larger space with many users while enjoying some degree of separation and privacy. For airlines, the extra large seats and leg room in business class partially explains the relatively high ticket price. For any shared facility, housekeeping is a routine activity performed between periods of customer usage (e.g., trash pickup upon landing for an airline flight and changing linen upon departure of a hotel guest).

Management of queues and crowd control is a challenge for managers of physical facilities that are shared by a large population of customers. Disney, for example, has made a science of controlling waiting lines using multiple techniques that include diversions and allowing guests to reserve time slots for rides hours in advance. Availability is critical for network services because customers depend upon and expect access 24/7 (24 hours per day, 7 days per week). Thus, continuous availability is essential, but because usage varies depending on time-of-day and day-of-week, pricing for the service must be creative and flexible.

The Service Package

Service managers have difficulty describing their product. This problem is partly a result of the intangible nature of services, but it is the presence of the customer in the process that creates a concern for the total service experience. Consider the following examples. For a sit-down restaurant, atmosphere is just as important as the meal because many diners regard the occasion as a way to get together with friends. A customer's opinion of a bank can be formed quickly on the basis of a teller's cheerfulness or the length of the waiting line.

The *service package* is defined as a bundle of goods and services with information that is provided in some environment. This bundle consists of five features (as shown in Figure 1.6) in the shape of an onion with the service experience at the core.

FIGURE 1.6
Service Package

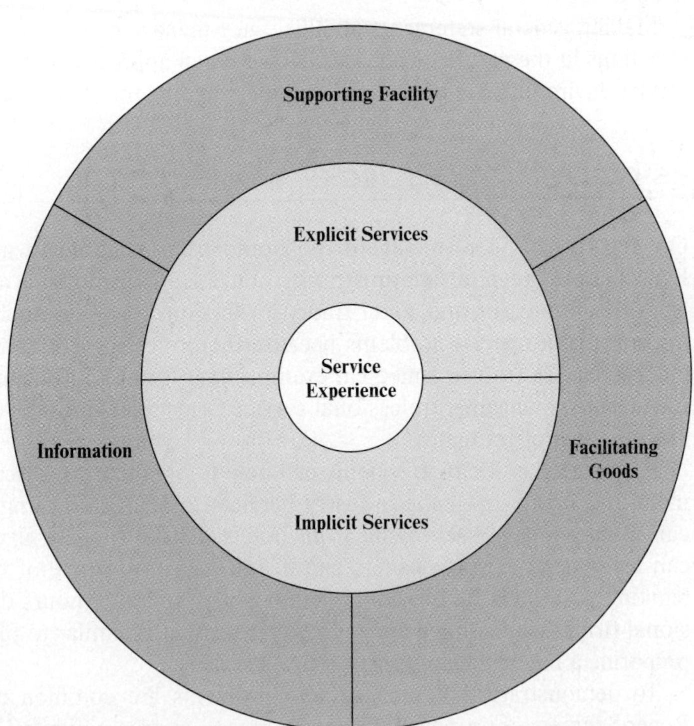

1. *Supporting facility.* The physical resources that must be in place before a service can be offered. Examples are a golf course, a ski lift, a hospital, and an airplane.
2. *Facilitating goods.* The material purchased or consumed by the buyer, or the items provided by the customer. Examples are golf clubs, skis, food items, replacement auto parts, legal documents, and medical supplies.
3. ***Information.*** Data that is available from the customer or provider to enable efficient and customized service. Examples include electronic patient medical records, airline showing seats available on a flight, customer preferences from prior visits, GPS website location of customer to dispatch a taxi, and Google map link on a hotel website.
4. *Explicit services.* The benefits that are readily observable by the senses and that consist of the essential or intrinsic features of the service. Examples are the absence of pain when a tooth is repaired, a smooth-running automobile after a tuneup, and the response time of a fire department.
5. *Implicit services.* Psychological benefits that the customer may sense only vaguely, or the extrinsic features of the service. Examples are the status of a degree from an Ivy League school, the privacy of a loan office, and worry-free auto repair.

All of these features are experienced by the customer and form the basis of his or her perception of the service. It is important that the service manager offer a total experience for the customer that is consistent with the desired service package. Take, for example, a budget hotel. The supporting facility is a concrete-block building with austere furnishings. Facilitating goods are reduced to the minimum of soap, towels, and tissue paper. Information on room availability is used to book a reservation. The explicit service is a comfortable bed in a clean room, and implicit services might include a friendly desk clerk and the security of a well-lighted parking area. Deviations from this service package, such as adding bellhops, would destroy the bargain image. Table 1.7 lists criteria (with examples) for evaluating the service package.

The importance of facilitating goods in the service package can be used to classify services across a continuum from pure services to various degrees of mixed services. For example, psychiatric counseling with no facilitating goods would be considered a "pure" service. Automobile maintenance usually requires more facilitating goods than a haircut does.

Making general statements about service management is difficult when there are such variations in the nature of services. However, an appreciation of the unique features of the service environment is important for understanding the challenges facing service managers.

Grouping Services by Delivery Process

Concepts of service management should be applicable to all service organizations. For example, hospital administrators could learn something about their own business from the restaurant and hotel trade. Professional services such as consulting, law, and medicine have special problems because the professional is trained to provide a specific clinical service (to use a medical example) but is not knowledgeable in business management. Thus, managing professional service firms offers attractive career opportunities for business school graduates.

A service classification scheme can help to organize our discussion of service management and break down the industry barriers to shared learning. As suggested, hospitals can learn about housekeeping from hotels. Less obviously, dry-cleaning establishments can learn from banks—cleaners can adapt the convenience of night deposits enjoyed by banking customers by providing laundry bags and after-hours dropoff boxes. For professional firms, scheduling a consulting engagement is similar to planning a legal defense or preparing a medical team for open-heart surgery.

To demonstrate that management problems are common across service industries, Roger Schmenner proposed the *service process matrix* in Figure 1.7. In this matrix, services

TABLE 1.7 Criteria for Evaluating the Service Package

Supporting Facility

1. *Location:*
   Is it accessible by public transportation?
   Is it centrally located?
2. *Interior decorating:*
   Is the proper mood established?
   Quality and coordination of furniture.
3. *Supporting equipment:*
   Does the dentist use a mechanical or air drill?
   What type and age of aircraft does the charter airline use?
4. *Architectural appropriateness:*
   Renaissance architecture for university campus.
   Unique recognizable feature of a blue tile roof.
   Massive granite facade of downtown bank.
5. *Facility layout:*
   Is there a natural flow of traffic?
   Are adequate waiting areas provided?
   Is there unnecessary travel or backtracking?

Facilitating Goods

1. *Consistency:*
   Crispness of french fries.
   Portion control.
2. *Quantity:*
   Small, medium, or large drink.
3. *Selection:*
   Variety of replacement mufflers.
   Number of menu items.
   Rental skis available.

Information

1. *Accurate:*
   Up-to-date customer addresses.
   Correct credit report.
2. *Timely:*
   Severe storm warning.
3. *Useful:*
   X-ray to identify a broken bone.
   Inventory status.

Explicit Services

1. *Training of service personnel:*
   Is the auto mechanic certified by the National Institute for Automotive Service Excellence (NIASE)?
   To what extent are paraprofessionals used?
   Are the physicians board certified?
2. *Comprehensiveness:*
   Discount broker compared with full service.
   General hospital compared with clinic.
3. *Consistency:*
   Airline's on-time record.
   Professional Standards Review Organization (PSRO) for doctors.
4. *Availability:*
   Twenty-four-hour ATM service.
   Is there a website?
   Is there a toll-free number?

Implicit Services

1. *Attitude of service:*
   Cheerful flight attendant.
   Police officer issuing traffic citation with tact.
   Surly service person in restaurant.
2. *Atmosphere:*
   Restaurant decor.
   Music in a bar.
   Sense of confusion rather than order.
3. *Waiting:*
   Joining a drive-in banking queue.
   Being placed on hold.
   Enjoying a martini in the restaurant bar.
4. *Status:*
   Flying first-class.
   Box seats at sports event.
5. *Sense of well-being:*
   Large commercial aircraft.
   Well-lighted parking lot.
6. *Privacy and security:*
   Attorney advising client in private office.
   Magnetic key card for hotel room.
7. *Convenience:*
   Use of appointments.
   Free parking.

are classified across two dimensions that significantly affect the character of the service delivery process. The vertical dimension measures the degree of labor intensity, which is defined as the ratio of labor cost to capital cost. Thus, capital-intensive services such as airlines and hospitals are found in the upper row because of their considerable investment in plant and equipment relative to labor costs. Labor-intensive services such as schools and legal assistance are found in the bottom row because their labor costs are high relative to their capital requirements.

FIGURE 1.7
The Service Process Matrix

Source: From "How Can Service Businesses Survive and Prosper?" by Roger W. Schmenner, *Sloan Management Review*, vol. 27, no. 3, Spring 1986, p. 25, by permission of publisher.

Degree of labor intensity	Degree of interaction and customization: Low	Degree of interaction and customization: High
Low	*Service factory:* • Airlines • Trucking • Hotels • Resorts and recreation	*Service shop:* • Hospitals • Auto repair • Other repair services
High	*Mass service:* • Retailing • Wholesaling • Schools • Retail aspects of commercial banking	*Professional service:* • Physicians • Lawyers • Accountants • Architects

The horizontal dimension measures the degree of customer interaction and customization, which is a marketing variable that describes the ability of the customer to affect personally the nature of the service being delivered. Little interaction between customer and service provider is needed when the service is standardized rather than customized. For example, a meal at McDonald's, which is assembled from prepared items, is low in customization and served with little interaction occurring between the customer and the service providers. In contrast, a doctor and patient must interact fully in the diagnostic and treatment phases to achieve satisfactory results. Patients also expect to be treated as individuals and wish to receive medical care that is customized to their particular needs.

The four quadrants of the service process matrix have been given names, as defined by the two dimensions, to describe the nature of the services illustrated. *Service factories* provide a standardized service with high capital investment, much like a line-flow manufacturing plant. *Service shops* permit more service customization, but they do so in a high-capital environment. Customers of a *mass service* will receive an undifferentiated service in a labor-intensive environment, but those seeking a *professional service* will be given individual attention by highly trained specialists.

Managers of services in any category, whether service factory, service shop, mass service, or professional service, share similar challenges, as noted in Figure 1.8. Services with high capital requirements (i.e., low labor intensity), such as airlines and hospitals, require close monitoring of technological advances to remain competitive. This high capital investment also requires managers to schedule demand to maintain utilization of the equipment. Alternatively, managers of highly labor-intensive services, such as medical or legal professionals, must concentrate on personnel matters. The degree of customization affects the ability to control the quality of the service being delivered and the perception of the service by the customer. Approaches to addressing each of these challenges are topics that will be discussed in later chapters.

Open-Systems View of Service Operations Management

Service organizations are sufficiently unique in their character to require special management approaches that go beyond the simple adaptation of the management techniques found in manufacturing a product. The distinctive characteristics suggest enlarging the system view to include the customer as a participant in the service process. As Figure 1.9 shows, the customer is viewed as an input that is transformed by the service process into an output with some degree of satisfaction.

The role of the service operations manager includes the functions of both production and marketing in an open system with the customer as a participant. The traditional

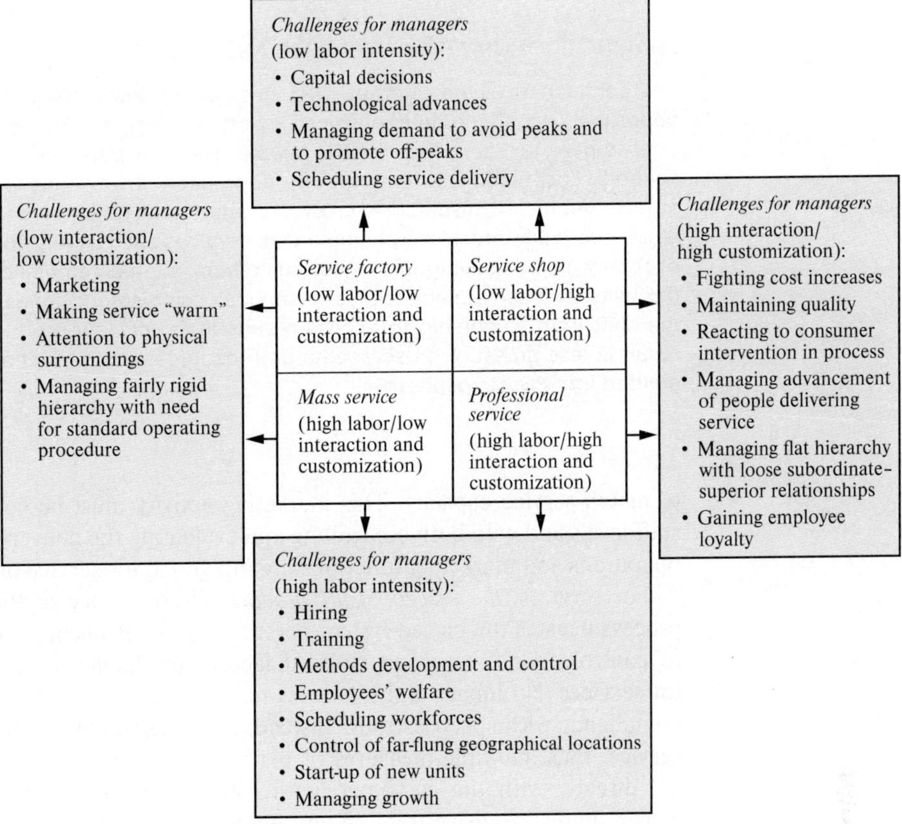

FIGURE 1.8
Challenges for Service Managers

Source: From "How Can Service Businesses Survive and Prosper?" by Roger W. Schmenner, *Sloan Management Review,* vol. 27, no. 3, Spring 1986, p. 27, by permission of publisher.

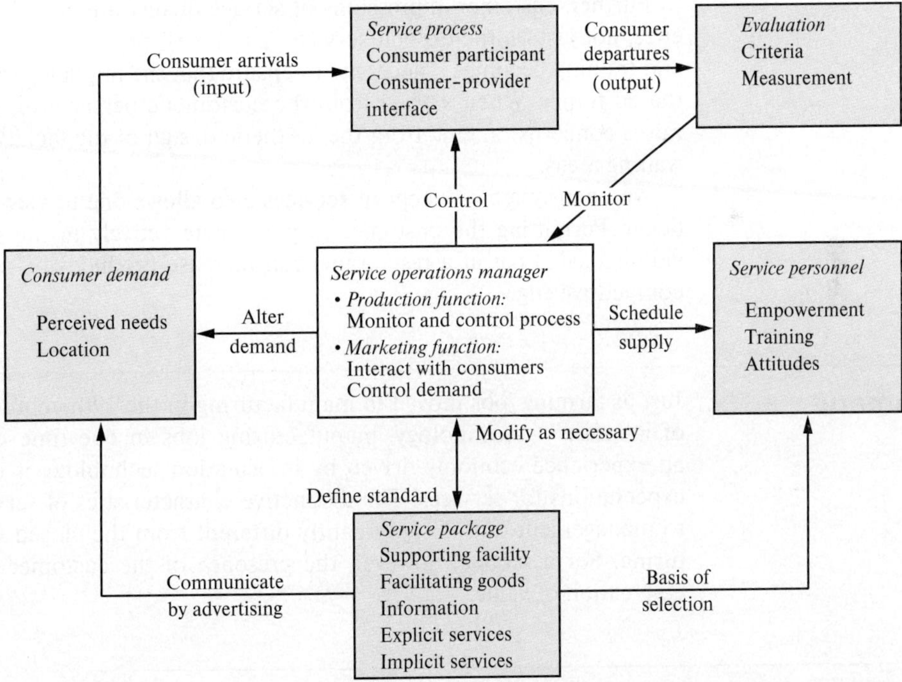

FIGURE 1.9
Open-Systems View of Service Operations

manufacturing separation of the production and marketing functions, with finished-goods inventory as the interface, is neither possible nor appropriate in services. Marketing performs two important functions in daily-service operations: (1) educating the consumer to play a role as an active participant in the service process and (2) "smoothing" demand

Service Benchmark

SHARING ECONOMY PIONEERS UBER AND AIRBNB

The confluence of the Internet, GPS positioning, and smartphones has given people the opportunity to share their physical assets for income. For example, Uber represents a peer-to-peer taxi service in which people use their personal vehicles to ferry paying passengers. Location-aware smartphone apps allow drivers and passengers to connect with an Internet-based dispatcher. Likewise, apartment dwellers and homeowners share their residences with travelers by using online services such as Airbnb. Advantages of the sharing economy include saving money for customers, supplemental income for providers, lifestyle flexibility, and convenient access to services using smartphones. For the economy at large, the shift from ownership to access results in fewer new products sold, which in turn can result in less pressure on scarce natural resources and reduction of global warming gases emitted into the atmosphere.

to match service capacity. This marketing activity must be coordinated with scheduling staff levels and with both controlling and evaluating the delivery process. By necessity, the operations and marketing functions are integrated for service organizations.

For services, *the process is the product.* The presence of the customer in the service process negates the closed-system perspective that is taken in manufacturing. Techniques to control operations in an isolated factory producing a tangible good are inadequate for services. No longer is the process machine-paced and the output easily measured for compliance with specifications. Instead, customers arrive with different demands on the service; thus, multiple measures of performance are necessary. Service employees interact directly with the customer, with little opportunity for management intervention. This requires extensive training and empowerment of employees to act appropriately in the absence of direct supervision.

Further, customer impressions of service quality are based on the total service experience, not just on the explicit service that is performed. A concern for employee attitudes and training becomes a necessity to ensure that the implicit service is also appreciated by the customer. When viewed from the customer's perspective, the entire service process raises concerns ranging from the aesthetic design of the facility to pleasant diversions in waiting areas.

An open-system concept of services also allows one to view the customer as a coproducer. Permitting the customer to participate actively in the service process (e.g., providing a salad bar at a restaurant) can increase productivity, which in turn can create a competitive edge.

Summary

Just as farming jobs moved to manufacturing in the 19th century under the driving force of labor-saving technology, manufacturing jobs in due time moved to services. Today an experience economy driven by information technology is emerging to satisfy rising expectations for services. The distinctive characteristics of services require an approach to management that is significantly different from the closed system found in manufacturing. For a service, however, the presence of the customer in the process allows for co-creation of value.

Key Terms and Definitions

Experience economy a stage of economic evolution in which added value is created by engaging and connecting with the customer in a personal and memorable way. *pg. 9*

Explicit services the essential or intrinsic features readily observable by the senses (e.g., on-time departure, quality of meal). *pg. 18*

Facilitating goods material purchased or consumed by the buyer, or items provided by the customer (e.g., food, golf clubs). *pg. 18*

Implicit services psychological benefits or extrinsic features the customer may sense only vaguely (e.g., security of a well-lighted parking lot, privacy of a loan office). *pg. 18*

Industrial society a society dominated by factory work in mass-production industries. *pg. 7*

Postindustrial society a service society in which people are engaged in information, intellectual, or creatively intensive activities. *pg. 7*

Preindustrial society an agrarian society structured around farming and subsistence living. *pg. 6*

Service-dominant logic a view that all economies are service economies in which value is always co-created in the exchange of doing something for another party. *pg. 12*

Service package five components describing a service: supporting facility, facilitating goods, information, explicit service, and implicit service. *pg. 17*

Service process matrix a classification of services based on the degree of interaction and customization and the degree of labor intensity that results in four categories: service factory, service shop, mass service, and professional service. *pg. 18*

Service science a field of study of the transfer and sharing of resources within and among service systems. *pg. 13*

Servitization revenue enhancement by bundling service with sale of a product (e.g., financing new car sale). *pg. 5*

Supporting facility the physical resources that must be in place before a service can be offered (e.g., golf course, hospital building, airplane). *pg.18*

Topics for Discussion

1. Illustrate how the type of work one does influences a person's lifestyle. For example, contrast a farmer, a factory worker, and a schoolteacher.
2. Is it possible for an economy to be based entirely on services?
3. What is the value of self-service in an economy?
4. Determine if the service sector is currently expanding or contracting based upon the Non-Manufacturing Index (NMI) found at the ISM (Institute of Supply Management) Report on Business website: https://www.instituteforsupplymanagement.org/ISMReport/
5. What are challenges of the sharing economy with respect to regulation, insurance, and trust issues?
6. Critique the distinctive characteristics of service operations by arguing that the characteristics of customer participation, simultaneity, perishability, intangibility, heterogeneity, and nontransferable ownership may apply to goods as well.

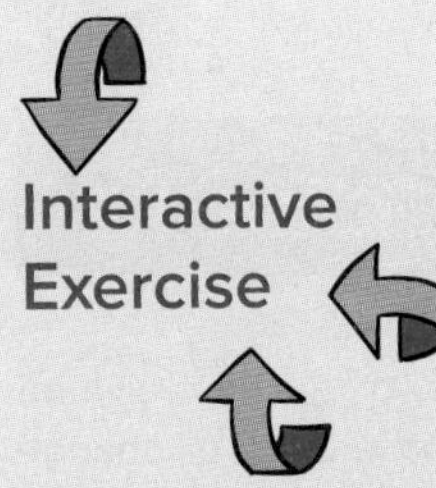

Interactive Exercise

The class breaks into small groups. Each group identifies service firms that should be listed in the Fortune 100 and places them in rank order of estimated annual revenue.

Village Volvo — CASE 1.1

Village Volvo is the "new kid in town." It represents an effort by two former authorized Volvo dealer mechanics to provide quality repair service on out-of-warranty Volvos at a reasonable cost. On the basis of their 22 combined years of training and experience with the local Volvo dealer, they have earned a respected reputation and a following of satisfied customers, which make an independent service operation feasible. Village Volvo occupies a new Butler building (i.e., a prefabricated metal structure) that has four work bays in addition to an office, waiting area, and storage room.

The owners feel they have designed their operation to provide clients with a custom car care service that is unavailable at the local dealer. They have set aside specific times each week when clients may drive in for quick, routine services such as tune-ups and oil changes, but they encourage clients to schedule appointments for the diagnosis and repair of specific problems.

At the time of the appointment, the mechanic who will be working on the vehicle and the client discuss the problems the client has noticed. On occasion, the mechanic may take a short test drive with the client to be certain that both understand the area of concern.

Another source of information for the mechanic is the Custom Care Vehicle Dossier (CCVD). Village Volvo maintains a continuing file on each vehicle it services. This history can help the mechanic to diagnose problems and also provides a convenient record if a vehicle is returned for warranty service on an earlier repair. The owners are considering use of the CCVD as a way of "reminding" customers that routine maintenance procedures may be due.

After the mechanic has made a preliminary diagnosis, the service manager gives the vehicle owner an estimate of the cost and the approximate time when the repair will be completed if no unexpected problems arise. Company policy states that the owner will be consulted before any work other than the agreed-on job is done. Although the customer may speak with the mechanic during the repair process, the service manager is the main point of contact. It is the service manager's responsibility to be sure the customer understands the preliminary diagnosis, to advise the customer of any unexpected problems and costs, and to notify the customer when the vehicle is ready for pickup.

Village Volvo has no provisions for alternate transportation for customers at this time. A shuttle service two or three times a day is being considered, because the owners think their suburban location may deter some clients. The waiting room is equipped with a television set, comfortable chairs, coffee, a soft-drink vending machine, magazines, and the local newspaper. This facility is used almost exclusively by clients who come during the "drop-in" times (3 to 5 PM Wednesdays and 8 to 10 AM Thursdays) for quick, routine jobs such as tune-ups and buyer checks of used cars.

The owner-mechanics do no repairs between 7 and 8 AM and 5 and 6 PM, because these are heavy customer contact hours. They believe it is just as important to discuss with the client the repairs that have been done as it is to discuss what problems exist before that work is done. As repairs are made, the owner-mechanic notes any other problems that might need attention in the future (e.g., fan and alternator belts show some wear and may need to be replaced in about 6,000 miles). These notes are brought to the customer's attention at pickup time and also are recorded in the CCVD for future use, perhaps in the form of a reminder postcard to the owner.

All small worn-out parts that have been replaced are put in a clean box inside the car. More cumbersome replaced parts are identified and set aside for the client's inspection. Care is taken throughout the repair process to keep the car clean, and the inside is vacuumed as a courtesy before pickup. After the repairs are finished, the vehicle is taken for a short test drive. Then it is parked, ready for pickup.

The Village Volvo owners see their responsibility as extending beyond immediate service to their clients. The owners have developed a network of other service providers who assist in recycling used parts and waste products and to whom they can refer clients for work that is not part of Village Volvo's services (e.g., body work, alignments, and reupholstering). The owners also are considering the possibility of offering a minicourse one Saturday morning each month to teach clients what they can do to attain their 200,000-mile Volvo medals.

Questions

1. Describe Village Volvo's service package.
2. How are the distinctive characteristics of a service firm illustrated by Village Volvo?
3. How could Village Volvo manage its back office (i.e., repair operations) like a factory?
4. How can Village Volvo differentiate itself from Volvo dealers?

Xpresso Lube[5] CASE 1.2

Charlie Green, owner of Xpresso Lube, is not your typical car repairman. A man of many talents, Charlie gained valuable knowledge of the oil-change business while working in the Special Mixtures Division of Goodyear. Charlie also learned from his father and brother while working on cars when he was growing up and later supplemented this knowledge by taking formal automotive courses. All similarities between Charlie and his fellow mechanics end there, however. Charlie also is a professional musician. He plays an upright bass and sings and owns a coffee plantation in Costa Rica.

When it's time to get your oil changed, you have only two choices—change it yourself or pay someone else (e.g., dealership, independent auto mechanic, or a quick oil-lube station) to do it for you. Many people choose quick oil-change stations because it is easier than doing it themselves and it is usually quicker and cheaper than going to a dealer or an independent mechanic.

Folks just want to get in and out as fast and economically as possible. Most companies that provide oil-change service are indistinguishable. They charge about the same price and are found on almost every major street. Most people pick one that is close to home and that has a short waiting line. The challenge faced by the quick-change services is to manage demand. Most customers want service during the lunch hour, after work, or on Saturdays. An oil-change business, therefore, wants to move customers in and out as quickly as possible. Speed of service is the way they try to differentiate themselves from their competitors.

Charlie remembers the last time he paid to have his car's oil changed. He was in the waiting room with several other customers when a lube technician came in to discuss a problem with an elderly lady. "Ma'am, you see this?" The technician held a PCV valve in his hand and shook it, producing a rattle. "You hear that? That's trouble. We're gonna have to replace this PCV valve." The woman looked puzzled, but she agreed with the mechanic. Unfortunately, she didn't know that the PCV in any car is *supposed* to rattle. This event dismayed Charlie. He believed that customers deserved good service and honesty, and he was tired of seeing people get "ripped off." He decided to do something about this problem by opening his own business, Xpresso Lube, which would specialize in oil changes.

No one likes to wait a long time to have his or her oil changed, especially because the facilities usually are not very pleasant. The waiting rooms are small, dirty, and furnished with uncomfortable chairs. If a television set is available, it has a small screen and reception is poor. Any magazines are probably car-related and months old. If there is coffee to drink, it has been sitting in an old pot since early that morning!

Charlie designed the environment for his business to be different from that of the traditional oil-change station. He chose not to compete with the other oil-change companies head to head, but instead changed "the game." When he converted an old gas/service station into Xpresso Lube, people told him that it would never work. They said he had too much waiting area and the stalls had lifts instead of the usual pits—so it would take too long to change a car's oil. Charlie used these unusual features to his advantage.

During the development phase of his business, Charlie noticed two things about the local and national economies—both the espresso bar and oil-change markets were saturated. Consumers viewed these services as commodities and based their purchase decision on price. Charlie considered that factor and the unappealing environment of existing oil-change facilities—and, in a moment of entrepreneurial revelation, decided to combine the coffee bar craze with an oil-change business.

Xpresso Lube was started with the purpose of providing a unique, pleasant, and honest experience. Charlie had thorough knowledge of both the coffee and oil-change business, so the merger of these two experiences came naturally to him. In fact, when Xpresso Lube first opened, he also drew on his musician roots and brought in bands to play in the evenings. As Xpresso Lube's success grew, Charlie had to phase out the live music because he was too busy with the other aspects of the business.

Charlie never forgot the experience of seeing others get treated dishonestly. Today, the majority of his customers are women, who frequently have been the victims of dishonest repairmen, and college students. "Little old ladies love me," Charlie says, "because we have earned their trust."

The large waiting area was transformed into a coffee bar with a number of amenities to make his customers' waits very enjoyable. He offered a variety of coffees and an atmosphere that doesn't make the customers feel as if they are in a waiting room. In fact, some customers come in just for the coffee. The floors are carpeted and there are numerous tables and chairs. An outside area is covered for use when the weather is pleasant. A stereo system provides music and the reading material is current and appealing to different interests.

Because of the atmosphere he has created, Charlie does not have to compete on speed, which allows Xpresso Lube to use lifts and only two stalls. Furthermore, using lifts gives employees an opportunity to show the customer when something is wrong with his or her car. The customer can go under the car with the technician and actually see the problem. Other oil-change stations do not have this luxury—they cannot allow their customers to go down into the pit to look at their cars. Pits are dirty and unsafe places for any customer. Consequently, a customer must take the employee's advice about extra work that needs to be done—and hope he or she is not being ripped off.

When a customer does not want to wait, Xpresso Lube provides transportation to and from work. This service helps smooth demand during the weekday afternoons, so customers will not all come after 5 PM during the week or on Saturdays. The transport service is provided by the automotive service center right behind Xpresso Lube, which is also owned by Charlie. University Automotive was the precursor to Xpresso Lube, which Charlie opened in 1984. University Auto provides car repair services for many makes and models of cars. A gas station was located in a lot adjacent to University Auto; when the station went out of business in the early nineties, Charlie bought the property and opened Xpresso Lube on the site in 1996. Xpresso Lube now provides 30 percent of the revenues for the joint businesses.

Austin is home to the University of Texas, a thriving high-tech business community, and arguably the nation's best live music. All of these factors give Austin a very diverse population. Xpresso Lube's location on a main street near the university attracts a broad spectrum of customers, but also it means customers can walk to many local shops while their cars are being serviced. Half-Price Bookstore, Wheatsville Coop food store, Amy's Ice Cream, and Toy Joy are all within easy walking distance. The business provides a great deal of fulfillment for Charlie. "I love coming to work because every day brings new and different customers into our shop."

Questions

1. Describe Xpresso Lube's service package.
2. How are the distinctive characteristics of a service operation illustrated by Xpresso Lube?
3. What elements of Xpresso Lube's location contribute to its success?
4. Given the example of Xpresso Lube, what other services could be combined to "add value" for the customer?

Selected Bibliography

Chase, Richard B., and Uday M. Apte. "A History of Research in Service Operations: What's the Big Idea?" *Journal of Operations Management* 25, no. 2 (March 2007), pp. 375–86.

Ehret, Michael, and Jochen Wirtz. "Division of Labor between Firms: Business Services, Non-Ownership-Value and the Rise of the Service Economy." *Service Science* 2, no. 3 (Sept 2010), pp. 136–45.

Enz, Cathy A., and Rohit Verma. "Introduction to the Cornell Hospitality Research Summit Special Issue: The New Science of Service Innovation in a Multipartner World." *Service Science* 8, no. 2 (June 2016), pp. iv–ix.

Feng, Cong, and K. Sivakumar. "The Role of Collaboration in Service Innovation Across Manufacturing and Service Sectors." *Service Science* 8, no. 3 (September 2016), pp. 263–81.

Froehle, Craig, Anita Tucker, and Stefanos Zenios (eds.). "Special Issue on Healthcare Operations Management." *Production and Operations Management* 20, no. 3 (May–June 2011), pp. 303–488.

Hatzakis, Emmanuel D., Suresh K. Nair, and Michael L. Pinedo (eds.). "Special Issue on Operations in Financial Services." *Production and Operations Management* 19, no. 6 (Nov–Dec 2010), pp. 633–779.

Heineke, Janelle, and Mark M. Davis. "The Emergence of Service Operations Management as an Academic Discipline." *Journal of Operations Management* 25, no. 2, (March 2007), pp. 364–74.

Kastall, Ivanka Visnjic, and Bart Van Looy. "Servitization: Disentangling the Impact of Service Business Model Innovation on Manufacturing Firm Performance." *Journal of Operations Management* 31, no. 4 (2013), pp. 169–80.

Kwortnik, Robert Jr., and Gary M. Thompson. "Unifying Service Marketing and Operations with Service Experience Management." *Journal of Service Research* 11, no. 4 (May 2009), pp. 389–406.

Machuca, Jose A. D., Maria del Mar Gonzalez-Zamora, and Victor G. Aguilar-Escobar. "Service Operations Management Research." *Journal of Operations Management* 25, no. 3 (April 2007), pp. 585–603.

Medina-Borja, Alexandra. "Editorial Column-Smart Things as Service Providers: A Call for Convergence of Disciplines to Build Research Agenda for the Service Systems of the Future." *Service Science* 7, no. 1 (March 2015), pp. ii–v.

Ostrom, Amy L., et al. "Moving Forward and Making a Difference: Research Priorities for the Science of Service." *Journal of Service Research* 13, no. 1 (February 2010), pp. 4–36.

Sampson, Scott E., and Craig M. Froehle. "Foundations and Implications of a Proposed Unified Services Theory." *Production and Operations Management* 15, no. 2 (Summer 2006), pp. 329–42.

Spohrer, Jim, and Paul P. Maglio. "The Emergence of Service Science: Towards Systematic Service Innovations to Accelerate Co-creation of Value." *Production and Operations Management* 17, no. 3 (May–June 2008), pp. 238–46.

Endnotes

1. Colin Clark, *The Conditions of Economic Progress,* 3rd ed. (London: Macmillan Co., 1957).
2. Daniel Bell, *The Coming of Post-Industrial Society: A Venture in Social Forecasting* (New York: Basic Books, 1973).
3. From Steven L. Vargo and Melissa Archpru Akaka, "Service-Dominant Logic as a Foundation for Service Science: Clarifications," *Service Science* 1, no. 1 (2009), pp. 32–41.
4. From Christopher Lovelock and Evert Gummesson, "Whither Services Marketing? In Search of a New Paradigm and Fresh Perspectives," *Journal of Service Research* 7, no. 1 (August 2004), pp. 34–46.
5. Prepared by Rich Ellis, Thomas Prudhomme, and Marly Yanaza under the supervision of Professor James A. Fitzsimmons. Thirty-two years after Charlie began Xpresso Lube, the business is now closed.

Chapter 2

Service Strategy

Learning Objectives

After completing this chapter, you should be able to:

1. Formulate a strategic service vision.
2. Describe how a service competes using the three generic service strategies.
3. Perform a SWOT and Five Forces Analysis.
4. Explain what is meant by qualifiers, service winners, and service losers.
5. Discuss the competitive role of information in services and its limits.
6. Explain the concept of the virtual value chain and its role in service innovation.
7. Discuss service firm sustainability and the triple bottom line impact.
8. Explain what features of a service firm lead to economics of scalability.
9. Categorize a service firm according to its stage of competitiveness.

As machine technology once changed an agricultural economy into an industrial economy, today's information technology has transformed our industrial economy into a service economy. The availability of computers and global communication technologies has created industries for collecting, processing, and communicating information. Today everyone on the globe can be in instant communication with everyone else, and this revolution is changing world society in many ways. Consider the impact of the private satellite network industry, which provides uplinks and downlinks for personnel training, product introductions, credit checks, billing, financial exchanges, and overall telecommunications.

Kmart was among the first retail box stores to establish a private satellite network using the new small-dish antenna VSAT (Very Small Aperture Terminal) placed on store roofs to receive and transmit masses of data. The VSAT at each Kmart is linked to the company's Hoffman Estates, Illinois, headquarters and is operated by Hughes Network.[1] The communication network has allowed Kmart to coordinate its multisite operations better and to realize substantial benefits, such as improved data transmission about the rate of sales, inventory status, product updates, and, most important, credit authorizations for customers. The instant accessibility of credit histories can significantly lower the risk of nonpayment that credit card companies face, thus lowering the discount rate that reverts back to the retailer. Such savings alone can help to pay for the cost of the satellite network.

Chapter Preview

Service strategy begins with a vision of the place and purpose of the enterprise. A strategic service vision is formulated by addressing questions about the target market, service concept, operating strategy, and delivery system. However, the competitive environment of services presents challenges such as low entry barriers, product substitution, and limited opportunities for economies of scale that must be overcome.

Three generic strategies have been found successful in formulating strategies that allow a firm to outperform competitors. The strategies of overall cost leadership, differentiation, and market focus are approaches that service firms have adopted in various ways to gain competitive advantage. With each of these strategies, however, management must not lose sight of the fact that only a focus on the customers and on satisfying their needs will result in a loyal customer base.

Before entering a market, an analysis of a company's position relative to its competitors and other players is advisable. Such an analysis begins with the well-known *five forces model* to gain an appreciation of the competitive nature of the industry. A SWOT analysis to assess strengths, weakness, opportunities, and threats follows.

Winning customers in the marketplace means competing on several dimensions. Customers base their purchase decisions on many variables, including price, convenience, reputation, and safety. The importance of a particular variable to a firm's success depends on the competitive marketplace and the preferences of individual customers.

A framework for viewing the contribution of information to the competitive strategy of the service firm also is presented. Using the dimensions of strategic focus both external and internal and competitive use of information both online and offline, four strategic roles of information are identified: creation of barriers to entry, revenue generation, database asset, and productivity enhancement. Industry examples for each role illustrate how firms have used information effectively.

Service product innovation is driven by an appreciation of the virtual value chain that assembles information on customer needs based on changing demographics and lifestyles. This database can be mined to develop new service offerings targeted at an existing customer base. However, there are limits to the use of information including questions of privacy, fairness, reliability, and data accuracy.

The chapter concludes with a framework that categorizes service firms according to their level of competitiveness with respect to key operational dimensions.

The Strategic Service Vision

The purpose and place of a service firm in the market begins with an entrepreneur's idea and an unmet need. Table 2.1 presents a framework in the form of questions one should ask in formulating a *strategic service vision*. The basic categories presented from left to right are: service delivery system, operating strategy, service concept, and target market segments. Within each category questions are offered to help in the development of the category. As one moves between categories a question is posed to assess how well the category has achieved the strategic service vision. For example, the between-category question "does the service delivery system support the operating strategy?" addresses the appropriateness of the service delivery system for the intended operating strategy. Table 2.1 is limited to a U.S. domestic service. Additional questions are necessary to account for cultural elements when applied in a global context. The international elements that need to be added to the strategic service vision shown here can be found in Table 10.1 in the Globalization of Services chapter.

To demonstrate the effectiveness of this framework, Table 2.2 illustrates the initial strategic service vision of Southwest Airlines when it served only three cities in Texas (i.e., Dallas, Houston, and San Antonio). With start-up firms such as Southwest Airlines, it is best to apply the strategic service vision from right to left beginning with the target market.

TABLE 2.1 Elements of the Strategic Service Vision

Source: Adapted and reprinted by permission of J. L. Heskett, W. E. Sasser, and L. A. Schlesinger, *The Service Profit Chain* (New York: The Free Press, 1997), p. 9.

Service Delivery System	Operating Strategy	Service Concept	Target Market Segment
• What are the important delivery system features (i.e., people, technology, etc.)? • What is the system capacity? • How does the system differentiate itself from competitors (i.e., quality, price, convenience)? • Are barriers to entry created?	• What are important business features (i.e., operations, finance, marketing, organization) • Where are effort and investments focused? • How will quality and cost be controlled? • What results will be expected versus competition?	• How are the results stated in terms of the customer? • How is the system supposed to be perceived by the target markets (i.e., customers and employees)? • How do customers perceive the service concept? • What efforts are required in terms of the manner the service is designed, delivered, and marketed?	• What are common characteristics of the target market? • How can the target market be segmented (i.e., demographic)? • How important are various segments and their needs? • How well are these needs being served (i.e., in what manner and by whom)?

TABLE 2.2 Southwest Airlines Strategic Service Vision

Service Delivery System	Operating Strategy	Service Concept	Target Market Segment
• Fun cabin atmosphere to differentiate service • Use only Boeing 737 aircraft to control maintenance and operating costs • Hire cabin crew based on attitude	• Quick turnaround at gate results in high utilization of aircraft • No assigned seating rewards punctuality and promotes on-time performance	• Short flights with frequent departures • Serves peanuts and soft drinks only • Use of inner-city or low traffic airports avoids congestion • Carry-on luggage	• State of Texas residents • Business traveler who drives because of inadequate airline service • Inexpensive family travel on weekends

Understanding the Competitive Environment of Services

In general, service firms compete in a difficult economic environment, and there are many reasons for this difficulty:

- *Relatively low overall entry barriers.* Service innovations are not patentable, and in most cases, services are not capital-intensive. Thus, innovations can easily be copied by competitors. However, other types of entry barriers exist, such as locating a resort hotel on the best beach on an island (e.g., Club Med's former location on the island of Moorea in French Polynesia).
- *Minimal opportunities for economies of scale.* The necessity of physical travel for many services limits the market area and results in small-scale outlets. Franchised firms can realize some economies of scale by sharing purchasing or advertising costs; in other instances, using the Internet can be a substitute for physical travel (e.g., ordering from Amazon.com).

- *Erratic sales fluctuations.* Service demand varies as a function of the time of day and the day of the week (and sometimes seasonally), with random arrivals. Can you think of some exceptions?
- *No advantage of size in dealing with buyers or suppliers.* The small size of many service firms places them at a disadvantage in bargaining with powerful buyers or suppliers. Many exceptions should come to mind, however, such as McDonald's buying beef and Marriott buying mattresses.
- *Product substitution.* Product innovations can be a substitute for services (e.g., the home pregnancy test). Thus, service firms must not only watch other service competitors but also anticipate potential product innovations that might make their services obsolete.
- *Customer loyalty.* Established firms can use personalized service to create a loyal customer base, which becomes a barrier to entry by new services. For example, a hospital supply firm may place its own ordering computer terminals at customers' sites. These terminals then facilitate the placement of new orders to the extent that competitors are effectively excluded.
- *Exit barriers.* Marginal service firms may continue to operate despite low, or even nonexistent, profits. For example, a privately held firm may have employment of family members rather than maximizing profit as its goal. Other service firms, such as antique stores or scuba diving shops, have a hobby or romantic appeal that provides their owners with enough job satisfaction to offset low financial compensation. Thus, profit-motivated competitors would find it difficult to drive these privately held firms from the market.

For any particular service industry, there are firms that have overcome these competitive difficulties and prospered. For example, McDonald's has achieved a dominant position in the fast-food industry by overcoming many of the difficulties listed here. New entrants, however, must develop a service strategy that will address the important competitive features of their respective industries. Three generic strategies have been successful in providing a competitive advantage, and illustrations of how service firms have used these strategies will be our next topic.

Competitive Service Strategies[2]

There are three generic competitive strategies: overall cost leadership, differentiation, and focus. Each strategy will be described in turn, with examples of how service firms use them to outperform their competition.

Overall Cost Leadership

An *overall cost leadership* strategy requires efficient-scale facilities, tight cost and overhead control, and often innovative technology as well. Having a low-cost position provides a defense against competition, because less efficient competitors will suffer first from competitive pressures. Implementing a low-cost strategy usually requires high capital investment in state-of-the-art equipment, aggressive pricing, and start-up losses to build market share. A cost leadership strategy sometimes can revolutionize an industry, as illustrated by the success of McDonald's, Walmart, and Southwest Airlines. Moreover, service firms have been able to achieve low-cost leadership using a variety of approaches.

Seeking Out Low-Cost Customers

Some customers cost less to serve than others, and they can be targeted by the service provider. For example, the United Services Automobile Association (USAA) occupies a preeminent position among automobile insurers because it serves only military personnel and their families. This group also entails lower cost because its members, who are relatively nomadic, are accustomed to and willing to do business by telephone, mail, or online. Consequently, USAA is able to eliminate any need for the extensive sales force employed by traditional insurers. Another example of this strategy is provided by low-cost retailers such as Sam's Wholesale Club and Costco, which target customers who are willing to buy in quantity, do without frills, and serve themselves.

Standardizing a Custom Service

Typically, income tax preparation is considered to be a customized service. H&R Block, however, has been successful in serving customers nationwide when only routine tax preparation is required. Also, storefront legal services and urgent care clinics are attractive means of delivering routine professional services at low cost. The key word here is *routine.* However, product substitution always is a danger (e.g., Turbo Tax).

Reducing the Personal Element in Service Delivery

The potentially high-risk strategy of reducing the personal element in service delivery can be accepted by customers if increased convenience results. For example, convenient access to ATMs has weaned customers from personal interaction with live tellers and, consequently, has reduced transaction costs for banks.

Reducing Network Costs

Unusual start-up costs are encountered by service firms that require a network to knit together providers and customers. Electric utilities, which have substantial fixed costs in transmission lines, provide the most obvious example. Federal Express conceived a unique approach to reducing network costs by using a hub-and-spoke network. By locating a hub in Memphis with state-of-the-art sorting technology, the overnight air-package carrier was able to serve the United States with no direct routes between the cities that it served. Each time a new city is added to the network, Federal Express only needs to add one more route to and from the hub instead of adding routes between all the cities served. The efficiency of the hub-and-spoke network strategy has not been lost on passenger airline operators, either.

Taking Service Operations Offline

Many services, such as surgery and passenger transportation, are inherently "online," because they can be performed only with the customer present. For services in which the customer need not be present, the service transaction can be "decoupled," with some content performed "offline." For example, a shoe repair service could locate dispersed kiosks for customer drop-off or pickup, thus consolidating orders for delivery to an off-site repair factory, which even could be located offshore. Performing services offline represents significant cost savings because of economies of scale from consolidation, low-cost facility location (e.g., American Airlines has a call center located in the Caribbean), and absence of the customer in the system. In short, the decoupled service operation is run like a factory.

Differentiation

The essence of the *differentiation* strategy lies in creating a service that is perceived as being unique. Approaches to differentiation can take many forms: brand image (e.g., McDonald's golden arches), technology (e.g., Sprint's fiber-optic network), features (e.g., American Express's travel services), customer service (e.g., Nordstrom's reputation among department stores), dealer network (e.g., Century 21's nationwide real estate presence), and other dimensions. A differentiation strategy does not ignore costs, but its primary thrust lies in creating customer loyalty. As illustrated here, differentiation to enhance the service often is achieved at some cost that the targeted customer is willing to pay.

Making the Intangible Tangible

By their very nature, services often are intangible and leave the customer with no physical reminder of the purchase. Recognizing the need to remind customers of their stay, many hotels now provide complimentary toiletry items with the hotel name prominently affixed.

The Hartford Steam Boiler Inspection and Insurance Company (now part of Munich Re) writes insurance on industrial power plants, but this company has enhanced its service to include regular inspections and recommendations to managers for avoiding potential problems.

Customizing the Standard Product

Providing a customized touch may endear a firm to its customers at very little cost. A hotel operator who is able to address a guest by name can make an impression that translates into repeat business. Hair salons have added many personalizing features (e.g., personal stylist, juice bar, relaxed surroundings, mood music) to differentiate themselves from barbershops. Burger King's efforts to promote a made-to-order policy is an attempt to differentiate itself from McDonald's classic make-to-stock approach to fast-food service.

Reducing Perceived Risk

Lack of information about the purchase of a service creates a sense of risk-taking for many customers. Lacking knowledge or self-confidence about services such as auto repair, customers will seek out providers who take the extra time to explain the work to be done, present a clean and organized facility, and guarantee their work (e.g., Village Volvo). Customers often see the "peace of mind" that is engendered when this trusting relationship develops as being worth the extra expense.

Giving Attention to Personnel Training

Investment in personnel development and training that results in enhanced service quality is a competitive advantage that is difficult to replicate. Firms that lead their industries are known among competitors for the quality of their training programs. In some cases, these firms have established college-like training centers (e.g., McDonald's Hamburger University in Oak Brook, Illinois, near Chicago).

Controlling Quality

Delivering a consistent level of service quality at multiple sites with a labor-intensive system is a significant challenge. Firms have approached this problem in a variety of ways, including personnel training, explicit procedures, technology, limits on the scope of the service, direct supervision, and peer pressure, among others. For example, to ensure consistency, the Magic Pan chain of restaurants designed a foolproof machine to produce its famous crêpes. The question of service quality is further complicated by the potential gap between customer expectations and experiences. Influencing customer quality expectations thus becomes an issue, which is explored in Chapter 6, Service Quality.

Focus

The *focus* strategy is built around the idea of servicing a particular target market very well by addressing customers' specific needs. The market segment could be a particular buyer group (e.g., USAA and the military community), service (e.g., Shouldice Hospital and patients with inguinal hernias), Motel 6 (budget travelers), Federal Express (people who need guaranteed overnight package delivery), or geographic region (e.g., community college or neighborhood restaurant). The focus strategy rests on the premise that the firm can serve its narrow target market more effectively and/or efficiently than other firms trying to serve a broad market. As a result, the firm achieves competitive advantage in its market segment by meeting specific customer needs and/or by lower costs through specialization. Thus, the focus strategy is the application of differentiation and/or overall cost leadership to a particular market segment rather than the entire market.

Davidow and Uttal argue how important customer selection is to achieving a successful focus strategy.[3] They relate how one bank in Palo Alto, California, targets wealthy individuals and discourages others by policies such as closing an account after two checks have bounced. Davidow and Uttal's three-step approach to focus includes segmenting the market to design core services, classifying customers according to the value they place on service, and setting expectations slightly below perceived performance.

Strategic Analysis

Strategic analysis begins with a stated objective, such as "should we enter an industry with a new service offering?" Two popular planning tools include (1) Porter's five forces analysis of the target industry structure and (2) SWOT analysis to assess the organization's strengths, weaknesses, opportunities, and threats in a market.

Porter's Five Forces Analysis[4]

The five forces model is used at the industry level (e.g., airlines) to determine the competitive intensity and, therefore, attractiveness of a market. The five forces affect the ability of a firm to attract customers and make a profit. Figure 2.1 shows a model of the five forces with example issues to consider in each case.

Consider Netflix as an example firm entering the video rental industry. Our discussion begins with the center block (Competitive Rivalry within Industry) upon which the external forces act.

- *Competitive Rivalry within Industry.* Often this factor is the major determinant of industry competitiveness. Rivals might be aggressive price competitors or they might use nonprice strategies such as innovation, branding, or superior quality. Industry capacity relative to total customer demand is an important indicator of whether a new entrant will find customers. An exception was Southwest Airlines, which entered the Texas market offering low-cost fares and frequent departures that tapped a latent demand of business commuters who usually traveled by car. When Netflix entered the market offering DVDs exclusively by mail, its only rivals were rental stores such as Blockbuster.
- *Potential New Entrants.* Profitable markets that yield high returns invite new competitors. For example, at one time Walmart challenged Netflix, but subsequently left the field because it was unable to overcome Netflix's established brand.
- *Threat of Substitutes.* For services, substitutes often take the form of a product. For example, Turbo Tax software is a substitute for the services of a tax accountant. Netflix is somewhat immune from product substitution but faces competition from the likes of Amazon Prime movie streaming on Internet-enabled smart TVs.
- *Bargaining Power of Suppliers.* Suppliers of inputs can be a source of power over the firm because of product uniqueness or monopoly source. The most important suppliers

FIGURE 2.1
Porter's Five Forces Model

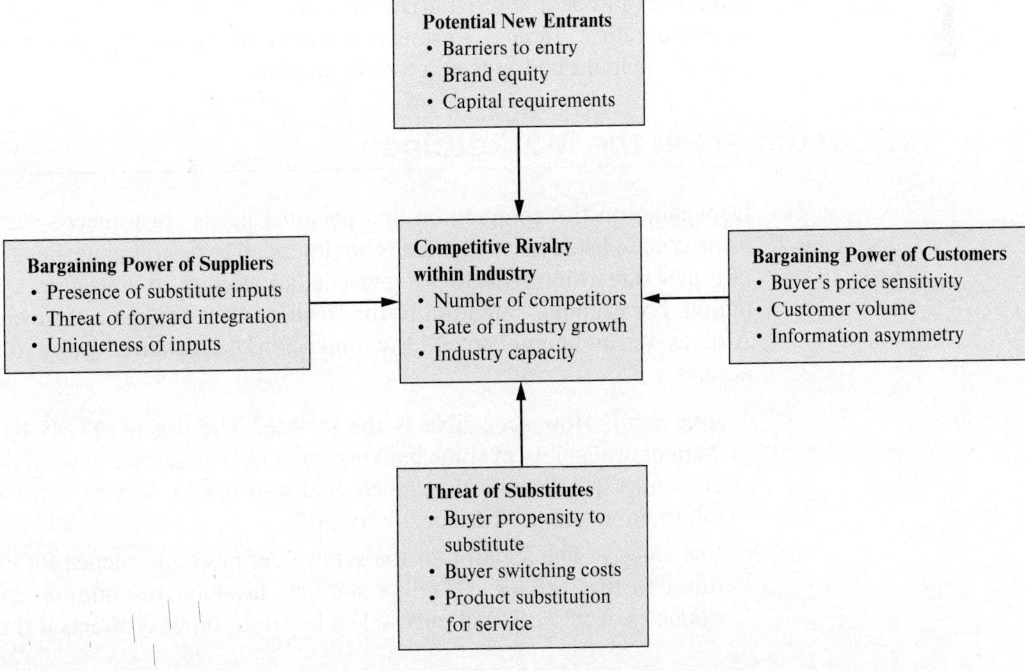

TABLE 2.3
SWOT Analysis

Strengths	Weaknesses
• What are your company's advantages? • What do you do better than anyone else? • What unique resources do you have? • What do people in your market see as your strengths?	• What could you improve? • What should you avoid? • What factors lose sales? • What are people in your market likely to see as a weakness?
Opportunities	**Threats**
• What are your competitors' vulnerabilities? • What are the current market trends? • Does technology offer new service options? • Are there niches in the market your organization can fill?	• What obstacles do you face? • What are your competitors doing? • Is changing technology threatening your position? • Do you have cash-flow problems?

to Netflix are the DVD distributors, but Netflix has considerable leverage because of volume purchases.

- *Bargaining Power of Customers.* Netflix customers might be able to exert price pressure and, thus, restrict high margins. In the travel industry the use of Priceline.com and Hotwire.com has shifted the information asymmetry to the advantage of the customer. However, Netflix uses information about customer purchases to recommend other movies with similar themes, thereby stimulating demand.

SWOT Analysis: Strengths, Weaknesses, Opportunities, Threats

Following the industry level of analysis, using the five forces model, SWOT analysis is conducted at the individual firm level. A *SWOT analysis* identifies an organization's internal strength and weakness as well as threats and opportunities in the external environment. The aim of the analysis is to reveal competitive advantages, analyze prospects, prepare for problems, and allow for development of contingency plans. A SWOT analysis begins with a stated objective and concludes with a summary of strengths to be maintained, built upon, or leveraged; weaknesses to be remedied; opportunities to be prioritized, captured, or built upon; and threats to be countered, minimized, or managed. A SWOT analysis is subjective, and people often arrive at different final versions, thus emphasizing the value of collaboration. Table 2.3 presents a sample of typical questions that might be asked in each of the four quadrants of a SWOT analysis.

Winning Customers in the Marketplace

Depending on the competition and personal needs, customers select a service provider using criteria listed here. This list is not intended to be complete, because the very addition of a new dimension by a firm represents an attempt to engage in a strategy of differentiation. For example, initiation of the frequent flyer program "AAdvantage" by American Airlines was an attempt to add the dimension of customer loyalty to competition among airlines.

- *Availability.* How accessible is the service? The use of ATMs by banks has created 24-hour availability of some banking services (i.e., service beyond the traditional "banker's hours"). Use of 800 numbers and websites by service firms facilitates access to information and personal accounts 24/7.
- *Convenience.* The location of the service defines convenience for customers who must travel to that service. Gasoline stations, fast-food restaurants, and dry cleaners are examples of services that must select locations on busy streets if they are to succeed.

- *Dependability.* How reliable is the service? For example, once the exterminator is gone, how soon do the bugs return? A major complaint regarding automobile repair services is the failure to fix the problem on the first visit. For airlines, on-time performance is a statistic collected by the FAA.
- *Personalization.* Are you treated as an individual? For example, hotels have discovered that repeat customers respond to being greeted by their name. The degree of customization allowed in providing the service, no matter how slight, can be viewed as more personalized service.
- *Price.* Competing on price is not as effective in services as it is with products, because it often is difficult to compare the costs of services objectively. Comparing costs in the delivery of routine services such as an oil change might be easy, but in professional services, competition on price can be considered counterproductive because price often is viewed as being a surrogate for quality.
- *Quality.* Service quality is a function of the relationship between a customer's prior expectations of the service and his or her perception of the service experience both during and after the fact. Unlike product quality, service quality is judged by both the process of service delivery and the outcome of the service.
- *Reputation.* The uncertainty that is associated with the selection of a service provider often is resolved by talking with others about their experiences before a decision is made. Unlike a product, a poor service experience cannot be exchanged or returned for a different model. Positive word-of-mouth is the most effective form of advertising.
- *Safety.* Well-being and security are important considerations because in many services, such as air travel and medicine, the customers are putting their lives in the hands of the service provider.
- *Speed.* How long must I wait for service? For emergency services such as fire and police protection, response time is the major criterion of performance. In other services, waiting sometimes might be considered a trade-off for receiving more personalized services, or in reduced rates.

Writing about manufacturing strategy, Terry Hill used the term *order-winning criteria* to refer to competitive dimensions that sell products.[5] He further suggested that some criteria could be called *qualifiers*, because the presence of these dimensions is necessary for a product to enter the marketplace. Finally, Hill said that some qualifiers could be considered *order-losing sensitive.*

We will use a similar logic and the service criteria listed earlier to describe the service purchase decision. The purchase decision sequence begins with qualifying potential service firms (e.g., is there a fast-food restaurant nearby?), followed by making a final selection from this subset of service firms using a service winner (e.g., are their burgers known to be good?). After the initial service experience, a return will be based on whether a "service loser" has occurred (e.g., disappointment in burger quality).

Qualifiers

Before a service firm can be taken seriously as a competitor in the market, it must attain a certain level for each service-competitive dimension, as defined by the other market players. For example, in airline service, we would name safety, as defined by the airworthiness of the aircraft and by the rating of the pilots, as an obvious *qualifier.* In a mature market such as fast foods, established competitors may define a level of quality, such as cleanliness, that new entrants must at least match to be viable contenders.

Service Winners

Service winners are dimensions such as price, convenience, or reputation that are used by a customer to make a choice among competitors. Depending on the needs of the customer at the time of the purchase, the service winner may vary. For example, seeking a restaurant for lunch might be based on convenience, but a dinner date could be influenced by reputation. For fast food, a dimension that once was a service winner, such as a drive-in window, over time could become a qualifier because some customers will not stop otherwise.

Service Losers

Failure to deliver at or above the expected level for a competitive dimension can result in a dissatisfied customer who is lost forever. For various reasons, the dimensions of dependability, personalization, and speed are particularly vulnerable to becoming *service losers.* Some examples might be failure of an auto dealer to repair a mechanical problem (i.e., dependability), rude treatment by a doctor (i.e., personalization), or failure of an overnight service to deliver a package on time (i.e., speed).

Sustainability in Services

Most casual observers might wonder why a service firm needs to worry about sustainability because no pollution-making fumes come out of a typical service facility. But when looked at thoughtfully, service firms have as big a role to play in the sustainability movement as manufacturing plants. Responsibilities of service firms go far beyond recycling their papers and reducing energy usage. A wide range of opportunities and threats in sustainability efforts can affect a service operation significantly.

For most service firms, environmental, social, and economic *sustainability* are essential features for the long-term viability of operations. Designing efficient processes and practices—as well as cultivating corporate cultures that eliminate negative environmental and social impacts and improve corporate image—requires significant organizational commitment to sustainability.[6]

Several forces that motivate a service firm to consider sustainability as a strategy include:

- *Regulations/legislation:* The U.S. Environmental Protection Agency (EPA) outlines regulations to protect human health and the environment. Directives from the Waste Electrical and Electronic Equipment (WEEE) and Restriction of Hazardous Substances (RoHS) set targets for collection, recycling, and recovery for all types of electrical and other hazardous materials. Also, international standards such as ISO 14000 and ISO 26000 exist for environmental protection and social responsibility.
- *Perception/image building:* Many of the sustainability efforts by service firms cater to public relations. Customers often seek out providers that are leaders in the sustainability movement.
- *Economic:* Certain aspects of sustainable operations actually save money for a firm, for example, waste reduction (as a part of lean operation) and value recovery.

Triple Bottom Line (TBL)

The term *triple bottom line* (TBL or 3BL) was coined to evaluate a firm on social, economic, and environmental criteria in relation to sustainability.[7] Different forms of triple bottom line concepts are possible. Shell Oil Company, for example, popularized the model, "People, Planet, and Profit." The 20th-century urban planner and educator, Patrick Geddes, used the phrase "Folk, Work and Place" in the same vein as today's 3BL.

Social issues include labor practices, workforce diversity, human rights, and community outreach. Economic issues include capital efficiency, growth enhancement, cost reduction, and risk management. Environmental issues include clean air, water and land, emission control, and waste management. In addition to these issues, we also can find overlapping criteria. Socioeconomic issues include job creation, skill enhancement, and business ethics. Eco-efficiency refers to resource efficiency and life-cycle management. Social-environmental issues include global climate change, environmental justice, and health safety. As shown in Figure 2.2, when all three basic criteria are satisfied, true sustainability can be achieved.

FIGURE 2.2 The Triple Bottom Line in Relation to Sustainability

Source: http://www.conocophillips.com/EN/susdev/commitments/Page/ApproachCommitments.aspx

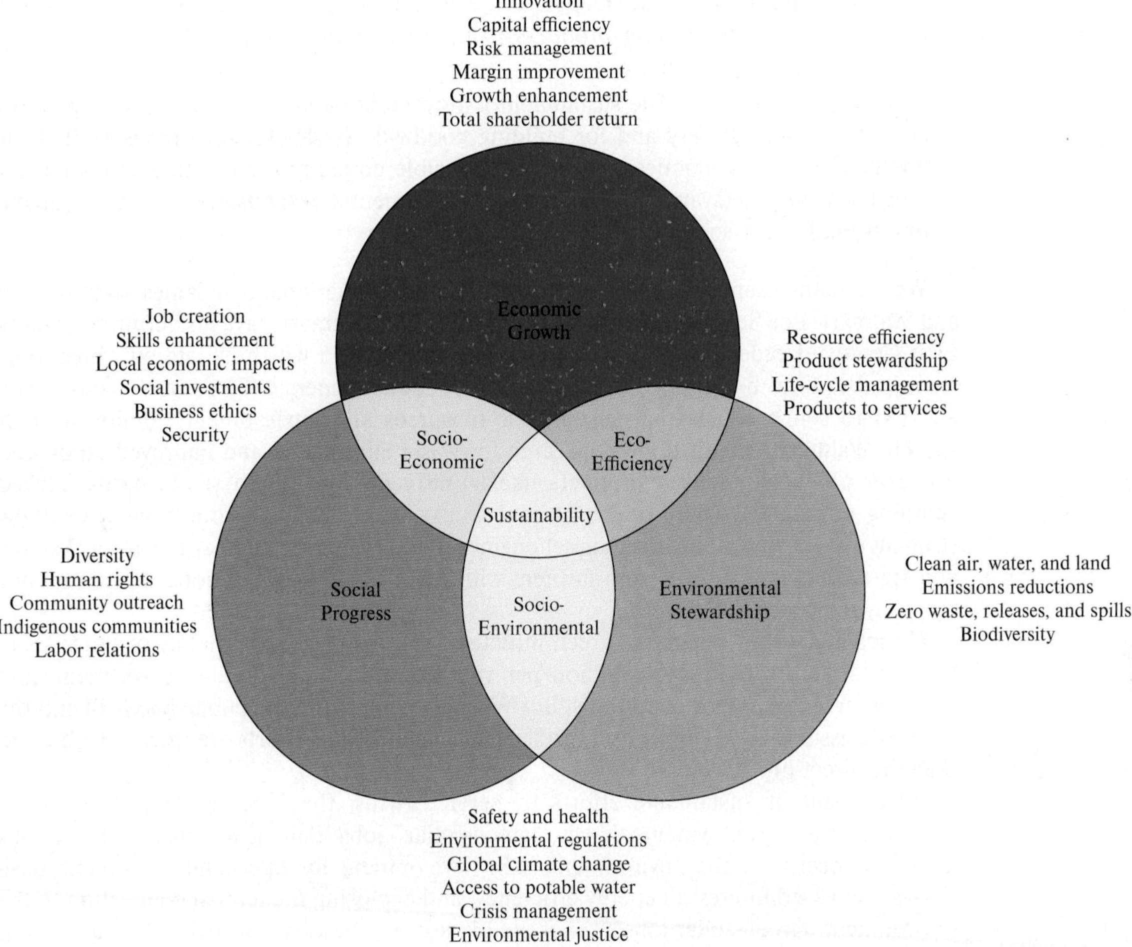

Some factors that support a movement to sustainability in service operations include:

- Labor, material, and energy costs will continue to grow.
- Public pressure for environmental, health, and safety performance is likely to remain strong.
- Consumer demand for services offered by 3BL companies is likely to grow.
- Strong nongovernmental organization (NGO) activities concerning sustainable business practices exist.

Beyond its internal sustainable efforts, a service firm needs to consider the following external factors:[8]

- *Ripple effect:* Often the biggest impact a service firm has is not its service offerings themselves, but how the firm affects the behavior and choices of its customers. When a bank approves a mortgage for a homebuyer, its influence goes beyond the financial aspects and includes factors that could affect the quality of life in the community, local traffic flow, diversity of residents, home-insurance costs, and even the national economy (recall the 2008 financial crisis).
- *Strategic threats:* Sustainability-related trends can threaten the foundation of a business. Global warming has resulted in lack of snow at several ski resorts, which in

turn shortens the ski season and decreases profits. Extreme climate concerns the insurance industry because it generates severe losses from more devastating storms. Nongovernmental organizations (NGOs) are known to call out service firms for unethical practices. Home Depot, for example, was criticized by the Rainforest Action Network for selling products from old-growth forests that are ecologically sensitive and illegally logged.

- *Emerging opportunities:* The sustainability movement opens doors for making positive contributions to society and for building goodwill. Starbucks, sometimes vilified for unethical business practices, attracts responsible coffee growers with premium-price, long-term contracts and guidelines for environmental responsibilities (shade-grown, bird-friendly) and social concerns (labor practices).

We see many examples of sustainable efforts by multinational companies such as Nike and Walmart. Lee Scott, former president and CEO of Walmart, gave his defining "Twenty First Century Leadership" speech on October 24, 2005, in which he laid out three long-term goals: (1) to be supplied 100 percent by renewable energy, (2) to create zero waste, and (3) to sell products that sustain our resources and environment.[9] Following that speech, Walmart embarked upon a search for waste elimination and improved efficiency. For example, it condensed products like laundry detergent into small, easily packed shipping containers; retrofitted long-haul trucks with small air conditioners to allow sleeping drivers to turn off their diesel engines; reduced plastic and cardboard packaging; and started buying directly from farmers with emphasis on organic food. Saving money by being green was the objective.

Critics argue that Walmart's green initiatives are unsustainable, mainly owing to exorbitant cost (more than $500 million per year), a suboptimal product assortment, and criticism of factory labor conditions. But Walmart claims that the public goodwill and the improved assurance of supply as a result of its sustainability efforts are worth much more than the direct profit generated.[10]

As a result of sustainable efforts by service firms, the U.S. economy has seen a new area of job employment, that is, "green-collar" jobs. Salient features for these jobs include concern for the environment, skill development for operating sustainable businesses, increased interest in energy efficiency, and exploring the human connection to the environment. Green-collar jobs are not the highest paying jobs, but their attraction lies in social responsibility. As the motto goes: *Green, Not Greed, Is Good!!*

The Competitive Role of Information in Services[11]

For service management, information technology is helping to define the competitive strategy of successful firms. Figure 2.3 illustrates the different roles in which information technology can support a service firm's competitive strategy. We shall explore each of these roles in turn with illustrations from successful applications.

Creation of Barriers to Entry

As noted earlier, many services exist in markets that have low entry barriers. However, barriers to entry can be created by using economies of scale, building market share, creating switching costs, investing in communications networks, and using databases and information technologies to strategic advantage. We will discuss three uses of information for creating barriers to entry: reservations systems, frequent flyer or similar programs to gain customer loyalty, and development of customer relationships to increase switching costs.

Reservation Systems

A barrier to entry can be created by investing in online reservations systems that are provided to sales intermediaries such as Expedia. American Airline's SABRE system is an example of the kind of subtle barrier to entry that is created by a comprehensive

FIGURE 2.3
Strategic Roles of Information in Services

Source: Adapted from James A. Fitzsimmons, "Strategic Role of Information in Services," in Rakesh V. Sarin (ed.), *Perspectives in Operations Management: Essays in Honor of Elwood S. Buffa,* Norwell, Mass: Kluwer Academic Publishers, 1993, p. 103.

Competitive use of information

	Online (Real Time)	Offline (Analysis)
External (Customer)	*Creation of barriers to entry:* Reservation system Frequent user club Switching costs	*Database asset:* Selling information Development of services Micromarketing
Internal (Operations)	*Revenue generation:* Yield management Point of sales Expert systems	*Productivity enhancement:* Inventory status Data envelopment analysis (DEA)

information system. United and Delta have duplicated this reservations system at great cost, but most smaller carriers use these existing systems for a fee. The competitive importance of online reservations systems became evident in late 1982. At this time, the Civil Aeronautics Board (CAB) and the U.S. Department of Justice began a joint investigation of possible antitrust violations by airline reservations systems. In this investigation, Frontier Airlines filed charges accusing United of unfairly restricting competition in the use of its Apollo computerized reservations system.

Frequent User Club

It was a small step for American Airlines, given its massive reservations system, to add passenger accounts to accumulate travel credit for frequent flyer awards. These programs, which award free trips and other awards, create strong brand loyalty among travelers, particularly business travelers who are not paying their own way. Thus, the discount fares of a new competitor have no appeal to these travelers. In recent years, however, the frequent-user benefits for airlines in particular have become very restricted; for example, credits that are generated by a given trip are greatly reduced, credits that are needed for a "free" flight are greatly increased, short expiration dates are implemented (a boon for magazine publishers), and availability of seats for free travel are sharply reduced and often relegated to undesirable times and connections. Therefore, the advent of online search engines that identify bargain fares might cause the restrictive frequent-user benefits to erode customer loyalty.

Switching Costs

Establishing customer relationships creates a cost in the form of a *switching cost*, an inconvenience for the customer to switch to another provider. Think of the hassle of changing your bank after you have arranged for automatic bill payment from your checking account.

Information technology in the form of online computer terminals has been used in the medical supplies industry to link hospitals directly to the suppliers' distribution networks. Both American Hospital Supply and the drug distributor McKesson have installed their online terminals in hospitals so that supplies and drugs can be purchased as the need arises. Significant switching costs are built into this arrangement, because the hospital is able to reduce inventory carrying costs and has the convenience of online ordering for replenishments. The supplier benefits by a reduction in selling costs because it is difficult for a competitor to entice away a customer who is already co-opted into its system.

Revenue Generation

Real-time information technologies with a focus on internal operations can play a competitive role in increasing revenue opportunities. The concept of *yield management* is best understood as a revenue-maximizing strategy to make full use of service capacity (e.g., seats on an airline flight). The advent of smartphones and tablets has created opportunities for innovative point-of-sale suggestions, and the use of expert systems resident on servers and accessible by laptop computers in the field allows maintenance personnel to provide on-site customer service.

Yield Management

Through the use of its SABRE reservations system, American Airlines was the first to realize the potential of what is now called yield management. By constantly monitoring the status of both its upcoming flights and competitors' flights on the same route, American makes pricing and allocation decisions on unsold seats. Thus, the number of Supersaver fares allocated to a particular flight can be adjusted to ensure that remaining empty seats have a chance of being sold, but not at the expense of a full-fare seat. This real-time pricing strategy maximizes the revenue for each flight by ensuring that no seat goes empty for want of a bargain-seeking passenger while holding some seats in reserve for late arrivals who are willing to pay full fare.

Thus, yield management is the application of information to improve the revenue that is generated by a time-perishable resource (e.g., airline seats, hotel rooms). The success of yield management for American has not gone unnoticed by other service industries; for example, Marriott Hotels has a nationwide yield management system to increase occupancy rates. In addition, American Airlines is capitalizing on its innovation by selling its yield management software to noncompetitive industries such as the French national railroad. The topic of yield management is covered in more detail in Chapter 11, Managing Capacity and Demand.

Point of Sale

In China, Walmart introduced a new toy for the discount shopper: the VideOcart. As the shopper pushes the VideOcart through the store, nearby items on sale flash onto the attached video screen. The cart also helps customers find items in the store by listing hundreds of products by department and then displaying a map of the store. For another example, consider a commercial application for the iPad. With this device, a server in a restaurant can transmit an order directly to the kitchen monitor and the bill to the cashier at the same time. This saves unnecessary steps and allows more time for suggestive selling.

Expert Systems

Otis Elevator Company puts an *expert system* together with laptop or tablet computers in the hands of its maintenance staff to speed repairs in the field. Collecting information on the behavior of its elevators over the years has led to a knowledge base that is incorporated into the expert system. Using the computer, a repair person in the field can access the system that is resident on a server and receive diagnostic help in identifying the source of a problem. As a result, elevators are placed back in service quickly, and fewer repair people are needed. Some of the earlier applications of expert systems have been in the medical field, to aid in disease diagnosis. As another example, an oil exploration expert system was able to identify promising drilling sites for a major oil company.

Database Asset

The database a service firm possesses can be a hidden asset of strategic importance. The expense of assembling and maintaining a large database is itself a barrier to entry by competitors. More important, however, the database can be mined for profiles of customers' buying habits, and these present opportunities for developing new services.

Rental car employees use handheld computers to speed up the car drop-off process, allowing customers to avoid missing flights.
©Comstock/Stockbyte/Getty Images RF

Selling Information

Dun & Bradstreet created a business by selling access to its database of business credit information. American Home Shield, a provider of service contracts for individual home heating, plumbing, and electrical systems, also discovered that it had a valuable asset in its database, accumulated over many years of repair experience; manufacturers now are invited to access this database to evaluate the performance patterns of their products. American Express has detailed information about the spending habits of its cardholders and now offers breakdowns of customer spending patterns to its retail customers.

Developing Services

Club Med, an all-inclusive resort company with locations worldwide, has evolved to reflect the maturing of its membership. Studying the database of member characteristics, Club Med realized that over time its once swinging singles members have become married with children. In order to continue capturing future vacation visits, Club Med modified some of its locations to accommodate families with young children. Now parents can enjoy the beach and water sports while their children are supervised by Club Med counselors at a children's park nearby. More recently, Club Med has added cruise ships to its vacation possibilities to attract the more senior members who are no longer interested in water sports. As this example illustrates, service firms that capture customer data at the time of the initial purchase have the opportunity to establish a lifetime relationship, with the potential for creating new or modified services for future purchase.

Micromarketing

Today, we can see a truly focused service strategy that can target customers at the micro level. Bar coding and checkout scanner technology create a wealth of consumer buying information that can be used to target customers with precision. Analysis of this database allows marketers to pinpoint their advertising and product distribution. To increase sales, Borden Inc. has used such information to select stores in which to feature its premium pasta sauce. Kraft USA saw its sales of cream cheese increase after targeting its flavors to the tastes of a particular store's shoppers. American Express, by analyzing information about its customers and their changing spending patterns in meticulous detail, can even tell when they get married.

Productivity Enhancement

New developments in the collection and analysis of information have increased our ability to manage multisite service operations. Through use of bar code information, retail inventory can be managed on a daily basis to make better use of shelf space by matching displayed products with sales. Information collected on the performance of multisite units can be used to identify the most efficient producers, and productivity is enhanced systemwide when the sources of these successes are shared with other sites. The foundation for a learning organization is then established.

Inventory Status

Using a tablet computer, Frito-Lay sales representatives have eliminated paper forms. They download the data collected on their routes each day via the Internet to the Plano, Texas, headquarters, and the company then uses these data to keep track of inventory levels, pricing, product promotions, and stale or returned merchandise. These daily updates on sales, manufacturing, and distribution keep fresh products moving through the system, matching consumer demands. For a perishable product like potato chips, having the right product at the right place and in the proper amount is critical to Frito-Lay's success.

Data Envelopment Analysis

Data envelopment analysis (DEA) is a linear programming technique developed by Abraham Charnes, William W. Cooper, and Edwardo Rhodes to evaluate nonprofit and public sector organizations. Subsequently, it has found applications in for-profit service organizations. DEA compares each service delivery unit with all other service units for a multisite organization, and it computes an efficiency rating that is based on the ratio of resource inputs to outputs. Multiple inputs (e.g., labor-hours, materials) and multiple outputs (e.g., sales, referrals) are possible and desirable in measuring a unit's efficiency. The linear programming model uses this information to determine the efficiency frontier on the basis of those units producing at 100 percent efficiency. Areas for improvement can be identified by comparing the operating practices of efficient units with those of less efficient units. Sharing management practices of efficient units with less efficient units provides an opportunity for the latter's improvement and enhancement of total system productivity. Repeated use of DEA can establish a climate of organizational learning that fuels a competitive strategy of cost leadership.

In one case, applying DEA to a 60-unit fast-food restaurant chain found 33 units to be efficient. Three outputs (i.e., food sales for breakfast, lunch, and dinner) and six inputs (i.e., supplies and materials, labor, age of store, advertising expenditures, urban versus rural location, and existence of a drive-in window) were used. It is interesting to note that the inputs included both discretionary and uncontrollable variables (e.g., the demographic variable of urban/rural locations, whether or not the unit had a drive-in window). The topic of data envelopment analysis is covered in more detail as a supplement to Chapter 7, Process Improvement.

The Internet of Things (IoT)

Welcome to your new world. Your alarm rings this morning, but it rings 15 minutes before the time you set. What is going on? While you slept, your clock monitored traffic along your route to work and determined that you will have to leave 15 minutes earlier than usual to get to work on time. Before you leave home, you add water and rice to your rice cooker. As you start home from work tonight, your cooker will note the time and then determine the time to turn itself on so that your rice is ready when you arrive home. As you approach your front door to leave home, the handle of your umbrella stand blinks a blue color, which tells you that it will rain today (a red light indicates hot weather, white indicates snow, and green tells you that the weather will be clear). You take your umbrella.

Once upon a time, this scenario would have been science fiction, but today it is technology in action thanks to the *Internet of Things (IoT)*. The Internet of Things is the internetworking of physical devices, vehicles, buildings, and many other items that are embedded with electronics, software, sensors, actuators, and network connectivity. These embedded capabilities enable objects to collect and exchange data via the Internet, which allows them to be remotely sensed and controlled. Consequently, they create opportunities for more direct integration of the physical world with the virtual world of cloud-based computing. As shown in Figure 2.4 the Internet of Things is built on a trajectory of advances in communications technology beginning with radio frequency identification (RFID), first used at the turn of the century to tag inventory in supply chains.

The idea behind IoT is to create an environment where everything is connected to the Internet, creating "swarm intelligence" from otherwise ordinary devices such as umbrella holders, toasters, rice cookers, microwave ovens, and your car. Such devices are able to talk directly to each other using sensors and actuators. Sensors are the devices that collect information and then send data over the Internet for processing. Actuators are the devices that produce outputs that are triggered by instructions sent from the sensors.

IoT involves a convergence of multiple technologies, including wireless communication, real-time analytics, machine learning, commodity sensors, and embedded systems. Using IoT, businesses can bring products to the marketplace faster, adapt to regulatory requirements amidst highly mobile workforces, and also adapt to evolving customer needs and changing supply chain dynamics.

FIGURE 2.4
Internet of Things Trajectory

Source: https://en.wikipedia.org/wiki/Internet_of_things

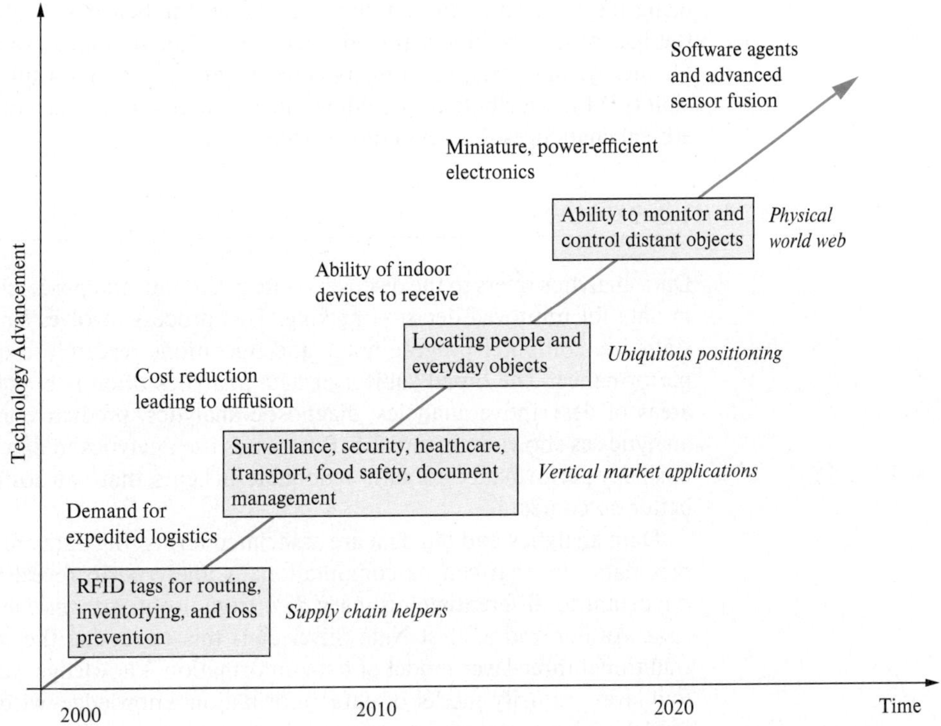

In the field of health care, Internet of Medical Things (IoMT) is gaining ground. This capability involves medical devices and applications that connect to health care IT systems through online computer networks. Medical devices equipped with Wi-Fi allow machine-to-machine communication that is linked to cloud platforms such as Amazon Web Services, on which captured data can be stored and analyzed.[12]

Examples of IoMT include remote monitoring of patients with chronic conditions, tracking patient medication orders, and locating patients admitted to hospitals. Patients wear devices such as wrist bands that can send information to caregivers. Infusion pumps that connect to analytics dashboards and hospital beds that are rigged with sensors to measure patients' vital signs are other examples of IoMT technology. The practice of using IoMT devices to monitor patients in their homes remotely is also known as telemedicine. Use of telemedicine spares patients from traveling to a hospital or physician's office whenever they have a medical situation or a change in health condition.

Drawbacks of IoMT include overloading physicians with too much data and distracting them from treating patients. In addition, hospitals and insurance agencies must tweak their security policies continuously to keep up with technological advancements.

IoT involves privacy concerns because it opens your personal activities to public access through the Internet, which is a massive open-publishing platform. While technology, by itself, is simply an enabler, it can definitely be misused by third parties with ulterior motives. Massive storage capabilities, especially in the cloud, and the advent of strong data mining tools allow personal data to be searched and exposed for the entire world to see. Posting your party photographs on Facebook is one thing, but it is a completely different story for an unsolicited third party to dig into your intimate lifestyle and medical history.

Recent stories on computer hacking via the Internet and leaking of personal information by groups such as Wikileaks demonstrate that IoT remains a risky venture. Contractual obligation clauses are included in most business ventures on how much information can be shared with outside parties, even including the government and the police. Can giving up some control on the privacy of personal information be justified in the face of terrorist threats or the safety of the country? Legal, social, and ethical discussions on this subject are sure to continue.

Determining what level of Internet of Things is appropriate will be the subject of much debate in coming years. Just because technology exists to control your household devices using the Internet from remote locations, do the benefits truly exceed the risks? Should the fear of misuse hinder the advancement of technology toward a better life? In today's technological world, practitioners of IoT might have an opportunity (and perhaps a responsibility?) to contribute to providing moral leadership in many of the upcoming social and ethical challenges that technology offers.

Data Analytics in Services

Data analytics refers to the discovery, interpretation, and processing of meaningful patterns in data for improved decision making. This process involves simultaneous application of statistics, computer programming, and operations research to quantify an organization's performance. The broad subject of data analytics often is broken down into subordinate areas of descriptive analytics, diagnostic analytics, predictive analytics, and prescriptive analytics as shown in Figure 2.5. Businesses use analytics to describe, analyze, and predict business performance to gain actionable insights that can foster smarter decisions and better outcomes.

Data analytics and big data are associated terms. Big data are extremely large and complex data sets that can be computationally analyzed to reveal patterns and trends. It is important to differentiate ordinary *data* from useful *information* to obtain relevant *knowledge.* Author and analyst Nate Silver calls this extracting the *signal* from the *noise.* The traditional three-layer model of data-information-knowledge was extended to the current four-layer maturity model of data-information-knowledge-wisdom. We offer a five-layer model of data-information-knowledge-fact-evidence. This five-layer model screens ordinary *data* to obtain *information* that can be used to create new *knowledge.* Computational methods then are used to establish *facts* that can be proven quantitatively and offered as *evidence* for business purposes.

As shown in Table 2.4, use of analytics has become commonplace across industries. For a Hollywood example, recall the use of analytics to draft players for the Oakland A's in the book and movie *Moneyball.*

Analytics can be challenging because a business must keep up with the four components of big data—volume, variety, velocity, and variability. These components change fast and require special optimization techniques and computational capabilities to manage them.

In the customer service domain, the use of data analytics is far from optimal for several reasons, including lack of integration of different phases of customer service and

FIGURE 2.5
Big Data

Source: http://www.fdot.gov/planning/statistics/symposium/2014/bigdata-industry.pdf, p.10.

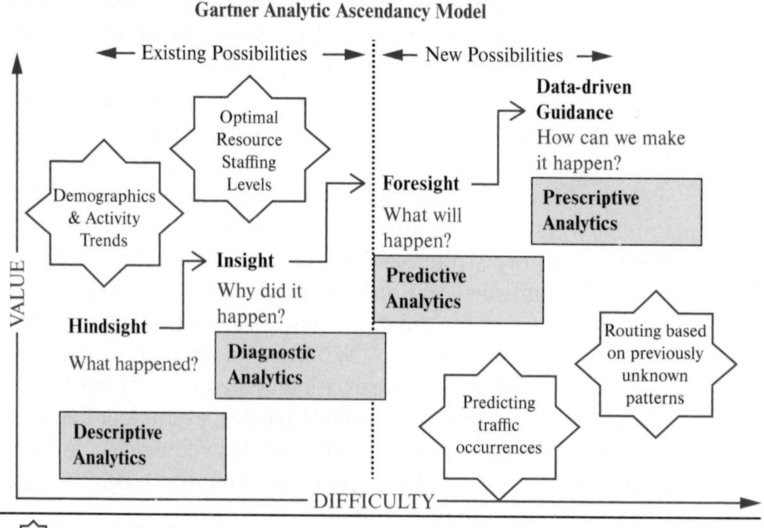

TABLE 2.4
Application of Data Analytics by Service Industry

Service Industry	Data Analytics Application
Airlines	Operational performance and pricing models
Investment Banks	Portfolio management and risk assessment
Insurance	Health assessment
Hospitals	In-patient care
Hotels/Restaurants	Revenue management
Marketing Firms	Sales and profitability improvement
Casinos	Customer loyalty programs
Retailers	Supply chain management
Sports Franchises	Drafting athletes and play-making during game

duplication of efforts. For example, good use of data analytics by a call center allows for personalization of the customer experience, which in turn can lead to improvements in customer satisfaction and cost efficiency. Analytics can be used to best advantage by including data collection that spans the entire customer journey, understanding customer needs better, using predictive analytics and machine-learning to anticipate important events, and using customer feedback to tune the analytics platform continuously.[13]

In a typical firm, some minimal level of data analysis is necessary for day-to-day activities–*to keep the lights on.* For example, in health care this analysis will include areas such as the human resource system, basic patient records, parts supply, and patient billing. The true benefits of higher-level analytics, however, are realized if a health care firm can leverage technology and quantitative analysis to achieve transformational changes by using capabilities such as an electronic health record (EHR) integrated system (e.g., EPIC software), telemedicine, mobile medical devices, surgical suite monitoring, and real-time medical alerts. The area of health analytics has the potential to reduce treatment costs, predict outbreaks of epidemics, avoid preventable diseases, and improve quality of life in general. The nature of such complexities makes big data and business analytics the next frontier for innovation, competition, and productivity.

The Virtual Value Chain[14]

Today, businesses compete in two worlds: a physical world of people and things called a *marketplace* and a virtual world of information called a *marketspace.* For example, after Barnes and Noble opened a website it established a presence in the virtual marketspace created by the Internet, but it also continued its competitive position as the leading bookstore in the marketplace. The nature of the marketspace that requires customer information for order fulfillment also enables the service provider to collect useful information such as customer buying behavior and addresses. The marketspace information also can be used to improve the service delivery process and create customer value.

The process of creating value has long been described as stages linked together to form a *value chain.* The traditional physical value chain, as shown at the top of Figure 2.6, consists of a sequence of stages beginning with manufacturing and ending with sales to a customer. The *virtual value chain,* as shown at the bottom of Figure 2.6, traditionally has been treated as information supporting physical value-adding elements, but not as a source of value itself. For example, managers use information on inventory levels to monitor the process, but they rarely use information itself to create new value for the customer. This is no longer the case for breakthrough service companies. For example, FedEx now exploits its information database by allowing customers to track packages themselves using the company's website on the Internet. UPS and the USPS have followed suit. Now customers can locate a package in transit by entering the airbill number, and they can even identify the name of the person who signed for it when delivered. Convenient tracking of a package added customer value and initially differentiated FedEx from its competitors.

FIGURE 2.6
Exploiting the Virtual Value Chain

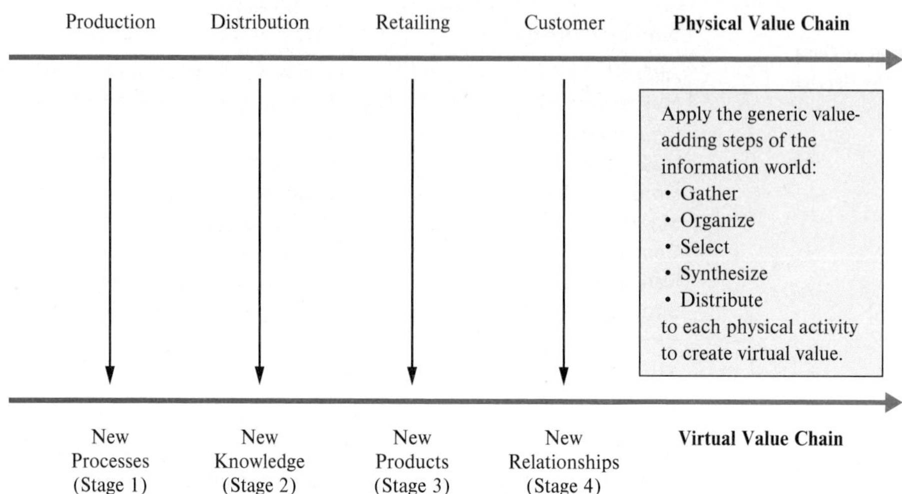

To create value with information, managers must look to the marketspace. Although the value chain of the marketspace can mirror that of the marketplace, the value-adding process first must gather raw information that is processed and finally distributed. The value-adding steps are virtual in that they are performed through and with information. Creating value in any stage of a virtual value chain involves a sequence of five activities: gathering, organizing, selecting, synthesizing, and distributing information.

The United Services Automobile Association (USAA), which provides financial services to military personnel and their families, has become a world-class competitor by exploiting the virtual value chain. USAA moved from the marketplace to marketspace in a four-stage evolution.

First Stage (New Processes)

The first stage involves seeing the physical operations more effectively with information. USAA became a "paperless operation," as it moved from a manual paper-based filing system to one based on a central computerized database with access via desktop terminals.

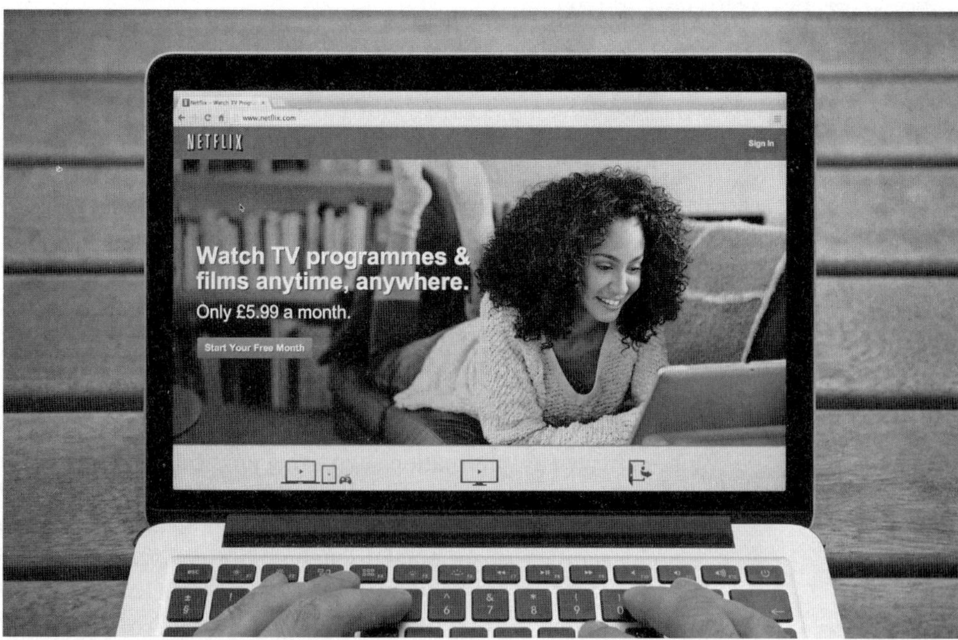

Collecting feedback on movies viewed allows for targeted recommendations.

Second Stage (New Knowledge)

In the second stage, virtual alternatives substitute for physical activities. At USAA, information systems were installed to automate the core business of insurance sales and underwriting. In the process, USAA captured significant amounts of information about customers who are members of the association. Unlike a typical insurance company, USAA has no traveling sales force and all of its business is conducted by telephone, mail, or Internet. All member-contact employees are trained to evaluate members' needs and provide appropriate products and services. Consequently, USAA has been able to build a database on its members who are accustomed to doing business with relatively little human interaction.

Third Stage (New Products)

In this stage, member information is analyzed to discover new product needs and methods to deliver value. As the database accumulated, USAA prepared member risk profiles and customized policies. Analyzing the flow of information harvested along the virtual value chain, in particular the aging of its members, USAA instituted products targeted to members' evolving needs, such as property and casualty insurance, banking products and services, life and health insurance, mutual funds, and retirement communities. The "event-oriented service" anticipates individual member needs such as a teenage child requiring auto insurance. Today, members can manage their financial portfolios using the USAA website.

Fourth Stage (New Relationships)

In the final stage, opportunities for customer collaboration in the co-creation of value are explored. Retired and active duty members of USAA need financial planning. In response, USAA created web-based investment planning tools and frequent online interactive seminars dealing with current financial issues.

Economics of Scalability

Scalability is the ability of a firm to improve contribution margins (Revenue – Variable costs) as its sales volume increases. Infinite scalability can occur *only* when the variable cost of serving an additional customer is zero. There are three sources of scalability: (1) conduct only information or data-transfer services (e.g., online encyclopedia), (2) allow customers to serve themselves (e.g., online reservations), and (3) let customers serve other customers (e.g., online auctions).

As shown in Table 2.5, the features of a service determine the extent of scalability that is possible. Note that Kbb represents Kelly Blue Book, a source for new and used car prices. InfoHub serves as a liaison between those who want "special-interest" travel and providers. BlueApron is a meal-service company that delivers to subscribers packets of meal-sized ingredients and recipes to transform those ingredients into a dinner. Amazon has taken retailing farther with its ability to facilitate business management in the cloud.

Scalability is not enough because, without differentiation, the service can lead to commoditization with only the price leader surviving. Differentiation can be accomplished by capitalizing on the "network effect." When the value for any one customer increases with the growth in total number of customers such as in online auctions (e.g., eBay), a network effect is experienced. Also, cultivating a reputation for effective human intervention can lead to a strategic advantage. Because customers often need help, a staff of responsive, effective, and empathetic call-center agents can foster customer loyalty.

Internet-enabled service is, of course, self-service delivered at home. We might be surprised at just how satisfied customers are with Internet service. In Table 2.6, the Internet services (Internet Retail, Internet Travel, and Internet Investments) are in good company

TABLE 2.5 Scalability and E-Commerce

Dimensions	High ⟵		Scalability ⟶	Low
E-commerce continuum	Selling Information (e-service)	Selling value-added service	Selling services with goods	Selling goods (e-commerce)
Information vs. goods content	Information dominates	Information with some service	Goods with support services	Goods dominate
Degree of customer content	Self-service	Call center backup	Online ordering	Call center order processing
Standardization vs. customization	Mass distribution	Some personalization	Limited customization	Fill individual orders
Shipping and handling costs	Digital asset	Mailing	Shipping	Shipping, order fulfillment, and warehousing
After-sales service	None	Answer questions	Meal credit	Returns possible
Example service	Used car prices	Online leisure travel agent	Meal ingredients and recipe	Online retailer
Example firm	Kbb.com	InfoHub.com	BlueApron.com	Amazon.com

TABLE 2.6 Customer Satisfaction Scores

Source: American Customer Satisfaction Index, University of Michigan, Ann Arbor, Michigan, http://www.theacsi.org.

Rank	Service Industry	Customer Satisfaction Scale of 0–100
1	Limited service restaurant (Chick-fil-A)	86
	Supermarkets (Wegmans)	86
2	Full service restaurants (Cracker Barrel)	83
	Internet retail (Amazon.com)	83
3	Consumer shipping (FedEx)	82
	Department stores (Nordstrom)	82
4	Hotels (Hilton)	81
	Internet travel (Priceline)	81
	Specialty stores (Costco and L Brands)	81
5	Airlines (JetBlue)	80
	Internet investment services (Vanguard)	80

with other service firms because of their reputation for exceptional service. The firms selected for inclusion in Table 2.6 are the leaders in customer satisfaction in their respective industries. Self-service has become an established and appreciated delivery mode for digital services.

Limits in the Use of Information

So far only the benefits of using information as a competitive strategy have been addressed. Some of these strategies, however, raise questions of fairness, invasion of privacy, and anticompetitiveness. Also, if these strategies were abused, the result could harm consumers.

Anticompetitive

To create entry barriers, the use of reservation systems and frequent user programs has been identified as potentially anticompetitive. For example, how should a frequent flyer's free-trip award be considered, particularly when the passenger has been traveling on business at corporate expense? The IRS is considering taxing the free trip as income in kind, and corporations believe that the free tickets belong to the company. The long-run implication, however, is the removal of price competition in air travel.

Fairness

Perhaps the easiest way to start a riot is asking airline passengers on a flight how much their tickets cost. Under yield management, ticket prices can change every hour; therefore, price is a moving target and the ticketing process a lottery. At the extreme, is yield management fair and equitable to the public, or has every service price always been negotiable? Are customers only now becoming aware of their buying power?

Invasion of Privacy

The concept of micromarketing has the potential to create the most violent backlash from consumers because of the perceived invasion of privacy. When a record of your every purchase at the local supermarket is shared with eager manufacturers, very manipulative sales practices, such as targeting buyers of a competitor's soft drink with enticements to buy an alternative, could result. Lotus Development Corporation felt the sting of consumer displeasure after announcing the availability of its MarketPlace household database to anyone with a PC and modem. Lotus received more than 30,000 requests from irate persons wanting to be removed from this database. Lotus subsequently withdrew its offer of general availability, but continued to sell access to the database to large corporations. The company was acquired by IBM in 1995.

Data Security

Allowing information to get into the hands of others for inappropriate use is a significant problem for government agencies such as the IRS; however, releasing personal medical records to insurance firms or potential employers without the consent of the patient is far more common–and damaging. Some businesses market lists of people who have filed worker compensation claims or medical malpractice suits, and such databases can be used to blackball prospective employees or patients.

Reliability

Are the data accurate? Data kept on individuals can be corrupted and create havoc in people's lives. For example, a new law ameliorates such dilemmas by requiring credit-report agencies to allow individuals to review their credit records for accuracy.

Using Information to Categorize Customers[15]

Service firms have become sophisticated in the use of information to target those customers who are worth extra pampering because of heavy purchases while ignoring others who are only casual users. The following popular techniques are used to serve customers based on their profitability to the company:

- *Coding* grades customers based on how profitable their business is. Each account is given a code with instructions for service staff on how to handle each category.
- *Routing* is used by call centers to place customers in different queues based on a customer's code. Big spenders are whisked to high-level problem solvers. Others may never speak to a live person at all.
- *Targeting* allows choice customers to have fees waived and get other hidden discounts based on the value of their business. Less valuable customers may never even know the promotions exist.
- *Sharing* corporate data about your transaction history with other firms is a source of revenue. You can be slotted before you even walk in the door, because your buying potential has already been measured.

Stages in Service Firm Competitiveness[16]

If a service firm is to remain competitive, continuous improvement in productivity and quality must be part of its strategy and corporate culture. The framework shown in Table 2.7 was developed by Chase and Hayes to describe the role of operations in the strategic development of service firms. This framework also is useful as an illustration of the many sources of productivity and quality improvement (i.e., new technology is only one source). In addition, the framework provides a way to measure and evaluate a firm's progress in the development of its service delivery system. It organizes service firms into four different stages of development according to their competitiveness in service delivery, and for each stage, the management practices and attitudes of the firm are compared across key operational dimensions.

It should be noted that services need not start at stage 1, but during their life cycle, they could revert to stage 1 out of neglect. For example, one might argue that FedEx began service as a stage 3 competitor because of its innovative hub-and-spoke network concept, whereby all sorting is accomplished at the single Memphis hub (thus guaranteeing overnight delivery).

Available for Service

Some service firms—and, often, government services in particular—fall into this category because they view operations as a necessary evil to be performed at minimum cost. There is little motivation to seek improvements in quality because the customers often have no alternatives. Workers require direct supervision because of their limited skills and the potential for poor performance that results from minimal investment in training. Investment in new technology is avoided until it is necessary for survival (e.g., consider the long-overdue adoption of Doppler radar by the Federal Aviation Administration for air traffic control). These firms are essentially noncompetitive, and they exist in this stage only until they are challenged by competition.

Journeyman

After maintaining a sheltered existence in stage 1, a service firm may face competition and, thus, may be forced to reevaluate its delivery system. Operations managers then must adopt industry practices to maintain parity with new competitors and avoid a significant loss of market share. For example, if all successful fast-food restaurants have drive-thru windows, then a new entrant might be inclined to do the same. The contribution of operations in this situation becomes competitive-neutral, because all the firms in the industry have adopted similar practices and even look like each other.

When firms do not compete on operations effectiveness, they often are creative in competing along other dimensions (e.g., breadth of product line, peripheral services, advertising). The workforce is disciplined to follow standard procedures and is not expected to take any initiative when unusual circumstances arise. These firms have not yet recognized the potential contribution of operations to a firm's competitiveness.

Distinctive Competence Achieved

Firms in stage 3 are fortunate to have senior managers with a vision of what creates value for the customer and who understand the role that operations managers must play in delivering the service. For example, Jan Carlzon, former CEO of Scandinavian Airlines (SAS), realized that recapturing the business-traveler market, which had been lost to aggressive competition, required improving on-time departure performance. To achieve this goal, he had to provide a leadership role that fostered operations innovations, like not allowing late passengers to board an aircraft even if it had not yet departed the gate.

Operations managers are the typical advocates of continuous improvement (Six Sigma) in their firms and take the lead in instituting service guarantees, worker empowerment, and service-enhancing technologies. Workers in these organizations often are cross-trained and encouraged to take the initiative when necessary to achieve operational goals that are

TABLE 2.7 Four Stages of Service Firm Competitiveness

Reprinted from "Operations' Role in Service Firm Competitiveness," by R. B. Chase and R. H. Hayes, *Sloan Management Review* 33, no. 1 (Fall 1991), p. 17 by permission of publisher.

	1. Available for Service	2. Journeyman	3. Distinctive Competence Achieved	4. World-Class Service Delivery
Reputation	Customers patronize service firms for reasons other than performance.	Customers neither seek out nor avoid the firm.	Customers seek out the firm on the basis of its sustained reputation for meeting customer expectations.	The company's name is synonymous with service excellence. Its service doesn't just satisfy customers; it *delights* them and thereby expands customer expectations to levels its competitors are unable to fulfill.
Operations	Operations is reactive, at best.	Operations functions in a mediocre, uninspired fashion.	Operations continually excels, reinforced by personnel management and systems that support an intense customer focus.	Operations is a quick learner and fast innovator; it masters every step of the service delivery process and provides capabilities that are superior to competitors.
Service quality	Is subsidiary to cost, highly variable.	Meets some customer expectations; consistent on one or two key dimensions.	Exceeds customer expectations; consistent on multiple dimensions.	Raises customer expectations and seeks challenges; improves continuously.
Back office	Counting room.	Contributes to service, plays an important role in the total service, is given attention, but still is a separate role.	Is equally valued with front office; plays integral role.	Is proactive, develops its own capabilities, and generates opportunities.
Customer	Unspecified, to be satisfied at minimum cost.	A market segment whose basic needs are understood.	A collection of individuals whose variation in needs is understood.	A source of stimulation, ideas, and opportunities.
Introduction of new technology	When necessary for survival under duress.	When justified by cost savings.	When promises to enhance service.	Source of first-mover advantages, creating ability to do things your competitors can't do.
Workforce	Negative constraint.	Efficient resource; disciplined; follows procedures.	Permitted to select among alternative procedures.	Innovative; creates procedures.
First-line management	Controls workers.	Controls the process.	Listens to customers; coaches and facilitates workers.	Is listened to by top management as a source of new ideas. Mentors workers to enhance their career growth.

Service Benchmark

OUTSIDE THE BOX

You might think Herb Kelleher, founder and former CEO of Southwest Airlines, had all the answers. His company is the most successful airline in the United States by almost every measure: profitable, on-time departures, fewer bags lost, most passenger miles flown, and high customer satisfaction.

Southwest Airlines didn't obtain this lofty position, however, simply by having board meetings and brainstorming sessions within the privacy of its own walls. Company planners also went "outside the box." For example, to improve the turnaround time of flights, they went to the races—the Indianapolis 500 in particular. Instead of watching the race, however, they watched the pit crews fuel and service the competing cars. Their observations gave them insights into equipment, handling parts, and teamwork that translated into better on-time service. These were insights that could not be gained just by observing the operations of other airlines. Oftentimes, the race is won in the pits.

stated clearly (e.g., overnight delivery for FedEx). Legend has it that a FedEx employee, knowing that a downed communication tower would disrupt operations, hired a helicopter and flew to the top of a snow-packed Colorado mountain to make repairs.

World-Class Service Delivery

Not satisfied with just meeting customer expectations, world-class firms expand on these expectations to levels that competitors find difficult to meet. Management is proactive in promoting higher standards of performance and identifying new business opportunities by listening to customers. World-class service firms such as Disney and Marriott define the quality standards by which others are judged.

New technology no longer is viewed only as a means to reduce costs; it is considered to be a competitive advantage that is not easily duplicated. For example, FedEx developed COSMOS (*C*ustomer *O*perations *S*ervice *M*aster *O*n-line *S*ystem) to provide a system that tracks packages from pickup to delivery. Customers, using the Internet and the FedEx website, can receive information on the exact location of their packages. This system also can be used to tell a driver en route to make customer pickups.

Working at a world-class firm is considered to be something special, and employees are encouraged to identify with the firm and its mission. For example, a Disney trash collector is considered to be a "cast member" who helps visitors to enjoy the experience.

Sustaining superior performance throughout the delivery system is a major challenge. Duplicating the service at multiple sites, however, and in particular overseas, is the true test of a world-class competitor.

Summary

We first looked at the strategic service vision and answered a number of questions before implementing the service. Our discussion then turned to the economic nature of competition in the service sector. The fragmented nature of service industries populated with many small- to medium-sized firms suggests a rich environment for the budding entrepreneur.

The three generic competitive strategies of overall cost leadership, differentiation, and focus were used to outline examples of creative service strategies. Because of the transferability of concepts among service firms, strategies that are successful in one industry may find application in firms seeking a competitive advantage in another service industry.

Next, we looked at several dimensions of service competition and examined the concepts of service winners, qualifiers, and losers as competitive criteria.

The strategic role of information in service strategies is organized into four categories: creation of barriers to entry, revenue generation, database asset, and productivity enhancement. Information-based competitive strategies were illustrated for each category.

The concept of a virtual value chain provides a view of service innovation that creates value by using information gathered while serving customers. The discussion of the limits in the use of information suggests that service managers always must be sensitive to the perceptions of their actions by the public they serve.

The chapter concluded with a discussion of the stages in a service firm's competitiveness based on operational dimensions.

Key Terms and Definitions

Data envelopment analysis a linear programming technique that measures the performance of service units to determine an efficiency frontier for internal benchmarking. *pg. 42*

Differentiation a competitive strategy that creates a service that is perceived as being unique. *pg. 31*

Expert system a computer program that can make inferences using a knowledge base and decision rules. *pg. 40*

Five forces model an analysis of an industry structure that considers competitive rivalry, new entrants, substitutes, and bargaining power of suppliers and customers. *pg. 28*

Focus a competitive strategy built around the concept of serving a particular target market very well by addressing the customers' specific needs. *pg. 32*

Internet of Things (IoT) internetworking of physical devices with electronic actuators controlled through the Internet. *pg. 42*

Overall cost leadership a competitive strategy based on efficient operations, cost control, and innovative technology. *pg. 30*

Qualifiers criteria used by a customer to create a subset of service firms meeting minimum performance requirements. *pg. 35*

Service losers criteria representing failure to deliver a service at or above the expected level, resulting in a dissatisfied customer who is lost forever. *pg. 36*

Service winners criteria used by a customer to make the final purchase decision among competitors that have been previously qualified. *pg. 36*

Strategic service vision formulated by addressing questions about the target market, service concept, operating strategy, and delivery system. *pg. 28*

Sustainability the long-term viability of a service firm. *pg. 36*

Switching cost inconvenience cost for the customer to switch to another provider. *pg. 39*

SWOT analysis assesses a firm's strengths, weaknesses, opportunities, and threats. *pg. 34*

Triple bottom line an evaluation of a firm on social, economic, and environmental criteria. *pg. 36*

Virtual value chain stages in the customer relationship where information is gathered, organized, selected, synthesized, and distributed to create a virtual delivery platform. *pg. 45*

Yield management an information system that attempts to maximize revenue for services with time-perishable capacity (e.g., airlines, hotels). *pg. 40*

Topics for Discussion

1. Give examples of service firms that use both the strategy of focus and differentiation and the strategy of focus and overall cost leadership.
2. What ethical issues are associated with micromarketing?
3. For each of the three generic strategies (i.e., cost leadership, differentiation, and focus), which of the four competitive uses of information is most powerful?
4. Give an example of a firm that began as world-class and has remained in that category.
5. Could firms in the "world-class service delivery" stage of competitiveness be described as "learning organizations"?
6. Compare and contrast the sustainability efforts in service operations and manufacturing.
7. Conduct a triple bottom line evaluation for a hospital by identifying its social, economic, and environmental attributes that enhance the sustainability movement.

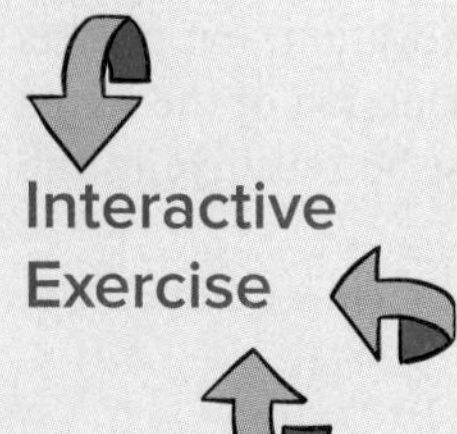

The class divides and debates the proposition "Frequent flyer award programs are anticompetitive."

United Commercial Bank and El Banco[17] CASE 2.1

This telling of the story of two special banks originally was prepared by students in 2007 who were engaged by the notion of two banks that had developed separate strategies for serving two niche markets. As you first read the students' story, ask yourself, what could have gone wrong with each bank? Also, as you read, keep a list of the factors that you see (with the advantage of hindsight) that might have contributed to the present status of these two banks. You will learn how the story played out at the end of the case.

THE STUDENTS' STORY

As the United States grows more diverse, tailoring service offerings to the needs and preferences of specific ethnic groups becomes more important. In fact, the nation's largest retail bank, Bank of America, was founded as the Bank of Italy by A.P. Gianini shortly after San Francisco's 1906 earthquake in order to serve the Italian American community.

Today, two of the most creative service offerings in banking that target ethnic communities are located in the United States. United Commercial Bank is the largest bank serving San Francisco's Asian American community and focuses on business and real estate lending within this famously entrepreneurial group. More recently, El Banco de Nuestra Comunidad has designed a unique retail banking operation for the burgeoning Latino community in Atlanta. Both of these communities are characterized by rapid growth, unique product needs, and a cultural identity separate from that of the general banking market.

SERVING THE CHINESE COMMUNITY: UNITED COMMERCIAL BANK

United Commercial Bank (UCB), a San Francisco-based bank that focuses on the Chinese American community, has $6.32 billion in assets and a market capitalization of approximately $1.4 billion. This bank has 46 branches in California, representative offices in Taiwan and China, and a branch in Hong Kong. Competitors serving the Asian market include East West Bancorp, Nara Bancorp, Hanmi Bancorp, Cathay General Bancorp, and Wilshire Bancorp.

UCB was founded in 1974 as a thrift operation with a focus on time deposits as its primary product. The bank has grown to become the largest (and perhaps the best run) bank serving the Asian community, with branches mainly in San Francisco and greater Los Angeles. The mission statement reads in part:

> *All of us at UCB share your values of dedication to hard work, savings, and education. We are committed to providing highly personalized service and a wide range of consumer and commercial banking products and services to help you, your family, and your business to achieve your "American Dream"*

United Commercial focuses on loans to businesses owned by Chinese Americans and their families. Almost 90 percent of its loans are real estate loans (40 percent multifamily and 60 percent commercial). The remaining 10 percent are mainly commercial and industrial loans (i.e., normal corporate lending). The average real estate loan at UCB is about $960,000 and the average multifamily loan is $600,000.

UCB has an unusually high proportion of savings accounts and time deposits as shown in Figure 2.7 This strategy is in response to the Chinese American desire to save in banks, instead of at brokerage firms. The reliance on savings accounts and CDs places UCB above the 95th percentile among banks overall. Not surprisingly, United Commercial's interest expense stands at the 71st percentile for large banks overall.

These financial facts highlight the unique service offerings of United Commercial. In the first place, Chinese American customers primarily demand savings accounts and CDs with high rates of interest. Non-interest bearing deposit accounts are only a small fraction of UCB's assets.

This customer focus on savings accounts and CDs also places a premium on the perception of overall bank soundness and safety. United Commercial answers this by favoring a highly conservative lending strategy on the real estate loans it underwrites. For example, the average loan-to-value ratio for the bank's commercial real estate loans is 58 percent, versus around 80 percent on average for other banks.

United Commercial effectively wins the safest and best customers in the Chinese American community because it charges much lower account fees than other banks. Banks classify fee income from commercial or retail accounts as "non-interest income" and this forms a major part of the income of most banks. United Commercial collects fee income equal to 0.32 percent of assets, while the average large bank collects fees equal to 1.70 percent of assets. UCB non-interest income is accordingly in the 5th percentile for banks overall. By rarely charging fees and often refunding fees previously charged, UCB differentiates its banking services to the point where it is very successful in winning customers.

Recognizing that many Chinese American businesses are involved in importing goods from China, UCB offers a full-featured trade finance department that issues letters of credit and provides other services to facilitate import–export businesses.

FIGURE 2.7
United Commercial Bank Deposits

Deposit Analysis (As of Dec 31, 2004)	United Commercial Amount	United Commercial Percent	All Banks* Percent
Total deposits	5,222,672	100.0	100.0
Transaction accounts	133,083	2.5	14.6
Money market accounts	1,288,595	24.7	34.3
Savings accounts	946,165	18.1	15.2
Total MMA and savings	2,234,760	42.8	49.5
Time deposits under $100k	916,077	17.5	16.8
Time deposits over $100k	1,610,270	30.8	17.4
Total time deposits	2,526,347	48.4	34.2
Deposits in foreign offices	328,572	6.3	1.7

** All commercial banks with assets between $1B and $10B.*

Finally, United Commercial has a well-articulated cultural focus on South Asia. Customers opening checking or savings accounts with relatively high balances receive tea caddies or gift tea sets. The bank's website allows visitors to send an animated, Chinese New Year-themed e-card to friends. Most important of all, every customer of UCB knows that each branch employs numerous Chinese-speaking representatives with whom to conduct business.

SERVING THE LATINO MARKET: EL BANCO

El Banco de Nuestra Comunidad is an offering of Nuestra Tarjeta de Servicios, Inc., which provides financial services in a bank setting to Hispanic customers. El Banco is a franchise that existing banks can license. El Banco was launched in January of 2002 as a branch of Flag Bank in Atlanta, Georgia. The idea resulted from the partnership of an individual with a check-cashing business and a Latino banker. El Banco branches offer a range of retail financial services including bank accounts, check cashing, and mortgage lending. Currently, there are six El Banco branches in Atlanta, which implies rapid growth from the company's first branch in 2002.

El Banco's physical setting is oriented toward Hispanics. In the words of CEO Drew Edwards, "The El Banco concept is designed to appeal to Latino customers from floor to ceiling, with bright color schemes, Spanish-language newspapers, lively Latin music, comfortable sitting areas, children's play areas, snacks, telephones, e-mail stations and, of course, Spanish-speaking bank employees (many of whom don't speak English at all)." This stands in contrast to traditional retail banks that aim for a conservative, business-like atmosphere suggesting solidity and wealth. El Banco branches are storefronts in strip centers frequented by Latinos. The branches do not provide drive-thru facilities because commercial customers are not targeted. For Latinos who feel uncomfortable in a foreign land, El Banco's informal atmosphere is an attractive feature.

El Banco is focused on fee-based services. Most retail banks occasionally cash third-party checks as a courtesy, but this service is not intended as a revenue-generating service. El Banco, however, focuses on this need, which is a basic financial service desired by Hispanics whether or not they have bank accounts. Fees for check cashing start at 1.5 percent for certain types of checks (e.g., high-security payroll checks); this line of business earns one-third of El Banco's revenues. The company also earns fees on other services, such as bounced checks and low account balances. Overall, service fees account for more than 50 percent of El Banco's revenue, versus less than 30 percent for retail banks in general.

El Banco also offers home mortgage financing to undocumented individuals (illegal aliens). Very few financial service providers will finance homes for illegal aliens—Banco Popular is the only bank that offers this service for most of the country. The Latino community is predominantly lower-income, but the community nonetheless includes thousands of individuals who could purchase $100,000–$150,000 homes but for their status as undocumented aliens. El Banco addresses this market by basing mortgage applications on "Individual Taxpayer Identification Numbers" (ITINs). Consequently the rates for El Banco's ITIN mortgages range from 8.0–9.5 percent, versus an average of about 4.86 percent in Georgia according to Bankrate.com.

Finally, as a customer acquisition strategy, El Banco has chosen to mimic Western Union. One of the most trusted financial services brands among Hispanics, Western Union won deep customer loyalty by completing international funds transfers from Hispanics in the United States to relatives and friends abroad on a reliable basis. El Banco has consciously attempted to piggyback on Western Union, both by offering primarily fee-based services and by emulating its logo.

Shown in Figure 2.8, El Banco acquires customers earlier than traditional banks. Customers are first attracted to El Banco's check-cashing service, a service that is usually offered only by nonbank retailers. As these customers grow in affluence, they seek more banking services (e.g., saving accounts, credit cards, financing), and El Banco is prepared to meet these growing needs to avoid losing customers to other institutions.

FIGURE 2.8
El Banco Customer Lifetime Value Progression

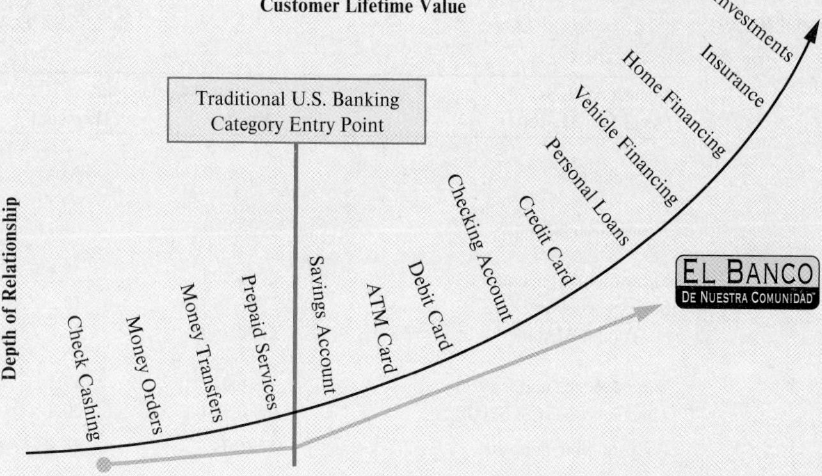

EPILOGUE

Here is the bottom line first—one of the two banks failed. Which one do you think failed and why? Your list probably includes many observations, among them the following:

- *UCB offered high interest rates and many "perks"—could these be continued, especially during the developing bank crisis of 2008–2009, and, if not, would its affluent clientele stick with the bank?*
- *El Banco serves a clientele that, mostly, is less-than-affluent and in some cases is undocumented in the United States—does this clientele have enough resources to support a bank that serves this niche market exclusively?*

In 2016, El Banco survives, perhaps by its collective fingernails, but it survives. Since its founding, El Banco has relied upon partnerships with other financial institutions for most of that span. As the student paper indicates, El Banco began its life to serve "underbanked" Hispanic clients, whose primary need at first was a check-cashing service. El Banco filled this need and developed other services for its particular population, including a cash-banking entity that, in 2007, became a separate business called CHEXAR® (name changed to Ingo Money in 2014).

The San Francisco Division of the Federal Bureau of Investigation (FBI) announced on August 11, 2011, that two executive officers of United Commercial Bank had been indicted on charges that they "conspired to hide loan losses, lied to their outside auditors, and misled regulators and the investing public."[18] They also were accused of violations by the U.S. Securities and Exchange Commission (SEC). In 2009, the two officers resigned and the FDIC merged the bank into East West Bank of Pasadena, California. Both officers pleaded not guilty in their initial court appearances and a status report on the case was scheduled for June 7, 2012, in the Northern District of California (San Francisco) of the U.S. District Court. In 2014 one of the two officers agreed to a plea deal[19] and in 2015 the other was convicted of seven felonies.[20]

Questions

1. Compare and contrast the strategic service vision of El Banco and United Commercial Bank.
2. Identify the service winners, qualifiers, and service losers for El Banco and United Commercial Bank.
3. What are the differentiating features of banks that target ethnic communities?

The Alamo Drafthouse[21] — CASE 2.2

The Alamo Drafthouse is a different kind of business, whether you call it a bar, a restaurant, or a movie theater. Is it a movie theater that serves burgers or a bar that shows movies? The Alamo combines multiple services and makes compromises on several fronts to make the combination work. Alamo customers eat and drink while watching movies. Tim, who owns and operates the business with his wife Carrie, candidly admits that the service is bad at his establishment: "Our service is pretty bad, but intentionally so. It's a compromise, because we want our service to be as minimal as possible. It's different from a restaurant, where you want the waiter to ask you if you need anything. We depend on customers to tell us."

HISTORY

Tim and Carrie met at Rice University in Houston, Texas, where he was majoring in mechanical engineering and art, and she was studying biology and French. After graduation and marriage, the two started their first movie theater in Bakersfield, California. This first venture showed art films and featured live music. Although it was not originally the main focus, the live music made a lot more money than the films. The theater was a failure—Bakersfield did not have a large enough art film audience, and the theater's location "on the wrong side of the tracks" contributed to its failure as well. Eventually the business was sold to an Evangelical church.

With this lesson under their belts, the couple moved to Austin, Texas, and decided to try again with a new approach—a theater that served food and alcohol.

Movie theaters that serve beer are very common in Europe, but much less so in the United States, which in general has more restrictive drinking laws. Nevertheless, they have been cropping up in many cities including Dallas, Washington, DC, and Portland, Oregon.

Before opening the Alamo, Tim and Carrie visited several of these theaters. The enterprising couple noticed several problems at these theaters. Some offered no in-theater service, forcing patrons who wanted drinks or food to go to the lobby. Other theaters offered too much service and waitstaff constantly asked customers if they needed anything. These interruptions bothered many customers. Tim and Carrie recognized that moviegoers wanted to see a movie first and foremost, and that good service meant that they would have to design a better system.

FACILITY LAYOUT AND DELIVERY SYSTEM

The Alamo Drafthouse opened in 1996 in downtown Austin's entertainment district. The Alamo Drafthouse is a single-screen movie theater that serves an assortment of beer and wine and offers a food menu of appetizers, hot sandwiches, individual pizzas, pasta, and dessert. Waiters take orders, serve the food, and collect the bill before and during a movie showing. Traditional movie theater snacks are also available, and patrons can choose self-service in the lobby for all offerings.

The Alamo Drafthouse, like most theaters, has rows of seats. Unlike most theaters, however, there are fewer rows so there is enough space between rows to accommodate long skinny tables where customers can place their food and drinks. Enough space also exists so that personnel can take orders and serve unobtrusively, and customers can slip out to the lobby if desired. Because of this layout, the Alamo offers about half the seating of most auditoriums of similar size and has a capacity of 215 customers.

Before each showing, waitstaff visit customers and explain to them how the Alamo's service system works. Paper, pencil, and menu are provided along the tables so customers can write their orders on the paper and place the slip of paper in a metal stand where it can be seen by waitstaff who patrol the ends of the aisles. The waiter slips in, picks up the paper, and then goes out to the kitchen to fill the order for the customer. When the order is ready, the waitperson delivers it to the customer. All of this can be done without a single word being exchanged and minimizes disruption to film viewers.

Austin is a fast-growing high-tech town with an extremely young and educated workforce. The film industry–focused Austin Film Festival, which coincides with the live music festival, South-by-Southwest, takes place primarily in downtown Austin every March during the University of Texas at Austin's spring break holiday.

The theater is located close to the center of downtown nightlife activity and requires only a short walk from one of the main club and restaurant areas. The theater does not have adjacent or free parking for customers, nor is there significant street parking in the vicinity. Most of the other movie theaters in town are located in huge megaplexes in suburbs or in shopping malls.

PROGRAMMING

The Alamo's programming is divided into two categories, second-run features and special events. Second-runs account for the majority of the Alamo's programming, about 20 of the 25 screenings per week. These movies are carefully picked to appeal to the Alamo's customer demographic: smart 25–40-year-olds who have a sophisticated taste in film. Examples of films that fall into this category are *Bowling for Columbine, The Italian Connection,* and the original *The Manchurian Candidate*. Unfortunately, the Alamo is somewhat at the mercy of Hollywood for this programming and is occasionally forced to play movies that don't appeal to its demographic as much as Tim and Carrie would like. At the end of each week Tim and Carrie pick the films that will play for the following week.

Special events are programmed in three-month blocks. These fall into two categories: Austin Film Society events (generally classics or art films) and cult films. The Film Society events usually replace a second-run showing during the week, and cult films play Thursday, Friday, and Saturday at midnight. The cult films appeal to a different (but overlapping) demographic: 18–30-year-olds, predominantly male, who are regular alcohol consumers and are customers of less mainstream, specialty-independent video rental stores such as Vulcan Video and I Luv Video. Special events account for about 5 of the Alamo's average 25 weekly screenings. Tim sees the special events as a creative outlet, for example, Italian Westerns (commonly known as "spaghetti Westerns"), which feature all-you-can-eat spaghetti, and silent films with live accompaniment by local bands.

Austin's thriving filmmaking community has been a major boon for special-events programming. Tim regularly gets filmmakers to speak at special engagements. Some guests to the theater include Robert Rodriguez, who hosted a special double feature of *El Marciachi* and a Hong Kong takeoff of that film. Quentin Tarantino, director of *Pulp Fiction,* hosts an annual festival of cult movies at the Alamo.

REVENUES AND COSTS

Tim sees the Alamo's ticket sales as a loss leader to get people into the establishment to consume food and drink, and he keeps ticket prices low, typically $4.00. This price point is below the cost of seeing a first-run film at most typical Austin theaters ($6.50–$7.00), but it is above the price of going to a bargain theater to see a second-run film ($1.00–$1.50). The average Alamo customer spends a total of $5 to $12 per showing. After the ticket is purchased, customers spend about 55 percent of this on food and 45 percent on alcohol. In order to increase spending, they have raised menu prices occasionally since opening and added more high-dollar items to the available selections. Special events account for one-third of revenues.

Although customers are spending more than they do when they go to a typical theater, the Alamo's profits are limited by its smaller capacity and high labor costs. On a typical Friday night a staff of 15 to 17 people is required, many more than are required to operate a standard theater.

ADVERTISING AND PROMOTION

To promote the Alamo, Tim and Carrie use several low-cost methods. They take advertisements out in the three most read Austin papers including the *Daily Texan,* the University of Texas student newspaper. They also create three-month calendars that list special events. Upcoming showings are announced before every feature. They have formed a close relationship with the Austin *Chronicle,* an entertainment publication, and consequently get a lot of free public relations exposure in the form of articles previewing their special events.

Tim also engages in some inexpensive but effective loyalty building. He manages the Alamo's website and answers every piece of e-mail personally. He also announces upcoming films and special events before every show and hangs around after shows to answer questions and talk to his customers. He is very open to suggestions and has used them to plan special events and to modify the menu. He notes that loyalty building has been a lot more effective with the Austin Film Society and cult film crowds.

Questions

1. Marketing analysts use market position maps to display visually the customers' perceptions of a firm in relation to its competitors regarding two attributes. Prepare a market position map for Alamo Drafthouse using "food quality" and "movie selection" as axes.
2. Use the "Strategic Service Vision" framework to describe Alamo Drafthouse in terms of target market segments, service concept, operating strategy, and service delivery system.
3. Identify the service qualifiers, winners, and service losers for Alamo Drafthouse. Are the Alamo purchase decision criteria appropriate for the multiplex movie theater market? What do you conclude?
4. Use Porter's Five Forces Model to assess the strategic position of Alamo Drafthouse in the "entertainment industry."
5. Conduct a SWOT analysis to identify internal strengths and weaknesses as well as threats and opportunities in the external environment.

Selected Bibliography

Christensen, Clayton M., et al. *Competing Against Luck: The Story of Innovation and Customer Choice.* New York: Harper Business, 2016.

Da Xu, We He, and Shancang Li. "Internet of Things in Industries: A Survey." *IEEE Transactions of Industrial Informatics* 10, no. 4 (2014), pp. 2233–43.

Diao, Y., et al. "Service Analytics for IT Service Management." *IBM Journal of Research and Development* 60, no. 2-3 (2016), pp. 1–13.

Goyal, Praveen, Zillur Rahman, and A.A. Kazmi. "Corporate Sustainability Performance and Firm Performance Research: Literature Review and Future Research Agenda." *Management Decision* 51, no. 2 (2013), pp. 361–79.

Jung, Hosang, Chi-Guhn Lee, and Chelsea C. White III. "Socially Responsible Service Operations Management: An Overview." *Annals of Operations Research* 230, no. 1 (2015), pp. 1–16.

Katzan, Harry Jr. "Cloud Software Service: Concepts, Technology, Economics." *Service Science* 1, no. 4 (Winter 2009), pp. 256–69.

Kumar, Vikas, Luciano Batista, and Roger Maull. "The Impact of Operations Performance on Customer Loyalty." *Service Science* 3, no. 2 (Summer 2011), pp. 158–71.

McEwen, Adrian, and Hakim Cassimally. *Designing The Internet of Things.* United Kingdom: John Wiley, 2014.

Rosenzweig, Eve D., Timothy M. Laseter, and Aleda V. Roth. "Through the Service Operations Strategy Looking Glass: Influence of Industrial Sector, Ownership, and Service Offerings on B2B E-Marketplace Failures." *Journal of Operations Management* 29, no.1 (January 2011), pp. 33–48.

Rowley, Jennifer. "The Wisdom Hierarchy: Representations of the DIKW Hierarchy." *Journal of Information and Communications Science* 33, no. 2 (2007), pp. 163–80.

Voss, Christopher, Aleda V. Roth, and Richard B. Chase. "Experience, Service Operations Strategy, and Services as Destinations: Foundations and Exploratory Investigation." *Production and Operations Management* 17, no. 3 (May–June 2008), pp. 247–66.

Wolfson, Adi, et al. "Better Place: A Case Study of the Reciprocal Relations between Sustainability and Service." *Service Science* 3, no. 2 (Summer 2011), pp. 172–81.

Zhang, Jie, Nitin R. Joglekar, and Rohit Verma. "Exploring Resource Efficiency Benchmarks for Environmental Sustainability in Hotels." *Cornell Hospitality Quarterly* 53, no. 3 (2012), pp. 229–41.

Endnotes

1. http://www.prnewswire.com/news-releases/hughes-network-systems-provides-kmart-with-the-broadband-direcpc-enterprise-system-to-upgrade-corporate-network-73559002.html
2. Adapted from James L. Heskett, "Positioning in Competitive Service Strategies," in *Managing in the Service Economy* (Boston: Harvard Business School Press, 1986).
3. William H. Davidow and Bro Uttal, "Service Companies: Focus or Falter," *Harvard Business Review,* July–August 1989, pp. 77–85.
4. Michael E. Porter, *Competitive Advantage: Creating and Sustaining Superior Performance* (New York: The Free Press, 1985).
5. Terry Hill, *Manufacturing Strategy* (Homewood, Ill: Irwin 1989), pp. 36–46.
6. Paul Kleindorfer, Kalyan Singhal, and Luk N. Van Wassenhove, "Sustainable Operations Management." *Production and Operations Management* 14, no. 4 (December 2005), pp. 482–92.
7. John Elkington, "Towards the Sustainable Corporation: Win-Win-Win Business Strategies for Sustainable Development." *California Management Review* 36, no. 2 (1994), pp. 90–100.
8. Darcy Hitchcock and Marsha Willard, *The Business Guide to Sustainability,* 2nd ed. (London: Earthscan, 2009).
9. Orville Schell. "How Walmart Is Changing China," *The Atlantic,* December 2011, p. 86.
10. Erica Plambeck. "The Greening of Wal-Mart's Supply Chain," *Supply Chain Management Review,* July 1, 2007, pp. 18–25.
11. Adapted from James A. Fitzsimmons. "Strategic Role of Information in Services." In Rakesh V. Sarin (ed.), *Perspectives in Operations Management: Essays in Honor of Elwood S. Buffa* (Norwell, MA: Kluwer Academic Publishers, 1993).
12. http://internetofthingsagenda.techtarget.com/definition/IoMT-Internet-of-Medical-Things, October, 2016
13. https://www.altocloud.com/blog/four_steps_using_data_analytics_in_customer_solutions, April 2014.
14. Adapted from Jeffrey F. Rayport and John J. Sviokla, "Exploiting the Virtual Value Chain," *Harvard Business Review,* November–December 1995, pp. 75–85.
15. Adapted from Diane Brady, "Why Service Stinks," *BusinessWeek,* October 23, 2000, p. 124.
16. Adapted from Richard B. Chase and Robert H. Hayes, "Operations' Role in Service Firm Competitiveness," *Sloan Management Review* 33, no. 1 (Fall 1991), pp. 15–26.
17. Prepared by Bryan R. Bradford, Will Reale, Brian Barrow, Jason Dillee, and Chris McClung under the supervision of Professor James A. Fitzsimmons.
18. Press Release, San Francisco Division, Federal Bureau of Investigation, October 11, 2011.
19. http://www.sfgate.com/business/networth/article/Ex-United-Commercial-Bank-officer-agrees-to-plea-5742713.php
20. https://www.justice.gov/opa/pr/former-united-commercial-bank-chief-sentenced-over-eight-years-felony-fraud
21. Prepared by Robert Ferrell, Greg Miller, Neil Orman, and Trent Reynolds under the supervision of Professor James A. Fitzsimmons.

Part 2

Designing the Service Enterprise

Now that the service vision and competitive strategy have been articulated, we direct our attention to issues of service design. Chapter 3, New Service Development, begins with a discussion of the new service development process. Service blueprinting is presented as a method to diagram a service process that separates the front- and back-office operations with a line of visibility. We also explore generic approaches to service design including information empowerment.

The relationship among customer, service organization, and contact personnel is depicted as a triad in Chapter 4, The Service Encounter. A service profit chain links the internal customers (employees) to satisfied and loyal external customers. The aesthetics and environment created by the facility structure itself is addressed using the servicescape framework found in Chapter 5, Supporting Facility and Process Flows. Service quality, which is measured by the gap between customer expectations and perceptions of the delivered service, is the topic of Chapter 6, Service Quality. We examine several approaches to managing service quality, including measurement issues, designing quality into the service, and service recovery when a failure occurs. Chapter 7, Process Improvement, describes the tools for continuous improvement in quality and productivity with an emphasis on Lean Service and Six Sigma approaches.

The question of location is critical for services delivered from physical facilities because the site determines the market that is served. Location models to minimize travel times or maximize revenue in the presence of competitors are presented in Chapter 8, Service Facility Location, that concludes Part 2.

Chapter 

New Service Development

Learning Objectives

After completing this chapter, you should be able to:

1. Describe the sources of service sector growth.
2. Describe the fundamental characteristics of service innovation.
3. Describe the managerial issues associated with the adoption of new technology.
4. Explain and differentiate what is meant by the divergence and the complexity of a service process.
5. Describe the sequence of stages and the enablers of the new service development process cycle.
6. Prepare a service blueprint.
7. Compare and contrast the four approaches to service system design: production-line, customer as coproducer, customer contact, and information empowerment.
8. Explain how intellectual property rights protect a service brand.

Designing a service delivery system is a creative process that begins with a service concept and strategy to provide a service with features that differentiate it from the competition. The various alternatives for achieving these objectives must be identified and analyzed before any decisions can be made. Designing a service system involves issues such as location, facility design and layout for effective customer and work flow, procedures and job definitions for service providers, measures to ensure quality, extent of customer involvement, equipment selection, and adequate service capacity. The design process never is finished; once the service becomes operational, modifications in the delivery system are introduced as conditions warrant.

Consider FedEx as an example of innovative service system design. The concept of guaranteed overnight air-freight delivery of packages and letters was the subject of a college term paper by the company's founder, Frederick W. Smith. As the story is told, the term paper received a "C" because the idea was so preposterous, but the business now defines an industry.

Air freight was slow and unreliable in those early days, an ancillary service provided by airlines that primarily were interested in passenger service. The genius of Smith, an electrical engineer, was in recognizing the analogy between freight transport and an electrical network connecting many outlets through a junction box. From this insight was born the hub-and-spoke network of FedEx, with Memphis serving as the hub and sorting center for all packages. Arriving at night from cities throughout the United States, planes unload their packages and wait approximately two hours before returning to their home cities with packages ready for delivery the next morning. Thus, in the early days of the company a package from Los Angeles destined for San Diego traveled from Los Angeles to Memphis on one plane, then from Memphis to San Diego on another. With the exception of severe weather grounding an aircraft or a sorting error, the network design guaranteed that a package reached its destination overnight. The design of the service delivery system itself, therefore, contained the strategic advantage that differentiated FedEx from the existing air-freight competitors. Today, FedEx has expanded to several hubs (e.g., Newark and Los Angeles) and uses trucks to transport packages between nearby large urban centers (e.g., Boston and New York).

Chapter Preview

We begin with a discussion of the sources of service sector growth and note the unique challenges for service innovation. We consider a model of the new service development process that defines the service product to include the elements of technology, people, and systems. Next, technology innovation in services is addressed with a discussion of the challenges of adoption and readiness to embrace new technology. Service design consists of four structural and four managerial elements, each linked to a future chapter in the text. A customer value equation is used to keep a customer-centric focus to the development process. Service process structure can be manipulated to achieve strategic positioning in the marketplace.

The service blueprint is an effective technique to describe the service delivery process in visual form. Using a line of visibility, we differentiate between the front-office and back-office operations. The front-office portion of the system is where customer contact occurs and is concerned with ambiance and effectiveness (e.g., a bank lobby). The back-office is hidden from the customer and often operates as a factory for efficiency (e.g., check-sorting operations of the bank).

Following a taxonomy for service process design, four generic approaches for viewing service system design–the production-line approach, customer as coproducer, customer contact, and information empowerment–are presented. Each approach advocates a particular philosophy, and the features of these approaches will be examined.

Sources of Service Sector Growth

Service sector growth is fueled by advances in information technology, innovation, and changing demographics that create new demands. Information technology has a substantial and indispensable impact on the growth of digital services. Figure 3.1 shows how information (digital) services have grown to the point that this "information sector" dominates the U.S. economy, contributing 53 percent to the GDP (gross domestic product). The arrows on the two axes show the direction of projected growth in the services and information components of the economy. Notice how information services (quadrant D) is growing at the expense of physical products (quadrant A).

Information Technology

The drive to miniaturize information technology devices such as the smartphone for Internet connectivity removes the need for physical proximity for service delivery and permits alternative delivery formats. Banking, for example, has become an electronic service with online access to personal accounts for activities such as transfer of funds, payment of bills, or managing personal finances. In health care, X-rays are digitized and transmitted offshore for interpretation by a radiologist. Information technology has thus affected the process of service delivery and created new service value chains with new business opportunities as creative intermediaries. Uday Karmarkar and Uday Apte make the following three propositions:[1]

- In the future, the major part of the U.S. GDP will be generated by "information chains" rather than supply chains, and most managers will be employed in information sectors.

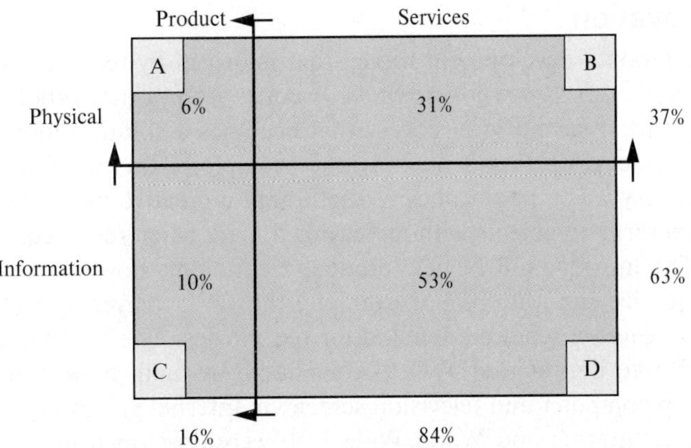

Sector	Description	Example
A	Physical products	Automotive, steel, chemicals
B	Physical services	Transportation, retailing
C	Digital products	Computers, DVDs, TVs, phones
D	Information services	Finance, telecommunications

FIGURE 3.1
Distribution of GDP in the U.S. Economy, 2007

Source: Karmarkar Uday and Uday M. Apte. "Operations Management in the Information Economy: Information Products, Processes, and Chains," *Journal of Operations Management* 25 no. 2 (January 2007), p 440.

- Management of these information chains and sectors has a great deal to do with process economics and its impact on the configuration and operation of information chains and processes.
- Technological developments underlie and drive the economics of processes and value chains.

The Internet as a Service Enabler

The Internet is the worldwide, publicly accessible network of interconnected computer networks that transmits data using the standard Internet protocol (IP). The "Net" is a "network of networks" that consists of, for example, academic (.edu), business (.com), nonprofit (.org), and government (.gov) networks, which together carry various information and services, such as electronic mail, online chat, file transfer, streaming media, Voice over Internet Protocol (VoIP), and access to the World Wide Web (www).[2]

The Internet and the World Wide Web are not synonymous: the Internet is a collection of interconnected computer networks, linked by copper wires, fiber-optic cables, and wireless connections; the web is a collection of interconnected documents and other resources, joined by hyperlinks and uniform resource locators (URLs). The web runs on top of the Internet protocol using hypertext transfer protocol (HTTP) that links and provides access to the files, documents, and other resources of the World Wide Web.

From a service provider's perspective, the Internet is an ideal vehicle for connecting with its customers in a cost-effective manner. Until recently, the only connection was via a desktop computer with Internet access using phone, cable, or satellite. The advent of modern wireless communications (smartphones and tablets) and social networking (Facebook, YouTube, LinkedIn, and Twitter) has provided a wealth of new opportunities for connecting with customers or finding new ones.

Also available is a new communications technology, General Packet Radio Service (GPRS), a packet-oriented mobile data service available to users of the 3G-to-5G cellular communications systems. As of late 2016, 6G and 7G systems are being developed. The GPRS system can deliver data directly to handsets, which are, in essence, always connected. These newer handsets (e.g., iPhones) are suitable for instant messaging (e.g., a Starbucks is just around the corner) or alerts (e.g., your flight has been delayed or your car is parked two blocks straight ahead). In the future, service firms can *push* information to customers rather than passively waiting for an inquiry. How this intrusion will be received is another matter!

Innovation

The product development model that is driven by technology and engineering could be called a *push theory of innovation.* A concept for a new product germinates in the laboratory with a scientific discovery that becomes a solution looking for a problem. The 3M experience with Post-it notes is one example of this innovation process. The laboratory discovery was a poor adhesive that found a creative use as glue for notes to be attached temporarily to objects without leaving a mark when removed.

The introduction of new product technology, however, does have an ancillary effect on service innovation. For example, the DVD player spawned a video rental business and created a renewed demand for old movies. The next innovation was the creation of Netflix to deliver the DVD to your home by mail. Now movies can be viewed on your laptop computer and television screen via Internet streaming.

The Internet and World Wide Web were developed originally as a robust network of linked computers for military and scientific file sharing. Since its humble beginning, however, the web has become the essential enabler for e-commerce and, more recently, the platform for social networks such as Facebook and LinkedIn and, of course, an ability to search the world of knowledge with Google.

For services, the cash management account introduced by Merrill Lynch is an example of the *pull theory of innovation.* During a period of high interest rates in the 1980s, a need arose to finance short-term corporate cash flows because individual investors were interested in obtaining an interest rate that was higher than those currently available on passbook bank deposits.

Unexpected events can generate innovative services. The Arab Spring uprising in Egypt in early 2011 left many travelers "trapped" in that country far beyond their scheduled departure dates. Such civil unrest around the globe has created a niche for some insurance businesses to provide their clients with "security evacuation" from dangerous situations, which can include areas of natural disasters, also.

A new service concept often originates with an observant contact employee who identifies an unmet customer need. For example, a hotel might institute an airport shuttle service because a concierge noticed a high demand for taxi service.

Service innovation also can arise from exploiting information available from other activities. For example, records of sales by auto parts stores can be used to identify frequent failure areas in particular models of cars. This information has value both for the manufacturer, who can accomplish engineering changes, and for the retailer, who can diagnose customer problems. In addition, the creative use of information can be a source of new services or it can add value to existing services. For example, an annual summary statement of transactions furnished by one's financial institution adds value at income tax time.

Service innovators face a difficult problem in testing their service ideas. The process of product development includes building a laboratory prototype for testing before full-scale production is initiated. One example of an effort in this direction is provided by Burger King, which acquired a warehouse in Miami to enclose a replica of its standard outlet. This mock restaurant was used to simulate changes in layout that would be required for the introduction of new features such as drive-through window service and a breakfast menu.

Changing Demographics

The French Revolution provides an interesting historical example of how a social change resulted in a new service industry. Before the revolution, only two restaurants were in existence in Paris; shortly afterward, there were more than 500. The dispossessed nobility had been forced to give up their private chefs, who found that opening their own restaurants was a logical solution to their unemployment.

A major influence on future service needs is the aging of the U.S. population. As the baby boom generation in the United States enters retirement, demand for health care and financial services will increase. People are living longer and placing increased demand on health care services to maintain active lifestyles. The replacement of pension plans with defined contribution plans [401(k) plans] creates a demand for investment counseling and financial management services. Finally, the new time available for leisure activities will be reflected in demand for airline travel, ocean cruises, restaurants, and hotel rooms.

Innovation in Services

The National Science Foundation has defined research and development into three categories:

- *Basic research* is research directed toward increases in the knowledge or understanding of fundamental aspects of phenomena and of observable facts without specific application toward process or products. This type of research is limited to the federal, university, and nonprofit sectors.
- *Applied research* is research directed toward gaining knowledge that will meet a specific need. This includes research for specific commercial objectives.
- *Development* is the systematic use of knowledge directed toward the production of a product, service, or method. This includes the design and development of prototypes and processes. However, it excludes quality control, routine product testing, and production.[3]

Based on the NSF's definitions, service innovation is the output of applied research and development efforts that have one or more of the following goals:

- Pursue a planned search for new knowledge, regardless of whether or not the search has reference to a specific application.
- Apply existing knowledge to problems involved in creating a new service or process, including work to evaluate feasibility.
- Apply existing knowledge to problems related to improving a current service or process.

The nonmanufacturing share of total industry R&D was about 31 percent for the United States in 2013 according to a report by the National Science Foundation.[4] This seemingly large percentage for service firms is partially explained by the increased use of outsourcing. For example, pharmaceutical companies use service companies to conduct testing for drug development and most manufacturing companies outsource software development to information service providers.

Many of the fundamental characteristics of the innovation process differ between products and services. The unique challenges for service innovation include:[5]

- *Ability to protect intellectual and property technologies:* The transparency of service systems makes imitation simpler, and patents are difficult to obtain.
- *Incremental nature of innovation:* Because customers participate in service systems, innovation tends to be evolutionary rather than radical to allow for acceptance.
- *Degree of integration required:* Service innovation requires interactions among people, products, and technology and thus requires systems integration.
- *Ability to build prototypes or conduct tests in a controlled environment:* Services, with the exception of the Burger King example, cannot be tested realistically in an isolated laboratory, so they run the risk of failure or poor performance upon launch.

Innovation is viewed both as the process of creating something new and also as the actual product or outcome. For services the outcome need not be a new service product but rather some degree of modification to an existing service. Table 3.1 presents a classification of service innovations within two major categories. Radical innovations are offerings not previously available to customers or new delivery systems for existing services (e.g., the Barnes & Noble website). Incremental innovations are changes to existing services that are valued as improvements (e.g., the addition of playscapes at fast-food restaurants).

Innovation is a destroyer of tradition; thus, careful planning is required to ensure success. By necessity, the productivity benefits of new technology will change the nature

TABLE 3.1 Levels of Service Innovation

Source: Reprinted with permission from S. P. Johnson, L. J. Menor, A. V. Roth, and R. B. Chase, "A Critical Evaluation of the New Service Development Process," in J. A. Fitzsimmons and M. J. Fitzsimmons (eds.), *New Service Development* (Thousand Oaks, Calif.: Sage, 2000), p. 4.

New Service Category	Descriptions	Examples
	Radical Innovations	
Major innovation	New services for markets as yet undefined. These innovations are usually driven by information- and computer-based technologies.	Wells Fargo Internet banking launched in May 1995.
Start-up business	New services in a market that already is served by existing services.	Mondex USA, a subsidiary of MasterCard International, that designs and distributes smart cards for retail transactions.
New services for the market presently served	New service offerings to existing customers of an organization (although the services might be available from other companies).	Freestanding bank branches or kiosks in supermarkets or other retail establishments (e.g., Wells Fargo kiosks in Starbucks coffee shops).
	Incremental Innovations	
Service line extensions	Augmentations of the existing service line such as adding new menu items, new routes, and new courses.	Singapore Airlines' first-class airport check-in in an exclusive lounge.
Service improvements	Changes in features of services that currently are offered.	Delta Airlines' use of ATM-like kiosks to issue boarding passes to passengers.
Style changes	The most common of all "new services," these are modest forms of visible changes that have an impact on customer perceptions, emotions, and attitudes. Style changes do not change the service fundamentally, only its appearance.	Funeral homes, such as Calvary Mortuary in Los Angeles, now offer abbreviated ceremonies that celebrate life instead of mourn death, full-service flower shops, and facilities with more pastels, brighter walls, and more windows and lights.

of work. Any introduction of new technology should include employee familiarization to prepare workers for new tasks and to provide input into the technology interface design (e.g., will typing skill be required, or will employees just point and click?). For services, the impact of new technology might not be limited to the back office. A change in the role that customers play in the service delivery process could be required. Customer reaction to the new technology–determined through focus groups or interviews–also provides input into the design to avoid future problems of acceptance (e.g., consider the need for surveillance cameras at automated teller machines). Speculate on the impact of blockchains (an emerging disruptive technology), as described in Example 3.1, on the delivery of services in the digital age.

Example 3.1 Blockchains[6]

Blockchain is the technical innovation and foundation underlying the digital currency Bitcoin, where it serves as the public ledger for all transactions or *blocks*. An analogy is the double-entry accounting system, where at least two accounting entries (a credit and a debit) are required to record each financial transaction. To insure integrity, total debits must equal total credits for each transition.

Consider the process of buying a house, a complex transaction involving banks, attorneys, title companies, insurers, surveyors, appraisers, and building inspectors. They all maintain separate records, and it's costly to verify and record each step resulting in the average closing taking about two months time. Blockchain offers a trusted, immutable digital ledger, visible to all participants, that shows every transaction.

A blockchain is a secure globally distributed ledger running on millions of individual computer devices (with no central computer to hack) and open to anyone with access to the Internet. Each transaction is linked to another in an ever-growing chain. Each data record or *block* contains a timestamp and a link to a previous block. The ledger contains not just financial data but anything of value (e.g., titles, deeds, music, or art) and can be moved and stored securely and privately. With a blockchain, peer-to-peer trust is established, not by powerful intermediaries like banks or governments (both of which have been hacked) but through mass collaboration, clever code, and the extreme difficulty, if not impossibility, of tampering with a block. Blockchains ensure integrity and trust between strangers because an individual block cannot be altered without altering each successive block in the chain, which can go on indefinitely.

Blockchain technology has gone beyond digital currency and now is finding its way into all transactions of value. For example, smart contracts (software programs that self-execute complex transactions) on a blockchain will reduce the costs of contracting, enforcing contracts, and making payments. Autonomous agents (bundles of smart contracts) on a blockchain hold the promise of eliminating agency and coordinating costs, and perhaps even lead to highly distributed enterprises with little or no management.

The application of blockchain has not been lost on the financial services industry. For example, Bank of America/Merrill Lynch has partnered with Microsoft to create a platform for more efficient trade transactions.[7] Settlement times for traditional stock trades can take a week or more to complete and leave behind a vulnerable trail.

The schematic of a three transaction blockchain shown in Figure 3.2 will be used to simplify the technical aspects of blockchains. Each transaction (block) includes the *hash* (cryptographic function) of the prior block in the blockchain, linking the two. The links in turn form a chain. A cryptographic hash function is a mathematical algorithm that maps data of arbitrary size to a bit-string of a fixed size, which is designed to be a one-way function (i.e., a function that is infeasible to invert). Every block contains a hash of the previous block. This has the effect of creating a chain of blocks from the genesis block to the current block. Each block is guaranteed to come after the previous block chronologically because the previous block's hash would not be known otherwise. Each block is also computationally impractical to modify once it has been in the chain for a while because every block after it would also have to be regenerated.

Each owner of the transaction creates a pair of cryptographic keys: *public keys* that may be disseminated widely and *private keys* that are known only to the owner. This arrangement (similar to the 2-key system to access a safety deposit box) supports two functions: (1) using a public key to authenticate that a message originated with a holder of the paired private key and (2) encrypting a message with a public key to ensure that only the holder of the paired private key can decrypt it. In a public-key encryption system, any person can encrypt a message using the public key of the receiver, but such a message can be decrypted only with the receiver's private key. For this to work it must be computationally easy for a user to generate a public and private key-pair to be used for encryption and decryption. The strength of a private/public-key cryptography system relies on the degree of difficulty (computational impracticality) for a properly generated private key to be determined from its corresponding public key. Security then depends only on keeping the private key private, and the public key may be published without compromising security. The owner signs any transaction using an electronic signature function.

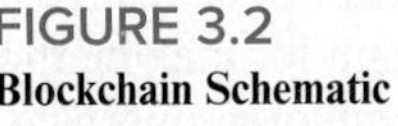

FIGURE 3.2
Blockchain Schematic

Source: Satoshi Nakamoto, Bitcoin: "A Peer-to-Peer Electronic Cash System," posted on the internet November 2008, p.2. https://ihb.io/2015-08-11/news/word-cloud-the-original-satoshi-nakamoto-bitcoin-white-paper-5638

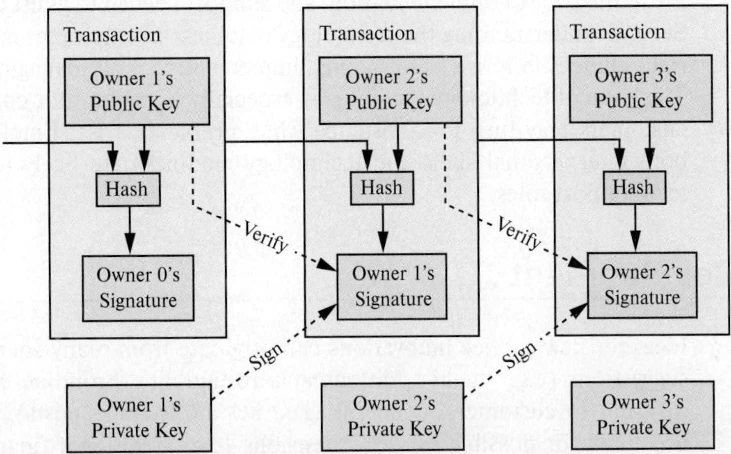

Challenges of Adopting New Technology in Services

For services, "the process is the product" because customers participate directly in the service delivery. Therefore, the success of technological innovations, particularly for the front office, depends on customer acceptance. The impact on customers is not always limited to a loss of personal attention. Customers also might need to learn new skills (e.g., how to operate an automatic teller machine or pump gasoline), or they might have to forgo some benefit (e.g., loss of float through the use of electronic funds transfer). The contribution of customers as active participants or coproducers in the service process must be considered when making changes in the service delivery system.

As internal customers, employees also are affected by new technology and often need retraining. The example of scanning in retail stores was minor compared with the adoption of word processing by secretaries, who were used to typewriters.

Back-office innovation that does not affect the customer directly might raise complications of a different sort. For example, consider the use of magnetic ink character recognition (MICR) equipment in banking. This technological innovation did not affect the customer at all; instead, it made the "hidden" check-clearing process more productive. The full benefits, however, could not be realized until all banks agreed to imprint their checks using a universal character code. Without such an agreement, the checks of uncooperative banks would need to be sorted by hand, which would limit the effectiveness of this technology severely. When all banks in the United States finally agreed on the use of the same MICR imprints on checks, the check-clearing process became much more efficient. Bank of America took a leadership role in gaining acceptance for the concept, but the self-interest of banks was a principal motivation. The volume of check processing had exceeded their manual sorting capacity.

The incentive to innovate in services is hampered, however, because many ideas cannot be patented. The prospective rewards for innovations are diminished because many innovations can be imitated freely and implemented quickly by the competition.

Readiness to Embrace New Technology[8]

Technology readiness refers to a person's propensity to embrace and use new technologies for accomplishing goals in his or her life at home or at work. Research on people's reactions to technology identified eight technology-related paradoxes: control/chaos, freedom/enslavement, new/obsolete, competence/incompetence, efficiency/inefficiency, fulfills/creates needs, assimilation/isolation, and engaging/disengaging. These paradoxes imply that technology can trigger both positive and negative feelings. For example, the paradox of competence/incompetence can facilitate feelings of intelligence and efficacy or lead to feelings of ignorance and ineptitude.

Managers face challenges when introducing new technology. First, what is the overall level of readiness of the customer base affected by the new technology-based service? Once this level of readiness is assessed, the extent and appropriate technology to implement, the pace of implementation, and support needed to assist customers will be realized. Second, understanding the technology readiness of employees is important for making the right choices in terms of designing, implementing, and managing the employee interface. The issue of technology readiness is especially important for contact employees to whom customers may turn for assistance when problems arise. Employees who rate highly on both interpersonal skills and technology readiness are likely to be good candidates for tech-support roles.

New Service Development

Ideas for new service innovations can originate from many sources. Customers can offer suggestions (e.g., menu additions at a restaurant). Frontline employees can be trained to listen to customers' concerns (i.e., act as listening posts). Customer databases can be mined for possible service extensions (e.g., additional financial services). Trends in

FIGURE 3.3 **The NSD Process Cycle**

Source: S. P. Johnson, L. J. Menor, A. V. Roth, and R. B. Chase, "A Critical Evaluation of the New Service Development Process," in J. A. Fitzsimmons and M. J. Fitzsimmons (eds.), *New Service Development* (Thousand Oaks, Calif.: Sage, 2000), p. 18.

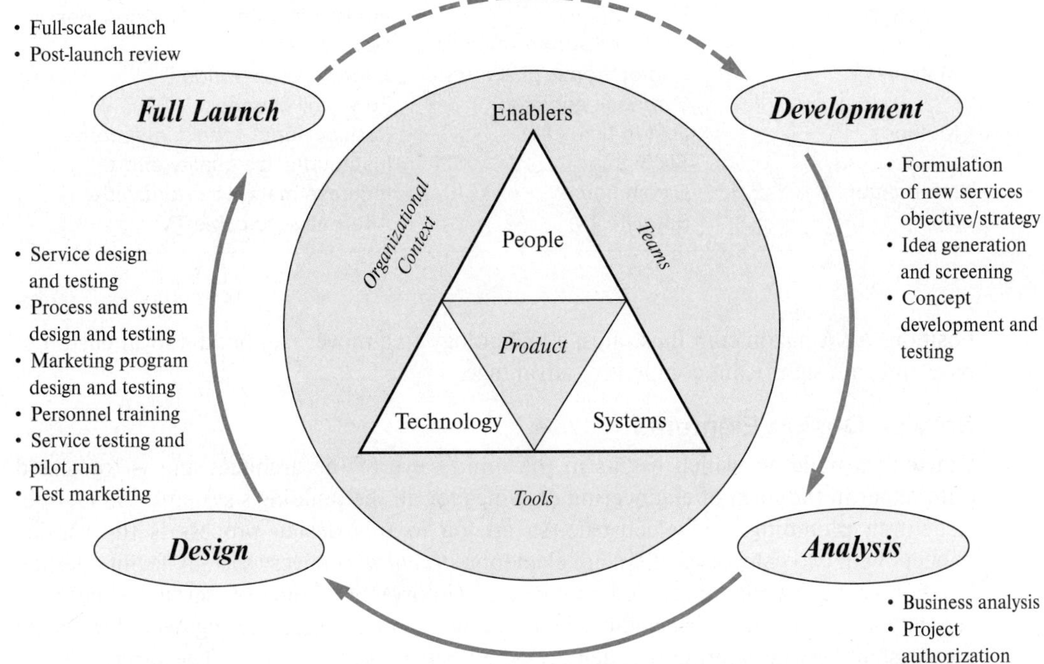

customer demographics can suggest new services (e.g., long-term health care) and new advances in technology. These ideas form the input to the "development" stage of the new service development (NSD) cycle shown in Figure 3.3.

In the development stage of a new service, new ideas are screened, and winning concepts are developed and tested for feasibility. Concepts that pass the development hurdle are then considered in the "analysis" stage to determine their potential as part of a profitable business venture. After project authorization, successful concepts move to the "design" phase. Considerable time and money are expended in design to create a new service product and process that can be field tested with appropriate personnel training and a marketing campaign in a given city or region. Finally, a proven new service is given a "full launch" that could be available nationwide or worldwide.

The NSD process is driven by enablers: teams that are cross-functional, tools such as spreadsheets, and an organization context that includes a culture of accepting innovation.

In the center of Figure 3.3 is the service product consisting of people, systems, and technology. The *people* component consists of both employees and customers. Employees must be recruited, trained, and empowered (e.g., computer access to books in print at Barnes & Noble) to deliver service excellence embodied in the product. The role of customers needs to be defined with appropriate motivation to foster the desired behavior (e.g., use of self-serve check-in at the Hyatt Regency hotel).

Notice in both cases the need for *systems* to accomplish the required tasks. Some systems (e.g., patient records system for a health clinic) are found in the back office to assist customer-facing employees in service delivery. Online hotel booking is an example of a front-office system because it interfaces directly with the customer.

Technological advances often are the basis for service innovation. Table 3.2 presents examples and industry impact of technology-driven service innovations from various sources (i.e., power/energy, physical design, materials, methods, and information). Thus, a service firm must include technology monitoring as an activity to protect its competitive

TABLE 3.2
Technology-Driven Service Innovation

Source of Technology	Service Example	Service Industry Impact
Power/energy	Jet aircraft	International flight is feasible
	Nuclear energy	Reduced dependence on fossil fuel
Facility design	Hotel atrium	Feeling of grandeur/spaciousness
	Enclosed sports stadium	Year-round use
Materials	Photochromic glass	Energy conservation
	Synthetic engine oil	Fewer oil changes
Methods	Just-in-time (JIT)	Reduce supply-chain inventories
	Six Sigma	Institutionalize quality effort
Information	E-commerce	Increase market to worldwide
	Satellite TV	Alternative to cable TV

position. As Amazon.com illustrates, a technology first-mover can build a loyal customer base and gain significant competitive advantage.

Service Design Elements

Consider a building, which begins in the mind's eye of the architect and is translated onto paper in the form of engineering drawings for all the building's systems: foundation, structural, plumbing, and electrical. An analog to this design process is the service concept with two categories of system elements: *structural* (delivery system, facility design, location, capacity planning) and *managerial* (information, quality, service encounter, capacity and demand management). These design elements must be engineered to create a consistent service offering that achieves the strategic service vision. The service design elements become a template that communicates to customers and employees alike what service they should expect to give and to receive.

A successful hospital located in Toronto, Canada, that performs only inguinal hernia operations will be used to illustrate how each element of the service concept contributes to the strategic mission. Shouldice Hospital is privately owned and uses a special operating procedure to correct inguinal hernias that has resulted in an excellent reputation because its recurrence rate is low.

The structural elements of Shouldice's service concept that support its strategy to target customers suffering only from inguinal hernias are:

- *Delivery system.* A hallmark of the Shouldice approach is patient coproduction in all aspects of the process. For example, patients shave themselves before the operation and walk from the operating table to the recovery area.
- *Facility design.* The facility is intentionally designed to encourage exercise and rapid recovery within four days, providing a return-to-normal-activity time that is approximately one-half the time at traditional hospitals. Hospital rooms are devoid of amenities, such as telephones or TVs, and patients must walk to lounges, showers, and the cafeteria. The extensive hospital grounds are landscaped to encourage strolling, and the interior is carpeted and decorated to avoid any typical hospital "associations."
- *Location.* Being located in a large metropolitan community with excellent air service gives Shouldice access to a worldwide market. The large local population also provides a source of patients who can be scheduled on short notice to fill any canceled bookings.
- *Capacity planning.* Because hernia operations are elective procedures, patients can be scheduled in batches to fill the operating time available; thus, capacity is utilized to its maximum. This ease in scheduling operations allows Shouldice to operate like a fully occupied hotel; thus, the supporting activities, such as housekeeping and food service, also can be employed fully.

The managerial elements of the Shouldice service concept also support the strategy of delivering a quality medical procedure:

- *Information.* A unique feature of the Shouldice service is the annual alumni reunion, which represents a continuing relationship of the hospital with its patients. Keeping information on patients allows Shouldice to build a loyal customer base that is an effective word-of-mouth advertising medium. Providing free annual check-ups also allows Shouldice to build a unique database on its procedure.
- *Quality.* The most important quality feature is the adherence of all physicians to the Shouldice method of hernia repair, which results in the low recurrence rate of inguinal hernias among these patients. In addition, patients with difficulties are referred back to the doctor who performed the procedure. Perceived quality is enhanced by the Shouldice experience, which is more like a short holiday than a typical hospital stay.
- *Service encounter.* A service culture that fosters a family-type atmosphere is reinforced by communal dining for both staff and patients. All employees are trained to encourage patient activity, which promotes rapid recovery. Patients who have had surgery that morning are encouraged to discuss during dinner their experience with patients who are scheduled for surgery the next day and, thus, alleviate preoperative fears.
- *Managing capacity and demand.* Patients are screened by means of a mail-in questionnaire and are admitted by reservation only. Thus, the patient demand in terms of timing and appropriateness can be controlled effectively. Walk-in patients or local residents on a waiting list are used to fill vacancies created by canceled reservations; thus, full use of hospital capacity is ensured.

Strategic Positioning through Process Structure

In a service process, the number and intricacy of the steps represent the *degree of complexity* of the service delivery structure. For example, preparation of a take-out order at a fast-food restaurant is less complex than preparation of a gourmet dinner at a fine French restaurant. The amount of discretion or freedom that the server has to customize the service is the *degree of divergence* that is allowed at each service process step. For example, the activities of an attorney, as contrasted with those of a paralegal, are highly divergent, because interaction with the client requires judgment, discretion, and situational adaptation.

Firms like H&R Block have sought high-volume, middle-class taxpayers by creating a *low-divergence* tax service for those seeking help in preparing standard tax returns. With low divergence, the service can be provided with narrowly skilled employees performing routine tasks, and the result is consistent quality at reduced cost.

A hair-styling salon for men represents a *high-divergence* strategy reshaping the traditional barbering industry. High divergence is characterized as a niche strategy that seeks out customers who are willing to pay extra for the personalization.

Narrowing the scope of a service by specializing is a focused strategy that results in *low complexity.* Retailing recently has seen an explosion of specialty shops selling only one product, such as ice cream, cookies, or coffee. For such a strategy to succeed, the service or product must be perceived as being unique or of very high quality.

To gain greater market penetration or maximize the revenue from each customer, a strategy of adding more services can be initiated, thereby creating a structure with *high complexity.* For example, supermarkets have evolved into superstores through the addition of banking services, pharmacies, flower shops, books, video rentals, and food preparation.

Repositioning need not be limited to changes in only one dimension of the process structure (i.e., level of divergence or complexity). For a family restaurant seeking a strategy combining changes in levels of both complexity and divergence, consider Table 3.3.

TABLE 3.3 Structural Alternatives for Family Restaurant

Source: Reprinted with permission of the American Marketing Association: G. Lynn Shostack, "Service Positioning through Structural Change," *Journal of Marketing* 51, January 1987, p. 41.

Lower Complexity/Divergence	Current Process	Higher Complexity/Divergence
No reservations	Take reservations	Specific table selection
Self-seating; menu on blackboard	Seat guests; give menus	Recite menu; describe entrées and specials
Self-serve water	Serve water and bread	Assortment of hot breads and hors d'oeuvres
Customer fills out form	Take orders	At table; taken personally by maitre d'
Pre-prepared; no choice	Salad bar	Salad (4 choices)
Limit entrée to 4 choices	Entrée (6 choices)	Expand to 10 choices; add flaming dishes; bone fish at table
Sundae bar; self-service	Dessert (6 choices)	Expand to 12 choices
Coffee, tea, milk only	Beverage (6 choices)	Add exotic coffees, wine list, liqueurs
Serve salad and entrée together; bill and beverage together	Serve orders	Separate-course service; sorbet between courses; hand-grind pepper
Cash only; pay when leaving	Cash or credit card	Choice of payment, including house accounts; serve mints

Service Blueprinting[9]

Developing a new service based on the subjective ideas contained in the service concept can lead to costly trial-and-error efforts to translate the concept into reality. For example, when a building is developed, the design is captured on architectural drawings called *blueprints,* because the reproduction is printed on special paper, creating blue lines. These blueprints show what the building should look like and all of the specifications needed for its construction. Likewise, a service delivery system can be captured in a similar manner with a focus on the customer process flow showing the interactions among staff and support services. As an example, consider attending a San Francisco Giants baseball game. To attend a Giants game driving from north of San Francisco, one has the option of parking at Larkspur and riding the Golden Gate Ferry directly across the bay to the AT&T Park on the San Francisco waterfront. We begin by developing the sequence of events experienced by the customer.

Example 3.2 Attending a San Francisco Giants Game

All *service blueprints* begin with a template as shown in Figure 3.4. The top line describes the "Physical Evidence" that customers will see (e.g., signage) and experience (e.g., smooth sailing). The second line "Customer Actions" is filled-in *first* because this is the customer process flow that drives the blueprint from beginning to end of the service experience. Arrows are omitted between the activities to save space but the actions follow left to right in a single sequence to create columns to be acted upon from below.

A dashed *line of interaction* between the Customer Actions and Onstage Contact Person shows the points of customer-facing activity (e.g., food vendor). A dotted *line of visibility* beyond which a customer cannot see is shown in the middle of the blueprint separating "Onstage Contact Person" (e.g., ticket collector) from "Backstage Contact Person" (e.g., grounds keeper). A final dashed *line of internal interaction* separates the activity above from the "Support Processes" (e.g., website).

Figure 3.5 shows the completed blueprint for the experience of attending a San Francisco Giants game. When building the blueprint, one proceeds from the top line down the template. When the Customer Actions and Physical Evidence are completed, we then insert Onstage Contact Person activities that are in full view of the customer. Vertical flow lines cross the "line of interaction" as two-way arrows depicting direct contact between the customer and the organization's staff (e.g., take food order). Next we proceed to activities below the "line of visibility" to show activities by Backstage Contact Persons out of sight of the customer

FIGURE 3.4 **Blueprint of San Francisco Giants Game (Template and First Stage)**

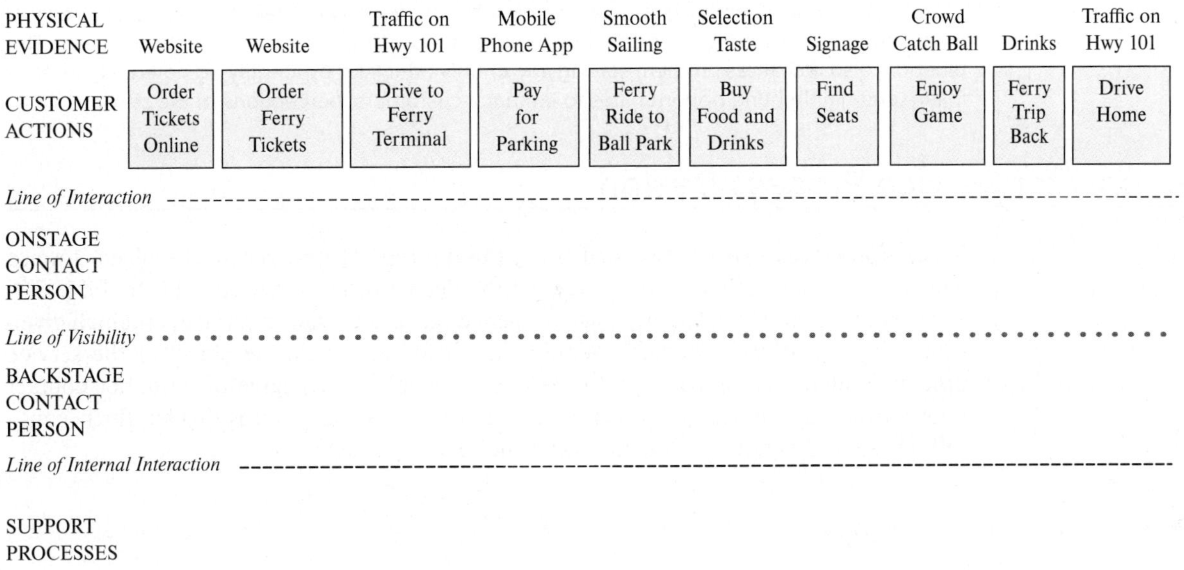

PHYSICAL EVIDENCE	Website	Website	Traffic on Hwy 101	Mobile Phone App	Smooth Sailing	Selection Taste	Signage	Crowd Catch Ball	Drinks	Traffic on Hwy 101
CUSTOMER ACTIONS	Order Tickets Online	Order Ferry Tickets	Drive to Ferry Terminal	Pay for Parking	Ferry Ride to Ball Park	Buy Food and Drinks	Find Seats	Enjoy Game	Ferry Trip Back	Drive Home
Line of Interaction										
ONSTAGE CONTACT PERSON										
Line of Visibility										
BACKSTAGE CONTACT PERSON										
Line of Internal Interaction										
SUPPORT PROCESSES										

FIGURE 3.5 **Blueprint of San Francisco Giants Game (Final Product)**

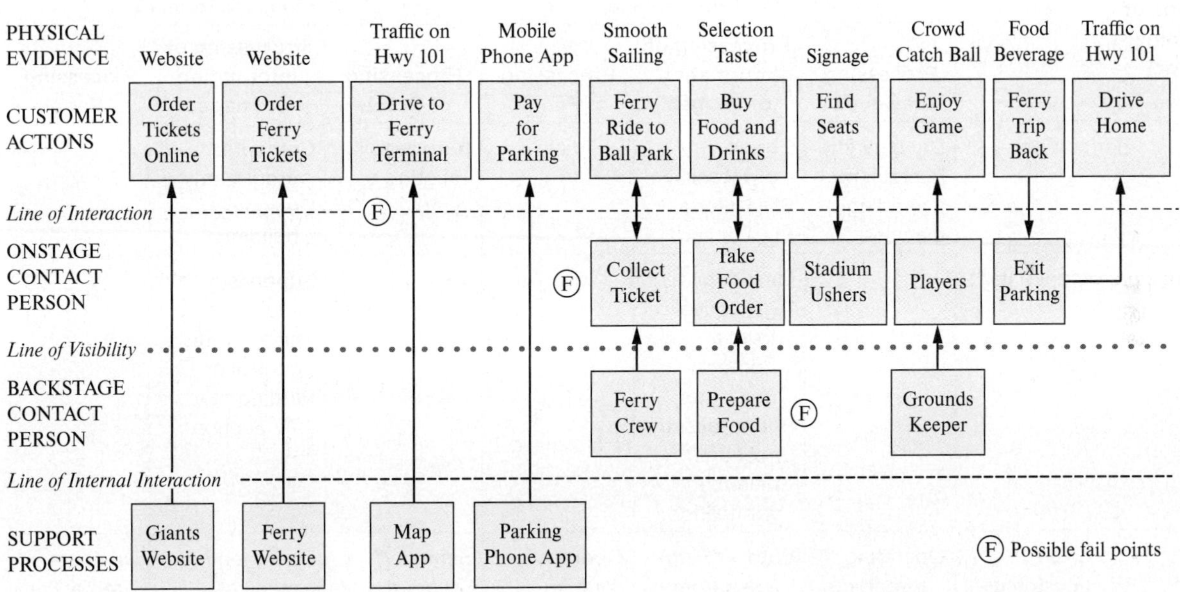

(e.g., food preparation) with arrows to appropriate activities higher up in the blueprint. Activities below the "line of internal interaction" consist of Support Processes (e.g., parking phone-app). Finally a "possible fail point" is shown next to an activity where problems could occur (e.g., ferry departure missed—bummer).

The service blueprint is a useful management tool to assess the service process and suggest possible improvements in the customer experience. Beginning with Physical Evidence, one might ask if the evidence is consistent with customer's expectations (e.g., is the website easy to navigate?). Are there Customer Actions that could be eliminated (e.g., combine ticket and ferry sales on the same website) or made self-service (e.g., exit from parking). For Onstage Contact Persons, are different interpersonal skills required of the ticket collector, food dispenser, and players? Questions for Backstage Contact Persons concern appropriate staffing to avoid unnecessary delays onstage. Fail points draw attention to the need for preemptive planning for the unexpected.

In summary, a blueprint is a precise definition of the service delivery system that allows management to test the service concept on paper before any final commitments are made. The blueprint also facilitates problem solving and creative thinking by identifying potential points of failure and highlighting opportunities to enhance customers' perceptions of the service.

Taxonomy for Service Process Design

Service processes can be classified using the concept of divergence, the object toward which the service activity is directed, and the degree of customer contact. In Table 3.4, services are broadly divided into low divergence (i.e., standardized service) and high divergence (i.e., customized service). Within these two categories, the object of the service process is identified as goods, information, or people. The degree of customer contact ranges from no contact to indirect contact to direct contact (and is divided further into self-service and personal interaction with the service worker).

TABLE 3.4 Taxonomy of Service Processes

Source: Reprinted with permission from Urban Wemmerlov, "A Taxonomy for Service Process and Its Implications for System Design," *International Journal of Service Industry Management* 1, no. 3 (1990), p. 29.

Degree of Customer Contact		Low Divergence (Standardized Service)			High Divergence (CustomizedService)		
		Processing of Goods	Processing of Information or Images	Processing of People	Processing of Goods	Processing of Information or Images	Processing of People
No customer contact		Dry cleaning Restocking a vending machine	Check processing Billing for a credit card		Auto repair Tailoring a suit	Computer programming Designing a building	
Indirect customer contact			Ordering groceries from a home computer Phone-based account balance verification			Supervision of a landing by an air-traffic controller Bidding at a TV auction	
Direct customer contact	No customer-service worker interaction (self-service)	Operating a vending machine Assembling premade furniture	Withdrawing cash from an automatic bank teller Taking pictures in a photo booth	Operating an elevator Riding an escalator	Sampling food at a buffet dinner Bagging of groceries	Documenting medical history at a clinic Searching for information in a library	Driving a rental car Using a health club facility
	Customer-service worker interaction	Food-serving in a restaurant Car washing	Giving a lecture Handling routine bank transactions	Providing public transportation Providing mass vaccination	Home carpet cleaning Landscaping service	Portrait painting Counseling	Haircutting Performing a surgical operation

Degree of Divergence

A standardized service (i.e., low divergence) is designed for high volume with a narrowly defined and focused service. The tasks are routine and require a workforce with relatively low levels of technical skills. Because of the repetitive nature of the service, opportunities to substitute automation for labor abound (e.g., use of vending machines, automatic car wash). Reducing the discretion of service workers is one approach to achieving consistent service quality, but one that also has possible negative consequences. These concepts will be referred to later as the *production-line approach* to service design.

For customized services (i.e., high divergence), more flexibility and judgment are required to perform the service tasks. In addition, more information is exchanged between the customer and the service worker. These characteristics of customized services require high levels of technical and analytic skills, because the service process is not programmed and not well defined (e.g., counseling, landscaping). To achieve customer satisfaction, decision making is delegated to service workers who can perform their tasks with some autonomy and discretion (i.e., the workers are empowered).

Object of the Service Process

When goods are processed, a distinction must be made between goods that belong to the customer and goods that are provided by the service firm (i.e., *facilitating goods*). For services such as dry cleaning or auto repair, the service is performed on the property of the customer; in this case, the property must be secured from damage or loss. Other services such as restaurants supply facilitating goods as a significant part of the service package. Therefore, appropriate stock levels and the quality of these facilitating goods become a concern, as illustrated by McDonald's attention to the purchase of food items.

Processing information (i.e., receiving, handling, and manipulating data) occurs in all service systems. In some cases, this is a back-office activity, such as check processing at a bank. For other services, the information is communicated indirectly by electronic means, as with telephone-based account balance verification. Customer service representatives in call centers might spend hours performing routine tasks in front of a video screen, and motivation becomes a challenge. There are services such as counseling, however, in which information is processed through direct interactions between the client and the project team. For highly skilled employees in these services, the challenge of dealing with unstructured problems is important to job satisfaction.

Processing people involves physical changes (e.g., a haircut or a surgical operation) or geographic changes (e.g., a bus ride or a car rental). Because of the "high-touch" nature of these services, workers must possess interpersonal as well as technical skills. Attention also must be paid to service facility design and location, because the customer is physically present in the system.

Type of Customer Contact

Customer contact with the service delivery system can occur in three basic ways. First, the customer can be present in the system physically and interact directly with the service providers in the creation of the service. In this instance, the customer has full sensory awareness of the service surroundings. Second, the contact may be indirect and occur via the Internet from the customer's home or office. Third, some service activities can be performed with no customer contact at all. Banking provides an example where all three options occur: making an application for an automobile loan requires an interview with a loan officer, payment on the loan can be accomplished by electronic funds transfer, and the financial record keeping for the loan is conducted in a back office of the bank.

Direct customer contact is subdivided into two categories: no interaction with service workers (i.e., self-service) and customer interaction with service workers. Self-service often is particularly attractive because customers provide the necessary labor at the appropriate time. Many cost-effective applications of technology in services, such as boarding-pass kiosks and automatic teller machines, rely on a market segment of customers who are willing to learn how to interact with machines. When customers desire direct interaction

Fast-food restaurants want customers to see the cleanliness of the kitchen.
©Dynamic Graphics Group/Creatas/Alamy

with service providers, all of the issues addressed earlier concerning the processing of people (i.e., training in interpersonal skills and facility issues of location, layout, and design) become important to ensure a successful service experience. When customers are in the service process physically, additional management problems arise (e.g., managing queues to avoid creating a negative image).

Service processes with indirect customer contact or with no customer contact need not be constrained by issues that arise from the physical presence of the customer in the system. Because the customer is decoupled from the service delivery system, a more manufacturing type of approach can be taken. Decisions regarding site location, facility design, work scheduling, and training of employees all can be driven by efficiency considerations. In fact, the no-customer-contact and goods-processing combination creates categories that normally are thought of as manufacturing. For example, dry cleaning is a *batch process,* and auto repair is a *job shop.*

This taxonomy of service processes presents a way to organize the various types of processes that are encountered in service systems and helps us to understand the design and management of services. This taxonomy also serves as a strategic positioning map for service processes and, thus, as an aid in the design or redesign of service systems.

Generic Approaches to Service System Design

In Chapter 1, we defined the service package as a bundle of attributes that a customer experiences. This bundle consists of five features: supporting facility, facilitating goods, information, explicit services, and implicit services. With a well-designed service system, these features are coordinated harmoniously in light of the desired service package. Consequently, the definition of the service package is key to designing the service system itself. This design can be approached in several ways.

Routine services can be delivered through a *production-line approach.* With this approach, services are provided in a controlled environment to ensure consistent quality and efficiency of operation. Another approach is to encourage active customer participation in the process. Allowing the customer to take an active role in the service process can result in many benefits to both the consumer and the provider. An intermediate approach divides the service into high and low-customer-contact operations. This allows the low-contact operations to be designed as a technical core that is isolated from the customer. Advances in information technology have driven the *information empowerment approach.*

We note that combinations of these approaches also can be used. For example, banks isolate their check-processing operation, use self-serve automated tellers, and provide personalized loan service.

Production-Line Approach

We tend to see service as something personal—it is performed by individuals directly for other individuals. This humanistic perception can be overly constraining, however, and therefore can impede development of an innovative service system design. For example, we sometimes might benefit from a more technocratic service delivery system. Manufacturing systems are designed with control of the process in mind. The output often is machine-paced, and jobs are designed with explicit tasks to be performed. Special tools and machines are supplied to increase worker productivity. A service taking this production-line approach could gain a competitive advantage with a cost leadership strategy.

McDonald's provides the quintessential example of this manufacturing-in-the-field approach to service. Raw materials (e.g., hamburger patties) are measured and prepackaged off-site, leaving the employees with no discretion as to size, quality, or consistency. In addition, storage facilities are designed expressly for the predetermined mix of products. No extra space is available for foods and beverages that are not called for in the service.

The production of french fries illustrates attention to design detail. The fries come precut, partially cooked, and frozen. The fryer is sized to cook a correct quantity of fries. This is an amount that will be not so large as to create an inventory of soggy fries or so small as to require making new batches very frequently. The fryer is emptied into a wide, flat tray near the service counter. This setup prevents fries from an overfilled bag from dropping to the floor, which would result in wasted food and an unclean environment. A special wide-mouthed scoop with a funnel in the handle is used to ensure a consistent measure of french fries. The thoughtful design ensures that employees never soil their hands or the fries, that the floor remains clean, and that the quantity is controlled. Further, a generous-looking portion of fries is delivered to the customer by a speedy, efficient, and cheerful employee.

This entire system is engineered from beginning to end, from prepackaged hamburgers to highly visible trash cans that encourage customers to clear their table. Every detail is accounted for through careful planning and design. The production-line approach to service system design attempts to translate a successful manufacturing concept into the service sector, and several features contribute to its success.

Limited Discretionary Action of Personnel

A worker on an automobile assembly line is given well-defined tasks to perform along with the tools to accomplish them. Employees with discretion and latitude might produce a more personalized car, but uniformity from one car to the next would be lost. Standardization and quality (defined as consistency in meeting specifications) are the hallmarks of a production line. For standardized routine services, consistency in service performance is valued by customers. For example, specialized services like muffler replacement and pest control are advertised as having the same high-quality service at any franchised outlet. Thus, the customer can expect identical service at any location of a particular franchise operation (e.g., one Big Mac is as desirable as another), just as one product from a manufacturer is indistinguishable from another. If more personalized service is desired, however, the concept of employee empowerment becomes appropriate. The idea of giving employees more freedom to make decisions and to assume responsibility is discussed in Chapter 4, The Service Encounter.

Division of Labor

The production-line approach suggests that the total job be broken down into groups of simple tasks. Task grouping permits the specialization of labor skills (e.g., not everyone at McDonald's needs to be a cook). Further, the division of labor allows one to pay only for the skill that is required to perform the task. Of course, this raises the criticism of many service jobs as being minimum-wage, dead-end, and low-skill employment. Consider, for example, a concept in health care where patients are processed through a fixed sequence of medical tests, which are part of the diagnostic work-up. Tests are performed by medical technicians using sophisticated equipment. Because the entire process is divided into routine tasks, the examination can be accomplished without an expensive physician.

Substitution of Technology for People

The systematic substitution of equipment for people has been the source of progress in manufacturing. This approach also can be used in services, as seen by the acceptance of automated teller machines in lieu of bank tellers. A great deal can be accomplished by means of the "soft" technology of systems, however. Consider, for example, the use of mirrors placed in an airplane galley. This benign device provides a reminder and an opportunity for flight attendants to maintain a pleasant appearance in an unobtrusive manner. Another example is the greeting card display that has a built-in inventory replenishment and reordering feature; when the stock gets low, a colored card appears to signal a reorder. Using a laptop computer, insurance agents can personalize their recommendations and illustrate the accumulation of cash values.

Service Standardization

The limited menu at McDonald's guarantees a fast hamburger. Limiting service options creates opportunities for predictability and preplanning; the service becomes a routine process with well-defined tasks and an orderly flow of customers. Standardization also helps to provide uniformity in service quality, because the process is easier to control. Franchise services take advantage of standardization to build national organizations and thus overcome the problem of demand being limited only to the immediate region around a service location.

Customer as Coproducer

For most service systems, the customer is present when the service is being performed. Instead of being a passive bystander, the customer represents productive labor just at the moment it is needed, and opportunities exist for increasing productivity by shifting some of the service activities onto the customer (i.e., making the customer a *coproducer*). Further, customer participation can increase the degree of customization. For example, Pizza Hut's lunch buffet permits customers to make their own salads and select pizza-by-the-slice while the cooks work continuously at restocking only the pizzas that are selling rather than at filling individual orders. Thus, involving the customer in the service process can support a competitive strategy of cost leadership with some customization if it is focused on customers who are interested in serving themselves.

Depending on the degree of customer involvement, a spectrum of service delivery systems, from self-service to complete dependence on a service provider, is possible. For example, consider the services of a real estate agent. A homeowner has the option of selling the home personally or staying away from any personal involvement by engaging a real estate agent for a significant commission. An intermediate alternative is the "Gallery of Homes" approach. For a fixed fee that is significantly lower than the conventional 6 percent commission for a full-service realtor, the homeowner lists the home with the Gallery. Home buyers visiting the Gallery are interviewed concerning their needs and are shown pictures and descriptions of homes that might be of interest. Appointments for visits with homeowners are made, and an itinerary is developed. The buyers provide their own transportation, the homeowners show their own homes, and the Gallery agent conducts the final closing and arranges financing as usual. Productivity gains are achieved by a division of labor. The real estate agent concentrates on duties requiring special training and expertise, while the homeowner and the buyer share the remaining activities.

The following features illustrate some of the contributions that customers can make in the delivery of services.

Self-Service

The substitution of customer labor for personalized service is the highest level of coproduction. For example, Alaska Airlines turned to self-service technology in response to competition from the encroachment of low-cost provider Southwest Airlines into its Pacific coast network. Alaska is credited as the first airline to introduce automatic check-in kiosks and to sell e-tickets over the Internet.

The modern customer has become a coproducer, receiving benefits for his or her labor in the form of convenience. Interestingly, a segment of the customer population actually appreciates the control aspects of self-service. For example, the popularity of salad bars is a result of allowing the customer to individualize his or her salad in terms of quantity and items selected. Finally, coproduction addresses the problem of matching supply with demand in services, because the customer brings the extra service capacity at the time when it is needed.

Smoothing Service Demand

Service capacity is a time-perishable commodity. For example, in a medical setting, it is more appropriate to measure capacity in terms of physician-hours rather than in terms of the number of doctors on staff. This approach emphasizes the permanent loss to the service provider of capacity whenever the server is idle through lack of customer demand. The nature of demand for a service, however, is one of pronounced variation by the hour of the day (e.g., restaurants), the day of the week (e.g., theaters), or the season of the year (e.g., ski resorts). If variations in demand can be smoothed, the required service capacity will be reduced, and fuller, more uniform utilization of capacity can be realized. The result is improved service productivity.

To implement a demand-smoothing strategy, customers act as passive coproducers, adjusting the timing of their demand to match the availability of the service. Typical means of accomplishing this are appointments and reservations; in compensation, customers expect to avoid waiting for the service. Customers also might be induced to acquire the service during off-peak hours by price incentives (e.g., midweek discounts on lift tickets at ski resorts).

If attempts to smooth demand fail, high utilization of capacity still can be accomplished by requiring customers to wait for service. Thus, customer waiting contributes to productivity by permitting greater utilization of capacity. Perhaps a sign such as the following should be posted in waiting areas: "Your waiting allows us to offer bargain prices!"

The customer might need to be "trained" to assume a new, and perhaps more independent, role as an active participant in the service process. This educational role for the provider is a new concept in services. Traditionally, the service provider has kept the consumer ignorant and, thus, dependent on the server.

Customer-Generated Content

The Internet has opened a new opportunity for customer coproduction–the actual generation of content used by others. For example, consider the online encyclopedia, Wikipedia.com that draws on a virtual community for its content. The website is self-monitoring as individuals add and critique material to produce a far richer presentation of material than is found in a traditional published encyclopedia for which each entry is only *one* person's view. Another example is Craigslist.com, a successful business model that competes directly with newspaper want-ads by offering an online platform for customers to post photos and descriptions of items for sale in their local communities at no cost.

Customer Contact Approach

The manufacture of products is conducted in a controlled environment. The process design is totally focused on creating a continuous and efficient conversion of inputs into products without consumer involvement. Using inventory, the production process is decoupled from variations in customer demand and, thus, can be scheduled to operate at full capacity.

How can service managers design their operations to achieve the efficiencies of manufacturing when customers participate in the process? One approach is to separate the service delivery system into high- and low-contact customer operations. The low-contact, or back-office, operation is run as a plant, where all of the production management concepts and automation technology are brought to bear. This separation of activities can result in a customer perception of personalized service while in fact achieving economies of scale through volume processing.

The success of this approach depends on the required amount of customer contact in the creation of the service, and on the ability to isolate a technical core of low-contact operations. In our taxonomy of service processes, this approach to service design would seem to be most appropriate for the processing-of-goods category (e.g., dry cleaning, where the service is performed on the customer's belongings).

Degree of Customer Contact

Customer contact refers to the physical presence of the customer in the system. The degree of customer contact can be measured by the percentage of time that the customer is in the system relative to the total service time. In high-contact services, the customer determines the timing of demand and the nature of the service by direct participation in the process. The perceived quality of service is measured to a large extent by the customer's experience. Customers have no direct influence on the production process of low-contact systems, however, because they are not present. Even if a service falls into the high-contact category, it still might be possible to seal off some operations to be run as a factory. For example, the maintenance operations of a public transportation system and the laundry of a hospital are plants within a service system.

Separation of High- and Low-Contact Operations

When service systems are separated into high- and low-contact operations, each area can be designed separately to achieve improved performance. Obviously, high-contact operations require employees with excellent interpersonal skills. The service tasks and activity levels in these operations are uncertain, because customers dictate the timing of demand and, to some extent, the service itself. However, low-contact operations can be separated physically from customer contact operations, although there is some need for communication across the line of visibility to track progress of customer orders or property (e.g., shoes dropped off at a kiosk for repair at a distant factory). The advantage of separation occurs because these back-office operations can be scheduled like a factory to obtain high utilization of capacity.

Airlines have used this approach effectively in their operations. Flight attendants wear uniforms designed in Paris and attend training sessions on the proper way to serve passengers. Baggage handlers seldom are seen, and aircraft maintenance is performed at a distant depot and run like a factory.

Sales Opportunity and Service Delivery Options

The service design matrix shown in Figure 3.6 shows the trade-off between operations efficiency and sales opportunity. Sales opportunity is a measure of the probability of add-on sales and, thus, of increasing the revenue that is generated from each customer contact. The implications are most dramatic at the extremes. Face-to-face customized services require highly trained employees, but the opportunity to develop loyal customer relationships is great (e.g., financial planners). A website, however, can reach many potential customers at low cost, but the opportunity for a sale is limited to the patience of the customer and the quality of the website. Even self-serve checkout using electronic scanning technology has been found to reduce the incidence of impulse sales.

We should not conclude that only one service delivery option must be selected. To avoid omitting certain market segments, multiple channels of service should be considered. For example, retail banks use all of the delivery options in Figure 3.6.

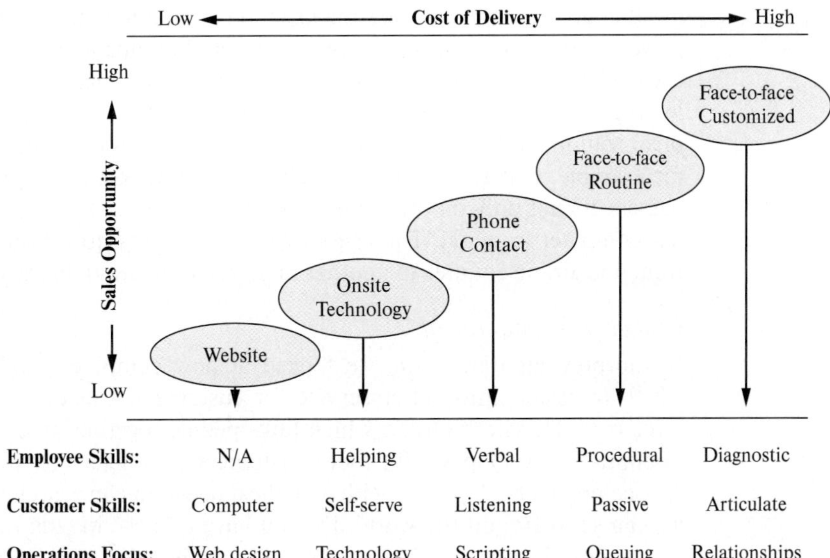

FIGURE 3.6
Sales Opportunity and Service Design

Source: Adapted from R. B. Chase and N. J. Aquilano, "A Matrix for Linking Marketing and Production Variables in Service System Design," *Production and Operations Management,* 6th ed., Richard D. Irwin, Inc., Homewood, IL, 1992, p. 123.

Information Empowerment

Forget the "Age of Aquarius"–this is the age of information, and like it or not, we all are a part of it. Information technology (IT) is no longer just for computer "nerds." IT touches all of us every day, even those who grew up with rattles and a fist full of marbles instead of electronic communication devices. The breakfast cereal on your table represents more than puffs, flakes, or shreds of grain. You can safely assume that three funny-looking little guys named Snap, Crackle, and Pop are not actually responsible for processing and packaging your rice, nor does a little sprite cavort around putting two scoops of raisins in each box of Raisin Bran. IT can be seen all the way from the rice paddy or wheat field, where it helps to manage the planting, propagating, harvesting, and transportation of the grain, to the processing and packaging facility, to your market, and even to your table (e.g., those traffic lights you passed between market and home are operated by information-based technology). Essential services such as fire and police protection demand the use of IT, and the electricity and running water in our homes are brought to us by IT. In fact, IT is such a fundamental part of daily life throughout the entire world that the challenge is to find some aspect not touched by it.

Certainly, no service today could survive without use of IT, and successful managers see that IT offers much more than simply a convenient way to maintain records. Indeed, one of its most important functions is to empower both employees and customers.

Employee Empowerment

The earliest use of IT was in record keeping. A business might have had a computerized database of customer names and addresses, and perhaps another database of the names and addresses for suppliers of essential goods and services. These various databases made it a little easier to keep the shareholders–and the IRS–happy. They made record keeping a little faster and a little more accurate, but secretaries still just entered data, procurement clerks just ordered supplies or services, frontline service people smiled a lot, and production-floor workers still went about their routine duties. Top management held the task of juggling these diverse activities.

The development of *relational databases,* however, changed everything. Relational, or integrated, databases meant that information from all aspects of an operation could be used by anybody. A service worker could call for necessary supplies from inventory and even initiate an order for replacement inventory without having to go through the procurement office. The day of the empowered employee had arrived.

Of course, computers were the key to maintaining these databases. The machines were powerful tools for keeping track of names and numbers, but when they began "talking to each other," another revolution was in store. Now employees of one organization could interact with each other across functional boundaries, and even with those in other organizations in "real time" and without the need to be together physically. This means, for example, that when a Delta flight is canceled, a Delta agent can book the stranded passengers not only on other Delta flights but also on those of other carriers from his or her computer terminal. The agent or the passengers no longer have to scurry frantically from one airline counter to another in search of an available seat.

Customer Empowerment

In the previous discussion, we looked at how computers and IT empower employees, which translates into better service for customers. Customers, too, can be empowered directly by IT. The Internet, which links people together around the entire world, is one example of a very powerful tool. Customers no longer are dependent entirely on local service providers. A person with a medical question can search the world for answers, and we can shop around the world. Do you have a "sick" Mazda that defies the best of local mechanics? Just get on the Internet and ask the folks at http://www.mx6.com/forums to suggest solutions.

IT provides customers with other ways of taking an active part in the service process. For example, we can go to FedEx's home page, enter the tracking number of a package sent through FedEx, and find out exactly where the package is at that moment. If it has been delivered, we can find out who signed for it. We also can make our own travel reservations online and get information about our destination, which can enhance our trip immeasurably.

Our daily lives surely will be affected more and more by IT, and the impact will be measured in days and weeks rather than in years. Right now, customers in many supermarkets can speed up their checkout time by weighing and labeling their own produce. In some cases, the customer takes a sticky, bar-coded label from a dispenser over the cucumbers, and the integrated scale/checkout register automatically weighs the produce, reads the bar code, and prices the purchase. In other cases, the customer places lemons on a scale in the produce department. A sign over the lemons gives an item number, which the buyer enters on a number pad on the scale, and the scale spits out a sticky label with the total cost. Some scales are extremely user-friendly and have labeled buttons for different items so that the customer does not have to remember the code number from the item's bin to the scale. Now, many of us engage in a "total" shopping experience. In addition to weighing and pricing our own produce, we scan all of our supermarket purchases ourselves, scan our credit card, and bag our groceries, too. (Some may think that's carrying customer empowerment too far!)

Intellectual Property

New service development often results in innovations that need protection from competitors copying the creation. Without this protection the benefits of creativity will not be realized by the inventor. *Intellectual property rights* are exclusive rights over creations of the mind such as inventions, literary and artistic works, symbols, names, images, and designs used in commerce. These rights allow the owners of intellectual property to reap monopoly profits for a period of time as an incentive for the creative activity and recover costs associated with research and development.

Intellectual property is divided into categories: (1) industrial properties are inventions (e.g., artificial heart) for commercial purpose and protected by patents granted for a certain period of time to prevent others from using the invention without license; (2) a trademark (e.g., McDonald's golden arches) is a distinctive sign that is used to prevent

Service Benchmark

TEN THINGS GOOGLE HAS FOUND TO BE TRUE

1. **Focus on the user and all else will follow.**
   Any change must benefit the user.
2. **It's best to do one thing really, really well.**
   Focus on your competence and practice continuous improvement.
3. **Fast is better than slow.**
   Customers want results now without delay.
4. **Democracy on the web works.**
   Let the community of users be the judge of service value.
5. **You don't need to be at your desk to need an answer.**
   Web mobile technology now allows information to come to the user.
6. **You can make money without doing evil.**
   Advertising can be useful if relevant to the viewer.
7. **There's always more information out there.**
   It takes creativity to find information that is not readily available.
8. **The need for information crosses all borders.**
   We live in a global community with many languages.
9. **You can be serious without a suit.**
   Work should be fun and challenging.
10. **Great just isn't good enough.**
    Through innovation and iteration, improve upon what works well.

Source: http://www.google.com/corporate/tenthings.html/

confusion among products in the marketplace; (3) industrial design rights (e.g., Starbucks' store ambience) protect the appearance, style, or design from infringement; and (4) a trade secret (e.g., KFC's recipe for fried chicken batter) is information concerning the practices or proprietary knowledge of a business.

A service firm's reputation and brand are protected by defending the intellectual property rights that define the service that customers expect to receive. For example, McDonald's is famous for bringing a lawsuit against a competitor that had taken advantage of the "golden arches" signature trademark. This is serious business because a duped customer who visits the competitor and receives poor service might attribute the experience to McDonald's.

Summary

In addition to changing demographics and information technology, the Internet has been an enabler of service sector growth and innovation. Service innovation can be either radical or incremental and often arises from advances in technology. Following service development, the design of the service delivery system is captured in a visual diagram called a service blueprint. The line of visibility in this diagram introduced the concept of a front-office and back-office partition of the service system. Competitive positioning of the service delivery system was accomplished using the dimensions of complexity and divergence to measure structural differentiation. We also looked at classifying services according to the concept of divergence, the object of the service, and the degree of customer contact. Four generic approaches to the design of service delivery systems were considered: production-line approach, customer coproduction, customer contact, and information empowerment.

Key Terms and Definitions

Applied research activity directed toward gaining knowledge that will meet a specific need. *pg. 67*

Blockchain a distributed database that maintains a continuously growing list of linked records (blocks) secure from tampering and revision. *pg. 68*

Basic research activity directed toward increases in knowledge without specific application. *pg. 67*

Complexity a dimension of service process structure that measures the number and intricacy of steps in the process. *pg. 73*

Coproducer the productive role a customer can play in the service delivery process. *pg. 80*

Customer contact a measure of the physical presence of the customer in the system as a percentage of the total service time. *pg. 82*

Development systematic use of knowledge directed toward the production of a product, service, or method. *pg. 67*

Divergence a dimension of service process structure that measures the degree of customization or decision making permitted of service employees. *pg. 73*

Intellectual property rights legal rights over creations of the mind both artistic and commercial. *pg. 84*

Line of visibility a line drawn on the service blueprint showing separation of front-office and back-office activities. *pg. 74*

Production-line approach a service design analogous to that in a manufacturing system with tight control, use of low-skilled labor, and the offering of a standard service. *pg. 77*

Service blueprint a diagram of the service process showing activities, flows, physical evidence, and lines of visibility and interaction. *pg. 74*

Topics for Discussion

1. What are the limits to the production-line approach to service?
2. Give an example of a service in which isolation of the technical core would be inappropriate.
3. What are some drawbacks of increased customer participation in the service process?
4. What ethical issues are raised in the promotion of sales during a service transaction?

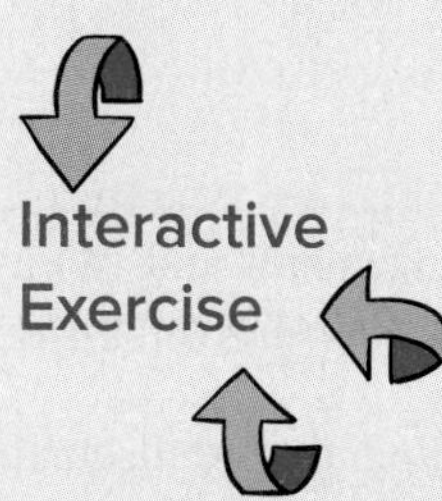

Interactive Exercise

The class breaks into small groups and prepares a service blueprint for Village Volvo.

100 Yen Sushi House[10] CASE 3.1

Sang M. Lee tells of a meeting with two Japanese businessmen in Tokyo to plan a joint U.S.–Japanese conference to explore U.S. and Japanese management systems. As lunchtime drew near, his hosts told him with much delight that they wished to show him the "most productive operation in Japan."

Lee describes the occasion: "They took me to a sushi shop, the famous 100 Yen Sushi House, in the Shinzuku area of Tokyo. Sushi is the most popular snack in Japan. It is a simple dish, vinegared rice wrapped in different things, such as dried seaweed, raw tuna, raw salmon, raw red snapper, cooked shrimp, octopus, fried egg, and so on. Sushi is usually prepared so that each piece will be about the right size to be put into the mouth with chopsticks. Arranging the sushi in an appetizing and aesthetic way with pickled ginger is almost an art in itself.

"The 100 Yen Sushi House is no ordinary sushi restaurant. It is the ultimate showcase of Japanese productivity. As we entered the shop, there was a chorus of *Iratsai,* a welcome from everyone working in the shop—cooks, waitresses, the owner, and the owner's children. The house features an ellipsoid-shaped serving area in the middle of the room, where inside three or four cooks were busily preparing sushi. Perhaps 30 stools surrounded the serving area. We took seats at the counters and were promptly served with a cup of *Misoshiru,* which is a bean paste soup, a pair of chopsticks, a cup of green tea, a tiny plate to make our own sauce, and a small china piece to hold the chopsticks. So far, the service was average for any sushi house. Then, I noticed something special. There was a conveyor belt going around the ellipsoid service area, like a toy train track. On it I saw a train of plates of sushi. You can find any kind of sushi that you can think of—from the cheapest seaweed or octopus kind to the expensive raw salmon or shrimp dishes. The price is uniform, however, 100 yen per plate. On closer examination, while my eyes were racing to keep up with the speed of the traveling plates, I found that a cheap seaweed plate had four pieces, while the more expensive raw salmon dish had only two pieces. I sat down and looked around at the other customers at the counters. They were all enjoying their sushi and slurping their soup while reading newspapers or magazines.

"I saw a man with eight plates all stacked up neatly. As he got up to leave, the cashier looked over and said, '800 yen, please.' The cashier had no cash register, since she can simply count the number of plates and then multiply by 100 yen. As the customer was leaving, once again we heard a chorus of *Arigato Gosaimas* (thank you) from all the workers."

Lee continues his observations of the sushi house operations: "In the 100 Yen Sushi House, Professor Tamura [one of his hosts] explained to me how efficient this family-owned restaurant is. The owner usually has a superordinate organizational purpose such as customer service, a contribution to society, or the well-being of the community. Furthermore, the organizational purpose is achieved through a long-term effort by all the members of the organization, who are considered 'family.'

"The owner's daily operation is based on a careful analysis of information. The owner has a complete summary of demand information about different types of sushi plates, and thus he knows exactly how many of each type of sushi plate he should prepare and when. Furthermore, the whole operation is based on the repetitive manufacturing principle with appropriate just-in-time and quality control systems. For example, the store has a very limited refrigerator capacity (we could see several whole fish or octopus in the glassed chambers right in front of our counter). Thus, the store uses the just-in-time inventory control system. Instead of increasing the refrigeration capacity by purchasing new refrigeration systems, the company has an agreement with the fish vendor to deliver fresh fish several times a day so that materials arrive just-in-time to be used for sushi making. Therefore, the inventory cost is minimum.

". . . In the 100 Yen Sushi House, workers and their equipment are positioned so close that sushi making is passed on hand to hand rather than as independent operations. The absence of walls of inventory allows the owner and workers to be involved in the total operation, from greeting the customer to serving what is ordered. Their tasks are tightly interrelated and everyone rushes to a problem spot to prevent the cascading effect of the problem throughout the work process.

"The 100 Yen Sushi House is a labor-intensive operation, which is based mostly on simplicity and common sense rather than high technology, contrary to American perceptions. I was very impressed. As I finished my fifth plate, I saw the same octopus sushi plate going around for about the 30th time. Perhaps I had discovered the pitfall of the system. So I asked the owner how he takes care of the sanitary problems when a sushi plate goes around all day long, until an unfortunate customer eats it and perhaps gets food poisoning. He bowed with an apologetic smile and said, 'Well, sir, we never let our sushi plates go unsold longer than about 30 minutes.' Then he scratched his head and said, 'Whenever one of our employees takes a break, he or she can take off unsold plates of sushi and either eat them or throw them away. We are very serious about our sushi quality.'"

Questions

1. Prepare a service blueprint for the 100 Yen Sushi House operation.
2. What features of the 100 Yen Sushi House service delivery system differentiate it from the competition, and what competitive advantages do they offer?
3. How has the 100 Yen Sushi House incorporated the just-in-time system into its operation?
4. Suggest other services that could adopt the 100 Yen Sushi House service delivery concepts.

Commuter Cleaning—A New Venture Proposal[11] CASE 3.2

The service vision of Commuter Cleaning is to provide dry cleaning services for individuals with careers or other responsibilities that make it difficult for them to find the time to go to traditional dry cleaners. The company's goal is to provide a high-quality dry cleaning service that is both reliable and convenient.

The targeted market consists of office workers who live in the suburbs of large metropolitan areas. The service will be marketed primarily to single men and women as well as dual-career couples, because this segment of the population has the greatest need for a quality dry cleaning service but does not have the time to go to the traditional dry cleaners. The targeted cities are those surrounded by suburbs from which many people commute via mass transit.

The facilities where customers will drop-off and pickup their dry cleaning will be located at sites where commuters meet their trains or buses into the downtown area (i.e., park-and-ride locations and commuter train stations). For each city, it will be necessary to determine who owns these transit stations and how land can be rented from the owner. In some locations, facilities where space could be rented already exist. In other locations, there might not be any existing facilities, and the pickup and drop-off booths will need to be built.

The facilities for laundry pickup and drop-off need not be large. The building or room at the station need only be large enough to accommodate racks for hanging the finished dry cleaning.

Initially, it might be necessary to restrict the service to laundering business-wear shirts, because these are the easiest of all clothing articles to clean and also will allow the operations to be simplified. Typically, a man or woman will need a clean shirt for each workday, so a large demand exists. One drawback would be the diminished customer convenience, because dry cleaning of garments would necessitate a separate trip to a traditional dry cleaner. If dry cleaning were outsourced, however, it would be possible to offer full-service cleaning very quickly, because a plant and equipment need not be purchased.

A decision also needs to be made about providing same-day or next-day service. One factor in this decision will be whether competitors in the area offer same-day service. These cleaners represent a serious threat only if they open early enough and close late enough to be convenient and accessible to customers. Most important, same-day service should be provided only where it is feasible to deliver on this promise consistently.

All advertisements will include a phone number that potential customers can call to inquire about the service. When a customer calls, he or she can request the service. That same day, the customer will be able to pick up a Commuter Cleaning laundry bag with the customer's name and account number on it and a membership card that is coded with the account number.

The delivery system will be a hub-and-spoke system, similar to the one that FedEx uses for package handling. Customers will have the convenience of dropping off their laundry at numerous neighborhood commuter stations. All dry cleaning will be picked up and delivered to one central plant, and once the shirts are clean they will be returned to the customer's drop-off point. Same-day service is possible with pickups beginning at 8:00 AM and returns completed by 5:00 PM.

The customer will place the dirty shirts in the bag at home and simply leave the bag at the station on the way to work. The station worker will attach a color-coded label on the bag to identify the location where the shirts were dropped off so that they can be returned to the same station. A laundry pickup route will be established to bring bags from each location to the central cleaning plant. Once the bag reaches the central plant, the items will be counted and the number entered into the billing database. After the shirts have been cleaned, they will be put on hangers with the customer's laundry bag attached. The cleaned shirts will be segregated according to the location to which they need to be returned and then placed on a truck in reverse order of the delivery route. The customer will provide the station worker with his or her membership card, which will be used to identify and retrieve the customer's clothing and bag. Because all customers will be billed monthly, the time to pick up the laundry should be expedited and waiting lines avoided.

Initially, cleaning will be outsourced to a large dry cleaner with excess capacity. A favorable rate should be negotiated because of the predictable volume, convenience of aggregating the demand into one batch, and performing the pickup and delivery service. Contracting for the cleaning will reduce the initial capital investment required to build a plant and buy equipment, and it also will provide time for the business to build a customer base that would support a dedicated cleaning plant. Further, contracting will limit the financial risk exposure if the concept fails. If the cleaning is outsourced, there will be no need to hire and manage a workforce to perform the cleaning; therefore, management can focus on building a customer base instead of supervising back-office activities. Also, with contract cleaning, it is more feasible to offer dry cleaning services in addition to laundering business shirts.

In the long run, however, contract cleaning may limit the potential profitability, expose the business to quality problems, and prevent the opportunity to focus cleaning plant operations around the pickup-and-delivery concept. Ideally, once Commuter Cleaning has built a large client base and has access to significant capital, all cleaning will be done internally.

Most of the hiring will be targeted to area college students. Initially, two shifts of workers will be needed for the transit station facilities but just one van driver at any given time. As business expands, additional vans will be acquired and additional drivers hired. The first shift of drop-off station workers will begin at 6:00 AM and finish at 9:00 AM, at which time the van driver will transport the items from the drop-off sites to the cleaning site. The number of drivers needed and the hours they work will depend on how many pickup and drop-off sites exist, their proximity to each other, the cleaning plant location, and the ability to develop efficient routing schedules. The second shift of drivers will deliver the cleaning from the plant to the transit stations from about 3:30 to 5:00 PM. The second shift of transit-site workers will begin at 5:00 PM and end when the last train or bus arrives, usually about 8:30 PM. Once cleaning is done internally, it will be possible to have plant employees also pick up the laundry and deliver it to the stations each day. This will allow Commuter Cleaning to hire some full-time workers, and it also will bring the back-office workers closer to the customers so that they can be more aware of problems and customer needs.

College students will be the best candidates for workers, because their schedules vary and classes usually are held in the middle of the day, from about 10 AM to 3 PM. Also, depending on course loads, some students might have time to work only three hours a day, while others can choose to work both the first and second shifts. The starting salary will be set slightly above the wage for typical part-time service jobs available to college students to discourage turnover.

When Commuter Cleaning is first introduced into a city, additional temporary workers will be needed to manage the customer inquiries for initiating the service. The week before introduction of the service, representatives will be at the station facilities to answer questions and perform the paperwork necessary to initiate service for interested customers. Because all advertisements will include the customer service number, it will be necessary to have additional representatives manning the phones to handle the inquiries. All employees will have the title "customer service representative" to stress the function of their jobs. These workers will be encouraged to get to know their customers and reach a first-name basis with them.

When customers initiate service, they will be encouraged to open an account for monthly billing rather than to pay each time that items are picked up. At this time, the customer service representative will collect all the necessary information, including name, address, phone number, location from where they commute, and credit card number. If a customer desires, the amount owed will be charged to the credit card each month. This is the most desirable form of payment, because it is efficient and involves no worry of delayed payments. This method also is becoming more common, and people generally now are comfortable having their

TABLE 3.5 Commuter Cleaning Economic Analysis

Expense Item	Monthly Amount	Assumptions
Transit station rent	$ 2,800	7 locations at $400 each
Delivery van	500	1 minivan (includes lease payment and insurance)
Station customer service representatives	5,544	7 locations, 2 shifts averaging 3 hours per shift at $15 per hour
Driver	528	1 driver, 2 shifts averaging 2 hours per shift at $15 per hour
Fuel	165	30 miles per shift at 12 mpg and $2.75 per gallon
Business insurance	100	
Office customer service representatives	4,000	2 office workers each paid $24,000 a year
Laundry bags	167	Cost of 1,000 laundry bags at $2 each, amortized over one year
Total monthly expenses	$13,804	22-day month

credit cards billed automatically. Each month, statements will be sent to all customers with transactions to verify the bill and request payment from those who do not use a credit card. If a customer is late in paying, a customer service representative will call and ask if he or she would like to begin paying with a credit card. Repeatedly delinquent customers will be required to pay at the time of pickup, a stipulation that will be included in the customer's initial agreement for service. The customer service representatives will be responsible for answering all customer inquiries, including the initiation of service, and one customer service representative will be responsible for customer billings. Each day, the laundry delivered to the plant will be entered into a database that accumulates each customer's transactions for the month.

A smooth demand throughout the week is desirable to create a stable workload; however, actions likely will be needed to control fluctuations in demand and to avoid imbalances in the workload. One method of controlling demand is through price specials and promotions. Offering a discount on certain days of the week is common practice for dry cleaners, and one approach would be to offer special prices to different customer segments to entice them to bring in their laundry on a certain day. For example, Friday might be the busiest day of the week and Monday and Tuesday the slowest. In this case, the customer base could be divided (e.g., alphabetically) and each segment offered a discount price on a particular day. Other ideas include providing a complimentary cup of coffee to anyone bringing in laundry on Monday. These promotions can be implemented once demand fluctuations are observed. Attention also must be given to holidays, which might create temporary surges or lulls in business.

Questions

1. Prepare a service blueprint for Commuter Cleaning.
2. What generic approach to service system design is illustrated by Commuter Cleaning, and what competitive advantages does this design offer?
3. Using the data in Table 3.5, calculate a break-even price per shirt if monthly demand is expected to be 20,000 shirts and the contract with a cleaning plant stipulates a charge of $0.50 per shirt.
4. Critique the business concept, and make suggestions for improvement.

Amazon.com[12] — CASE 3.3

Like many entrepreneurs, Jeffrey Bezos, founder of Amazon.com had an idea, did his homework, and developed a new service. Amazon opened its virtual doors in July 1995. Since then, the retailer has served millions of customers worldwide and, in 2015, generated more than $100 billion in annual sales through its retailing operation and nearly $10 billion through its Web Services (AWS) operation.[13] Many people regard Amazon as the "golden child" of the Internet. Unlike many entrepreneurs, however, Bezos was not content with just gaining market share for his initial concept. More than 20 years after opening its doors, Amazon still is developing new services.

The young CEO started Amazon with the intention of establishing a strong brand name that he could leverage into other products. He marketed books first, because he believed they were ideal cyberspace products. Customers do not need much physical interaction with the product or with a salesperson to purchase books. Books, therefore, are well suited to marketing over the web.

A key success factor for Amazon is that it captures market share and fosters brand loyalty by focusing on customer needs. Bezos believes that paying too much attention to short-term gains means forgetting about long-term customer satisfactions. Loss of this long-term customer focus comes at a price, however.

Despite impressive sales growth, Amazon did not turn a profit quickly, but that didn't stop it from becoming a dominant force in online retailing. In addition to books, the Amazon website now includes products and services such as electronics, music, software, toys, clothing, and B2B services for other businesses. Some items are available from Amazon's inventory, and other products and services are supplied by third-party sellers through its Marketplace capability. These sellers, in turn, pay a portion of their revenues to Amazon. Amazon also manufactures and sells several versions of its Kindle e-book reader, which has made Amazon the leader in e-book sales.

AMAZON'S GUIDING FORCE—THE CUSTOMER

Amazon's guiding philosophy is to provide superior service to its customers. Bezos and his management team spent one year creating the website and database programs that drove Amazon in the beginning. They sought to create a friendly site that would not demand a high level of computer literacy.

Bezos recognized that Internet commerce would shift the balance of power toward consumers. Consequently, Amazon built customer relationships by customizing its service, involving its website visitors in the service, and creating a communal spirit. Focus on the consumer still is the cornerstone for developing customer loyalty.

CUSTOMER AS COPRODUCER AND SERVICE CUSTOMIZATION

Amazon integrates customers into the service delivery process in several ways. Customers can review items they have purchased and answer other customers' questions. The "wish list" is another service that Amazon offers. For example, a customer can enter titles of books he or she would like to have into a personal wish list. A friend who wants to give that customer a book as a gift then can make a selection from the wish list.

Amazon also makes personalized recommendations to individual customers. Some of these recommendations are based on the customer's past purchases, and other recommendations are based on the behavior of past customers who have made purchases similar to those of the customer. If a consumer purchases a book on Amish quilts, for example, Amazon's software will search for all of the people who purchased this same book. Using a mathematical process developed by Amazon called *item-based collaborative filtering,* the software determines what other books are popular with people who read the Amish quilt book. The customer then receives a list of proposed titles based on this information. Amazon uses this technique to provide the same friendly and personalized reading advice that a local bricks-and-mortar bookstore operation can, but it achieves greater accuracy and convenience at a fraction of the cost.

One flaw of this early collaborative filtering was its inability to distinguish gift purchases. Someone buying his or her mother a book on quilting, for example, would receive recommendations on this topic despite a lack of personal interest. Amazon solved this problem by including a check box on the order page so the customer can indicate if the item is a gift. Another problem can arise because the power of collaborative filtering is based on the customer's history. If a person changes e-mail addresses frequently and uses a new Amazon identification, all of the data are lost.

In addition to collaborative filtering, the company uses other strategies to achieve its mission. When repeat customers log on to the website, a personalized web page greets the customer by name and allows him or her to view the new recommendations made by the collaborative filtering tool. Bezos compares this personalized front page with "walking into your favorite store and finding only items that you want on the shelves near the door." Amazon also allows customers to store information on the company's secure server.

Customers can authorize Amazon to keep a record of their credit cards and mailing addresses, for example. This technology, called 1-Click, streamlines the service so that customers don't have to reenter the information every time they make purchases.

Amazon doesn't wait for customers to come to its site to provide its service. Customers receive periodic e-mails encouraging them to visit Amazon.com and giving a list of recommendations for items to check out on the next visit.

OTHER UNIQUE USES OF TECHNOLOGY FOR THE CUSTOMER

Amazon not only has used technology to personalize the customer experience, but also has designed its site with customers in mind. The pages are easy to understand and use. The website avoids large graphics, which can take a long time to load.

A powerful search engine is another unique feature of Amazon. The company employs a "do what I mean" (DWIM) search function. The site recognizes the misspellings that customers make frequently and changes the search function to account for these mistakes. If a customer misspells the author's name Fitzsimmons as Fitzsimons, for example, Amazon still displays the book *Service Management.*

MORE THAN JUST FRIENDLY TECHNOLOGY

Amazon's technology has helped to create loyal customers who not only visit the site, but, as we have noted, also interact with it. Amazon is an active virtual community that involves the customer.

As noted, the company encourages visitors and customers to post reviews of any book or product on the site. This review process involves the customers in developing the content on the website and creates an information tool for other website visitors. To help its Kindle users, Amazon hosts a customer forum website where customers can ask and answer questions and participate in online discussions.

Amazon employees go to great lengths for the customers and consider them as part of a community. One customer reported with joy that a copy of his father's book, 20 years out of print, had been located for him by Amazon.

The Associates Program expands this "community" beyond the websites under Amazon's direct control. Amazon allows registered websites, such as Yahoo.com, Drugstore.com, and Zappos.com, to recommend specific books, CDs, videos, and other Amazon products to their visitors using a hyperlink. If customers follow the hyperlink and purchase the product on Amazon.com, these associates receive a modest commission.

Amazon claims "tens of thousands" of associates are participating in its programs, which expands Amazon's presence and publicity on the web, but it also means that Amazon could lose some control of its brand and image. Amazon has encountered some other problems in the past. A reporter once revealed that Amazon was selling space to publishers on a list of favorite books. Amazon also was accused of selling authors extra e-mail support on the website for various titles.[14] The company was flooded with outraged e-mails and stopped all paid promotions in response to the outcry. This incident raises the question: Will the loyal customer base of Amazon or any other electronic service tolerate being used for financial gain?

The ability to provide the broad spectrum of services for millions of customers seamlessly and consistently depends on very sophisticated technology, much of which was pioneered by Amazon engineers and architects. The highly personalized page that greets a returning customer contains hundreds of bits of software logic, and is a testament to their work. Referring to software and technology capabilities, Bezos says in a 2010 letter to shareholders issued in early 2011, "Many of the problems we face have no textbook solutions, and so we—happily—invent new approaches."[15]

NOT JUST A BOOKSELLER ANYMORE

Amazon Web Services (AWS) is a pivotal addition to the company's offerings. This program, which began about 10 years ago as a simple cloud storage system, supplies other businesses with a web-based platform for all of their operations. In fact, Amazon is the single largest supplier of cloud support technology for businesses, large and small. The company's cloud computing services are available in 2015 in 12 geographic regions of the world. In addition to basic infrastructure technology, Amazon's 2015 Annual Report says that the company offers more than 70 related services. Among these services are a new database engine, Aurora, and Redshift, a managed data warehouse service. Other new offerings include QuickSight, a new Business Intelligence computing capability; EC2 Container Service; and Lambda, a pioneering serverless computing service.[16] Amazon states that "developers and systems administrators can . . . collect and track metrics, gain insight, and react immediately to keep their applications and businesses running smoothly."[17]

An alliance with Viacom, a company that provides online access to many entertainment venues, was announced in early 2012.[18] This alliance allows Amazon Prime members to stream movies and television programs instantly and commercial-free.[19] Amazon has gone beyond this service and is producing its own video programming for customers to stream.

In accordance with his firm belief that successful entrepreneurs must take a long-term view of their businesses and the world, Bezos founded Blue Origin, a company dedicated (and determined) to provide affordable suborbital and orbital space travel.[20] Early in 2016 Bezos predicted that the company might be taking paying tourists for short trips as early as 2018.[21] In its short life thus far, Blue Origin has enjoyed the taste of success and failure, and researchers look forward—and upward—to matching Amazon's achievements.

IT'S A BIRD, IT'S A PLANE, NO—IT'S AMAZON

Amazon has been a leader in retailing and customer service from its very beginning. Since those early days it has pioneered a host of services, most recently its AmazonWebServices (AWS) that provides cloud technology for businesses and some brick-and-mortar stores. What more can it possibly do? Think drones. We can chuckle at the idea of a drone delivering a book or dog food to our doorstep, but Amazon is not laughing about that possibility. Shipping is the backbone of Amazon's retail success, so it is not surprising that much attention goes into facilitating that part of the company's operation. Amazon now has its own fleet of delivery trucks, robot-powered warehouses, and the first of a fleet of transport planes. These new capabilities might represent a threat to UPS's long-time dominance in the field of home delivery. And, the company really is exploring ways to use drones, also.

AS AMAZON LOOKS TO THE FUTURE—WILL IT BECOME THE WALMART OF THE INTERNET?

Amazon has been very successful turning a profit since 2004. Amazon's personalized customer service and online community strategy work well. The company claims its sales of electronic books have surpassed the sales of its printed books, and it is the largest seller of videos and music on the web.[22] Early skeptics suggested that price-sensitive buyers would constantly search the net for the lowest prices and leave companies without any pricing power or brand loyalty. Amazon has not suffered this predicted pattern in part because it has taken a long-range view of the business and invested heavily in creating a loyal customer base.

Fast expansion into a variety of retailing areas reinforces Amazon's goal to be a one-stop shopping site on the Internet. In 2012 some sources suggested that Amazon might venture into the brick-and-mortar arena by establishing Apple-type stores to sell its Kindle e-readers, and, also, might introduce a smartphone.[23] This prediction has come true. Amazon's first brick-and-mortar store is located in Seattle, WA, and a second store will be opened in San Diego, CA. The Seattle store sells books and electronic devices including Kindles and Echo, which is sort of a home companion who can answer your questions, make dinner reservations at your favorite restaurant, but who doesn't need care or watering. Future stores might sell other types of products.[24] As for the smartphone, the Amazon culture values failures as well as successes.

Questions

1. How does Amazon.com illustrate the sources of service sector growth? Comment on information technology, the Internet as an enabler, innovation, and changing demographics.
2. What generic approach(s) to service design does Amazon.com illustrate, and what competitive advantages does this design offer?
3. Is Amazon.com a model for the future of retailing?

Selected Bibliography

Chen, Ja-Shen, Hung Tai Tsou, and Astrid Ya-Hui Huang. "Service Delivery Innovation: Antecedents and Impact on Firm Performance." *Journal of Service Research* 12, no.1 (August 2009), pp. 36–55.

Eisingerich, Andreas, Gaia Rubera, and Matthias Seifert. "Managing Service Innovation and Interorganizational Relationships for Firm Performance: To Commit or Diversify?" *Journal of Service Research* 11, no. 4 (May 2009), pp. 344–56.

Frei, Francis X. "Four Things a Service Business Must Get Right." *Harvard Business Review* 86, no. 4 (April 2008), pp. 28–41.

Lim, Chie-Hyeon, and Kwang-Jae Kim. "Information Service Blueprint: A Service Blueprinting Framework for Information-Intensive Services." *Service Science* 6, no. 4 (December 2014), pp. 296–312.

Menor, L. J., et al. "New Service Development Competence and Performance: An Empirical Investigation in Retail Banking." *Production and Operations Management* 17, no. 3 (May–June 2008), pp. 267–84.

Patricio, Lisa, Raymond P. Fisk, and Joao Falcao e Cunha. "Designing Multi-Interface Service Experiences: The Service Experience Blueprint." *Journal of Service Research* 10, no. 4 (May 2008), pp. 318–34.

Tang, Christopher S. "The Past, Present, and Future of Manufacturing & Service Operations Management." *Manufacturing & Service Operations Management* 17, no. 1 (2015), pp. 1–3.

Tapscott, Don, and Alex Tapscott. *Blockchain Revolution.* New York: Penguin, 2016.

Trinh, T. H., Voratas Kachitvichyanukul, and D. B. Khang. "The Coproduction Approach to Service: A Theoretical Background." *Journal of the Operations Research Society* 65, no. 2 (2014), pp. 161–68.

Endnotes

1. Uday S. Karmarkar and Uday M. Apte, "Operations Management in the Information Economy: Information Products, Processes, and Chains," *Journal of Operations Management,* 25, no. 2, (March 2007), p. 438–53.
2. Adapted from http://en.wikipedia.org/wiki/Internet.
3. http://www.nist.gov/director/prog-ofc/report05-1.pdf Planning Report 05-1, "Measuring Service-Sector Research and Development," prepared for National Science Foundation and National Institute of Standards & Technology by Research Triangle Institute, March 2005, p. 2.2.
4. Company R&D expenditures in the United States increased 6.7 percent in 2013. August 21, 2015, Press Release 15-094, https://www.nsf.gov/news/news-summ.jsp?ntn_id=136026.
5. "Planning Report 05-1, Measuring Service-Sector Research and Development," prepared for National Science Foundation and National Institute of Standards & Technology by Research Triangle Institute, March 2005, pp. 3.3–3.4, http://www.nist.gov/director/prog-ofc/report05-1.pdf.
6. Don Tapscott and Alex Tapscott. "The Impact of the Blockchain Goes Beyond Financial Services," *Harvard Business Review* (May 2016).
7. https://www.thestreet.com/story/13753305/1/bofa-merrill-lynch-bac-stock-rises-developes-block chain-platform-with -microsoft.html
8. Adapted from A. Parasuraman, "Technology Readiness Index (TRI): A Multiple-Item Scale to Measure Readiness to Embrace New Technologies," *Journal of Service Research* 2, no. 4 (May 2000), pp. 307–21.
9. Mary Jo Bitner, Amy L. Ostrom, and Felicia N. Morgan, "Service Blueprinting: A Practical Technique for Service Innovation," *California Management Review* (Spring 2008), pp. 66–94.
10. Reprinted with permission from Sang M. Lee, "Japanese Management and the 100 Yen Sushi House," *Operations Management Review* (Winter 1983), pp. 46–48.
11. Prepared by Mara Segal under the supervision of Professor James A. Fitzsimmons.
12. Students Laura Bennett, Sarah Bird, and Matt Rhone contributed to this case under the supervision of Professor James A. Fitzsimmons.

13. http://phx.corporate-ir.net/phoenix.zhtml?c=97664&p=irol-reportsAnnual. April 2015 Annual Report.
14. Peter DeJonge, "Riding the Perilous Waters of Amazon.com," *New York Times Magazine,* March 14, 1999.
15. 2010 Letter to Shareholders, April 27, 2011, http://phx.corporate-ir.net/phoenix.zhtml?c=97664&p=irol-reportsAnnual.
16. April 2015 Annual Report, http://phx.corporate-ir.net/phoenix.zhtml?c=97664&p=irol-reportsAnnual,
17. http://aws.amazon.com/cloudwatch/, © 2012, Amazon Web Services LLC.
18. http.//phx.corporate-ir.net/phoenix.zhtml?c=176060&p=irol-newsArticle&ID=165838.
19. The Amazon Prime membership is available for an annual fee and provides several perks in addition to the LiveVideo streaming, such as free two-day shipping for product purchases.
20. http://www.blueorigin.com/about/about.html
21. http://www.nytimes.com/2016/03/09/science/space/jeff-bezos-lifts-veil-on-his-rocket-company-blue-origin.html?emc=etal
22. http://businessweek.com/news/2011-05-19/amazon-com-says-kindle-e-book-sales-surpass-printed-books.html.
23. "Taking the Long View," *The Economist Technology Quarterly,* March 3, 2012.
24. http://www.nytimes.com/2016/03/12/business/media/a-virtual-trip-through-amazons-physical-store.html?emc=etal

Chapter 

The Service Encounter

Learning Objectives

After completing this chapter, you should be able to:

1. Describe the five roles of technology in the service encounter.
2. Use the service encounter triad to describe a service firm's delivery process.
3. Differentiate four organizational control systems for employee empowerment.
4. Prepare abstract questions and write situational vignettes to screen service recruits.
5. Describe the classification of customers into four groups based on their attitudes and expectations.
6. Describe how the creation of an ethical climate leads to job satisfaction and service quality.
7. Discuss the role of scripts in customer coproduction.
8. Describe how the elements of the service profit chain lead to revenue growth and profitability.

Most services are characterized by an encounter between a service provider and a customer. This interaction, which defines the quality of the service in the mind of the customer, is called a "moment of truth." The often brief encounter is a moment in time when the customer is evaluating the service and forming an opinion of its quality. A customer experiences many encounters with a variety of service providers, and each moment of truth is an opportunity to influence the customer's perceptions of the service quality. For example, an airline passenger experiences a series of encounters, beginning with purchasing the ticket (online encounter with a website), and continuing with baggage check-in at the airport, in-flight service, baggage claim on arrival, and, finally, the award of frequent flyer credit.

Realizing that such moments of truth are critical in achieving a reputation for superior quality, Jan Carlzon, the CEO of Scandinavian Airlines System (SAS), focused on these encounters in the reorganization of SAS to create a distinctive and competitive position in terms of quality of service. According to Jan Carlzon's philosophy, the organization exists to serve the frontline workers who have direct customer contact. His revolutionary thinking stood the old organization chart on its head, placing the customer-encounter personnel (formerly at the bottom) now at the top of the chart. It then became everyone else's responsibility to serve those frontline personnel, who in turn served the customer. Changing the organization chart signaled a move to refocus on satisfying the customer and managing moments of truth. It is interesting that this implementation required dividing the company into various profit centers down to the route level and allowing managers (now close to the customers) the authority to make decisions on their own.[1]

Chapter Preview

The chapter begins with a discussion of the role of customer-facing technology in the service encounter. The service encounter itself is depicted as a triangle formed by the interacting interests of the customer, service organization, and contact personnel. Each participant in the service encounter attempts to exert control over the transaction, leading

A moment of truth occurs during every customer-employee interaction.
©Rob Melnychuk/Getty Images RF

to the need for flexibility and the empowerment of contact personnel. A discussion of service organization culture follows, with examples of how the founders of successful service firms established a set of values and expectations that encourages their employees to focus on delivering exceptional service.

The activities of selecting and training contact personnel are addressed next. Then, the many expectations and attitudes of customers are explored, as well as the role of scripts in customer coproduction. The high correlation of service quality perceptions that are shared by contact personnel and customers leads to a desire to foster a customer service orientation among employees. Investment in contact personnel creates a service profit chain that links perceived service value to customer loyalty to eventual profitability.

Technology in the Service Encounter[2]

Advances in communications and information technology have a profound effect on ways customers interface with service providers. For example, the Internet and airport kiosks have changed the expectations and behavior of airline passengers. Customers no longer need to wait on hold to reach a reservation clerk or wait in line at the airline counter to receive a boarding pass. These trivial face-to-face interactions have been replaced with technology. Figure 4.1 displays the five modes of technology's contribution to the service encounter.

The A mode is called *technology-free service encounter,* where the customer is in physical proximity to and interacts with a human service provider. This mode represents the traditional high-touch service that we experience at a hairdresser salon or chiropractor in which technology does not play a *direct* role. Most personal care services fall into this category, along with some professional services such as law, consulting, and psychiatry.

The B mode is called *technology-assisted service encounter,* because *only* the service provider has access to the technology to facilitate the delivery of face-to-face service. Many health care procedures fall in this category, such as an eye exam during a visit to an optometrist's business place or a full mouth X-ray at the dentist. In the "old" days, airline representatives used a computer terminal to check in all passengers, represented by mode B, but today passengers are encouraged to use check-in kiosks or online represented by mode E.

FIGURE 4.1
Role of Technology in the Service Encounter

Adapted from James A. Fitzsimmons, Mona J. Fitzsimmons, Sanjeev Bordoloi, *Service Management Operations, Strategy, Information Technology,* 8th edition, (2014).

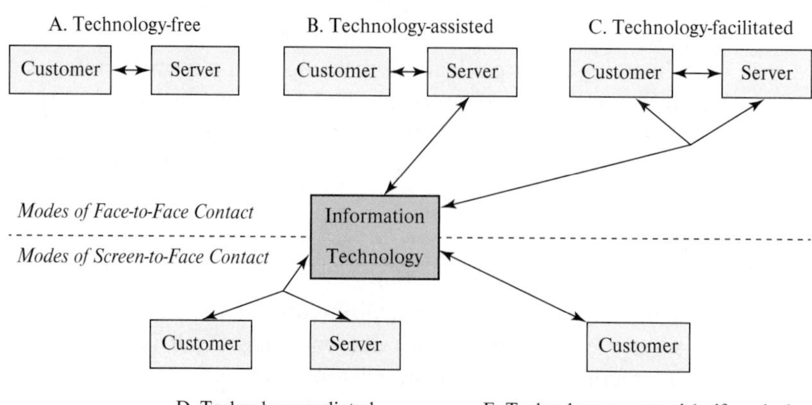

The C mode is called *technology-facilitated service encounter,* because *both* the customer and service provider have access to the same technology. For example, a financial planner in consultation with a client can refer to a financial model on a personal computer to illustrate projected returns for different risk profiles.

Beginning with the D mode, called *technology-mediated service encounter,* the customer and human service provider are not *colocated* physically and, thus, the service encounter no longer is the traditional "face-to-face" contact. Communication usually is enabled by voice telephone call to access services such as making a restaurant reservation or getting technical help from a distant call center. Consider, also, how General Motors has bundled a remote monitoring service in its automobiles called "OnStar" that uses GPS (global positioning satellite) technology to reassure stranded motorists that assistance is on the way.

In mode E, called *technology-generated service encounter,* the human service provider is replaced entirely with technology that allows the customer to *self-serve* (i.e., outsourcing the job to the customers). This mode is becoming more common as firms attempt to reduce the cost of providing service. Examples are ubiquitous–bank ATMs, checkout scanning, airport check-in kiosks, online reservations, and interactive voice response (IVR) technology in call centers.

The Emergence of Self-Service

Example 4.1 Self-Service Vignette[3]

The alarm rings and Emma's day begins with a shower followed by a breakfast of frozen waffles heated in the toaster. Before leaving for the airport, she goes to the airline's web page, where weeks before she had purchased the ticket and made seat selections, and prints her boarding pass. At the entrance to the tollway on the way to the airport, a scanner reads the bar code on her windshield for later billing. At the airport, she uses a credit card to pass through the gate to the airport long-term parking structure. Inside the airport, she attaches a baggage claim tape to a package she is checking and places it on the conveyor into the X-ray machine. After landing at her destination, she looks on the message board at the car rental and picks up her reserved car in the lot. On the way into town, she uses a cell phone to direct-dial business appointments and leaves several messages on answering machines. She purchases a drink and sandwich at a vending machine for lunch. Dinner is at a cafeteria where she selects meal items, places them on a tray, pays with a credit card, and finds an empty table. When she finishes eating, she buses her dishes. After the day's business meetings, she leaves the rental car at its drop-off point, proceeds to the airport terminal, and uses the airline kiosk to print her boarding pass. Arriving home, she picks up her car at the parking lot where a scanner reads the ticket and debits her credit card. She stops at a grocery store to pick up a few items on the way home and uses the self-checkout station and credit card. At home, she checks her investments and sells shares of a poor-performing stock.

The vignette of a typical business trip illustrates many opportunities for self-service and suggests that provider motivation and customer benefits can drive the growth of self-service. Elimination of labor costs for nonproductive activity is the principal driver for the service provider. For example, it costs $7 to answer a query through a call center, but only 10 cents to deal with one online. Customer acceptance and, often, preference result from increased opportunity for customization, accuracy, convenience, and speed.

Service has migrated from human interaction to substitution of machines for service employees or, where feasible, to anywhere–anytime electronic service. This trajectory is similar to the past experience in the agricultural and manufacturing sectors of the economy where human labor has been driven out of the production process relentlessly. Table 4.1 gives examples of the inroads that self-service technology (SST) has made in the service sector.

The initial targets of SST were service transactions that did not add value or have revenue-enhancing opportunity because the substitution of technology for employee labor achieved cost savings. For example, the introduction of ATMs by banks a quarter century ago saved teller costs but also provided customers with place-and-time convenience. Retailers are adopting readers for a new technology called near-field communication (NFC),

TABLE 4.1
Evolution of Self-Service

Source: James A. Fitzsimmons, "Is the Future of Services Self-service?" Managing Service Quality 13, no. 6 (2003), p. 444.

Service Industry	Human Contact	Machine Assisted	Internet Facilitated
Banking	Teller	ATM	Online banking
Grocery	Checkout clerk	Self-checkout station	Online order/pickup
Airlines	Ticket agent	Check-in kiosk	Print boarding pass
Restaurants	Wait person	Vending machine	Online order/delivery
Movie theater	Ticket sale	Kiosk ticketing	Pay-per-view
Bookstore	Information clerk	Stock-availability terminal	Online shopping
Education	Teacher	Computer tutorial	Distance learning
Gambling	Poker dealer	Computer poker	Online poker

which stores credit card information in mobile devices that allow customers to use smartphones instead of credit cards. The technology helps retailers to keep track of customer spending habits and advertise special offers. Customers gain the convenience that frequent purchases (e.g., personalized latte at Starbucks) can be ordered and paid for without joining the waiting line, thereby speeding service.

By definition, high-touch services such as health care, fire fighting, and dentistry remain immune to self-service, but some inroads are possible. For example, a patient at home can use a blood pressure machine to record a vital activity that can be sent by telephone to a remote receiver in the doctor's office.

The proliferation of self-service has many implications for society. Low-wage, unskilled, non-value-added service jobs are bound to disappear. The emergence of a self-service sector means that the growth in service jobs will be limited to highly skilled (e.g., health care), intellectual (e.g., professional), and creative (e.g., entertainment) pursuits. Finally, the question of what constitutes economic activity will need to be redefined to account for the value of self-service labor.

The Service Encounter Triad

One of the unique characteristics of services is the active participation of the customer in the service production process. Every moment of truth involves an interaction between a customer and a service provider; each has a role to play in an environment staged by the service organization. The *service encounter triad* shown in Figure 4.2 captures the relationships between the three parties in the service encounter and suggests possible sources of conflict.

Managers of for-profit service organizations have an interest in delivering service as efficiently as possible to protect their margins and remain competitive. Nonprofit service organizations might substitute effectiveness for efficiency, but they still must operate under the

FIGURE 4.2
The Service Encounter Triad

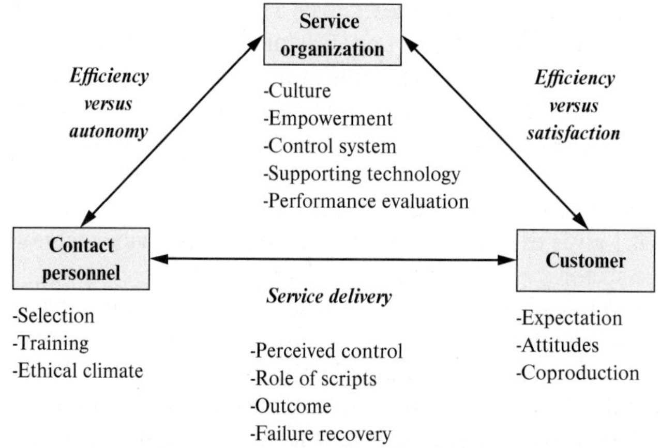

The convenience of the check-in kiosk was welcomed by business travelers.

limits imposed by a budget. To control service delivery, managers tend to impose rules and procedures on the contact personnel to limit their autonomy and discretion when serving the customer. These same rules and procedures also are intended to limit the extent of service provided for the customer and the resulting lack of customization that might result in a dissatisfied customer. Finally, the interaction between contact personnel and the customer has the element of perceived control by both parties. The contact people want to control the behavior of the customer to make their own work more manageable and less stressful; at the same time, the customer is attempting to gain control of the service encounter to derive the most benefit from it.

Ideally, the three parties gain much by working together to create a beneficial service encounter. The moment of truth can be dysfunctional, however, when one party dominates the interaction by focusing solely on his or her own control of the encounter. The following examples illustrate the conflict that arises when each party in turn dominates control of the encounter.

Encounter Dominated by the Service Organization

To be efficient and, perhaps, to follow a cost leadership strategy, an organization might standardize service delivery by imposing strict operating procedures and, thus, severely limit the discretion of the contact personnel. Customers are presented with a few standard service options from which to choose, and personalized service is not available. Many franchise services such as McDonald's, Jiffy Lube, and H&R Block have been successful with a structural organization and environment that dominates the service encounter. Much of their success has resulted from teaching customers what *not* to expect from their service; however, much of the frustration that customers experience with other institutions, labeled pejoratively as "bureaucracies," is the result of contact personnel having no autonomy to deal with an individual customer's needs. Contact personnel in such organizations may sympathize with the customer but are forced to go "by the book," and their job satisfaction is diminished in the process.

Contact Personnel–Dominated Encounter

In general, service personnel attempt to limit the scope of the service encounter to reduce their own stress in meeting demanding customers. When contact personnel are placed in an autonomous position, they may perceive themselves as having a significant degree of control over customers. The customer is expected to place considerable trust in the contact person's judgment because of the service provider's perceived expertise. The relationship between physician and patient best illustrates the shortcomings of the contact personnel-dominated encounter. The patient, who is not even referred to as a "customer," is placed in a subordinate position with no control over the encounter. Further, an allied organization, such as a hospital in this case, is subjected to tremendous demands placed on it by individual staff physicians with no regard for matters of efficiency.

Customer-Dominated Encounter

The extremes of standardized and customized services represent opportunities for customers to control the encounter. For standardized services, self-service is an option that gives customers complete control over the limited service that is provided. For example, at a self-service gasoline station that is equipped with a credit card reader, the customer need not interact with anyone. The result can be very efficient and satisfying to the customer who needs or desires very little service. For a customized service such as legal defense in a criminal case, however, all of the organization's resources might be needed, at great cost in efficiency.

The online encounter is an increasing popular variation on Figure 4.2 where the "contact personnel" box is replaced with a website. Designing a website that will attract repeat customers is a challenge for the service organization. In an effort to measure the effectiveness of websites, a survey instrument called E-S-QUAL was developed.[4] The 22-item survey consists of four dimensions: efficiency (e.g., the site is easy to navigate), system availability (e.g., site does not crash), fulfillment (e.g., ordered items arrive quickly), and privacy (e.g., one's credit card information is protected).

A satisfactory and effective service encounter should balance the need for control by all three participants. The organization's need for efficiency to remain economically viable can be satisfied when contact personnel are trained properly and the customer's expectations and role in the delivery process are communicated effectively. Our discussion of approaches to managing the service encounter begins with the service organization.

The Service Organization

The service organization establishes the environment for the service encounter. The interaction between customer and contact personnel occurs within the context of an organization's culture as well as its physical surroundings.

Culture

Why do we choose employment or seek service at one firm versus another? Often the choice is based on the firm's reputation as a good place to work or shop. This reputation is based upon the organization's *culture* or identity. The following definitions of culture share the idea that beliefs and traditions create a unique identity for an organization:

- Culture is a pattern of beliefs and expectations that is shared by the organization's members and produces norms that powerfully shape the behavior of individuals or groups in organizations.
- Culture is the traditions and beliefs of an organization that distinguish it from other organizations and infuse a certain life into the skeleton of structure.
- Organizational culture is a system of shared orientations that hold the unit together and give a distinctive identity.

The founders and/or senior managers of a service organization establish, whether purposely or unintentionally, a climate or culture that prescribes a norm of behavior or set of values to guide employee decision making in the firm. Consider, for example, ServiceMaster, a very profitable company that provides hospitals and other organizations with housekeeping services. Writing about ServiceMaster, Carol Loomis discovered that the company's name embodied its value of "Service to the Master."

> Founded by a devout Baptist, the late Marion E. Wade, the company has always described itself as driven by religious principle. The first of its corporate objectives is "to honor God in all we do." The cafeteria wall at ServiceMaster's suburban headquarters proclaims that "Joy cometh in the morning," and although there are no "Cleanliness is next to Godliness" signs around, the neatness and shine of the office project the thought.[5]

Choice of language is another approach to communicate values, as illustrated by the Walt Disney Corporation. At Disney theme parks, show business terms are used because they are in the entertainment business. Instead of Personnel there is Casting. Employees

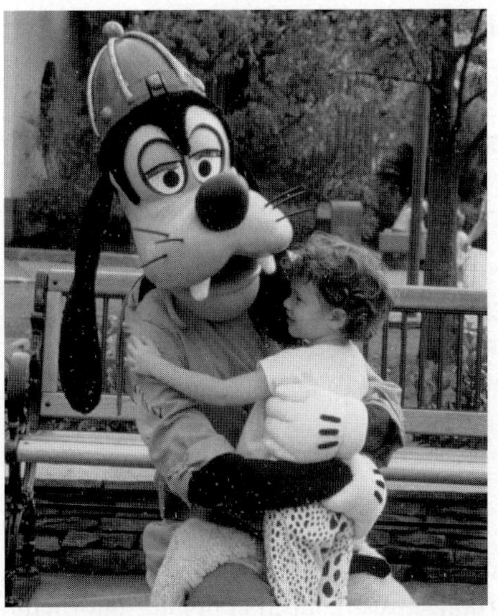

The use of language and symbols communicates the culture of organization. ©Carl & Ann Purcell/ CORBIS via Getty Images FR

are referred to as "cast members" to instill the appropriate frame of mind. Cast members work either "onstage" or "backstage," but both kinds of employees are required to "put on the show."

The examples above illustrate how an organization's values, when consistently communicated by management, permit contact personnel to act with considerable autonomy, because their judgment is founded on a shared set of values. These values often are communicated by stories and legends about individual risk-taking on behalf of the organization and its customers. Federal Express, with a motto of "absolutely positively overnight," has many stories of extraordinary employee feats to safeguard that service guarantee. Consider, for example, the pickup driver who was faced with a collection box he was unable to open–instead of leaving it standing on the street corner until someone could come out to repair it, he wrestled the entire box into his vehicle so that the packages it contained could be liberated and delivered the next day.

The organization benefits from a shared set of values, because contact personnel are empowered to make decisions without the need for the traditional level of supervision, which assumes that only management is vested with authority to act on behalf of the organization.

Empowerment

Empowerment does not begin with delegation, but by trusting unconditionally the inherent power within employees to evaluate choices and competently execute creative decisions. Empowerment unleashes within each person the opportunity to make a difference that cannot be given or taken away. Delegation is acting upon another's behalf as a surrogate to perform a particular task. It is not power, but rather permission given as often as taken away.

A new model of service organization that has a structure best described as an inverted T has emerged. In this organization, the layers of supervision are drastically reduced because contact personnel are trained, motivated, and supplied with timely, computer-based information that enables them to manage the service encounter at the point of delivery.

Jan Carlzon, the innovative president of SAS, is quoted as saying:

> Instructions only succeed in providing employees with knowledge of their own limitations. Information, on the other hand, provides them with a knowledge of their opportunities and possibilities. . . . To free someone from rigorous control by instructions, policies and orders, and to give that person freedom to take responsibility for his ideas, decisions and actions, is to release hidden resources which would otherwise remain inaccessible to both the individual and the company. . . . A person who has information cannot avoid taking responsibility.[6]

Perhaps it is surprising that Taco Bell has become the new service model of employee *empowerment*. Other firms adopting this new model include ServiceMaster, Marriott, and Dayton Hudson. Senior managers of these firms all share a belief that people want to do good work–and will do so if given the opportunity. Consequently, they have made the following commitments: (1) to invest in people as much as, or more than, in machines; (2) to use technology to support contact personnel rather than to monitor or replace them; (3) to consider the recruitment and training of contact personnel as critical to the firm's success; and (4) to link compensation to performance for employees at all levels. In this type of organization, a much-reduced middle management no longer has the traditional

TABLE 4.2 Organizational Control Systems for Employee Empowerment

Adapted from James A. Fitzsimmons, Mona J. Fitzsimmons, Sanjeev Bordoloi, *Service Management Operations, Strategy, Information Technology,* 8th edition, (2014).

Control System	Belief	Boundary	Diagnostic	Interactive
Objective	Contribute	Compliance	Achieve	Create
Employee Challenge	Uncertainty about purpose	Pressure or temptation	Lack of focus	Lack of opportunity or risk averse
Management Challenge	Communicate core values and mission	Specify and enforce rules	Build and support clear targets	Critical performance variables
Key Issues	Identify core values	Risks to be avoided	Critical performance variables	Strategic uncertainties

supervisory role; instead, middle managers become facilitators for the frontline or contact personnel. More important, investment in computer information systems is necessary to supply the frontline personnel with the ability to resolve problems as they arise and to ensure a quality service encounter.

Control Systems

Table 4.2 describes four organizational control systems to encourage creative employee empowerment. The belief system is facilitated by a well-articulated organizational culture. A boundary system defines limits to employee initiative (e.g., do not commit the organization to a financial liability in excess of $1,000) without creating an environment of negative thinking that can be generated by using standard operating procedures. Diagnostic systems define measurable goals to achieve (e.g., 90 percent on-time performance). The interactive control system is most appropriate for "knowledge industries" such as consulting firms, because the organization's very survival depends on delivering creative solutions for its customers.

Empowered contact personnel must be motivated, informed, competent, committed, and well-trained. Frontline personnel should exhibit the ability to take responsibility, manage themselves, and respond to pressure from customers.

Customer Relationship Management

Systems have been developed to help organizations to manage the interactions with their customers and sales prospects. Customer relationship management (CRM) is an information industry term for methodologies, software, and Internet capabilities that help an enterprise to manage its relationships in an organized way. For example, an enterprise can build a database about its customers that describes relationships and permits management, salespeople, and service providers–even the customers themselves–to access information directly that matches customer needs with product offerings, reminds customers of service requirements, and lists other products the customer has purchased already. The overall goals are to find, attract, and win new clients, nurture and retain those the company already has, entice former clients back into the fold, and reduce the cost of marketing and client service. CRM systems offer the following capabilities:

- Enabling marketing departments to identify and target their best customers, manage marketing campaigns, and generate quality leads for the sales team.
- Allowing the formation of individualized relationships with customers, in order to improve customer satisfaction and maximize profits by identifying the most profitable customers and providing them with the highest level of service.
- Providing employees with the information and processes necessary to know their customers; understand and identify customer needs; and effectively build relationships among the company, its customer base, and distribution partners.

- Assisting the organization to improve sales management by optimizing information shared by multiple employees, preparing metrics on sales effectiveness, and monitoring social media sites as a vehicle for crowd-sourcing solutions to client-support problems.

Contact Personnel

Ideally, customer contact personnel should have personality attributes that include flexibility, tolerance for ambiguity, an ability to monitor and change behavior on the basis of situational cues, and empathy for customers. The last attribute (i.e., empathy for customers) has been found to be more important than age, education, sales-related knowledge, sales training, and intelligence.

Some individuals may find frontline service to be boring and repetitive, whereas others see the job as providing an opportunity to meet and interact with a variety of people. Those with the necessary interpersonal skills may gravitate toward high-contact service jobs, but a selection process still is required to ensure high-quality moments of truth.

Selection

No reliable tests exist to measure a person's service orientation; however, a variety of interviewing techniques have proven to be useful. Abstract questioning, the situational vignette, and role playing all have been used in evaluating potential frontline employees.

Abstract Questioning

The questions asked in the abstract interview are open-ended. They provide insights regarding an applicant's ability to relate the immediate service situation to information collected from past experience. An example of a question that assesses an applicant's attention to the details of an encounter would be "From your past work experience, what type of customer was most difficult for you to deal with and why?" To determine if an applicant actively collects information, a questioner might ask, "What was the customer's primary complaint?" Some final questions to evaluate the applicant's interpersonal style could be "How did you handle the customer?" and "What would be the ideal way to deal with that type of customer?"

Abstract questioning also can be used to reveal a person's willingness to adapt. An effective employee will take notice of details in his or her personal life as well as on the job. People who consider the events around them and can describe their significance usually are able to learn more as well as faster.

Because of their nature and preparation for the interview, some applicants will be better able than others to talk extensively about their past experiences. Careful listening and probing by the interviewer for the substance of an answer to an abstract question will lessen the possibility of being deceived with "puffery." Finally, there is no assurance that the ability to reflect on past events necessarily will guarantee that such perceptiveness and flexibility will transfer to the job.

Situational Vignette

A *situational vignette* interview requires the applicant to answer questions regarding a specific situation. For example, consider the following situational vignette:

> The day after a catering service has catered a large party, a customer returns some small cakes, claiming they were stale. Although the man is demanding a refund, he is so soft spoken and timid that you can hardly hear him across the counter. You know that your business did not make those cakes, because they don't look like your chef's work. What would you do?

Presenting a situation like this may reveal information regarding an applicant's instincts, interpersonal capabilities, common sense, and judgment. To gain more information about a candidate's creativity and adaptability, further questions about the situation can be asked: "How would you handle the man if, suddenly, he were to become irate and insistent? What steps would you take to remedy the situation?"

Situational vignettes provide an opportunity to determine whether applicants are able to "think on their feet." An applicant with good communication skills, however, still might not indicate clearly a genuine desire to serve customers or display empathy. Again, the interviewer must pay close attention to the substance of an applicant's response in addition to the way it is delivered.

Role Playing

Role playing is an interviewing technique that requires applicants to participate in a simulated situation and to react as if this service environment were real. Role playing often is used in the final phase of recruitment, and others in the organization are asked to cooperate by posing as "actors" for the situation.

Role playing provides a way for an interviewer to observe an applicant under stress. Interviewers using this technique can probe and change the situation as the session progresses. This method allows for more realistic responses than either the abstract questioning or situational vignette interviews; applicants are required to use their own words and react to the immediate situation instead of describing them.

Although role playing provides an excellent opportunity to observe a candidate's strengths and weaknesses in a realistic customer encounter, direct comparison of applicants is difficult. Role playing does require careful scripting, and the "actors" need to rehearse their roles before the interview.

Training

Most training manuals and employee handbooks for customer-contact personnel are devoted to explaining the technical skills that are needed to perform the jobs. For example, they often detail explicitly how to fill out guest reports, use cash registers, dress properly, and enforce safety requirements, but customer interaction skills are often dismissed with a simple comment to be pleasant and smile.

Difficulties with interactions between customers and contact personnel fall into two categories: problem customers and service failure. These are shown in Table 4.3.[7]

Unrealistic Customer Expectations

Approximately 75 percent of the reported communication difficulties arise from causes other than a breakdown in the technical service delivery. These difficult encounters involve customers with unrealistic expectations that cannot be met by the service delivery system. Examples include passengers who bring oversized luggage aboard an airplane or diners who snap fingers and yell at servers. Unrealistic customer expectations can be broken down into five challenges:

1. *Unreasonable demands.* Services that the firm cannot offer or customer demands that require inappropriate time and attention (e.g., "I want to carry all my luggage on board," or "Please sit with me; I'm afraid of flying").
2. *Abusive or hostile attitude.* Customers treatment of employee with verbal or physical abuse (e.g., "You idiot! Where is my drink?" or a diner pinching a waitress).
3. *Inappropriate behavior.* Customers becoming intoxicated or acting inappropriately (e.g., an inebriated passenger trying to exit the plane while in flight or guests swimming nude in the hotel pool).

TABLE 4.3
Challenges Facing Customer Contact Personnel

Problem Customers	Service Failure
1. Unreasonable demands	1. Unavailable service
2. Abusive or hostile attitude	2. Slow performance
3. Inappropriate behavior	3. Unacceptable service
4. Unanticipated demands	
5. Demands contrary to policies	

4. *Unanticipated demands.* Special attention to customers with medical or language difficulties (e.g., "My wife is in labor," or "Wieviel kostet das?").
5. *Demands contrary to policies.* Requests that are impossible to fulfill because of safety regulations, laws, or company policies (e.g., "We've been waiting an hour for takeoff, and I must have my smoke," or "Our party of 10 wants separate checks for the meal").

Service Failure

A failure in the service delivery system places a communication burden on the contact personnel. Service failures, however, provide a unique opportunity for contact personnel to demonstrate innovation and flexibility in their recovery. Three types of service failures can be identified:

1. *Unavailable service.* Services that normally are available or expected are lacking (e.g., "I reserved a table by the window," or "Why is the ATM out of order?").
2. *Slow performance.* Service is unusually slow, creating excessive customer waiting (e.g., "Why hasn't our plane arrived?" or "We've been here for an hour, and no one has taken our order").
3. *Unacceptable service.* Service does not meet acceptable standards (e.g., "My seat doesn't recline," or "There's a hair in my soup!").

Communication with difficult customers requires contact personnel whose training and interpersonal skills can prevent a bad situation from becoming worse. Programs can be developed to train contact personnel to use prescribed responses in given situations. For example, when faced with unreasonable demands such as "Please sit with me; I'm afraid of flying" the flight attendant can appeal to the customer's sense of fairness by pointing out that the needs of other customers would be jeopardized. Actual scripts also can be developed and rehearsed for each anticipated situation. For example, in response to "I want to carry all my luggage on board," the boarding attendant need only say, "I'm very sorry, but federal safety regulations permit a passenger only two carry-on pieces small enough to be stored under the seat or overhead. May I check your larger pieces all the way to your final destination?"

Role playing can provide an ideal setting for gaining experience in dealing with service failures. This approach should help contact personnel to anticipate the types of exchanges they might encounter, expand their repertoire of possible responses, and develop decision rules for choosing appropriate responses to a given situation. Contact personnel who are well trained will be able to control the service encounter in a professional manner, and the results will be increased satisfaction for the customer and decreased stress and frustration for the provider.

Creating an Ethical Climate

A shift has occurred in society away from the past expectation of organizational self-regulation in the marketplace. Once financial firms such as banking and insurance, in addition to the professions of law, medicine, and accounting, viewed themselves as private-sector participants with public responsibilities. In fact, lawyers still are called "officers of the court." Historically, they acted with a sense of stewardship, thinking not only about advancing their firm but what was appropriate action for the entire legal system. For lawyers, that meant advising their clients against time-consuming litigation or mindless mergers. Elihu Root, a leader of the New York bar in the late 19th century, once said, "About half the practice of a decent lawyer consists of telling would-be clients that they are dammed fools and should stop."[8]

Customer-contact employees working without close supervision often are placed in situations where ethical standards might be compromised in an effort to serve multiple conflicting demands at the same time. Table 4.4 illustrates how employees might engage in unethical behaviors to cover their mistakes, to increase the firm's revenues (e.g., inappropriate cross-selling), or to satisfy a demanding customer. To prevent the negative consequences of unethical opportunism and build a culture of trust and integrity, managers must have a means of instilling ethical behavior in their employees.

TABLE 4.4 Examples of Unethical Behaviors in Customer-Contact Settings

Source: Adapted from Charles H. Schwepker, Jr. and Michael D. Hartline, "Managing the Ethical Climate of Customer-Contact Service Employees," *Journal of Service Research* 7, no. 4 (May 2005), p. 378.

Misrepresenting the Nature of the Service	Customer Manipulation	General Honesty and Integrity
• Promising a nonsmoking room when none is available	• Giving away a guaranteed reservation	• Treating customers unfairly or rudely
• Using bait-and-switch tactics	• Performing unnecessary services	• Being unresponsive to customer requests
• Creating a false need for service	• Padding a bill with hidden charges	• Failing to follow stated company policies
• Misrepresenting the credentials of the service provider	• Hiding damage to customer possessions	• Stealing customer credit card information
• Exaggerating the benefits of a specific service offering	• Making it difficult to invoke a service guarantee	• Sharing customer information with third parties

Schwepker and Hartline propose that both formal controls (enforcement of ethical codes and punishment for ethical violations) and informal controls (discussion of ethics, internalization of a code of ethics, and ethical climate) are central to promoting ethical behavior and will lead to a commitment to service quality and job satisfaction. Formal controls are necessary to set boundaries for what is considered acceptable behavior. The social and cultural climate created via informal controls ensures that employees monitor and regulate their ethical behavior individually and within work groups.[9]

The Customer

Every purchase is an event of some importance for the customer, whereas the same transaction usually is routine for the service provider. The emotional involvement that is associated with the routine purchase of gasoline at a self-serve station or a hamburger and fries at a drive-thru restaurant is minor, but consider the very personal and dramatic roles played by a customer taking an exotic vacation or seeking medical treatment. Unfortunately, it is very difficult for bored contact personnel, who see hundreds of customers a week, to maintain a corresponding level of emotional commitment.

Expectations and Attitudes

Service customers are motivated to look for a service much as they would for a product; similarly, their expectations govern their shopping attitudes. Gregory Stone developed a now-famous topology in which shopping-goods customers were classified into four groups.[10] The definitions that follow have been modified for the service customer:

1. *The economizing customer.* This customer wants to maximize the value obtained for his or her expenditures of time, effort, and money. He or she is a demanding and sometimes fickle customer who looks for value that will test the competitive strength of the service firm in the market. Loss of these customers serves as an early warning of potential competitive threats.
2. *The ethical customer.* This customer feels a moral obligation to patronize socially responsible firms. Service firms that have developed a reputation for community service can create such a loyal customer base; for example, the Ronald McDonald House program for the families of hospitalized children has helped the image of McDonald's in just this way.
3. *The personalizing customer.* This customer wants interpersonal gratification, such as recognition and conversation, from the service experience. Greeting customers on a first-name basis always has been a staple of the neighborhood family restaurant, but

computerized customer files can generate a similar personalized experience when used skillfully by frontline personnel in many other businesses.

4. *The convenience customer.* This customer has no interest in shopping for the service; convenience is the secret to attracting him or her. Convenience customers often are willing to pay extra for personalized or hassle-free service, witness the success of Amazon Prime service.

The attitude of customers regarding their need to control the service encounter was the subject of a study investigating customers' decision-making processes when they were confronted with the choice between a self-service option and the traditional full-service approach.[11] Customers who were interviewed appeared to be using the following dimensions in their selection: (1) amount of time involved, (2) customer's control of the situation, (3) efficiency of the process, (4) amount of human contact involved, (5) risk involved, (6) amount of effort involved, and (7) customer's need to depend on others.

It is not surprising that customers who were interested in the self-service option found the second dimension (i.e., customer's control of the situation) to be the most important factor in choosing that option. The study was conducted over a variety of services, ranging from banks and gas stations to hotels and airlines. Services competing on a cost leadership strategy can make use of this finding by engaging the customer in *coproduction* to reduce costs.

The Role of Scripts in Coproduction

In the service encounter, both the provider and the customer have roles to play in transacting the service. Society has defined specific tasks for service customers to perform, such as the procedure required for cashing checks at a bank. Diners in some restaurants might assume a variety of productive roles, such as assembling their meals and carrying them to the table in a cafeteria, serving themselves at a salad bar, or busing their own tables. In each case, the customer has learned a set of behaviors that is appropriate for the situation. The customer is participating in the service delivery as a partial employee with a role to play and is following a script that is defined by societal norms or implied by the particular design of the service offered.

Customers possess a variety of scripts that are learned for use in different service encounters. Following the appropriate script allows both the customer and the service provider to predict the behavior of each other as they play out their respective roles. Thus, each participant expects some element of perceived control in the service encounter. Problems can arise if customers abuse their script. For example, upon finishing a meal at a fast-food restaurant, a customer is expected to clear his or her table, but if this script is not followed, an employee must do the task.

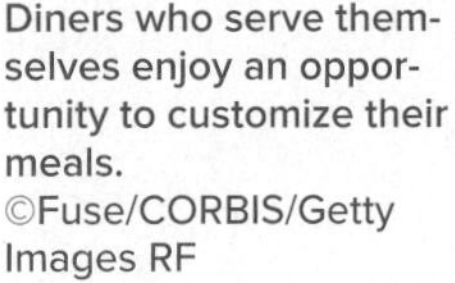

Diners who serve themselves enjoy an opportunity to customize their meals.
©Fuse/CORBIS/Getty Images RF

Acceptance of new technology that replaces a human service encounter can take time while customers learn the new script. What once was a "mindless" routine service encounter now requires some effort to learn a new role. For example, the introduction of self-scanning checkout machines at supermarkets and home improvement stores requires an attendant nearby to help customers through the new process. When customers learn their new script and grow to appreciate the reduced checkout lines, the dedicated attendant might no longer be needed and the full benefit of the self-checkout investment will be realized.

Teaching customers a new role can be facilitated if the transition becomes a logical modification of past behavior. Public acceptance of the Windows operating system for PCs can be attributed to the fact that all applications share the same interface; thus, only one script must be learned.

Creating a Customer Service Orientation[12]

A study of 23 branch banks revealed a high correlation between customers' and employees' perceptions of service quality. Each dot in Figure 4.3 represents data from a different branch bank. Employees were asked: "How do you think the customers of your bank view the general quality of the service they receive in your branch?" Customers were asked: "Describe the general quality of the service received in your branch." Both groups graded service on the same six-point scale.

Further analysis showed that customers perceived better service in branches where employees reported the following:

1. There is a more enthusiastic service emphasis.
2. The branch manager emphasizes service as personnel perform their roles.
3. There is an active effort to retain all customer accounts, not just those of large-account holders.
4. The branch is staffed with sufficient and well-trained tellers.
5. Equipment is well maintained, and supplies are plentiful.

In addition, when employees described their branch as one in which the manager emphasized customer service, customers not only reported that service was superior but, more specifically, that:

1. Tellers were courteous and competent.
2. Staffing levels were adequate.
3. The branch appeared to be well administered.

FIGURE 4.3
Relationship between Customer and Employee Perceptions of Customer Service

Source: Benjamin Schneider, "The Service Organization: Climate Is Crucial," *Organizational Dynamics*, Autumn 1980, p. 62.

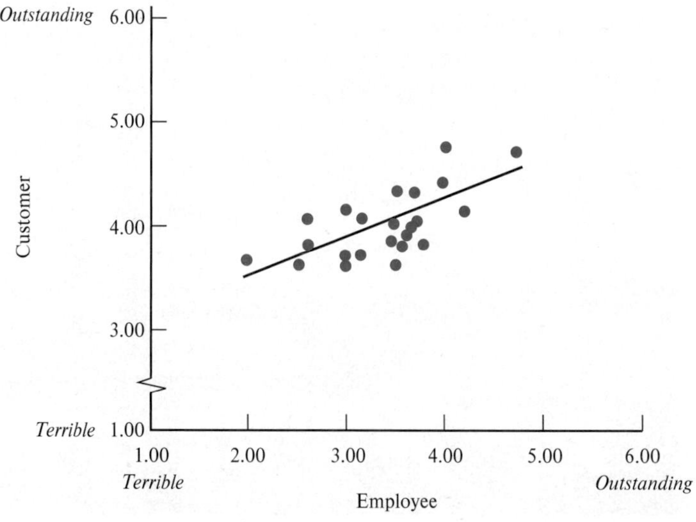

TABLE 4.5
Satisfaction Duality

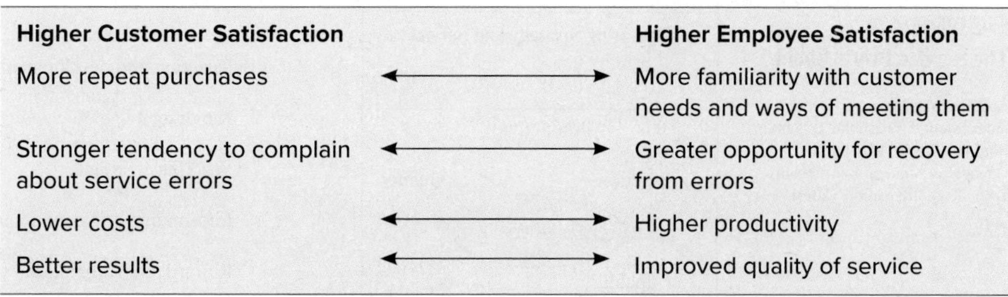

Higher Customer Satisfaction		Higher Employee Satisfaction
More repeat purchases	←→	More familiarity with customer needs and ways of meeting them
Stronger tendency to complain about service errors	←→	Greater opportunity for recovery from errors
Lower costs	←→	Higher productivity
Better results	←→	Improved quality of service

4. Teller turnover was low.
5. The staff had positive work attitudes.

From this study, it appears that when employees perceive a strong service orientation, customers report superior service. Creating a customer service orientation results in superior service practices and procedures that are observable by customers and, further, seem to fit employee views of the appropriate style for dealing with customers. Thus, even though employees and customers view service from different perspectives, their perceptions of organizational effectiveness are positively related.

This relationship that develops between the customer and the employee is shown in Table 4.5 as a satisfaction duality. For example, after a bank employee gets to know a customer, the cost of serving that customer decreases because time is saved in identity verification and needs can be anticipated (e.g., purchase of a certificate of deposit when money market balance becomes excessive). The loyal customer values this improved productivity and more personalized service. Both parties enjoy the satisfaction of a more human relationship.

The satisfaction duality also suggests a lesson for management. The way management relates to the contact personnel (or internal customers) is reflected in how the external customers are treated.

Service Profit Chain[13]

The service profit chain proposes a relationship that links profitability, customer loyalty, and service value to employee satisfaction, capability, and productivity. Figure 4.4 shows that profitability and revenue growth are derived from loyal customers. Loyal customers, in turn, result from satisfaction that is influenced by the perceived value of the service. Satisfied, committed, capable, and productive employees create service value. Satisfied and loyal employees begin with selection and training, but require investment in information technology and other workplace support that allow decision-making latitude to serve customers.

1. *Internal quality drives employee satisfaction.* Internal service quality describes the environment in which employees work and includes employee selection and development, rewards and recognition, access to information to serve the customer, workplace technology, and job design. At USAA, a financial services company serving the military community, for example, a telephone service representative is supported by a sophisticated information system that puts complete customer information files on his or her monitor when a customer gives a membership number. The facility is headquartered in suburban San Antonio and resembles a small college campus. Using 75 classrooms, state-of-the-art job-related training is an expected part of everyone's work experience.
2. *Employee satisfaction drives retention and productivity.* In most service jobs, the real cost of employee turnover is the loss of productivity and decreased customer satisfaction. In personalized service firms, low employee turnover is linked closely to high customer satisfaction. The cost of losing a valued broker at a securities firm, for example, is measured by the loss of commissions during the time a replacement is building relationships with

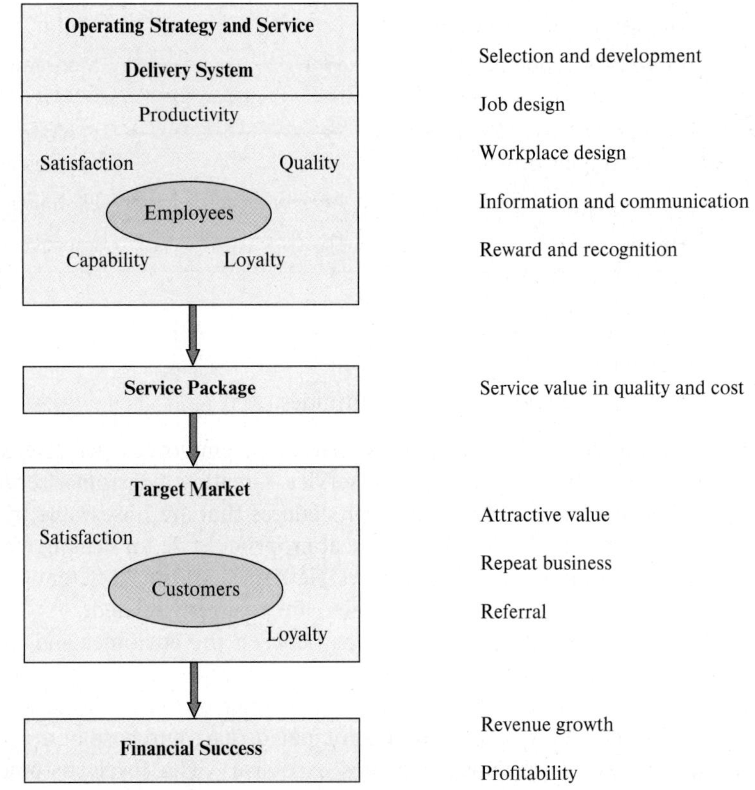

FIGURE 4.4
The Service Profit Chain

Adapted from James A. Fitzsimmons, Mona J. Fitzsimmons, Sanjeev Bordoloi, Service Management Operations, Strategy, Information Technology, 8th edition, (2014).

customers. Employee satisfaction also can contribute to productivity. Southwest Airlines has been the most profitable airline consistently owing in part to its high rate of employee retention. Its turnover rate of less than 5 percent per year is the lowest in the industry.

3. *Employee retention and productivity drive service value.* At Southwest Airlines, customer perceptions of value are very high, even though the organization does not assign seats, offer first-class seating, or integrate its reservation system with other airlines. Customers place high value on frequent departures, on-time service, friendly employees, and competitive fares. Southwest fares are possible in part because highly trained flexible employees can perform several jobs and because they can turn around an aircraft at the gate in fewer than 15 minutes.
4. *Service value drives customer satisfaction.* Customer value is measured by comparing results received to the total costs incurred in obtaining the service. Progressive Corporation, the casualty insurance company, creates customer value by processing and paying claims quickly and with little policyholder effort. Progressive, for example, flies a team to the scene of major catastrophes and is able to process claims immediately, provide support services, reduce legal costs, and actually place more money in the hands of injured parties.
5. *Customer satisfaction drives customer loyalty.* When Xerox polled its customers using a five-point scale ranging from "extremely dissatisfied" to "very satisfied," it discovered that "very satisfied" customers were six times more likely to repurchase Xerox products and services than those who were just "satisfied." Xerox called these very satisfied customers "apostles," because they would convert the uninitiated to their product. At the other extreme are the "terrorists," customers who are so unhappy that they speak out against the firm.
6. *Customer loyalty drives profitability and growth.* Because a 5 percent increase in customer loyalty can produce a profit increase from 25 to 85 percent, the *quality* of market share, measured in terms of customer loyalty, deserves as much attention as the *quantity* of share. For example, Banc One, which merged with J.P. Morgan Chase in 2004, was a profitable bank based in Columbus, Ohio, that developed a sophisticated system to track customer loyalty by measuring the number of services that customers used and the depth of their relationship with Banc One.

Service Benchmark

MISS MANNERS ON COMPLAINT HANDLING

In the standard exchange involving a person making a complaint and one who is receiving the complaint, usually on behalf of a commercial establishment, there are, Miss Manners has observed, two obligatory roles.

One person must say something along the lines of: "This is the most outrageous thing that ever happened. I can't imagine how anyone could be so stupid. I'm going to find out exactly how this came about, and believe me, I'm going to do something about it right away."

And the other must say: "Look, mistakes happen. This is just not all that important. There's no use getting upset, because these things happen all the time. It's not really anybody's fault."

Now here comes the peculiar part: The person at whom the complaint is directed gets to choose which role he or she wants to play, and the complainer has to take the other.

Miss Manners realizes that this is a difficult concept. It must be, because those who are obliged to receive complaints, either occasionally or as a wearisome way to earn a living, don't seem to have caught on to the possibilities of the *switcheroo.*

Here is the way the standard exchange goes:

Complainer (in more or less normal voice, with just a small edge to it): "This is an outrage."

Complainee (in bored tone): "Oh, calm down. It's nobody's fault; it just happens occasionally. It's really too late to do anything about it."

Complainer (shrieking): "You mean it's happened before? Is everyone here an idiot? I've never seen such bungling in all my life. There is no excuse for this, none whatsoever." And so on and on and on.

But here is the same situation, except that the complainee has decided not to take abuse, and so has preempted that function.

Complainee (with note of abject desperation): "It certainly is. I can't imagine how this could have happened, but you may be sure I'm going to do something about it. I can't apologize to you enough. We pride ourselves on getting things right, and this is intolerable. Please give us another chance—let me see what I can do to make it up to you."

Complainer (grudgingly at first, but warming up to the subject to counter threat of Complainee continuing in the same vein): "Oh, that's OK. We all make mistakes. It's not all that important."

The essential ingredients to pull off the switch are the apology and the promise to do something, but what makes it work is the tone. Two people can't keep up an argument in which both are carrying on like that.

Miss Manners is astonished that so few people avail themselves of this simple technique to neutralize what is otherwise a nasty exchange.

Source: Judith Martin, "Complaint-Handling Requires a Deft 'Switcheroo,'" Associated Press as printed in *Austin American Statesman,* November 1, 1992, p. E14.

Summary

The Internet and other technologies have had a profound effect on the customer interface with service firms resulting in the emergence of self-service.

The service encounter is viewed as a triad, with the customer and contact personnel both exercising control over the service process in an environment defined by the service organization. The importance of flexibility in meeting customer needs has prompted many service organizations to empower their contact personnel to exercise more autonomy.

Giving employees more discretion requires a selection process that identifies applicants with the potential for adaptability in their interpersonal behaviors. Communication difficulties with customers will arise even in the best of circumstances, however. Unrealistic customer expectations and unexpected service failures must be dealt with by the contact personnel as they arise. Training to anticipate possible situations and developing "scripts" to respond to problems are two important measures that can contribute to the professionalism of the service providers.

Customers can be classified by their service expectations. Those who have a need for control are candidates for self-service options. Viewing customers as coproducers suggests the use of customer "scripts" that facilitate the service delivery and provide some behavioral predictability in the encounter.

The concept of creating a customer service orientation was discussed with reference to a study of branch banks. In this study it was discovered that customers and contact personnel share similar views of the quality of service delivered.

The chapter concludes with a discussion of the service profit chain, which provides an explanation for a firm's profitability and growth that result from the selection and development of the internal capability of the service providers and in satisfied and loyal customers.

Key Terms and Definitions

Abstract questioning an open-ended question used to screen potential employees by revealing a candidate's ability to adapt and use interpersonal skills. *pg. 103*

Coproduction viewing the customer as a productive resource in the service delivery process, which requires roles to play (e.g., busing his or her lunch table) and scripts to follow (e.g., using an ATM). *pg. 107*

Culture the shared beliefs and values of an organization that guide employee decision making and behavior in the firm. *pg. 100*

Empowerment providing contact personnel with the training and information to make decisions for the firm without close supervision. *pg. 101*

Service encounter triad a triangle depicting the balance of goals among the service organization, the contact personnel, and the customer. *pg. 98*

Situational vignette a service encounter situation that can test a candidate's ability to "think on her or his feet" and to use good judgment. *pg. 103*

Topics for Discussion

1. How can we design for self-recovery when self-service failure occurs?
2. What are the organizational and marketing implications of considering a customer as a "partial employee"?
3. Comment on the different dynamics of one-on-one service and group service in regard to perceived control of the service encounter.
4. How does use of a "service script" relate to service quality?
5. If the roles played by customers are determined by cultural norms, how can services be exported?

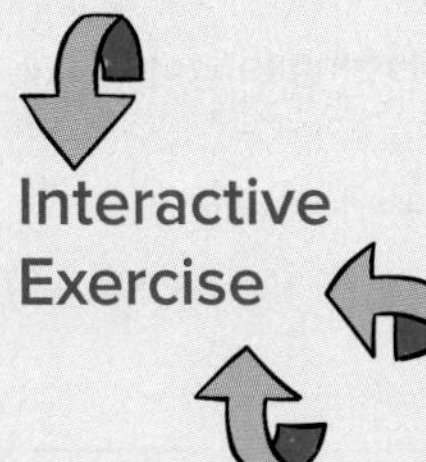

Interactive Exercise

The class breaks into small groups and each group comes up with an example from each of the four organizational control systems (i.e., belief, boundary, diagnostic, and interactive).

Amy's Ice Cream[14] CASE 4.1

Amy's Ice Cream is a business that was founded in Austin, Texas, and now has 12 locations in Austin and one each in Houston and San Antonio. When asked about the driving force behind it, Phil Clay, the production manager, explained that "while the product is of excellent quality and does come in some unique flavors, ultimately ice cream is ice cream. One can just as easily go to Swensen's or the Marble Slab to get great ice cream. Service is what differentiates Amy's from other ice cream stores and keeps customers coming back again and again." And indeed, the service at Amy's is unique.

Amy Miller, the owner and founder, got her start in the ice cream business when she worked for Steve's Ice Cream in Boston, a store whose gimmick was mashing toppings into ice cream. She recalls how Harvard and M.I.T. students would work at the store—obviously for reasons other than the great salary and fringe benefits. She quickly realized that this was a business that instantly made its customers happy. Working in an ice cream store was a "feel-good" occupation, which lured such bright workers who could easily make much more money working almost anywhere else.

When she opened the first Amy's Ice Cream in October 1984, she had two philosophies: one that an employee should enjoy what he or she does, and another that the service as well as the ice cream should make the customer smile. These philosophies have provided the foundation for a business that two decades later is firmly established and thriving.

In the beginning, theater majors and artists often were hired as servers, because the idea of enjoying what they were doing was just as appealing to them as making money. These outgoing and creative employees were very skilled at projecting their colorful personalities across the counter. They joked and interacted with customers while filling their orders. Customers were drawn to the fun and variety of the service, which might be described as "ice cream theater," and once drawn, the customers returned again and again for repeat performances.

How does Amy's recruit employees who are up to "performing"? Originally, the employment application form was rather casual, simply handwritten and mimeographed. Mr. Clay recalls, however, that one day he was out of forms when a very large man asked for a copy. The man became somewhat belligerent at being told none was available, so Mr. Clay whipped out a white paper bag—the only writing surface under the counter—and offered it as an "alternate" form. The applicant was satisfied and carried away his form to complete! When Mr. Clay relayed this story to Amy, she said the white paper bag would work just fine, and it became the new "official" application form. In fact, it has proven to be a very good indicator of whether an applicant is willing and able to express herself or himself both easily and creatively. A person who uses the bag just to write down the usual biographical information (i.e., name, address, Social Security number, and so on) probably will not be as entertaining a scooper as one who makes it into a puppet or hot air balloon. Getting "the sack" at Amy's takes on a whole new meaning. Applicants who pass the sack test then are interviewed.

New employees go through an on-the-job training process. One part of this training concerns ice cream procedures so that servers can deliver a consistent product. The other part teaches them to express themselves from behind the counter, which includes recognizing which customers enjoy the revelry and which just want to be left alone, as well as how far the kidding can be taken with different customers. In general, employees are free to interact theatrically with those customers who want to do so.

In the early days Amy's operated on an approximate 3 percent profit margin. Consequently, the servers were minimum wage, and about 80 percent of them were part-time workers who received no additional benefits. In fact, most managers made less than $15,000 per year, and there was a $30,000 cap for all employees—including Amy. In view of the low remuneration that still exists, how is Amy's Ice Cream always able to recruit the high-quality help that translates into satisfied customers?

Well, they do get Amy's Ice Cream T-shirts at cost and all the ice cream they can eat! Perhaps the major reason, however, is that Amy's is freedom-oriented rather than rules-oriented. The only "uniform" an employee must wear is an apron, whose primary function is to project a sense of continuity behind the counter. A hat also is de rigueur, but the employee is free to choose any hat as long as it effectively restrains the hair. In addition, the employee may wear any clothing that suits his or her mood that day as long as it is not soiled, political, or excessively revealing.

Employees can bring their own music, keeping in mind their type of clientele, to play in their stores. For example, an Amy's located in a downtown nightspot district draws a young, exuberant crowd that would appreciate lively music, whereas an Amy's located in an upscale shopping mall attracts a clientele whose musical tastes might be a bit more quiet.

The design of each store and the artwork displayed there tend to be colorful and eclectic, but again, the employees are free to make contributions. Amy's employs a local artist to decorate all stores; still, the individual managers have considerable say in what they feel is desirable for their own location. Often, the artwork is an exhibition of local artists' efforts.

Everyone does everything that needs to be done in the store. If the floor needs to be cleaned, the manager is just as likely to do it as a scooper. There is a very strong sense of teamwork and camaraderie. Employee meetings are usually held at 1 AM, after the last Amy's Ice Cream has closed for the night. Door prizes are offered to encourage attendance.

Apparently, it is a lifestyle choice to work for Amy's. These employees are people who do not want a "real job" in which they would have to wear certain clothes, work certain hours, and not have nearly as much fun. Obviously, money is not the major motivation, and it might be that the lack of big money is one of the unifying forces among employees.

Amy's Ice Cream has created what is definitely a "nonmainstream environment," which many feel is responsible for the legions of happy customers who keep the business merrily dipping along.

Questions

1. Describe the service organization culture at Amy's Ice Cream.
2. What are the personality attributes of the employees who are sought by Amy's Ice Cream?
3. Design a personnel selection procedure for Amy's Ice Cream using abstract questioning, a situational vignette, and/or role playing.

Enterprise Rent-A-Car[15] CASE 4.2

Enterprise Rent-A-Car (ERAC) maintains a unique selling proposition in the rental automobile industry, describing its "greatest idea [as] personal service." This proposition is built into every facet of ERAC's operations, from point-to-point car delivery to a 427,000 rental-vehicle fleet. This is clearly seen in president Andy Taylor's welcoming message on the company's website (www.enterprise.com):

> They say the greatest ideas are the simplest ones. They're right, and our greatest idea was personal service. It was so

> easy because it simply required people to act like people. To treat people in a business environment the way you'd treat them if they were your neighbors. You see, our business has been shaped by this very concept. Treating our customers like good friends and neighbors has enabled us to grow to a point where our automotive operations have annual revenues in the billions, a fleet of cars and trucks numbering hundreds of thousands, and thousands of employees—each dedicated to providing personal service.[16]

BACKGROUND

Enterprise Rent-A-Car began life in 1957 as a leasing company in St. Louis, Missouri, with a fleet of 17 cars. Founder Jack Taylor soon found that his customers needed short-term rentals to cover times when their leased vehicles were in for maintenance or repairs. Although it was a relatively successful operation, it wasn't until the 1970s that the business took off. That was when a court ruling held casualty insurers liable for an insured motorist's loss from being without a car. ERAC became a major player almost overnight, and rapidly grew to a 10,000-vehicle fleet by 1977. By 1993, ERAC began serving Canada and competing internationally. At this time ERAC had more than 200,000 units covering 1,500 locations. Overseas expansion continued in the United Kingdom a year later, bringing the total operation to more than 300,000 rental units and 50,000 lease units in more than 2,500 locations. Today, ERAC operates 7,200 offices in 30 countries around the world. The company has a domestic rental fleet of almost 1.2 million vehicles and annual revenues of $13,880 million.

Now that ERAC has become the industry leader in terms of fleet size and market presence, management faces the challenge of maintaining its performance level as the company's domestic markets approach saturation.

SERVICE CONCEPT

Andrew Taylor, the second CEO and son of the founder, said, "My father instilled his business philosophy in me, and it's very simple. When my father started the business, he said that you put customers first because if they are satisfied, they'll come back. Then come the employees. By making sure they are happy, well informed, and part of a team atmosphere, they will provide the best service possible. If you put the customers and the employees first, the bottom line will happen."[17]

Enterprise claims to offer the perfect rental package, as symbolized by its now-famous wrapped car. The focus is on three key benefits for the customer:

1. Extraordinary convenience in the form of nearby locations and picking up and dropping off customers at their homes, offices, or repair shops free of charge.
2. Excellent rates made possible by the operating strategy.
3. Exceptional selection of vehicles with something for every occasion.

From the first days of the rental business, ERAC's market focus has been on the local rental segment rather than following the "suits & shorts" emphasis on the business and holiday segment of the established players. This "hometown" rental market now includes the replacement segment (i.e., customers who need a car because of an accident, routine maintenance, or theft) and the discretionary segment (i.e., short business and leisure trips and other special occasions). ERAC relied on the pickup and drop-off components of its service to help set the company apart from the competition. This focus on convenience is now facilitated by a network of offices located within 15 minutes of 90 percent of the U.S. population.

As ERAC began to take on the commercial market, the company maintained some airport locations, especially through its acquired holdings of Alamo Rent A Car and National Car Rental. Consistent with its original market focus, customers are picked up and taken back to the office to settle the paperwork and take possession of the car. Still, according to Taylor, the focus is on the customer: "After all, other companies rent, lease and sell pretty much the same cars as Enterprise. The difference is, their business is cars and ours is people, which explains why so much of our energy goes into recruiting, hiring, and training."[18]

CULTURE

A combination of unusual hiring practices and relatively strict promotion-from-within drives the company's culture. Virtually every employee is a college graduate; Enterprise claims to be the top recruiter of college graduates in the United States. This factor is out of sync with the labor-intensive car rental industry that seeks to keep employee wages of a unionized workforce low.

The recruiting itself is rather nontraditional, also. "Brainy introverts need not apply," says Donald L. Ross, ERAC's chief operating officer. "We hire from the half of the college class that makes the upper half possible," he adds wryly. "We want athletes, fraternity types—especially fraternity presidents and social directors. People people."[19] The company finds that social directors make good salespeople because they are more readily able to chat up service managers and to calm someone who has just been in a car wreck.

The focus on athletes also has a noticeable impact on the company's culture because it fosters a competitive atmosphere to go along with the emphasis on teamwork. Starting pay varies around the country, and ERAC's reward system feeds this competitive drive because employees don't receive regular pay raises. They are compensated in part according to the profit earned at their particular location. Financial results by location and region are made available for everyone to see, which further fuels the competition.

The "bottom half of the class" also tends to bring a work ethic akin to the zeal of a reformed smoker, because its alumni have been sobered by a scarcity of career opportunities. Jeffrey M. Brummett, vice president for daily rental operations and a onetime semipro baseball player, comments, "Nobody ever went to college planning to go into the car rental business [an often repeated comment among Enterprise employees]. Then a time comes when that's the opportunity that presents itself, and you grab it."[20]

New management trainees are welcomed by long, grueling hours, during which they spend most of their time cleaning cars and shuttling vehicles to customers. Still, almost every employee, including top executives, start this way. Conscious of the bond this creates, senior officers routinely get involved in the dirty work, and even CEO Andy Taylor used a vacuum. "We were visiting an office in Berkeley and it was mobbed, so I started cleaning cars," he says. "As it was happening, I wondered if it was a good use of my time, but the effect on morale was tremendous."[21] Still, many quit after just a few weeks.

At the corporate level, Taylor left many of the decisions to Donald L. Ross, senior executive VP and COO, and to William F. Holekamp, executive VP. Ross and Holekamp served as role models for new recruits, as both men started by washing cars and serving customers. In time, each decided to take the risk and open an ERAC office in a new location, and their success with these operations proved that they could help guide the company, according to the Taylor philosophy.

GROWTH

ERAC's focus on the local market continues to pay off as it takes an increasingly larger share. While the airport market has grown annually at about 3 to 5 percent, the local market has grown at 10 to 15 percent. According to Jon LeSage, managing editor of *Auto Rental News,* "The local car rental market is a lot more significant than the public would assume. The real growth in this business is going to be in the local market."[22]

ERAC likely will continue to benefit from this growth, because the company has so many rental locations spread around the world. CEO Taylor saw no sign of a slowdown. Moreover, the company has grown at an annual rate of more than 20 percent for the past several years.

Two-income families also are helping to drive the market: When both partners of a couple work, each depends on his or her car, and when one of the cars falls out, ERAC's lower price makes it a natural choice. Moreover, people are renting from ERAC even when the family car runs just fine. "We call it the Virtual Car," said Taylor. "Small-business people who have to pick up clients call us when they want something better than their own car. So do people who have to take a long trip and don't trust, or just don't want to use, the family car."[23]

A new office is opened usually as soon as adjacent offices have reached a 100-vehicle inventory. After a new office opens, employees move into the surrounding community to develop relationships with the service managers of every good-size repair facility in the area. ERAC knows that the recommendations of service managers carry a great deal of weight with repair customers who are busy dealing with the confusion of the moment. It has become a national Wednesday ritual for ERAC employees to bring pizza and doughnuts to workers at nearby garages. Indeed, a large portion of recent growth has come from auto dealers who offer customers a free or cheap replacement while their cars are in the shop. ERAC has agreements with many dealers to provide these replacement vehicles, but at major accounts, ERAC staffs an office on the premises for several hours a day and keeps cars parked outside. According to one Porsche, Audi, and Rover dealer in West Long Branch, New Jersey: "The Enterprise people are practically part of my staff."[24]

OPERATIONS

ERAC operations are separated along its two primary lines of business: rental vehicles and corporate fleet management. Enterprise buys cars from a wide variety of American, Japanese, and European automakers. To reduce costs, it keeps its cars on the road up to six months longer than do either Hertz or Avis.

Rental Operations

ERAC's 7,200 offices are connected via an exclusive 1-800 number that links customers to the world's most advanced and most convenient office locator system. It allows customers to contact any of the North American offices via one simple number. This is supplemented by ARMS (automated rental management system), which provides an electronic interface that allows major clients, such as insurance companies, to manage bookings, billings, and payments in the most efficient manner possible.

ERAC's service concepts are evident in the rental operations. Whether at home or at the repair shop, ERAC delivers the vehicle to the customer. Despite this highly personalized service, ERAC offers rates that are often 30 percent lower than those of its competitors. From Chevy Aveo to Lincoln Towncar, from Ford Escape to Cadillac Escalade, ERAC provides a selection from more than 60 vehicles, including electric/hybrid cars, to meet a wide range of customer needs. Variety is also a primary profit driver in the replacement market. ERAC is betting that customers who are stuck for transportation won't be in the mood to quibble about prices. While the tiny GEO Metro is available for about $30 a day (i.e., the amount many insurance policies pay for replacement rentals), about 90 percent of people pay more to get a bigger car.

Fleet Management Operations

Its origin was leasing, but ERAC has expanded the scope of its fleet management services by providing complete, end-to-end fleet management, which allows client companies to outsource their entire vehicle departments. A dedicated, local Enterprise Account Services representative manages every aspect of the client's fleet including acquisition, insurance services, registration, after-market equipment, financing, fuel management and reporting, full maintenance management, corporate rental programs, and disposal.

COMPETITION

ERAC faces competition from a variety of sources, most notable of which are the traditional airport car rental companies such as Avis, Hertz, and Budget. Nevertheless, ERAC focuses on a different segment of the rental car market than do these companies. Traditional companies are dedicated to short-term, on-site rental for travelers, but ERAC focuses on the "hometown" market. Consequently, its most direct competition comes from the service loaner fleets of car dealerships. When a customer brings a car in for service, many dealerships now provide a service loaner, which eliminates the opportunity for ERAC to provide service.

The shape of the competitive field also is changing with a reviving auto industry and rising car prices. Consolidation is ongoing, as the smaller players are finding themselves unable to withstand the higher capital outlays. One of the biggest threats to the independents is the cash reserve of the allied players like Hertz and Budget, both of which are owned by Ford. Still, lacking debt, outside ownership, or red ink, ERAC is one of the most secure companies in a very insecure business.

Questions

1. How has Enterprise Rent-A-Car (ERAC) defined its service differently than that of the typical national car rental company?
2. What features of its business concept allow ERAC to compete effectively with the existing national rental car companies?
3. Use the service profit chain to explain the success of ERAC.

Selected Bibliography

Ba, Sulin, and Wayne C. Johansson. "An Exploratory Study of the Impact of e-Service Process on Online Customer Satisfaction." *Production and Operations Management* 17, no. 1 (January-February 2008), pp. 107-19.

Bone, Sterling A., and John C. Mowen. "'By-the-Book' Decision Making: How Service Employee Desire for Decision Latitude Influences Customer Selection Decisions." *Journal of Service Research* 13, no. 2 (May 2010), pp. 184-97.

Buell, Ryan W., Dennis Campbell, and Frances X. Frei. "Are Self-service Customers Satisfied or Stuck? *Production and Operations Management* 19, no. 6 (November-December 2010), pp. 679-97.

Coelho, Filipe, and Mario Augusto. "Job Characteristics and the Creativity of Frontline Service Employees." *Journal of Service Research* 13, no. 4 (Nov 2010), pp. 426-38.

Czepiel, J. A., M. R. Solomon, and C. F. Surprenant (eds). *The Service Encounter.* Lexington, MA: Lexington, 1985.

Evanschitzky, Heiner, et al. "How Employer and Employee Satisfaction Affect Customer Satisfaction: An Application to Franchise Services." *Journal of Service Research* 14, no. 2 (May 2011), pp. 136-48.

Grandey, Alicia A., Lori S. Goldberg, and S. Douglas Pugh. "Why and When Do Stores with Satisfied Employees Have Satisfied Customers?: The Roles of Responsiveness and Store Busyness." *Journal of Service Research* 14, no. 4 (November 2011), pp. 397-409.

Grougiou, Vassiliki, and Simone Pettigrew. "Senior Customers' Service Encounter Preferences." *Journal of Service Research* 14, no. 4 (November 2011), pp. 475-88.

Henning-Thurau, Thorsten, et al. "The Impact of New Media on Customer Relationships." *Journal of Service Research* 13, no. 3 (August 2010), pp. 311-30.

Heskett, James L., W. Earl Sasser, Jr., and Leonard A. Schlesinger. *The Service Profit Chain.* New York: Free Press, 1997.

Lariviere, Bart. "Linking Perceptual and Behavioral Customer Metrics to Multiperiod Customer Profitability: A Comprehensive Service-Profit Chain Application." *Journal of Service Research* 11, no. 1 (August 2008), pp. 8-21.

Osarenkhoe, Aihie, et al. "Technology-Based Service Encounter–A Study of the Use of E-Mail as a Booking Tool in Hotels." *Journal of Service Science and Management* 7, no. 6 (2014), pp. 419-29.

Porath, Christine, Deborah Macinnis, and Valerie S. Folkes. "It's Unfair: Why Customers Who Merely Observe an Uncivil Employee Abandon the Company." *Journal of Service Research* 14, no. 3 (August 2011), pp. 302-17.

Reinders, Machiel J., Pratibha A. Dabholkar, and Ruud T. Frambach. "Consequences of Forcing Consumers to Use Technology-Based Self-Service." *Journal of Service Research* 11, no. 4 (May 2009), pp. 107-23.

Robertson, Nichola, and Robin H. Shaw. "Predicting the Likelihood of Voiced Complaints in the Self-Service Technology Context." *Journal of Service Research* 12, no. 1 (August 2009), pp. 100-16.

Roels, Guillaume. "Optimal Design of Coproductive Services: Interaction and Work Allocation." *Manufacturing & Service Operations Management* 16, no. 4 (2014), pp. 578–94.

Schneider, Benjamin, and David E. Bowen. "Modeling the Human Side of Service Delivery." *Service Science* 1, no. 3 (Fall 2009), pp. 154–68.

Seck, Anne Marianne, and Jean Philippe. "Service Encounter in Multichannel Distribution Context: Virtual and Face-to-Face Interactions and Consumer Satisfaction." *The Service Industries Journal* 33, no. 6 (2013), pp. 565–79.

Sharma, Piyush, Jackie L. M. Tam, and Namwoon Kim. "Demystifying Intercultural Service Encounters: Toward a Comprehensive Conceptual Framework." *Journal of Service Research* 12, no. 2 (November 2009), pp. 227–42.

van Beuningen, Jacqueline, Ko de Ruyter, and Martin Wetzels. "The Power of Self-Efficacy Change During Service Provision: Making Your Customers Feel Better About Themselves Pay Off." *Journal of Service Research* 14, no. 1 (February 2011), pp. 108–25.

Verhoef, Peter C., Werner J. Reinartz, and Manfred Krafft. "Customer Engagement as a New Perspective in Customer Management." *Journal of Service Research* 13, no. 3 (August 2010), pp. 247–52.

Yee, Rachel W. Y., Andy C. L. Yeung, and T. C. Edwin Cheng. "The Impact of Employee Satisfaction on Quality and Profitability in High-Contact Service Industries." *Journal of Operations Management* 26, no. 5 (September 2008), pp. 651–68.

Endnotes

1. Jan Carlzon, *Moments of Truth* (Cambridge, MA: Ballinger, 1987).
2. Adapted from Craig M. Froehle and Aleda V. Roth, "New Measurement Scales for Evaluating Perceptions of the Technology-Mediated Customer Service Experience," *Journal of Operations Management* 22, no. 1 (February 2004), pp. 1–21.
3. Adapted from James A. Fitzsimmons, "Is Self-Service the Future of Services?" *Managing Service Quality* 13, no. 6 (2003), pp. 443–44.
4. A. Parasuraman, Valarie A. Zeithaml, and Arvind Malhotra, "E-S-QUAL: A Multiple-Item Scale for Assessing Electronic Service Quality," *Journal of Service Research* 7, no. 3 (February 2005), pp. 213–33.
5. Carol J. Loomis, "How the Service Stars Managed to Sparkle," *Fortune,* June 11, 1984, p. 117.
6. W. E. Sasser, Jr., C. W. L. Hart, and J. L. Heskett, *The Service Management Course* (New York: The Free Press, 1991), p. 97.
7. Adapted from J. D. Nyquist, M. J. Bitner, and B. H Booms, "Identifying Communication Difficulties in the Service Encounter: A Critical Incident Approach," in J. A. Czepiel, M. R. Solomon, and C. F. Surprenant (eds.), *The Service Encounter* (Lexington, MA: Lexington Books, 1985), chap. 13, pp. 195–212.
8. Cited by Fareed Zakaria, "The Capitalist Manifesto: Greed is Good (To a Point)," *Newsweek,* June 22, 2009, p. 44.
9. Adapted from Charles H. Schwepker, Jr. and Michael D. Hartline, "Managing the Ethical Climate of Customer-Contact Service Employees," *Journal of Service Research* 7, no. 4 (May 2005), pp. 377–97.
10. Gregory P. Stone, "City Shoppers and Urban Identification: Observations on the Social Psychology of City Life," *American Journal of Sociology,* July 1954, pp. 36–43.
11. John E. G. Bateson, "The Self-Service Consumer: Empirical Findings," in L. Berry, L. Shostack, and G. Upah (eds.), *Marketing of Services* (Chicago: American Marketing Association, 1983), pp. 76–83.
12. Adapted from Benjamin Schneider, "The Service Organization: Climate Is Crucial," *Organizational Dynamics,* Autumn 1980, pp. 52–65.
13. Adapted from J. L. Heskett, T. O. Jones, G. W. Loveman, W. E. Sasser, Jr., and L. A. Schlesinger, "Putting the Service-Profit Chain to Work," *Harvard Business Review,* March–April 1994, pp. 164–74.
14. Prepared by Bridgett Gagne, Sandhya Shardanand, and Laura Urquidi under the supervision of Professor James A. Fitzsimmons.
15. Prepared by Yair Almagor, Jason Hearnsberger, Gijun Kim, and Michael Sebold under the supervision of Professor James A. Fitzsimmons.

16. Andrew C. Taylor, "Welcome Message," http://www.enterprise.com, accessed on March 20, 1998.
17. "Enterprising Growth with a Hometown Flavor," *St. Louis Commerce,* June 1996.
18. Dan Callahan, "Enterprise's Strategy of Local Domination," *Auto Rental News,* December/ January 1994.
19. Brian O'Reilly, "The Rent-A-Car Jocks Who Made Enterprise #1," *Fortune,* October 28, 1996.
20. Ibid.
21. Ibid.
22. Ibid.
23. Ibid.
24. Ibid.

Chapter 5

Supporting Facility and Process Flows

Learning Objectives

After completing this chapter, you should be able to:

1. Describe the impact of the "servicescape" on the behavior of customers and employees.
2. Identify and discuss the three environmental dimensions of servicescapes.
3. Identify the six critical design features of a service supporting facility.
4. Draw a swim lane flowchart, process flow diagram, and a Gantt chart of a service process.
5. Calculate performance metrics such as throughput time and direct labor utilization.
6. Identify the bottleneck operation in a product layout, and regroup activities to create new jobs that will increase the overall service capacity.
7. Use operations sequence analysis to determine the relative locations of departments in a process layout that minimize total flow-distance.

Subtle differences in facility design are important. Consider the rivalry between the home improvement stores, Home Depot and Lowe's. Home Depot, the senior citizen of the pair, conveys a "roll up your sleeves and let's get at it" message . . . the aisles are narrow and lined with ceiling-high stores of merchandise, lighting is industrial, and lines at the checkout counters usually are long. The newcomer, Lowe's, began by copying its rival, but since then it has taken a different approach. A shopper at today's Lowe's finds wide aisles, bright lighting, and merchandise that is displayed in a way that encourages browsing and inspires many project ideas. Lowe's strategy worked for a time, but the competition has evolved to the point that both firms now move in lock step performance.[1]

Lowe's used facility design successfully for many years to differentiate itself from its competitors. Using facility design as part of a differentiation strategy is very common. For example, the A-frame structure and blue roof of IHOP (International House of Pancakes) attract travelers to a pancake breakfast just as the "golden arches" of McDonald's signal a hamburger lunch.

Using a standard, or "formula," facility design is an important feature in the overall cost leadership strategy of many companies. Major gasoline retailers have perfected the design of their service stations to facilitate construction (often completed within two weeks) and lower costs, and to create a consistent image awareness that will attract customers.

For theme restaurants and bars (e.g., a western bar, an Irish pub), facility design is central to the focus strategy of targeting a particular market and creating a unique ambiance. A retail store first must attract customers and then guide them through the store with eye-catching products in a pleasant environment that holds their attention. For example, the Apple Store is designed like a modern art museum with white walls and a bright, uncluttered floor plan that displays the entire product line as exhibits. Unlike a museum, however, passing visitors are invited to touch, pick up, and experiment with the product because all of the computers are running and connected to the Internet. A "Genius Bar" at the rear of the store is staffed with highly skilled folks who answer questions and provide short tutorials for new computer buyers.

Chapter Preview

The chapter begins with the topic of environmental psychology as applied to facility design and layout to avoid customer disorientation and frustration upon entering an unfamiliar structure. The concept of servicescapes is based on the idea that the physical environment influences the behavior and perception of the service for both customers and workers. Facility design issues are addressed with respect to objectives of the service, its space requirements, flexibility, aesthetic factors, and the environment. Facility layout is discussed with attention to traffic flow, space planning, and the need to avoid unnecessary travel. The concept of process flow analysis used by industrial engineers is modified for service operations and illustrated by a mortgage service in which all the process analysis terms are evaluated.

The traditional product and process layouts from manufacturing are shown to have service counterparts and can be studied using the techniques of assembly-line balancing and relative location analysis.

Environmental Psychology and Orientation[2]

Orientation is the first behavioral need of an individual on entering a place. It includes questions of place orientation (e.g., "Where am I?") as well as of function orientation (e.g., "How does this organization work, and what do I do next?"). On entering a physical setting, customers gain control when they can use spatial cues, along with previous experience, to identify where they are, where they should go, and what they need to do. Anxiety and a sense of helplessness can result if spatial cues are not present or previous experience cannot be used to avoid disorientation. The causes of disorientation in service settings can be reduced by a facility design that incorporates the following: previous experience, design legibility, and orientation aids.

Using formula facilities, franchised services have removed the anxiety of disorientation so that customers know exactly what to do. Holiday Inn took this concept a step further by advertising that a guest will find no surprises at any of its locations, capitalizing on the need for familiarity to attract repeat customers.

Orientation also can be aided by facility designs that allow customers to see both into and through the space. The layout of a Hyatt hotel uses an interior atrium that allows the entire space to be viewed and conceptualized at a glance. In addition, such a layout allows customers to observe the actions of others for behavioral cues.

Orientation aids and signage such as "You Are Here" maps, if properly aligned with the user's perspective (i.e., "up" on the sign equates to straight ahead for the user) and complete with environmental landmarks, can be effective as well. Strategically located plants and artwork can act as points of reference. Color-coded subway routes with corresponding color-coded connecting arrows represent an excellent use of signage to assist visitors and to promote smooth flow of traffic.

Servicescapes[3]

The physical environment or *servicescape* of the supporting facility influences both customer and employee behavior and should be designed with an image and feel that is congruent with the service concept. A typology of servicescapes shown in Figure 5.1

FIGURE 5.1
Typology of Servicescapes

Source: Adapted from Mary Jo Bitner, "Servicescapes: The Impact of Physical Surroundings on Customers and Employees," *Journal of Marketing* 56, April 1992, p. 59.

Who Performs within a Servicescape	Physical Complexity of the Servicescape	
	Elaborate	**Lean**
Self-service (customer only)	Golf course Museum	Driving range Gallery
Interpersonal services (both customer and employee)	Resort hotel Theme restaurant Disneyland Airline terminal	Budget motel Fast-food takeout County fair Bus station
Remote service (employee only)	Professor's office	TA's cubicle

is organized according to who participates within the service environment and the degree of complexity of the servicescape.

Because of the absence of employees, the servicescape for a self-service operation plays a central role in guiding customer behavior through the use of signage (e.g., direction to the next golf tee) and intuitive design of interfaces (e.g., hot buttons on a website). For remote services, the primary physical design objectives are employee satisfaction, motivation, and operational efficiency because customers do not visit the site physically. Offices of professional services such as those of lawyers and physicians, however, should project competence and authority. Interpersonal services are the most challenging because social interaction between employees and customers and among customers should be facilitated by the servicescape. For example, the servicescape at Disneyland is famous for creating a fantasy experience for customers and a stage for employees (i.e., cast members).

Consider the photographs of two restaurant servicescapes below. Note how the table settings, furniture, room decor, and even customer attire communicate distinct expectations for customers and employees alike.

Behaviors in Servicescapes

An organization's service facility reflects its values and is instrumental in executing its strategy. Without words, a building communicates a message to both its customers and employees. For example, the building may communicate modernity and progressiveness or other features such as pleasantness, safety, and convenience. Obviously facility design should support the goals of the institution and be deliberate because this is the place where service is delivered.

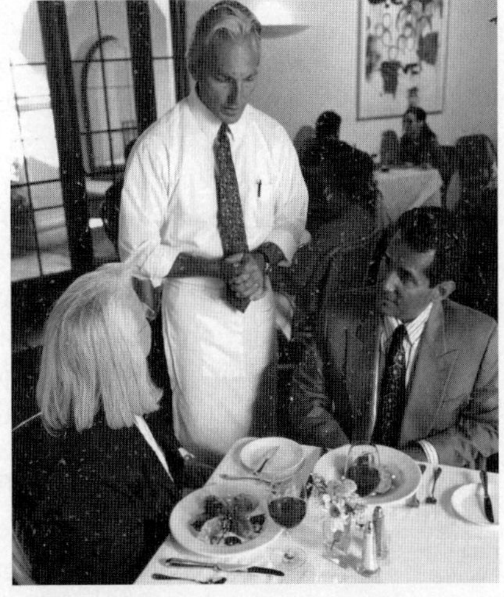

Restaurants use their servicescapes to create desired expectations and behaviors for employees and customers.

FIGURE 5.2 **Servicescape Framework**

Source: Adapted from Mary Jo Bitner, "Servicescapes: The Impact of Physical Surroundings on Customers and Employees," *Journal of Marketing* 56 (April 1992), p. 60.

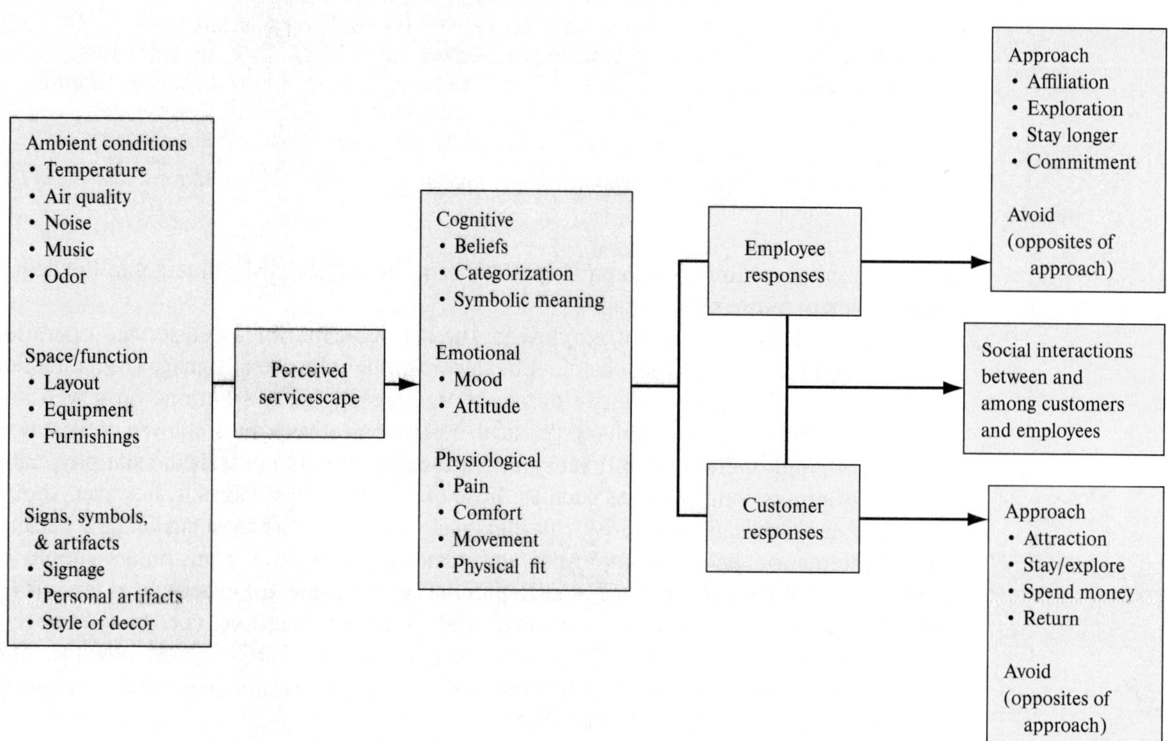

As shown in Figure 5.2, a mix of environmental dimensions consisting of ambient conditions, space/function, and signs/symbols/artifacts describes the servicescape, which is viewed as a holistic environment by customers and employees.

The employee or customer internal response to the servicescape is either approach or avoidance behavior. For example, arousal-seekers enjoy and look for high levels of stimulation (e.g., a bright and loud disco), whereas arousal-avoiders prefer lower levels of stimulation (e.g., a quiet museum). The internal response is moderated by psychological attributes that are cognitive (e.g., reassurance of signage), emotional (e.g., calming effect of music), and physiological (e.g., discomfort of poor lighting). The servicescape is designed to invoke social interaction between and among customers and employees.

A well-conceived servicescape will encourage an approach behavior for both employees (e.g., commitment and desire to remain with the firm) and customers (e.g., exploration, spending money, and returning).

Because the physical environment elicits an emotional response and influences behavior, the design of the service facility can mold the behavior of the participants to support the organization's goals. Thus, unpleasant environments that are also high in arousal (lots of stimulation, noise, confusion) are to be avoided.

Environmental Dimensions of Servicescapes

The dimensions of the physical environment surroundings include all of the objective factors that can be controlled by the firm to enhance employee and customer actions and perceptions of the service. Although these dimensions will be discussed independently, it is important to realize that people respond to their environment holistically; that is, the total combined effect on all of our senses defines our perception of the servicescape.

Ambient Conditions

The background of our environment, such as temperature, lighting, noise, music, and scent, affects all five of our senses. Music tempo, for example, can affect a customer's pace of shopping, length of stay, and amount of money spent. Consider a convenience store that played "elevator music" successfully to drive away teenagers who were loitering and discouraging paying customers from entering the store. A cookie shop in a busy mall can leave its doors open to invite customers with the fragrance of freshly baked cookies. All of these factors, including color of surroundings, also influence employee performance and job satisfaction.

Spatial Layout and Functionality

The arrangement of furnishings and equipment and the relationships among them create a visual and functional landscape for delivery of the service. This landscape can communicate order and efficiency (e.g., formal garden) or chaos and uncertainty for both employees and customers. For self-service activities, the functionality or ease of use of equipment is important to allow customers to perform unattended activities. Fast-food restaurants purposely design the facility to communicate visually the appropriate activities of diners. Menus are posted over the cash registers, self-serve drink machines are positioned between the counter and the tables, and waste containers are located near exits.

Signs, Symbols, and Artifacts

Many items in the physical environment serve as explicit or implicit signals that communicate acceptable norms of behavior. Explicit signs such as "no smoking" communicate rules of behavior, whereas "recycle bins" encourage responsible acts. The quality of the floor covering, artwork, and furnishings can create an overall aesthetic impression for the visitor and a pleasant workplace for the employee. Professional services can use interior decorating to communicate competence and enhance their professional image with clients. Restaurants communicate full service and high prices with signs such as pictures of famous diners, symbols such as tablecloths, and artifacts such as antiques or pottery. Studies of faculty offices indicate that desk placement, selection of wall pictures or posters, and tidiness of the office influence students' beliefs about the person who occupies the office.

Our discussion of servicescapes suggests that the physical environment may assume a variety of strategic roles in support of the service concept. First, the servicescape provides a visual metaphor for an organization's offering. The environmental dimensions of the servicescape create a package, similar to the packaging of a product that conveys an image suggesting relative quality, potential usage, and target market segment. For example, consider a comparison of Home Depot and Lowe's. A visit to Home Depot with its orange colors, bare floors, industrial lighting, and generally cluttered look conveys a masculine image of the construction industry. However, Lowe's with soft blues, tidy aisles, and attractively displayed merchandise projects a more female-friendly image for the home improvement customer.

Second, the servicescape can facilitate customer orientation by incorporating "wayfinding" techniques that people use to navigate from place to place. Wayfinding, as used in architectural design, includes signage and other graphic communications (e.g., color-coded subway lines), clues inherent in a building's physical space (e.g., carpet and plantings), logical flow planning, audible assistance, and provision for special-needs users. Appropriate attention to wayfinding can reduce customer anxiety and improve the overall service experience. When Google maps are embedded in retail websites, wayfinding becomes a visual exercise rather than written directions that sometimes are hard to follow. In the virtual world, wayfinding facilitates navigation around a website and minimizes the number of keystrokes needed to reach a search topic.

The American Institute for Graphic Arts (AIGA), the professional association for design, together with the U.S. Department of Transportation has produced a set of passenger/pedestrian symbols designed and used internationally at the crossroads of modern life (i.e., airports, train stations, Olympic Games). The complete set of 50 symbols can be found at http://www.aiga.org/symbol-signs.

Third, the servicescape also can encourage social interaction among customers. For example, the layout of a waiting room that has chairs grouped together around tables encourages social interaction and makes time pass more pleasantly.

Finally, the physical environment can serve as a subtle method to focus employee behavior. The design of the Mid-Columbia Medical Center in Columbia River, Oregon, for example, gave much attention to the employee entrance. A special employee-only entrance was designed as an atrium that could grace a five-star hotel. Employees were greeted with a breakfast buffet in an environment of overstuffed chairs, potted plants, paintings, and inspiring music. The design was a deliberate attempt to foster a good mood for the day's work and encourage employees to leave personal cares and troubles at the door.

Facility Design

Service operations can be affected directly by the design of the facility. For example, a restaurant with inadequate ventilation for nonsmoking diners discourages many customers. Alternatively, a physical fitness center with easy wheelchair access might be able to enlarge its services to include a new clientele.

Design and layout represent the supporting facility component of the *service package*. Together, they influence how a service facility is used and, sometimes, if it is even used at all. Consider again Toronto's Shouldice Hospital (discussed in Chapter 3). A good portion of its success in repairing inguinal hernias results from thoughtful facility design and layout. For example, operating rooms are grouped together so that surgeons can consult with each other easily during procedures. Because early ambulation promotes faster healing, the hospital is designed to provide ample pleasant places to walk–and even to climb a few steps. Meals are served only in community dining rooms rather than in patient rooms, which requires more walking and, as an added benefit, allows patients to get together and "compare notes." While functional and comfortable, patient rooms are not equipped with "extras" such as television sets that might encourage patients to "lie around."

Other factors of design and layout can be "urgent." Consider the generally inadequate supply of restroom facilities for women in most public buildings, especially during mass entertainment events. During intermission at your next concert or play, observe how long it takes individual females and males to use the restrooms. Do you see any evidence of "potty parity" being designed into the building? In addition, count the number of restrooms for men and the number for women in your classroom building. Chances are that equal numbers exist for each gender, but this does not necessarily ensure equality of access.

Clearly, good design and layout enhance the service, from attracting customers to making them feel more comfortable to ensuring their safety (e.g., adequate lighting, fire exits, proper location of dangerous equipment). Facility design also has an impact on the implicit service component of the service package–in particular, on criteria like privacy and security, atmosphere, and sense of well-being.

Several factors influence design: (1) the nature and objectives of the service organization, (2) land availability and space requirements, (3) flexibility, (4) security, (5) aesthetic factors, and (6) the community and environment.

Nature and Objectives of Service Organizations

The nature of the core service should dictate the parameters of its design. For example, a fire station must have a structure that is large enough to house its vehicles and accommodate 24-hour shifts. Physicians' offices come in many shapes and sizes, but all must be designed to afford patients some degree of privacy.

Beyond such fundamental requirements, however, design can contribute much more to defining the service. For example, design can engender immediate recognition, as in the case of McDonald's arches or IHOP's blue roof. External design also can provide a clue about the nature of the service inside. One would expect to see well-manicured grounds, freshly painted or marble columns, and perhaps a fountain in front of a funeral home. A school, however, might have colorful tiles on its facade and certainly a playground or athletic field nearby.

Appropriateness of design is important as well. A gasoline service station can be constructed of brightly colored, prefabricated sheet metal; however, would you deposit money in a bank that was using a trailer on wheels for a temporary branch?

Land Availability and Space Requirements

The land that is available for a service facility often comes with many constraints, such as costs, zoning requirements, and actual area. Good design must accommodate all these constraints. In an urban setting, where land is at a premium, buildings only can be expanded upward, and organizations often must exhibit great creativity and ingenuity in their designs to use a relatively small space efficiently. For example, in some urban areas (e.g., in Copenhagen), McDonald's has incorporated a second-floor loft to provide eating space.

Suburban and rural areas frequently offer larger, more affordable parcels of land that ameliorate the space constraints of urban facilities. Many sites, however, and especially urban ones, might have strict zoning laws on land usage and ordinances governing the exterior appearance of structures. Space for off-street parking also is a requirement. In any event, space for future expansion always should be considered.

Flexibility

Successful services are dynamic organizations that can adapt to changes in the quantity and nature of demand. How well a service can adapt depends greatly on the flexibility that has been designed into it. Flexibility also might be called "designing for the future." Questions to address during the design phase might be: How can this facility be designed to allow for later expansion of present services, and how can we design this facility to accommodate new and different services in the future? For example, many of the original fast-food restaurants built for walk-in traffic have had to modify their facilities to accommodate customer demands for drive-through window service.

Several airports face facility problems today because designers failed to anticipate either the tremendous growth in the numbers of people flying or the advent of the hub-and-spoke airline network following deregulation. Consequently, passengers often must tote carry-on luggage through a maze of long passageways to reach the departure gates of their connecting flights. In addition, consider the frustration facing passengers trying to retrieve checked luggage from a baggage-handling operation that was designed for circa 1960s air travelers!

Designing for the future often can translate into financial savings. For example, consider a church that locates in a developing community but does not have the resources to build the sanctuary it would like plus the necessary ancillary facilities it needs. Good design might lead the congregation to build a modest structure that can be used as a temporary sanctuary but later adapted easily and economically to serve as a fellowship hall, a Sunday school, and even a day care facility to meet the needs of a growing community.

In other instances, designing for the future might require additional expenses initially, but will save financial resources in the long run. In fact, such foresight can provide for growth that might not be possible otherwise. For example, cities often invest in oversized water and wastewater treatment plants in anticipation of future growth.

Security

Anyone who has flown on a commercial airliner since the terrorist attack against the United States on September 11, 2001, has observed modifications in airports. Some of the security technology is obvious to the traveler (e.g., more sophisticated carry-on luggage

X-ray scanners, "wipes" or tissues that can detect residue of drugs or explosives on the surfaces of bags, and handheld magnetic detectors). Other airport security measures are less visible to travelers. Information technology plays a part in providing profiles of potential terrorists, although the use of profiling is problematical. By government mandate, all checked luggage in U.S. airports is screened, either by workers or by some type of automatic scanner. Some airlines are making use of "smart facilities" that recognize magnetic ID cards to control entrance or, recently, scans of eyes to establish identity.

Security in facilities can be enhanced by installing surveillance cameras. Banks and convenience stores, for example, use cameras to discourage would-be robbers or to identify those who aren't discouraged. "Granny cams" allow families to monitor the care that is given to a patient in a nursing home, and "nanny cams" allow parents to see the care their child receives from a babysitter in the home.

Another example of a security system for a facility can be seen at something as ordinary as a neighborhood pool. A high fence surrounds the pool and safety equipment such as a ring buoy and shepherd's hook is readily available at positions around the pool. Other examples of facilities adapted for security are jails and level-four labs, both of which have many levels of modifications to ensure that "bad things" don't get out.

Slightly less obtrusive security measures can be seen at many retail stores. Consider the row of concrete posts or "bollards" outside the entrance to some stores and the scanners and tags affixed to clothing items to discourage shoplifting. Consider, also, that "window shopping" might become a nostalgic pastime as more stores do away with big windows that invite burglaries. Imagine Macy's Department Store without holiday windows because our need for security has exploded.

Aesthetic Factors

Compare two shopping trips to successful, upscale clothing stores. First, we go to an upscale department store such as Nordstrom's. As we enter the women's fine dresses department, we are aware of the carpeting beneath our feet, the ample space between clothing racks, the lack of crowding of dresses on the racks, the complimentary lighting, and most certainly, the very well-groomed salesperson who is ready to serve us immediately. Fitting rooms are located in an area separate from the display area, are roomy and carpeted, and have mirrors on three sides so that you can appreciate every aspect of your appearance. Everything in the department is designed to give a sense of elegance and attention to our needs.

Our second trip takes us to an Eddie Bauer Factory Outlet store. Within just a few steps of the entrance, we are confronted by tables piled high with a vast assortment of clothing. Along the walls and among the tables are racks packed as full as possible with more clothing. Only a maze of narrow pathways is visible around the floor. Salespersons are stationed at cash-register counters and are available to help when you seek them out. Fitting rooms are small "stalls" on the showroom floor and are equipped with only one mirror. (It helps to shop here with a companion, who can give you the advantage of "hindsight.") This is a large warehouse type of store rather than a modest-sized, serene, elegant place to shop; however, the outlet store offers great bargains in exchange for sacrificing plushness and lots of personal attention.

Both stores offer attractive, quality clothing. We feel very different in each one, however, and their respective designs have played an important part in shaping our attitudes. Clearly, the aesthetic aspects of a design have a marked effect on the consumer's perceptions and behaviors, but they also affect the employees and the service they provide. Lack of attention to aesthetic factors during the design phase can lead to surly service rather than to "service with a smile."

The Community and Environment

The design of a service facility may be of greatest importance where it affects the community and its environment. Will the planned church allow enough space for parking, or will neighbors find it impossible to enter or exit their properties during church activities? Can Priscilla Price design a boarding kennel facility that will not "hound" neighboring businesses with undue noise and odor? How can a community design a detention facility that will provide adequately for the inmates' health and welfare yet still ensure the safety of the town's residents? Has the local dry cleaner designed his or her facility to keep hazardous chemicals out of the local environment?

These questions illustrate how crucial facility design can be in gaining community acceptance of a service. Zoning regulations and many public interest groups also can provide guidance in designing service facilities that are compatible with their communities and environment.

Process Analysis

Types of Processes

Students of manufacturing long ago found it useful to categorize processes in order to derive general management principles that would apply across industries sharing the same process. For example, all manufacturing assembly operations be they automobiles or personal computers share characteristics of a "flow" process. Using the traditional manufacturing process types listed in Table 5.1, we show that services also can be categorized by process type to identify management challenges. For example, any service that has a "batch" process shares the challenge of managing a perishable asset (unused capacity) such as an empty seat on an airplane, an unused hotel room, or an empty cabin on a cruise ship. After identifying the type of process, we then diagram the operations in a flowchart as the first step in process analysis.

Flowcharting

The ability to diagram a process, identify the bottleneck operation, and determine the system capacity are fundamental skills in managing service operations and making improvements. An acknowledged axiom is, "If you can't draw it, then you don't really understand it."

Our discussion begins with Figure 5.3, an example of a swim lane flowchart of a typical graduate school admissions process. Swim lane flowcharts diagram organizational activities that cross functional lines (i.e., the swim lanes) highlighting the handoffs between lanes. The hardest task in developing a flowchart is getting everyone to agree on what the process looks like. However, the final diagram is useful for training, helping to coordinate activities between functions, and facilitating creative ideas for improvement. For example, from an applicant's viewpoint, how could the process be improved? Perhaps an online inquiry system would allow the applicant to follow the process and thus reduce the need for the admissions clerk to "contact applicant" when a folder is incomplete.

TABLE 5.1 **Service Process Types with Management Challenges**

Process Type	Service Example	Characteristic	Management Challenge
Project	Consulting	One-of-a-kind engagement	Staffing and scheduling
Job Shop	Hospital	Many specialized departments	Balancing utilization and scheduling patients
Batch	Airline	Group of customers treated simultaneously	Pricing of perishable asset (seat inventory)
Flow	Cafeteria	Fixed sequence of operations	Adjust staffing to demand fluctuations
Continuous	Electric utility	Uninterrupted delivery	Maintenance and capacity planning

FIGURE 5.3 **Swim Lane Flowchart of Graduate School Admissions**

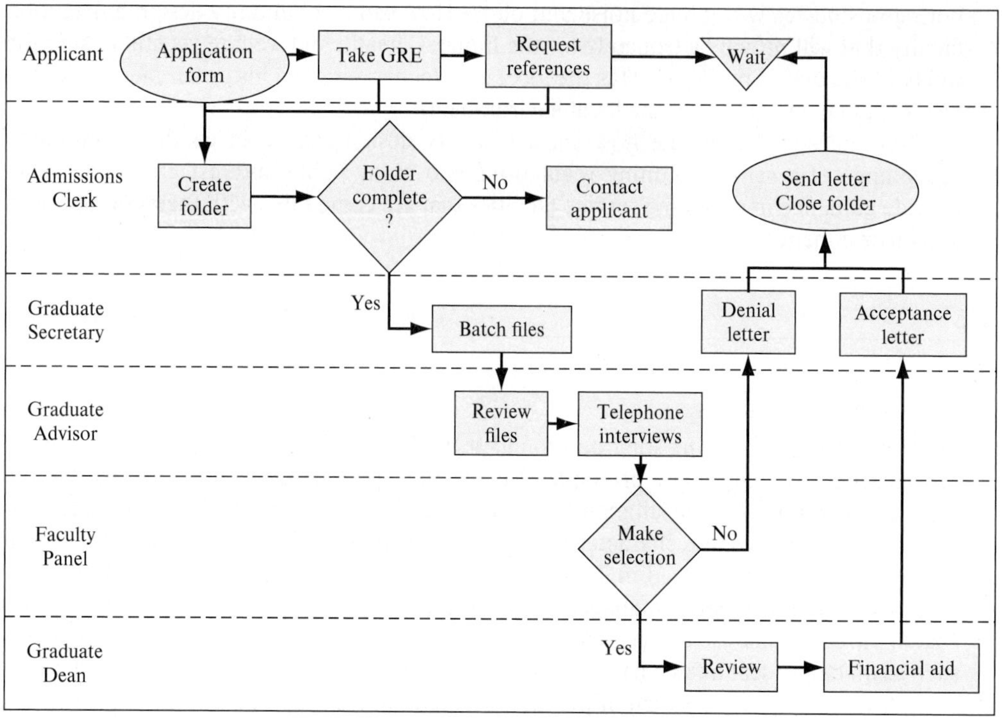

Applicant	Application form → Take GRE → Request references → Wait
Admissions Clerk	Create folder → Folder complete? — No → Contact applicant; Send letter Close folder
Graduate Secretary	Yes → Batch files; Denial letter; Acceptance letter
Graduate Advisor	Review files → Telephone interviews
Faculty Panel	Make selection — No → Denial letter
Graduate Dean	Yes → Review → Financial aid → Acceptance letter

The following standard symbols are used in flowcharting and illustrated in Figure 5.3:

Terminator: An *ellipse* represents a start or stop in a process.

Operation: A *rectangle* represents a process or action step.

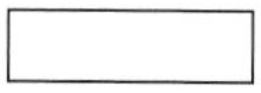

Decision: A *diamond* represents a question or branch.

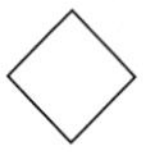

Wait: A *triangle* represents a delay (time in queue) or inventory of goods.

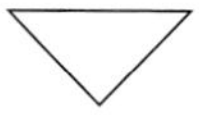

Flow: An *arrow* shows movement of customers, goods, or information.

Example 5.1 shows a process flow diagram for mortgage service. This example will be used as a basis for our discussion of process analysis.

Example 5.1 Mortgage Service

The purchase of real estate usually involves taking out a loan or "mortgage" on the property. The lending institution requires an accurate description of the property and proof that the title is clear of any outstanding liens. Furthermore, the creditworthiness of the buyer must be determined. Many independent mortgage service firms offer these services.

Figure 5.4 shows a simplified process flow diagram of the mortgage application process. Because we intend to use this example to illustrate process terminology such as the bottleneck operation and throughput time, we include the cycle time (CT) of each activity (i.e., the average time in minutes to perform the activity) in the diagram.

Gantt Chart

An activity-based schedule of the mortgage service process provides another visual representation for understanding and analysis. In Figure 5.5, we follow the progress of three applications through time. We see that "property survey" is an unusual activity because application 1 is immediately followed by application 2 and then by application 3 in unbroken procession. Because the "property survey" activity is never idle it is referred to

FIGURE 5.4 **Process Flow Diagram of Mortgage Service**

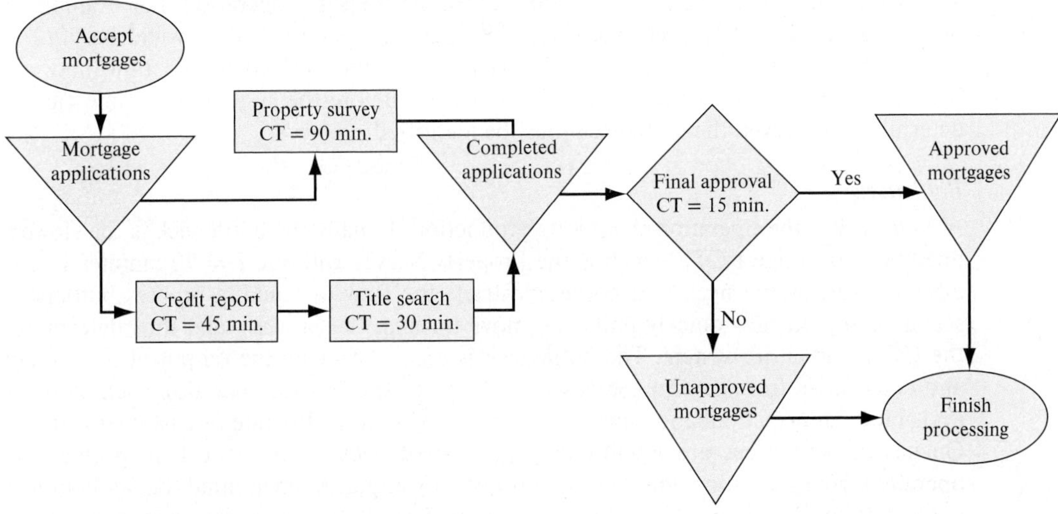

FIGURE 5.5 **Gantt Chart of Mortgage Service**

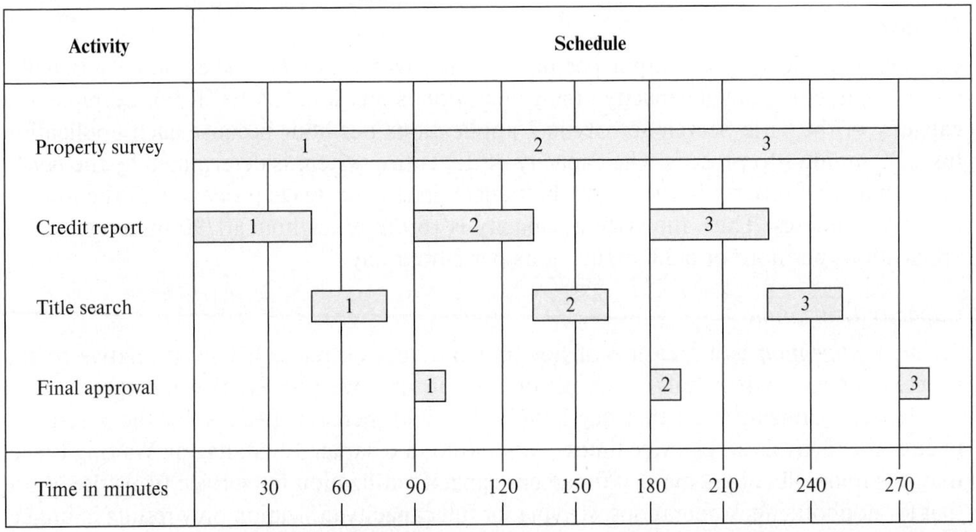

Activity	Schedule
Property survey	1 2 3
Credit report	1 2 3
Title search	1 2 3
Final approval	1 2 3
Time in minutes	30 60 90 120 150 180 210 240 270

as the *bottleneck* (an activity that constrains output) and its cycle time (CT) of 90 minutes defines the system output of one mortgage application completed every 90 minutes. Also, it can be observed that "credit report" and "title search" could be combined into one activity taking a total time of 75 minutes (45 min. + 30 min.) at no loss of system productivity because together these activities still have 15 minutes of idle time per each 90 minute cycle. The Gantt chart has many uses and will be seen again in Chapter 16, Managing Service Projects.

Process Terminology

The following process-analysis terms are defined and illustrated using Example 5.1, assuming one worker is assigned to each operation and an unlimited supply of mortgage applications.

Cycle Time

Cycle time (CT) is the average time between completions of successive units. For an operation, CT is the average service time to perform the activity. In our example, securing a

Credit Report requires 45 minutes on average. Cycle time, however, could also apply to a *work area* in which several servers are performing the same operation. For example, if two surveyors were employed, the CT for Property Survey *work area* would be 90/2 = 45 minutes. Finally the entire system has a cycle time defined as the time between successive customers exiting during a busy period. Before the system cycle time can be determined, however, the bottleneck must be identified.

Bottleneck

A *bottleneck* is the operation that limits production. Usually the bottleneck is the slowest operation (or longest CT), which is the Property Survey with a CT = 90 minutes in our example. Just as the neck of a bottle constricts the flow of liquid, a process bottleneck sets a ceiling on how quickly units can move through the process, and thus determines the CT of the entire system. The bottleneck is a constraint on the output of the system and could arise from several sources in addition to the slowest operation such as labor availability, information, and, most importantly for services, the rate of customer arrivals. Queues or wait areas are intentionally positioned *before* a bottleneck to protect the operation from starvation and thus compromise its output. Keep in mind that an hour lost at the bottleneck is an hour lost in system output. The role of the bottleneck in understanding processes is the central theme of *The Goal,* a novel by Eli Goldratt that is a "must read" for aspiring operations managers.

Capacity

Capacity is a measure of output per unit of time when *fully busy* (i.e., activity is never idle). The unconstrained capacity of any operation is measured as 1/CT. For example, the capacity of the Title Search activity is 2 applications per hour because each application takes 30 minutes to process. The capacity of the entire system is determined by the *bottleneck* capacity. Property Survey is the bottleneck in the mortgage process with the longest CT = 90 minutes. Thus, the system capacity is (60 minutes/hour)(1/90 minutes) = 2/3 applications per hour or 5.33 applications per 8-hour day.

Capacity Utilization

Capacity utilization is a measure of how much actual output is achieved relative to the process capacity when fully busy. If, for a given day, we process five mortgages, then the capacity utilization on that day is 5/5.33 = 93.8 percent. Because of the variability in customer arrivals and service times, we will find in Chapter 12, Managing Waiting Lines, that it is impossible to achieve 100 percent capacity utilization for service firms. Be aware that for nonbottleneck operations, striving for full capacity utilization only results in unnecessary work-in-process and not more system output. Capacity utilization, particularly of individual operations, is a *dangerous* management performance metric and should be used only with great caution.

Throughput Time

Throughput time is the time it takes to complete a process from time of arrival to time of exit. Throughput time is the sum of the *critical path* operation times plus the average time spent waiting. The critical path is defined in Chapter 16, Managing Service Projects, as the longest time path from beginning to end of a process flow diagram. For our mortgage example the critical path begins and ends with the terminator symbols Accept Mortgages and Finish Processing and includes only the Property Survey and Final Approval activities.

$$\begin{aligned}\text{Throughput time} = {} & \text{Average time waiting in Mortgage Applications} \\ & + \text{Property Survey (90 min.)} \\ & + \text{Average time waiting in Completed Applications} \\ & + \text{Final Approval (15 min.).}\end{aligned}$$

Note in Figure 5.5 that the operations of Credit Report and Title Search are performed concurrently with Property Survey and together sum to 75 minutes and thus are not on the critical path defined by the bottleneck operation, Property Survey. The average time waiting can be estimated using queuing formulas found in Appendix D or by computer simulation, but in any event, are very dependent on the rate of arrivals of mortgage applications.

Rush Order Flow Time

Rush order flow time is the time it takes to go through the system from beginning to end without any time in queue (i.e., throughput time with zero wait time). In our example the rush order flow time following the critical path is 105 minutes, the sum of Property Survey (90 min.) plus Final Approval (15 min.).

Total Direct Labor Content

Total direct labor content is the sum of all of the operations times (i.e., touch time) consumed in performing the service. In professional services this often is referred to as "billable" hours. Indirect labor hours and overhead (e.g., maintenance and management) are not included in the calculation. For the mortgage example the total direct labor content is $90 + 45 + 30 + 15 = 180$ minutes.

Direct Labor Utilization

Direct labor utilization is a measure of the percentage of time that workers actually contribute value to a fully busy service organization. Direct labor utilization for the mortgage service process is calculated as

$$\textit{Direct labor utilization} = \frac{\textit{Total direct labor content}}{(\textit{Process cycle time})\,(\textit{Number of workers})}$$

$$= \frac{180}{(90)\,(4)} = 50 \text{ percent}$$

Facility Layout

In addition to facility design, the layout, or arrangement, of the service delivery system is important for the convenience of the customer as well as the service provider. No customer should be subjected to unnecessary aggravation from a poorly planned facility. Further, a poor layout can be costly in time that is wasted when service workers are engaged in unproductive activity.

Flow Process Layout and the Work Allocation Problem

Some standard services can be divided into an inflexible sequence of steps or operations that all customers must experience. This is an example of a *flow process layout* most often associated with manufacturing assembly lines, where a product is assembled in a fixed sequence of steps. The most obvious service analogy is a cafeteria, where diners push their trays along as they assemble their meals. Staffing such a service requires allocating tasks among servers to create jobs that require nearly equal time. The job requiring the most time per customer creates a bottleneck and defines the capacity of the service line. Any change in the capacity of the service line requires that attention be given to the bottleneck activity. Several options are available: adding another worker to the job, providing some aid to reduce the activity time, or regrouping the tasks to create a new line balance with different activity assignments. A well-balanced line would have all jobs be of nearly equal duration to avoid unnecessary idleness and inequity in work assignments. A service-line approach has the additional advantage of allowing for division of labor and use of dedicated special equipment, as illustrated by Example 5.2.

Example 5.2 Automobile Driver's License Office

The state automobile driver's license office is under pressure to increase its productivity to accommodate 120 applicants per hour with the addition of only one clerk to its present staff. The license renewal process currently is designed as a service line, with customers being processed in the fixed sequence listed in Table 5.2. Activity 1 (i.e., review application for correctness) must be performed first, and activity 6 (i.e., issue temporary license) must be the last step and, by state policy, be handled by a uniformed officer. Activity 5 (i.e., photograph applicant) requires an expensive digital camera and color printer.

The process flow diagram for the current arrangement, as shown in Figure 5.6*a*, identifies the bottleneck activity (i.e., the activity with the slowest flow rate per hour) as activity 3 (i.e., check for violations and restrictions), which limits the current capacity to 60 applicants per hour. By focusing only on the bottleneck, one might think that assigning an additional clerk to perform activity 3 would double the flow through the bottleneck and achieve the goal of 120 applicants per hour. However, the flow for this system would be limited to 90 applicants per hour, because the bottleneck would shift to activity 4.

The proposed process design, as shown in Figure 5.6*b* with seven clerks, can achieve the desired capacity of 120 applicants per hour, because activities 1 and 4 have been grouped together to create a new job (i.e., review applications for correctness and conduct eye test) that better balances the work load among the staff. How did we know to group these two activities together? First, remember that a flow rate of at least 120 applicants per hour must be achieved at each step in the process. Because activities 2 and 6 already are being performed at this rate, they need not be considered further. An additional clerk is required to perform activity 3, however, because we can achieve a combined flow rate of 120 applicants per hour only if two clerks work in parallel. Next, we must ask if it is possible to combine activities requiring small amounts of time to arrive at a job that can be performed in 60 seconds or less (i.e., achieve a flow rate of at least 60 applicants per hour). By combining activity 1, which requires 15 seconds, with activity 4, which requires 40 seconds, we can achieve a combined

TABLE 5.2
License Renewal Process Times

Activity	Description	Cycle Time, Sec.
1	Review application for correctness	15
2	Process and record payment	30
3	Check for violations and restrictions	60
4	Conduct eye test	40
5	Photograph applicant	20
6	Issue temporary license (state trooper)	30

FIGURE 5.6*a*
(*a*) Present and (*b*) Proposed Process Flow Diagrams

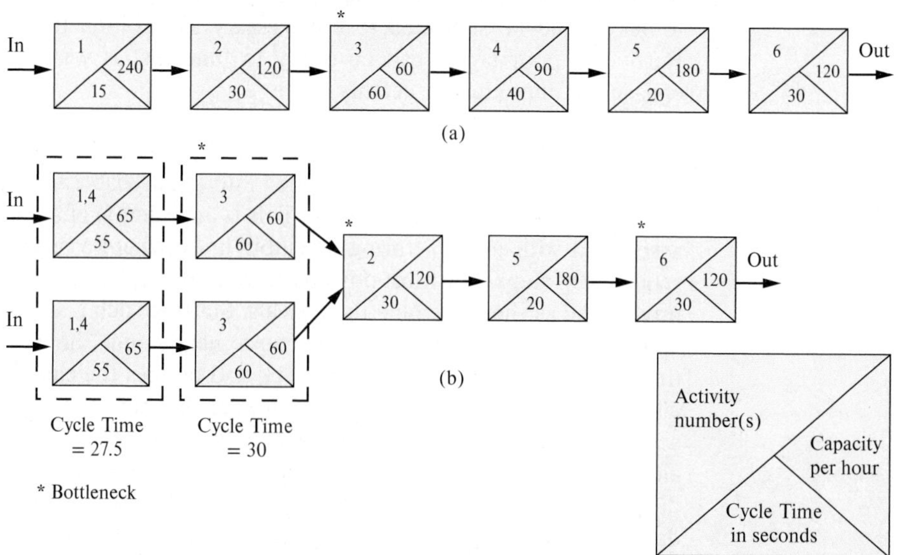

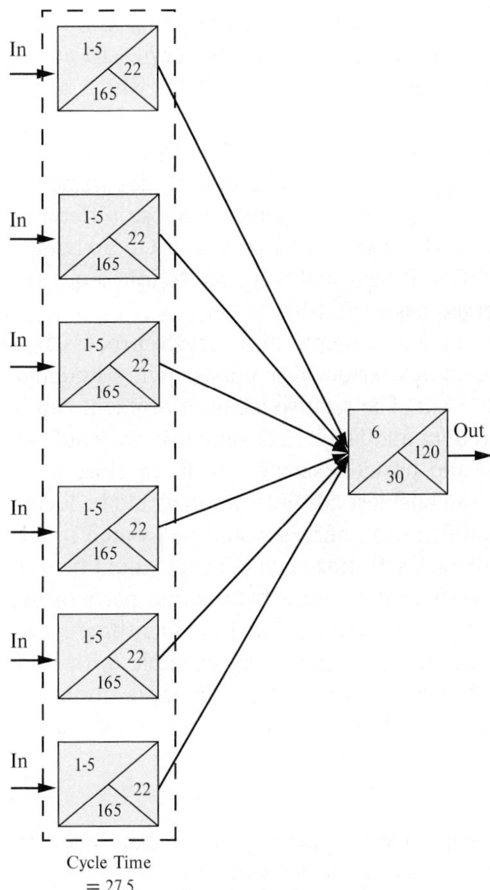

FIGURE 5.7
Reengineered Driver's License Office

job requiring 55 seconds per applicant (or a flow rate of 65 applicants per hour). Note that this solution requires the acquisition of one additional eye-testing machine. Another solution would be to combine activities 4 and 5 to create a job yielding a flow rate of 60 applicants per hour; however, an additional expensive camera would need to be purchased. Can you think of another process design that meets the capacity goal but could be viewed by customers and employees as offering more personalized service?

The example of the driver's license office lends itself to a radical rethinking of the product layout. If money were available to invest in computers, additional eye-testing equipment, and cameras, then the entire process could be reengineered. Consider training each clerk to perform all five activities with a combined time of 165 seconds, or an individual flow rate of approximately 22 customers per hour. Now, an arriving customer would be faced with choosing from among six clerks working in parallel, as shown in Figure 5.7. This system would be appealing to customers, however, because one clerk would handle all the transactions and, thus, customers would not be passed from one clerk to another and be required to wait in between. Further, one would expect that the total time could be shortened because information would not need to be repeated as before. Finally, staffing of the office would now be flexible because only the number of clerks required to meet anticipated demand need be on duty. This savings in labor could justify easily the investment in six work stations.

Job Shop Process Layout and the Relative Location Problem

In a *job shop process layout*, no fixed sequence of operations exists, so service can be customized to meet the needs of the customer. The flexibility of the layout allows the service to be tailored to the customer's specifications, thereby delivering personalized services. The ability to customize service requires more highly skilled service providers, who have discretion to personalize the service to customers' needs. Professional services such as law, medicine, and consulting, which are organized into specialties, provide examples.

From the service provider's perspective, the flow of customers appears to be intermittent, so there is a need for a waiting area in each department. The variability in demand at each department results when customers choose different sequences of services and place different demands on the service provided. On arriving at a particular department, customers often will find it busy and will need to join a queue, which usually operates on a first-come, first-served basis (FCFS).

A dramatic and physical example of a service process layout is a university campus with buildings dedicated to various disciplines, giving students the flexibility of choosing classes from among them. The relative location problem can be seen in the layout of the campus. For both student and faculty convenience, we would expect selected departments such as engineering and physical sciences to be in close proximity to each other, while perhaps economics and business administration would be located together in another area. The library and administration offices would be located in a central part of the campus. One possible objective for selecting such a layout would be to minimize the total distance traveled by faculty, staff, and students between all pairs of departments. Many different layouts are possible, however. In fact, if we have identified n departments to be assigned to n locations, then $n!$ layouts are possible. For example, with 10 departments $10! = 10 \times 9 \times 8 \times 7 \ldots$ yields 3,628,800 different layouts. Because finding the best layout among these possibilities is beyond complete enumeration, we will use a heuristic approach to finding a good layout in Example 5.3.

Example 5.3 Ocean World Theme Park

The architect for Ocean World is beginning to formulate plans for the development of property outside New Orleans, Louisiana, for a second marine theme park after the success of its Neptune's Realm on the West Coast. Because of the hot and humid gulf weather during the summer months, ways to minimize the visitors' total travel distance between attractions are being considered. Data showing a typical day's flow of visitors between attractions at San Diego are given in Table 5.3 and will be used in the layout planning.

A heuristic called *operations sequence analysis* will be used to identify a good layout for this relative location problem. This method uses as input the matrix of flows between attractions and a grid showing the geographic center location for attraction assignments. In Table 5.3, we have created a triangular form of the original flow matrix to sum the flows in either direction because we are interested only in the total.

The heuristic begins with an initial layout, shown on the grid in Figure 5.8*a*. This initial layout is arbitrary but could be based on judgment or past experience. Table 5.3 suggests that attractions with high daily flow between them should be placed adjacent to each other. For example, we cannot see a need to place A adjacent to D, but it would be appropriate to place A close to C.

For nonadjacent attractions, the flow between them is multiplied by the number of grid squares that separate the attractions. Note we have assumed that diagonal separation is

TABLE 5.3
Daily Flow of Visitors between Attractions, Hundreds*

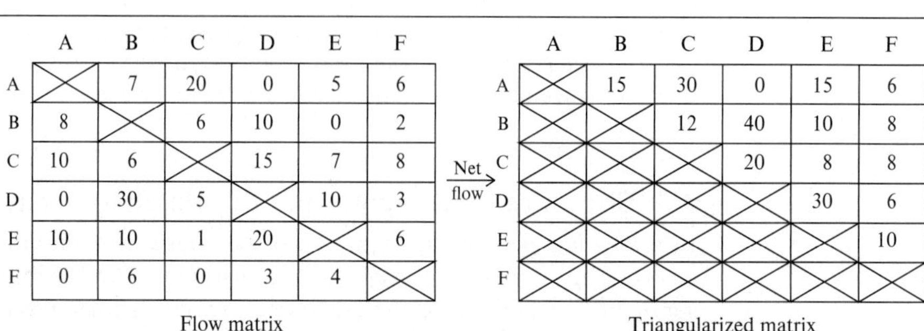

	A	B	C	D	E	F
A		7	20	0	5	6
B	8		6	10	0	2
C	10	6		15	7	8
D	0	30	5		10	3
E	10	10	1	20		6
F	0	6	0	3	4	

Flow matrix

Net flow →

	A	B	C	D	E	F
A		15	30	0	15	6
B			12	40	10	8
C				20	8	8
D					30	6
E						10
F						

Triangularized matrix

*Description of attractions: A = killer whale, B = sea lions, C = dolphins, D = water skiing, E = aquarium, F = water rides.

(*a*) **Intial layout**

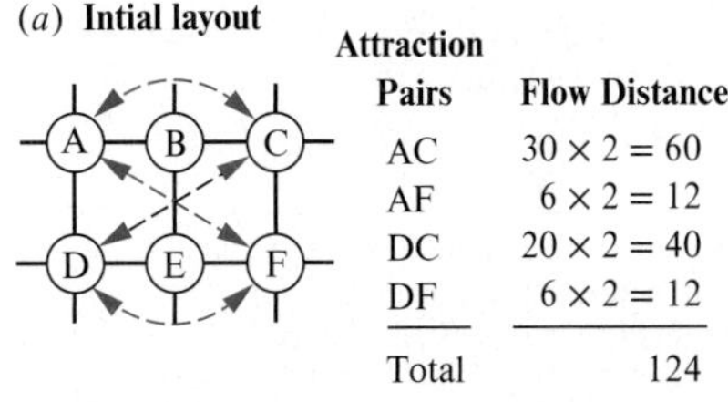

Attraction Pairs	Flow Distances
AC	30 × 2 = 60
AF	6 × 2 = 12
DC	20 × 2 = 40
DF	6 × 2 = 12
Total	124

(*b*) **Move C close to A**

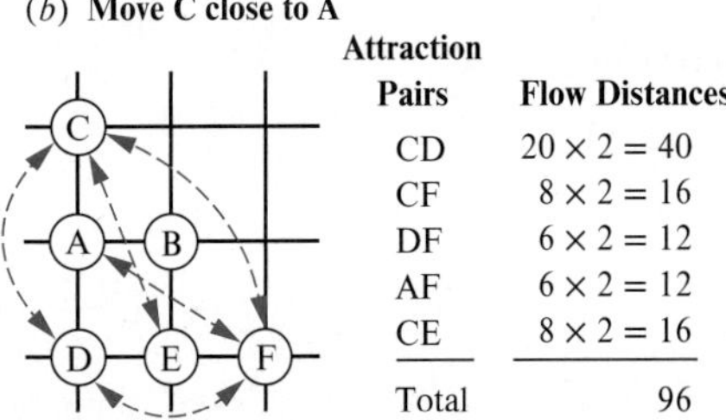

Attraction Pairs	Flow Distances
CD	20 × 2 = 40
CF	8 × 2 = 16
DF	6 × 2 = 12
AF	6 × 2 = 12
CE	8 × 2 = 16
Total	96

(*c*) **Exchange A and C**

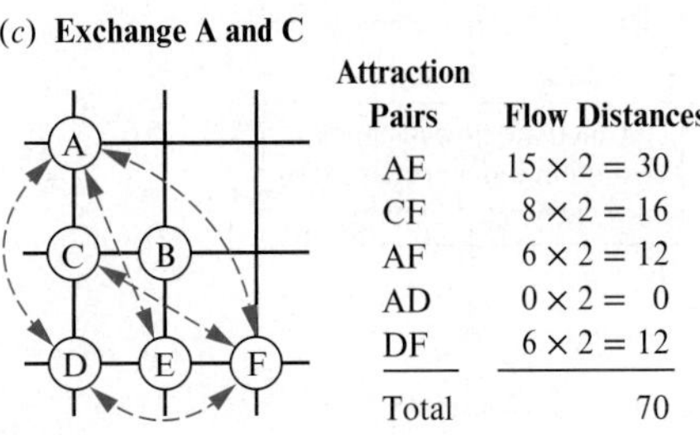

Attraction Pairs	Flow Distances
AE	15 × 2 = 30
CF	8 × 2 = 16
AF	6 × 2 = 12
AD	0 × 2 = 0
DF	6 × 2 = 12
Total	70

(*d*) **Exchange B and E and move F**

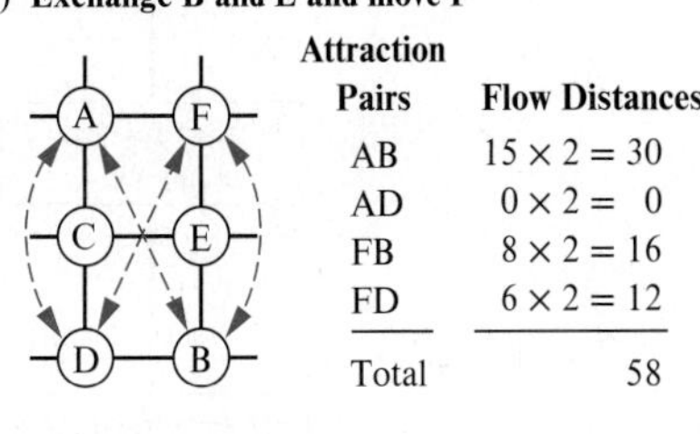

Attraction Pairs	Flow Distances
AB	15 × 2 = 30
AD	0 × 2 = 0
FB	8 × 2 = 16
FD	6 × 2 = 12
Total	58

FIGURE 5.8
Ocean World Site Planning Using Operations Sequence Analysis

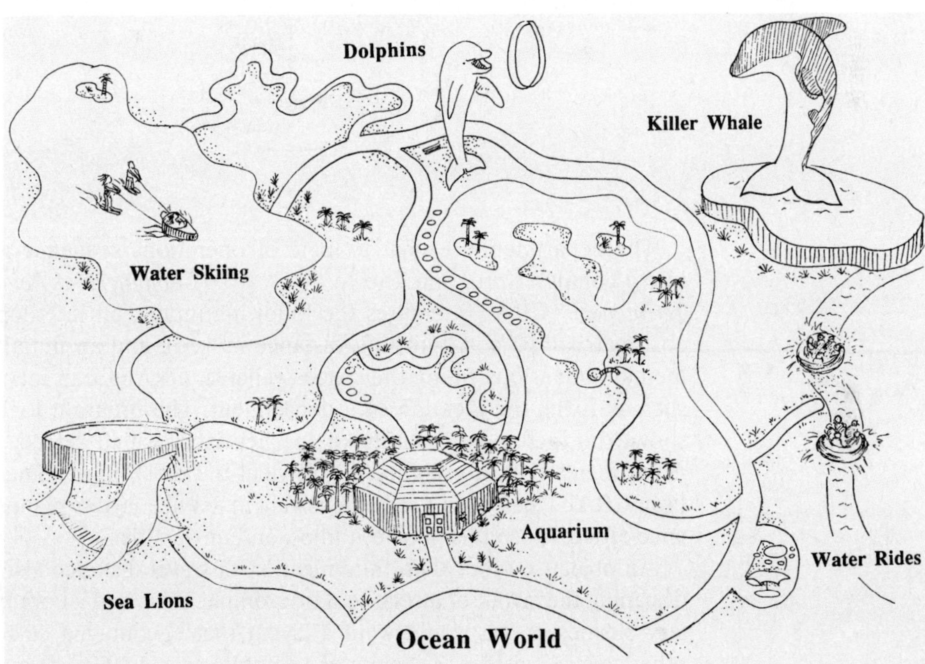

FIGURE 5.9
Final Site Plan for Ocean World Theme Park

Source: Map by Kate O'Brien, Desert Tale Graphics.

approximately equal to the distance of a grid side instead of using the Pythagorean theorem (in practice, distance would be measured using a plot plan). These products are summed to arrive at a total flow distance of 124 for this initial layout. Considering the large contribution made to this sum by the separation of attractions A and C, we decide to move C adjacent to A to form the revised layout shown in Figure 5.8*b*, with a total flow distance of 96. The revised layout shown in Figure 5.8*c* is the result of exchanging attractions A and C. This exchange has placed attraction C adjacent to attractions D, E, and F, thereby reducing the total flow distance to 70. However, the nonrectangular layout in Figure 5.8*c* is not acceptable for the real estate in question. Thus, the final layout, in Figure 5.8*d*, is created by exchanging attractions B and E and by moving attraction F to form a rectangular space; exchanging B and E keeps E and F adjacent as we move F to form a more compact space. By making high-flow attractions adjacent, we have reduced total nonadjacent flow distance to a value of 58 for our final site plan, which when rotated 90° to the right is shown in Figure 5.9.

FIGURE 5.10
Flow Diagram for CRAFT Logic

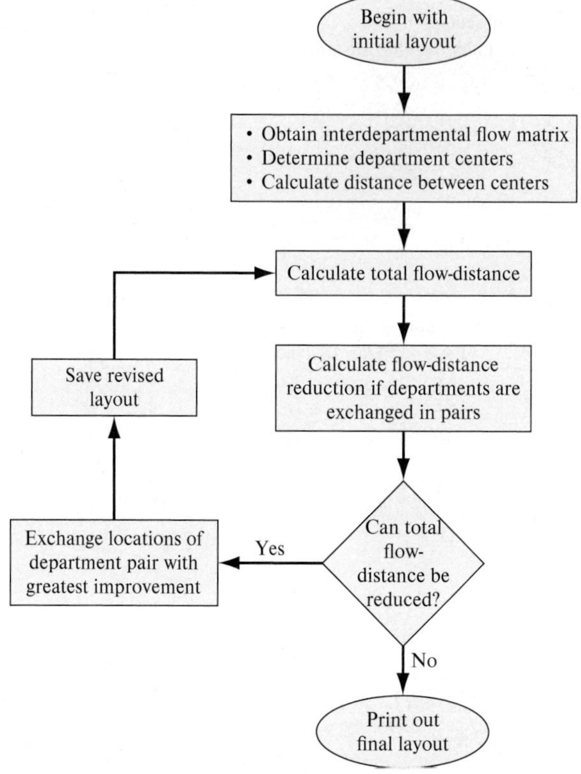

The departmental exchange logic of operations sequence analysis was incorporated into a computer program known as *CRAFT (Computerized Relative Allocation of Facilities Technique).*[4] CRAFT requires the following inputs: an interdepartmental flow matrix, a cost matrix (i.e., cost/unit/unit distance moved), and an initial layout with exact departmental dimensions filling the space available. CRAFT can incorporate some constraints, such as fixing the location of a department. The program logic depicted in Figure 5.10 shows the incremental nature of the heuristic, which selects at each iteration the two departments that, if exchanged, will yield the most improvement in flow distance reduction. CRAFT has been used extensively in service layout planning–for example, in insurance offices, hospitals, movie studios, and universities.

An objective other than minimization of travel distance also could be appropriate for designing the layout of a service. For example, if we had a core business with several ancillary businesses, we would want a layout that encouraged customers to browse in these other areas. Consider the layout of a gambling casino. Guests must walk through corridors lined with trendy shops and must always pass through the slot machine area to reach the hotel elevators or the restaurant.

Summary

The psychological implications of service facility design and layout were addressed to avoid customer disorientation and to mold behavior. The concept of a servicescape was used to illustrate the behavioral impact of environmental features in a service facility design on customers and employees. Facility design was seen as a package shaping the service experience and included features such as flexibility, security, and aesthetics. Process analysis begins with the construction of a process flow diagram that can be used to identify the system bottleneck and determine the throughput time. Facility layout was divided into product and process categories with graphic tools introduced for analysis.

Service Benchmark

WHERE, OH WHERE SHALL WE GO?

Airports are gateways to great adventures for millions of people around the world. Finding these gateways, however, can be adventures themselves.

Wall Street Journal reporter Bridget O'Brian explored the subject of signage outside airports.* She cites examples of problems such as a lack of necessary or helpful signs, ambiguous words or phrases, "inconspicuous" signs, and signs that are placed inappropriately. The consequences of poor signage can lead to bad tempers, missed flights, motor vehicle accidents, and deaths.

National standards for airport signage in the United States to cure these ills have been proposed. Such standards, if adopted, would represent an important service breakthrough.

Getting to the airport is only part of the adventure, however. Signage within airports often challenges the traveler. Consider two experienced passengers who are booked on a Delta Air Lines trip from Oakland, California, to Austin, Texas. They arrive at the Oakland International Airport and are told by the Delta agent that their Oakland–Dallas flight has been canceled. The agent gives them a voucher for an American Airlines flight and explains that they are still booked on Delta's Dallas–Austin flight, a 30-minute trip. They proceed to the American check-in counter where they receive their boarding passes. The trip is uneventful until they arrive in the Dallas–Fort Worth International Airport.

The travelers arrive at Gate 22, Concourse C, and quickly discover that the departure/arrival monitors display only American Airlines flights; the posted airport "maps" show Concourses A, B, and C—they do not indicate the existence of any other concourses. Signs for a train to the other two concourses direct the two passengers to a tram station on a lower level. They find that Concourses A and B also have gates—and monitors—for American Airlines flights only. They do not find a single sign for any airline or airport transportation service other than those for American Airlines. They finally ask for directions from an AA gate agent in Concourse A who tells them to leave the concourse opposite Gate 21A, go downstairs, and take the airport train (i.e., not the AA train) to Concourse E. Signs for a way downstairs are lacking and personnel at the concourse exit cannot speak English well enough to be helpful. Eventually they locate an elevator, descend to the lower level, and find that they must exit the building to get to the tram station. The tram station, however, is closed and a sign directs them to the next tram station to the right. They set off in that direction, although they cannot see another station. It is nighttime and the walk is deserted until a security guard comes in sight. He says the next open station is in the other direction. The transfer from an American Airlines gate to a Delta gate can be made in less than 10 minutes, but the complete absence of appropriate signs and knowledgeable personnel extends the transfer time to more than one hour.

Source: Bridget O'Brian, "Signs and Blunders: Airport Travelers Share Graphic Tales," *The Wall Street Journal,* March 28, 1995, p. B1.

Key Terms and Definitions

Bottleneck the activity in a product layout that takes the most time to perform and thus defines the maximum flow rate for the entire process. *pg. 130*

Capacity a measure of output per unit of time when *fully busy*. *pg. 130*

Capacity utilization a measure of how much output is actually achieved relative to the process capacity when fully busy. *pg. 130*

CRAFT (Computerized Relative Allocation of Facilities Technique) a computer program that uses the departmental exchange logic of operations sequence analysis to solve the relative location problem of process layouts. *pg. 136*

Cycle time the average time between completions of successive units. *pg. 129*

Direct labor utilization a measure of the percentage of time that workers are actually contributing value to the service. *pg. 131*

Flow process layout a standardized service performed in a fixed sequence of steps (e.g., cafeteria). *pg. 131*

Job shop process layout a service permitting customization because customers determine their own sequence of activities (e.g., an amusement park). *pg. 133*
Operations sequence analysis a procedure to improve the flow distance in a process layout by arranging the relative location of departments. *pg. 134*
Rush order flow time the time it takes to go through the system from beginning to end without any wait time in queue. *pg. 131*
Servicescape the physical environment of a service facility that influences the behavior and perceptions of the service for both the customers and the workers. *pg. 120*
Throughput time the time it takes to get completely through a process from time of arrival to time of exit. *pg. 130*
Total direct labor content the sum of all the operations times. *pg. 131*

Topics for Discussion

1. Compare the attention to aesthetics in waiting rooms that you have visited. How did the different environments affect your mood?
2. From a customer perspective, give an example of a servicescape that supports the service concept and an example that detracts from the service concept. Explain the success and the failure in terms of the servicescape dimensions.
3. Select a service and discuss how the design and layout of the facility meet the five factors of nature and objectives of the organization, land availability and space requirements, flexibility, aesthetics, and the community and environment.
4. For Example 5.3, the Ocean World theme park, make an argument for not locating popular attractions next to each other.
5. The CRAFT program is an example of a heuristic programming approach to problem solving. Why might CRAFT not find the optimal solution to a layout problem?

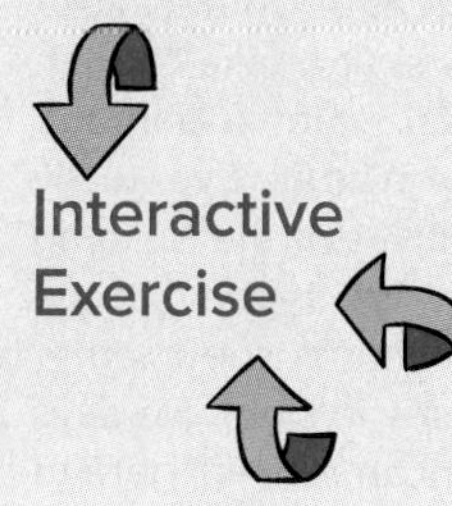

Interactive Exercise

The class divides into small groups. One-half of the groups produce examples based on work experience with *supportive* servicescapes in terms of job satisfaction and productivity. The other one-half of the groups provide examples of *poor* servicescapes in terms of job satisfaction and productivity.

Solved Problems

1. Work Allocation for Product Layout

Problem Statement

Arriving at JFK airport in New York from overseas requires a sequence of immigration and customs-clearing activities before a passenger can board a domestic flight for home. The table below lists the activities and their average times. Except for baggage claim, these activities must be performed in the sequence noted. What is the bottleneck activity and maximum number of passengers who can be processed per hour? What would you recommend to improve the balance of this process?

Activity	Average Time, Sec.
1. Deplane	20
2. Immigration	16
3. Baggage claim	40
4. Customs	24
5. Check baggage	18
6. Board domestic flight	15

Solution

First, draw the process flow diagram and identify the bottleneck activity. The slowest activity is "baggage claim," which results in a system capacity of 90 passengers per hour.

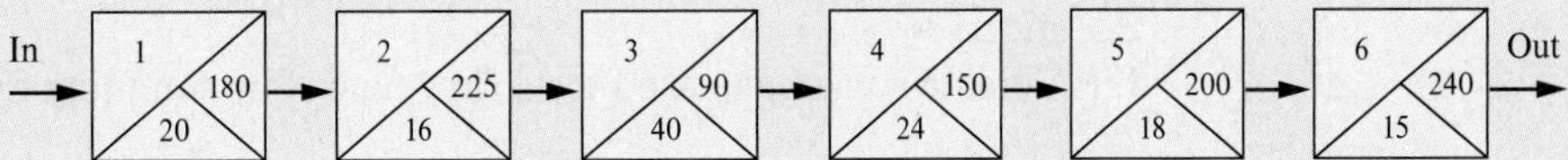

A recommendation for increasing system capacity could include doubling the capacity of the baggage claim area and combining the activities of the immigration and customs areas. This new product layout is shown in the process flow diagram below, with the result of doubling the system capacity to 180 passengers per hour.

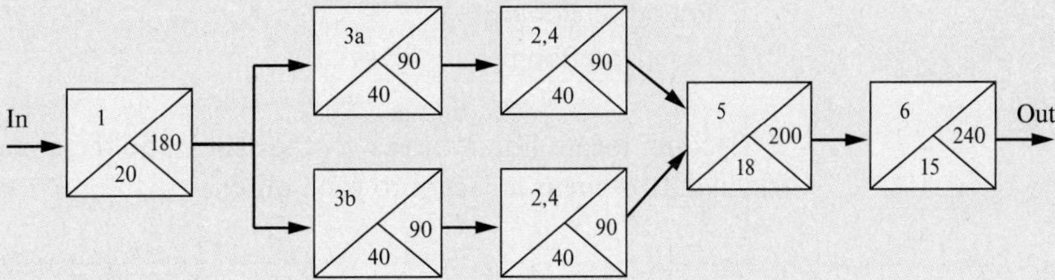

2 Process Analysis

Problem Statement

Consider the original process flow diagram shown above for overseas arrivals at JFK airport. Calculate the values for system capacity, total direct labor content, rush order flow time, and direct labor utilization.

Solution

The first step in process analysis is the identification of the *bottleneck* activity, which in this case is "baggage claim" with a CT of 40 seconds. The *system capacity* is determined by the bottleneck CT and is calculated as (60 minutes/hour)(60 seconds/minute)(1/40 seconds) = 90 passengers per hour. Assuming no waiting time between activities, the *rush order flow time* is the sum of all the activity times: 20 + 16 + 40 + 24 + 18 + 15 = 133 seconds. Because there is only one path in the process, *total direct labor content* is also the sum of all the activity times or 133 seconds. Direct labor utilization is total direct labor content divided by system process cycle time (bottleneck CT) multiplied by number of workers.

$$\textit{Direct labor utilization} = \frac{133}{(40)(6)}(100) = 55.4 \textit{ percent}$$

3. Relative Location for Process Layout

Problem Statement

The architect for the new undergraduate library is interested in a floor plan that would be viewed as convenient by users. Based on survey data from the old library, student movements between different areas in hundreds of trips per month are noted in the flow matrix below. Prepare a good initial rectangular layout that minimizes total flow distance between nonadjacent areas; then use operations sequence analysis to improve the layout.

Library Area	A	B	C	D	E	F
A Reserve Room	—	5	9	3	7	1
B Reference Room	3	—	8	2	6	2
C Copy Room	1	1	—	7	2	3
D Stacks	2	2	10	—	2	5
E Periodical Room	1	2	6	3	—	2
F Computer Room	1	1	1	4	2	—

Solution

First, create a triangularized total flow matrix by summing flows across the diagonal.

Library Area	A	B	C	D	E	F
A Reserve Room	—	8	10	5	8	2
B Reference Room	—	—	9	4	8	3
C Copy Room	—	—	—	17	8	4
D Stacks	—	—	—	—	5	9
E Periodical Room	—	—	—	—	—	4
F Computer Room	—	—	—	—	—	—

Second, locate library areas on the schematic rectangular layout shown below by placing high-flow areas adjacent to each other.

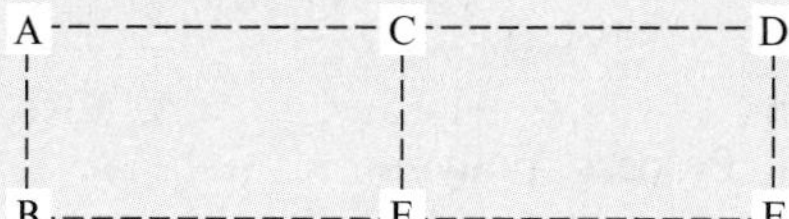

Next, calculate the total flow distance of nonadjacent pairs as shown below:

Nonadjacent Area Pairs	Flow		Distance		Total
AD	5	×	2	=	10
AF	2	×	2	=	4
BD	4	×	2	=	8
BF	3	×	2	=	6
					28

Finally, look for improvement by exchanging a pair of nonadjacent areas. Because no improvement is possible, accept the above layout.

Exercises

5.1. Passengers arriving at an airport departure gate must first wait for their row to be called before proceeding to the gate to have their boarding pass authenticated. If the boarding pass does not match the departing flight, the passenger is directed to the appropriate gate. A passenger attempting to carry on an excessively large bag is directed to check the luggage piece and return. Passengers with the proper boarding pass and appropriate sized carry-on are allowed to enter the jet way and board the plane. Draw a process flow diagram of the departure gate process. How might this process be improved to avoid delays?

5.2. Consider the Mortgage Service Process shown in Figure 5.4, and assume the Title Search cycle time has changed to 60 minutes.

a. What is the bottleneck operation and corresponding system capacity?

b. What is the rush order flow time?

c. What is the system capacity, if the same person performs Credit Report and Title Search?

5.3. Revisit the Automobile Driver's License Office example.

a. What is the direct labor utilization for the process shown in Figure 5.6*a*?

b. What is the direct labor utilization for the process shown in Figure 5.6*b*?

c. What is the direct labor utilization for the process shown in Figure 5.7?

d. What do you conclude from these calculations?

5.4. Revisit the Automobile Driver's License Office, and assume that some of our previous recommendations for investment have been implemented. For example, "checking for violations and restrictions" will be done on a computer terminal, with that activity now taking 30 instead of 60 seconds. However, no additional eye-test machines or cameras were purchased.

a. Assuming that one worker is assigned to each activity, what is the bottleneck activity and the maximum number of applicants who can be seen per hour?

b. Suggest a reallocation of activities among the six workers that would result in a service capacity of 120 applicants per hour. What investment would be required to implement your layout recommendation?

5.5. Getting a physical examination at a physician's office involves a series of steps. The table below lists these activities and their average times. The activities can occur in any order, but the doctor's consultation must be last. Three nurses are assigned to perform activities 1, 2, and 4.

Activity	Average Time, Min.
1. Blood pressure, wt., temp.	6
2. Medical history	20
3. Doctor's checkup	18
4. Lab work	10
5. Doctor's consultation	12

a. What are the bottleneck activity and the maximum number of patients who can be seen per hour?

b. Suggest a reallocation of nursing and/or doctor activities that would result in increased service capacity, and draw a product flow diagram. What is the capacity of your improved system?

5.6. A school cafeteria is operated by five persons performing the activities in the average times shown in the following chart.

Activity	Average Time, Sec.
1. Serve salad and dessert	10
2. Pour drinks	30
3. Serve entrèe	60
4. Serve vegetables	20
5. Tally and collect payment	40

a. What are the bottleneck activity and the maximum service capacity per hour?

b. Suggest a reallocation of activities that would increase capacity and use only four employees, and draw a product flow diagram. What is the capacity of your improved system?

c. Recommend a way to maintain the serving capacity found in part b using only three employees.

5.7. Every fall, volunteers administer flu vaccine shots at a local supermarket. The process involves the following four steps:

Activity	Average Time, Sec.
1. Reception	30
2. Drug allergy consultation	60
3. Fill out form and sign waiver	45
4. Administer vaccination	90

a. What are the bottleneck activity and maximum number of people who can be processed per hour?

b. If a fifth volunteer is assigned to help administer vaccinations, what activity now becomes the bottleneck? How has this arrangement influenced the capacity of the system?

c. Using five volunteers, suggest a reallocation of activities that would result in increased service capacity, and draw a product flow diagram. What is the capacity of your improved system?

5.8. Revisit the Ocean World Theme Park, and use the daily flow of visitors between attractions found in Example 5.3 for a different analysis.

a. Recommend a layout that would *maximize* the total travel distance between attractions.

b. What benefit would such a layout have for the owners of Ocean World Theme Park?

c. What reservations do you have about using the data from Table 5.3 for this new approach to the Ocean World Theme Park layout?

5.9. The Second Best Discount Store is considering rearranging its stockroom to improve customer service. Currently, stock pickers are given customer orders to fill from six warehouse areas. Movement between these areas is noted in the flow matrix below:

	A	B	C	D	E	F
A	—	1	4	2	0	3
B	0	—	2	0	2	1
C	2	2	—	4	5	2
D	3	0	2	—	0	2
E	1	4	3	1	—	4
F	4	3	1	2	0	—

Using the initial layout below, perform an operations sequence analysis to determine a layout that minimizes total flow between nonadjacent departments. Calculate your flow improvement.

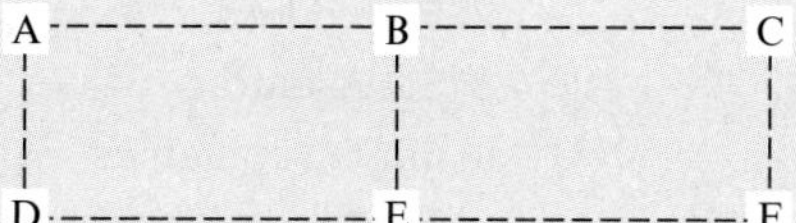

5.10. A convenience store is considering changing its layout to encourage impulse buying. The triangular flow matrix below gives the measure of association between different product groups (e.g., beer, milk, magazines). A plus sign (+) indicates a high association, such as between beer and peanuts; a minus sign (−) indicates a repulsion, such as between beer and milk; and a zero (0) indicates no association.

	A	B	C	D	E	F
A		+	+	0	0	−
B			+	0	−	−
C				+	+	0
D					+	+
E						+
F						

Using the initial layout below, perform an operations sequence analysis to determine a layout that will encourage impulse buying by placing high-association product groups close to one another.

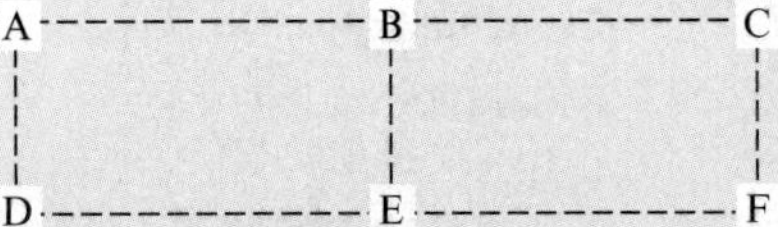

5.11. A community college that recently acquired a parcel of land is now preparing site plans. There is interest in locating academic departments in each of six buildings along a mall with three buildings on each side. Based on registration patterns, the daily flow of students between these six departments in hundreds is shown below.

	A	B	C	D	E	F
A. Psychology	—	6	4	8	7	1
B. English	6	—	2	3	9	5
C. Mathematics	6	1	—	12	2	4
D. Economics	3	2	10	—	3	5
E. History	7	11	2	1	—	6
F. Biology	6	2	8	10	3	—

Using the initial layout below, perform an operations sequence analysis to determine a site plan for the community college that will minimize the distance that students need to walk between classes.

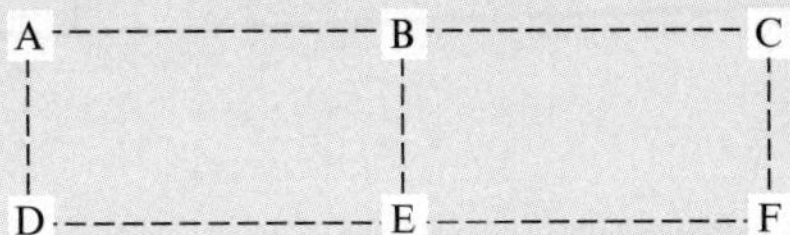

Health Maintenance Organization (A) CASE 5.1

In January 2012, Joan Taylor, the administrator of the Life-Time Insurance Company HMO in Buffalo, New York, was pleased with the Austin, Texas, location that was selected for a new ambulatory health center. (The process used to select this site is discussed in Chapter 8, Service Facility Location.) The center not only would serve as a clinic for the acutely ill but also as a center for preventive health services.

An important goal of the HMO was to offer programs that would encourage members to stay healthy. Various programs already had been planned, including those on smoking cessation, proper nutrition, diet, and exercise.

The clinic portion of the health center would be quite large; however, certain constraints in the layout would be necessary. Acutely ill patients would need to be separated from well patients. In addition, federal safety regulations prohibited the radiography department from being adjacent to the main waiting room.

It was very important to Ms. Taylor to minimize the walking distance for both the patients and the HMO personnel. The matrix below provides the expected flow between departments based on 35 patients per day.

Questions

1. Beginning with a good initial layout, use operations sequence analysis to determine a better layout that would minimize the walking distance between different areas in the clinic.
2. Defend your final layout based on features other than minimizing walking distance.

		A	B	C	D	E	F
Reception	A	—	30	0	5	0	0
Waiting room	B	10	—	40	10	0	0
Examination	C	15	20	—	15	5	5
Laboratory	D	5	18	8	—	6	3
X-ray	E	0	4	1	2	—	4
Minor surgery	F	2	0	0	0	1	—

Health Maintenance Organization (B) CASE 5.2

The administrator of the Life-Time Insurance Company HMO, Ms. Taylor, was anxious to solve potential problems before the new clinic opened in Austin, Texas. In Buffalo, New York, where the original clinic is located, the pharmacy had been extremely busy from the beginning, and long waiting times for prescriptions to be filled presented a very real problem.

The Buffalo HMO pharmacy was modern, spacious, and well designed. The peak time for prescriptions was between 10 AM and 3 PM. During this period, prescriptions would back up, and the waiting time would increase. After 5 PM, the staff would be reduced to one pharmacist and one technician, but the two had no trouble providing very timely service throughout the evening.

Ms. Taylor became acutely aware of the long waiting times after several complaints had been lodged. Each stated that the waiting time had exceeded 1 hour. The pharmacy is staffed with five persons on duty until 5 PM.

Ms. Taylor personally studied the tasks of all the pharmacy personnel. She noted the time required to accomplish each task, and results are listed in the chart. The prescriptions were filled in an assembly-line fashion by two technicians and three pharmacists, and each person performed only one task.

Activity	Time in Seconds
Receive prescriptions	24
Type labels	120
Fill prescriptions	60
Check prescriptions	40
Dispense prescriptions	30

Note: The activities of filling, checking, and dispensing prescriptions must be performed by a registered pharmacist.

Questions

1. Identify the bottleneck activity, and show how capacity can be increased by using only two pharmacists and two technicians.
2. In addition to savings on personnel costs, what benefits does this arrangement have?

Esquire Department Store CASE 5.3

Established by Arthur Babbitt, Sr., in 1996, Esquire Department Store has shown a recent decline in sales. The store manager, young Arthur Babbitt, Jr., has noticed a decrease in the movement of customers between departments. He believes that customers are not spending enough time in the store, and that this may result from the present layout, which is based on the concept of locating related departments close to each other. Babbitt, Sr., is not convinced. He argues that he has been in business for almost 20 years, and that the loyal customers are not likely to quit shopping here simply because of the layout. He believes they are losing customers to the new factory outlet mall outside town, which seems to attract them away with discount prices.

Babbitt, Jr., explains that the greater the distance the customer travels between departments, the more products the customer will see. Customers usually have something specific in mind when they go shopping, but exposure to more products might stimulate additional purchases. Thus, to Babbitt, Jr., it seems that the best answer to this problem is to change the present layout so that customers are exposed to more products. He feels the environment today is different from the environment of 1996, and that the company must display products better and encourage impulse buying.

At this point, Babbitt, Sr., interrupts to say, "Son, you might have a point here about the store layout. But before I spend money on tearing this place up, I need to see some figures.

Develop a new layout, and show me how much you can increase the time customers spend in the store."

Babbitt, Jr., returns to his office and pulls out some information that he has gathered about revising the store layout. He has estimated that, on average, 57 customers enter the store per hour. The store operates 10 hours a day, 200 days a year. He has a drawing of the present layout, which is shown in Figure 5.11, and a chart depicting the flow of customers between departments, which is shown in Table 5.4.

Questions

1. Use CRAFT logic to develop a layout that will maximize customer time in the store.
2. What percentage increase in customer time spent in the store is achieved by the proposed layout?
3. What other consumer behavior concepts should be considered in the relative location of departments?

FIGURE 5.11 Current Layout of Esquire Department Store figure (Figures in parentheses refer to a grid layout in rows and columns)

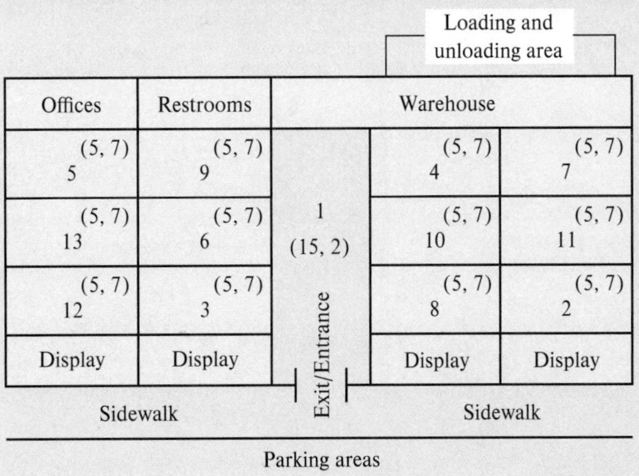

TABLE 5.4 Flow of Customers between Departments, in Thousands

	1	2	3	4	5	6	7	8	9	10	11	12	13
1	0	32	41	19	21	7	13	22	10	11	8	6	10
2	17	0	24	31	16	3	13	17	25	8	7	9	12
3	8	14	0	25	9	28	17	16	14	7	9	24	18
4	25	12	16	0	18	26	22	9	6	28	20	16	14
5	10	12	15	20	0	18	17	24	28	30	25	9	19
6	8	14	12	17	20	0	19	23	30	32	37	15	21
7	13	19	23	25	3	45	0	29	27	31	41	24	16
8	28	9	17	19	21	5	7	0	21	19	25	10	9
9	14	8	13	15	22	18	13	25	0	33	27	14	19
10	18	25	17	19	23	15	25	27	31	0	21	17	10
11	29	28	31	16	29	19	18	33	26	31	0	16	16
12	17	31	25	21	19	17	19	21	31	29	25	0	19
13	12	25	16	33	14	19	31	17	22	15	24	18	0

1. Exit-entrance
2. Appliances
3. Audio-stereo-TV
4. Jewelry
5. Housewares
6. Cosmetics
7. Ladies' ready-to-wear
8. Mens' ready-to-wear
9. Boys' clothing
10. Sporting goods
11. Ladies' lingerie
12. Shoes
13. Furniture

Central Market[5] CASE 5.4

The original Central Market grocery store, located in the Hyde Park area of Austin, Texas, is a radical departure from the usual corporate grocery chain stores, namely a standardized, undifferentiated place to shop that was designed for efficiency and offered similar products. Central Market attempts to change the entire grocery shopping experience from the products it stocks to the way people shop, the customer service, the store layout, and ancillary services offered. The founders wanted to create a farmers' market "look and feel" by offering only high-quality, fresh products while also providing a vibrant, interactive atmosphere. Central Market was designed to change the way people ate and how they prepared a meal. Exploration and discovery are encouraged as the customers make their way through, what some consider, a delectable labyrinth of displays.

FIGURE 5.12 **Central Market Floor Plan**

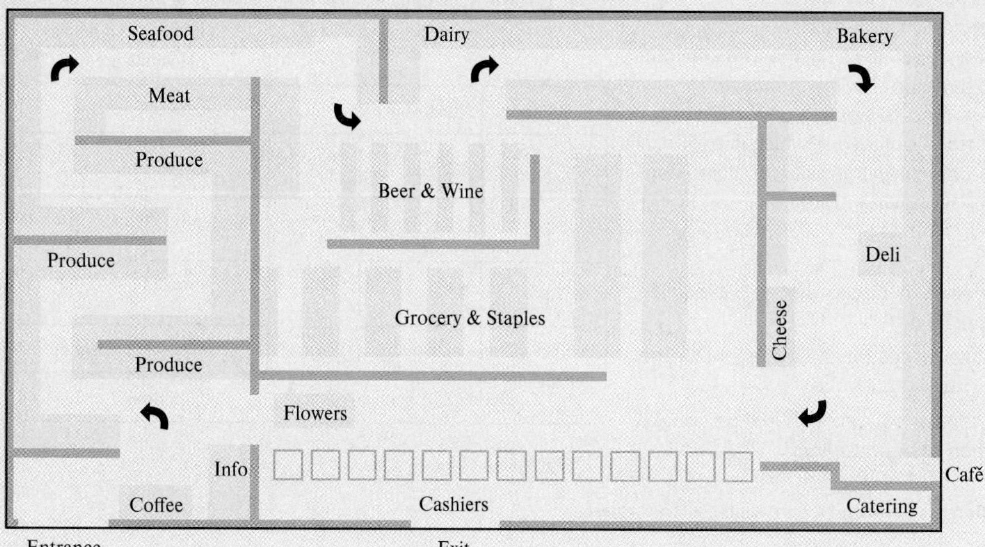

The entrance to Central Market leads into an atrium that contains an information desk and a small coffee bar. Customers then join a serpentine flow through a full-view European style city market. Central Market calls this a *force flow* as seen by the floor plan in Figure 5.12. Customers weave through winding aisles of fresh fruit and vegetables before entering "protein alley" where they can purchase assorted meats and seafood. A winery, bakery, deli, and *fromagerie* departments follow. Staples such as canned goods and bulk foods are housed in the center of the "maze." Escape passages throughout the store provide shortcuts to the checkout area.

The facility layout is analogous to the construct of a fine meal, that is, vegetables, meats, wine, bread and cheese in that order. Brian Cronin, general manager for Central Market, states the design is meant to "funnel people through the core products." The design, however, is just a small part of how Central Market delivers its service concept.

Central Market has achieved the look and feel similar to a farmers' market. Temperature is controlled primarily to ensure product quality. Produce and meat departments are kept at 68° F, while the temperature in the preparation areas is set at 50° F. The rest of the store has a slightly warmer environment of about 70° F. The aroma of coffee, fresh produce, fish, and baked goods greets customers as they walk through the store. Freshness is ensured because products are shipped in daily.

The spacing and functional landscape are also compatible with the farmers' market concept. Displays are arranged to emphasize an abundance of products. As products are sold, displays are rearranged to maintain visual aesthetics. Aisles are arranged to allow at least two carts to pass one another. One example of the way the floor plan helps to achieve strategic goals (i.e., increase profitability) is the location of alcoholic beverages in the forced flow model. The main thoroughfare divides the beer and wine section and creates an opportunity for browsing and impulse purchases.

The store design is remarkably flexible. Displays are added or removed dependent upon seasonality and customer demand. For example, the floral department can be expanded during February for Valentine's Day or reduced when customer count is expected to be high during holiday seasons.

A "café on the run" area is located near the express checkout. Customers who use this queue are likely to be time-sensitive and this queuing system reduces the average time to be served. Shoppers with more items use the standard multiqueue and can engage in *jockeying.* The perception of waiting in line is often more important than the actual delay; thus, the placement of the florist behind the cashiers provides an opportunity to distract customers and, also, make an impulse purchase.

Signs, symbols, and artifacts again are consistent with the farmers' market theme. Signs are handmade and painted by three people on the store art team. Pastel colors are used throughout the store, on signs and on the enormous cutlery sculptures in the café. Color-coding is used to identify organic and Texas-grown produce. These environmental dimensions are manipulated by Central Market to entice the customer to shop longer and buy more.

The Central Market experience is a wonderful assault on the senses. Customers can see, smell, feel, and even taste products. Variety is apparent as produce from all over the world is presented. Customers spend extra time in the store because they are presented with items they have never seen before and the facility design controls their travel path. The average shopper spends 45 minutes in Central Market, but on weekends customers frequently linger because of special displays and demonstrations, as well as increased congestion. The experience of shopping at Central Market appears to be addictive. Central Market is, in fact, the second-largest tour destination in Austin.

Shoppers also end up spending more than they planned even though Central Market does not stock standard grocery items such as soft drinks, chips, paper goods, and cleaning supplies. The average customer check is significantly higher when compared to the industry average of $20. Products cost more because of their uniqueness, freshness, and quality. Impulse purchasing is facilitated by numerous opportunities to sample products and because the facility design creates bottlenecks and waiting areas near appealing products such as flowers, wine, and baked goods.

Central Market customers' biggest complaint about the experience is the store layout, and they usually have to learn the location of different items through repeat visits. Orientation aids such as a store map and signs are scarce. Perhaps this lack of direction is not an oversight—after all, Central Market is about discovery. If customers know where everything is, how can they explore?

Questions

1. How do the environmental dimensions of the servicescape explain the success of Central Market?
2. Comment on how the servicescape shapes the behaviors of both customers and employees.

Selected Bibliography

Baron, Opher, et al. "Strategic Idleness and Dynamic Scheduling in an Open-Shop Service Network: Case Study and Analysis." *Manufacturing & Service Operations Management* 18 (October 2016).

Bordoloi, Sanjeev K. "Agent Recruitment Planning in Knowledge-Intensive Call Centers." *Journal of Service Research* 6, no. 4 (2004), pp. 309–23.

Chang, Kuo-Chien. "Effect of Servicescape on Customer Behavioral Intentions: Moderating Roles of Service Climate and Employee Engagement." *International Journal of Hospitality Management* 53 (February 2016), pp. 116–28.

Dean, Dwane H. "Visual Antecedents of Patronage: Personal and Professional Items in the Servicescape." *Services Marketing Quarterly* 35, no. 1 (2014), pp. 68–83.

Goldratt, Eliyahu M., and J. Cox. *The Goal.* New York: North River Press, 2004.

KC, Diwas Singh. "Does Multitasking Improve Performance? Evidence from the Emergency Department." *Manufacturing & Service Operations Management* 16, no. 2 (2013), pp. 168–83.

Nilsson, Elin, and David Ballantyne. "Reexamining the Place of Servicescape in Marketing: A Service-Dominant Logic Perspective." *Journal of Services Marketing* 28, no. 5 (2014): pp. 374–79.

Parish, Janet Turner, Leonard L. Berry, and Shun YinLam. "The Effects of the Servicescape on Service Workers." *Journal of Service Research* 10, no. 3 (February 2008), pp. 220–38.

Vilnai-Yavetz, Iris, and Anat Rafaeli. "Aesthetics and Professionalism of Virtual Servicescapes." *Journal of Service Research* 8, no. 3 (February 2006), pp. 245–59.

Wright, Juli, and Russ King. *We All Fall Down: Goldratt's Theory of Constrainst for Healthcare Systems.* London: Ashgate, 2006.

Endnotes

1. http://www.fool.com/investing/2016/09/16/better-buy-the-home-depot-inc-vs-lowes.aspx.
2. Richard E. Wener, "The Environmental Psychology of Service Encounters," in J. A. Czepiel, M. R. Solomon, and C. F. Surprenant (eds.), *The Service Encounter* (Lexington, MA: Lexington Books, 1985), pp. 101–13.
3. Mary Jo Bitner, "Servicescapes: The Impact of Physical Surroundings on Customers and Employees," *Journal of Marketing* 56 (April 1992), pp. 57–71.
4. E. S. Buffa, G. C. Armour, and T. E. Vollmann, "Allocating Facilities with CRAFT," *Harvard Business Review* 42, no. 2 (March–April 1964), pp. 136–59.
5. Prepared by Charles Morris, Allison Pinto, Jameson Smith, and Jules Woolf under the supervision of Professor James A. Fitzsimmons.

Chapter 

Service Quality

Learning Objectives

After completing this chapter, you should be able to:

1. Describe and illustrate the five dimensions of service quality.
2. Use the service quality gap model to diagnose quality problems.
3. Apply poka-yoke methods to a service.
4. Construct a "house of quality" as part of a quality function deployment project.
5. Construct a statistical process control chart for a service operation.
6. Describe the features of an unconditional service guarantee and its managerial benefits.
7. Perform a walk-through audit (WtA).
8. Explain what service recovery is and why it's important.

Service "with a smile" used to be enough to satisfy most customers. Today, however, some service firms differentiate themselves in the marketplace by offering a "service guarantee." Unlike a product warranty that promises to repair or replace the faulty item, service guarantees typically offer the dissatisfied customer a refund, discount, or free service. Take, for example, the First Interstate Bank of California (acquired by Wells Fargo & Co. in 1996). After interviewing its customers, the bank management discovered that they were annoyed by a number of recurring problems, such as inaccurate statements and broken automatic teller machines (ATMs). Account retention improved after the bank began to pay customers $5 for reporting each such service failure. What is surprising, however, is that the service guarantee also had a motivating effect on the employees. When an ATM failed at a branch, the employees, out of pride, decided to keep the branch open until the machine was repaired at 8:30 PM.

Another hidden benefit of a guarantee is customer feedback. Now customers have a reason and motivation to talk to the company instead of just to their friends.

In addition to advertising the firm's commitment to quality, a service guarantee focuses employees by defining performance standards explicitly and, more important, builds a loyal customer base. The experience of Hampton Inns, an early adopter of a "100 percent satisfaction guarantee," illustrates that superior quality is a competitive advantage. In a survey of 300 guests who invoked the guarantee, more than 100 already had stayed again at a Hampton Inn. The hotel chain figures that it has received $8 in revenue for every $1 paid to a disgruntled guest.[1]

Chapter Preview

Service quality is a complex topic, as shown by the need for a definition that includes five dimensions: reliability, responsiveness, assurance, empathy, and tangibles. We use these dimensions to introduce the concept of a service quality gap. This gap is based on the difference between a customer's expectations of a service and the perceptions of the service that is delivered. A survey instrument that measures service quality, called SERVQUAL, is based on implementing the service quality gap concept.

Quality begins with the design of the service delivery system. Thus, concepts borrowed from product design such as Taguchi methods, poka-yoke, and quality function deployment are applied to the design of service delivery systems. Statistical process control is used to monitor variation in service performance metrics and signal when intervention is necessary. A customer satisfaction survey instrument, called a *walk-through audit* (WtA), is built on the premise that each customer is a participant in the service process.

However, service failures do occur and the use of an unconditional service guarantee might be offered as the equivalent of a product warranty. Because the customer is present during service delivery, service recovery strategies can be planned in anticipation of a service failure.

Defining Service Quality

For services, the assessment of quality is made during the service delivery process. Each customer contact is referred to as a moment of truth, an opportunity to satisfy or dissatisfy the customer. Customer satisfaction with a service can be defined by comparing perceptions of service received with expectations of service desired. When expectations are exceeded, service is perceived to be of exceptional quality—and also to be a pleasant surprise. When expectations are not met, however, service quality is deemed unacceptable. When expectations are confirmed by perceived service, quality is satisfactory. As shown in Figure 6.1, these expectations are based on several sources, including word of mouth, personal needs, and past experience.

Dimensions of Service Quality

The dimensions of service quality as shown in Figure 6.1 were identified by marketing researchers studying several different service categories: appliance repair, retail banking, telephone service, securities brokerage, and credit card companies. They identified five principal dimensions that customers use to judge service quality—reliability, responsiveness, assurance, empathy, and tangibles, which are listed in order of declining relative importance to customers.[2]

Reliability. The ability to perform the promised service both dependably and accurately. Reliable service performance is a customer expectation and means that the service is accomplished on time, in the same manner, and without errors every time. For example, consider your expectation of a pizza delivered to you home. Reliability also extends into the back office, where accuracy in record keeping and billing is expected.

Responsiveness. The willingness to help customers and to provide prompt service. Keeping customers waiting, particularly for no apparent reason, creates unnecessary

FIGURE 6.1
Perceived Service Quality

Reprinted with permission of the American Marketing Association: adapted from A. Parasuraman, V. A. Zeithaml, and L. L. Berry, "A Conceptual Model of Service Quality and Its Implications for Future Research," *Journal of Marketing* 49, Fall 1985, p. 48.

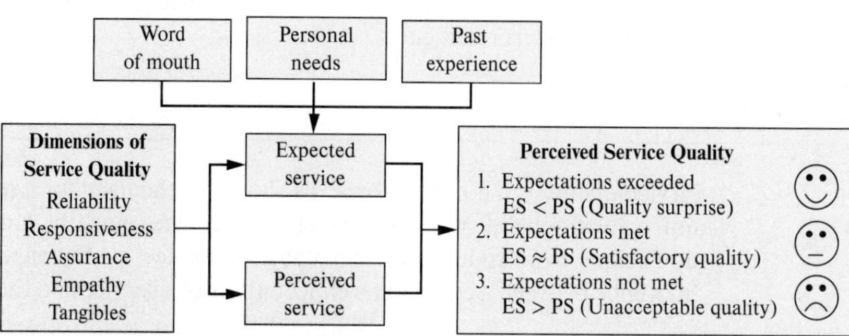

negative perceptions of quality. If a service failure occurs, the ability to recover quickly and with professionalism can create very positive perceptions of quality. For example, serving complimentary drinks on a delayed flight can turn a potentially poor customer experience into one that is remembered favorably.

Assurance. The knowledge and courtesy of employees as well as their ability to convey trust and confidence. The assurance dimension includes the following features: competence to perform the service, politeness and respect for the customer, effective communication with the customer, and the general attitude that the server has the customer's best interests at heart.

Empathy. The provision of caring, individualized attention to customers. Empathy includes the following features: approachability, sensitivity, and effort to understand the customer's needs. One example of empathy is the ability of an airline gate attendant to make a customer's missed connection the attendant's own problem and to find a solution.

Tangibles. The appearance of physical facilities, equipment, personnel, and communication materials. The condition of the physical surroundings (e.g., cleanliness) is tangible evidence of the care and attention to detail that are exhibited by the service provider. This assessment dimension also can extend to the conduct of other customers in the service (e.g., a noisy guest in the next room at a hotel).

Customers use these five dimensions to form their judgments of service quality, which are based on a comparison between expected and perceived service. The gap between expected and perceived service is a measure of service quality; satisfaction is either negative or positive.

Gaps in Service Quality

Measuring the gap between expected service and perceived service is a routine customer feedback process that is practiced by leading service companies. For example, Club Med, with resort villages worldwide, uses the questionnaire shown in Figure 6.2. This questionnaire is mailed to all guests immediately after their departure from a Club Med vacation to assess the quality of their experience. Note that the first question explicitly asks the guest to evaluate the gap between his or her expectations and the actual Club Med experience.

In Figure 6.3, the gap between customer expectations and perceptions is defined as GAP 5. Customer satisfaction is dependent on minimizing gaps 1 through 4 that are associated with delivery of the service.

The *market research* gap is the discrepancy between customer expectations and management perceptions of these expectations. GAP 1 arises from management's lack of full understanding about how customers formulate their expectations on the basis of a number of sources: advertising, past experience with the firm and its competitors, personal needs, and communications with friends. Strategies for closing this gap include improving market research, fostering better communication between management and its contact employees, and reducing the number of levels of management.

The *design* gap results from management's inability to formulate a service design that meets perceptions of customer expectations and translates these into workable service standards. GAP 2 might result from a lack of management commitment to service quality or a perception of the practicality of meeting customers' expectations; however, setting goals and standardizing service delivery tasks can close this gap.

The *conformance* gap occurs because actual delivery of the service does not meet the service standards set by management. GAP 3 can arise for a number of reasons, including lack of teamwork, poor employee selection, inadequate training, and inappropriate job design.

The *communication* gap results when customer perceptions are at odds with the intended service delivery. GAP 4 results when operations management fails to manage the evidence (all the aspects of what the customer experiences) at the point of service delivery. GAP 4 may result from lack of controls or poor employee training.

FIGURE 6.2 **Customer Satisfaction Questionnaire**

Source: Club Med, 40 West 57th Street, New York, NY 10019.

G.M. Questionnaire

Club Med Village: ____________________

Dates of your stay: From: ____________ to: ____________
Month/Day/Year Month/Day/Year

Name: ____________ Member # ____________

Address: ____________________

City: ____________ State: ____________ Zip: ____________

	• OVERALL IMPRESSION	• ORGANIZATION	• TEAM OF G.O.s	• FOOD	• BAR	• SPORTS	• DAYTIME AMBIANCE	• EVENING ENTERTAINMENT	• MUSIC AND DANCE	• MINI CLUB	• EXCURSIONS	• ACCOMMODATIONS	• CLUB FLIGHTS AND TRANSFERS	• CLEANLINESS
EXCELLENT	6	6	6	6	6	6	6	6	6	6	6	6	6	6
VERY GOOD	5	5	5	5	5	5	5	5	5	5	5	5	5	5
GOOD	4	4	4	4	4	4	4	4	4	4	4	4	4	4
FAIR	3	3	3	3	3	3	3	3	3	3	3	3	3	3
POOR	2	2	2	2	2	2	2	2	2	2	2	2	2	2
VERY POOR	1	1	1	1	1	1	1	1	1	1	1	1	1	1

Your Comments: ____________________

1. Did Club Med meet your expectations?
   ☐ Far below expectations ☐ Surpassed expectations
   ☐ Fell short of expectations ☐ Far surpassed expectations
   ☐ Met expectations
2. If this was not your first Club Med, how many other times have you been to a Club Med village? ________
3. How did you make your Club Med reservations?
   ☐ Through a travel agent ☐ Through Club Med Reservations
4. Quality of your reservations handling (pre-travel information):
   ☐ Very poor ☐ Poor ☐ Fair ☐ Good ☐ Excellent
5. Which one factor was most important in your choosing Club Med for your vacation?
   ☐ Previous stay with us ☐ Advertisement ☐ Editorial Article
   ☐ Travel Agent Recommendation ☐ Friend/Relative Recommendation
6. Kindly indicate your age bracket:
   ☐ Under 25 ☐ 25–34 ☐ 35–44 ☐ 45–54 ☐ 55 or over
7. Kindly indicate your marital status: ☐ Married ☐ Single
8. Would you vacation with Club Med again? ☐ Yes ☐ No
9. If you answered yes to question 8, where would you like to go on your next Club Med vacation?
   ☐ U.S.A. ☐ Mexico ☐ French West Indies ☐ Caribbean ☐ Europe
   ☐ Other: ____________

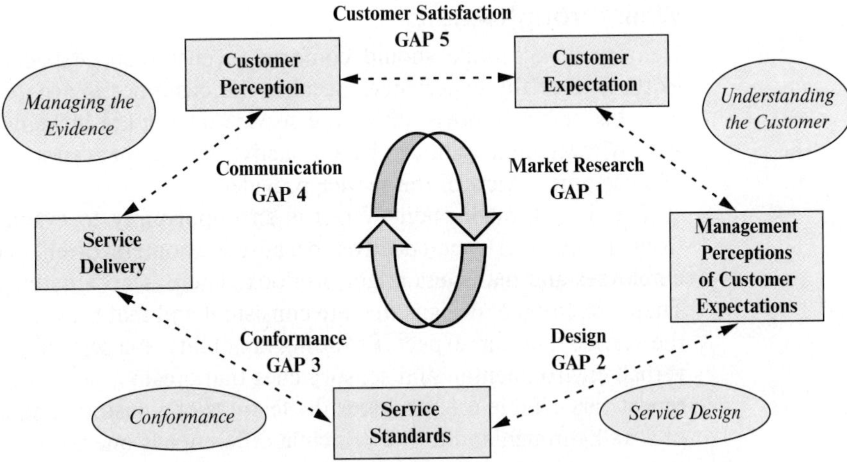

FIGURE 6.3
Service Quality Gap Model

Source: Reprinted with permission of Professor Uttarayan Bagchi, University of Texas at Austin.

The numbering of the gaps from 1 to 5 represents the sequence of steps (i.e., market research, design, conformance, communication, and customer satisfaction) that should be followed in new service process design. The remainder of this chapter will address ways of closing these gaps in service quality. We begin by considering approaches to measuring service quality.

Measuring Service Quality

Measuring service quality is a challenge because customer satisfaction is determined by many intangible factors. Unlike a product with physical features that can be measured objectively (e.g., the fit and finish of a car), service quality contains many psychological features (e.g., the ambiance of a restaurant). In addition, service quality often extends beyond the immediate encounter because, as in the case of health care, it has an impact on a person's future quality of life. The multiple dimensions of service quality are captured in the SERVQUAL instrument, which is an effective tool for surveying customer satisfaction that is based on the service quality gap model.

SERVQUAL[3]

The authors of the service quality gap model developed a multi-item scale called *SERVQUAL* for measuring the five dimensions of service quality (i.e., reliability, responsiveness, assurance, empathy, and tangibles). This two-part instrument, which can be found on McGraw-Hill's student resource website, pairs an *expectation* statement with a corresponding *perception* statement. Customers are asked to record their level of agreement or disagreement with the statements using a seven-point Likert scale. The 22 statements in the survey describe all aspects of the five dimensions of service quality.

A score for the quality of service is calculated by computing the differences between the ratings that customers assign to paired expectation and perception statements. This score is referred to as GAP 5, as was shown in Figure 6.3. Scores for the other four gaps also can be calculated in a similar manner.

This instrument has been designed and validated for use in a variety of service encounters. The authors have suggested many applications for SERVQUAL, but its most important function is tracking service quality trends through periodic customer surveys. For multisite services, SERVQUAL could be used by management to determine if any unit has poor service quality (indicated by a low score); if so, management can direct attention to correcting the source of customers' poor perceptions. SERVQUAL could be used in marketing studies to compare a service with a competitor's and again identify the dimensions of superior or inadequate service quality.

Walk-through Audit

Delivery of a service should conform to customers' expectations from the beginning to the end of the experience. Because the customer is a participant in the service process, his or her impressions of the service quality are influenced by many observations. An environmental audit can be a proactive management tool for the systematic evaluation of a customer's view of the service provided.

The walk-through audit (WtA) is an opportunity to evaluate the service experience from a customer's perspective, because customers often become aware of cues the employees and managers might overlook. There is no inherently superior service design. There are, instead, designs that are consistent and that provide a signal to customers about the service they can expect. Providing tangibility in a service involves giving the customer verbal, environmental, and sensory cues that create a pleasant experience and encourage repeat visits. Table 6.1 compares the features of a customer satisfaction survey with those of a walk-through audit. The principle difference is one of perspective. Customer satisfaction surveys are marketing oriented, seeking a measure of overall customer satisfaction. The walk-through audit, however, is operations or process oriented, with the objective of uncovering opportunities for improvement.

Fitzsimmons and Maurer developed such a walk-through audit for full-service sit-down restaurants.[4] The audit consisted of 42 questions spanning the restaurant dining experience. The questions begin with approaching the restaurant from the parking area, then walking into the restaurant and being greeted, waiting for a table, being seated,

TABLE 6.1 Comparison of Customer Satisfaction Survey with Walk-through Audit

Source: Elsa Lai-Ping Leong Koljonen and Richard A. Reid, "Walk-through Audit Provides Focus for Service Improvements for Hong Kong Law Firm," *Managing Service Quality* 10(1), 2000, p. 35.

	Customer Satisfaction Survey	Walk-through Audit
Purpose	Determine overall satisfaction associated with the current level of service quality.	Conduct a systematic assessment of the entire customer service experience from beginning to end.
Focus	Measure customer attitudes toward, opinions about, and perceptions of service quality.	Measure customer perceptions of the effectiveness of each stage of the service delivery process.
Process	1. Identify important customer service requirements or quality dimensions.	1. Flowchart the service delivery process from the customer's perspective.
	2. Design, test, and administer questionnaire to a sample of customers.	2. Design, test, and administer questionnaire to a sample of customers, management personnel, and/or customers at benchmark organizations.
	3. Summarize and analyze questionnaire results with emphasis on low ratings and changes relative to prior survey administrations.	3. Summarize and analyze survey results with emphasis on low rating relative to benchmark firms and gaps between management and customers.
	4. Determine areas needing improvements and implement change designed to correct deficiencies.	4. Determine deficiencies and implement improvements.
	5. Repeat for continuous quality improvement.	5. Repeat for ongoing improvement.
Features	1. Survey may be completed by customers at any time after receiving service.	1. Questionnaire is completed by customers during or immediately after receiving service.
	2. Management, with some customer input, designs/structures the survey around common service dimensions (e.g., *availability, timeliness, responsiveness, convenience*).	2. A comprehensive audit of the customer's total service experience of all five dimensions of the service package (i.e., *supporting facility, facilitating goods, information, explicit service, implicit service*).
	3. Often performed by marketing personnel.	3. Usually conducted by operations personnel.
	4. Primary emphasis is placed on assessing the determinants of the customer's overall impression of the service.	4. Emphasis is placed on the customer's evaluation of each stage of the service delivery process and his/her overall impression of the organization's performance.

FIGURE 6.4
Restaurant Satisfaction Survey

As Your Guest, I Would Like to Tell You . . .

____
____
____
____

	Great	Good	Fair	Poor
Food quality				
Service speed				
Service attentiveness				
Cleanliness				
Atmosphere				

Name ____________________
Address ____________________
City ____________________ State ______ Zip ________
Phone ____________________ Date ____________

ordering and receiving food and drinks, and finally receiving the check and paying the bill. The questions include nine categories of variables: (1) maintenance items, (2) person-to-person service, (3) waiting, (4) table and place settings, (5) ambiance, (6) food presentation, (7) check presentation, (8) promotion and suggestive selling, and (9) tipping. Thus, the entire customer experience is traced from beginning to end. Unlike the brief and overall customer satisfaction survey shown in Figure 6.4, the WtA is focused on the details of the service delivery process as seen in Figure 6.5. This audit can exceed an entire page of items with responses using a Likert scale.

Designing a Walk-through Audit

The first step in designing a WtA is the preparation of a flowchart of customer interactions with the service system. The WtA for the Helsinki Museum of Art and Design (shown in Figure 6.5) is divided into five major service delivery process sections

FIGURE 6.5 **Walk-through Audit for Helsinki Museum of Art and Design**

Source: Prepared by Eivor Biese, Lauren Dwyre, Mikes Koulianos, and Tina Hyvonen under the supervision of Professor James A. Fitzsimmons.

Hello, we are from the Helsinki School of Economics and Business Administration and we are conducting a survey to find out what you think about the service experience when visiting this museum. Please answer the following questions.

All information in this questionnaire is strictly confidential!

1. Was it easy getting to the Museum? ❑ Yes ❑ No

2. Are the Museum's opening hours acceptable? ❑ Yes ❑ No

3. Did you arrive alone or with others? ❑ Alone ❑ Others Number in Party: ____________

4. Where did you hear about this event: [Check all that apply]

❑ Newspaper ❑ Internet
❑ Magazine ❑ Friends or relatives
❑ Tourist/City guide ❑ Passing by
❑ Radio ❑ Other: (Specify) ________

5. Did you come here to see

❑ Brooching It Diplomacy
❑ Wine–Nectar of Gods
❑ The Holy Cross
❑ The permanent exhibition
❑ All exhibitions

continued

FIGURE 6.5 *(concluded)*

6. Which of the following facilities did you visit? ❑ Cafeteria ❑ Gift shop ❑ Restrooms

7. How many hours did you spend in the museum? ____________ hours

8. Ticketing	**Strongly Disagree**	**Disagree**	**Not Sure**	**Agree**	**Strongly Agree**
a. It is easy to find information about ticket prices.	1	2	3	4	5
b. The ticket price is a good value for the money.	1	2	3	4	5
c. You did not spend too much time by waiting in the ticket line.	1	2	3	4	5
d. You would like to purchase tickets ahead of time, via phone or Internet.	1	2	3	4	5

9. Information	**Strongly Disagree**	**Disagree**	**Not Sure**	**Agree**	**Strongly Agree**
a. Signs gave clear information about exhibits' locations.	1	2	3	4	5
b. After arriving at the exhibition, you found adequate information about the exhibition(s).	1	2	3	4	5
c. The information provided was in your language.	1	2	3	4	5
d. Guide services were available.	1	2	3	4	5
e. There was enough information about the objects.	1	2	3	4	5
f. The explanations provided on the objects were clear.	1	2	3	4	5
g. You would like to see a variety of media (video, etc.) providing explanations.	1	2	3	4	5
h. You would like to have access to self-guided material such as a cassette player.	1	2	3	4	5
i. You would like to have more information about the process for creating the objects.	1	2	3	4	5
j. You would like to learn more when visiting exhibits.	1	2	3	4	5
k. It was easy to get additional information from the staff.	1	2	3	4	5
l. The staff helping you was friendly.	1	2	3	4	5

10. The experience	**Strongly Disagree**	**Disagree**	**Not Sure**	**Agree**	**Strongly Agree**
a. There was a clear path in which you were guided through the exhibition.	1	2	3	4	5
b. There was enough room to move around the exhibits.	1	2	3	4	5
c. Lighting was adequate.	1	2	3	4	5
d. There was pleasant background music.	1	2	3	4	5
e. The background sounds were pleasant.	1	2	3	4	5
f. The objects on display were adequately spaced apart.	1	2	3	4	5
g. There is enough opportunity for interaction with the displayed objects.	1	2	3	4	5
h. Touching, smelling, and hearing make the experience memorable.	1	2	3	4	5
i. You would also like to touch the material.	1	2	3	4	5

11. Facilities	**Strongly Disagree**	**Disagree**	**Not Sure**	**Agree**	**Strongly Agree**
a. There were clear signs giving information about the facilities.	1	2	3	4	5
b. The toilettes were easily accessible.	1	2	3	4	5
c. The toilettes were clean.	1	2	3	4	5
d. The food was of good quality.	1	2	3	4	5
e. There was enough variety of food and beverages.	1	2	3	4	5
f. The food was of good value for the money.	1	2	3	4	5
g. Smoking should be allowed in the restaurant.	1	2	3	4	5
h. The selection of gifts (including books) met your needs.	1	2	3	4	5
i. The gifts were of good value for the money.	1	2	3	4	5

12. Satisfaction	**Strongly Disagree**	**Disagree**	**Not Sure**	**Agree**	**Strongly Agree**
a. The services met my needs.	1	2	3	4	5
b. I found the overall service outstanding.	1	2	3	4	5
c. I am likely to use this service again.	1	2	3	4	5
d. I would recommend this museum to my friend.	1	2	3	4	5
e. Could we improve the service to better meet your expectations?	1	2	3	4	5

13. Comments

____

____

____

____

(i.e., ticketing, information, experience, facilities, and satisfaction). Within each section a number of statements are made concerning observations that a customer would make (e.g., signs give clear information about exhibits' locations). The statements must be phrased as declarative sentences rather than questions. A five-point Likert scale is used to gauge customer perceptions (i.e., 1 = strongly disagree to 5 = strongly agree). As this WtA illustrates, other questions of interest to management are included such as "Where did you hear about the event" to gauge the effectiveness of advertising. A final section for "comments" can provide customer insights not anticipated in the questions asked. To avoid overwhelming the customer, the WtA should be limited to two pages printed back-to-back.

The WtA can be administered in several ways (e.g., mail, telephone interview, in person) but the most effective method is in person immediately following the service experience. Rewarding the customer with a gift certificate or money off on a return visit has significantly increased participation. Survey design issues such as sample size and stratifying the sample to poll all customer segments should be considered.

The Walk-through Audit as a Diagnostic Instrument

The walk-through audit can be a useful diagnostic instrument for management to evaluate the gaps in perception between customers and managers of the service delivery system. Customers visit a site less frequently than do managers and, thus, are more sensitive to subtle changes (e.g., peeling paint or worn rugs). Managers who see the facility every day are likely to overlook gradual deterioration of the supporting facility. The quality of customer service also can deteriorate and be less noticeable to employees as well as managers.

To test this use of a WtA, the same Helsinki Museum of Art and Design audit that was given to customers was also given to the managers and employees. The responses for each item on the audit were averaged for the three groups and are shown in Figure 6.6. This figure highlights the gaps in service perceptions among management, employees, and customers. Some of the gaps are not surprising, such as "There was enough information about the objects," because the employees are quite familiar with the exhibits. Other gaps suggest

FIGURE 6.6 Helsinki Museum of Art and Design Service Audit Gaps

Source: Prepared by Eivor Biese, Lauren Dwyre, Mikes Koulianos, and Tina Hyvonen under the supervision of Professor James A. Fitzsimmons.

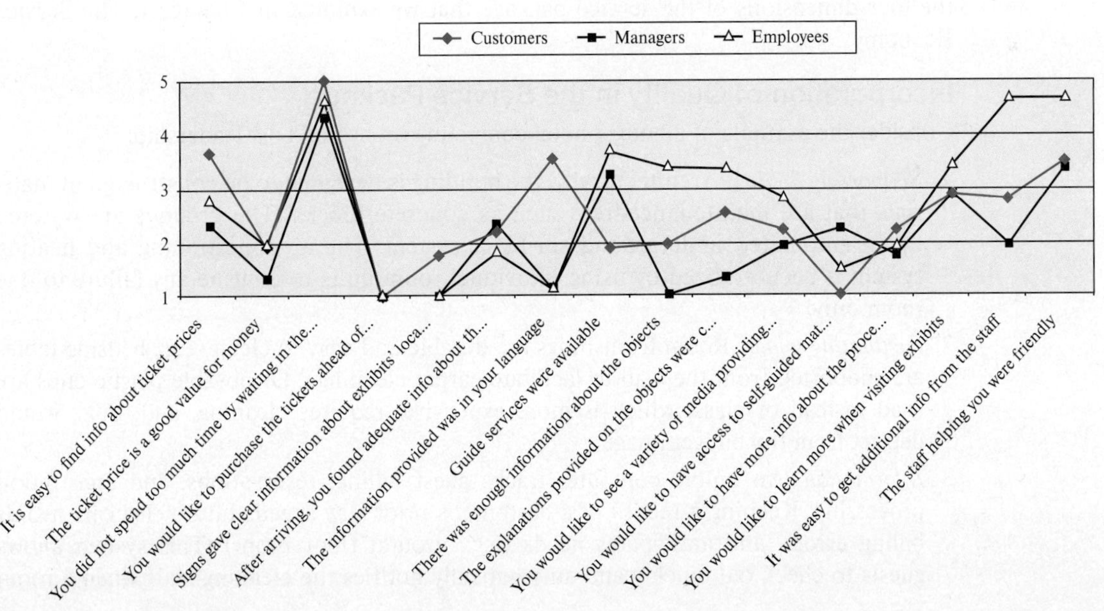

continued

FIGURE 6.6 *(concluded)*

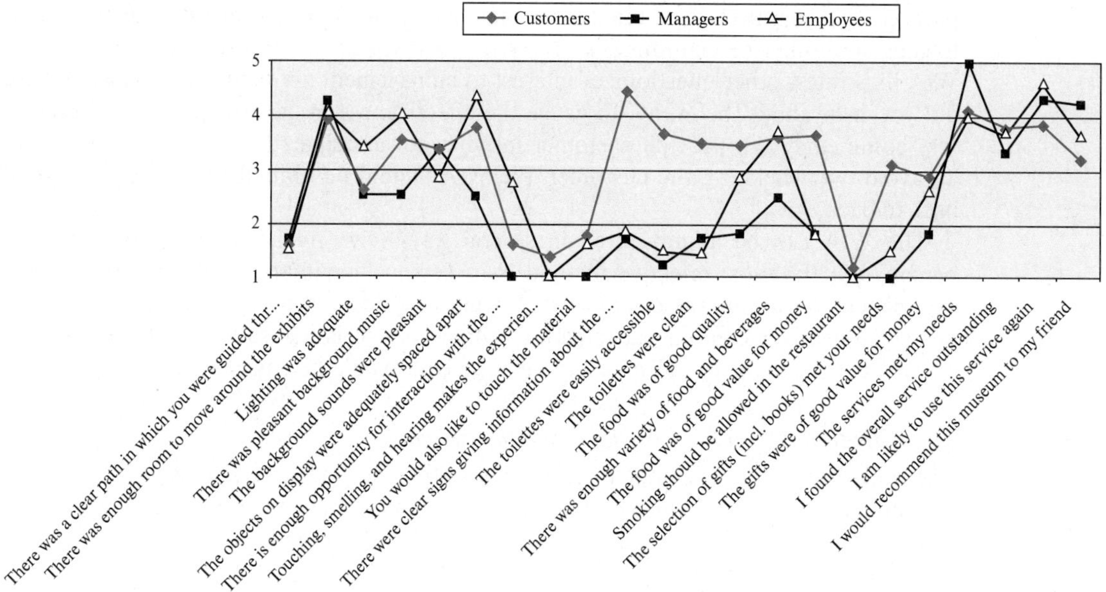

some improvements are in order; for example, "It was easy to get additional information from the staff" and "The staff helping you are friendly." It is interesting to note where management and employee perceptions deviated, such as "The explanations provided on the objects were clear" and "There is enough opportunity for interaction with the displayed objects." In both cases, employees were more in agreement with the statements than customers and management agreed least.

Quality Service by Design

Quality can neither be inspected into a product nor somehow added on, and this same observation applies to services. A concern for quality begins with the design of the service delivery system. How can quality be designed into a service? One approach is to focus on the four dimensions of the service package that we explored in Chapter 1, The Service Economy.

Incorporation of Quality in the Service Package

Consider the example of a budget hotel competing on overall cost leadership:

1. *Supporting facility.* Architecturally, the building is designed to be constructed of materials that are maintenance-free, such as concrete blocks. The grounds are watered by an automated underground sprinkler system. The air-conditioning and heating system is decentralized by using individual room units to confine any failure to one room only.
2. *Facilitating goods.* Room furnishings are durable and easy to clean (e.g., bedside tables are supported from the wall to facilitate carpet cleaning). Disposable plastic cups are used instead of glass, which is more expensive, requires cleaning, and, thus, would detract from the budget image.
3. *Information.* An online computer tracks guest billing, reservations, and registration processing. Keeping a record of a customer's prior stay speeds future check-in, avoids billing errors, and anticipates needs (e.g., ground floor room). This system allows guests to check out quickly and automatically notifies the cleaning staff when a room

is free to be cleaned. Noting time of check-out allows for scheduling early maid service and inventorying available rooms for early arrivals.

4. *Explicit services.* Every room has the same essential furnishings including a flat panel TV mounted to the wall, desk-side telephone, open clothes rack, and chest of drawers. Maids are trained to clean and make up rooms in a standard manner.
5. *Implicit services.* Individuals with a pleasant appearance and good interpersonal skills are recruited as desk clerks. Training in standard operating procedures (SOPs) ensures uniform and predictable treatment for all guests.

Table 6.2 illustrates how the budget hotel has taken these design features and implemented a quality system to maintain conformance to the design requirements. The approach is based on the definition of quality as "conformance to requirements." This example illustrates the need to define explicitly, in measurable terms, what constitutes conformance to requirements. Quality is seen as an action-oriented activity requiring corrective measures when nonconformance occurs.

Taguchi Methods

The budget hotel example illustrates the application of *Taguchi methods*, which are named after Genichi Taguchi, who advocated "robust design" of products to ensure their proper functioning under adverse conditions.[5] The idea is that for a customer, proof of a product's quality is in its performance when abused. For example, the desk-side telephone is designed to be far more durable than necessary because more than once it will be pulled off the desk and dropped to the floor. In our budget hotel example, the building is constructed of concrete blocks and furnished with durable furniture.

Taguchi also applied the concept of robustness to the manufacturing process (i.e., being able to tolerate changes in the environment). For example, the recipe for caramel candy was reformulated to make plasticity, or chewiness, less sensitive to fluctuations in cooking temperature. Similarly, our budget hotel uses an online computer to notify the cleaning staff automatically when a room has been vacated. Keeping the maids posted on which rooms are available for cleaning allows this task to be spread throughout the day, thus avoiding a rush in the late afternoon that could result in quality degradation.

TABLE 6.2 Quality Requirements for Budget Hotel

Service Package Feature	Attribute or Requirement	Measurement	Nonconformance Corrective Action
Supporting facility	Appearance of building	No flaking paint	Repaint
	Grounds	Green grass	Water grass
	Air-conditioning and heating	Temperature maintained at $68° \pm 2°$	Repair or replace
Facilitating goods	TV operation	Reception clear in daylight	Repair or replace
	Soap supply	Two bars per bed	Restock
	Ice	One full bucket per room	Restock from ice machine
Information	Guest preferences	Complete	Update
Explicit services	Room cleanliness	Stain-free carpet	Shampoo
	Swimming-pool water purity	Marker at bottom of deep end visible	Change filter and check chemicals
	Room appearance	Drapes drawn to width of 3 ft	Instruct maid
Implicit services	Security	All perimeter lights working	Replace defective bulbs
	Pleasant atmosphere	Telling departing guests "Have a nice day"	Instruct desk clerk
	Lobby congestion	No customer having to wait for a room	Review room cleaning schedule

Taguchi believed that product quality was achieved best by focusing on a specified goal, rather than just being satisfied with performance within an acceptable range about the target specification. The customer cost function in Figure 6.7 shows that any deviation from the target performance level within the customer's acceptance range is assigned zero cost (performance between lower limit and upper limit). However, using the Taguchi quadratic cost function, an internal cost is assigned based upon deviation from the performance target—that is, the internal cost of poor quality is measured by the square of the deviation from the target.

For our budget hotel example, if we used the performance measure of wait time for a room (with a target of zero minutes) we would use only the *right half* of Figure 6.7 because customer waiting cannot be less than zero. The upper limit could be set at a wait time that would cause a customer to leave with a cost equal to the revenue forgone (e.g., a 20-minute upper limit would translate to $69, the cost of a room for one night).

The corresponding Taguchi quadratic cost function would be of the form $C(y) = y^a$ using logarithms $[a = \log C(y)/\log(y)]$ and solving for the intersection of $[C(y) = 69, y = 20]$ yields the quadratic cost function $C(y) = y^{1.414}$ to measure internal cost of quality. Either cost penalty can serve as an incentive for front desk staff to avoid customer delays at check-in. This explains the attention to standard operating procedures (SOPs) used by the budget hotel to promote uniform treatment of guests and expedient preparation of vacated rooms.

Poka-Yoke (Failsafing)

Shigeo Shingo believed that low-cost, in-process, quality-control mechanisms and routines used by employees in their work could achieve high quality without costly inspection. He observed that errors occurred, not because employees were incompetent, but because of interruptions in routine or lapses in attention. He advocated the adoption of *poka-yoke* methods, which translates roughly as "foolproof" devices. Poka-yoke methods use checklists or manual devices that do not let the employee make a mistake.[6] As noted by Chase and Stewart and summarized in Table 6.3, service errors can originate from both the server and the customer. Poka-yoke methods therefore should address both sources.[7]

Service provider errors fall into three categories: tasks, treatments, and tangibles. The use of a french fry scoop at McDonald's to measure out a consistent serving of potatoes is an example of a *task* poka-yoke device that also enhances cleanliness and, hence, the implicit quality of the service as well. A novel *treatment* poka-yoke devised by a bank for tellers to ensure customer eye contact requires them to enter the customer's eye color on a checklist at the start of the transaction. An example of a *tangible* poka-yoke is the placement of mirrors in employee break rooms to promote appropriate appearance upon returning to the customer area. The automatic spell check feature of Microsoft Outlook assures that an e-mail is not sent until it has been proofed for spelling errors but not for misuse of words (e.g., cam vs can).

FIGURE 6.7
Taguchi Cost of Quality Functions

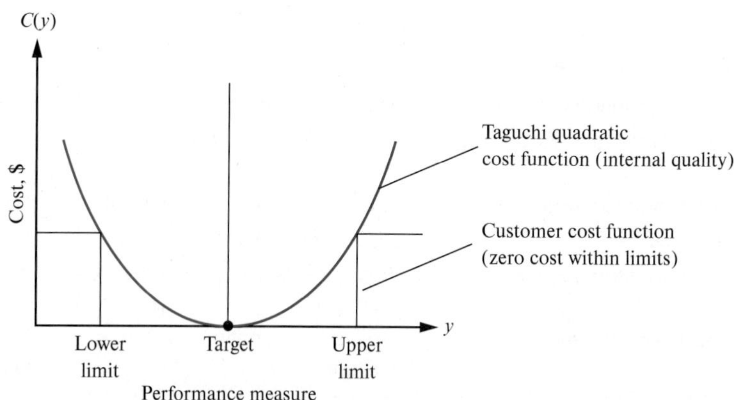

TABLE 6.3
Classification of Service Failures

Server Errors	Customer Errors
Task:	*Preparation:*
• Doing work incorrectly	• Failure to bring necessary materials
• Doing work not required	• Failure to understand role in transaction
• Doing work in the wrong order	• Failure to engage the correct service
• Doing work too slowly	
Treatment:	*Encounter:*
• Failure to acknowledge the customer	• Failure to remember steps in process
• Failure to react appropriately	• Failure to follow system flow
• Failure to listen to the customer	• Failure to specify desires sufficiently
Tangible:	• Failure to follow instructions
• Failure to clean facilities	*Resolution:*
• Failure to provide clean uniforms	• Failure to signal service failure
• Failure to control environmental factors	• Failure to learn from experience
• Failure to proofread documents	• Failure to adjust expectations
	• Failure to execute post-encounter action

Airlines use this poka-yoke device to alert passengers to the size limits of carry-on luggage. Courtesy of Mona Fitzsimmons

Because customers play an active role in the delivery of services, they also need help to avoid errors. These errors fall into three categories: preparation, encounter, and resolution. Shouldice Hospital located in Toronto, Canada, performs only inguinal hernia operations. All potential patients are required to fill out a comprehensive medical survey, that is, a *preparation* poka-yoke, to ensure that the medical condition is appropriate for the standardized treatment at Shouldice. Many *encounter* poka-yokes are unobtrusive, such as the use of height bars at amusement rides to ensure that riders exceed size limitations. *Resolution* poka-yokes help mold the behavior of customers as they exit the service. Fast-food restaurants strategically locate tray-return stands and trash bins at the exits.

Using physical design to control employee and customer discretion is an important preemptive strategy to avoid mistakes. Because it is difficult for management to intervene in the service process and impose a quality appraisal system (i.e., inspection and testing), limiting discretion and incorporating poka-yoke methods facilitate mistake-free service. It is interesting to note how these unobtrusive design features channel service behavior without a suggestion of coercion, such as a "beep" from our word processor to warn us that an invalid keystroke has been made.

Quality Function Deployment

To provide customer input at the product design stage, a process called *quality function deployment* (QFD) was developed in Japan and used extensively by Toyota and its suppliers. The process results in a matrix, referred to as a "house of quality," for a particular product that relates customer attributes to engineering characteristics. The central idea of QFD is the belief that products should be designed to reflect the customers' desires and tastes; thus, the functions of marketing, design engineering, and manufacturing must be coordinated. The "house of quality" provides a framework for translating customer satisfaction into identifiable and measurable conformance specifications for product or service design.[8]

Although QFD was developed for use in product planning, its application to the design of service delivery systems is very appropriate, as shown by Example 6.1.

Example 6.1 Quality Function Deployment for Village Volvo

Recall the Village Volvo case from Chapter 1, The Service Economy. Village Volvo is an independent auto service garage that specializes in Volvo auto maintenance and competes with Volvo dealers for customers. Village Volvo has decided to assess its service delivery system in comparison with that of the Volvo dealer to determine areas for improving its competitive position. The steps in conducting the QFD project and constructing a "house of quality" follow:

1. *Establish the aim of the project.* In this case, the objective of the project is to assess Village Volvo's competitive position. QFD also could be used when a new service delivery system is being considered for the first time.
2. *Determine customer expectations.* Based on the aim of this project, identify the customer group to be satisfied and determine the expectations of its members. For Village Volvo, the target customer group is Volvo owners with nonroutine repairs (i.e., exclude routine maintenance for this study). Customer expectations could be solicited by interviews, focus groups, or questionnaires. In this example, we will use the five dimensions of service quality to describe customer expectations. As shown in Figure 6.8, these are the *rows* of the house of quality. In a more sophisticated QFD project, customer expectations are broken down into primary, secondary, and tertiary levels of detail; for example, the primary expectation of "reliability" could be specified further with "accuracy" at the secondary level and "correct problem diagnosed" as the tertiary level of detail.
3. *Describe the elements of the service.* The *columns* of the house of quality matrix contain the service elements that management can manipulate to satisfy customer expectations. For Village Volvo, we have selected training, attitudes, capacity, information, and equipment.
4. *Note the strength of relationship between pairs of service elements.* The *roof* of the house of quality provides an opportunity to note the strength of correlation between pairs of service elements. We have noted three levels of strength of relationship: * = strong, • = medium, and Ø = weak. As you might expect, we note a strong relationship between training and attitudes. Noting these relationships between elements can provide useful points of leverage to improve service quality.
5. *Note the association between customer expectations and service elements.* The *body* of the matrix contains numbers between 0 and 9 (9 indicating a very strong link) to indicate the strength of the link between a service element and a corresponding customer expectation. These numbers would follow a discussion by the project team about how various service elements affect the firm's capacity to satisfy the different customer expectations.

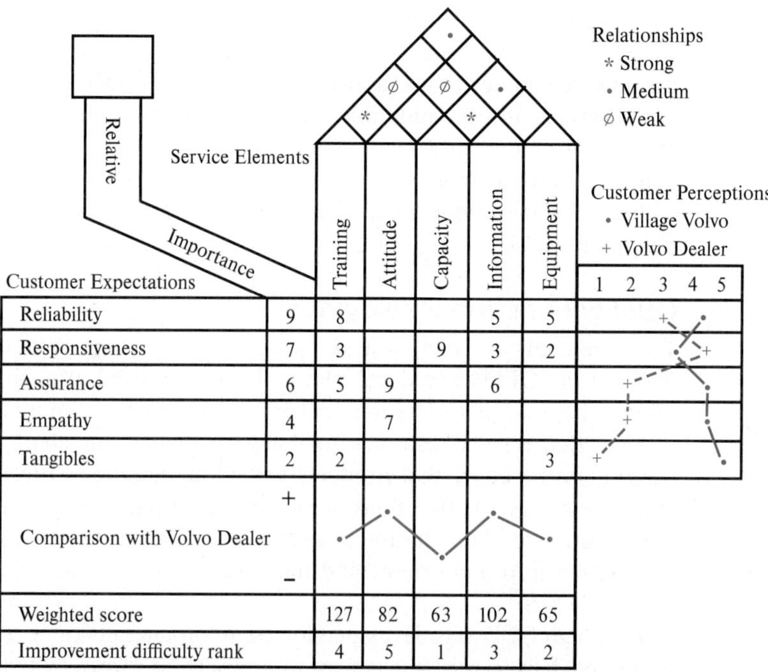

FIGURE 6.8
"House of Quality" for Village Volvo

6. *Weighting the service elements.* This step is taken to measure the importance of a customer's assessment of the service element. The *chimney* of the house of quality contains a listing of the relative importance of each customer expectation. These weights on a scale of 1 to 9 indicate the importance that customers place on each of their expectations and could be determined by a customer survey. The relative importance will be multiplied by the strength of the link number in the body of the matrix under each service element to arrive at a weighted score for that element. For example, the training element would have a weighted score calculated as

$$(9)(8) + (7)(3) + (6)(5) + (4)(0) + (2)(2) = 127$$

   The weighted scores are entered in the *basement* of the house of quality and represent a measure of each service element's importance to satisfying customer needs. These weighted results should be treated with caution and common sense, however, because they depend on uncertain estimates of relative importance and relationship scores.
7. *Service element improvement difficulty rank.* In the basement of the house is a ranking for the difficulty of improving each service element, with a rank of 1 being the most difficult. Capacity and equipment have a high rank because of their capital requirements. This exercise demonstrates that even though customers give a service element a high rank, the firm might be unable to deliver it.
8. *Assessment of competition.* A study of the Volvo dealer is made to assess customers' perceptions of service at the dealer compared with that at Village Volvo. The result of a customer survey (using customers who have experienced both providers) using a five-point scale is plotted to the *right* of the matrix. Based on knowledge of the dealer (perhaps from mechanics), a relative comparison of the level (plus or minus) of each service element is plotted at the *bottom* of the matrix. This information will be used to assess the competitive strengths and weaknesses of Village Volvo.
9. *Strategic assessment and goal setting.* Looking at the completed house of quality, Village Volvo can see some strengths and weaknesses in its strategic position relative to the Volvo dealer. Except for responsiveness, it is viewed favorably by its customers. This result must be viewed with caution, however, because these data were obtained from a survey of Village Volvo customers and, thus, were not unexpected. The comparison of service elements with the Volvo dealer and weighted scores yields some possible directions for improvement in service. In the area of attitudes and information, Village Volvo is in a superior position, but there appears to be a problem with capacity, training, and equipment. The high-weighted score given to training suggests that a first-priority goal of an investment in training might be in order. In addition, leverage would be achieved because training has relationships, from strong to weak, with attitudes, capacity, and equipment. Finally, the improvement difficulty rank for training is fourth out of five.

Achieving Service Quality

Services are difficult for customers to evaluate before the fact. As we have already noted, they are intangible and consumed simultaneously with production. This presents a challenge to the service manager because quality-inspection intervention between the customer and the contact employee is not an option as in manufacturing (e.g., no slip of paper can be placed in the box by Inspector Number 12).

Cost of Quality

Caveat emptor–"let the buyer beware"–has become obsolete. As American automobile manufacturers discovered in the late 1980s and early 1990s, impersonal service, faulty products, and broken promises all carry a price by inviting competition from abroad. A very visible example of this reality today is the extensive fines paid by banks following the 2008 financial crash. Poor quality can lead to severe loss of market share as experienced by Chipotle following an outbreak of food poisoning traced to contaminated salad ingredients. Unethical behavior can ruin a reputation as witnessed by Wells Fargo following the revelation of inappropriate cross-selling of products to customers.

Products can be returned, exchanged, or fixed, but what recourse does the customer of a faulty service have? Legal recourse! No service has immunity from prosecution. For example, a Las Vegas hotel was sued for failing to provide proper security when a guest was assaulted in her room. An income tax preparer can be fined up to $500 per return if a taxpayer's liability is understated because of the preparer's negligence or disregard of Internal Revenue Service rules and regulations.

A noted quality expert, Joseph M. Juran, has advocated a cost-of-quality accounting system to convince top management of the need to address quality issues.[9] He identified four categories of costs: internal failure costs (from defects discovered before shipment), external failure costs (from defects discovered after shipment), detection costs (for inspection of purchased materials and during manufacture), and prevention costs (for keeping defects from occurring in the first place). Juran found that in most manufacturing companies, external and internal failure costs together accounted for 50 to 80 percent of the total cost of quality. Thus, to minimize this total cost, he advocated that more attention be paid to prevention. Suggestions have been made that $1 invested in prevention is worth $100 in detection costs and $10,000 in failure costs.

In Table 6.4, we have adapted Juran's cost-of-quality system for use by service firms with a banking example. For prevention, recruitment and selection of service personnel are viewed as ways to avoid poor quality. Identifying people with appropriate attitudes and interpersonal skills can result in hiring contact persons with the natural instincts that are needed to serve customers well. Inspection is included under detection, but generally it is impractical except in the back-office operations of a service. Because service is an experience for the customer, any failure becomes a story for that customer to tell others. Service managers must recognize that dissatisfied customers not only will take their future business elsewhere but also will tell others about the unhappy experience, thus resulting in a significant loss of future business.

Statistical Process Control

The performance of a service often is judged by key indicators. For example, the educational performance of a high school is measured by the Scholastic Aptitude Test (SAT) scores of its students. The effectiveness of a police department's crime-prevention program is judged by the crime rate, and a bank teller's performance is judged by the accuracy of his or her end-of-day balances.

What happens if the service process is not performing as expected? Generally, an investigation is conducted to identify the cause of the problem and to suggest corrective action;

TABLE 6.4
Costs of Quality for Services

Source: Adapted from C. A. Aubry and D. A. Zimbler, "The Banking Industry: Quality Costs and Improvement," *Quality Progress*, December 1983, pp. 16–20.

Cost Category	Definition	Bank Example
Prevention	Costs associated with operations or activities that keep failure from happening and minimize detection costs	Quality planning Recruitment and selection Training programs Quality improvement projects
Detection	Costs incurred to ascertain the condition of a service to determine whether it conforms to safety standards	Periodic inspection Process control Checking, balancing, verifying Collecting quality data
Internal failure	Costs incurred to correct nonconforming work prior to delivery to the customer	Scrapped forms and reports Rework Machine downtime
External failure	Costs incurred to correct nonconforming work after delivery to the customer or to correct work that did not satisfy a customer's special needs	Payment of interest penalties Investigation time Legal judgments Negative word-of-mouth Loss of future business

TABLE 6.5
Risks in Quality-Control Decisions

	Quality-Control Decision	
True State of Service	**Take Corrective Action**	**Do Nothing**
Process in control	Type I error (producer's risk)	Correct decision
Process out of control	Correct decision	Type II error (consumer's risk)

however, performance variations may result from random occurrences and not have a specific cause. The decision maker wants to detect true degradation in service performance and avoid the failure costs that are associated with poor service. On the other hand, making an unnecessary change in a system that is performing correctly should be avoided. Thus, two types of risks are involved in controlling quality, as shown in Table 6.5. These risks have been given names to identify the injured party. If a process is deemed to be out of control when it in fact is performing correctly, a Type I error has occurred, which is the producer's risk. If a process is deemed to be functioning properly when it in fact is out of control, a Type II error has occurred, which is the consumer's risk.

Statistical process control is the use of a control chart to monitor a process performance measure that signals when intervention is needed. A visual display called a *control chart* is used to plot average values of a measure of performance (e.g., ambulance response time) over time to determine if the process remains in control (i.e., the performance mean and variance have not changed). Figure 6.9 shows an $\overline{X}$-chart that is used to monitor emergency ambulance response time. This chart is a daily plot of mean response time that permits monitoring performance for unusual deviations from the norm. When a measurement falls outside the control limits–that is, above the upper control limit (UCL) or below the lower control limit (LCL)–the process is considered out of control; consequently, the system is in need of attention. For our ambulance example, the first seven days represent the expected variation about the mean of all observations within the control limits. However, in day 10 our observation exceeds the UCL, a very unusual occurrence, signaling a need for root-cause analysis.

Constructing a control chart is similar to determining a confidence interval for the mean of a sample. Recall from statistics that sample means tend to be distributed normally according to the central-limit theorem (i.e., although the underlying statistic may be distributed in any manner, mean values drawn from this statistic have a normal distribution). We know from standard normal tables that 99.7 percent of the normal distribution falls within 3 standard deviations of the mean. Using representative historical data, both the mean and the standard deviation for some system performance measure are determined. These parameters then are used to construct a 99.7 percent confidence interval for the mean of the performance measure. We expect future sample means that are collected at random to fall within this confidence interval; if they do not, then we conclude that the process has changed and the true mean has shifted.

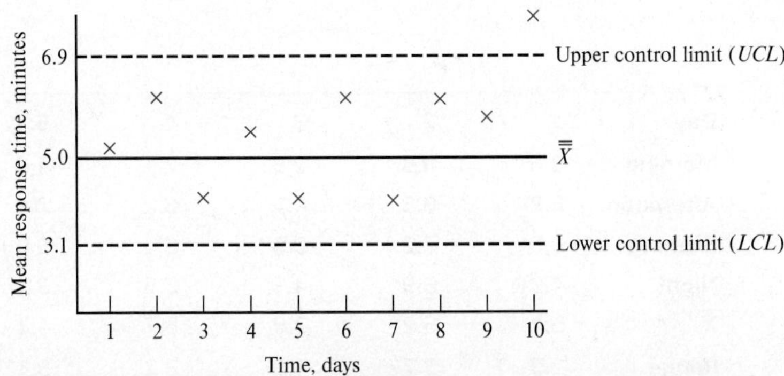

FIGURE 6.9
$\overline{X}$-chart for Ambulance Response

The steps in constructing and using a quality-control chart can be summarized as:

1. Decide on some measure of service system performance.
2. Collect representative historical data from which estimates of the population mean and variance for the system performance measure can be made.
3. Decide on a sample size, and using the estimates of population mean and variance, calculate (by convention) ± 3 standard deviation control limits.
4. Graph the control chart as a function of sample mean values versus time.
5. Plot sample means collected at random on the chart, and interpret the results as follows:
   i. Process in control (i.e., sample mean falls within control limits).
   ii. Process out of control (i.e., sample mean falls outside control limits, or a run of seven means falling either above or below the average). In this case:
      a. Evaluate the situation.
      b. Take corrective action.
      c. Check results of action.
6. Update the control chart on a periodic basis, and incorporate recent data.

Control charts for means fall into two categories based on the type of performance measure. Variable control charts $\overline{X}$ and (*R*-chart), illustrated in Example 6.2, record measurements that permit fractional values, such as length, weight, or time. An attribute control chart (*p*-chart), illustrated in Example 6.3, records discrete data, such as the number of defects or errors as a percentage.

Example 6.2 Control Chart for Variables ($\overline{X}$-chart and *R*-chart)

The purpose of the $\overline{X}$-chart is to detect changes in the process mean of a continuous variable (e.g., ambulance response time). The *R*-chart for the continuous variable measures the process dispersion. Table 6.6 contains data on response time for an emergency ambulance collected over a historically representative seven days. Four response calls were picked at random each day, one each during the morning, afternoon, evening, and night shifts. For each day the average response (based on the sample of four observations) and range (i.e., the difference between the highest and lowest values) are calculated and noted in the last two rows.

The estimate of population mean response and range are calculated as

$$\overline{\overline{X}} = \frac{5.1 + 6.2 + 3.9 + 5.7 + 4.1 + 6.1 + 4.3}{7} = 5.0$$

$$\overline{R} = \frac{2.9 + 2.7 + 1.8 + 3.2 + 3.1 + 2.0 + 2.8}{7} = 2.6$$

The *R*-chart frequently is constructed prior to determining the $\overline{X}$-chart in order to ensure that the process variability is under control. The control chart for the range is constructed using the following formulas:

$$\text{Upper Control Limit (UCL)} = D_4\overline{R} \quad (1)$$

$$\text{Lower Control Limit (LCL)} = D_3\overline{R} \quad (2)$$

TABLE 6.6
Ambulance Response Times, minutes

Day	1	2	3	4	5	6	7
Morning	3.6	4.5	2.9	7.1	4.3	6.7	2.8
Afternoon	5.2	6.3	4.7	6.2	2.8	5.8	5.6
Evening	6.5	7.2	3.8	3.9	5.9	6.9	3.8
Night	4.9	6.9	4.3	5.6	3.2	4.9	4.9
$\overline{X}$	5.1	6.2	3.9	5.7	4.1	6.1	4.3
Range	2.9	2.7	1.8	3.2	3.1	2.0	2.8

where $\overline{R}$ = estimate of population range
D_4 = UCL value from Table 6.7 for sample size *n*
D_3 = LCL value from Table 6.7 for sample size *n*

For our ambulance case, the range control limits are calculated using the control chart constants in Table 6.7 for a daily sample size of four:

$$(UCL) = D_4\overline{R} = (2.282)(2.6) = 6.0$$

$$(LCL) = D_3\overline{R} = (0)(2.6) = 0$$

Because all the range values in the last column of Table 6.6 fall within the UCL and LCL of *R*-chart for the seven day period, the process variability is in control and thus we can proceed to the construction of the $\overline{X}$-chart.

Appropriate formulas for calculating the control limits for an $\overline{X}$-chart use A_2 found in Table 6.7 and $\overline{R}$ as a measure of process dispersion.

$$(UCL) = \overline{\overline{X}} + A_2\overline{R} \quad (3)$$

$$(LCL) = \overline{\overline{X}} - A_2\overline{R} \quad (4)$$

The control limits for our sample size of four are calculated as follows:

$$UCL = \overline{\overline{X}} + A_2\overline{R} = 5.0 + (0.729)(2.6) = 6.9$$

$$LCL = \overline{\overline{X}} - A_2\overline{R} = 5.0 - (0.729)(2.6) = 3.1$$

Figure 6.9 shows the $\overline{X}$-chart for ambulance response with the mean $\overline{\overline{X}}$ = 5.0, UCL = 6.9, and LCL = 3.1. The sample means $\overline{X}$ for the first seven days from Table 6.6 are plotted on the chart to describe visually the week's performance to ascertain that the process is in control before placing the control chart in use. As seen for the first seven days all observations fall between the UCL and LCL and thus the process is in control. However, on day 10 the sample average exceeds the UCL; consequently, the system is in need of attention. Assume our ambulance example represents data from the city of Fort Lauderdale, Florida, and spring break began on day eight. The longer response times, therefore, could be explained by extended trips to the beaches. Prepositioning an ambulance on the beach during spring break might improve performance.

TABLE 6.7
Variable Control Chart Constants

Source: Adapted from Table 27 of *ASTM Manual on Presentation of Data and Control Chart Analysis,* copyright 1976, Philadelphia; American Society for Testing and Materials.

Sample Size	($\overline{X}$-chart)	(*R*-chart)	
n	A_2	D_3	D_4
2	1.880	0	3.267
3	1.023	0	2.574
4	0.729	0	2.282
5	0.577	0	2.114
6	0.483	0	2.004
7	0.419	0.076	1.924
8	0.373	0.136	1.864
9	0.337	0.184	1.816
10	0.308	0.223	1.777
12	0.266	0.283	1.717
14	0.235	0.328	1.672
16	0.212	0.363	1.637
18	0.194	0.391	1.608
20	0.180	0.415	1.585
22	0.167	0.434	1.566
24	0.157	0.451	1.548

Example 6.3 Control Chart for Attributes (*p*-chart)

In some cases, system performance is classified as either "good" or "bad." Of primary concern is the percentage of bad performance. For example, consider the operator of a mechanized sorting machine in a post office. The operator must read the ZIP code on a parcel and, knowing its location in the city, divert the package by conveyor to the proper route truck. From past records, the error rate for skilled operators is about 5 percent, or a fraction defective of 0.05. Management wants to develop a control chart to monitor new operators to ensure that personnel who are unsuited for the job can be identified. Equations (5) and (6) below are used to construct a percentage or *p*-chart. These formulas should be familiar because they represent the ±3 standard deviation confidence interval for a percentage.

$$\text{UCL} = \bar{p} + 3\sqrt{\frac{\bar{p}(1-\bar{p})}{n}} \tag{5}$$

$$\text{LCL} = \bar{p} + 3\sqrt{\frac{\bar{p}(1-\bar{p})}{n}} \tag{6}$$

where

$$\sqrt{\frac{\bar{p}(1-\bar{p})}{n}} = \text{standard error of percentage}$$

$$\bar{p} = \text{estimate of population percentage}$$

$$n = \text{sample size}$$

The *p*-chart control limits for the sorting operation are calculated using equations (5) and (6) and random samples of 100 parcels drawn from the route trucks. Note that if the calculation of an *LCL* results in a negative number, then *LCL* is set equal to zero.

$$\text{UCL} = 0.05 + 3\sqrt{\frac{(0.05)(0.95)}{100}} = 0.05 + 3(0.0218) = 0.1154 \approx 0.11$$

$$\text{LCL} = 0.05 - 3\sqrt{\frac{(0.05)(0.95)}{100}} = 0.05 - 3(0.0218) = -0.0154 \text{ [set} = 0.0\text{]}$$

The *p*-chart for this operation is shown in Figure 6.10. Given this 9-day probationary experience for the new employee, would you conclude that the person is suitable for the sorting position?

Unconditional Service Guarantee[10]

Whenever you buy a product, a warranty to guarantee its performance is expected—but to guarantee a service? Impossible! Not so, according to Christopher Hart, who writes that *unconditional service guarantees* such as the example shown in Figure 6.11 have five important features:

1. *Unconditional.* Customer satisfaction is unconditional, without exceptions. For example, L.L. Bean, a Maine mail-order house, accepts all returns without question and provides a replacement, refund, or credit.

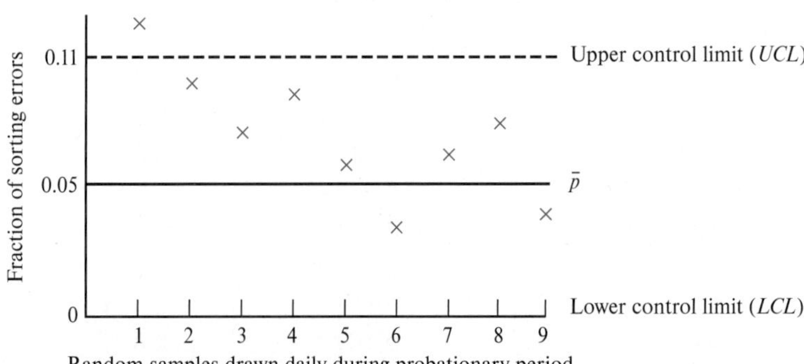

FIGURE 6.10 **p-chart for ZIP Code Sorting Operator**

FIGURE 6.11
Seller's Realty Group Unconditional Service Guarantee

Used with permission of Seller's Realty Group.

Seller's Realty Group is so certain that our service is superior, we proudly back our services with an unconditional guarantee.

This guarantee allows you to cancel your listing agreement at any time for any reason.

Upon receiving your request to cancel our agreement, within one business day, we will remove your home from all marketing and multiple listing services and our lawn sign.

2. *Easy to understand and communicate.* Customers should know precisely what to expect from a guarantee in measurable terms. For example, Bennigan's promises that if a lunch is not served within 15 minutes, the diner receives a free meal.
3. *Meaningful.* The guarantee should be important to the customer in financial as well as in service terms. Domino's Pizza guarantees that if an order is not delivered within 30 minutes, the customer gets $3 off rather than a free pizza, because its customers consider a rebate to be more reasonable.
4. *Easy to invoke.* A dissatisfied customer should not be hassled with filling out forms or writing letters to invoke a guarantee. Cititravel, a service of Citibank, guarantees the lowest airfares or a refund of the difference; a toll-free call to an agent is all that is necessary to confirm a lower fare and get a refund.
5. *Easy to collect.* The best guarantees are resolved on the spot, as illustrated by Domino's Pizza and Bennigan's.

A service guarantee has obvious marketing appeal. More important, however, the service guarantee can redefine the meaning of service for an industry by setting quality standards. For example, Federal Express defined small-parcel delivery with its overnight delivery guarantee. A service guarantee promotes organizational effectiveness in several ways:

1. *Focuses on customers.* A guarantee forces a company to identify its customers' expectations. In a survey of its passengers, British Airways found that passengers judged its service on four dimensions: care and concern, initiative, problem solving, and–to the airline's surprise–recovery when things go wrong.
2. *Sets clear standards.* A specific, unambiguous guarantee for the customer also sets clear standards for the organization. The Federal Express guarantee of delivery "absolutely positively by 10:30 AM" defines the responsibilities of all of its employees.
3. *Guarantees feedback.* Customers invoking a guarantee provide valuable information for quality assessment. Dissatisfied customers now have an incentive to complain and

to get management's attention. ManpowerGroup, a temporary-worker agency, takes a proactive approach by calling the client after the first day to get feedback on customer satisfaction.

4. *Promotes an understanding of the service delivery system.* Before a guarantee is made, managers must identify the possible failure points in their system and the limits to which these can be controlled. "Bugs" Burger Bug Killers, Inc., a Florida exterminator, will not guarantee or accept a job unless the client adheres to recommended facility improvements such as sealing doors and windows from insect penetration. Federal Express originally adopted a hub-and-spoke network to ensure that all packages would be brought to Memphis in the evening for sorting and flown out that very night for delivery by 10:30 the next morning.
5. *Builds customer loyalty.* A guarantee reduces the customer's risk, makes expectations explicit, and builds market share by retaining dissatisfied customers who otherwise would leave for the competition.

Stages in Quality Development

In this section, we looked at the most important issues of incorporating quality into the delivery of services. Some aspects of quality assurance in a service organization might occur simultaneously, but it is useful to look at the development in a systematic way. The service quality ladder shown in Figure 6.12 summarizes the progressive steps in quality development. Inspection is shown as the first rung because organizations usually begin here with their first attempts to address quality problems (e.g., checking hotel rooms after cleaning). Quality function deployment is shown as the top rung because quality should be recognized as a basic customer requirement that must be incorporated into the design of the service delivery process.

Service Recovery

Even with the best quality intentions, service failures do occur. What to do then? Table 6.8 contains some statistics on the behavior of dissatisfied customers that suggest a quick resolution to service failure is an important way to create loyal customers. Because customers participate in the service delivery process, an alert employee trained in *service recovery* techniques can turn a potential disaster into a loyal customer.

A service failure can be turned into a service delight by empowering frontline employees with the discretion to "make things right." For example, when an airplane full of anxious passengers is delayed for some minor mechanical problem, it's time to break out complimentary drinks. More heroic efforts become legends, such as the story of a FedEx employee who hired a helicopter to repair a downed telephone line during a snowstorm. Expenses incurred to accomplish a recovery are "pennies on the dollar" compared with the possible adverse "word-of-mouth" stories that now are turned into good stories of how an employee went the extra mile to accommodate a customer. Training employees in approaches to service recovery should be the first line of defense against defections and "poor word-of-mouth."

The phases in service recovery shown in Figure 6.13 is illustrated by the example of Club Med, an all-inclusive resort for guests who want to worry about nothing except relaxing and enjoying themselves. However, weather is an uncontrollable variable for Club Med, and storms can put a damper on expectations of sunbathing on the beach.

In the *pre-recovery phase* that occurs following a service failure but before the provider becomes aware of the problem, the customer's service recovery expectations are set. The recovery expectation is formed by several factors: severity of failure, previous experience with service quality, customer loyalty, and service guarantee. With dark clouds forming in

FIGURE 6.12
The Service Quality Ladder

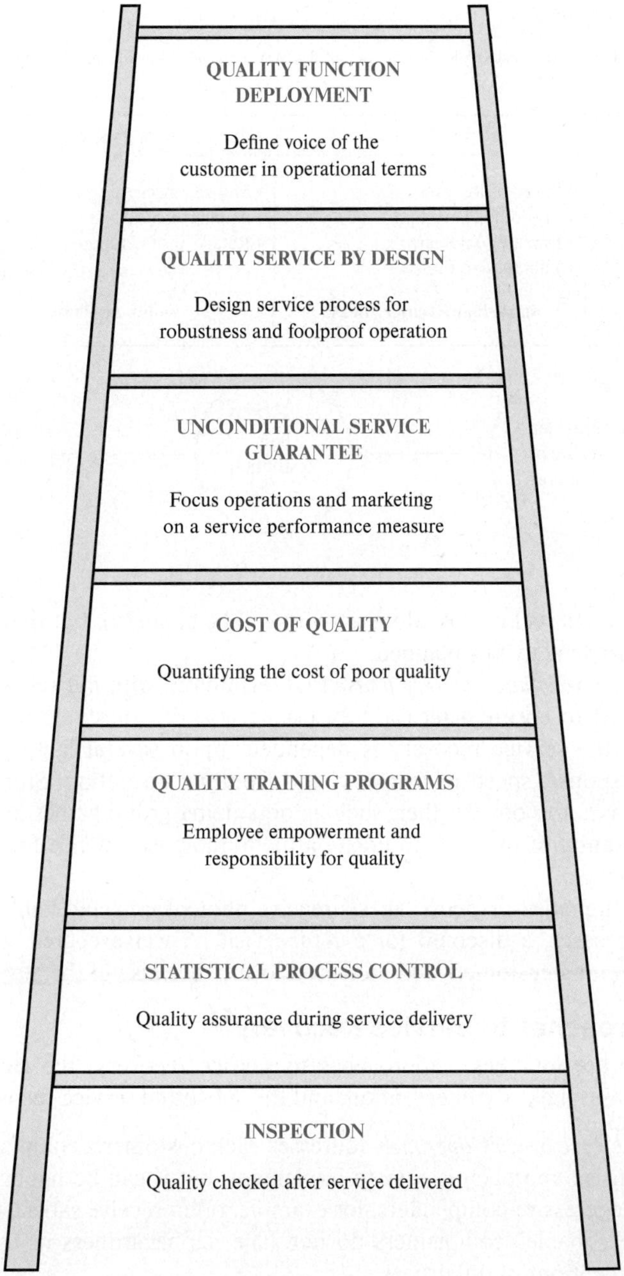

TABLE 6.8
Customer Feedback and Word of Mouth

- The average business only hears from 4 percent of its customers who are dissatisfied with the products or services. Of the 96 percent who do not bother to complain, 25 percent of them have serious problems.
- The 4 percent who complain are more likely to stay with the supplier than are the 96 percent who do not complain.
- About 60 percent of the complainers would stay as customers if their problem were resolved and 95 percent would stay if the problem were resolved quickly.
- A dissatisfied customer will tell from 10 to 20 other people about his or her problem.
- A customer who has had a problem resolved by a company will tell approximately 5 people about her or his situation.

FIGURE 6.13 **Phases in Service Recovery**

Source: Adapted from Janis L. Miller, Christopher W. Craighead, and Kirk R. Karwan, "Service Recovery: A Framework and Empirical Investigation," Journal of Operations Management 18, 2000, p. 388.

Service Recovery Expectations	Service Recovery	Follow-up Recovery
• Customer Loyalty • Service Guarnatee • Perceived Quality • Service of Failure	• Speed of Recovery • Frontline Discretion • Empathy/apology • Value-added Fix	• Show Concern • Apology • Return Visit Coupon
Pre-recovery Phase	**Immediate Recovery Phase**	**Follow-up Phase**

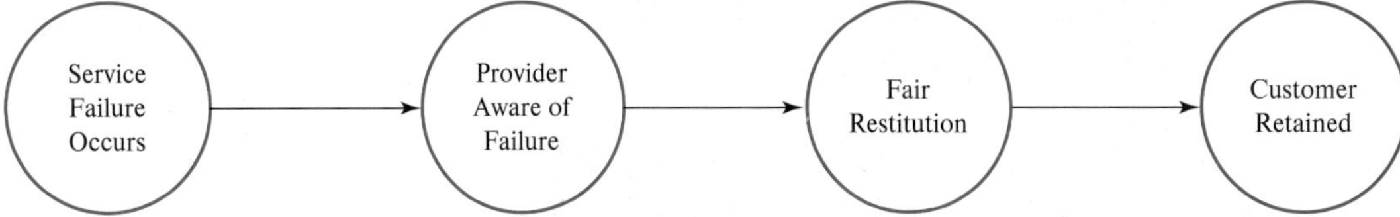

the sky, guests know outdoor activity will be canceled, but they expect Club Med to have alternative activities planned.

The *immediate recovery phase* that terminates with fair restitution requires initiative by the staff to ensure a pleasant experience for the guests despite poor weather. The quality of the service recovery is dependent upon several factors: staff empathy, appropriate response, speed of recovery, and frontline discretion. Stories abound about creative responses to poor weather, such as organizing group games and putting on stage shows. This ability of the staff to create a memorable experience for guests is called "the Club Med magic."

In the *follow-up phase,* guests receive photographs and trinkets of the vacation and, in severe cases, a discount for a return visit. A well-executed service recovery can result in retaining customers and increased loyalty because of the attention they received.

Approaches to Service Recovery[11]

There are four basic approaches to service recovery: the case-by-case, the systematic-response, the early intervention, and the substitute-service recovery approaches.

1. The *case-by-case approach* addresses each customer's complaint individually. This inexpensive approach is easy to implement, but it can be haphazard. The most persistent or aggressive complainers, for example, often receive satisfactory responses while more "reasonable" complainers do not. The haphazardness of this approach can generate perceptions of unfairness.
2. The *systematic-response approach* uses a protocol to handle customer complaints. This technique is more reliable than the case-by-case approach because it is a planned response based on identification of critical failure points and prior determination of appropriate recovery criteria. As long as the response guidelines are continuously updated, this approach can be very beneficial because it offers a consistent and timely response.
3. An *early intervention approach* adds another component to the systematic-response approach by attempting to intervene and fix service-process problems before they affect the customer. A shipper who realizes that a shipment is being held up by a truck breakdown, for example, can choose to notify the customer immediately so the customer can develop alternative plans if necessary.
4. An alternate approach capitalizes on the failure of a rival to win the competitor's customer by providing a *substitute service recovery.* At times the rival firm may support this approach. A check-in employee at an overbooked hotel, for example, might send

Service Benchmark

BRONSON METHODIST HOSPITAL

Bronson Methodist Hospital (BMH), a regional hospital that serves southwest Michigan, is a cut above most such institutions . . . the Malcolm Baldrige National Quality Program says so; the U.S. Department of Health and Human Services (HHS) says so; HealthGrades, the nation's leading health care ratings company, says so; the Thomas Reuters health care ratings organization says so; the American Hospital Association says so; *Fortune* magazine says so; and, most important, its patients say so.

This innovative hospital combines its vision of providing excellent health care, its philosophy of nursing, and its three corporate strategies (clinical excellence, corporate effectiveness, and customer and service excellence) to be a national leader in health care delivery. Bronson is consistently named as a "best practice" health care organization in different measures of quality care. For example, the hospital received a nationwide 5-star ranking, the highest possible, for its heart attack and hip replacement practices.

A Gallup poll reports that patient satisfaction ranks in the 97th percentile or better for inpatients, outpatient surgery, and outpatient testing. This remarkable achievement is the result of several efforts to focus on patient needs: patient surveys, post-discharge telephone calls, focus groups, community surveys, hospital "rounds" conducted by BMH leaders and patient-relations staff members, and a significant commitment to employee support.

BMH maintains a program for Customer Service Standards and Expectations that outlines each staff member's personal responsibility to provide excellent care for each patient. Employees are regarded as valuable resources; for example, the hospital has a formal plan to develop and retain its workforce and includes strategies such as supporting continuing education for the employee and awarding higher-education scholarships to children of employees. Employees also receive reimbursable wellness benefits in the form of personal trainers, massage therapy, smoking cessation, and weight-loss programs. The hospital's employee-supportive culture has resulted in significantly low employee turnover rates; for example, in one recent reporting period the rate of vacant positions for registered nurses was less than one-half of a national best practices comparison.

In addition to being a national leader in providing excellent health care, Bronson also leads in its commitment to its environment and community. Hospital staff volunteer an extraordinary number of hours to community health-related needs, and the hospital has received an environmental leadership award for reducing waste and pollution.

Sources: http://www.quality.nist.gov/PDF_files/Bronson_Profile.pdf; http://100tophospitals.com/top-national-hospitals/; http://www.bronsonhealth.com/AboutUs/page5345

a customer to a rival hotel. The rival hotel then might be able to capitalize on such an opportunity if it can provide a timely and quality service. This approach is difficult to implement because information about a competitor's service failures usually is closely guarded.

Complaint Handling Policy[12]

A customer complaint should be treated as a gift. A complaining customer is volunteering her time to make the firm aware of an error because she cares. This opportunity should be seized upon not just to satisfy the customer but also to create a relationship with someone who will become an advocate for the firm. A complaint-handling policy should be incorporated into the training of all customer-contact employees. An example policy might include the following features:

- Every complaint is treated as a gift.
- We welcome complaints.
- We encourage customers to complain.
- We make it easy to complain.
- We handle complaints fast.

- We treat complaints in a fair manner.
- We empower our employees to handle complaints.
- We have customer- and employee-friendly systems to handle complaints.
- We reward employees who handle complaints well.
- We keep records of complaints and learn from them.

Summary

We began our study of quality issues in services by noting that customers are the ultimate judges of a service's value. Market researchers have identified five principal dimensions that customers use to judge service quality. Customers use those dimensions to make their assessments, which are based primarily on a comparison of their expectations for the service desired with their perceptions of the service delivered. We then looked at the different types of gaps that can occur when customers' expectations do not meet their perceptions of the service.

Next we turned to the problem of measuring service quality. The walk-through audit and SERVQUAL are two useful approaches that can be used to measure quality in a variety of services.

We noted the necessity of "designing in" quality and examined the Taguchi concept of robustness, poka-yoke fail-safe strategies, and quality function deployment methods of incorporating customer requirements in design for quality.

The costs of quality are categorized as failure costs, detection costs, and prevention costs. We illustrated the application of statistical process control to avoid high failure costs in service operations.

Finally, because service failures do occur, we examined the concept of service recovery and unconditional guarantee programs.

Key Terms and Definitions

Control chart a chart with an upper control limit and a lower control limit on which sample means are plotted periodically to show visually when a process is out of control. *pg. 165*

Poka-yoke a "foolproof" device or checklist to assist employees in avoiding a mistake. *pg. 160*

Quality function deployment a process in which a "house of quality" is constructed to incorporate customer needs into the design of a service process. *pg. 161*

Service recovery converting a previously dissatisfied customer into a loyal customer. *pg. 170*

SERVQUAL a customer survey instrument used to measure service quality gaps. *pg. 153*

Statistical process control the use of a control chart to monitor a process performance measure that signals when intervention is needed. *pg. 165*

Taguchi methods approaches to service process design that ensure "robustness" or an ability to function under adverse conditions. *pg. 159*

Unconditional service guarantee a service warranty that provides a customer focus for the firm. *pg. 168*

Walk-through audit a process-oriented survey given to customers, employees, and managers to evaluate the perception of the customer service experience. *pg. 150*

Topics for Discussion

1. How do the five dimensions of service quality differ from those of product quality?
2. Why is measuring service quality so difficult?
3. Illustrate the four components in the cost of quality for a service of your choice.
4. Why do service firms hesitate to offer a service guarantee?
5. How can recovery from a service failure be a blessing in disguise?

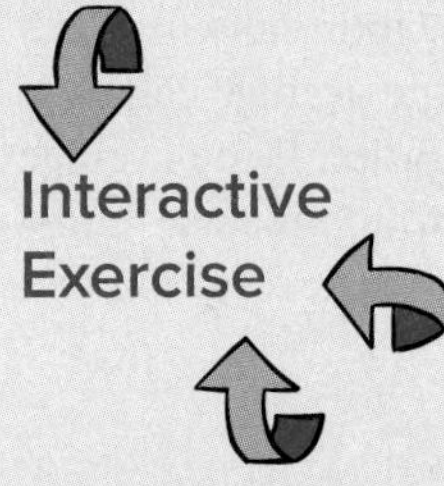

Interactive Exercise

The class breaks into small groups. Each group identifies the *worst* service experience and the *best* service experience that any member has had. Return to class and discuss what has been learned about service quality.

Solved Problems

1. Control Chart for Variables ($\overline{X}$-chart and R-chart)

Problem Statement

To become productive, Resort International is interested in setting standards for the time that telephone reservation clerks spend with vacationers making tour arrangements. Collecting data on the amount of time the reservation clerks spend with customers has been proposed to determine the mean time and average range as well as to establish a process control chart for this operation. The following table records the time in minutes that reservation clerks spent answering calls as found by observing one call at random each day during a typical week. The fifth row contains the $\overline{X}$ values for each day. The last row contains the range (i.e., high-low) values for each day (e.g., the high for Monday was 14 and the low was 5, yielding a range of 9).

Clerk	Mon.	Tue.	Wed.	Thru.	Fri.
Alice	5	11	12	13	10
Bill	6	5	12	10	13
Janice	14	13	10	9	9
Mike	8	6	9	12	14
$\overline{X}$	8.25	8.75	10.75	11.0	11.5
Range	9	8	3	4	5

Solution

First, we establish the population mean and range using the sample results from the five days shown above:

$$\overline{\overline{X}} = \frac{8.25 + 8.75 + 10.75 + 11.0 + 11.5}{5} = 10.05$$

$$\overline{R} = \frac{9 + 8 + 3 + 4 + 5}{5} = 5.8$$

Second, we establish limits for the range of call times for these samples of four calls each by constructing an R-chart using equations (1) and (2).

$$UCL = D_4\overline{R} = (2.282)(5.8) = 13.2$$

$$LCL = D_3\overline{R} = (0)(5.8) = 0$$

Third, we establish the control limits for an $\overline{X}$-chart using equations (3) and (4) when sampling four random calls each day for each clerk. The sample size of 4 was selected for convenience.

$$UCL = \overline{\overline{X}} + A_2\overline{R} = 10.05 + (0.729)(5.8) = 14.28$$

$$LCL = \overline{\overline{X}} - A_2\overline{R} = 10.05 - (0.729)(5.8) = 5.82$$

Plotting the average call time, which is based on a random sample of four calls for each clerk for each day, provides a record of performance for each clerk. If the average call time for any clerk falls outside the control limits, then an explanation is in order. If the average is above the UCL, too much time is being spent taking reservations, which results in lost productivity. If the average falls below the LCL, the clerk might be too curt, resulting in a customer perception of unresponsiveness.

2. Control Chart for Attributes (p-chart)

Problem Statement

A regional airline is concerned about its record of on-time performance. The Memphis hub experiences 20 flight operations each day of the week, with the following record of on-time departures for the previous 10 days: 17, 16, 18, 19, 16, 15, 20, 17, 18, and 16. Prepare a p-chart to monitor daily on-time performance.

First, we calculate the expected population fraction of on-time departures, which is the sum of the 10-day experience divided by a total of 200 flights:

$$\bar{p} = \frac{17 + 16 + 18 + 19 + 16 + 15 + 20 + 17 + 18 + 16}{(10)(20)} = 0.86$$

Then, the control limits are determined using equations (5) and (6) with a sample size of 7:

$$\text{UCL} = \bar{p} + 3\sqrt{\frac{\bar{p}(1-\bar{p})}{n}} = 0.86 + 3\sqrt{\frac{0.86(1-0.86)}{20}}$$

$$= 0.86 + 3(0.078) = 1.09[\text{set} = 1.00]$$

$$\text{LCL} = \bar{p} - 3\sqrt{\frac{\bar{p}(1-\bar{p})}{n}} = 0.86 - 3(0.078) = 0.63$$

As often is the case for p-charts, one limit is set equal to the extreme value (i.e., UCL = 1.00 or LCL = 0.0). In this case, the percentage of on-time departures for the day would be calculated, and only if this is found to be less than 63 percent (or 13 out of 20 departures late) would action be taken to investigate the abnormal occurrence for cause.

Exercises

6.1. In Example 6.1, Village Volvo wants to test the results of the QFD exercise for sensitivity to changes in the relative importance of customer expectations. Recalculate the weighted scores for the QFD exercise when customer expectations are given equal relative importance (e.g., five). Has this changed the previous recommendation to focus on training?

6.2. In Example 6.2, the ambulance supervisor now has decided to double the response time sample size to 8 calls per day. Calculate the new UCL and LCL for a revised $\bar{X}$-chart. For the next week, you record the following sample of daily mean response times: 5.2, 6.4, 6.2, 5.8, 5.7, 6.3, and 5.6. Would you be concerned?

6.3. The time to make beds at a motel should fall into an agreed-on range of times. A sample of four maids was selected, and the time needed to make a bed was observed on three different occasions:

	Service Time, Sec.		
Maid	**Sample 1**	**Sample 2**	**Sample 3**
Ann	120	90	150
Linda	130	110	140
Marie	200	180	175
Michael	165	155	140

a. Determine the upper and lower control limits for an $\overline{X}$-chart and an R-chart with a sample size of four.

b. After the control chart was established, a sample of four observations had the following times in seconds: 185, 150, 192, and 178. Is corrective action needed?

6.4. The management of the Diners Delight franchised restaurant chain is in the process of establishing quality-control charts for the time that its service people give to each customer. Management thinks the length of time that each customer is given should remain within certain limits to enhance service quality.

A sample of six service people was selected, and the customer service they provided was observed four times. The activities that the service people were performing were identified, and the time to service one customer was recorded.

	Service Time, Sec.			
Service Person	**Sample 1**	**Sample 2**	**Sample 3**	**Sample 4**
1	200	150	175	90
2	120	85	105	75
3	83	93	130	150
4	68	150	145	175
5	110	90	75	105
6	115	65	115	125

a. Determine the upper and lower control limits for an $\overline{X}$-chart and an R-chart with a sample size of 6.

b. After the control chart was established, a sample of six service personnel was observed, and the following customer service times in seconds were recorded: 180, 125, 110, 98, 156, and 190. Is corrective action called for?

6.5. After becoming familiar with their jobs, the sorting machine operators of Example 6.3 now average only two address errors per 100 parcels sorted. Prepare a p-chart for experienced sorting operators.

6.6. Several complaints recently have been sent to the Gotham City police department regarding the increasing incidence of congestion on the city's streets. The complaints attribute the cause of these traffic tie-ups to a lack of synchronization of the traffic lights. The lights are controlled by a main computer system, and adjusting this program is costly. Therefore, the controllers are reluctant to change the situation unless a clear need is shown.

During the past year, the police department has collected data at 1,000 intersections. The data were compiled on a monthly basis as shown below:

Month	Congestion Incidence
January	14
February	18
March	14
April	12
May	16
June	8
July	19
August	12
September	14
October	7
November	10
December	18

a. Construct a *p*-chart based on the above data.

b. Should the system be modified if, during the next 3 months, reports of congestion at these 1,000 intersections indicate the following:

Month	Congestion Incidence
January	15
February	9
March	11

6.7. The Speedway Clinical Laboratory is a scientific blood-testing facility that receives samples from local hospitals and clinics. The blood samples are passed through several automated tests, and the results are printed through a central computer that reads and stores the information about each sample that is tested.

Management is concerned about the quality of the service it provides and wants to establish quality-control limits as a measure for the quality of its tests. Such managerial practice is viewed as significant, because incorrect analysis of a sample can lead to a wrong diagnosis by the physician, which in turn might cost the life of a patient. For this reason, 100 blood samples were collected at random each day after they had gone through testing. After retesting was performed manually on this sample, the results were:

Day	Incorrect Analysis	Day	Incorrect Analysis
1	8	11	4
2	3	12	6
3	1	13	5
4	0	14	10
5	4	15	2
6	2	16	1
7	9	17	0
8	6	18	6
9	3	19	3
10	1	20	2

a. Construct a *p*-chart to be used in assessing the quality of the service described above.

b. On average, what is the expected number of incorrect tests per 100 samples?

c. Later, another sample of 100 was taken. After the accuracy of the tests was established, 10 samples were found to have been analyzed incorrectly. What is your conclusion about the quality of this service?

6.8. The Long Life Insurance Company receives applications to buy insurance from its salespeople, who are specially trained in selling insurance to new customers. After the applications are received, they are processed through a computer. The computer is programmed so that it prints messages whenever it runs across an item that is not consistent with company policies. The company is concerned with the accuracy of the training that its salespeople receive, and it contemplates recalling them for more training if the quality of their performance is below certain limits. Five samples of 20 applications received from specific market areas were collected and inspected with the following results:

Sample	No. of Applications with Errors
1	2
2	2
3	1
4	3
5	2

a. Determine the upper and lower control limits for a *p*-chart using a sample size of 20.

b. After the control limits were established, a sample was taken and four applications were found to have mistakes. What can we conclude from this?

Clean Sweep, Inc. — CASE 6.1

Clean Sweep, Inc. (CSI), is a custodial-janitorial services company specializing in contract maintenance of office space. Although not a large company compared with its primary competitors, CSI does have several major contracts to service some of the state government's offices. To enter and stay in the custodial service business, CSI adopted the strategy of having a small workforce that performs high-quality work at a reasonably rapid pace. At present, management feels that CSI has a staff that is more productive on an individual basis than those of its competition. Management recognizes that this single factor is the key to the company's success, so maintaining a high worker productivity level is critical.

Within the staff, the organizational structure is divided into four crews, each of which is composed of a crew leader and six to nine other crew members. All crews are under the direction of a single crew supervisor.

Nine buildings within the state building complex are included in CSI's contracts, and the custodial assignments have been distributed as shown in Table 6.9 to balance the work-load distribution among the crews (on the basis of gross square feet of floor space per member).

The responsibilities of each crew involve the following general tasks, which are listed in no order of importance: (1) vacuum carpeted floors, (2) empty trash cans and place trash in industrial waste hoppers, (3) dry-mop and buff marble floors, (4) clean rest rooms, (5) clean snack bar area(s), and (6) dust desk tops.

Each crew works an 8½-hour shift, during which it gets two 15-minute paid rest breaks and one 30-minute lunch break, which is unpaid. There is some variation among the crews in choosing break and lunch times, however, primarily because of the personalities of the crew leaders. The leaders of crews 2 and 3 are the strictest in their supervision, whereas the leaders of crews 1 and 4 are the least strict, according to the crew supervisor.

CSI's management is aware that the department of the state government overseeing the custodial service contracts makes periodic random inspections and rates the cleaning jobs that CSI does. This department also receives any complaints about the custodial service from office workers. Table 6.10 contains the monthly ratings and number of complaints received (by building) during CSI's current contracts. Because the

TABLE 6.9 Custodial Assignments

Crew	No. of Members*	Buildings Assigned and Gross ft^2	Total ft^2 Assigned
1	6	Bldg. A, 30,000; Bldg. C, 45,000; Bldg. F, 35,000	110,000
2	8	Bldg. B East, 95,000; Bldg. H, 55,000	150,000
3	9	Bldg. B West, 95,000; Bldg. G, 85,000	180,000
4	8	Bldg. D, 40,000; Bldg. E, 75,000; Bldg. I, 42,000	157,000

*Excludes crew leader.

TABLE 6.10 Complaints and Ratings of Cleaning Crews

	Building									
Month	**A**	**Be**	**Bw**	**C**	**D**	**E**	**F**	**G**	**H**	**I**
1	2	5	7	3	2	3	2	4	3	4
	7	5	3	6	7	5	6	5	4	5
2	1	6	8	2	1	1	2	3	2	5
	7	5	3	6	6	5	6	5	5	4
3	0	6	8	1	0	2	2	4	0	1
	8	5	4	6	8	5	6	6	6	7
4	1	5	4	1	0	1	1	4	1	3
	7	5	5	8	8	6	7	5	6	6
5	1	3	2	2	0	1	1	3	1	2
	6	6	6	7	8	6	7	5	6	6
6	2	5	3	0	1	0	0	2	1	0
	7	6	6	7	7	8	6	5	5	7
7	0	4	2	1	0	0	0	0	0	1
	8	7	7	6	6	8	8	6	7	7
8	1	2	4	2	1	0	1	2	1	1
	6	6	5	7	7	8	7	5	6	7
9	1	2	4	1	1	0	1	1	3	0
	7	7	5	6	7	8	6	5	5	8

First-row numbers for each month represent total number of complaints. Second-row numbers for each month represent ratings on a 1-to-10 scale; any rating under 5 is felt to be poor, and 8 or above is good.

renegotiation of CSI's contracts is several months away, company management would like to maintain a high level of quality during the remaining months to improve its competitive stance.

Questions

1. Prepare an $\overline{X}$-chart and *R*-chart for complaints, and plot the average complaints for each crew during the nine-month period. Do the same for the performance ratings. What does this analysis reveal about the service quality of CSI's crews?
2. Discuss possible ways to improve service quality.
3. Describe some potential strategies for reducing CSI's staffing problems.

The Complaint Letter — CASE 6.2

Most service problems are solved by direct communication between the server and the customer during the moment of service. Occasionally, however, a customer may be motivated to communicate some thoughtful and detailed feedback to a service provider after the encounter, as illustrated in the following letter:

THE COMPLAINT LETTER

October 13, 1986
123 Main Street
Boston, Massachusetts

Gail and Harvey Pearson
The Retreat House on Foliage Pond
Vacationland, New Hampshire

Dear Mr. and Mrs. Pearson:

This is the first time that I have ever written a letter like this, but my wife and I are so upset by the treatment afforded by your staff that we felt compelled to let you know what happened to us. We had dinner reservations at the Retreat House for a party of four under my wife's name, Dr. Elaine Loflin, for Saturday evening, October 11. We were hosting my wife's brother and his wife, visiting from Atlanta, Georgia.

We were seated at 7:00 PM in the dining room to the left of the front desk. There were at least four empty tables in the room when we were seated. We were immediately given menus, a wine list, ice water, dinner rolls, and butter. Then we sat for 15 minutes until the cocktail waitress asked us for our drink orders. My sister-in-law said, after being asked what she would like, "I'll have a vodka martini straight-up with an olive." The cocktail waitress responded immediately, "I'm not a stenographer." My sister-in-law repeated her drink order.

Soon after, our waiter arrived, informing us of the specials of the evening. I don't remember his name, but he had dark hair, wore glasses, was a little stocky, and had his sleeves rolled up. He returned about 10 minutes later, our drinks still not having arrived. We had not decided upon our entrees, but requested appetizers, upon which he informed us that we could not order appetizers without ordering our entrees at the same time. We decided not to order appetizers.

Our drinks arrived and the waiter returned. We ordered our entrees at 7:30. When the waiter asked my wife for her order, he addressed her as "young lady." When he served her the meal, he called her "dear."

At 10 minutes of 8 we requested that our salads be brought to us as soon as possible. I then asked the waiter's assistant to bring us more rolls (each of us had been served one when we were seated). Her response was, "Who wants a roll?" upon which, caught off guard, we went around the table saying yes or no so she would know exactly how many "extra" rolls to bring to our table.

Our salads were served at five minutes of eight. At 25 minutes past the hour we requested our entrees. They were served at 8:30, one and one-half hours after we were seated in a restaurant which was one-third empty. Let me also add that we had to make constant requests for water refills, butter replacement, and the like.

In fairness to the chef, the food was excellent, and as you already realize, the atmosphere was delightful. Despite this, the dinner was a disaster. We were extremely upset and very insulted by the experience. Your staff is not well trained. They were overtly rude, and displayed little etiquette or social grace. This was compounded by the atmosphere you are trying to present and the prices you charge in your dining room.

Perhaps we should have made our feelings known at the time, but our foremost desire was to leave as soon as possible. We had been looking forward to dining at the Retreat House for quite some time as part of our vacation weekend in New Hampshire.

We will be hard-pressed to return to your establishment. Please be sure to know that we will share our experience at the Retreat House with our family, friends, and business associates.

Sincerely,
Dr. William E. Loflin

Martin R. Moser, "Answering the Customer's Complaint: A Case Study," *Cornell HRA Quarterly,* May 1987, p. 11.

Experience has shown that complaint letters receive "mixed reviews." Some letters bring immediate positive responses from the providers, whereas other letters bring no response or resolution. The restaurateur's response to the complaint letter in this case was:

THE RESTAURATEUR'S REPLY

The Retreat House on Foliage Pond
Vacationland, New Hampshire
November 15, 1986

Dr. William E. Loflin
123 Main Street
Boston, Massachusetts

Dear Dr. Loflin:

My husband and I are naturally distressed by such a negative reaction to our restaurant, but very much appreciate your taking the time and trouble to apprise us of your recent dinner here. I perfectly understand and sympathize with your feelings, and would like to tell you a little about the circumstances involved.

The Lakes Region for the past four or five years has been notorious for its extremely low unemployment rate and resulting deplorable labor pool. This year local businesses found that the situation had deteriorated to a really alarming nadir. It has been virtually impossible to get adequate help, competent or otherwise! We tried to overhire at the beginning of the season, anticipating the problems we knew would arise, but were unsuccessful. Employees in the area know the situation very well and use it to their advantage, knowing that they can get a job anywhere at any time without references, and knowing they won't be fired for incompetency because there is no one to replace them. You can imagine the prevailing attitude among workers and the frustration it causes employers, particularly those of us who try hard to maintain high standards. Unhappily, we cannot be as selective about employees as we would wish, and the turnover is high. Proper training is not only a luxury, but an impossibility at such times.

Unfortunately, the night you dined at the Retreat House, October 11, is traditionally one of the busiest nights of the year, and though there may have been empty tables at the time you sat down, I can assure you that we served 150 people that night, despite the fact that no fewer than four members of the restaurant staff did not show up for work at the last minute, and did not notify us. Had they had the courtesy to call, we could have limited reservations, thereby mitigating the damage at least to a degree, but as it was, we, our guests, and the employees who were trying to make up the slack all had to suffer delays in service far beyond the norm!

As to the treatment you received from the waitress and waiter who attended you, neither of them is any longer in our employ, and never would have been had the labor situation not been so desperate! It would have indeed been helpful to us had you spoken up at the time—it makes a more lasting impression on the employees involved than does our discussing it with them after the fact. Now that we are in a relatively quiet period we have the time to properly train a new and, we hope, better waitstaff.

Please know that we feel as strongly as you do that the service you received that night was unacceptable, and certainly not up to our normal standards.

We hope to be able to prevent such problems from arising in the future, but realistically must acknowledge that bad nights do happen, even in the finest restaurants. Believe me, it is not because we do not care or are not paying attention!

You mentioned our prices. Let me just say that were you to make a comparative survey, you would find that our prices are about one half of what you would expect to pay in most cities and resort areas for commensurate cuisine and ambience. We set our prices in order to be competitive with other restaurants in this particular local area, in spite of the fact that most of them do not offer the same quality of food and atmosphere and certainly do not have our overhead!

I hope that this explanation (which should not be misconstrued as an excuse) has shed some light, and that you will accept our deep regrets and apologies for any unpleasantness you and your party suffered. We should be very glad if someday you would pay us a return visit so that we may provide you with the happy and enjoyable dining experience that many others have come to appreciate at the Retreat House.

Sincerely,
Gail Pearson

Martin R. Moser, "Answering the Customer's Complaint: A Case Study," *The Cornell HRA Quarterly,* May 1987, p. 11.

Questions

1. Briefly summarize the complaints and compliments in Dr. Loflin's letter.
2. Critique the letter of Gail Pearson in reply to Dr. Loflin. What are the strengths and weaknesses of the letter?
3. Prepare an "improved" response letter from Gail Pearson.
4. What further action should Gail Pearson take in view of this incident?

The Helsinki Museum of Art and Design[13] CASE 6.3

The Museum of Art and Design is a small privately owned museum located in the center of Helsinki, Finland. It occupies a beautiful three-story 19th century building that used to be a school. It specializes in design and industrial art. The museum was founded in the early 20th century and its original goal was to educate the public about design. During the big era of Finnish design in the 1950s, the museum focused on Finnish design. Recently, however, the museum has become more outward looking and frequently organizes international exhibits. On one occasion, for example, the museum brought the Dalai Lama to Finland to view an extravagant Tibet exhibit.

The museum themes bridge both the past and the future. The museum produces its own exhibits and hosts exhibits from other museums, both foreign and Finnish. It strives to have three or four major exhibits per year, in addition to devoting space to a number of smaller exhibits and its own private collection. The museum has a private café and a gift shop owned by the museum foundation. Customers include professional design people as well as lay people. The typical museum visitor was a middle-aged woman, but the increased cultural emphasis has been attracting a wider audience. Recently, after the building had undergone significant renovation, the new managing director hired a communications manager. The museum had never had a public relations person before. The advertising that was done in this year alone equaled the amount of advertising that had been done in the past 20 years. As a result of the new effort to increase the visibility of the museum, and the popular Tibet exhibit, the museum had a record number of visitors—more than 100,000 people. Only 5 of Finland's 1,000 museums attracted that many people.

The museum is privately owned by a foundation, but does receive 60 percent of its budget from government funding. Forty percent of its budget is derived from operating revenues. In addition to admission tickets sold, other revenue comes from the café, the gift shop, and events that the museum organizes in connection with exhibits. Lectures on wine and wine-tasting evenings, for example, were offered in conjunction with an exhibit on wines. The museum also has a closed society called Friends of the Museum, which provides the museum with funding to buy more objects for its private collection. The museum's major competition comes from the specialist museums: Design Forum, the University of Design Museum, and the Finnish National Museum, which is going to open a new museum of ethnography in Helsinki.

WALK-THROUGH AUDIT

A walk-though audit (WtA) of the Museum of Art and Design was conducted by a team of students from the MBA program at the Helsinki School of Economics and Business Administration. The WtA is a survey questionnaire used to evaluate a service from the perspective of the customer's experience. The same survey also is given to managers and staff to identify "gaps" between the perceptions of managers and customers. The WtA is used as a diagnostic tool to uncover misconceptions in the perceptions of what customers are experiencing during the service delivery process.

The team interviewed four members of the museum staff and then prepared a questionnaire for visitors to fill out. Thirty-two visitors responded to the questionnaire, shown in Figure 6.5. Museum management and contact personnel (i.e., primarily guides) filled out the same questionnaire, responding as if they were customers. The team did a statistical analysis of the questionnaire results to identify gaps between museum personnel's (i.e., both management and contact personnel) perceptions of the services offered and visitors' perceptions.

GAP ANALYSIS

On the basis of the questionnaire responses, the team found several categories of gaps between the museum personnel's perceptions and visitors' perceptions. The gaps were related to how visitors heard of the exhibits, information, experience, whether or not visitors come alone, and facilities. A graph showing the gaps was presented in Figure 6.6 earlier in this chapter.

Awareness of Exhibits

Visitors to the museum obtained information about exhibits primarily from newspapers, but also from magazines and by word-of-mouth. Management, however, thought newspapers played a smaller role in creating awareness but they were accurate about the influence of magazines. Management also thought word-of-mouth was significantly more important than it was and that the radio was a more important source of information than it was.

Information

Two types of gaps related to information were identified. The first gap concerns the museum management and contact personnel who believe that visitors are highly aware of their services. The management and contact personnel also believed they were an easy source of information for customers. The visitors, however, did not agree. This gap might exist because the contact personnel do not perceive that visitors would have any problem identifying or having contact with them.

In the second gap, management was more critical in its assessment of clarity and adequacy of information and explanations about exhibited objects. The visitors in turn were more positive about these issues. Visitors did not seem to have an interest in self-guided material (e.g., headphones), but the museum staff thought that it might be worthwhile to look into the possibility of having such material. Perhaps we can conclude that visitors might have a preference for human contact.

Experience

Visitors appreciated the multidimensional aspects of exhibits, such as music, but managers underestimated how much the visitors noticed and appreciated them. Contact personnel were more in touch than management with visitors' views on the spacing of displays. Both the visitors and the museum staff were not sure about experimenting with new experiences, such as those involving the senses, having more interactions, and demonstrating processes. Perhaps this factor is explained by lack of familiarity with these types of interaction.

Visitor Habits

The museum staff believed that visitors came alone more often than they did. In fact, a large number came in twos or threes. Museum staff also had a different perception of visitors' interests in exhibit offerings. Even though the management thought most visitors went to all of the exhibits, only 38 percent of the visitors saw all of the exhibits. The remaining visitors came for one of the main exhibits and did not spend time at the others. The permanent exhibit received the smallest number of visitors (i.e., 13 percent including three foreign visitors). We might conclude that each exhibit attracts different visitors.

Facilities

Visitors generally had a more favorable opinion of the facilities than did the museum management and personnel. Specifically, visitors rated food value, gift selection, signage, and cleanliness of restrooms favorably. Perhaps the expectations of visitors were not as high as museum management and personnel thought.

Language

Museum managers and contact personnel are aware that information is presented primarily in Finnish and Swedish. Of the 32 visitors surveyed, only three were nonnative speakers and, therefore, the majority did not identify language as a problem area. During the summer tourist season, more visitors probably would identify the limitations of information that is available only in Finnish or Swedish.

Questions

1. Critique the WtA gap analysis. Could there be other explanations for the gaps?
2. Make recommendations for closing the gaps found in the WtA.

Selected Bibliography

Basfirinci, Cigdem, and Amitava Mitra. "A Cross-Cultural Investigation of Airlines Service Quality Through Integration of SERVQUAL and the Kano model." *Journal of Air Transport Management* 42 (2015), pp. 239–48.

Choo, Adrian S., Kevin W. Linderman, and Roger G. Schroeder. "Method and Context Perspectives on Learning and Knowledge Creation in Quality Management." *Journal of Operations Management* 25, no. 4 (June 2007), pp. 918–31.

Collier, Joel E., and Carol C. Bienstock. "Measuring Service Quality in E-Retailing." *Journal of Service Research* 8, no. 3 (February 2006), pp. 260–75.

Dagger, Tracey S., and Jillian C. Sweeney. "Service Quality Attribute Weights: How Do Novice and Longer-Term Customers Construct Service Quality Perceptions?" *Journal of Service Research* 10, no. 1 (August 2007), pp. 22–42.

—, —, and Lester W. Johnson. "A Hierarchical Model of Health Service Quality: Scale Development and Investigation of an Integrated Model." *Journal of Service Research* 10, no. 2 (November 2007), pp. 123–42.

DeWitt, Tom, Doan T. Nguyen, and Roger Marshall. "Exploring Customer Loyalty Following Recovery: The Mediating Effects of Trust and Emotions." *Journal of Service Research* 10, no. 3 (February 2008), pp. 269–87.

Eisingerich, Andreas B., and Simon J. Bell. "Perceived Service Quality and Customer Trust: Does Enhancing Customers' Service Knowledge Matter?" *Journal of Service Research* 10, no. 3 (February 2008), pp. 256–68.

Evanschitzky, Heiner, Christian Brock, and Markus Blut. "Will You Tolerate This? The Impact of Affective Commitment on Complaint Intention and Post-Recovery Behavior." *Journal of Service Research* 14, no. 4 (November 2011), pp. 410–25.

Gabbott, Mark, Yelena Tsarenko, and Wai Hoe Mok. "Emotional Intelligence as a Moderator of Coping Strategies and Service Outcomes in Circumstances of Service Failure." *Journal of Service Research* 14, no. 2 (May 2011), pp. 234–48.

Hays, Julie M., and Arthur V. Hill. "An Extended Longitudinal Study of the Effects of a Service Guarantee." *Production and Operations Management* 15, no. 1 (Spring 2006), pp. 117–31.

Heim, Gregory R., and Joy M. Field. "Process Drivers of E-Quality: Analysis of Data from an Online Rating Site." *Journal of Operations Management* 25, no. 5 (August 2007), pp. 962–84.

Hogreve, Jens, and Dwayne D. Gremler. "Twenty Years of Service Guarantee Research: A Synthesis." *Journal of Service Research* 11, no. 4 (May 2009), pp. 322–43.

Karande, Kiran, Vincent P. Magnini, and Leona Tam. "Recovery Voice and Satisfaction after Service Failure: An Experimental Investigation of Mediating and Moderating Factors." *Journal of Service Research* 10, no. 2 (November 2007), pp. 187–203.

Lapre, Michael A. "Reducing Customer Dissatisfaction: How Important Is Learning to Reduce Service Failure?" *Production and Operations Management* 20, no. 4 (July–Aug 2011), pp. 491–507.

Măgdoiu, Alex, and Constantin Oprean. "Broadening the Concept of Poka-Yoke Beyond the Automotive Industry." *ACTA Universitatis Cibiniensis* 65, no. 1 (2014), pp. 52–57.

Molina, Luis M., Javier Llorens-Montes, and Antonia Ruiz-Moreno. "Relationship between Quality Management Practices and Knowledge Transfer." *Journal of Operations Management* 25, no. 3 (April 2007), pp. 682–701.

Parasuraman, A., Valarie A. Zeithaml, and Arvind Malhotra. "E-S-QUAL: A Multiple-Item Scale for Assessing Electronic Service Quality." *Journal of Service Research* 7, no. 3 (February 2005), pp. 213–33.

Posselt, Thorsten, Eitan Gerstner, and Dubravko Radic. "Rating E-Tailers' Money Back Guarantees." *Journal of Service Research* 10, no. 3 (February 2008), pp. 207–19.

Rafaeli, Anat, Lital Ziklik, and Lorna Doucet. "The Impact of Call-Center Employees' Customer Orientation Behaviors in Service Quality." *Journal of Service Research* 10, no. 3 (February 2008), pp. 239–55.

Reimann, Martin, Ulrich F. Lunemann, and Richard B. Chase. "Uncertainty Avoidance as a Moderator of the Relationship between Perceived Service Quality and Customer Satisfaction." *Journal of Service Research* 11, no. 1 (August 2008), pp. 63–73.

Sajtos, Laszio, Roderick J. Brodie, and James Whittome. "Impact of Service Failure: The Protective Layer of Customer Relationships." *Journal of Service Research* 13, no. 2 (May 2010), pp. 216–29.

Shanmugasundaram, Palani, and Prathyusha Vikram. "Total Quality Management, Process Analytical Technology, Five Basic Principles, and the Pharmaceutical Industry: An Overview." *Total Quality Management* 8, no. 6 (2015), pp. 178–85.

Sila, Ismail. "Examining the Effects of Contextual Actors on TQM and Performance through the Lens of Organizational Theories: An Empirical Study." *Journal of Operations Management* 25, no. 1 (January 2007), pp. 83–109.

Smith, Jeffery S., and Kirk R. Karwan. "Empirical Profiles of Service Recovery Systems: The Maturity Perspective." *Journal of Service Research* 13. no. 1 (February 2010), pp. 111–25.

–, –, Gavin L. Fox, and Edward Ramirez. "An Integrated Perspective of Service Recovery: A Socio-Technical Systems Approach." *Journal of Service Research* 13, no. 4 (November 2010), pp. 439–52.

Theokary, Carol, and Zhon Justin Ren. "An Empirical Study of the Relations between Hospital Volume, Teaching Status, and Service Quality." *Production and Operations Management* 20, no. 3 (May–June 2011), pp. 303–18.

Endnotes

1. Daniel Pearl, "More Firms Pledge Guaranteed Service," *The Wall Street Journal,* July 17, 1991, p. B1.
2. A. Parasuraman, V. A. Zeithaml, and L. L. Berry, "SERVQUAL: A Multiple-Item Scale for Measuring Consumer Perceptions of Service Quality," *Journal of Retailing* 64, no. 1 (Spring 1988), pp. 12–40.
3. Ibid.
4. J. A. Fitzsimmons and G. B. Maurer, "Walk-through Audit to Improve Restaurant Performance," *Cornell HRA Quarterly,* February 1991, pp. 95–99.
5. G. Taguchi and D. Clausing, "Robust Quality," *Harvard Business Review,* January–February 1990, pp. 65–75.
6. Shigeo Shingo, *Zero Quality Control: Source Inspection and the Poka-Yoke System* (Stanford, CT: Productivity Press, 1986).
7. R. B. Chase and D. M. Stewart, "Make Your Service Fail-Safe," *Sloan Management Review,* Spring 1994, pp. 35–44.
8. J. R. Hauser and D. Clausing, "The House of Quality," *Harvard Business Review,* May–June 1988, pp. 63–73.
9. J. M. Juran and F. M. Gryna, Jr., *Quality Planning and Analysis* (New York: McGraw-Hill, 1980).
10. From Christopher W. L. Hart, "The Power of Unconditional Service Guarantees," *Harvard Business Review,* July–August 1988, pp. 54–62.
11. T. C. Johnston and M. A. Hewa, "Fixing Service Failures," *Industrial Marketing Management* 26, 1997, pp. 467–77.
12. Private communication from Ms. Jeanne Zilmer, lecturer at Copenhagen Business School, Denmark.
13. Prepared by Eivor Biese, Lauren Dwyre, Mikes Koulianos, and Tina Hyvonen under the supervision of Professor James A. Fitzsimmons.

Chapter 7

Process Improvement

Learning Objectives

After completing this chapter, you should be able to:

1. Use quality tools for process analysis and problem solving.
2. Describe and contrast corporate quality improvement programs.
3. Lead a team in a process improvement initiative.
4. Measure the capability of a process.
5. Conduct a Six Sigma process analysis.
6. Describe the philosophy of lean service.
7. Conduct a data envelopment analysis (DEA).

Process improvement is the bed rock principle of a cost leadership strategy. Consider the labor-saving ideas that have been incorporated by the Sleep Inn chain to reduce the labor costs of operating a hotel unit. For example, clothes washers and dryers are located behind the front desk, so the night clerk can load and unload laundry while on duty. To help reduce housekeeping chores, nightstands are bolted to the wall so that maids need not vacuum around legs, and the shower stall is round to prevent dirt from collecting in corners. In addition, the computerized electronic security system has eliminated room keys: guests use their own credit cards to enter their rooms. Also, to reduce energy costs, heat or air-conditioning is turned on or off automatically when the guest checks in or out. In addition, the computer records the time that maids spend cleaning each room. Thus, creative facility design, effective use of labor, and innovative use of computers can have a major impact on increasing service productivity.[1]

Chapter Preview

The focus of this chapter is on continuous improvement in service organizations using productivity and quality initiatives. World-class service firms are noted by their commitment to ongoing improvement in customer service, thus raising the bar of excellence for the industry. Continuous improvement is a way of thinking that needs to be incorporated into a firm's culture.

The philosophy of continuous improvement is captured in the plan-do-check-act (PDCA) cycle proposed by W. Edwards Deming. Quality tools for analysis and problem solving are described and illustrated using an example in the airline industry. At the corporate level, organizations embrace continuous improvement through personnel development programs, competing for the Baldrige National Quality Award, adopting process quality captured in ISO 9000 standards, and adopting programs such as Six Sigma and Lean Service.

Finally, a linear programming model referred to as data envelopment analysis (DEA) is found in the chapter supplement. DEA is an empirical method of measuring the efficiency of service delivery units by comparing one unit against all others. This comparative analysis of unit performance provides an opportunity to promote continuous improvement through shared learning.

Quality and Productivity Improvement Process

Foundations of Continuous Improvement

Continuous improvement is based on the teachings and philosophy of W. Edwards Deming. Deming is credited with helping Japanese industry recover from WWII and pursue a strategy of exporting goods of high quality at affordable prices. This combination of quality and low cost was thought impossible because people took for granted that quality was achieved only at high cost. The foundations of Deming's teachings consisted of three principles:

1. *Customer satisfaction.* Focusing on satisfying customers' needs should be paramount in workers' minds. This requires an attitude of putting the customer first and a belief that this principle is the object of one's work.
2. *Management by facts.* To encourage scientific thinking, objective data must be collected and presented to management for decision making. This approach requires formal data gathering and statistical analysis of the data by the quality improvement teams.
3. *Respect for people.* A companywide quality-improvement program assumes that all employees have a capacity for self-motivation and for creative thought. Employees are given support, and their ideas are solicited in an environment of mutual respect.

Plan-Do-Check-Act (PDCA) Cycle[2]

Deming's approach to quality recognizes that checking or inspecting for quality is too late and instead one should focus on the process. Deming's approach, represented by a wheel, consists of four steps: *plan,* select and analyze the problem; *do,* implement the solution; *check* the results of the change; and *act* to standardize the solution and reflect on the learning. These four steps are called a *PDCA cycle.* As shown in Figure 7.1, the Deming wheel is a repetitive cycle with quality improving incrementally with each turn of the wheel.

Plan. Planning begins with the selection of the problem. Problems will appear as changes to important customer indicators, such as rate of defections or complaints. Narrow the project focus and describe the improvement opportunity. The current process is documented, perhaps with a flowchart, and data are collected.

The possible causes are brainstormed and, using data, agreement is reached on the root cause(s). Develop an action plan that includes a workable solution, measures of success, and the implementation targets agreed upon.

Do. Implement the solution or process change perhaps on a trial basis. Monitor the implementation plan by collecting data on performance measures and noting progress against milestones.

Check. Review and evaluate the result of the change. Check that the solution is having the intended effect and note any unforeseen consequences.

Act. Reflect and act on learning from the experience. If successful, the process changes are standardized and communicated to all involved workers with training in

FIGURE 7.1
Deming's Quality-Improvement Wheel

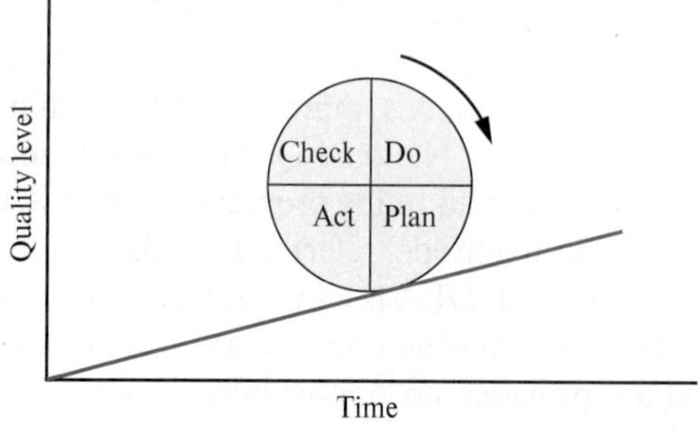

the new methods as needed. In some cases this could include external participants such as customers and suppliers. Celebrate the success and repeat the PDCA cycle on another problem.

Problem Solving

A systematic approach to solving problems is central to a worker-empowered program of continuous improvement in quality and productivity. The principal objective of continuous improvement is eliminating the cause of problems so they do not recur. A problem-solving approach based on Deming's PDCA cycle is described in Table 7.1.

TABLE 7.1 Problem-Solving Steps in the PDCA Cycle

Source: From D. C. S. Summers, *Quality*, 2nd ed., Upper Saddle River, N.J.: Prentice Hall, 2000, pp. 64–109.

Step 1	**Recognizing the Problem and Establishing Priorities** During the recognition stage, the problem is outlined by management in very general terms based on information from many sources.
Step 2	**Forming Quality Improvement Teams** An interdisciplinary team of individuals close to the problem is created and given a mandate to address the problem. Management involvement sets the team focus and shows buy-in on finding a solution that will be implemented.
Step 3	**Defining the Problem** The team first must define the problem and its scope clearly. Pareto analysis often can point to significant areas to investigate.
Step 4	**Developing Performance Measures** The effect of changes on the process can be verified only by taking before- and after-measures of performance.
Step 5	**Analyzing the Problem/Process** Flowcharting the process is often the first step at this stage to get a full understanding of all the intricacies involved. Information gathered at this stage will help determine potential solutions.
Step 6	**Determining Possible Causes** The cause-and-effect diagram is particularly helpful in identifying possible causes of the problem. The team can use the diagram to brainstorm ideas for the root cause. In a brainstorming session the team members are encouraged to throw out ideas without comment from the other members. Absolutely no arguing, criticism, or evaluation of ideas is allowed during this session, which is devoted to generating possible causes. After the possible causes are identified, data are organized using check sheets, scatter diagrams, histograms, and run charts to discover the root cause.
Step 7	**Selecting and Implementing the Solution** This is the most exciting stage, but temptation to propose solutions immediately must be curtailed. The criteria for selecting a solution include focus on the root cause, prevention of problem recurrence, cost-effectiveness, and timeliness.
Step 8	**Evaluating the Solution: The Follow-Up** Once the solution has been implemented and time has passed, the process is checked to verify that the problem has been solved. Run charts are useful for comparing prior data with current performance.
Step 9	**Ensuring Permanence** New methods need to be established and workers must be trained. Control charts can be used to monitor the process to ensure that the process remains stable.
Step 10	**Continuous Improvement** As the Deming wheel in Figure 7.1 suggests, quality and productivity are ramped up only with repetitions of the PDCA cycle. Once a problem is solved, another opportunity is identified for a new round of improvement analysis.

Quality Tools for Analysis and Problem Solving[3]

Quality improvement teams use many tools in the PDCA process. The tools aid in data analysis and provide a foundation for decision making. In the following section, eight tools are described with an example application to a problem that Midway Airlines faced. Midway Airlines, a regional carrier, served business travelers from a hub at the Midway Airport in Chicago until taken over by Southwest Airlines in 1991. The hub-and-spoke network required on-time departures to avoid delays that would compromise the efficient transfer of passengers during their multileg journeys. Midway monitored departure delays and found its systemwide on-time performance had deteriorated, causing irritation among its business passengers. The quality tools are presented next in the sequence in which they would be used in the problem-solving process.

Check Sheet

A check sheet is a historical record of observations and represents the source of data to begin the analysis and problem identification. Originally a check sheet simply was a sheet of paper listing potential problems, and each day workers would place check marks in the appropriate column to tally the frequency of occurrence. Today, data on problem frequency are entered online in an Excel spreadsheet to facilitate data interpretation. Figure 7.2 is based on an Excel spreadsheet record of problems faced by Midway during the prior year.

Run Chart

A run chart tracks change in an important process variable over time to detect trends, shifts, or cycles in performance. Run charts are easy to interpret and useful in predicting trends. Teams can use run charts to compare a performance measure before and after implementation of a solution. As shown in Figure 7.3, Midway experienced a steady increase in the number of departure delays.

Histogram

A histogram presents data collected over a period of time as a frequency distribution in bar-chart form. Using the chart command in Excel, data from the check sheet can be presented visually to obtain a sense of the distribution. Unusual features become obvious,

FIGURE 7.2
Excel Check Sheet

	Problem Area				
Month	**Lost Luggage**	**Departure Delay**	**Mechanical**	**Overbooked**	**Other**
January	1	2	3	3	1
February	3	3	0	1	0
March	2	5	3	2	3
April	5	4	4	0	2
May	4	7	2	3	0
June	3	8	1	1	1
July	6	6	3	0	2
August	7	9	0	3	0
September	4	7	3	0	2
October	3	11	2	3	0
November	2	10	1	0	0
December	4	12	2	0	1
Total	44	84	24	16	12

FIGURE 7.3
Run Chart of Departure Delays

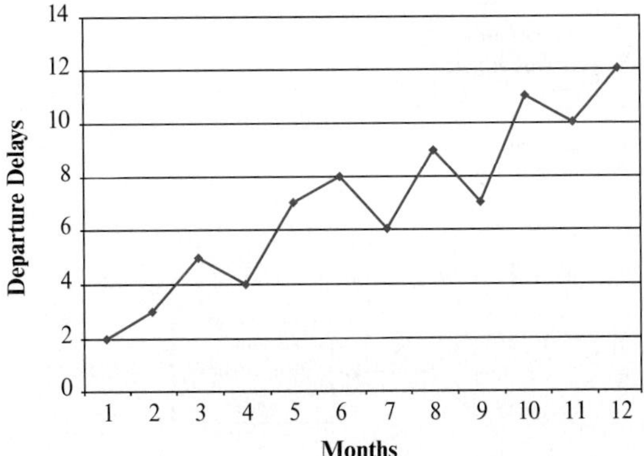

such as lack of symmetry, or skewness. A distribution with two peaks, or bimodal, suggests that two distributions with different means underlie the data. For airlines, a bimodal distribution of departure delays could be explained by a seasonality effect based upon weather conditions. In Figure 7.4 we selected "lost luggage" for our histogram. Note that the distribution is not symmetrical but skewed toward the fewer occurrences.

Pareto Chart

A *Pareto chart* orders problems by their relative frequency in a descending bar graph to focus efforts on the problem that offers the greatest potential improvement. Vilfredo Pareto, a 19th-century Italian economist, observed that relatively few factors usually account for a large percentage of the total cases (e.g., 80 percent of a country's wealth resides with 20 percent of its citizens). This principle, known as the *80/20 rule,* has been observed in many situations. For example, 80 percent of a retailer's sales are generated by 20 percent of the customers. Figure 7.5 presents the total number of problem occurrences for the year as a Pareto chart to identify "departure delay" as the most serious customer-related problem to address.

Flowchart

Flowcharts are visual representations of the process and help team members to identify points where problems might occur or intervention points for solution. Flowcharting conventions use diamonds to represent decision points, rectangles for activities, and ovals for beginning and ending points. All symbols are connected with arrows to represent the

FIGURE 7.4 **Histogram of Lost Luggage**

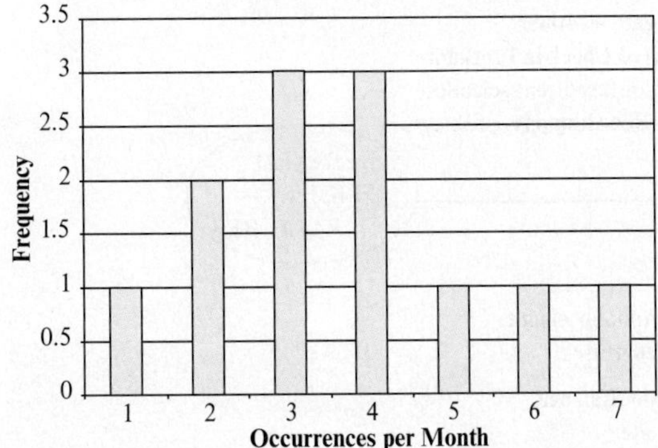

FIGURE 7.5 **Pareto Chart**

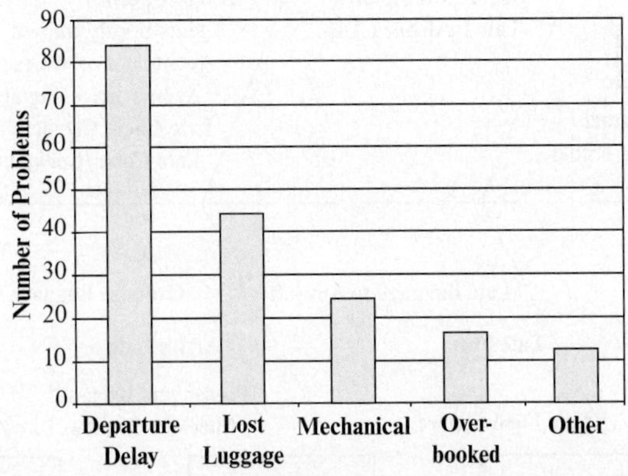

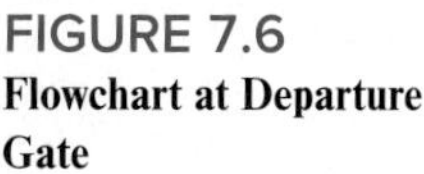

FIGURE 7.6 Flowchart at Departure Gate

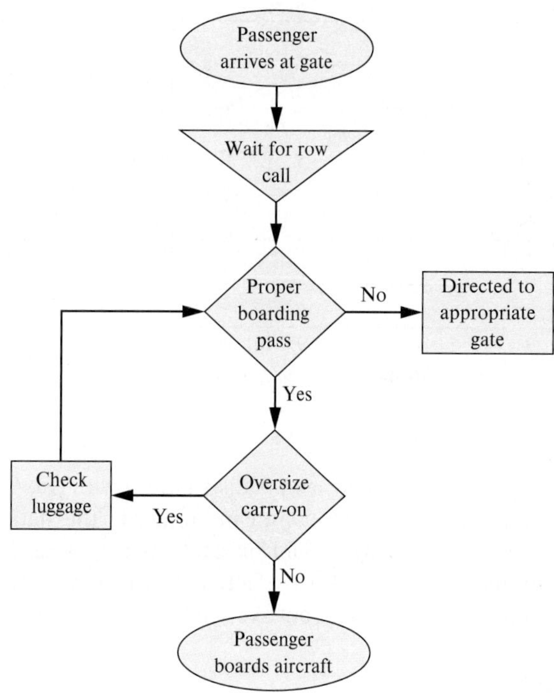

sequence of activities. In Figure 7.6 we provide a flowchart of the process at the departure gate to capture possible sources of delay, such as customers attempting to board with oversized luggage.

Cause-and-Effect Diagram

Cause-and-effect analysis offers a structured approach for a team to identify, explore, and display graphically, in increasing detail, all of the possible causes related to a problem in order to discover the root cause. The cause-and-effect diagram is also known as a *fishbone chart,* owing to its skeletal shape, or an Ishikawa chart, named after its originator. Figure 7.7

FIGURE 7.7 Cause-and-Effect Diagram for Delayed Flight Departures

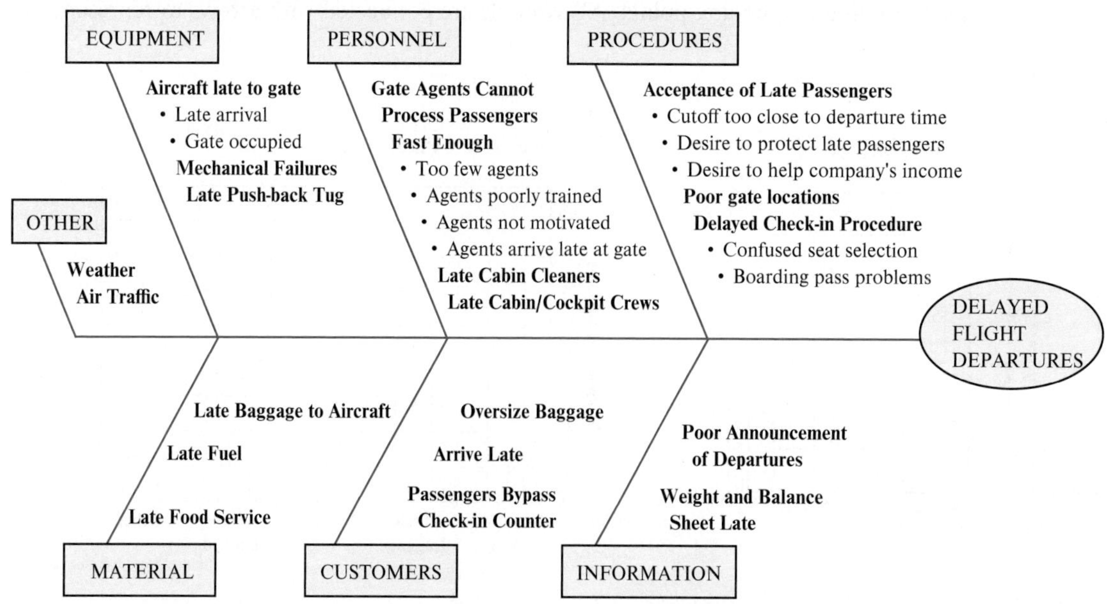

contains a cause-and-effect diagram for departure delays. The construction of the chart begins with the problem at the head and traces the major categories of causes back along the spine. For services, categories such as information, customers, material, procedures, personnel, and equipment are typical. Using the brainstorming technique, the detailed causes are filled in under each category and subcategory. Often causes are uncovered by asking the *who, what, where, when, why,* and *how* questions. The fishbone chart now can be used to eliminate the causes of delayed departure through a process of discussion and consensus; the remaining possibilities are targeted for additional data gathering.

Table 7.2, for example, shows a Pareto chart of the possible causes. Note that approximately 88 percent of the departure delays are accounted for by four root causes. Finally, fishbone charts become records of cause-and-effect relationships and often are posted in work areas for consultation.

Scatter Diagram

A scatter diagram visually shows the relationship between two variables. Plotting possible-cause variables against the problem can identify where a strong correlation exists (i.e., scatter points form a tight trend line). As shown in Figure 7.8, the scatter diagram of late passengers versus departure delays confirms the identification of a root cause.

Acceptance of late passengers, thus, was shown to be the major root cause of departure delays. Because gate agents were anxious to avoid antagonizing latecomers, they delayed flight departures, and, consequently, inconvenienced punctual passengers. As a solution, Midway established and advertised a policy of on-time departures that would be implemented by refusing late passengers to board even if the plane was still at the gate. After passengers realized that Midway was serious, the incidence of late arrivals declined significantly. Other causes of delay (e.g., waiting for pushback or fueling) were then addressed.

Control Chart

Control charts are used to monitor a process. As shown in Figure 7.9, a control chart shows when a process is out of control (i.e., the plot did not remain within the boundaries

TABLE 7.2
Pareto Analysis of Flight Departure Delay Causes

Cause	Percentage of Incidents	Cumulative Percentage
Late passengers	53.3	53.3
Waiting for pushback	15.0	68.3
Waiting for fuel	11.3	79.6
Late weight and balance sheet	8.7	88.3

FIGURE 7.8 Scatter Diagram

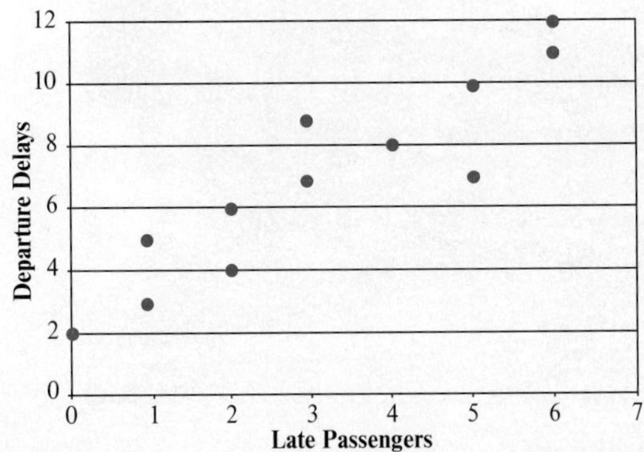

FIGURE 7.9 Control Chart of Midway Departure Delays

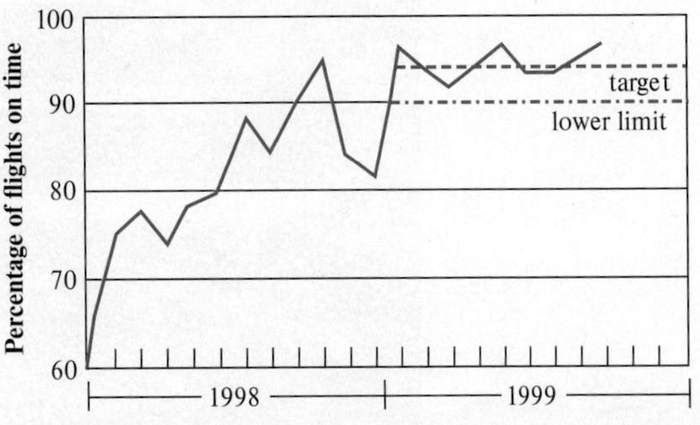

during the prior year). After the problem solution is implemented, the control chart is a check that the process is under control (e.g., percentage of on-time departures remains above 90 percent with a target of 95 percent). For the current year, the process is in control and the solution appears permanent.

Benchmarking

The measure of the quality of a firm's performance can be made by comparison with the performance of other companies known for being "best in class," which is a process known as *benchmarking*. For example, Singapore Airlines has a reputation for outstanding cabin service, FedEx for consistent overnight delivery, Hampton Inns for clean rooms, and Nordstrom's department store for attentive salespersons. For every performance dimension, some firm has earned the reputation for being "best in class" and, thus, is a benchmark for comparison. Benchmarking, however, involves more than comparing statistics. This measure also includes visiting the leading firm to learn firsthand how management has achieved such outstanding performance. For obvious proprietary reasons, this often requires going outside one's own field. Some manufacturers, for example, have visited the pit stops at automobile races to learn methods of reducing the time for production-line changeovers. Others have visited Domino's Pizza to understand how it delivers customized products within 30 minutes.

The benchmarking process involves five steps: (1) select a critical process that needs improvement; (2) identify an organization that excels in the process; (3) contact the benchmark firm, make a visit, and study the process; (4) analyze the findings; and (5) improve your process accordingly.

For a typical example, consider an electronics company seeking to improve its purchasing function. This company formed a study team that visited Ford to learn how it reduced the number of its suppliers, talked with Toyota about vendor relationships, and observed the buying process at Reliance Electric. The team returned with quantifiable measures that benchmarked the superior performance of these leading firms and with knowledge of how these gains were accomplished.

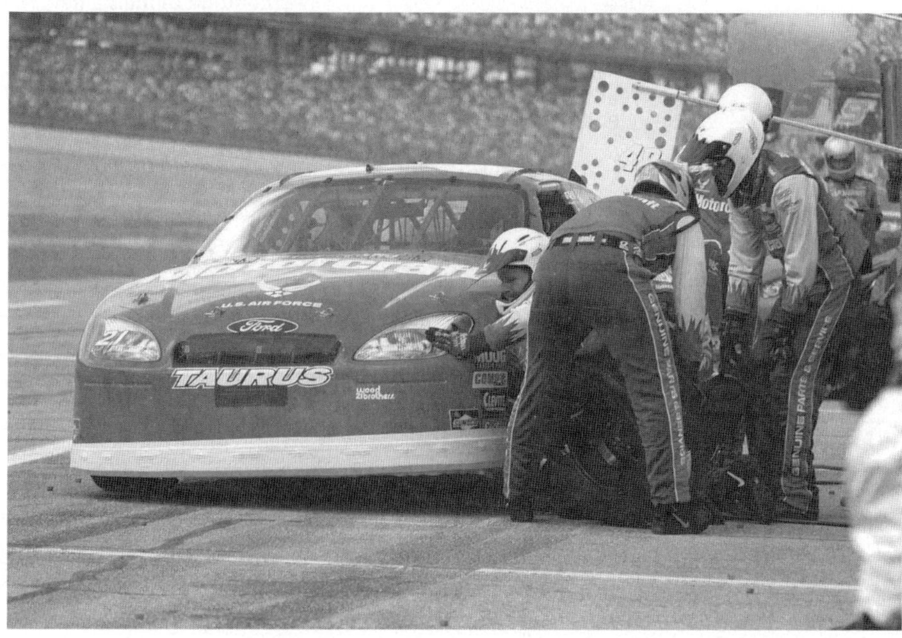

Airlines have learned to reduce turnaround time at the gate by observing the teamwork at automobile racetracks. Source: U.S. Air Force/Senior Airman Mike Meares

Improvement Programs

Service quality begins with people. All of our measurements to detect nonconformance do not produce a quality service; instead, quality begins with the development of positive attitudes among all people in the organization. How is this accomplished? Positive attitudes can be fostered through a coordinated program that begins with employee selection and progresses through training, initial job assignments, and other aspects of career advancements. To avoid complacency, an ongoing quality-improvement program is required. These programs emphasize preventing poor quality, taking personal responsibility for quality, and building an attitude that quality can be made certain.

Deming's 14-Point Program

W. Edwards Deming generally is credited with initiating the highly successful Japanese quality revolution. In Deming's view, management was responsible for 85 percent of all quality problems and, therefore, had to provide the leadership in changing the systems and processes that created them. Management needed to refocus attention on meeting customer needs and on continuous improvement to stay ahead of the competition. His philosophy is captured in a 14-point program:[4]

1. *Create constancy of purpose for improvements of product and service.* Management must stop its preoccupation solely with the next quarter and build for the future. Innovation in all areas of business should be expected.
2. *Adopt the new philosophy.* Refuse to allow commonly accepted poor levels of work, delays, and lax service.
3. *Cease dependence on mass inspection.* Inspection comes too late and is costly. Instead, focus on improving the process itself.
4. *End the practice of awarding business on price tag alone.* The purchasing department should buy on the basis of statistical evidence of quality, not on the basis of price. Reduce the number of vendors, and reward high-quality suppliers with long-term contracts.
5. *Constantly and forever improve the system of production and service.* Search continually for problems in the system, and seek ways of improvement. Waste must be reduced and quality improved in every business activity, both front office and back office.
6. *Institute modern methods of training on the job.* Restructure training to define acceptable levels of work. Use statistical methods to evaluate training.
7. *Institute modern methods of supervising.* Focus supervision on helping workers to do a better job. Provide the tools and techniques to promote pride in one's work.
8. *Drive out fear.* Eliminate fear by encouraging the communication of problems and expression of ideas.
9. *Break down barriers between departments.* Encourage problem solving through teamwork and use of quality-control circles.
10. *Eliminate numerical goals for the workforce.* Goals, slogans, and posters cajoling workers to increase productivity should be eliminated. Such exhortations cause worker resentment, because most of the necessary changes are outside their control.
11. *Eliminate work standards and numerical quotas.* Production quotas focus on quantity, and they guarantee poor quality in their attainment. Quality goals such as an acceptable percentage of defective items do not motivate workers toward improvement. Use statistical methods for continuing improvement of quality and productivity.
12. *Remove barriers that hinder hourly workers.* Workers need feedback on the quality of their work. All barriers to pride in one's work must be removed.
13. *Institute a vigorous program of education and training.* Because of changes in technology and turnover of personnel, all employees need continual training and retraining. All training must include basic statistical techniques.

14. *Create a structure in top management that will push every day on the above 13 points.* Clearly define management's permanent commitment to continuous improvement in both quality and productivity.

ISO 9001

The *ISO 9001* series of quality management system standards has become a de facto requirement for doing business in many industries, despite the fact that it is a voluntary standard. ISO (derived from the Greek word for "same") is a series of quality standards defined by the International Organization for Standardization, which is a consortium of the world's industrialized nations. The sheer extent of its global adoption makes it a critical business standard and it assumes the status of a "qualifier." Firms therefore seek certification regardless of whether they expect to achieve or believe in the need for improvements in quality.

Certification to an ISO 9001 standard signals that the firm has a quality management system in place that ensures consistency of output quality. The system is embedded in procedures, hence the common paraphrasing of the ISO 9001 requirements as "say what you do, and do what you say." ISO 9001 has several important characteristics. First, it does not prescribe specific practices. Second, it does not say anything directly about the quality of the product or service itself. Third, certification is provided by a highly decentralized system of auditors and accreditation bodies. ISO itself is involved only in design and updating of the standards, not in certification.

Documentation of processes and consistent performance are the key features of ISO standards. ISO 9001 seeks to achieve this by requiring that businesses implement a three-component cycle:

1. *Planning.* Activities affecting quality must be planned to ensure that goals, authority, and responsibility are both defined and understood.
2. *Control.* Activities affecting quality must be controlled to ensure that specified requirements at all levels are met, problems are anticipated and averted, and corrective actions are planned and carried out.
3. *Documentation.* Activities affecting quality must be documented to ensure an understanding of quality objectives and methods, smooth interaction within the organization, feedback for the planning cycle, and to serve as objective evidence of quality system performance.

The motivation for considering ISO 9001 arises from the fact that the European Economic Community has adopted this certification as a requirement for doing business in its member countries. Many companies follow and implement the ISO 9001 quality standards for reasons other than compulsory requirements, however. Companies have found that the very process of implementing the standard and the benefits from quality improvement are significant enough to justify this effort.

Six Sigma

In the mid-1980s, Motorola engineers wanted to highlight quality problems to drive process improvement and decided to report quality levels in defects per million of output. Motorola adopted this new standard and implemented a methodology called *Six Sigma* that, with top level management leadership, created a culture change within the organization. As a result of these efforts, Motorola documented $16 billion in savings that fell directly to the bottom line, unlike an equal increase in revenues from which cost of goods must be subtracted. This financial performance did not go unnoticed; hundreds of firms around the world have adopted Six Sigma as a way of doing business. For example, rumor has it that Larry Bossidy of Allied Signal (now Honeywell) and Jack Welch of General Electric were playing golf one day and Jack bet Larry that he could implement Six Sigma faster and with greater results at GE than Larry could at Allied Signal. The financial results for GE far exceeded expectations, and Six Sigma became the cornerstone of the Jack Welch legend. Six Sigma has evolved over time to become more than just a quality

FIGURE 7.10
Distribution of On-Time Arrivals

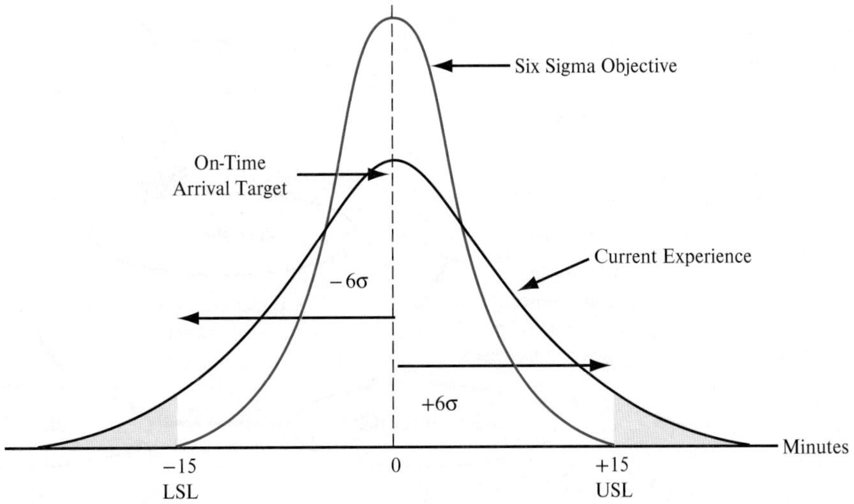

system, but a way of doing business that can be seen as a vision, a philosophy, a symbol, a metric, a goal, and a methodology.[5]

Variation is part of any process—just look at an airline's on-time arrivals in Figure 7.10. Organizations typically describe their efforts in terms of "averages" such as average wait time that can hide problems by ignoring variation. The objective of Six Sigma is to reduce or narrow variation in performance to such a degree that six standard deviations can be squeezed within the limits defined by the customer's expectations. These limits are defined as an upper specification limit (USL) and a lower specification limit (LSL). Figure 7.10 shows that the current variation far exceeds the customer expectation of a plus or minus 15-minute deviation from scheduled departure or arrival. A Six Sigma objective is achieved when sufficient variation is removed from the process such that the plus or minus 15-minute range would span plus or minus 6 standard deviations (σ) of the on-time arrival target.

The effort to reduce the variability requires a measure of progress in reaching the specification objective. A *process capability index* is a statistical measure of how much the process variability has been reduced in achieving the goal. When the mean is centered between the specification limits the, C_p process capability index is used:

$$C_p = \frac{USL - LSL}{6\sigma} \tag{1}$$

The value of $C_p \geq 2.0$ is considered the acceptable level of process capability for Six Sigma standards. For our example on-time arrival distribution illustrated in Figure 7.10, we see that a $\sigma = 15/6 = 2.5$ is required to meet the minimum level of variation for the Six Sigma objective.

$$C_p = \frac{USL - LSL}{6\sigma} = \frac{+15 - (-15)}{6(2.5)} = 2.0$$

When the mean is not centered between the specification limits, the C_{pk} process capability index is used:

$$C_{pk} = \min\left[\frac{USL - \mu}{3\sigma}, \frac{\mu - LSL}{3\sigma}\right] \tag{2}$$

Returning to our Figure 7.10, let us assume the on-time mean has shifted from $\mu = 0$ to $\mu = +1$ and the standard deviation σ has remained at 2.5.

$$C_{pk} = \min\left[\frac{USL - \mu}{3\sigma}, \frac{\mu - LSL}{3\sigma}\right] = \min\left[\frac{15 - 1}{3(2.5)}, \frac{1 - (-15)}{3(2.5)}\right] = \min[1.87, 2.13] = 1.87$$

FIGURE 7.11
Six Sigma Organization Roles and Responsibilities

Source: Paul Fox, "Six Sigma Deployment," presented at session Driving Improvement through Six Sigma, National Quality Conference of the European Society for Quality in Healthcare, Dublin, Ireland, November 8, 2001.

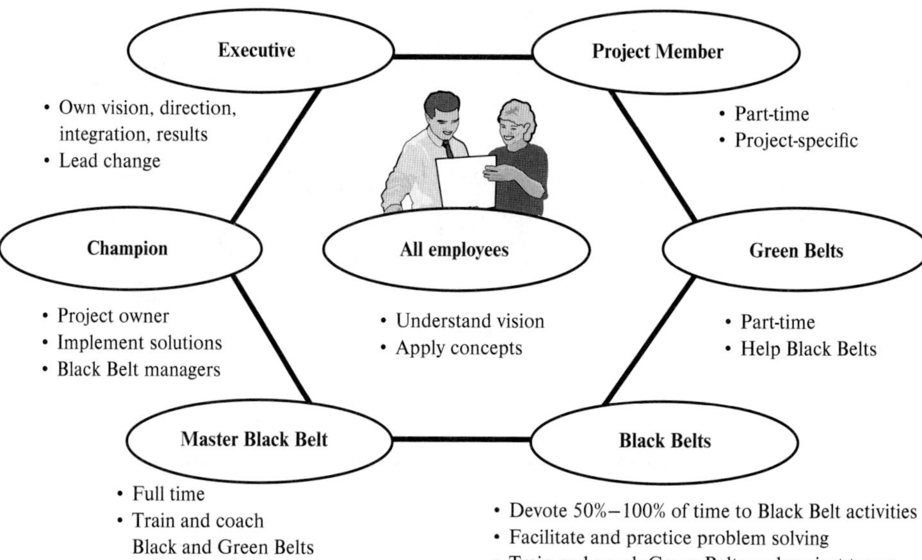

We no longer have a process that meets the Six Sigma expectation of $C_{pk} \geq 2.0$ unless we increase the value for USL to 16 to reflect the new mean.

Six Sigma is a rigorous and disciplined methodology that uses data and statistical analysis to measure and improve a company's operational performance by identifying and eliminating defects to enhance customer satisfaction. Six Sigma requires that an organization adopt a culture whereby everyone at all levels embraces a passion for continuous improvement with the ultimate aim of achieving virtual perfection equal to 3.4 errors per million customer encounters. In statistical terms, if one assumes process variation has a normal distribution, then six standard deviations (6σ) define a probability of 0.0000034 in the tail of the distribution. The focus of Six Sigma is on reporting errors, which is more motivating than stating performance in terms of percent success. For example, an overnight package delivery firm, such as FedEx, could take pride in delivering 99.9 percent of packages correctly. However, if it processes approximately one million packages per day, the result is 1,000 errors per day! Interestingly one-half of these errors could be customer-induced and, thus, the process never will reach a Six Sigma objective unless the quality of customer input is improved–a typical problem for service firms.

Six Sigma is project oriented with emphasis on top-down support and leadership that identifies targets of opportunity to maximize financial benefits. The objective of a Six Sigma project could be the reduction of defects (service failures), costs, or process variability, the increase of productivity, or the improvement of customer satisfaction. Six Sigma project responsibilities are structured by the use of a hierarchy for training and assignment of responsibilities. Figure 7.11 shows the roles and assigned responsibilities that in hierarchical order consist of executive, champion, master black belt, black belt, green belt, and project member. Skill development is encouraged; for example, a project member can advance with training to become a green belt, and then later to higher levels of responsibility in the organization's Six Sigma program. As shown in Table 7.3, Six Sigma uses a

TABLE 7.3
Six Sigma DMAIC Process Steps

Step	Definition
Define	Define project objectives, internal, and external customers.
Measure	Measure current level of performance.
Analyze	Determine causes of current problems.
Improve	Identify how the process can be improved to eliminate the problems.
Control	Develop mechanisms for controlling the improved process.

DMAIC (Define, Measure, Analyze, Improve, Control) cycle, illustrated in Example 7.1, to structure the improvement efforts for existing processes that are not performing as well as desired.

Example 7.1
Big Tex Burgers

Big Tex Burgers is a fast-food restaurant chain famous for its giant burger, the "belt-busting one-pounder." Recently, a consumer organization criticized the restaurant claiming that its burgers contain fewer than 16 ounces of meat. You are the quality assurance manager for the restaurant and your boss asks you to investigate the matter. This is your opportunity to shine, so you decide to use the DMAIC steps of Six Sigma to evaluate the situation.

Step 1: Define

The weight of the meat patty is defined as the critical quality characteristic.

Step 2: Measure

To evaluate the extent of the problem, we first need to set acceptable limits for the quality characteristic—that is, the weight of the meat patty. Therefore, set the quality limits at $\pm$ 5 percent of the advertised weight.

$$\text{Upper Tolerance Limit} = 16 + (0.05)(16) = 16.8$$

$$\text{Lower Tolerance Limit} = 16 - (0.05)(16) = 15.2$$

The next question to answer is what percentage of the burgers has fewer than 15.2 ounces of meat. Note, even though customers might not object to receiving more than 16.8 ounces of meat in the burger (i.e., above the upper tolerance limit), you must count that as an internal error because of its effect on profits.

Step 3: Analyze

Next, a random sample of burgers is collected and weighed. You find that the average of the sample is 15.8 ounces with a standard deviation of 0.5 ounce. Even though the average of 15.8 ounces is lower than the advertised weight of 16 ounces, we cannot imply automatically that the error is significant and that the system should be considered "defective." To classify the system as defective, you need to determine if a significant percentage of burgers fall below the acceptable limit of 15.2 ounces.

Using the standard normal distribution,

$$Z = \frac{x - \mu}{\sigma} = \frac{(15.2 - 15.8)}{0.5} = -1.2$$

Using the Areas of Standard Normal Distribution table in Appendix A, or the Excel command, we find the area in the negative tail to be

NORMSDIST (Z) = NORMSDIST (−1.2) = 0.1151

Now, you can infer that 11.51 percent of the burgers are likely to weigh fewer than 15.2 ounces.

Step 4: Improve

Your boss concludes that an 11.51 percent defective rate is unacceptable and the company's performance needs to be improved. You identify three ways to achieve the desired improvement:

a. Decrease variation.

b. Center or adjust the process about the 16-ounce target.

c. Increase specifications.

First, assume that by doing process improvement, the standard deviation can be reduced from 0.5 ounce to 0.4 ounce. Then,

$$Z = \frac{x - \mu}{\sigma} = \frac{(15.2 - 15.8)}{0.4} = -1.5$$

NORMSDIST (−1.5) = 0.0668 or 6.68 percent

Alternatively, with the current standard deviation at 0.5 ounce, assume that the process can be adjusted (centered) so that the new mean is exactly 16 ounces. Then,

$$Z = \frac{x - \mu}{\sigma} = \frac{(15.2 - 16)}{0.5} = -1.6$$

NORMSDIST (−1.6) = 0.0548 or 5.48 percent

The third possibility is to negotiate with the consumer organization to widen the acceptable range to between 15 ounces and 17 ounces. Then,

$$Z = \frac{x - \mu}{\sigma} = \frac{(15 - 15.8)}{0.5} = -1.6$$

NORMSDIST (−1.6) = 0.548 or 5.48 percent

Therefore, you discover that using any one of the three options, the "defect" rate can be brought down from current 11.51 percent to a range of 5 to 7 percent. If all three options are used simultaneously, then

$$Z = \frac{x - \mu}{\sigma} = \frac{(15 - 16)}{0.4} = -2.5$$

NORMSDIST (−2.5) = 0.0062 or 0.62 percent

This combined effort results in less than 1 percent of the burgers falling outside the lower acceptable limit.

Step 5: Control

After the desired improvements are obtained, the quality standards must be controlled on a continuous basis. Recall from Chapter 6, Service Quality, that statistical quality control of a process is achieved by using control charts. Because you are interested in controlling the weight of the burger, the use of an $\overline{X}$-chart and *R*-chart is appropriate. You decide to construct a control chart with an expected weight $\overline{X}$ of 16 ounces and expected range *R* of 2 ounces. Four burgers will be sampled each hour with a mean and range calculated. Using Table 6.7 from Chapter 6 with a sample size of 4, we find $A_2 = 0.729$, $D_3 = 0$, and $D_4 = 2.282$. Using equations (1) and (2) from Chapter 6, you find the control limits for the range are

$$UCL = D_4R = (2.282)(2) = 4.6$$

$$LCL = D_3R = (0)(2) = 0$$

Using equations (3) and (4), from Chapter 6, you find the control limits for the sample mean are

$$UCL = \overline{X} + A_2\,R = 16 + (0.729)\,(2) = 17.5$$

$$LCL = \overline{X} - A_2\,R = 16 - (0.729)\,(2) = 14.5$$

As a result of your work, Big Tex Burgers will implement a practice of sampling four burgers each hour at random times, recording the range of weights, and calculating the mean value. This information will be recorded on two separate charts, a range chart and a weight chart, on which UCL and LCL lines have been drawn. A recorded value that falls outside of these control limits indicates that action should be taken to find the root cause of the loss-of-weight control.

Lean Service

Lean Service is an extension of lean principles pioneered by the Toyota Production System (TPS) with a focus on waste elimination, continuous flow, and customer demand pull, and is referred to in manufacturing as Just-in-Time production. The objective of a Lean Service process is a continuous rapid flow of value-adding activities to satisfy customer needs. The lean philosophy has three guiding principles:

1. Satisfy the needs of the customer by performing only those activities that add value in the eyes of the customer.
2. Define the "value stream" by flowcharting the process to identify both value-added and non-value-added activities.
3. Eliminate waste. Waste in the value stream is any activity for which the customer is not willing to pay.

Lean Service is an approach to achieving the perfect process with three goals: the right purpose (value); the best method (process); and the highest sense of accomplishment (people). The right purpose is driven by a focus on customer-valued activities that are achievable (e.g., Six Sigma), available (e.g., staffing level), adequate (e.g., trained staff), and flexible (e.g., employee discretion). The best process has a flow capable of low volume with high variety and is responsive to customer demand pull. The process is satisfying for workers because they have a sense of providing a valuable service and personal fulfillment.

Value-stream mapping (VSM) is a tool central to Lean Service that maps out a process to uncover opportunities for improvement by using lean management concepts. This tool identifies value-adding processes (e.g., waiter delivering a meal to the table) and non-value-adding processes (e.g., waiter walking to cashier to process credit card). Overall efficiency of the service delivery system is calculated as the ratio of total value-added time divided by throughput time. The benefits of value-stream mapping include viewing the system from a customer's perspective, capturing the key processes and activity times in a graphical presentation, and identifying opportunities for improvement.[6]

Example 7.2 Small Business Loan Approval

A regional bank in a rural community offers small business loans to customers who walk into the branch. The current state value-stream map shown in Figure 7.12 captures the sequence of activities a customer experiences from entering the bank to leaving with a loan account established. Analysis of the VSM yields the following:

- The total value-added time is 95 minutes
- The total non-value-added time is 45 minutes
- The throughput time (95 + 45) for processing a loan is 140 minutes.
- Overall efficiency (total value-added/throughput time) 95/140 = 68 percent

Assume the bank is considering using an online application that would eliminate the "fill-out application" step in the branch office. This would also eliminate the waiting time of 15 minutes before "fill-out application" and the 5 minutes wait time before "create customer profile"

FIGURE 7.12
Value Stream Map of Small Business Loan Approval

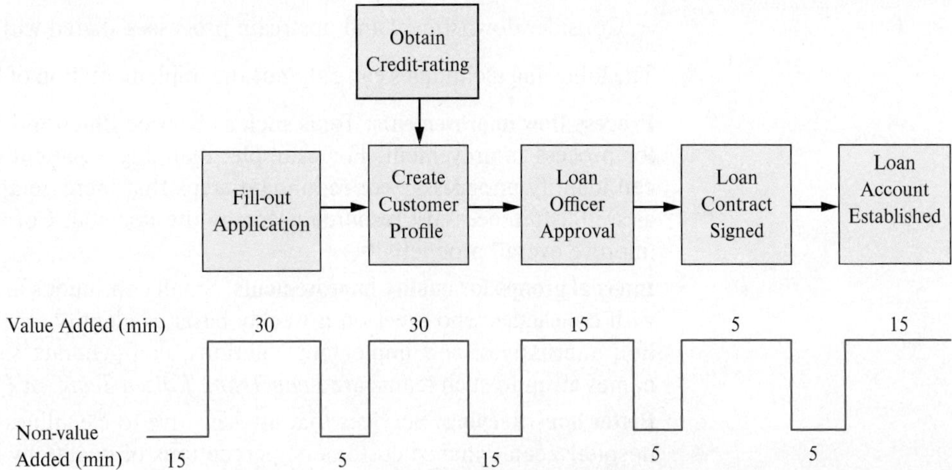

because the loan applicant would be invited to the branch to meet with the loan officer after the customer profile has been prepared. The revised value-stream map would yield the following:

- The total value-added time is now 95 − 30 = 65 minutes
- The total non-value-added time now is 45 − 15 − 5 = 25 minutes
- The throughput time (65 + 25) for a processing a loan now is 90 minutes
- Overall efficiency 65/90 = 72 percent, a 4 percent improvement!

The following steps provide a guide to achieving a Lean Service.[7]

1. Identify the key processes in your organization.
   - Which are primary?
   - Which are support?
   - Which are most important to the customer?
   - Which are most important to the success of the organization?
   - Which are most troubling to your people?
2. Select the most important processes and order by importance.
   - Form a team of people involved in the process including customers.
   - Create a "current state" value-stream map of the process.
3. Analyze how the process can be changed to move toward perfection.
   - Create a "future state" value-stream map of the improved process.
4. Ask what changes will be needed to sustain the "future state" process.
   - Establish a new process manager position?
   - Rearrange existing departments and functions?
   - Introduce new metrics to align department and function performance?
5. Implement the necessary changes to create the "future state" process.
   - Measure the performance compared with the "current state."
   - Introduce necessary changes to adjust the process.
   - Determine whether the adjusted process is stable and sustainable.
6. When the "future state" process has been proven:
   - Determine what you will do with excess people and assets.
7. When all processes have been improved:
   - Start the cycle again.
   - Consider downstream and upstream processes shared with other organizations.

The following techniques can enhance the implementation of Lean concepts in services:

- **Process flow improvements:** Tools such as Service Blueprinting reveal potential sources for process improvement. For example, mapping a patient's flow through a hospital can identify unnecessary or redundant steps that increase a patient's throughput time as well as unnecessary resource usage by the hospital. Correcting such problems will improve overall productivity.
- **Internal groups for quality improvements:** Small continuous-improvement teams, formed with colleagues who meet on a weekly basis to identify local problems, evaluate solution alternatives, and implement solutions, can generate significant savings. Typical names given to such teams are *Lean Team, Kaizen Team,* or *Quality Circle.*
- **Better housekeeping:** Services that are sensitive to cleanliness, such as restaurants and hospitals, can enhance customers' perceptions of quality by achieving superior housekeeping. For example, to promote pride in the presentation and maintenance of their property, a number of cities recognize establishments with a Golden Broom Award.

Service Benchmark

WHEN SOMETHING DOESN'T WORK— SOMETIMES JUST HIT IT WITH A HAMMER!

My husband has a small rolling suitcase that we bought from L.L.Bean a couple of years ago. It is a great little case, but recently the "telescoping" handle got jammed down in the case and wouldn't pull out. We tried yanking on it with various levels of force and poked around to see if we could get at the mechanism without having to cut something open, with no success. Today he e-mailed L.L.Bean to ask about repair/replacement of the case. Here is the answer that he received:

"Thank you for contacting L.L.Bean regarding our rolling luggage. The best way to fix the problem with the handle is to give it a good whack. Seriously, sometimes the extension poles can get wedged together during baggage handling. I recommend to first try a rubber mallet and if that doesn't work then to return the luggage to us for an exchange or refund. Our products are guaranteed to give 100% satisfaction in every way. Return anything purchased from us at any time if it proves otherwise. We do not want you to have anything from L.L.Bean that is not completely satisfactory. Thank you for contacting L.L.Bean today. I know that my response might sound a bit crazy but it works."

We were of course happy to know we could return it, but first he did indeed give the back of the case one "good whack" with a rubber mallet . . . and presto, the handle works again. Anyway, kudos to L.L.Bean for (a) great return service and (b) having a sense of humor.

Source: Private communication from a customer.

- **Quality improvement in service delivery:** Food chains such as McDonald's and hotel chains such as Marriott aim at consistency as a quality measure by standardizing the service delivery process across the chain. The subsequent predictability results in service offerings and resource efficiencies that make the firm much leaner.
- **Resource flexibility:** Flexibility in resource usage gives a firm the ability to utilize a common resource for multiple operations. The challenge lies in quick changeovers between operations to avoid delay. This capability results in *economies of scope* that can be achieved through flexible process technology. For example, operating rooms in a hospital often need to be set up with different types of medical technology between patients.
- **Pull-system implementation:** A lean service firm can adopt a customer-driven demand pull-system. For example, the kitchens of some Wendy's restaurants face the parking entry, so that the cooks can start processing fresh beef patties on the grill as cars enter the parking lot.
- **Line balancing:** Service firms can level resource utilization by managing supply and demand appropriately. For example, McDonald's offers a limited breakfast menu that utilizes its human resources better and results in shorter customer waits.
- **Layout improvements:** Lean implementations in services typically lead to better space management. In a hospital, a better layout plan improves both patient and staff flow as well as material flow, resulting in savings in throughput time and patient waiting.
- **Superior vendor management:** A service firm vendor could be a supplier of human resources with the necessary skills to perform a particular operation. For example, a supplier of temporary help should check early on with the client to determine that its employee performance is acceptable.
- **Looking for *mudas* in services:** *Muda* is a Japanese term for wastes of different types. For example, in a hospital wastes could be identified as excessive patient waiting and poor information exchange.

Summary

The foundation of continuous process improvement rests upon Deming's incremental approach to problem solving captured in the PDCA cycle. The improvement process uses the seven quality tools: check sheet, run chart, histogram, Pareto chart, flowchart, scatter diagram, and fishbone chart. These tools can be used by anyone in the organization to make a contribution to process improvement. However, senior management needs to show leadership as Jack Welch did at General Electric promoting the adoption of Six Sigma. The most recent improvement programs, Lean Service and Six Sigma, are credited with significant results at firms such as Motorola, Allied Signal, and General Electric.

Key Terms and Definitions

Benchmarking the practice of comparing one's performance with that of other firms that are known as "best in class." *p. 194*
Cause-and-effect analysis a process using a chart shaped like a fishbone to discover the root cause of a service quality problem. *p. 192*
ISO 9001 an international program that certifies a firm as having a quality management system to ensure consistent output quality. *p. 196*
Lean Service a process-improvement philosophy based on eliminating non-value-added activities. *p. 200*
Pareto chart presents problems in a bar graph by their relative frequency in descending order. *p. 191*
PDCA cycle a process of continuous improvement consisting of four steps: plan, do, check, and act. *p. 188*
Process capability index measures the ability of a process to meet specifications. *p. 197*
Six Sigma a rigorous and disciplined methodology to improve a firm's operational performance by eliminating process defects. *p. 196*
Value-stream mapping distinguishes between value-adding activities and non-value-adding activities in a service process. *p. 201*

Topics for Discussion

1. Discuss why Deming's 14-point program was rejected by U.S. firms but embraced by the Japanese following World War II.
2. Explain how the application of the PDCA cycle can support a competitive strategy of low cost leadership.
3. What are the limitations of "benchmarking"?
4. Explain why the introduction of Six Sigma at 3M was blamed for stifling creativity.
5. Reconsider Figure 7.12, the value-stream map of the small business loan approval process. If the process was conducted entirely online, what value-added activities could be eliminated? What is the overall efficiency of an online process?

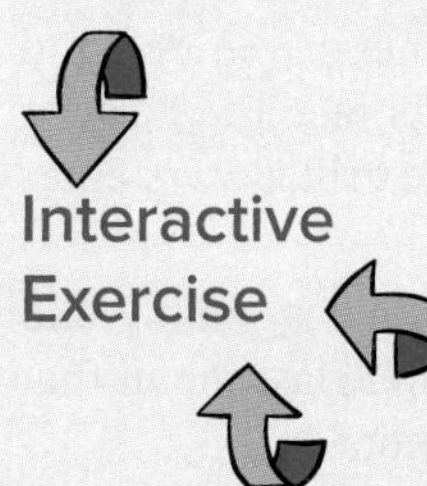

Interactive Exercise

Have the class prepare a process flow chart (value-stream map) of a familiar service and identify the non-value-added activities. Make suggestions for elimination of waste.

Sonora County Sheriff — CASE 7.1

Sonora County is located in northern California and is known for its wine country and rugged Pacific coast line. Sonora is a rural county with only one major city, Santa Rita, which has a population of approximately 150,000. Sonora State University is located in Santa Rita and has a student population of approximately 12,000. The county sheriff keeps a monthly record of her department's law enforcement activities by incident as shown in Figure 7.13 for the prior year. She is troubled by an apparent recent increase in burglaries.

Questions

1. Prepare a run chart on each of the incident categories. Does she have reason to be concerned about burglaries? What variable might you plot against burglaries to create a scatter diagram to determine a possible explanation?
2. What is unusual about the pattern of reported disorderly and DUI incidents by month? What could be an explanation for this behavior? How could the sheriff address this pattern and reduce the number of incidents?
3. Would you recommend preparing control charts for assault and theft incidents? Why or why not?
4. Prepare a Pareto chart based on the total of last year's incidents. Why might the sheriff not prioritize efforts on incident reduction according to the results of the Pareto chart?

FIGURE 7.13
Incident Check Sheet

Month	Incident: Assault	Burglary	Disorderly	DUI	Theft
January	2	2	3	6	6
February	2	1	1	2	4
March	1	3	2	4	5
April	2	2	1	2	6
May	2	4	2	3	7
June	3	5	4	4	5
July	2	4	5	3	3
August	1	7	4	4	6
September	3	9	2	3	5
October	2	8	1	2	4
November	1	10	2	4	5
December	1	13	1	7	6

Mega Bytes Restaurant[8] CASE 7.2

Mega Bytes is a restaurant that caters to business travelers and has a self-service breakfast buffet. To measure customer satisfaction, the manager constructs a survey and distributes it to diners during a three-month period. The results, as summarized by the Pareto chart in Figure 7.14, indicate that the restaurant's major problem is customers waiting too long to be seated.

A team of employees is formed to work on resolving this problem. The team members decide to use the Seven-Step Method (SSM), which is a structured approach to problem solving and process improvement originally developed by Joiner Associates, Inc., of Madison, Wisconsin. The SSM leads a team through a logical sequence of steps that forces a thorough analysis of the problem, its potential causes, and its possible solutions. The structure imposed by the SSM helps the team to focus on the correct issues and avoid diffusing its energy on tangential or counterproductive efforts. The SSM is directed at analytic rather than enumerative studies. In general, analytic studies are interested in cause and effect and in making predictions, whereas enumerative studies are focused on an existing population.

The steps in this method are shown in Table 7.4 and applied here to the case of Mega Bytes.

Step 1: Define the project. The results of the Mega Bytes survey indicate that customers wait too long to be seated. Most customers are business travelers who want to be served promptly or have an opportunity to discuss business during their meal. The team considers several questions such as "When does the wait start? When does it end? How is it measured?" and then arrives at an operational definition of the problem it must solve as "waiting to be seated."

Step 2: Study the current situation. The team collects baseline data and plots them as shown in Figure 7.15. At the same time, a flowchart for seating a party is developed, and the team also diagrams the floor plan of Mega Bytes as shown in Figure 7.16.

The baseline data indicate that the percentage of people who must wait is higher early in the week than it is late in the week. This finding is to be expected, however, because most Mega Bytes customers are business travelers. The size of the party does not appear to be a factor, and no surprises were found when a histogram of the number of people waiting in excess of one minute was plotted against the time of the morning: more people wait during the busy hours than during the slow hours.

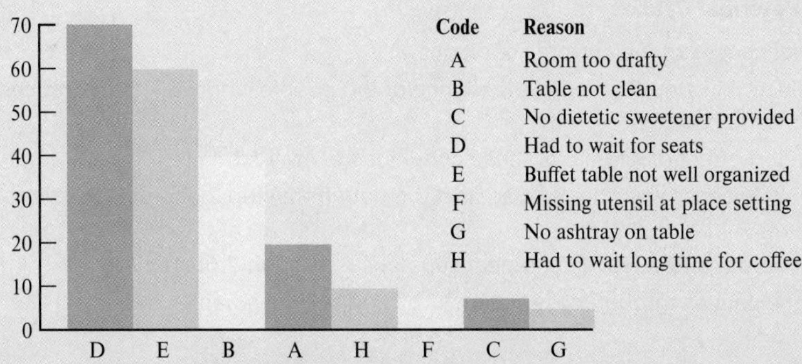

FIGURE 7.14
Pareto Chart of Complaints

Reprinted with permission from M. Gaudard, R. Coates, and L. Freeman, "Accelerating Improvement," *Quality Progress* 24, no. 10, October 1991, p. 83.

FIGURE 7.15
Run Chart of Percent of Customers Waiting More Than One Minute to Be Seated

Reprinted with permission from M. Gaudard, R. Coates, and L. Freeman, "Accelerating Improvement," *Quality Progress* 24, no. 10, October 1991, p. 83.

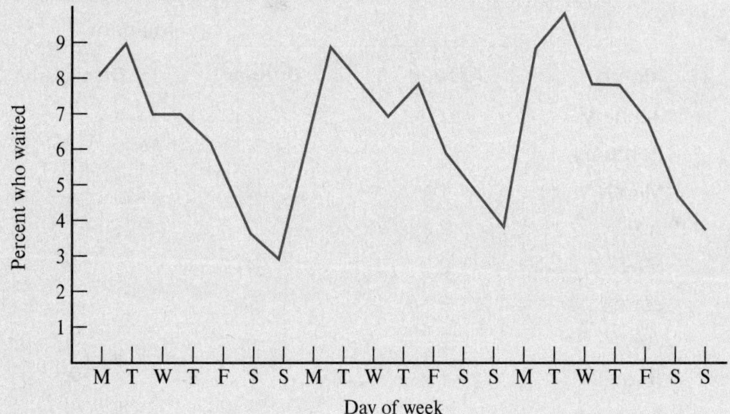

TABLE 7.4 The Seven-Step Method

Reprinted with permission from M. Gaudard, R. Coates, and L. Freeman, "Accelerating Improvement," *Quality Progress* 24, no. 10, October 1991, p. 82.

Step 1 Define the Project

1. Define the problem in terms of a gap between what is and what should be. (For example, "Customers report an excessive number of errors. The team's objective is to reduce the number of errors.")
2. Document why it is important to be working on this particular problem:
   - Explain how you know it is a problem, providing any data you might have that support this.
   - List the customer's key quality characteristics. State how closing the gap will benefit the customer in terms of these characteristics.
3. Determine what data you will use to measure progress:
   - Decide what data you will use to provide a baseline against which improvement can be measured.
   - Develop any operational definitions you will need to collect the data.

Step 2 Study the Current Situation

1. Collect the baseline data and plot them. Sometimes historical data can be used for this purpose. A run chart or control chart usually is used to exhibit baseline data. Decide how you will exhibit these data on the run chart. Decide how you will label your axes.
2. Develop flowcharts of the processes.
3. Provide any helpful sketches or visual aids.
4. Identify any variables that might have a bearing on the problem. Consider the variables of what, where, to what extent, and who. Data will be gathered on these variables to localize the problem.
5. Design data collection instruments.
6. Collect the data and summarize what you have learned about the variables' effects on the problem.
7. Determine what additional information would be helpful at this time. Repeat substeps 2 through 7, until there is no additional information that would be helpful at this time.

Step 3 Analyze the Potential Causes

1. Determine potential causes of the current conditions:
   - Use the data collected in step 2 and the experience of the people who work in the process to identify conditions that might lead to the problem.
   - Construct cause-and-effect diagrams for these conditions of interest.
   - Decide on most likely causes by checking against the data from step 2 and the experience of the people working in the process.
2. Determine if more data are needed. If so, repeat substeps 2 through 7 of step 2.
3. If possible, verify the causes through observation or by controlling variables directly.

(continued)

TABLE 7.4 *(continued)*

Step 4 Implement a Solution

1. Develop a list of solutions to be considered. Be creative.
2. Decide which solutions should be tried:
   - Carefully assess the feasibility of each solution, the likelihood of success, and potential adverse consequences.
   - Clearly indicate why you are choosing a particular solution.
3. Determine how the preferred solution will be implemented. Will there be a pilot project? Who will be responsible for the implementation? Who will train those involved?
4. Implement the preferred solution.

Step 5 Check the Results

1. Determine whether the actions in step 4 were effective:
   - Collect more data on the baseline measure from step 1.
   - Collect any other data related to the conditions at the start that might be relevant.
   - Analyze the results. Determine whether the solution tested was effective. Repeat prior steps as necessary.
2. Describe any deviations from the plan and what was learned.

Step 6 Standardize the Improvement

1. Institutionalize the improvement:
   - Develop a strategy for institutionalizing the improvement and assign responsibilities.
   - Implement the strategy and check to see that it has been successful.
2. Determine whether the improvement should be applied elsewhere and plan for its implementation.

Step 7 Establish Future Plans

1. Determine your plans for the future:
   - Decide if the gap should be narrowed further and, if so, how another project should be approached and who should be involved.
   - Identify related problems that should be addressed.
2. Summarize what you learned about the project team experience and make recommendations for future project teams.

FIGURE 7.16
Restaurant Floor Plan

Reprinted with permission from M. Gaudard, R. Coates, and L. Freeman, "Accelerating Improvement," *Quality Progress* 24, no. 10, October 1991, p. 83.

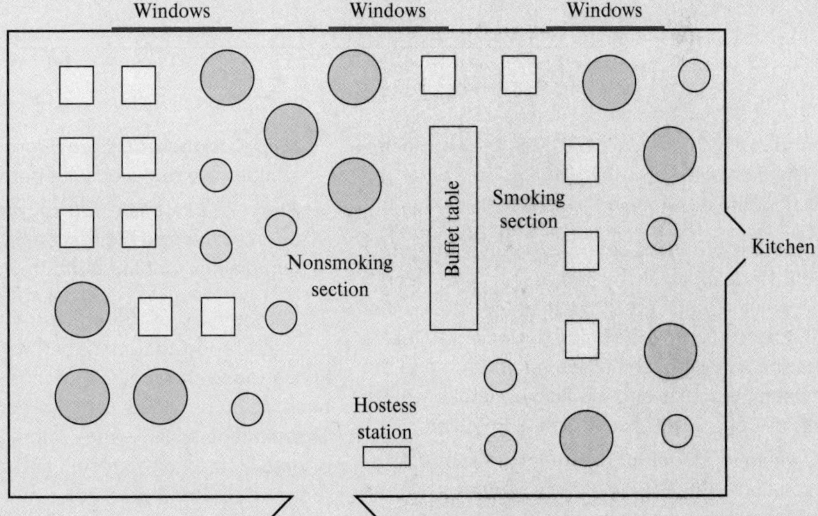

The reason for the waiting, however, is interesting. Most people are kept waiting either because no table is available or no table in the area of their preference is available. Customers seldom have to wait because a host or hostess is not available to seat them or others in their party have not yet arrived. At this point, it would be easy to jump to the conclusion that the problem could be solved just by adding more staff early in the week and during the busy hours.

The team members decide, however, that they need additional information on why these tables are not available and how seating preferences affect the waiting time. Subsequent data indicate that "unavailable" tables usually are unavailable

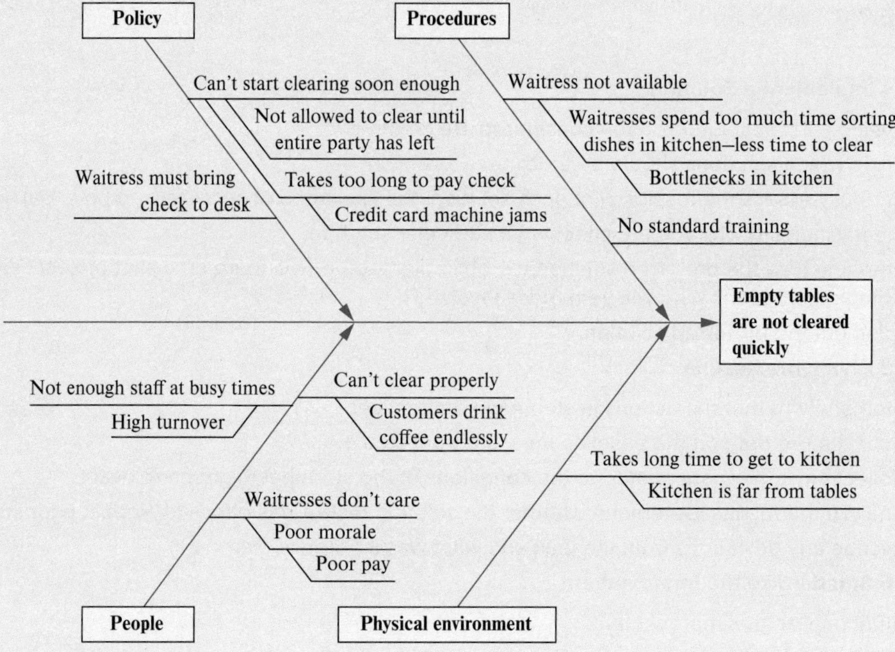

FIGURE 7.17
Cause-and-Effect Diagram Describing Why Tables Are Not Cleared Quickly

Reprinted with permission from M. Gaudard, R. Coates, and L. Freeman, "Accelerating Improvement," *Quality Progress* 24, no. 10, October 1991, p. 82.

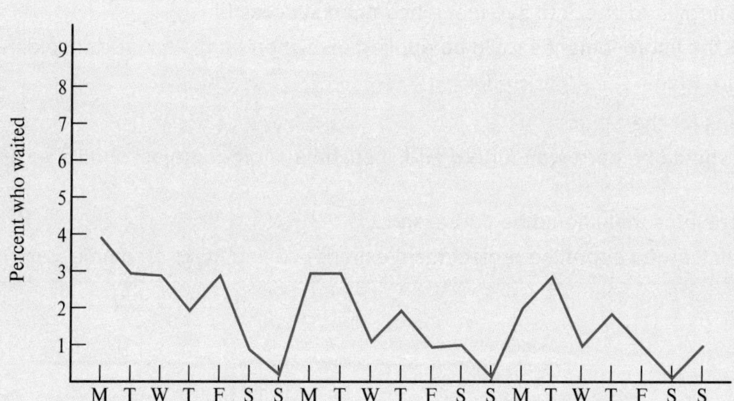

FIGURE 7.18
Run Chart of Percent of Customers Waiting More Than One Minute to Be Seated after Implementation of Solution

Reprinted with permission from M. Gaudard, R. Coates, and L. Freeman, "Accelerating Improvement," *Quality Progress* 24, no. 10, October 1991, p. 85.

because they need to be cleared, not because they are occupied by diners. The data also show that most people who wait have a preference for the nonsmoking section.

Step 3: Analyze the potential causes. A cause-and-effect diagram is constructed for "why tables are not cleared quickly," as shown in Figure 7.17. The team concludes that the most likely cause of both problems (i.e., uncleared tables and waiting for nonsmoking tables) can be attributed to the distance between the tables and the kitchen and, perhaps, to the current ratio of smoking-to-nonsmoking tables.

Step 4: Implement a solution. The team develops a list of possible solutions. Because the team cannot verify its conclusion by controlling variables, it chooses a solution that can be tested easily: set up temporary work stations in the nonsmoking area. No other changes are made, and data on the percentage of people now waiting longer than one minute to be seated are collected.

Step 5: Check the results. The team analyzes the results of data collected for one month in step 4 of the study. As Figure 7.18 shows, the improvement is dramatic.

Step 6: Standardize the improvement. The temporary work stations are replaced with permanent ones.

Step 7: Establish future plans. The team decides to address the next highest bar in the Pareto chart of customer complaints: that the buffet table is not well organized.

The authors of the article on which our Mega Bytes case is based report that managers who used SSM in various situations found the method's focus and restraint to be valuable because it provided organization, logic, and thoroughness. The managers also were impressed with the method's use of data instead of opinions, and they credited this factor with reducing territorial squabbles and promoting both cooperation and trust among team members.

While very valuable, SSM does entail some difficulties. For example, project teams have found several concepts in the first two steps very difficult to formulate. In particular, a team might have trouble developing a problem statement, because the tendency is to frame a solution as a problem. In the case of Mega Bytes, the team had to avoid identifying the problem as "There are too few servers," "There aren't enough tables," or

"The servers need to work faster." The real problem was identified correctly as "The customers must wait too long."

Another concept that has been difficult for study teams is localization, which is a process of focusing on smaller and smaller vital pieces of the problem. This concept initially proved difficult because team members had not yet internalized the idea that improvement should be driven by customer requirements.

Some study teams have experienced an assortment of other difficulties. Occasionally, team members could not see the benefit of collecting data accurately, or they did not understand how baseline data would be used to validate a solution. Some members had trouble keeping an open mind and, consequently, resisted investigating the effects of variables they felt to be irrelevant. In some cases, members had to learn new skills, such as how to obtain information in a nonthreatening way from workers in the system. Finally, organizational problems such as arranging meeting times and getting support from coworkers had to be resolved as well.

Questions

1. How is SSM different from Deming's PDCA cycle?
2. Prepare a cause-and-effect or fishbone diagram for a problem such as "Why customers have long waits for coffee." Your fishbone diagram should be similar to that in Figure 7.17, using the main sources of cause: policy, procedure, people, and physical environment.
3. How would you resolve the difficulties that study teams have experienced when applying SSM?

Chapter 7 Supplement

Data Envelopment Analysis (DEA)

How can corporate management evaluate the productivity of a fast-food outlet, a branch bank, a health clinic, or an elementary school? The difficulties in measuring productivity are threefold. First, what are the appropriate inputs to the system (e.g., labor hours, material dollars) and the measures of those inputs? Second, what are the appropriate outputs of the system (e.g., checks cashed, certificate of deposits) and the measures of those outputs? Third, what are the appropriate ways of measuring the relationship between these inputs and outputs?

Measuring Service Productivity

The measure of an organization's productivity, if viewed from an engineering perspective, is similar to the measure of a system's efficiency. It can be stated as a ratio of outputs to inputs (e.g., miles per gallon for an automobile).

To evaluate the operational efficiency of a branch bank, for example, an accounting ratio such as cost per teller transaction might be used. A branch with a high ratio in comparison with those of other branches would be considered less efficient, but the higher ratio could result from a more complex mix of transactions. For example, a branch opening new accounts and selling CDs would require more time per transaction than another branch engaged only in simple transactions such as accepting deposits and cashing checks. The problem with using simple ratios is that the mix of outputs is not considered explicitly. This same criticism also can be made concerning the mix of inputs. For example, some branches might have automated teller machines in addition to live tellers, and this use of technology could affect the cost per teller transaction.

Broad-based measures such as profitability or return on investment are highly relevant as overall performance measures, but they are not sufficient to evaluate the operating efficiency of a service unit. For instance, one could not conclude that a profitable branch bank is necessarily efficient in its use of personnel and other inputs. A higher than-average proportion of revenue-generating transactions could be the explanation rather than the cost-efficient use of resources.

The DEA Model

Fortunately, a technique has been developed with the ability to compare the efficiency of multiple service units that provide similar services by explicitly considering their use of multiple inputs (i.e., resources) to produce multiple outputs (i.e., services). The technique, which is referred to as *data envelopment analysis (DEA),* circumvents the need to develop standard costs for each service, because it can incorporate multiple inputs and multiple outputs into both the numerator and the denominator of the efficiency ratio without the need for conversion to a common dollar basis. Thus, the DEA measure of efficiency explicitly accounts for the mix of inputs and outputs and, consequently, is more comprehensive and reliable than a set of operating ratios or profit measures.

DEA is a linear programming model that attempts to maximize a service unit's efficiency, expressed as a ratio of outputs to inputs, by comparing a particular unit's efficiency with the performance of a group of similar service units that are delivering the same service. In the process, some units achieve 100 percent efficiency and are referred to as the *relatively efficient units,* whereas other units with efficiency ratings of less than 100 percent are referred to as *inefficient units.*

Corporate management thus can use DEA to compare a group of service units to identify relatively inefficient units, measure the magnitude of the inefficiencies, and by comparing the inefficient with the efficient ones, discover ways to reduce those inefficiencies.

The DEA linear programming model is formulated according to Charnes, Cooper, and Rhodes, and is referred to as the CCR Model.[9]

Definition of Variables

Let E_k, with $k = 1, 2, \ldots, K$, be the efficiency ratio of unit k, where K is the total number of units being evaluated.

Let u_j, with $j = 1, 2, \ldots, M$, be a coefficient for output j, where M is the total number of output types considered. The variable u_j is a measure of the relative decrease in efficiency with each unit reduction of output value.

Let v_i, with $i = 1, 2, \ldots, N$, be a coefficient for input i, where N is the total number of input types considered. The variable v_i is a measure of the relative increase in efficiency with each unit reduction of input value.

Let O_{jk} be the number of observed units of output j generated by service unit k during one time period.

Let I_{ik} be the number of actual units of input i used by service unit k during one time period.

Objective Function

The objective is to find the set of coefficient u's associated with each output and of v's associated with each input that will give the service unit being evaluated the highest possible efficiency.

$$\max E_e = \frac{u_1 O_{1e} + u_2 O_{2e} + \cdots + u_M O_{Me}}{v_1 I_{1e} + v_2 I_{2e} + \cdots + v_N I_{Ne}} \qquad \textbf{(3)}$$

where e is the index of the unit being evaluated.

This function is subject to the constraint that when the same set of input and output coefficients (u_j's and y_i's) is applied to all other service units being compared, no service unit will exceed 100 percent efficiency or a ratio of 1.0.

Constraints

$$\frac{u_1 O_{1e} + u_2 O_{2e} + \cdots + u_M O_{Me}}{v_1 I_e + v_2 I_{2e} + \cdots + v_N I_{Ne}} \leq 1.0 \qquad k = 1, 2, \ldots, K \qquad \textbf{(4)}$$

where all coefficient values are positive and nonzero.

To solve this fractional linear programming model using standard linear programming software requires a reformulation. Note that both the objective function and all constraints are ratios rather than linear functions. The objective function in equation (3) is restated as a linear function by arbitrarily scaling the inputs for the unit under evaluation to a sum of 1.0.

$$\max E_e = u_1 O_{1e} + u_2 O_{2e} + \cdots + u_M O_{Me} \tag{5}$$

subject to the constraint that

$$v_1 I_{1e} + v_2 I_{2e} + \cdots + v_N I_{Ne} = 1 \tag{6}$$

For each service unit, the constraints in equation (2) are similarly reformulated:

$$u_1 O_{1k} + u_2 O_{2k} + \cdots + u_M O_{Mk} - (v_1 I_{1k} + v_2 I_{2k} + \cdots + v_N I_{Nk}) \leq 0 \qquad k = 1, 2, \ldots, K \tag{7}$$

where

$$u_j \geq 0 \qquad j = 1, 2, \ldots, M$$
$$v_i \geq 0 \qquad i = 1, 2, \ldots, N$$

Sample Size

A question of sample size often is raised concerning the number of service units that are required compared with the number of input and output variables selected in the analysis. The following relationship relating the number of service units K used in the analysis and the number of input N and output M types being considered is based on empirical findings and the experience of DEA practitioners:

$$K \geq 2(N + M) \tag{8}$$

Example 7.3 Burger Palace

An innovative drive-in-only burger chain has established six units in several different cities. Each unit is located in a strip shopping center parking lot. Only a standard meal consisting of a burger, fries, and a drink is available. Management has decided to use DEA to improve productivity by identifying which units are using their resources most efficiently and then sharing their experience and knowledge with the less efficient locations. Table 7.5 summarizes data for two inputs: labor-hours and material dollars consumed during a typical lunch hour period to generate an output of 100 meals sold. Normally, output will vary among the service units, but in this example, we have made the outputs equal to allow for a graphical presentation of the units' productivity. As Figure 7.19 shows, service units S_1, S_3, and S_6 have been joined to form an efficient-production frontier of alternative methods of using labor hours and material resources to generate 100 meals. As can be seen, these efficient units have defined an envelope that contains all the inefficient units—thus the reason for calling the process "data envelopment analysis."

For this simple example, we can identify efficient units by inspection and see the excess inputs being used by inefficient units (e.g., S_2 would be as efficient as S_3 if it used $50 less in

TABLE 7.5
Summary of Outputs and Inputs for Burger Palace

Service Unit	Meals Sold	Labor-Hours	Material Dollars
1	100	2	200
2	100	4	150
3	100	4	100
4	100	6	100
5	100	8	80
6	100	10	50

FIGURE 7.19
Productivity Frontier of Burger Palace

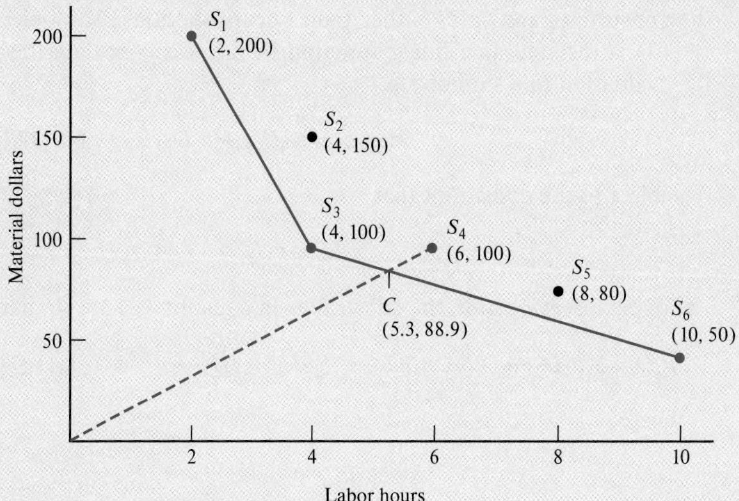

materials). To gain an understanding of DEA, however, we will proceed to formulate the linear programming problems for each unit, then solve each of them to determine efficiency ratings and other information.

We begin by illustrating the LP formulation for the first service unit, S_1, using equations (5), (6), and (7).

$$
\begin{aligned}
&\max E(S_1) = u_1 100\\
&\text{subject to}\\
&u_1 100 - v_1 2 - v_2 200 \leq 0\\
&u_1 100 - v_1 4 - v_2 150 \leq 0\\
&u_1 100 - v_1 4 - v_2 100 \leq 0\\
&u_1 100 - v_1 6 - v_2 100 \leq 0\\
&u_1 100 - v_1 8 - v_2 80 \leq 0\\
&u_1 100 - v_1 10 - v_2 50 \leq 0\\
&v_1 2 + v_2 200 = 1\\
&u_1, u_2, v_2 \geq 0
\end{aligned}
$$

Similar linear programming problems are formulated (or, better yet, the S_1 linear programming problem is edited) and solved for the other service units by substituting the appropriate output function for the objective function and substituting the appropriate input function for the last constraint. Constraints 1 through 6, which restrict all units to no more than 100 percent efficiency, remain the same in all problems.

This set of six linear programming problems was solved with Excel Solver 7.0 in fewer than five minutes by editing the data file between each run. Because the output is 100 meals for all units, only the last constraint must be edited by substituting the appropriate labor and material input values from Table 7.5 for the unit being evaluated.

The data file for unit 1 of Burger Palace using a linear programming Excel add-in is shown in Figure 7.20. The linear programming results for each unit are shown in Table 7.6 and summarized in Table 7.7.

In Table 7.6, we find that DEA has identified the same units shown as being efficient in Figure 7.19. Units S_2, S_4, and S_5 all are inefficient in varying degrees. Also shown in Table 7.6 and associated with each inefficient unit is an *efficiency reference set*. Each inefficient unit will have a set of efficient units associated with it that defines its productivity. As Figure 7.19 shows for inefficient unit S_4, the efficient units S_3 and S_6 have been joined with a line defining the efficiency frontier. A dashed line drawn from the origin to inefficient unit S_4 cuts through this frontier and, thus, defines unit S_4 as inefficient. In Table 7.7, the value in parentheses that is associated with each member of the efficiency reference set (i.e., .7778 for S_3 and .2222 for S_6) represents the relative weight assigned to that efficient unit in calculating

TABLE 7.6 LP Solutions for DEA Study of Burger Palace

Summarized results for unit 1 — Page: 1

Variables No.	Variables Names	Solutions	Opportunity costs	Variables No.	Variables Names	Solutions	Opportunity costs
1	U1	+1.0000000	0	6	S3	0	0
2	V1	+.16666667	0	7	S4	+33.333336	0
3	V2	+.00333333	0	8	S5	+60.000000	0
4	S1	0	+1.0000000	9	S6	+83.333336	0
5	S2	+16.666670	0	10	A7	0	+100.00000

Maximized objective function = 100 Iterations = 4

Summarized results for unit 2 — Page: 1

Variables No.	Variables Names	Solutions	Opportunity costs	Variables No.	Variables Names	Solutions	Opportunity costs
1	U1	+.85714287	0	6	S3	0	+.71428573
2	V1	+.14285715	0	7	S4	+28.571430	0
3	V2	+.00285714	0	8	S5	+51.428574	0
4	S1	0	+0.28571430	9	S6	+71.428574	0
5	S2	+14.285717	0	10	A7	0	+85.714287

Maximized objective function = 85.71429 Iterations = 4

Summarized results for unit 3 — Page: 1

Variables No.	Variables Names	Solutions	Opportunity costs	Variables No.	Variables Names	Solutions	Opportunity costs
1	U1	+1.0000000	0	6	S3	0	+1.0000000
2	V1	+.06250000	0	7	S4	+12.500000	0
3	V2	+.00750000	0	8	S5	+10.000001	0
4	S1	+62.500000	0	9	S6	0	0
5	S2	+37.500008	0	10	A7	0	+100.00000

Maximized objective function = 100 Iterations = 3

Summarized results for unit 4 — Page: 1

Variables No.	Variables Names	Solutions	Opportunity costs	Variables No.	Variables Names	Solutions	Opportunity costs
1	U1	+.88888890	0	6	S3	0	+.77777779
2	V1	+.05555556	0	7	S4	+11.111112	0
3	V2	+.00666667	0	8	S5	+8.8888893	0
4	S1	+55.555553	0	9	S6	0	+.22222224
5	S2	+33.333340	0	10	A7	0	+88.888885

Maximized objective function = 88.88889 Iterations = 3

Summarized results for unit 5 — Page: 1

Variables No.	Variables Names	Solutions	Opportunity costs	Variables No.	Variables Names	Solutions	Opportunity costs
1	U1	+.90909088	0	6	S3	0	+.45454547
2	V1	+.05681818	0	7	S4	+11.363637	0
3	V2	+.00681818	0	8	S5	+9.0909100	0
4	S1	+56.818180	0	9	S6	0	+.54545450
5	S2	+34.090916	0	10	A7	0	+90.909088

Maximized objective function = 90.90909 Iterations = 4

(continued)

TABLE 7.6 *(continued)*

Summarized results for unit 6							Page: 1
Variables				Variables			
No.	Names	Solutions	Opportunity costs	No.	Names	Solutions	Opportunity costs
1	U1	+1.0000000	0	6	S3	0	0
2	V1	+.06250000	0	7	S4	+12.500000	0
3	V2	+.00750000	0	8	S5	+10.000001	0
4	S1	+62.500000	0	9	S6	0	+1.0000000
5	S2	+37.500008	0	10	A7	0	+100.00000
		Maximized objective function = 100				Iterations = 4	

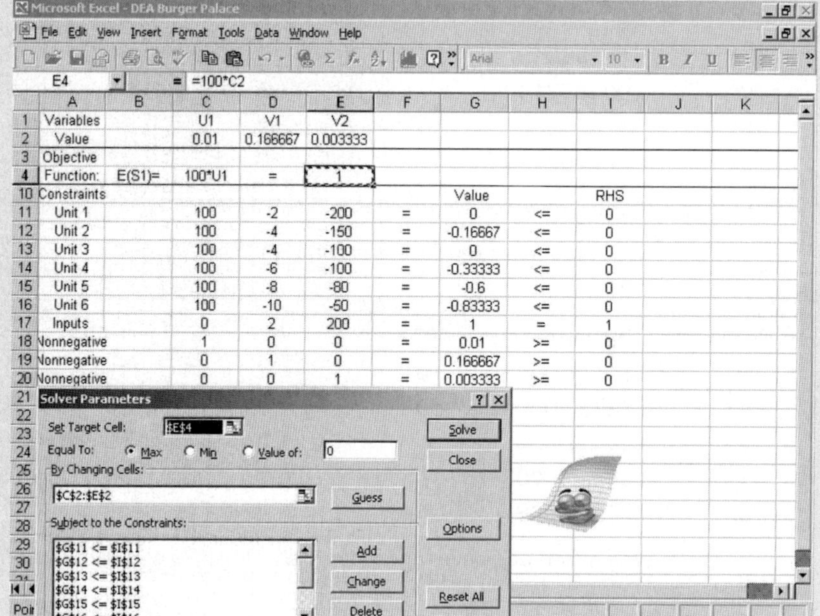

FIGURE 7.20
Excel Data File for DEA Analysis of Burger Palace Unit 1

the efficiency rating for S_4. These relative weights are the shadow prices that are associated with the respective efficient-unit constraints in the linear programming solution. (Note in Table 7.6 that for unit 4, these weights appear as opportunity costs for S_3 and S_6.)

The values for v_1 and v_2 that are associated with the inputs of labor-hours and materials, respectively, measure the relative increase in efficiency with each unit reduction of input value. For unit S_4, each unit decrease in labor-hours results in an efficiency increase of 0.0555. For unit S_4 to become efficient, it must increase its efficiency rating by 0.111 points. This can be accomplished by reducing labor used by 2 hours (i.e., 2 hours $\times$ 0.0555 = 0.111). Note that with this reduction in labor-hours, unit S_4 becomes identical to efficient unit S_3. An alternative approach would be a reduction in materials used by $16.57 (i.e., 0.111/0.0067 = 16.57). Any linear combination of these two measures also would move unit S_4 to the productivity frontier defined by the line segment joining efficient units S_3 and S_6.

Table 7.8 contains the calculations for a hypothetical unit C, which is a composite reference unit defined by the weighted inputs of the reference set S_3 and S_6. As Figure 7.19 shows, this composite unit C is located at the intersection of the productivity frontier and the dashed line drawn from the origin to unit S_4. Thus, compared with this reference unit C, inefficient unit S_4 is using excess inputs in the amounts of 0.7 labor-hour and 11.1 material dollars.

TABLE 7.7
Summary of DEA Results

Service Unit	Efficiency Rating (E)	Efficiency Reference Set	Relative Labor-Hour Value (V_1)	Relative Material Value (V_2)
S_1	1.000	N.A.	0.1667	0.0033
S_2	0.857	S_1 (0.2857)	0.1428	0.0028
		S_3 (0.7143)		
S_3	1.000	N.A.	0.0625	0.0075
S_4	0.889	S_3 (0.7778)	0.0555	0.0067
		S_6 (0.2222)		
S_5	0.901	S_3 (0.4545)	0.0568	0.0068
		S_6 (0.5454)		
S_6	1.000	N.A.	0.0625	0.0075

TABLE 7.8
Calculation of Excess Inputs Used by Unit S_4

Outputs and Inputs	Reference Set		Composite Reference Unit C	S_4	Excess Inputs Used
	S_3	S_6			
Meals	(0.7778) × 100	+ (0.2222) × 100 =	100	100	0
Labor-hours	(0.7778) × 4	+ (0.2222) × 10 =	5.3	6	0.7
Material ($)	(0.7778) × 100	+ (0.2222) × 50 =	88.9	100	11.1

DEA offers many opportunities for an inefficient unit to become efficient regarding its reference set of efficient units. In practice, management would choose a particular approach on the basis of an evaluation of its cost, practicality, and feasibility; however, the motivation for change is clear (i.e., other units actually are able to achieve similar outputs with fewer resources).

DEA and Strategic Planning

When combined with profitability, DEA efficiency analysis can be useful in strategic planning for services that are delivered through multiple sites (e.g., hotel chains).

Figure 7.21 presents a matrix of four possibilities that arise from combining efficiency and profitability.

Considering the top-left quadrant of this matrix (i.e., underperforming potential stars) reveals that units operating at a high profit may be operating inefficiently and, thus, have unrealized potential. Comparing these with similar efficient units could suggest measures that would lead to even greater profit through more efficient operations.

FIGURE 7.21
DEA Strategic Matrix

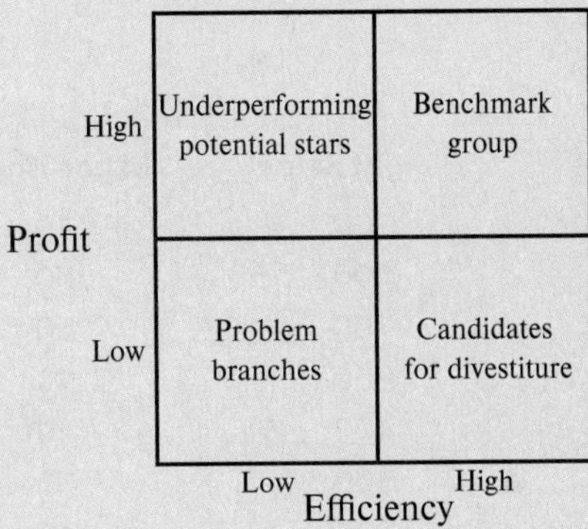

Star performers can be found in the top-right quadrant (i.e., benchmark group). These efficient units also are highly profitable and, thus, serve as examples for others to emulate in both operations efficiency and marketing success in generating high revenues.

The lower-right quadrant (i.e., candidates for divestiture) contains efficient but unprofitable units. These units are limited in profit potential, perhaps because of a poor location, and should be sold to generate capital for expansion in new territories.

It is not clear which strategy to employ with the lower-left quadrant units (i.e., problem branches). If profit potential is limited, investments in efficient operations might lead to a future candidate for divestiture.

Exercises

7.1. For the Burger Palace example, perform a complete analysis of efficiency improvement alternatives for unit S_2, including determination of a composite reference unit.

7.2. For the Burger Palace example, perform a complete analysis of efficiency improvment alternatives for unit S_5, including determination of a composite reference unit.

7.3. For the Burger Palace example, what is the effect of removing an inefficient unit from the analysis (e.g., S_2)?

7.4. For the Burger Palace example, what is the effect of removing an efficient unit from the analysis (e.g., S_6)?

Mid-Atlantic Bus Lines — CASE 7.3

Mid-Atlantic Bus Lines was founded by a group of managers from Trailways when that company was acquired by Greyhound. They launched a first-class, express bus service operating between the major coastal cities from Philadelphia, Pennsylvania, to Jacksonville, Florida. By hiring laid-off Trailways drivers and leasing buses, they established franchises in each city with local entrepreneurs, who were given the right to operate a Mid-Atlantic bus terminal. A percentage of the passenger ticket sales and freight sales would be kept by the terminal operator to cover his or her costs and profit.

After several months of operation, some franchisees complained about inadequate profits and threatened to close their terminals. Because other franchisees were pleased with their experiences, however, a study of all terminal operations in the system was undertaken. The information in Table 7.9 was collected over several weeks and represents a typical day's operation.

Questions

1. Use DEA to identify efficient and inefficient terminal operations. Formulate the problem as a linear programming model, and solve using computer software such as Excel Solver that permits input file editing between runs.
2. Using the appropriate reference set of efficient terminals, make recommendations for changes in resource inputs for each inefficient terminal.
3. What recommendations would you have for the one seriously inefficient terminal in regard to increasing its outputs?
4. Discuss any shortcomings in the application of DEA to Mid-Atlantic Bus Lines.

TABLE 7.9 **Outputs and Inputs for Mid-Atlantic Bus Lines**

Bus Depot	City Served	Ticket Sales	Freight Sales	Labor-Hours	Facility Dollars
1	Philadelphia, PA	700	300	40	500
2	Baltimore, MD	300	600	50	500
3	Washington, DC	200	700	50	400
4	Richmond, VA	400	600	50	500
5	Raleigh, NC	500	400	40	400
6	Charleston, SC	500	500	50	500
7	Savannah, GA	800	500	40	600
8	Jacksonville, FL	300	200	30	400

Selected Bibliography

Anand, Alan Gopesh, Peter T. Ward, and Mohan V. Tatikonda. "Role of Explicit and Tacit Knowledge in Six Sigma Projects: An Empirical Examination of Different Project Success." *Journal of Operations Management* 28, no. 4 (July 2010), pp. 303–15.

Banker, Rajiv D., A. Charnes, and W. W. Cooper. "Some Models for Estimating Technical and Scale Inefficiencies in Data Envelopment Analysis." *Management Science* 30, no. 9 (September 1984), pp. 1078–92.

Brenner, Mary J., and Francisco M. Veloso. "ISO 9000 Practices and Financial Performance: A Technology Coherence Perspective." *Journal of Operations Management* 26, no. 5 (September 2008), pp. 611–29.

Chakraborty, Ayon, and Tan Kay Chuan. "An Empirical Analysis on Six Sigma Implementation in Service Organisations." *International Journal of Lean Six Sigma* 4, no. 2 (2013), pp. 141–70.

Cooper, W. W., L. M. Seiford, and K. Tone. *Introduction to Data Envelopment Analysis with DEA-Solver Code and References.* New York: Springer, 2006.

Drotz, Erik, and Bozena Poksinska. "Lean in Healthcare from Employees' Perspectives." *Journal of Health Organization and Management* 28, no. 2 (2014), pp. 177–95.

Gabow, Patricia A., and Philip L. Goodman. *The Lean Prescription: Powerful Medicine for Our Ailing Healthcare System.* London: CRC Press, 2014.

George, Michael L., David Rowlands, and Bill Kastle. *What Is Lean Six Sigma?* New York: McGraw-Hill, 2003.

LaGanga, Linda R. "Lean Service Operations: Reflections and New Directions for Capacity Expansion in Outpatient Clinics." *Journal of Operations Management* 29, no. 5 (July 2011), pp. 422–33.

Martinez-Costa, Micaela, et al. "ISO 9000/1994, ISO 9001/2000 and TQM: The Performance Debate Revisited." *Journal of Operations Management* 27, no. 6 (December 2009), pp. 495–511.

Nair, Anand, Manoj K. Malhotra, and Sanjay L. Ahire. "Toward a Theory of Managing Context in Six Sigma Process-Improvement Projects: An Action Research Investigation." *Journal of Operations Management* 29, no. 5 (July 2011), pp. 529–48.

Psychogios, Alexandros G., Jane Atanasovski, and Loukas K. Tsironis. "Lean Six Sigma in a Service Context: A Multifactor Application Approach in the Telecommunications Industry." *International Journal of Quality & Reliability Management* 29, no. 1 (2012), pp. 122–39.

Schroeder, Roger G., et al. "Six Sigma: Definition and Underlying Theory." *Journal of Operations Management* 26, no. 4 (July 2008), pp. 536–54.

Shah, Rachna, and Peter T. Ward. "Defining and Developing Measures of Lean Production." *Journal of Operations Management* 25, no. 4 (June 2007), pp. 785–805.

Singh, Prakash J., Damien Power, and Sum Chee Chuong. "A Resource Dependence Theory Perspective of ISO 9000 in Managing Organizational Environment." *Journal of Operations Management* 29, no. 1 (January 2011), pp. 49–64.

Staats, Bradley R., David James Brunner, and David M. Upton. "Lean Principles, Learning, and Knowledge Work: Evidence from a Software Service Provider." *Journal of Operations Management* 29, no. 5 (July 2011), pp. 376–90.

White, Sheneeta W., and Sanjeev K. Bordoloi. "A Review of DEA-based Resource and Cost Allocation Models: Implications for Services." *International Journal of Services and Operations Management* 20, no. 1 (2014), pp. 86–101.

Wickramasinghe, Nilmini. "Lean Principles for Healthcare." In *Lean Thinking for Healthcare.* Eds. Nilmini Wickramasinghe et al. New York: Springer, 2014. pp. 3–11.

Zu, Xingxing, Lawrence D. Fredendall, and Thomas J Douglas. "The Evolving Theory of Quality Management: The Role of Six Sigma." *Journal of Operations Management* 26, no. 5 (September 2008), pp. 630–50.

Endnotes

1. David Wessel, "With Labor Scarce, Service Firms Strive to Raise Productivity," *The Wall Street Journal,* June 1, 1989, p. 1.
2. Michael Brassard and Diane Ritter, *The Memory Jogger II* (Methuen, MA: GOAL/QPC 1994), pp. 115–31.
3. D. Daryl Wyckoff, "New Tools for Achieving Service Quality," *Cornell HRA Quarterly* 25, no. 3 (November 1984), pp. 78–91.
4. W. Edwards Deming, *Quality, Productivity, and Competitive Position* (Cambridge, MA: MIT Center for Advanced Engineering Study, 1982).
5. http://www.isixsigma.com.
6. http://www.leanmanufacturingtools.org/551/creating-a-value-stream-map/.
7. James P. Womack, "An Action Plan for Lean Services," presentation at Lean Service Summit, Amsterdam, June 23, 2004.
8. Reprinted and selectively adapted with permission from M. Gaudard, R. Coates, and L. Freeman, "Accelerating Improvement," *Quality Progress* 24, no. 10 (October 1991), pp. 81–88.
9. A. Charnes, W. W. Cooper, and E. Rhodes, "Measuring the Efficiency of Decision Making Units," *European Journal of Operations Research* 2, no. 6 (November 1978), pp. 429–44. (The "CCR" Model.)

Chapter 

Service Facility Location

Learning Objectives

After completing this chapter, you should be able to:

1. Explain the difference between competitive clustering and saturation marketing.
2. Explain the impact of the Internet on location decisions.
3. Describe how a geographic information system is used in service location decisions.
4. Differentiate between a Euclidian and metropolitan metric approach to measuring travel distance.
5. Locate a single facility using the cross-median approach.
6. Use the Huff retail location model to estimate revenue and market share for a potential site.
7. Locate multiple facilities using the set covering model.

The ability to take organizational data and apply geographic location empowers decision making and becomes what MapInfoPro™ [a geographic information system (GIS) offered by Pitney Bowes] calls *location intelligence.* The integration of location into daily operations helps organizations to achieve significant analytical and operational advantage. Location intelligence can help answer questions such as where the next store should be located, where the markets are vulnerable to competition, and where assets like cell towers or ATM machines should be placed.

When a franchisee invests in a new business, the contract will set out the territory and number of homes within that territory. Franchise areas and associated purchase prices are determined by the number of reachable households, overlaid with socioeconomic data. However, accurate geographical data is essential to resolve disputes over territory infringement. For example, MapInfoPro™ is able to validate address accuracy quickly and defuse franchisee disputes. Also, up-to-date street information allows Domino's to increase delivery reach by accounting for new housing and thus to focus direct marketing efforts. Using up-to-date address information, a Domino's dispatcher can direct telephone orders to the nearest store thereby reducing delivery times. Implementation of the program has allowed Domino's to manage and update territories quickly. Unknown addresses are now a thing of the past. The real winner is the customer with improved ordering experience and fast delivery.[1]

Chapter Preview

This chapter begins with a discussion of strategic location considerations. For example, the strategies of competitive clustering or saturation marketing are used to attract customers to a service site. Other service delivery strategies, such as using marketing intermediaries and the Internet, remove the need for customer travel and, thus, a decision on site location can be based on other considerations, such as cost or availability of skilled labor. Geographic information (i.e., demand and its characteristics distributed across a market area) is an essential input to location models. The chapter concludes with a discussion of modeling considerations and a review of several facility location techniques for both single- and multiple-facility situations.

Strategic Location Considerations

In a study of La Quinta Motor Inns to learn why some inns were successful and others not, several strategic location dimensions were discovered including flexibility, competitive positioning, demand management, and focus.[2]

Flexibility of a location is a measure of the degree to which the service can react to changing economic situations. Because location decisions are long-term commitments with capital-intensive aspects, it is essential to select locations that can be responsive to future economic, demographic, cultural, and competitive changes. For example, locating sites in a number of states could reduce the overall risk of a financial crisis resulting from regional economic downturns. This portfolio approach to multisite location could be augmented by selecting individual sites near inelastic demand (e.g., locating a hotel near a convention center).

Competitive positioning refers to methods by which the firm can establish itself relative to its competitors. Multiple locations can serve as a barrier to competition through building a firm's competitive position and establishing a market awareness. Acquiring and holding prime locations before the market has developed can keep the competition from gaining access to these desirable locations and create an artificial barrier to entry (analogous to a product patent).

Demand management is the ability to control the quantity, quality, and timing of demand. For example, hotels cannot manipulate capacity effectively because of the fixed nature of the facility; however, a hotel can control demand by locating near a diverse set of market generators that supply a steady demand regardless of the economic condition, the day of the week, or the season.

Focus can be developed by offering the same narrowly defined service at many locations. Many multisite service firms develop a standard (or formula) facility that can be duplicated at many locations. While this "cookie-cutter" approach makes expansion easier, sites that are located in close proximity could siphon business from each other. This problem of demand cannibalization can be avoided if a firm establishes a pattern of desired growth for its multisite expansion.

In the following discussion, we will look at additional strategic location considerations beginning with the concept called competitive clustering, which is used for shopping goods, as well as a strategy called saturation marketing that defies the curse of cannibalization. Other strategies extend the service market beyond the confines of geography using *marketing intermediaries*, substitution of communication for travel, physical separation of front from back office operations, and finally the use of the Internet to reach a global audience.

Competitive Clustering

Competitive clustering is a reaction to observed consumer behavior when they are choosing among competitors. When shopping for items such as new automobiles or used cars, customers like to make comparisons and, for convenience, seek out the area of town where many dealers are concentrated (i.e., the so-called motor mile).

Motel chains such as La Quinta have observed that inns located in areas with many nearby competitors experience higher occupancy rates than those located in isolation. Sometimes, locating near the competition is a surprising strategy that yields profitable counterintuitive results for some services.

Saturation Marketing

Au Bon Pain, a café known for its gourmet sandwiches, French bread, and croissants, has embraced the unconventional strategy of *saturation marketing* popularized in Europe.

Auto dealers that locate in clusters attract customers from afar because of the convenience of one-stop comparison shopping. ©Bob Daemmrich/The Image Works

The idea is to group outlets of the same firm tightly in urban and other high-traffic areas. Au Bon Pain has clustered about 25 cafés in the Boston area alone, with many of them fewer than 100 yards apart–in fact, one group of five shops operated on different floors of the old Filene's department store. Although modest cannibalization of sales was reported, the advantages of reduced advertising, easier supervision, and customer awareness, when taken together, overwhelm the competition and far outweigh the drawbacks. This strategy works best in high-density, downtown locations, where shops can intercept impulse customers with little time to shop or eat.[3]

The success of this approach became apparent to the authors during a summer visit to Helsinki, Finland, where we noticed ice cream vendors from the same firm with carts on nearly every corner of the downtown walking streets. The sight of a vendor seems to plant the idea of a treat in the mind of a passerby, who then takes advantage of the next, nearby opportunity.

Marketing Intermediaries

The idea that services are created and consumed simultaneously does not seem to allow for the "channel-of-distribution" concept as developed for goods. Because services are intangible and cannot be stored or transported, the geographic area for service would seem to be restricted. However, service channels of distribution have evolved that use separate organizational entities as intermediaries between the producer and the consumer.

James H. Donnelly provides a number of examples that illustrate how some services have created unlimited geographic service areas.[4] The retailer who extends a bank's credit to its customers is an intermediary in the distribution of credit. Citibank does not limit use of its Visa card to purchases at Costco; it is honored by merchants worldwide. A health maintenance organization (HMO) performs an intermediary role between the practitioner and the patient by increasing the availability and convenience of "one-stop" shopping, and group insurance written through employers and labor unions is an example of how the insurance industry uses intermediaries to distribute its service.

Substitution of Communication for Travel

An appealing alternative to moving people from one place to another is the use of telecommunications. One proposal that has met with some success is the use of telemetry to extend health care services into remote regions. Sometimes paramedics or nurse practitioners can use communication with a distant hospital to provide health care without transporting the patient. In addition, the banking industry has promoted direct payroll

TABLE 8.1
Considerations in Locating the Front and Back Office

	Front Office	Back Office
External Customer (consumer)	Is travel out to customer or customer travel to site?	Is service performed on person or property?
	Is location a barrier to entry? Can electronic media substitute for physical travel?	Is colocation necessary? How is communication accomplished?
Internal Customer (employee)	Availability of labor?	Are economies of scale possible?
	Are self-service kiosks an alternative?	Can employees work from home?
		Is offshoring an option?

deposit, which permits employees to have their pay deposited directly into their checking accounts. By authorizing employers to deposit salaries, the employees save trips to the bank; bankers also benefit through reduced check-processing and less congestion at their drive-in teller facilities.

Separation of Front from Back Office

For many services the front and back office need not be colocated (e.g., dry cleaning, shoe repair, and store front banks). As shown in Table 8.1, thinking in terms of separating the front from the back office can yield strategic benefits.

If the front office and back office need not be colocated, opportunities exist for creative service design. When you place a drive-in order at a Texas McDonald's, for example, the order taker might be located at a call center in Iowa. Taking orders from several stores at a central location allows the local employees to concentrate on filling the order. Viewing location decisions from both an internal (employee) and external (customer) perspective also highlights opportunities for self-service and substitution of electronic media for physical travel. Notice the strategic role of front office location in creating a barrier to entry and the back office location in achieving cost economies.

Impact of the Internet on Service Location

With the advent of the Internet, the potential for electronic commerce has become a reality–customers shop from a desk at home and surf the web for interesting sites to visit. A website has become the virtual location of pure e-commerce firms (e.g., Amazon.com) or an alternative channel of distribution for established click-and-mortar retailers (e.g., Barnes & Noble). The limits of a market area once were defined by how far a customer would travel to the site, but physical travel is irrelevant in the virtual world of the Internet. Location, however, is still a concern for e-commerce retailers that must ship a product. This aspect of a business is now driven by access to overnight shippers (e.g., locating a warehouse in Memphis for access to FedEx). Internet providers of electronic services, such as brokers (e.g., Fidelity.com), are less reliant on physical offices, and the location of an auction facilitator (e.g., eBay.com) can be based on personal preference of the owners or on access to talented employees. Finally, the Internet facilitates 24/7 access to call centers located strategically around the world. Each center (e.g., India, Ireland, and Jamaica) operates a normal daylight shift staffed with educated English literate low-wage labor.

The concept of *e-distance*, the barrier created by internal and external navigation, arises from the desire to attract customers to a website. For example, an undiscovered website is infinitely distant and one that is five clicks away might rule out 90 percent of the public. Site navigation is a measure of distance, so web developers often use a two-click rule, that is, a customer's destination should be no more than two clicks away from the homepage. Locating and getting to the website is another form of distance. If a customer uses a search engine, he or she still needs to read, evaluate, and select a link to follow.

TABLE 8.2
Site Selection Considerations

1. *Access:* Convenient to freeway exit and entrance ramps Served by public transportation	5. *Expansion:* Room for expansion
2. *Visibility:* Set back from street Sign placement	6. *Environment:* Immediate surroundings should complement the service
3. *Traffic:* Traffic volume on street that may indicate potential impulse buying Traffic congestion that could be a hindrance (e.g., fire stations)	7. *Competition:* Location of competitors
4. *Parking:* Adequate off-street parking	8. *Government:* Zoning restrictions Taxes
	9. *Labor:* Available labor with appropriate skills
	10. *Complements:* Complementary services nearby

Julie Kendall reports on a study of small off-Broadway theaters in southern New Jersey that are unable to take advantage of the "competitive clustering" strategy because no central theater district exists.[5] Theaters are scattered across eight counties and getting potential audiences to realize they exist is a challenge. A shared website, however, allows a potential patron to browse the available plays with direct links to each theater for ticket purchase and seat selection. The shared website reduces the e-distance of theater patrons from that of searching several individual websites to visiting a single site. The result is a virtual application of the competitive clustering strategy in which the attraction of patrons is increased for all theaters.

Site Considerations

Available real estate represents a major constraint on the final selection of a site. Moreover, site selection requires a physical visit to assess the local environment (e.g., observing if the locale is upscale enough for a luxury hotel). Table 8.2 contains many physical attributes to consider such as access, visibility, and traffic that are important to attracting customers to the site. The nearby location of competitors often is desirable as noted in our discussion of competitive clustering. Another consideration is the existence of complementary services, such as locating a restaurant with motels nearby.

If customers do not need to travel to the site, these physical attributes may not be important, but, instead one might consider the availability of skilled labor. For example, we noted that it is common practice for service firms to locate call centers in Bangalore, India, because of the availability of low cost, talented, English-speaking employees.

Geographic Information Systems[6]

One dark and stormy night in The Sea Ranch (TSR), a water main ruptured. No big deal, you say . . . just fix it as quickly as possible so the 1,305 residents of this 10-square-mile environmentally planned community on California's northern coast can have their coffee or tea the next morning. The glitch, however, is that this event took place in 2007 instead of 2017. The rupture triggered an alarm in the office of The Sea Ranch Water Company, which in turn roused the company's head water wizard, Randy Burke. Mr. Burke and other strategic employees gathered at the office, stilled the alarm, and noted that the level of water in the community's storage tank was lowering dramatically. They then had to take to the field and explore more than 2,000 acres to locate the break . . . they piled into a 4-wheel-drive vehicle and criss-crossed the largely unpaved area, stopping periodically to listen for leaking water. Despite their heroic efforts, the residents missed their morning coffee or tea.

FIGURE 8.1
GIS Data Layers for The Sea Ranch

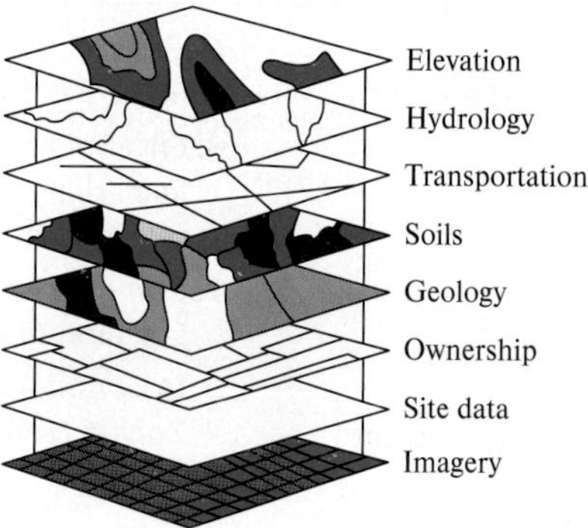

Fast forward to 2017. An event similar to the Great Break of 2007 still will trigger an alarm and Mr. Burke and his cohorts will gather at the Water Company office, but there the similarity ends. In the years since the Big Break, the community has embraced and integrated a geographic information system (GIS) across each of its operational spheres. As shown in Figure 8.1, when the entire system is up and running, it will include eight layers of data pertaining to elevation, hydrology, transportation, soils, geology, ownership, site data, and imagery.

Many years ago, the Environmental Research Institute, Inc. (ESRI; www.esri.com) introduced a GIS tool called ArcView, which transformed disparate demographic data into very useful data by plotting them on a map. For example, a business could use such mapped data to determine the location of a target market, analyze demand, and improve delivery service.

The great advances in information technology in recent decades, however, have led to much more sophisticated GIS tools. At ESRI, for example, ArcView has grown into ArcGIS, which has applications for all services, including those in private, public, non-profit, governmental, and military arenas. Today's GIS tools also have applications that span all operational areas within a single organization. Any data that can be put on a spreadsheet can be mapped.

Rejoining Mr. Burke for a hypothetical new Big Break, we see him and his team gather around the computer and bring up GIS maps that show the geographical coordinates of each water line and valve, and all of the other factors they need to consider in order to repair the leak. If Sea Ranch installs pressure-sensitive valves and data logic controls, the GIS maps would allow them to locate the leak precisely from the office. This mapping capability alone could save significant costs because of reduced worker-hours and far less water lost before the rupture is located and repaired. This is not the whole Sea Ranch story, however.

The community's Design, Construction, and Environmental Management (DCEM) committee is incorporating GIS into its operation. The DCEM is charged with reviewing all preliminary building plans and ensuring compliance with prescribed community standards. In addition to considering the design and appearance of a proposed structure itself, the committee also must consider "unseen" factors, such as the location of leach fields, storm drains, underlying geologic structures, and underground utilities. GIS maps of these disparate data can be overlaid to provide a comprehensive picture of the building site not only for the DCEM, but also for homeowners, architects, builders, and real estate people.

The DCEM also is involved in managing the landscape of 2,000 acres of commons property. Here, again, GIS proves to be a very useful and time/cost-saving tool because it puts precise data on boundaries of commons and private areas and all of the building-related information at the fingertips of decision makers. Other data—such as sites of nesting bird populations, plant diseases, and fuel management concerns—can be incorporated into the GIS instrument, also.

All of the integrated data that is so useful to the DCEM is vital to the community's Security and Emergency Management operation. In addition to handling day-to-day calls such as dogs off-leash, "sightseeing" motorists who do not have permits to use the community's private roads, and liaising with county sheriff personnel and federal fish and game agents who handle more serious transgressions, the security department also plays an integral role in the event of a disaster.

The Sea Ranch faces three primary disaster threats: wildfires, earthquakes, and tsunamis. First responders to such disasters include security personnel, TSR volunteer fire department personnel, CalFire (a state fire-fighting unit is located within TSR boundaries), and a cadre of medical and nonmedical Sea Ranchers who have been equipped, trained, and integrated into an immediate-response team.

During any of these disasters, information means lives saved. Think about finding underground utility lines (water or electric) that are torn asunder by an earthquake; selecting sites for storing medical supplies, potable water, and food; and providing evacuation routes from a wildfire or tsunami. Now think about addressing all of these factors in a community that is 10 miles long, measures just 1 mile wide from the ocean bluff to the redwood-forested ridge of the coastal mountains, and has only one major road, the Pacific Coast Highway (that's just two ways out, folks!) that might or (more likely) might not stay passable. A two-lane county road takes off from the highway and heads up to the ridge and a two-hour mountain drive out of the boonies. Those who choose to live at TSR know that fleeing a disaster might not always be an option, so they rely on the kind of preparations and response that GIS facilitates to survive for a few weeks without outside help.

Because of its reliance on new information technology, TSR has incorporated a three-tiered data security system. Backup data are maintained locally, at an off-site location, and in the cloud.

Our Sea Ranch example illustrates how organizations can use GIS in planning and analysis, asset/data management, promoting operational awareness across organizational boundaries, and facilitating the work of field units.

GIS uses spatial analysis to improve the ability to anticipate and manage change and provides a platform for viewing and disseminating results. A large volume of disparate data can be presented in an intuitive, map-based format. Data integrity can be maintained and templates of industry standards for organizations can be accessed. GIS applications can be configured for particular users from executives to field workers and also can provide live feeds of information, automated analyses, and alert tools. Such data are easy for field staff to use and can support a variety of field projects.

As seen in our TSR example, GIS fosters better decision making and enables better use of resources by making up-to-date information available to all users by way of online data maps.

Facility Location Modeling Considerations

Traditionally, location decisions have been based on intuition with mixed results. Although site selection often is based on opportunistic factors such as site availability and favorable leasing, a quantitative analysis can be useful to avoid a serious mistake. Many factors enter into the decision to locate a service facility. Figure 8.2 classifies location issues that will be used to guide our discussion. The broad categories are geographic representation, number of facilities, and optimization criteria.

Geographic Representation

The traditional classification of location problems is based on how the geography is modeled. Location options and travel distance can be represented on either a plane or a network. Location on a plane is characterized by a solution space that has infinite possibilities. Facilities may be located anywhere on the plane and are identified by an *x,y*

FIGURE 8.2
Classification of Service Facility Location Issues

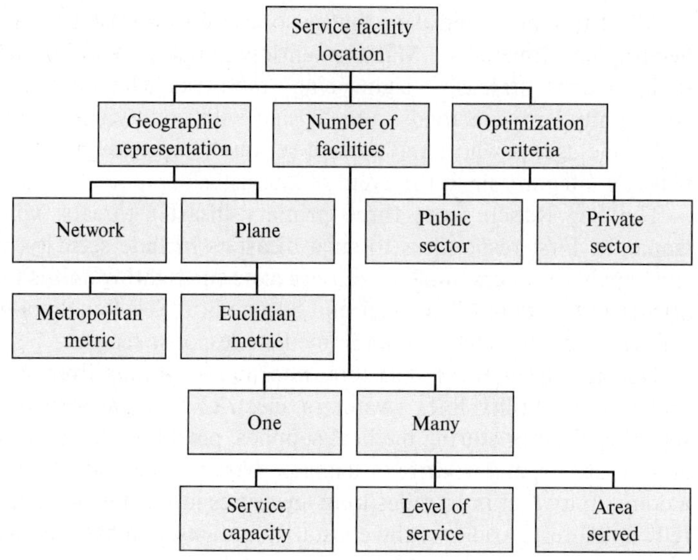

FIGURE 8.3
Geographic Structure

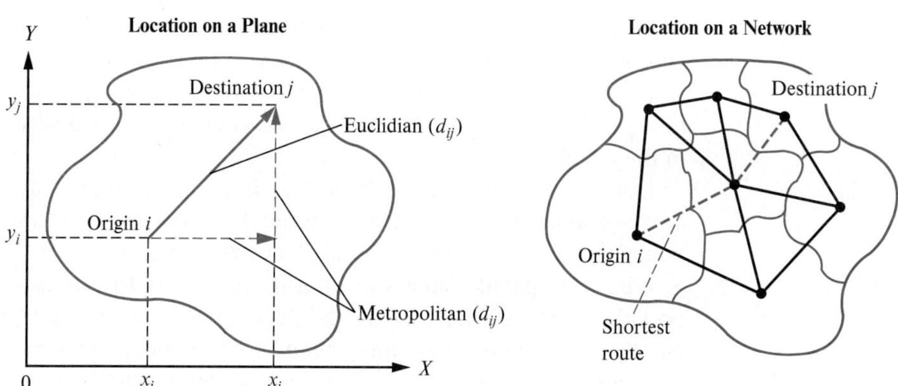

Cartesian coordinate (or, in a global context, by latitudes and longitudes), as shown in Figure 8.3. Distance between locations is measured at the extremes in one of two ways. One method is the *Euclidean metric,* or vector, travel distance (remember the Pythagorean theorem), which is defined as

$$d_{ij} = [(x_i - x_j)]^2 + (y_i - y_j)^2]^{1/2} \tag{1}$$

where

d_{ij} = distance between points i and j
x_i, y_i = coordinates of the ith point
x_j, y_j = coordinates of the jth point

For example, if

the origin $x_i, y_i = 2, 2$ and the destination $x_j, y_j = 4, 4$

then

$$d_{ij} = [(2 - 4)^2 + (2 - 4)^2]^{1/2} = 2.83$$

The other method is the *metropolitan metric*, or rectangular displacement, travel distance (i.e., north-south and east-west travel in urban areas), which is defined as

$$d_{ij} = |x_i - x_j| + |y_i - y_j| \tag{2}$$

Using the same example from above for the metropolitan metric:

$$d_{ij} = |2 - 4| + |2 - 4| = 4.0$$

Location on a network is characterized by a solution space that is restricted to the nodes of that network. For example, a highway system could be considered a network, with major highway intersections as nodes. The arcs of the network represent travel distance (or time) between pairs of nodes, calculated using the shortest route.

The selection of geographic representation and distance metric often is dictated by the economics of the data collection effort and the problem environment. Networks can represent more accurately the geographic uniqueness of an area (e.g., the travel restrictions caused by a river with few bridges or by mountainous terrain). Unfortunately, the cost of gathering the travel times between nodes can be prohibitive. When locating is done on a plane that represents an urban area, the metropolitan metric often is used, because streets for some cities are arranged in an east-west and north-south pattern. Both the metropolitan and Euclidean metrics require an estimate of the average speed to convert distance traveled to time.

Number of Facilities

The location of a single facility generally can be treated mathematically with little difficulty. Unfortunately, the methods used to site a single facility do not guarantee optimal results when they are modified and applied to multisite location problems. Finding a unique set of sites is complicated by assigning demand nodes to sites (i.e., defining service areas for each site), and the problem is complicated further if the capacity at each site varies. In addition, for some services such as health care, a hierarchy of service exists. Private physicians and clinics offer primary care, general hospitals provide primary care plus hospitalization, and health centers add special treatment capabilities. Thus, the selection of services provided also may be a variable in multisite location studies.

Optimization Criteria

Private and public sector location problems are similar in that they share the objective of maximizing some measure of benefit. The location criteria that are chosen differ, however, because the "ownership" is different. Within the private sector, the location decision is governed by either minimization of cost (e.g., in the case of distribution centers) or maximization of profit (e.g., in the case of retail locations). In contrast, we like to think that public facility decisions are governed by the needs of society as a whole. The objective for public decision making is to maximize a societal benefit that can be difficult to quantify.

Private Sector Criteria

Traditional private sector location analysis focuses on a trade-off between the cost of building and operating facilities and the cost of transportation. Much of the literature has addressed this problem, which is appropriate for the distribution of products (i.e., the warehouse location problem). These models might find some applications in services, however, when the services are delivered to the customers (e.g., consulting, auditing, janitorial, and lawn care services).

When the consumer travels to the facility, no direct cost is incurred by the provider. Instead, distance becomes a barrier restricting potential consumer demand and the corresponding revenue generated. Facilities such as retail shopping centers therefore are located to attract the maximum number of customers.

Public Sector Criteria

Location decisions in the public sector are complicated by the lack of agreement on goals and the difficulty of measuring benefits in dollars to make trade-offs with facility investment. Because the benefits of a public service are difficult to define or quantify directly, surrogate (or substitute) measures of utility are used.

The average distance traveled by users to reach the facility is a popular surrogate. The smaller this quantity, the more accessible the system is to its users. Thus, the problem becomes one of minimizing the total average distance traveled, with a constraint on the number of facilities. The problem is constrained additionally by some maximum travel distance for the user. Another possibility is the creation of demand. Here the user population is not considered fixed but is determined by the location, size, and number of facilities. The greater the demand created or drawn, the more efficient the system is in filling the needs of the region.

These utility surrogates are optimized with constraints on investment. Analysis of cost-effectiveness usually is performed to examine trade-offs between investment and utility. The trade-offs for the surrogates are (1) the decrease in average distance traveled per additional thousand-dollar investment and (2) the increase in demand per additional thousand-dollar investment.

Effect of Optimization Criteria on Location

The selection of optimization criteria influences service facility location. For example, William J. Abernathy and John C. Hershey studied the location of health centers for a three-city region.[7] As part of that study, they noted the effect of health-center locations with respect to the following criteria:

1. *Maximize utilization.* Maximize the total number of visits to the centers.
2. *Minimize distance per capita.* Minimize the average distance per capita to the closest center.
3. *Minimize distance per visit.* Minimize the average per-visit travel distance to the nearest center.

The problem was structured so that each city had a population with a different mix of health care consumption characteristics. These characteristics were measured along two dimensions: (1) the effect of distance as a barrier to health care use and (2) the utilization rate at immediate proximity to a health care center. Figure 8.4 shows a map of the three cities and the location of a single health care center under each of the three criteria. These criteria yield entirely different locations because of the different behavioral patterns of each city. For criterion 1 (maximize utilization), the center is located at city C, because this city contains a large number of elderly individuals for whom distance is a strong barrier. City B is selected under criterion 2 (minimize distance per capita), because this city is centrally located between the two larger cities. City A is the largest population center and has the most mobile and frequent users of health care; therefore, criterion 3 (minimize distance per visit) leads to this city being selected.

FIGURE 8.4
Location of One Health Center for Three Different Criteria

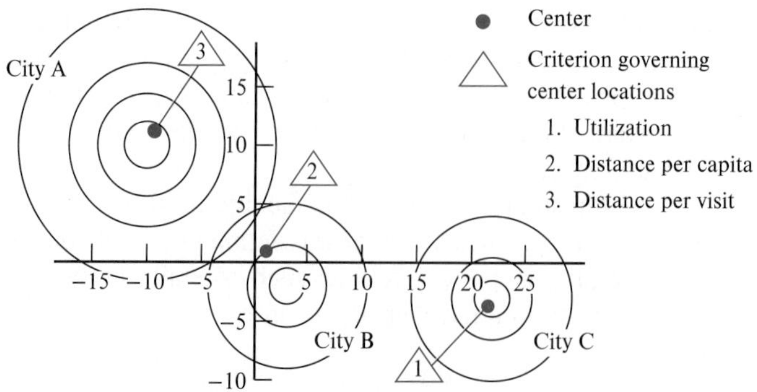

W. J. Abernathy and J. C. Hershey, "A Spatial-Allocation Model for Regional Health-Services Planning." Reprinted with permission from *Operations Research* 20, no. 3, 1972, p. 637, Operations Research Society of America.

Facility Location Techniques

An understanding of the facility location problem can be gained from the results of locating a single facility on a line. For example, consider the problem of locating a beach mat concession along the beachfront at Waikiki. Suppose you wish to find a location that would minimize the average walk to your concession from anywhere on the beach. Further, suppose you have data showing the density of bathers along the beachfront, which is related to the size and location of hotels. This distribution of bathers is shown schematically in Figure 8.5.

The objective is

$$\text{Minimize} \qquad z = \sum_{i=0}^{s} w_i(s - x_i) + \sum_{i=s}^{n} w_i(x_i - s) \tag{3}$$

where

w_i = weight of demand (bathers) attached to the ith location on the beach

x_i = location of the ith demand point on the beach in yards from the west end of the beach

s = site of the beach mat concession

The total-distance function Z is differentiated with respect to s and set equal to zero. This yields

$$\frac{dZ}{ds} = \sum_{i=0}^{s} w_i - \sum_{i=s}^{n} w_i = 0 \qquad \text{or} \qquad \sum_{i=0}^{s} w_i = \sum_{i=s}^{n} w_i \tag{4}$$

This result suggests that the site should be located at the median with respect to the density distribution of bathers. That is, the site is located so that 50 percent of the potential demand is to each side (i.e., 29 in Figure 8.5). We probably should have expected this, because the median has the property of minimizing the sum of the absolute deviations from it.

The result for locating a site along a line can be generalized for locating a site on a plane if we use the metropolitan metric. Total travel distance will be minimized if the coordinates of the site correspond to the intersection of the x and y medians for their respective density distributions. We will refer to this as the *cross-median* approach.

The selection of a solution technique is determined by the characteristics of the problem, as outlined in Figure 8.2. Our discussion of location techniques is not exhaustive, but a few techniques will be discussed to illustrate various approaches to the problem.

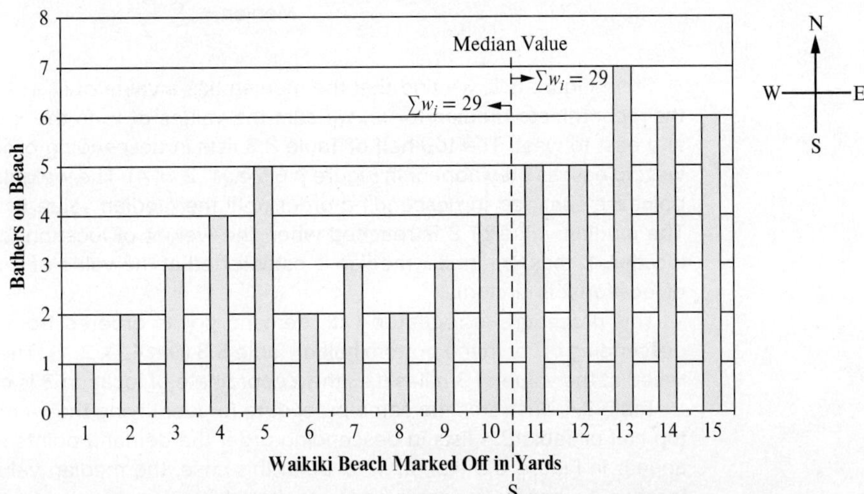

FIGURE 8.5
Location of Beach Concession

The selected techniques also represent approaches that deal with the various problem characteristics: single-facility versus multiple-facility location, location on a plane or a network, and public versus private optimization criteria.

Cross-Median Approach for a Single Facility

Locating a single facility on a plane to minimize the total travel distance Z by means of the metropolitan metric is straightforward using the cross-median approach. The objective is

$$\text{Minimize} \qquad Z = \sum_{i=1}^{n} w_i \{ |x_i - x_s| + |y_i - y_s| \} \tag{5}$$

where

w_i = weight attached to the ith point (e.g., trips per month)
x_i, y_i = coordinates of the ith demand point
x_s, y_s = coordinates of the service facility
n = number of demand points served

Note that the objective function can be restated as two independent terms.

$$\text{Minimize} \qquad Z = \sum_{i=1}^{n} w_i |x_i - x_s| + \sum_{i=1}^{n} w_i |y_i - y_s| \tag{6}$$

Recall from our beach mat concession example that the median of a discrete set of values is such that the sum of absolute deviations from it is a minimum. Thus, our optimum site will have coordinates such that (1) x_s is at the median value for w_i ordered in the x direction and (2) y_s is at the median value for w_i ordered in the y direction. Because x_s, y_s, or both can be unique or lie within a range, the optimal location might be at a point, on a line, or within an area. As an illustration, consider Example 8.1.

Example 8.1 Copying Service

A copying service has decided to open an office in the central business district of a city. The manager has identified four office buildings that will generate a major portion of its business, and Figure 8.6 shows the location of these demand points on an *xy* coordinate system. Weights are attached to each point and represent potential demand per month in hundreds of orders. The manager would like to determine a central location that will minimize the total distance per month that customers travel to the copying service.

Because of the urban location, a metropolitan metric is appropriate. A site located by the cross-median approach will be used to solve this problem. First, the median is calculated using equation (7):

$$\text{Median} = \sum_{i=1}^{n} \frac{w_i}{2} \tag{7}$$

From Figure 8.6, we find that the median has a value of (7 + 1 + 3 + 5)/2 = 8. To identify the x-coordinate median for x_s, we sum the values of w_i in the x direction both west to east and east to west. The top half of Table 8.3 lists in descending order the demand points from west to east as they appear in Figure 8.6 (i.e., 1, 2, 3, 4). The weights attached to each demand point are summed in descending order until the median value of 8 is reached or exceeded. The median value of 8 is reached when the weight of location 2 is added to the weight of location 1: thus, the first x median is established at the value of 2 miles (i.e., the x coordinate of location 2 is circled).

This procedure is repeated with demand points ordered from east to west, as shown in descending order in the bottom half of Table 8.3 (i.e., 4, 3, 2, 1). The second x median is established at the value of 3 miles (i.e., the x coordinate of location 3 is circled).

Table 8.4 illustrates the same procedure for identifying the y-coordinate median for y_s. The top half of Table 8.4 lists in descending order the demand points from south to north as they appear in Figure 8.6 (i.e., 4, 1, 2, 3). In this case, the median value of 8 is first exceeded at location 1 when its weight is added to that of location 4 to yield a total of 12. The y median is

FIGURE 8.6
Locating a Copying Service Using Cross-Median Approach

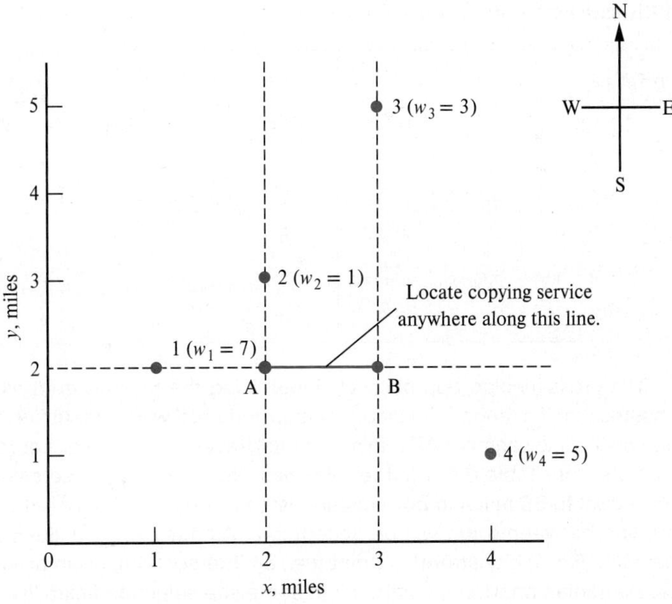

TABLE 8.3
Median Value for x_s

Point i	Location x_i	Σw_i
	Ordering west to east ⟶	
1	1	7 = 7
2	②	7 + 1 = 8
3	3	
4	4	
	Ordering east to west ⟵	
4	4	5 = 5
3	③	5 + 3 = 8
2	2	
1	1	

TABLE 8.4
Median Value for y_s

Point i	Location y_i	Σw_i
	Ordering south to north ↑	
4	1	5 = 5
1	②	5 + 7 = 12
2	3	
3	5	
	Ordering north to south ↓	
3	5	3 = 3
2	3	3 + 1 = 4
1	②	3 + 1 + 7 = 11
4	1	

established at the value of 2 miles (i.e., the *y* coordinate of location 1 is circled). At the bottom of Table 8.4, the demand points from north to south are listed in descending order as they appear in Figure 8.6 (i.e., 3, 2, 1, 4). Again, the median value is first exceeded at location 1 when its weight is added to those of locations 3 and 2 to yield a total of 11. Thus, we are left with only one *y* median at 2 miles.

TABLE 8.5 **Total Weighted Distance for Locations A and B**

Location A (2,2)							Location B (3,2)						
Office	Distance		Weight		Total		Office	Distance		Weight		Total	
1	1	×	7	=	7		1	2	×	7	=	14	
2	1	×	1	=	1		2	2	×	1	=	2	
3	4	×	3	=	12		3	3	×	3	=	9	
4	3	×	5	=	15		4	2	×	5	=	10	
					35							35	

The cross-median approach of determining the median from all four points of the compass ensures that if a range of locations is appropriate, it will be identified readily. In this case, any location on the line segment AB minimizes total travel distance (e.g., coordinates $2 = x_s = 3$ and $y_s = 2$).

Note from Table 8.5 that the total weighted travel distance calculated for point A and point B is equal to 35 miles in both instances; thus, any location at either point A or point B or along the line between them will be acceptable. As this example illustrates, a location solution can be a line (i.e., a city street), a point (i.e., an intersection), or an area (i.e., a city block). Thus, the cross-median approach can result in some site selection flexibility.

Huff Model for a Retail Outlet

When locating a retail outlet such as a supermarket, the objective is to maximize profit. In this case, a discrete number of alternative locations must be evaluated to find the most profitable site.

A gravity model is used to estimate consumer demand. This model is based on the physical analog that the gravitational attraction of two bodies is directly proportional to the product of their masses and inversely proportional to the square of the distance that separates them. For a service, the attractiveness of a facility may be expressed as

$$A_{ij} = \frac{S_j}{T_{ij}^{\lambda}} \tag{8}$$

where

A_{ij} = attraction to facility j for consumer i

S_j = size of the facility j

T_{ij} = travel time from consumer i's location to facility j

λ = parameter estimated empirically to reflect the effect of travel time on various kinds of shopping trips (e.g., where a shopping mall may have a $\lambda = 2$, convenience stores would have a $\lambda = 10$ or larger)

David L. Huff developed a retail location model, known as the *Huff model*, using this gravity model to predict the benefit that a customer would have for a particular store size and location.[8] Knowing that customers also would be attracted to other competing stores, he proposed the ratio P_{ij}. For n stores, this ratio measures the probability of a customer from a given statistical area i (e.g., census tract) traveling to a particular shopping facility j.

$$P_{ij} = \frac{A_{ij}}{\sum_{j=1}^{n} A_{ij}} \tag{9}$$

An estimate of E_{jk}, the total annual consumer expenditures for a product class k at a prospective shopping facility j, then can be calculated as

$$E_{jk} = \sum_{i=1}^{m} (P_{ij} C_i B_{ik}) \tag{10}$$

where

P_{ij} = probability of a consumer from a given statistical area i traveling to a shopping facility j, calculated by means of equation (9)

C_i = number of consumers at area i

B_{ik} = average annual amount budgeted by consumer at area i for a product class k

m = number of statistical areas

An estimate of M_{jk}, the market share captured by facility j of product class k sales, can be calculated as

$$M_{jk} = \frac{E_{jk}}{\sum_{i=1}^{m} C_i B_{ik}} \tag{11}$$

An exhaustive procedure is used to calculate the expected annual profit of each potential site for various possible store sizes at the site. Net operating profit before taxes is calculated as a percentage of sales adjusted for the size of the store. The result is a list of potential sites with the store size at each that maximizes profit. All that remains is to negotiate a real estate deal for the site that comes closest to maximizing annual profit. In Example 8.2, we revisit the Copying Service using Huff Analysis.

Example 8.2 Copying Service—Huff Analysis

Assume that the copying service in Example 8.1 has been established at (x = 2, y = 2), as shown by location A in Figure 8.6 at the far left end of the optimal line. Further, assume that each customer order represents an expenditure of approximately $10. Because convenience would be an important customer criterion, assume that $\lambda = 2$. If we wish to open a competing store at location (x = 3, y = 2) (i.e., at location B on the far right end of the optimal line) but with *twice* the capacity of the existing copy center, how much market share would we expect to capture? Using the travel distances in Table 8.6 as input to the Huff model, the calculations shown in Tables 8.7 to 8.9 are obtained.

This example illustrates the result of an aggressive location strategy as used by well-financed national retail chains. For example, as the name might imply, Blockbuster Video had a reputation of moving into a community with supersized stores and driving out small, locally operated video-rental establishments until Netflix, in turn, put them out of business.

TABLE 8.6
Travel Distance in Miles (T_{ij}) (Using Metropolitan Metric)

	Customer Location (i)			
Site (j)	**1**	**2**	**3**	**4**
Proposed (3, 2)	2	2	3	2
Existing (2, 2)	1	1	4	3

TABLE 8.7
Attraction (A_{ij})

	Customer Location (i)			
Site (j)	**1**	**2**	**3**	**4**
Proposed ($S_1 = 2$)	0.5	0.5	0.2222	0.500
Existing ($S_2 = 1$)	1.0	1.0	0.0625	0.111
Total attraction	1.5	1.5	0.2847	0.611

TABLE 8.8
Probability (P_{ij})

	Customer Location (i)			
Site (j)	**1**	**2**	**3**	**4**
Proposed	.33	.33	.78	.82
Existing	.67	.67	.22	.18

TABLE 8.9
Monthly Expenditures (E_{jk}) and Market Share (M_{jk})

	Customer Expenditures					
Site (*j*)	**1**	**2**	**3**	**4**	**Monthly Total**	**Market Share %**
Proposed	$2,333	$ 333	$2,340	$4,100	$ 9,106	0.57
Existing	4,667	667	660	900	6,894	0.43
Totals	$7,000	$1,000	$3,000	$5,000	$16,000	1.00

Location Set Covering for Multiple Facilities

The difficulty of evaluating decisions regarding public facility location has resulted in a search for surrogate, or substitute, measures of the benefit of the facility location. One such measure is the distance that the most distant customer would have to travel to reach the facility. This is known as the *maximal service distance.* We want to find the minimum number and location of facilities that will serve all demand points within some specified maximal service distance; this is known as the *location set covering* problem as illustrated in Example 8.3.

Example 8.3 Rural Medical Clinics

A state department of health is concerned about the lack of medical care in rural areas, and a group of nine communities has been selected for a pilot program in which medical clinics will be opened to serve primary health care needs. It is hoped that every community will be within 30 miles of at least one clinic. The planners would like to determine the number of clinics that are required and their locations. Any community can serve as a potential clinic site except for community 6, because facilities are unavailable there. Figure 8.7 shows a network identifying the cities as numbered circles; lines drawn between the sites show the travel distances in miles.

The problem is approached by first identifying for each community the other communities that can be reached from it within the 30-mile travel limit. Beginning with community 1, we see in Figure 8.7 that communities 2, 3, and 4 can be reached within the 30-mile distance limit. The results of similar inspections for each community are reported in the second column of Table 8.10 as the set of communities served from each site. An equivalent statement could be

FIGURE 8.7
Travel Network for a Rural Area

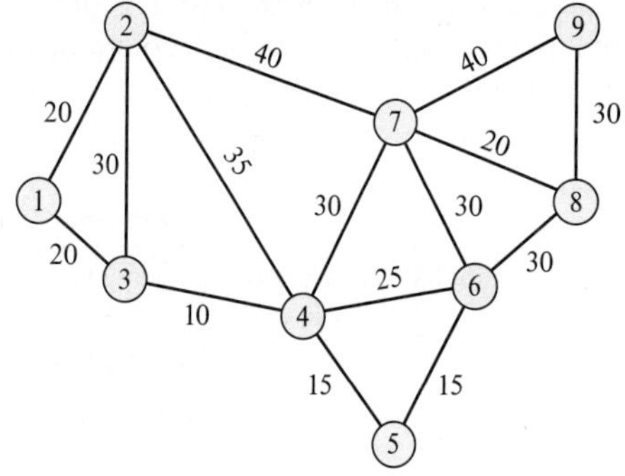

TABLE 8.10
Range of Service for Potential Sites

* Community 6 cannot serve as a clinic site.
† Subsets of potential sites.

Community	Set of Communities Served from Site	Potential Sites That Could Serve the Community
1	1,2,3,4	1,2,3,4
2	1,2,3	(1,2,3)†
3	1,2,3,4,5	1,2,3,4,5
4	1,3,4,5,6,7	1,3,4,5,7
5	3,4,5,6	(3,4,5)†
6*	N/A	4,5,7,8
7	4,6,7,8	(4,7,8)†
8	6,7,8,9	7,8,9
9	8,9	(8,9)†

made that this set, less any communities that could not serve as a site, represents the set of sites that could cover the community in question for service within 30 miles. Thus, for community 5, a clinic located at site 3, 4, or 5 meets the maximal travel limit.

The third column of Table 8.10 represents the set of potential sites that could cover a given community. Several of these sets have been placed in parentheses, however, because they represent subsets of other potential locations. For example, because community 2 can only be served by sites 1, 2, and 3, one of these sites must be selected for a clinic location. Identifying these subsets reduces the problem size while ensuring that restrictions are satisfied.

Note that because of our desire to minimize the number of clinics to cover all the communities, any site common to two or more of these subsets is an excellent candidate for selection. In this case, sites 3, 4, and 8 are candidates. From inspection, we see that if sites 3 and 8 are selected, all subsets are accounted for; thus, all communities can be covered with just these two clinics. We also have identified the service region for each clinic; the clinic located at community 3 will serve communities 1 through 5, and the clinic located at community 8 will serve communities 6 through 9.

The location set covering problem often can yield more than one solution. In this example, if the maximal travel distance were set at 40 miles, the following five pairs of clinic site locations would provide coverage: (3, 8), (3, 9), (4, 7), (4, 8), and (4, 9).

Regression Analysis in Location Decisions

When a firm with many facilities wants to expand, it can rely on the wealth of statistical information about existing facilities to forecast the performance of a candidate location. A regression model based on several independent variables, such as size, competitors nearby, and traffic, can be constructed to forecast performance (i.e., anticipated revenue).

As an example, the management of La Quinta Motor Inns, a national chain of hotels, commissioned a study to determine the direction of its expansion efforts.[9] It wanted to know which factors determined a profitable hotel location and, thus, would allow management to screen available real estate for new hotel sites. Investigators collected data on many factors at existing locations, such as traffic count, number of competitive rooms nearby, visibility of signs, local airport traffic, types of neighboring businesses, and distance to the central business district. In all, 35 factors, or independent variables, were considered.

The inn's operating margin, was chosen as the most reliable measure, or dependent variable *Y*, on which to base a forecast. A statistical evaluation of the data for all the variables in Table 8.11 allowed the investigators to identify four critical factors–STATE, PRICE, INCOME, and COLLEGE–to be used in the forecast model. The resulting regression model (1) contains several independent variables with negative coefficients that need explanation. The variable STATE, defined as state population per inn, is a measure of brand exposure. A small number for this variable represents a high density of La Quinta Motor Inns in the state and, thus, brand recognition is strong. The variable INCOME, defined as average family income, is a measure of the affluence of the area in which the inn is located. Because La Quinta Motor Inns targets the business traveler, locations in nonresidential areas are preferred.

Collecting data on the independent variables at a proposed hotel site and making appropriate transformations as needed allows investigators to forecast the operating margin.

$$\text{Operating margin } Y = 39.05 + (-5.41)\text{STATE} + (5.86)\text{PRICE} + (-3.09)\text{INCOME} + (1.75)\text{COLLEGE} \quad (12)$$

The results of this study proved the model to be very good in predicting the likelihood of success for a new inn at a proposed location.

TABLE 8.11
Independent Variables for Hotel Location

Reprinted by permission, S. E. Kimes and J. A. Fitzsimmons, "Selecting Profitable Hotel Sites at La Quinta Motor Inns," *Interfaces* 20, no. 2, March–April 1990, p. 14. Copyright 1990, the Operations Research Society of America and The Institute of Management Sciences, 290 Westminster Street, Providence, RI 02903.

Name	Description
Competitive factors	
INNRATE	Inn price
PRICE	Room rate for the inn
RATE	Average competitive room rate
RMS1	Hotel rooms within 1 mile
RMSTOTAL	Hotel rooms within 3 miles
ROOMSINN	Inn rooms
Demand generators	
CIVILIAN	Civilian personnel on base
COLLEGE	College enrollment
HOSP1	Hospital beds within 1 mile
HOSPTOTL	Hospital beds within 4 miles
HVYIND	Heavy industrial employment
LGTIND	Light industrial acreage
MALLS	Shopping mall square footage
MILBLKD	Military base blocked
MILITARY	Military personnel
MILTOT	MILITARY + CIVILIAN
OFC1	Office space within 1 mile
OFCTOTAL	Office space within 4 miles
OFCCBD	Office space in central business district
PASSENGER	Airport passengers enplaned
RETAIL	Scale ranking of retail activity
TOURISTS	Annual tourists
TRAFFIC	Traffic count
VAN	Airport van
Area demographics	
EMPLYPCT	Unemployment percentage
INCOME	Average family income
POPULACE	Residential population
Market awareness	
AGE	Years inn has been open
NEAREST	Distance to nearest inn
STATE	State population per inn
URBAN	Urban population per inn
Physical attributes	
ACCESS	Accessibility
ARTERY	Major traffic artery
DISTCBD	Distance to downtown
SIGNVIS	Sign visibility

Summary

Facility location plays an important role in the strategy of a service firm through its influence on the competitive dimensions of flexibility, competitive positioning, demand management, and focus. Strategies such as competitive clustering are common for shopping goods, and saturation marketing has been successful for some small retail outlets.

Service Benchmark

HERE A BUN, THERE A BUN, EVERYWHERE A BUN-BUN

The idea of clustering or saturation marketing has come of age and been embraced enthusiastically by many companies such as Au Bon Pain, Benetton, and Starbucks. At first blush, the notion of locating several shops from one company in a small geographical area, sometimes within one block of each other, seems risky. For Au Bon Pain, a chain known for its special sandwiches and baked goods, the advantages have outweighed the disadvantages.

Saturation marketing decreases the need for advertising—why advertise when prospective customers can't walk one block, or sometimes even just one floor in a department store, without passing a Benetton clothing shop or a Starbucks coffee shop? Au Bon Pain also has found that it is easier to supervise the shops when they are located close together. Saturation marketing is most successful in high-density, urban locations, particularly for businesses like Starbucks and Au Bon Pain, which are not destination shops. Customers usually stop at these places on their way to other destinations.

Clustering seems to work better with company-owned outlets rather than with independently owned franchises. If one company-owned outlet does siphon off a little business from another one, it does not affect the company's bottom line. If one independently owned franchise siphons business from another one, however, it is of concern to an independent owner who comes out on the shorter end.

In addition, use of marketing intermediaries can decouple the provider from the consumer. If the requirement for face-to-face interaction between server and customer is not necessary, as illustrated by Internet service providers, the substitution of electronic communication for physical transportation becomes possible.

The discussion of facility location techniques began with the single-facility problem. The cross-median approach identified an optimal location for minimizing the total distance traveled by customers. The location of a single retail outlet to maximize profit is an important decision that has been studied by David Huff using a gravity model to predict customer attractiveness to a store based on its size and location. For the multiple-facility location problem, the concept of location set covering uses maximal service distance as a constraint to identifying candidate locations.

Key Terms and Definitions

Competitive clustering the grouping of competitors (e.g., automobile dealerships) in close proximity for convenience in comparative shopping by customers. *p. 220*

Cross-median an approach to the location of a single facility using the metropolitan metric to minimize the total weighted distance traveled. *p. 229*

E-distance a barrier found in website design created by internal and external navigation. *p. 222*

Huff model a retail location model that is based on an analogy to celestial gravity to measure the attraction of a customer for a facility. *p. 232*

Location set covering an approach to finding the minimum number and location of facilities that will serve all demand points within a specified maximum travel distance. *p. 234*

Marketing intermediaries a business entity in the channel of distribution between the final customer and the service provider (e.g., a bank extending credit to a retailer through a credit card). *p. 220*

Metropolitan metric a measure of distance traveled assuming rectangular displacement (e.g., north-south and east-west travel in urban areas). *p. 227*

Saturation marketing the location of a firm's individual outlets (e.g., ice cream vendors) in close proximity to create a significant presence that attracts customer attention. *p. 220*

Topics for Discussion

1. Pick a particular service and identify shortcomings in its site selection.
2. How would you proceed to estimate empirically the parameter λ in the Huff retail location model for a branch bank?
3. What are the characteristics of a service that would make communication a good substitute for travel?
4. What are the benefits of using intermediaries in the service distribution channel?
5. Conduct a Google search and find the definition of "location intelligence." What use can be made of geographic information?

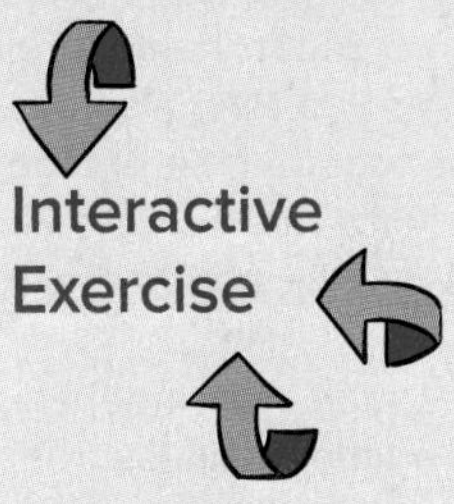

Interactive Exercise

The class discusses the business opportunities of using Google Earth.

Solved Problems

1. Cross-Median Location Problem

Problem Statement

A health clinic is being planned to serve a rural area in west Texas. The service area consists of four communities at the following *xy* coordinate locations in miles: A (6, 2), B (8, 6), C (5, 9), D (3, 4), with populations of 2,000, 1,000, 3,000, and 2,000, respectively. Recommend a cross-median location for the health clinic minimizing the total weighted metropolitan distance traveled.

Solution

First, calculate the median value in thousands:

$$\text{Median} = (2 + 1 + 3 + 2)/2 = 4$$

Second, plot the four communities on a grid with population in thousands as subscripts:

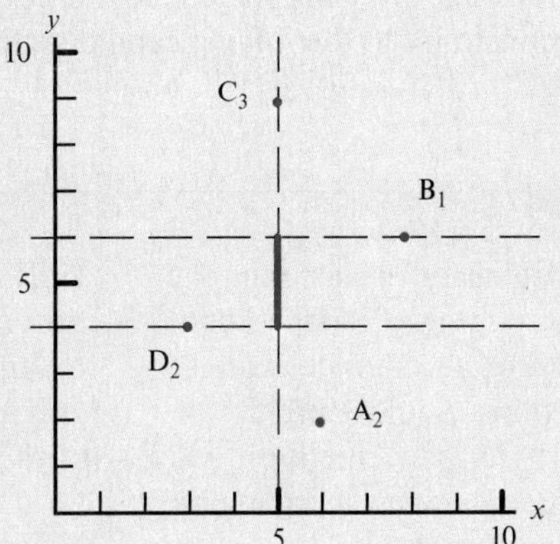

Third, draw the *x*-median dotted line (i.e., vertical line) on the plot by moving from left to right, adding the weights until the sum is equal to or exceeds the median (i.e., $D_2 + C_3 = 5$). The result is one vertical line at $x = 5$. Moving from right to left, add the weights until the sum is equal to or exceeds the median (i.e., $B_1 + A_2 + C_3 = 6$). The result is the same vertical line at $x = 5$.

Fourth, draw the *y*-median dotted line (i.e., horizontal line) on the plot by moving from top to bottom, adding the weights until the sum is equal to or exceeds the median (i.e., $C_3 + B_1 = 4$). The result is a horizontal line at $y = 6$. Moving from bottom to top, add the weights until the sum is equal to or exceeds the median (i.e., $A_2 + D_2 = 4$). The result is another horizontal line at $y = 4$. The recommended location results in a line segment shown as a dark line in the plot with xy coordinates of (5,4 to 5,6).

2. Retail Location Using the Huff Model

Problem Statement

The west Texas area in the plot above is served by a grocery store in community D. A proposed store with three times the floor space is being considered for location in community C. Assume that monthly expenditures per customer average about \$100. Then, using the metropolitan metric for travel and $\lambda = 2$, use the Huff model to estimate the impact on monthly expenditures and market share for the existing store in community D if the proposed store in community C is constructed.

Solution

First, determine the travel distances using the metropolitan metric:

Travel Distance in Miles (T_{ij}) (Using Metropolitan Metric)

	Community (i)			
Site (j)	**A (6, 2)**	**B (8, 6)**	**C (5, 9)**	**D (3, 4)**
Proposed C (5, 9)	8	6	0	7
Existing D (3, 4)	5	7	7	0

Second, using equation (8), calculate the attraction matrix with $\lambda = 2$. For example, the attraction of community A to the proposed location at C (with $S = 3$ to account for the larger floor space) would be calculated as

$$A_{ij} = \frac{S_j}{T_{ij}^{\lambda}} = \frac{S_1}{T_{11}^2} = \frac{3}{8^2} = \frac{3}{64} = 0.0469$$

Note that the attraction is given a value of ∞ where the store is located in the same community ($T_{ij} = 0$ in the denominator).

Attraction (A_{ij})

	Community Location (i)			
Site (j)	**A**	**B**	**C**	**D**
Proposed $S_1 = 3$	0.0469	0.0833	∞	—
Existing $S_2 = 1$	0.0400	0.0204	—	∞
Total attraction	0.0869	0.1037		

Third, using equation (9), calculate the probability using the total attraction as the denominator. For example, the probability of residents in community A traveling to the proposed grocery store location at C would be calculated as

$$P_{ij} = \frac{A_{ij}}{\sum_{j=1}^{n} A_{ij}} = \frac{A_{11}}{A_{11} + A_{12}} = \frac{0.0469}{0.0469 + 0.04} = 0.54$$

Probability (P_{ij})

	Community Location (i)			
Site (j)	**A**	**B**	**C**	**D**
Proposed	.54	.80	1.0	0
Existing	.46	.20	0	1.0

Fourth, using equation (10), the monthly expenditures are calculated, and using equation (11), the market shares are determined. For example, expenditures from residents of community A at the proposed grocery store location at C would be calculated as

$$E_{jk} = \sum_{i=1}^{m} (P_{ij} C_i B_{ik}) = P_{11} C_1 B_1 = (.54)(2000)(100) = \$108{,}000$$

Monthly Expenditures (E_{jk}) and Market Share (M_{jk})

	Community Expenditures					
Site (*j*)	**A**	**B**	**C**	**D**	**Monthly Total**	**Market Share %**
Proposed	$108,000	$ 80,000	$300,000	$ 0	$488,000	0.61
Existing	92,000	20,000	0	200,000	312,000	0.39
Totals	$200,000	$100,000	$300,000	$200,000	$800,000	1.00

Exercises

8.1. Revisit the copying service in Example 8.1 and assume that over the years, the monthly demand from the four customers has increased to the following weights: $w_1 = 7$, $w_2 = 9$, $w_3 = 5$, $w_4 = 7$. If we previously located the copying service at point A in Figure 8.6, should we now consider a relocation?

8.2. A temporary-help agency wants to open an office in a suburban section of a large city. It has identified five large corporate offices as potential customers. The locations of these offices in miles on an *xy* coordinate grid for the area are $c_1 = (4, 4)$, $c_2 = (4, 11)$, $c_3 = (7, 2)$, $c_4 = (11, 11)$, and $c_5 = (14, 7)$. The expected demand for temporary help from these customers is weighted as $w_1 = 3$, $w_2 = 2$, $w_3 = 2$, $w_4 = 4$, and $w_5 = 1$. The agency reimburses employees for travel expenses incurred by their assignments; therefore, recommend a location (i.e., *xy* coordinates) for the agency that will minimize the total weighted metropolitan distance for job-related travel.

8.3. Four hospitals located in one county are cooperating to establish a centralized blood-bank facility to serve them all. On an *xy* coordinate grid of the county, the hospitals are found at the following locations: $H_1 = (5, 10)$, $H_2 = (7, 6)$, $H_3 = (4, 2)$, and $H_4 = (16, 3)$. The expected number of deliveries per month from the blood bank to each hospital is estimated at 450, 1,200, 300, and 1,500, respectively. Using the cross-median approach, recommend a location for the blood bank that will minimize the total distance traveled.

8.4. A pizza delivery service has decided to open a branch near off-campus student housing. The project manager has identified five student apartment complexes in the northwest area of the city, the locations of which, on an *xy* coordinate grid in miles, are $C_1 = (1, 2)$, $C_2 = (2, 6)$, $C_3 = (3, 3)$, $C_4 = (4, 1)$, and $C_5 = (5, 4)$. The expected demand is weighted as $w_1 = 5$, $w_2 = 4$, $w_3 = 3$, $w_4 = 1$, and $w_5 = 5$. Using the cross-median approach, recommend a location for the pizza branch that will minimize the total distance traveled.

8.5. A small city airport is served by four airlines. The terminal is rather spread out, with boarding areas located on an *xy* coordinate grid at $A = (1, 4)$, $B = (5, 5)$, $C = (8, 3)$, and $D = (8, 1)$. The number of flights per day, of approximately equal capacity, is $A = 28$, $B = 22$, $C = 36$, and $D = 18$. A new central baggage claim area is under construction. Using the cross-median approach, recommend a location for the new baggage claim area that will minimize the total weighted distance from the boarding areas.

8.6. You have been asked to help locate a catering service in the central business district of a city. The locations of potential customers on an *xy* coordinate grid are $P_1 = (4, 4)$, $P_2 = (12, 4)$, $P_3 = (2, 7)$, $P_4 = (11, 11)$, and $P_5 = (7, 14)$. The expected demand is weighted as $w_1 = 4$, $w_2 = 3$, $w_3 = 2$, $w_4 = 4$, and $w_5 = 1$. Using the cross-median approach, recommend a location for the catering service that will minimize the total weighted distance traveled to serve the customers.

8.7. Revisit the copying service Huff analysis in Example 8.2. Recalculate the monthly customer expenditures and the market share for the proposed copying center at location B if the new store will be *three* times the capacity of the existing store at location A and the new demand weights from Exercise 8.1 above are used.

8.8. A locally owned department store samples two customers in each of five geographic areas to estimate consumer spending in its home appliances department. It is estimated that these customers are a good sample of the 10,000 customers the store serves. The number of customers in each area is $C_1 = 1{,}500$, $C_2 = 2{,}500$, $C_3 = 1{,}000$, $C_4 = 3{,}000$, and $C_5 = 2{,}000$. It is found that the two consumers have the following budgets in dollars for home appliances per year: $B_{11} = 100$, $B_{12} = 150$; $B_{21} = 75$, $B_{22} = 100$; $B_{31} = 125$, $B_{32} = 125$; $B_{41} = 100$, $B_{42} = 120$; and $B_{51} = 120$, $B_{52} = 125$.

a. Using the Huff retail location model, estimate annual home appliance sales for the store.

b. Bull's-Eye, a chain department store, opens a branch in a shopping complex nearby. The Bull's-Eye branch is three times larger than the locally owned store. The travel times in minutes from the five areas to the two stores ($j = 1$ for the locally owned store, $j = 2$ for Bull's-Eye) are $T_{11} = 20$, $T_{12} = 15$; $T_{21} = 35$, $T_{22} = 20$; $T_{31} = 30$, $T_{32} = 25$; $T_{41} = 20$, $T_{42} = 25$; and $T_{51} = 25$, $T_{52} = 25$. Use the Huff retail location model to estimate the annual consumer expenditures in the home appliance section of each store assuming that $\lambda = 1$.

8.9. A community is currently being served by a single self-serve gas station with six pumps. A competitor is opening a new facility with 12 pumps across town. Table 8.12 shows the travel times in minutes from the four different areas in the community to the sites and the number of customers in each area.

a. Using the Huff retail location model and assuming that $\lambda = 2$, calculate the probability of a customer traveling from each area to each site.

b. Estimate the proportion of the existing market lost to the new competitor.

8.10. Recall the rural medical clinics in Example 8.3 and suppose that each community were required to be 25 miles at most from the nearest clinic. How many clinics would be needed, and what would their locations be? Give all possible location solutions.

8.11. A bank is planning to serve the rural communities shown in Figure 8.8 with automated teller machines (ATMs). The travel time in minutes between communities in the service area is shown on the network in Figure 8.8. The bank is interested in determining the number and location of ATMs necessary to serve the communities so that a machine will be within 20 minutes' travel time of any community.

TABLE 8.12
Travel Times to Gas Stations

Area	1	2	3	4
Old station	5	1	9	15
New competitor	20	8	12	6
Number of customers	100	150	80	50

FIGURE 8.8
Service Area Network

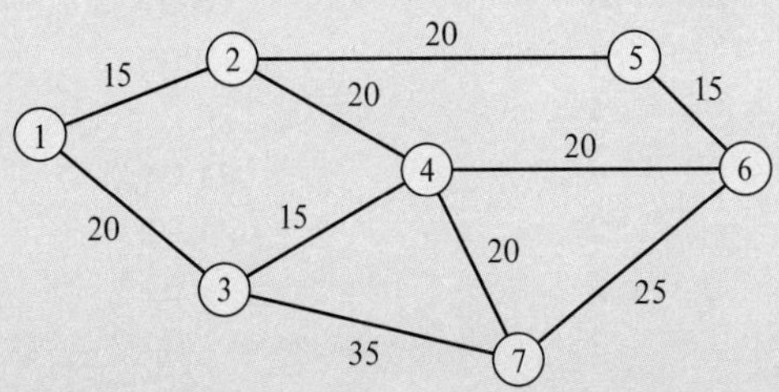

8.12. The volunteer fire department serving the communities in Figure 8.8 has just purchased two used fire engines auctioned off by a nearby city.

a. Select all possible pairs of communities in which the fire engines could be located to ensure that all communities can be reached in 30 minutes or less.

b. What additional consideration could be used to make the final site selection from the community pairs found in part a?

Health Maintenance Organization (C) — CASE 8.1

Joan Taylor, the administrator of Life-Time Insurance Company, which is based in Buffalo, New York, was charged with establishing a health maintenance organization (HMO) satellite clinic in Austin, Texas. The HMO concept would offer Austin residents an alternative to the traditional fee-for-service medical care. Individuals could enroll in the HMO voluntarily and, for a fixed fee, be eligible for health services. The fee would be paid in advance.

Ms. Taylor carefully planned the preliminary work that would be required to establish the new clinic in Austin, and when she arrived, most of the arrangements had been completed. The location of the ambulatory health center (clinic), however, had not been selected. Preliminary data on the estimated number of potential enrollees in the HMO had been determined by census tract, and these data are presented in Table 8.13. Using the cross-median approach and the census-tract map in Figure 8.9, recommend a location for the clinic.

Athol Furniture, Inc.[10] — CASE 8.2

Athol Furniture, Inc. (AFI), is a growing regional chain of discount furniture and large-appliance stores. Management has targeted the small city of Bluff Lake as the next location for a retail outlet. Although the total population is currently 21,000, Bluff Lake is expected to grow during the next decade because of increased mining in the surrounding hills.

AFI's marketing department did a general analysis of the potential of market expansion into Bluff Lake, but the task of locating the best site for a store has been given to Mr. Carlos Gutierrez. After obtaining the market data on Bluff Lake, Mr. Gutierrez decides it would be very appropriate to utilize the Huff location model in developing a recommendation for the company's management. This is because there are existing competitors and several potential sites under consideration.

Figure 8.10 is a map of Bluff Lake showing major streets and highways, the railway (AFI will ship its merchandise into the city by rail from a regional warehouse 800 miles away), Crystal River, Bluff Lake, and the census block groups (numbered 1 through 12). Table 8.14 gives the number of households, average annual income per household, and average annual furniture/large-appliance expenditure per household for each census block group.

In Figure 8.10, the letters A and B show the locations of AFI's existing competitors, and Table 8.15 indicates the sizes of

TABLE 8.13 **Estimated Number of Potential Enrollees per Census Tract**

Census Tract	Enrollees, in Thousands	Census Tract	Enrollees, in Thousands
1	5	13.02	4
2	4	14	5
3	3	15.01	6
4	1	15.02	4
5	2	15.03	5
6	1	16.01	3
7	4	16.02	2
8	1	18.03	5
9	2	20	2
10	4	21.01	4
11	2	21.02	3
12	2	23.01	4
13.01	3		

FIGURE 8.9
Census-Tract Map of Austin, Texas

Source: AustinTexas.gov

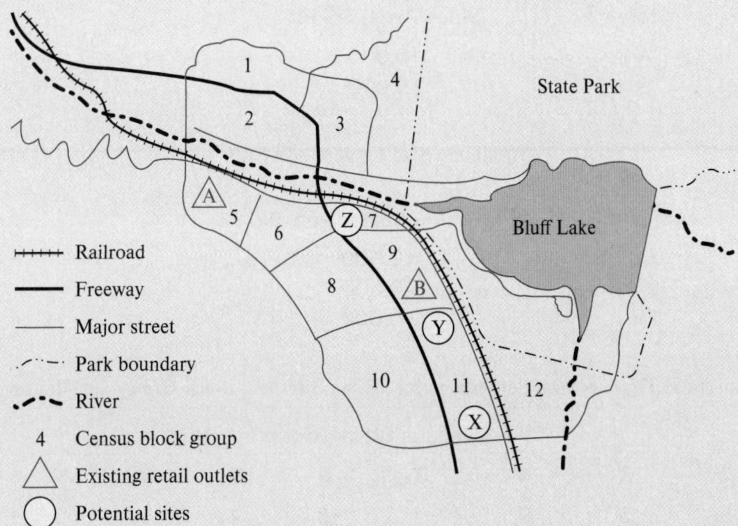

FIGURE 8.10
Bluff Lake

these existing stores to the nearest 5,000 square feet of sales area. The letters X, Y, and Z in Figure 8.10 show the possible sites that Mr. Gutierrez feels AFI could use for a retail store. The maximum size limit (i.e., sales area) of each potential location is given in Table 8.16.

On the basis of average speeds for the main streets and highways obtained from the city's planning department, Mr. Gutierrez has developed a matrix of travel times between the existing and potential retail sites and the center of each census block group. These travel times can be found in Table 8.17.

From experience with other AFI locations, Mr. Gutierrez has developed a fairly accurate portrayal of the relationship between store size (i.e., sales area) and margin on sales, expenses, and net operating profit before taxes. This information is shown in Table 8.18.

Questions

1. Utilizing a spreadsheet version of the Huff location model (with $\lambda = 1.0$), recommend a store size and location for AFI. Assuming that AFI does not wish to consider a store that

is smaller than 10,000 square feet, assess the store sizes (based on 5,000-square-foot increments) up to the maximum allowable sales area for each potential site.

2. What is the expected annual net operating profit before taxes and expected market share for the outlet you have recommended? Defend your recommendation.
3. Try two other values of λ (e.g., 0.5 and 5.0) to measure the sensitivity of customer travel propensity on your recommended location.
4. Briefly state any shortcomings you may perceive in this model.

TABLE 8.14 Market Data

Census Block Group	Number of Households	Avg. Annual Income	Avg. Annual Furniture/Large-Appliance Expenditures per Household
1	730	65,000–70,000	$180
2	1,130	45,000–50,000	125
3	1,035	80,000–85,000	280
4	635	150,000–over	350
5	160	25,000–30,000	75
6	105	20,000–25,000	50
7	125	20,000–25,000	60
8	470	40,000–45,000	115
9	305	30,000–35,000	90
10	1,755	85,000–90,000	265
11	900	75,000–80,000	215
12	290	150,000–over	370
	7,640		

TABLE 8.15 Competitors' Store Sizes

Store	Sales Area, Sq. Ft.
A	10,000
B	15,000

TABLE 8.16 Maximum Size Limit of AFI Sites

Site	Maximum Sales Area, Sq. Ft.
X	15,000
Y	20,000
Z	10,000

TABLE 8.17 Minimum Travel Time between Potential and Existing Sites and Block Groups in Minutes

	Census Block Group											
Site	1	2	3	4	5	6	7	8	9	10	11	12
A	7	5	5	9	1	3	4	5	7	10	14	17
B	10	8	8	10	7	3	3	2	1	4	2	5
X	16	14	14	16	13	8	7	6	4	3	2	2
Y	12	10	10	12	9	5	4	3	2	3	2	4
Z	7	5	5	7	4	2	1	4	3	8	10	13

TABLE 8.18 Relationship of Size of Store to Margin on Sales, Expenses, and Net Operating Profit as a Percent of Sales

	Operating Data		
Sales Area, Sq. Ft.	Margin on Sales	Expenses	Net Operating Profit before Taxes
10,000	16.2	12.3	3.9
15,000	15.6	12.0	3.6
20,000	14.7	11.8	2.9

Selected Bibliography

Baron, Opher, Joseph Milner, and Hussein Naseraldin. "Facility Location: A Robust Optimization Approach." *Production and Operations Management* 20, no. 5 (September-October 2011), pp. 772-85.

Castillo, Ignacio, Armann Ingolfsson, and Thaddeus Sim. "Social Optimal Location of Facilities with Fixed Servers, Stochastic Demand, and Congestion." *Production and Operations Management* 18, no. 6 (November-December 2009), pp. 721-36.

Chanta, Sunarin, Maria E. Mayorga, and Laura A. McLay. "Improving Emergency Service in Rural Areas: A Bi-objective Covering Location Model for EMS Systems." *Annals of Operations Research* 221, no. 1 (2014), pp. 133-59.

Ehsani, Amir, Abolfazl Danaei, and Mohammad Hemmati. "A Mathematical Model for Facility Location in Banking Industry." *Management Science Letters* 4, no. 9 (2014), pp. 2097-100.

Fernández, José, and Eligius MT Hendrix. "Recent Insights in Huff-like Competitive Facility Location and Design." *European Journal of Operational Research* 227, no. 3 (2013), pp. 581-84.

Fitzsimmons, James A., and B. N. Srikar. "Emergency Ambulance Location Using the Contiguous Zone Search Routine." *Journal of Operations Management* 2, no. 4 (August 1982), pp. 225-37.

Min, H. "Location Planning of Airport Facilities Using the Analytic Hierarchy Process." *Logistics and Transportation Review* 30, no. 1 (March 1995), pp. 79-94.

Schmenner, Roger W. "The Location Decisions of New Services." In *New Service Development,* Eds. J. A. Fitzsimmons and M. J. Fitzsimmons. Thousand Oaks, CA: Sage Publications, 2000, pp. 216-38.

Endnotes

1. http://www.pitney-bowes.com/us/location-intelligence/case-studies/dominos-pizza.html.
2. S. E. Kimes and J. A. Fitzsimmons, "Selecting Profitable Hotel Sites at La Quinta Motor Inns," *Interfaces* 20, no. 2 (March 1990), pp. 12-20.
3. Suzanne Alexander, "Saturating Cities with Stores Can Pay," *The Wall Street Journal,* September 11, 1989, p. B1.
4. James H. Donnelly, "Marketing Intermediaries in Channels of Distribution for Services," *Journal of Marketing* 40, January 1976, pp. 55-70.
5. Julie E. Kendall, "E-distance and the Theatres of South Jersey," *Decision Line,* March 2003, pp. 13-15.
6. Information provided by Michael Lane (geologist, PHD, TSRA GIS coordinator), Sara Windsor (information technology manager), Lisa Scott (DCEM director), Randy Burke (TSR Water Company director), and Louise deWilder (security and emergency management director).
7. W. J. Abernathy and J. C. Hershey, "A Spatial-Allocation Model for Regional Health Services Planning," *Operations Research* 20, no. 3 (May-June 1972), pp. 629-42.
8. David L. Huff, "A Programmed Solution for Approximating an Optimum Retail Location," *Land Economics,* August 1966, pp. 293-303.
9. S. E. Kimes and J. A. Fitzsimmons, "Selecting Profitable Hotel Sites at La Quinta Motor Inns," *Interfaces* 20, no. 2 (March 1990), pp. 12-20.
10. This case was prepared by James H. Vance under the supervision of Professor James A. Fitzsimmons.

Part 3

Managing Service Operations

We will discover that the service supply chain actually is a challenge in relationship management because of the nature of a customer–supplier duality. A discussion of the growth of services in today's global competitive environment follows. The day-to-day operation of a service is a constant challenge because the objectives of the organization, the needs of the customer, and attention to service providers must be managed simultaneously in an ever-changing environment. We explore strategies for matching capacity and demand with techniques such as overbooking, workshift scheduling, and yield management. A perfect match seldom is possible, however, and the result is waiting customers. Thus, the management of waiting lines to avoid customer perceptions of a poor service experience is an important skill. We conclude Part 3 with the application of queuing models to plan for adequate service capacity to balance the cost of customer waiting with the cost of providing service.

Chapter 

Service Supply Relationships

Learning Objectives

After completing this chapter, you should be able to:

1. Contrast the supply chain for physical goods with service supply relationships.
2. Describe the role played by an omnichannel supply chain in e-commerce.
3. Identify the sources of value in a service supply relationship.
4. Discuss the managerial implications of bidirectional relationships.
5. Identify the three factors that drive profitability for a professional service firm.
6. Classify a business service based on the focus of the service and its importance to the buyer.
7. Discuss the managerial considerations to be addressed in outsourcing services.

Supply chain management is a total systems approach to delivering manufactured products to the end customer. Using information technology to coordinate all elements of the supply chain from parts suppliers to retailers achieves a level of integration that is a competitive advantage not available in traditional logistics systems.

Consider, for example, the decision of Hewlett-Packard to manufacture a generic DeskJet printer and allow distributors the option to localize the printer by adding the proper manuals and power cords. The result was a significant reduction of finished goods inventory because demand was then consolidated into one generic printer, which eliminated the need for separate inventories for each country. This postponement strategy also produced unexpected savings in shipping costs because generic printers can be packed more densely.[1]

Taco Bell took an approach to its supply chain not unlike Hewlett-Packard. The first stage of Taco Bell's supply chain consists of the natural resources supplied from agriculture (e.g., meat, vegetables, spices, and grain). These ingredients are purchased in bulk and held at regional distribution centers for supply to the retail stores. Removing the kitchen from the retail store to a central location allowed for consolidation of demand and reduction of waste. The production process at the retail store is changed from make-to-order to assemble-to-order. Customers are delighted because wait times are shorter, the facility is cleaner, and extra room is allowed for dining-in.

Chapter Preview

Supply chain management for manufactured goods offers benefits obtained by taking a total systems view of the value chain from product design to after-sale customer service. Information technology has been the driving force behind the ability to coordinate the many interrelated activities commonly performed by independent companies. Service supply management, however, is best depicted as a relationship rather than a chain of activities because of the customer–supplier duality found in services, including the role of social media. An example of home health care is used to demonstrate the sources of value in a service supply relationship. The unique characteristics of professional services are explored and the chapter concludes with a discussion of service outsourcing and the related managerial considerations.

Supply Chain Management

The challenge of supply chain management is to balance the requirements of reliable and prompt customer delivery with manufacturing and inventory costs. Supply chain modeling enables managers to evaluate which options will provide the greatest improvement in customer satisfaction at reasonable costs. The supply chain is modeled as a network that captures the relationship between asset costs (i.e., inventory and capital equipment) and the time domain characteristics of customer service (i.e., responsiveness and reliability in customer delivery).

Network Model

The physical goods supply chain can be viewed as a network of value-adding material processing stages each defined with supply input, material transformation, and demand output. As shown in Figure 9.1, these stages (suppliers, manufacturing, distribution, retailing, and recycling) are connected with arrows depicting the flow of material with inventory stocks between each stage. The manufacturing stage represents the operation where raw material and parts arrive from external suppliers; the material is transformed or assembled to add value, creating an inventory of finished goods that is transported downstream to distributors and then to retailers where consumers purchase the item.

Concerns for environmental sustainability have awakened manufacturers to the need for product-life-cycle management. Thus, at end-of-life, we are seeing an increase in the number of products designed to be recycled or remanufactured rather than disposed of in a landfill. For example, spent products such as old printer cartridges are remanufactured and aluminum cans are recycled because of their inherent value. Several governments in Europe require automobiles to be designed for ease in recycling component materials.

Information transfer flows upstream as shown by dashed lines in Figure 9.1 and includes activities by suppliers, process and product design, and after-sales service. A significant benefit from supply chain coordination is utilization of downstream information. For example, automobile manufacturers often discover design flaws during after-sales service. Point-of-sale data at the retailer can be aggregated at the distributor level to alert manufacturing in planning production schedules that will avoid either inventory buildup or lost sales.

FIGURE 9.1 **Supply Chain for Physical Goods**

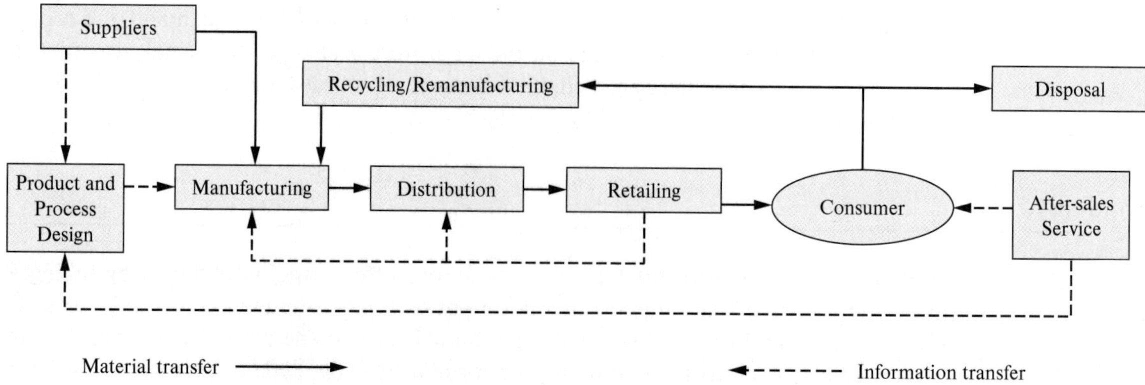

Success is achieved only with the formation of effective partnerships and cooperation among participants throughout the entire supply chain. In an uncoordinated supply chain, a *"bullwhip effect"* results in which a small change in retail orders is magnified as we move back up the supply chain to the distributor and finally to the manufacturer. The independent stages in the supply chain, unaware of the true nature of final demand, overreact to orders from downstream customers. Also, delays in orders being filled create oscillations in inventory stocks that are propagated upstream. The lack of supply chain coordination results in a self-imposed system destabilization that creates simultaneous overstocking of inventory at one point in time followed by later stockouts.

Managing Uncertainty

Managing a supply chain would be straightforward except for the uncertainty arising from three sources: supplier delivery performance, manufacturing reliability, and customer demand. Inventory is used as insurance in this uncertain world. To meet customer service level objectives (e.g., experience stockouts less than 5 percent of the time), a little extra material or safety stocks are held so that customer deliveries can be made when something goes wrong in an upstream process.

Any number of events can cause variability in supplier on-time deliveries: storms delaying a shipment, quality problems, machine failure, or late arrival of raw material supply. Over time, a distribution of delivery performance punctuality can be established for each supplier and used in purchasing negotiations, because the more reliable a supplier is, the smaller the safety stock of materials required to protect the downstream operation. Manufacturing reliability is influenced by the same problems facing suppliers and, also, by internal scheduling delays caused by several products competing for shared resources (e.g., an overhead crane in a machine shop). The overall uncertainty is captured by a historical probability distribution of on-time performance. Customer demand variability is the most difficult factor to determine. However, market research and past experience with similar products can be used to predict future demand distributions.

Strategic initiatives can lessen the impact of uncertainty and thus improve customer service. For example, implementation of total quality control techniques such as statistical process control can improve manufacturing reliability. More dependable transportation modes can be investigated, also. Changes in product design can allow the manufacturing operations to stock uncompleted products and postpone the final customization, thus increasing responsiveness to customer orders. Consider the strategies taken by Procter & Gamble and Walmart as shown in Example 9.1

Example 9.1 Procter & Gamble and Walmart

Procter & Gamble and Walmart both had the same goal of improving the effectiveness and profitability of their production/distribution system, but each, working independently in self-serving ways, temporarily damaged the industry. The "before" column in Table 9.1 captures many of the problems faced by supplier and retailer in the supply chain. For example, when Procter & Gamble initiated a price promotion on Pampers to boost market share, Walmart stocked up on Pampers at the low cost. Walmart's intention was to improve its margins by buying during a discount period and selling later at regular prices when the promotion ended (called "forward buying"). The result of such independent behavior is a self-induced "bullwhip effect" on the level of finished goods inventories in the supply chain. Forward buying created great swings in manufacturing volume, because stocked-up Walmart would not place another order for months. The added costs of holding inventory by Walmart and disruptions in manufacturing schedules led to collaboration between Walmart and Procter & Gamble to move the supply chain to the "after" column of Table 9.1. Procter & Gamble agreed to stop promotions and Walmart initiated the "everyday low prices" marketing slogan.

Omnichannel Supply Chain

Warehouses that historically have focused solely on store replenishment are now being used to support e-commerce. Companies increasingly seek to have visibility of the warehouse inventory regardless of channel. This not only allows for higher service levels at

TABLE 9.1 The Impact of Supply Chain Management at Walmart and Procter & Gamble

Element or Link	Before	After
Channel relationships	Independent/competitive; many competing suppliers and distributors	Interdependent; a few select suppliers and distributors as partners
Flow of goods	Push	Pull
Flow of information (upstream)	Pull, incomplete, partial, manual; encumbered by numerous human links in the chain; slow, on the order of weeks or months; most recent downstream demand data and production schedules not available	Push, planned, appropriate, automated; high level of connectivity and transparency for all players in the chain; fast, in some cases instantaneous; access to most recent downstream demand data and production schedules
Flow of information (downstream)	Little or no product-tracking information	Product tracking using RFID; advance shipping notices
Business processes	Predominantly in-house; locally optimized for efficiency	In-house for key processes, others outsourced for flexibility; integrated and synchronized to match supply with demand
Demand management	Reactive forecasting used for capacity planning; segmented	Proactive management to remove volatility; customer relationship management
Inventory	High; used as a buffer against uncertainty and lack of information; *bullwhip effect* common	Low; information connectivity reduces inventory buffers owing to transparency; delayed differentiation used more effectively to risk pool and reduce inventory further; better positioning of inventory further up the supply chain
Production	Inflexible; long lead times; dominated by material requirements planning (MRP); push; build-to-stock	Flexible; lead time reduction; pull (e.g., just-in-time); mass customization (products based on common components positioned at the right location in the supply chain to meet customer lead times); build-to-order
Distribution	Traditional warehousing network; extend MRP to distribution; distribution requirements planning; push	Pull ideas extended to distribution in such programs as quick response, continuous replenishment; vendor-managed inventory; distribution centers and cross docking; direct delivery more feasible
Product design	Product designed without input from manufacturing or distribution	Greater emphasis on designed for manufacturing and supply chain management
Pricing	Strong emphasis on promotional pricing	Greater emphasis on fixed pricing and everyday low pricing (EDLP)

lower cost because of demand consolidation and thus lower inventory levels, but also allows customers to check their order status. The customer experience of purchasing, tracking, and receiving goods from Amazon.com "the Amazon effect" has pressured retailers everywhere to adopt this *omnichannel supply chain*.

Figure 9.2 shows how an omnichannel supply chain uses a central stock pool or warehouse to control the process of stock management and fulfillment of orders. This puts the supply chain in the hands of customers because the central warehouse acts as a visible clearing house for orders from various sources and a distribution operation that uses many different channels. Omnichannel supply chains allow customers to browse, buy, and return goods through various channels instead of being limited to the traditional in-store experience.

FIGURE 9.2
Omnichannel Supply Chain

©NATUREWORLD/Alamy

Service Supply Relationships[2]

Customer–Supplier Duality

The nature of services creates a customer-supplier duality that results in service supply relationships rather than the supply chain found in manufactured goods that depicts a physical object passed from one entity to another. Services can be considered as acting on people's *minds* (e.g., education, entertainment, religion), *bodies* (e.g., transportation, lodging, health care), *belongings* (e.g., auto repair, dry cleaning, banking), and *information* (e.g., tax preparation, insurance, legal defense). Thus, all services act on something provided by the customer. The implication is that customers also are acting as suppliers in the service exchange, that is, the customer-supplier duality. The customer-supplier duality is shown in Figure 9.3 as *bidirectional* relationships between the service delivery firm, its supplier, and the customer.

Examples of elementary single-level service supply chains (i.e., no supplier is present) are shown in Table 9.2. In each case the service transaction is carried out directly between the customer and the service provider without the need for ancillary suppliers. For example, a patient sees a dentist for a toothache and has a filling prepared for the affected tooth.

FIGURE 9.3
Service Supply Bidirectional Relationships

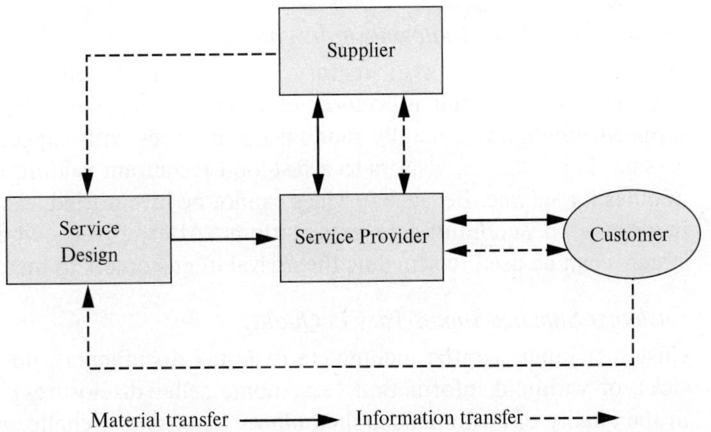

TABLE 9.2
Single-Level Bidirectional Service Supply Relationships

Service Category	Customer-Supplier	> *Input*/Output >	Service Provider
Minds	Student	> *Mind*/Knowledge >	Professor
Bodies	Patient	> *Tooth*/Filling >	Dentist
Belongings	Investor	> *Money*/Interest >	Bank
Information	Client	> *Documents*/1040 >	Tax preparer

TABLE 9.3 **Two-Level Bidirectional Service Supply Relationships**

Service Category	Customer-Supplier	> *Input*/Output >	Service Provider	> *Input*/Output >	Provider's Supplier
Minds	Patient	> *Disturbed*/Treated >	Therapist	> *Prescription*/Drugs >	Pharmacy
Bodies	Patient	> *Blood*/Diagnosis >	Physician	> *Sample*/Test result >	Lab
Belongings	Driver	> *Car*/Repaired >	Garage	> *Engine*/Rebuilt >	Machine shop
Information	Home buyer	> *Property*/Loan >	Mortgage company	> *Location*/Clear title >	Title search

Table 9.3 shows examples of two-level service supply chains as depicted in Figure 9.3. In each example, the service provider requires the assistance of a third-party supplier to complete the service. For example, a patient feeling ill sees a physician who draws blood that is sent to an off-site laboratory for analysis. Upon receiving the blood report from the laboratory the physician makes the diagnosis.

The customer–supplier duality and resulting bidirectional relationship are central to understanding the nature of service relationships. Several observations will be made that lead to implications for the management of service supply relationships.

Service Supply Relationships Are Hubs, Not Chains

For the most common supply relationship the concept of simultaneous production and consumption applies. For example, when one visits the dentist for teeth cleaning, the supply relationship is compressed to a single transaction between your teeth and the dental hygienist. As noted in Table 9.3, the supply chain can be extended to include a supplier to the service provider; however, service supply relationships extending beyond two levels are quite rare. In fact, the service supply relationship is more like a hub than a chain because the service provider acts as the agent for the customer when dealing with outside suppliers. Hubs are more desirable than chains because there are fewer opportunities for delays and information can be shared more easily. Partnering or sole-sourcing between a service provider and its supplier is common practice because both financial and process efficiencies are achieved (e.g., physician and lab).

Service Capacity Is Analogous to Inventory

For goods supply chains, inventory is used to buffer the variations in final customer demand and allow full utilization of productive capacity. For services, the customer-supplied inputs are generally random occurrences with expectations of immediate processing. For example, visitors to a fast-food restaurant seldom will wait more than a few minutes for service. Because services cannot be inventoried, excess capacity must be held in reserve to accommodate expectations. Alternatively, when possible, reservations systems can be used to schedule the arrival of customers to match capacity.

Customer-Supplied Inputs Vary in Quality

Customer inputs can be incomplete (e.g., tax documents), not well described (e.g., feel sick), or withhold information (e.g., home seller disclosures). This lack of consistency in the quality of customer-supplied inputs represents a challenge for the service provider to deliver on promises when inputs are questionable. This situation places a premium on effective communications. Explicitly communicating value-adding expectations with customers prior to service can avoid misunderstandings.

Managing Service Relationships

Example 9.2 Service Relationship Management in Home Health Care

The unrestrained rise in cost of health care has motivated creative alternative methods of providing care at lower cost. Home health care is one approach to managing the cost of care by treating patients in their home and thus avoiding hospitalization or nursing home care. The home health care service relationship has the additional property that service providers (i.e., nurses, dietitians, and therapists) are mobile servers because they travel to the customer.

TABLE 9.4 Impact of Service Relationship Management on Home Health Care

Source: James Fitzsimmons, Edward Anderson, Douglas Morrice, and G. Edward Powell, "Managing Service Supply Relationships," *International Journal of Services Technology and Management* 5, no. 3, 2004, pp. 221–32.

Element	Before	After
Service Recipient	Passive	Active as a coproducer
Flow of Service	Available waiting for demand	Activated upon demand
Flow of Information (upstream)	Pull: manual reporting of demand data results in delayed management response	Push: high level of connectivity and transparency with fast or instantaneous access to most recent demand data
Flow of Information (downstream)	Little or no knowledge of resource deployment	Real-time tracking and dispatching
Demand Management	Limited to use of appointments and reservations	Proactive involving customer in scheduling to achieve bidirectional optimization
Capacity Management	Limited to use of part-time employees	Creative use of cross-trained employees, outsourcing, and customer self-service
Service Delivery	Inflexible; standardized and impersonal	Flexible; personable with customization possible
Routing and Scheduling	Static; fixed daily schedules	Dynamic; based on system connectivity and process visibility
New Service Design	Marketing initiatives based on firm's perception of customer needs	Virtual value chain design with customer database information driving new services
Pricing	Fixed	Variable; yield management promotes off-peak demand and avoids idle capacity

Table 9.4 summarizes the features of a well-managed service relationship for mobile workers shown in the "after" column as compared to the traditional approach shown in the "before" column. Value in service supply relationship management arises from three sources: bidirectional optimization, management of productive capacity, and management of perishability.

Bidirectional Optimization

Bidirectional optimization implies the possibility of doing what is best from the customer's perspective while doing the best for the service enterprise. In home health care the patient is an active participant in the service. Direct customer involvement facilitates bidirectional optimization, a simultaneous optimization of both supply and demand for the service. This translates into providing a highly individualized service for the patient that is very cost-effective for the organization.

For mobile service, a "time window" is reserved for each customer to be available for a service worker to perform the requested service. Customers see generous time windows as a major inconvenience that wastes their time for the benefit of an inefficient service provider. Typically, managers of mobile workforces ask customers to be available for extended time windows (i.e., between noon and 5:00 PM) because routes, customer sequencing, and frequent service provider job status updates are not built into a functionally integrated information system. Service relationship management uses forecasting data to construct an initial daily plan for each worker. Customers then can select from several appointment choices based on a preoptimized calculation of an optimized solution for the whole group of service workers in a defined geographic area. The calculation of the optimized solution considers customer preferences and service requirements (i.e., language, worker skills, worker licensing, and supplies on the vehicle) along with geographical information such as where the service workers will be just prior to and just after a particular customer's appointment.

Home visits require dynamic routing to avoid unproductive travel time. ©Terry Vine/Blend Images LLC RF

Productive Capacity

A primary consideration of *productive capacity* for mobile workers is the amount of time spent between jobs, which correlates with the distance between jobs. Because value is created predominantly during the time that the mobile worker is at the customer site, time spent traveling between customer sites is lost productive capacity. This creates an opportunity to increase greatly the productive capacity of the workforce by better management of the service relationship resulting in more cumulative time for workers to be with customers. Strategies to improve productive capacity of the service worker include transfer, replacement, and embellishment.

Transfer is an approach to make knowledge available to customers so that value can be transferred with very low cost. One example is a web-based, frequently-asked-questions (FAQ) database. This information-transfer tool can be used instead of more expensive human resources and is available at all hours. For example, patients can access disease-specific areas of a website and obtain information about side effects of medicines, explanations of symptoms, or procedures to follow.

Replacement is a strategy of substituting technology for human resources. Blood pressure measurement is one example. For patients needing blood pressure measurements three times daily, an automated measurement system might be substituted for a nurse visit. A digital blood pressure measurement device is easy for patients to use and costs less than a single visit from a home health care nurse.

Embellishment of customer skills to enable self-service is a third strategy to enhance the productive capacity of the home health care system. Teaching a patient or family member to change a surgical dressing is appropriate in some circumstances. This embellishment of customer skills requires additional nursing time initially, but significantly decreases the subsequent use of nursing resources if, for example, a wound is chronic and requires daily changes of dressings for an extended period of time. In such a scenario, a nurse might check the healing wound every three days instead of daily, resulting in a 66 percent decrease in the amount of nursing time required to care for the patient.

Perishability

Management of *perishability* is the approach used in service relationship management to minimize the negative impact of idle time on the productive capacity of the distributed service workforce. The productive capacity of a service worker is limited to the time he or she is at the customer site with the right tools, skills, and knowledge of the customer's requirements and preferences.

For the mobile workforce, managing perishability has two foci. The first is a time allocation system that offers time windows to customers based on "best use" of workers. In service relationship management systems that use dynamic schedule optimization software, schedules are constructed and revised up until the very last possible moment before dispatch of a worker to a job. Service systems with no communication infrastructure are limited to creating a fixed schedule for each mobile worker at the beginning of the workday. Service systems with mobile data communications, however, can produce "real-time" schedules so that a worker learns of the next assignment only after completing the current job. The dynamic allocation of jobs among workers minimizes idle (i.e., perishable) time.

Managing perishability also involves the process of training, refining, and extending skills and capabilities of workers. When potential idle time of workers is identified and directed to training activities, productive capacity can be reclaimed prospectively. This service inventory-hedging strategy benefits the firm by directing skill-enhancing activities into idle time slots, which makes the worker available during the time when traditional training efforts otherwise would have consumed productive capacity. The mobile worker with mobile data communication tools can obtain modular, computer-based training, certification, and testing material "online" (using the mobile data terminal of the service vehicle), thereby maximizing this hedging strategy.

Social Media in Services

The emergence of social media has changed the way service firms run their businesses significantly. *Social media* refers to web-based and mobile technologies that turn communication into interactive dialogue. Social media helps to blend technology and social interaction for the co-creation of value. As of November 2016, Facebook had more than 1.79 billion users, topping Google in weekly traffic in the United States. One source claimed one out of every eight couples married in the United States met on social media.[3]

Social media, or Web 2.0, is being used by corporations in ways different from the first-generation Web 1.0 applications. For example, Walmart uses the Internet to hold down prices by improving its management of supply chain inventories, and banks eliminate clerical workers by using online accounts and e-mail correspondence. Whereas Web 1.0 was about automating routine processes, Web 2.0 is about building customer relationships, fostering connections in far-flung organizations, and embracing co-creation in product development.[4]

Characteristics of social media that are useful to service firms include

- A wide reach that is decentralized, less hierarchical, and has multiple points of production and consumption.
- Easy access that generally is available to the public at little or no cost.
- Ease of use that does not require specialized skills and training, or requires only modest reinterpretation of existing skills.
- Immediacy that allows instantaneous responses.
- Flexibility that allows information to be altered almost instantaneously by comments or editing.

Social media no longer are just a good option for a service firm to do business, but now are the first place customers turn to when they need to contact a service firm. A 2011 study, conducted by the customer experience analytics company ClickFox, identified the top five industry groups in which people have sought customer service using social media as retail, telephone, travel and hospitality, cable, and banks.[5]

When a customer purchases a shirt at Target, the retailer "listens" very carefully to any feedback or review that the customer may generate on the product. Customers find it very easy to provide feedback and seek information about most services on Twitter or other media without having to spend long times on telephone calls.

Effective use of social media and their marketing potential requires a deep understanding of where the customers are, what they are searching for, and what problems they have. One of the most important things that firms can do in social media is to provide resources and information about their services.

Social Media as a Competitive Strategy

Because service innovations usually are not patentable, the industry is very competitive in the social media space to learn from each other and outperform each other. Firms constantly check each other's online strategies and readjust their own when necessary. Another concern for firms that use social media involves advertisement and marketing regulations. A report by Onmark Solutions, a consultant in e-marketing services, recommends five strategies to move offline operations online to succeed in social media–based competition:[6]

- **Tune-up reminders:** Customers can benefit from regular tune-up reminders related to the service. The reminder might be for a tax filing date or dental appointment posted on Facebook or Twitter.
- **Cookie-cutter presence in cyberspace:** The more open channels of communication a firm offers, the better the service is perceived by customers. The firm needs to identify where customers go online when they have questions or feedback, and then use those social channels to respond.
- **Lead generation:** Firms can develop relationships outside of their services that will lead to referrals. Social media provide the fastest way to spread the good (and sometimes bad) word-of-mouth.
- **Customer education:** Instead of selling a service, a firm can educate its customers about a "lifestyle" that indirectly aligns with its service offerings. For example, an insurance company can use social media to promote safe driving.
- **Start online, finish offline:** Often, a customer might pose a question online that involves sensitive information. On such occasions, a service representative can call the customer directly and/or invite the customer to an office to discuss the response.

Social Media and Customer Convenience

Service firms have found innovative ways to use social media and technological advancements to add to customer convenience. Banks accept check deposits when customers snap a photo of a check on their smartphone and send it to the bank. Airlines send boarding passes to passengers' smartphones, which subsequently can be scanned at the airport security check without a need to print a boarding pass. Insurance companies data mine for customer information on Facebook, Twitter, and other sites, which enables underwriters and claims professionals to track individuals' lifestyles, experiences, and habits. The insurance industry, for example, can identify a link between consumers' payment histories and risky driving behavior.[7] The danger of such data mining is, of course, the compromise to consumer privacy. As the new saying goes: "What happens in Vegas stays on . . . Facebook, Twitter, Flickr, YouTube. . . ."

A social media service firm called "Flip.to" turns hotel guests into brand advocates.[8] Flip.to calls its service "Magnetic Marketing," which claims that the greatest bond between a brand and a consumer is when the customer is ready to confirm a sale. Flip.to utilizes social media during this stage of the buying cycle to understand consumer behavior and capitalize on customer engagement. The study shows that each positive post a customer makes at the time of booking a hotel room brought, on average, eight new bookings. Service firms now use the term *consumer-generated media* (CGM) to refer to the power of social media–based promotions. Radian6, a social media consultant, prepared an e-book for the financial sector to use social media. The consultant recommends social media "netiquettes" that ask service providers to avoid the "Three D's" (disclosure, defamation, and discrimination) and to promote the "Three R's" (reciprocation, respect, and reliability).[9]

Social Media for Organizing and Co-creation of Value

Using social media to enable connections across a geographically dispersed organization promotes learning and fosters creativity. For example, when Red Robin launched its Tavern Double burger, it turned to an internal social network instead of sending out spiral-bound books to its store managers. Personal visits by home office executives to store sites were replaced with open virtual discussions. These discussions and videos produced kitchen-tested recipes in days and significantly reduced the time involved in the idea-to-counter process. Companies are using social networks to solve problems, share information, and even use customers in product design. Dell Computers, for example, used its IdeaStorm site to reach customers for product improvements ideas such as backlit keyboards. The company also proposes ideas for new products on the site to solicit feedback from customers before launch.[10]

Social media are here to stay. The economics of social media have created a new field called "socialnomics."[11] Service firms find it necessary to use the social media for branding, recruiting, building awareness, information sharing, networking, and most importantly, for listening to the customers. Today's firms listen first and sell next. The social media generation no longer finds products and services themselves; they expect the products and services to find them.

Professional Service Firms[12]

Professional services are attractive because of the intellectual challenge, potential for job growth, and high income. Examples of professional service providers include architects, lawyers, consultants, accountants, and contracting engineers. Professionals command a specific body of knowledge and usually belong to a discipline that licenses its members (e.g., CPAs) based on demonstrated competence. Some professionals engage in solo practices, but many choose to participate in group practices of single or multidisciplinary nature. For the purposes of our discussion, professional service providers refer to partners who own and manage the firm and junior professional staff who are paid a salary and aspire to become partners.

Attributes of Professional Services

The term *professional services* describes a service delivered by knowledge workers and has four distinguishing features. First, the work involves a high level of specialization and customization. Such highly specialized and customized work creates management issues different from those that occur in a mass-market standardized approach of other services. Most important, managing a professional service requires the ability to manage activities and information without proven routines that are common in other businesses.

Second, the frequency and importance of face-to-face interactions with customers, often referred to as clients, require special attention. The face-to-face nature of the work changes the way quality and level of service are perceived and measured. In addition, a behavioral skill, such as customer management, can be as important as technical competence itself.

Third, professional services are delivered by highly educated professional people who represent the assets of the firm. The organization, therefore, must give careful attention to both the input (i.e., recruiting) and the output (i.e., clients) sides of the service.

Finally, according to James Brian Quinn, Philip Anderson, and Sydney Finkelstein, the true professional commands a body of knowledge that operates on four levels of increasing importance.[13]

Cognitive knowledge (know-what) is the basic mastery of a discipline achieved through extensive training and certification. This knowledge is necessary but not sufficient for commercial success.

Advanced skills (know-how) translate "book learning" into effective execution. The ability to apply the rules of a discipline to complex real-world problems is the most widespread value-creating professional skill level.

Systems understanding (know-why) is deep knowledge of the web of cause-and-effect relationships underlying the discipline. Professionals with know-why can anticipate subtle interactions and unintended consequences. The ultimate expression of a systems understanding is highly trained intuition.

Self-motivated creativity (care-why) consists of will, motivation, and adaptability for success. Without self-motivated creativity, intellectual leaders can lose their knowledge advantage through complacency.

Thus, staff mentoring by partners and investment in continuing education is an expectation of those who join a professional firm.

Service Consulting

The market for consulting in the service sector is growing steadily. Service consulting is sought when a firm faces challenges or opportunities that it cannot handle with its internal capabilities. The areas of the service industry where consulting is prevalent include health care, financial services, logistics, and hospitality (hotels, restaurants, and entertainment firms such as Disney). The scope of service consulting covers a wide range of operations such as staffing, billing, office automation, workforce scheduling, process improvement, quality assurance, waiting line management, and call center management. An increasing number of nonprofit institutions and government agencies also seek consulting services for outside advice. Major service consulting firms include Accenture, Bain, Booz Allen Hamilton, Deloitte Consulting (an affiliate of Deloitte Touché Tohmatsu), and IBM Global Services. The effectiveness of service consulting typically relies upon improving the efficiency of the firm's operations and its ability to maintain a steady flow of business.

Consider the following ways that service consulting businesses use the traditional 5 P's of operations in developing strategies:

- People: workforce management, productivity improvement, and staffing decisions.
- Processes: process improvement, office automation, and reengineering.
- Programs: quality improvement and Lean/Kaizen projects.
- Plant: service facility and layout planning.
- Planning and control systems: dispatching, enterprise resource planning (ERP) and closed-loop systems.

A typical service consulting project contains a combination of these components in different proportions. The stages of a typical consulting engagement are given in Figure 9.4.

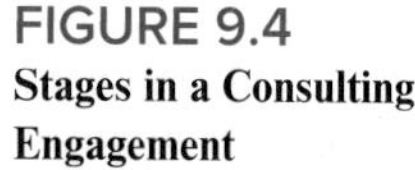
FIGURE 9.4
Stages in a Consulting Engagement

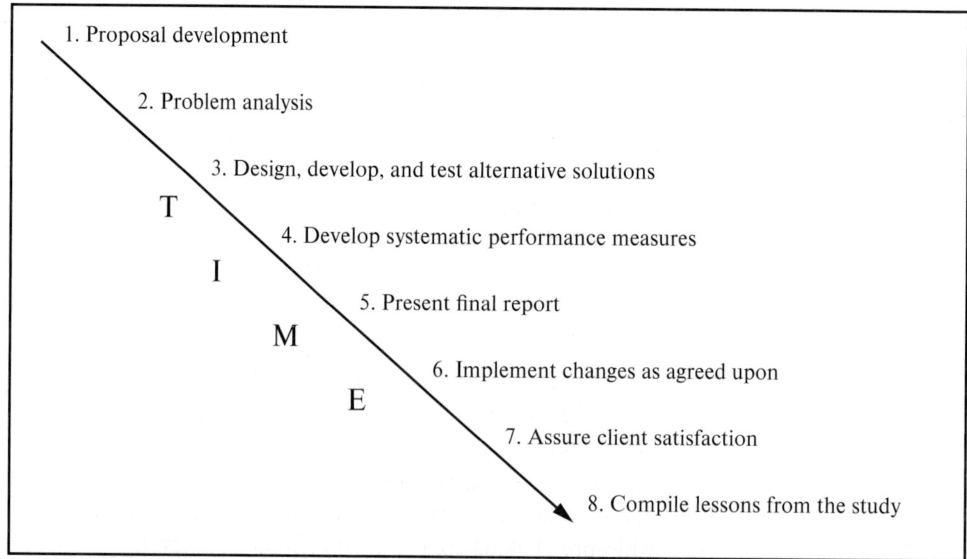

Regardless of the nature of the business, the general steps of this consulting cycle are very comparable, but the tools used and emphasis given at each stage might differ. Rasiel offers a few useful tips for successful consulting using the McKinsey model:[14]

- Underpromise and overdeliver–decide very carefully what you promise to your client.
- The 80-20 rule–80 percent of your problems come from 20 percent of your issues.
- "Don't boil the ocean"–pick the battle that you can win.
- Use the "elevator rule"–know your solution thoroughly so that you can explain it to your client in a 30-second elevator ride.
- Pluck the low-hanging fruit–make quick improvements with easy implementation even in the middle of a project.
- Hit singles–don't go for a home run in each stage; instead, take smaller steps toward your goal.
- Make a chart every day–illustrate your findings in a visual presentation.
- Engage your client–continuous engagement of your client keeps the project moving and avoids stalling.

A typical consulting firm can be thought of as a pyramid, with four levels named "finders," "minders," "binders," and "grinders." Finders are the firm's partners who secure new businesses opportunities. Minders are the middle-level managers who are involved throughout the project. A binder is someone with a very high level of people skills and is a whiz in client relationships, building trust, and maintaining fluid communications. Grinders are the entry-level or junior consultants who do much of the leg work.[15]

Operational Characteristics

Professional service firms often are organized as partnerships instead of corporations. The partners have equity in the firm and, as a group, represent the governing body. The day-to-day work of the firm is performed by a staff of junior professionals on salary.

The economic success of a partnership is measured by profit-per-partner, which is driven by three factors: margin, productivity, and leverage as shown in the relationship below:

$$\begin{aligned} Profit-per-Partner &= \left(\frac{Profit}{Fees}\right)\left(\frac{Fees}{Staff}\right)\left(\frac{Staff}{Partners}\right) \\ &= (Margin)(Productivity)(Leverage) \end{aligned}$$

Margins

Margins often are the most-utilized factor in measuring the profitability of departments within a professional services firm. Unfortunately, however, margins frequently are inaccurate and misleading indicators.

Margin is equal to the percent of profit for each dollar of fees charged (i.e., margin is equal to fees minus costs as a ratio of fees). This ratio is affected by many factors, including the *productivity* (i.e., fees-to-staff ratio) and *leverage* (i.e., staff-per-partner ratio) of the firm. For example, a more productive firm will incur less cost for each dollar of fees than will a less productive firm. Less cost translates to higher profit per dollar of fees, which means higher margins.

Aside from productivity and leverage, overhead costs (e.g., clerical support, office space, and equipment) influence margins. If these costs are not kept under control, margins will suffer. However, just cutting overhead costs cannot return desired results in the long run.

Productivity

Productivity can be broken down further into two factors that affect the short- and long-term success of the firm: realized fee-per-hour (value) and utilization of professional staff, as shown below.

$$\begin{aligned} Productivity &= \left(\frac{Fees}{Hours}\right)\left(\frac{Hours}{Staff}\right) \\ &= (Value)(Utilization) \end{aligned}$$

Utilization is the ratio of the number of hours billed to the number of possible billable hours. Assuming that most professionals work at least 40 hours per week, a week with 30 billed hours would have a utilization of 30/40 or 75 percent.

Utilization is affected by two aspects of the professional services business. First, balancing demand and capacity is especially challenging for professionals. The challenges stem from the fact that customers commonly desire immediate service from very specialized personnel. Whenever a project or contract is completed and no work is in backlog, the staff must use nonbillable time until more work is found. Because clients tend to be impatient, a backlog is difficult to maintain.

Several strategies are used to maximize utilization by matching capacity with demand. First, firms find ways to schedule future work into a backlog. Although clients want immediate attention, firms can give incentives or "lock" customers into a backlog. Incentives include price-differentiated levels of service and discounts for delays. Lock-ins include building a customer knowledge database, bundling service with products, and ownership of a customer's processes and designs.

Another strategy to maximize utilization is to spread personal knowledge and skill throughout the organization. This strategy is especially useful when a customer consistently asks for certain personnel, which constrains a firm's ability to manage capacity. A firm will be much more likely to maintain high coverage throughout the firm if it has cross-trained people available for any given assignment instead of having a high percentage of overutilized individuals.

A second fact that affects utilization is the importance of nonbillable activities. These activities include business development, training, and general management. None of these activities generates revenue, but all are vital to the future of the company. For example, consulting firms have functional groups consisting of six-to-ten billable staff members. If a dedicated manager is assigned to a group of nine billable personnel, the utilization of the group immediately falls to 9/10 or 90 percent at best. Without the manager, the group might be more profitable in the short term, but the group would quickly become disorganized and less competitive in the long term.

Another factor in the productivity of a professional services firm is the amount of *value* that they can provide and capture in the rates. Increasing the value of services can be attained through several value-building activities. First, a firm can identify the service offerings that customers value. This activity involves product development, market research, and customer feedback. Second, firms can demand higher fees by creating ways to specialize and differentiate themselves from their competitors. This requires investment in hiring and developing talent who can offer unique expertise.

Leverage

Leverage is the ratio of the number of professional staff members to the number of partners, an essential factor in determining the profit-per-partner. Partners get profit from two sources: the high rates a senior staff member charges for services, and, more important, the ability to hire professional staff and bill them to customers at multiples of their salary. A successful firm will maximize its leverage while still maintaining the ability to complete projects successfully.

Managing the leverage of a firm involves matching the skill level of the professional staff to the requirements of the contract or project. We will look at three common categories of projects:

- *Brains projects* involve solving client problems that are at the forefront of professional or technical knowledge. At a minimum, brains projects involve extreme complexity and need professional staff members who possess the ability to create, innovate, and pioneer new approaches to solving problems. A firm that targets these projects should market itself as being the most skilled and talented at its craft. In essence, the firm's appeal to the market is "hire us because we are smart."

  Brains projects seldom are standardized or repeatable. In addition, the skill-level requirements for the professional staff are high and the partners are the experts in their

TABLE 9.5
Profitability Tactics

TACTIC	CATEGORY
Lower Fixed (Overhead) Costs	**Margin**
Improve cash cycle	
Reduce office space and equipment	
Reduce administrative and support staff	
Raise Prices and Differentiate	**Productivity**
Specialize, innovate, add more value	
Target higher value work	
Invest in training	
Invest in higher value services	
Address Underperforming Projects	**Productivity**
Drop unprofitable services	
Drop unprofitable customers	
Increase Volume	**Productivity**
Increase utilization	
Lower Variable Costs	**Leverage**
Improve engagement management	
Increase leverage of professionals	
Increase the use of paraprofessionals	

profession. This inability to standardize and the high-skill requirements make leveraging difficult.

- *Grey hair projects* also require a high level of skill and customization, but they involve less creativity and innovation than brains projects. The challenge of managing a grey hair project is similar to that of managing a brains project, but marketing differs for the two types of projects.

  Grey hair projects require knowledge and judgment, but they can be standardized and repeated, especially when a firm specializes in a certain type of project, such as implementation of enterprise resource planning (ERP) systems. Because grey hair firms have done similar projects before, certain tasks can be predicted and delegated to junior staff. The marketing strategy is "hire us because we have done this before."
- *Procedure projects* involve a well-recognized and standardized project, such as conducting an audit. These projects involve some level of customization, but the execution has become so familiar that it can be seen as programmatic (i.e., the project has well-defined steps to complete the necessary analysis, diagnosis, and conclusions of the projects). These projects easily can be delegated to junior staff. Customers of procedure projects usually look for firms that can complete the work quickly and inexpensively. Firms marketing procedure projects usually sell their efficiency, accuracy, procedures, and availability. Their appeal to the market is "hire us because we know how to do this and we can deliver it effectively."

The key to managing the operations, and ultimately the profitability, of a professional services firm successfully is to manage margins, productivity, and leverage. Table 9.5 shows tactics for increasing profitability within these three factors.

Outsourcing Services

As noted earlier in Figure 9.3, service providers themselves have relationships with other service firms that contribute to satisfying the customer. For example, a physician who uses an independent laboratory to perform tests on blood drawn from a patient in the physician's office is using an *outsourcing* service.

However, a transaction cost is incurred in seeking and maintaining the outsourced relationship. There are three kinds of transaction costs:

- *Search* costs are incurred in finding a capable supplier.
- *Bargaining* costs are associated with reaching an acceptable agreement with the other party and drawing up a contract.
- *Enforcement* costs are incurred in making sure the other party sticks to the terms of the contract, and taking legal action if it does not.

Benefits and Risks of Outsourcing Services

There are many reasons to outsource a service activity rather than perform the task. Consider the following reasons and examples:

- Allows the firm to focus on its core competence. The volunteer U.S. Army, for example, no longer has KP (kitchen patrol) duty for its soldiers.
- Decreases costs by purchasing from an outside source rather than performing in-house. For example, janitorial services are a good candidate for outsourcing to a specialist provider because the cleaning service must remain competitive in the marketplace.
- Provides access to latest technology without investment. Local hospitals seldom invest in expensive diagnostic equipment such as an MRI but, instead, contract with an outside source to provide the specialized service.
- Leverages benefits from a supplier who has economies of scale. Automobile dealers seldom have an in-house collision repair capability because the demand faced by a dealer is erratic and keeping highly paid specialists busy all the time, therefore, is difficult.

Of course, outsourcing should be undertaken with caution because of the following considerations:

- Loss of direct control over quality.
- Jeopardizes employee loyalty because of job-loss fears.
- Exposure to data security and customer privacy issues.
- Dependence on one supplier compromises future negotiation leverage.
- Additional coordination expense and delays.
- Atrophy of in-house capability to perform outsourced service.

The outsourcing process model is diagrammed in Figure 9.5 and consists of need identification, information search, vendor selection, and performance evaluation. Outsourcing services in general, however, poses challenges because of the intangible nature of services. For example, the development of written specifications for the service desired is a challenge. Furthermore, it is difficult to judge if the services being delivered are meeting expectations, because they are not subject to close scrutiny. For example, how does one know if

FIGURE 9.5
Outsourcing Process

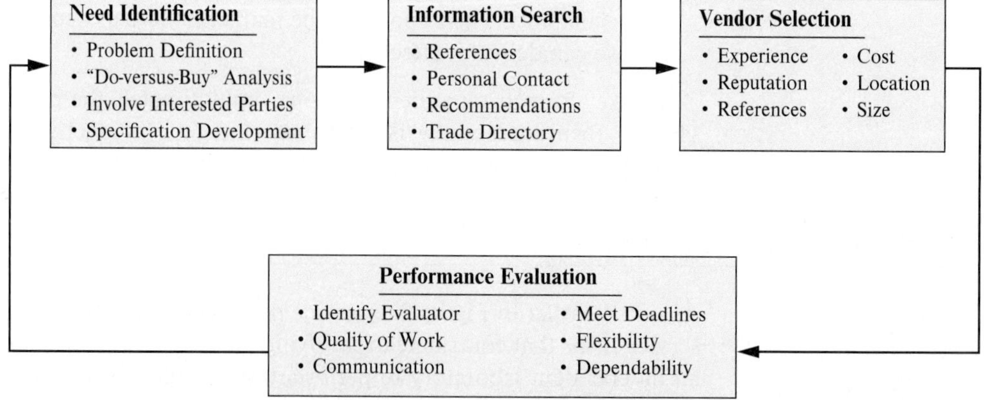

the contractor supplying plant security is being effective? Material goods can be inspected upon delivery, but this opportunity does not exist for purchased services.

The most important outsourcing challenge is supplier selection and performance evaluation. For example, multinational retailers such as Target and Walmart have very strict procedures for vendor selection and evaluation. In vendor selection, several factors come into play including experience, reputation, geographical proximity, and cost parameters. In performance evaluation of suppliers, relevant criteria include communication ability, dependability, flexibility in operation, and quality measures such as historical on-time delivery records.

Hayes et al. provide a structure for supplier relationships in the range from vertical integration to arm's-length relationships.[16] Typically, arm's-length relationships are better candidates for outsourcing. Coordination efforts with vendors for such arm's-length relationships require highly codified and standardized information on price, quantity, and delivery schedules. If more strategic control is desired, vertical integration is the preferred option. This option reduces the risk of termination because significant investments are needed in highly durable relationship-related assets for optimal execution of tasks. Another factor that plays a role in supplier selection is intellectual property. Arm's-length relationships need strong intellectual property protection with very clear boundaries among the different components.

The multinational apparel industry is a good example of a carefully developed supplier relationship. Sports jacket retailer and manufacturer Sport Obermeyer is such an example. Headquartered in Colorado, Sport Obermeyer has manufacturing units in Hong Kong and China. While the home office focuses on monitoring fashion trends, consumer preferences, and retailer management, the Asian units deal with fabric selection, dying and printing options, and managing suppliers for zippers, buttons, and labels. Sport Obermeyer has found controlling and monitoring for quality standards to be very important for a global supply chain.

Outsourcing is complicated also by the need to satisfy a larger number of affected personnel. Contracted services such as travel booking, janitorial services, and food services are examples that affect all employees personally, not in the detached way that material goods acquired for use in the production process are viewed.

Business services often need to be customized to meet an organization's needs, especially in the case of services in support of the manufacturing process. Business services also tend to be more technological in nature than consumer services because of the greater complexity of organizational needs.

The decision process might also differ depending upon the service to be purchased. For example, outsourcing computer software development must involve the active participation of the end users and the final selection will be based upon many attributes that are difficult to quantify, such as user friendliness. The outsourcing of waste disposal service, however, can be handled in a routine manner with cost being one important criterion. Because of the legal liability associated with waste disposal, the selection of a responsible vendor with knowledge and experience with your type of industrial waste is important. For this reason, we develop a classification of services to assist in the purchase process.

Classification of Business Services

Business services often are classified according to degree of tangibility. The degree of tangibility describes the extent to which the service has physically measurable output properties. Some services such as janitorial or laundry are highly tangible and have well-defined and measurable output. Other services such as public relations or advertising have output that is significantly less measurable and more difficult to define.

Differentiating services on the basis of tangibility does indicate the potential level of difficulty faced by the purchaser, but the degree of tangibility fails to provide the purchaser with sufficient information to assist in the service purchase decision. Thus, the focus of the business service (property, people, and process) is used as the principal dimension for the taxonomy. The degree of service tangibility will be an attribute to be considered when purchasing service in each of these categories. In general, however, service tangibility will decrease as the focus of the service moves from property to people to process.

A second dimension representing the criticality or importance of the service to the buying firm must be considered in the purchase decision. The importance of the service is considered either high or low depending upon the relationship of the service to the firm's core business activity. Services important to the core business will attract higher-level management involvement in the purchase decision, because the fit with corporate goals is critical and involves substantial exposure to risk if failure occurs. This is obvious for sensitive areas such as product testing, medical care, public relations, and advertising. Other services such as laundry, waste disposal, plant security, and travel booking might be considered less important to a firm's core business.

Considering a service as low in importance is a relative viewpoint, however. For example, the uniforms of personnel working in clean rooms of semiconductor manufacturers must be laundered under exacting conditions to avoid introducing contamination into the manufacturing process. Thus, a particular firm, based on its own circumstances, might modify the classification of a service according to importance.

Table 9.6 shows a six-cell matrix of this two-way classification. Each cell has a descriptive title for the business service category; that is, facility support, equipment support, employee support, employee development, facilitator, and professional.

Managerial Considerations with Service Outsourcing

The outsourcing considerations for each category of business service are found in Table 9.7 grouped by the focus of the service.

Facility Support Service (Property/Low Importance)

Services in the facility support category can be treated like the purchase of goods. Tight specifications can be prepared and vendor selection then is based on low bid. Even though the purchase of such services is straightforward, an interested person in the organization must be responsible for evaluating the performance of the service delivered with particular attention to quality and timeliness. For example, because of the higher level of tangibility, it is possible to measure performance on the basis of a before–after comparison (e.g., dirty-to-clean laundry or broken-to-repaired equipment). Purchasers place greater importance on price when evaluating less critical services and

TABLE 9.6
Taxonomy for Outsourcing Business Services

		Importance of Service	
		Low	**High**
Focus of Service	**Property**	**Facility support:** • Laundry • Janitorial • Waste disposal	**Equipment support:** • Repairs • Maintenance • Product testing
	People	**Employment support:** • Food service • Plant security • Temporary personnel	**Employee development:** • Training • Education • Medical care
	Process	**Facilitator:** • Bookkeeping • Travel booking • Call center	**Professional:** • Advertising • Public relations • Legal

TABLE 9.7
Outsourcing Considerations

Focus on Property

Facility support service
- Low cost
- Identification of responsible party to evaluate performance
- Writing of precise specifications

Equipment support service
- Experience and reputation of vendor
- Availability of vendor for emergency response
- Designation of person to make service call and to check that service is satisfactory

Focus on People

Employee support service
- Vendor clients contacted for references
- Specifications prepared with end-user input
- Performance evaluated on a periodic basis

Employee development service
- Experience with particular industry important
- Involvement of high levels of management in vendor identification and selection
- Vendor clients contacted for references
- Employees used to evaluate vendor performance

Focus on Process

Facilitator service
- Knowledge of alternate vendors important
- Involvement of end user in vendor identification
- References or third-party evaluations useful
- Detailed specifications written by user

Professional service
- Involvement of high-level management in vendor identification and selection
- High importance of reputation and experience
- Performance evaluation by top management

on quality for more critical services. Many noncritical services such as janitorial, food service, and bookkeeping can be considered as commodity services with price driving the purchase decision.

Equipment Support Service (Property/High Importance)

Equipment support services create an additional problem because the vendor should be located close enough to provide emergency service. Someone in the organization must be identified in the service contract as the person with the authority to request calls for emergency service. Because of the critical nature of maintenance and repair of industrial equipment or product testing, potential vendors should be limited to those with experience in the purchaser's industry. Vendor reputation and references are important selection criteria. In addition to quality of work performed, the performance evaluation will include an assessment of communication problems and dependability.

Employee Support Service (People/Low Importance)

For services that serve people, user input is important in defining the specifications for the service. Requests for employee support service usually originate from a functional department (e.g., a request for temporary personnel) and, thus, the need specification will be developed with department personnel input. Evaluation of the service provided should be made periodically by the same department and is a condition for contract renewal. The process of vendor selection should include obtaining references from vendor clients, a common practice with temporary help service.

Employee Development (People/High Importance)

Employee development service requests also originate within a functional department and usually involve the Personnel Department or a higher level of management. Employee development is an important investment in the firm's human capital that requires expertise to guide the purchase of the service. For example, changing the health insurance carrier for a firm's employees has many ramifications and vendor selection is not a trivial decision. High levels of management must be involved in developing the need specifications and vendor selection. Outside expertise often is sought and vendor reputation and experience with the particular industry are important considerations. Employees affected by the service also can be useful in the evaluation process.

Facilitator Service (Process/Low Importance)

The least tangible classification of business service deals with activities of an information processing nature that support the organization's mission or process. The facilitator service involves routine information processing such as bookkeeping and travel booking. End users should be able to write detailed need specifications and identify possible vendors. For example, the selection of a travel agency benefits from employee inputs about ancillary services (e.g., credit card payment). Online reviews (e.g., Yelp.com) or other sources of comparison among vendors are useful in identifying possible sources and selecting appropriate criteria.

When decision criteria are not well formulated, purchasers look for cues in the environment. In this case the final selection is more likely to be made on the basis of secondary considerations. For example, when selecting from several travel agencies that are all reputable and that provide the same basic service of booking travel, the final choice can be decided on the basis of ancillary services offered, such as delivery of tickets and monthly billing rather than payment at the time of purchase. Another secondary consideration involves the interpersonal relationship between the supplier and the buyer.

Professional Service (Process/High Importance)

Because professional service has significant impact on the strategic future of the organization, top management must be involved from the very beginning. The process starts with need identification and proceeds through all stages of the purchase process including, most importantly, performance evaluation. Trust in the supplier is a primary factor, so vendor reputation and experience might be the only important selection criteria. As customization increases, the delivery of a service such as consulting, public relations, or employee training is more likely to be extended over a period of time. As a result, the evaluation of the supplier's performance necessarily will be delayed.

Summary

The customer–supplier duality for services creates a network of relationships rather than a chain as found in manufacturing. We discovered that bidirectional optimization, management of productive capacity, and management of perishability are sources of value in service supply relationships. Professional services have unique characteristics that require creative leadership to achieve profitability. The increasing use of service outsourcing was explored with the help of a taxonomy for purchasing business services.

Service Benchmark

CITIZENS COME FIRST IN LYNCHBURG

Lynchburg, Virginia, has a before-and-after story. In the beginning, Lynchburg's 11 municipal departments worked independently and communicated with each other only with phone calls and written memos. Consequently, a citizen might wait weeks or months to learn the disposition of a request for a permit to remodel a home. Neither government personnel nor citizens were happy with the situation. The council, therefore, pledged to provide all of the services that the citizens needed.

The after story begins when the community started using the Service module of SuiteResponse. This software supported Lynchburg's Citizens First Information Center and empowered employees to foster the kind of customer service that generated compliments instead of complaints. The Service module enables employees in the call center to accumulate all of the necessary caller information and assign the task to appropriate departments quickly and also provides an electronic audit trail from the initial inquiry to the final resolution. Because the Service module is linked to the Internet, citizens can do their "city shopping" from home and get updates on the progress of their inquiry.

Lynchburg's citizens are living happily ever after.

Key Terms and Definitions

Bidirectional optimization occurs when the service provider and the customer agree on the time a service should be delivered, taking into account the needs of both parties. *p. 255*

Bullwhip effect a phenomenon observed in physical supply chains that occurs when a variation in final demand is propagated up the supply chain in ever-increasing amplitude. *p. 251*

Embellishment of customer skills to enable self-service is a strategy to enhance productive capacity. *p. 256*

Leverage the ratio of the number of professional staff members to the number of partners, an essential factor in determining the profit-per-partner. *p. 261*

Omnichannel supply chain uses a central stock pool to manage the fulfillment operation in a supply chain consisting of various ordering options and multiple distribution channels. *p. 252*

Outsourcing the decision to have an external vendor supply a service once accomplished in-house.

Perishability a result of the inability to inventory service worker productive capacity and a loss of capacity that occurs during periods of idleness. *p. 256*

Productive capacity measured by the worker-hours available to serve customers. *p. 256*

Replacement a strategy to substitute self-serve technology for customer use in lieu of personal attention. *p. 256*

Social media web-based and mobile technologies for interactive dialogue. *p. 257*

Transfer an approach to make knowledge available to customers at low cost. *p. 256*

Topics for Discussion

1. How can effective goods supply chain management support environmental sustainability?
2. Explain why the goods analogy of a supply chain is inappropriate for services.
3. Discuss the implications of service outsourcing on employees, stockholders, customers, and the host-country economy when a firm outsources a call center overseas?
4. How has social media affected the growth of the service industry?
5. What features of social media have service firms leveraged in developing their competitive strategies?
6. Identify areas within a few selected service industries (e.g., health care and hospitality) that can benefit from external consultants.
7. How would you train yourself to be a successful consultant in the service sector?
8. Identify activities that compare Walmart's vertical integration efforts with maintaining an arm's-length relationship with suppliers.

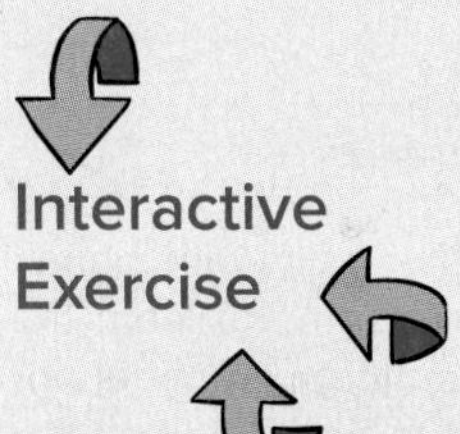

The class divides into small groups, and members come up with examples of multilevel bidirectional service relationships (i.e., service supplier relationships with three or more levels). Be prepared to argue why such service relationships are so rare.

Boomer Consulting, Inc.[17] CASE 9.1

Boomer Consulting, Inc. (BCI), began as a division of the small regional CPA firm of Varney & Associates. The division was headed by a single partner, L. Gary Boomer. In 1995, as the division's revenues grew, the firm separated the consulting and accounting practice, creating a wholly owned subsidiary, which was headed by Boomer and named Boomer Consulting. In 1997, Boomer bought out his partnership agreement and as CEO transformed BCI into an entrepreneurial company.

L. Gary Boomer is recognized in the accounting profession as the leading authority on technology and firm management. Since 1995, he has been named by *Accounting Today* as one of the 100 most influential people in accounting. He consults and speaks internationally on management and technology-related topics such as strategic and technology planning, compensation, and developing a training/learning culture. He acts as a planning facilitator, provides coaching, and serves on many advisory boards.

THE ACCOUNTING INDUSTRY

Until 1989, the accounting industry was viewed in terms of "The Big Eight" and "all others." Owing to industry consolidation and major scandals (most notably the Arthur Andersen and Enron events), the industry morphed into "The Big Four" and "all others." The recent scandals also resulted in increased regulation (e.g., Sarbanes–Oxley) and concern about litigation. These issues affected both the cost of doing business with a big four accounting firm and the workload required of the employees of those firms. As a result both clients and employees are moving to smaller national and regional firms (i.e., "all others").

The scandals also increased the industry's focus on ethics and management issues. Major issues in the industry include increasing corporate governance as firms shift from a partnership model to more of a corporate-management structure, document management and records retention, succession planning, offshoring tax-return preparation, strategic planning, and general management topics such as human resources and compensation. The industry also is notorious for being late adopters in terms of technology that stimulates considerable interest among clients in both hardware and software.

BCI EARLY OPERATIONS

Boomer Consulting, Inc.'s client base comprises a variety of CPA firms in terms of size and geography. Clients include firms as large as those just below "The Big Four" and as small as firms with just a handful of employees. Geographically, clients are spread throughout the United States, United Kingdom, Australia, Canada, and India. Clients typically call on BCI for a number of services ranging from traditional one-on-one engagements to membership in the Boomer Technology Circles. The wide range of services makes BCI an integral part of many firms' strategic planning processes and positions BCI as a coach to many in the industry.

In the early days of BCI, a Sunday afternoon flight out of Kansas City to New York was the norm for Boomer. Clients were dispersed primarily throughout the United States and Canada and he might be in New York on Monday and Tuesday, San Diego on Wednesday, Jackson, Mississippi, on Thursday, and back home late Friday night. This schedule was necessary to allow one-on-one consulting with clients at their office locations, the method of delivery for consulting services in those days. This was a tiring schedule for one person to maintain so Boomer contemplated ways to reduce the level of travel. Realizing that many of his clients, especially those of similar size, had shared issues, he looked for a way to standardize the delivery of his knowledge and experience.

BCI's services then evolved from one-on-one client-specific projects to a more standardized set of services. Today, these offerings are encapsulated in a five-phase process-oriented solution called The Technology Leadership Process shown in Figure 9.6.

BOOMER TECHNOLOGY CIRCLES—A SERVICE INNOVATION

In an effort both to reduce travel and standardize the process, Boomer developed a unique service offering that transformed the BCI business model. Instead of traveling constantly to the client site for one- or two-day projects, he created the Boomer Technology Circles (Circle) where the clients come to BCI.

The Boomer Technology Circles were built on the concept of "roundtables," where clients share common concerns and solutions. The circles are held at a hotel in Kansas City, Missouri, which provides a centralized location for the geographically dispersed client base. Circle members are placed into one of ten different circles, and each circle meets three times per year for a one and one-half day conference. Each circle consists of two employees from about 15–20 firms that are of similar size, increasing the probability of having common issues and concerns. BCI avoids placing clients who are direct competitors in a geographical region in the same circle unless all parties agree.

FIGURE 9.6 **The Technology Leadership Process**

Phase 1: Workshop	Phase 2: Review	Phase 3: Blueprint	Phase 4: Team	Phase 5: Coach
The Technology Leadership Workshop™ is a free, one-hour, one-on-one conference call with Boomer Consulting, Inc.'s consultants. During this call, we will address issues dealing with firm perceptions, requirements, and expectations.	**The Strategic Review**™ is designed to first identify your firm's dangers, opportunities, and strengths; and then to provide the vision and strategy necessary to ensure a return on your investment as well as provide your firm a tremendous advantage. **The Technical Review**™ assesses your current technology situation and provides feedback in areas that will help your firm be more productive and profitable. **The Executive Analysis**™ is a combination of the strategic and technical reviews. It is the best of the technical and management worlds. **The Consultants Training Program**™ will educate you on the components needed to create a consulting practice so your firm may become a leader in the use of technology.	**The Technology Leadership Blueprint**™ helps your firm map out a technology strategy. The final product is a written plan including objectives, priorities, strategies, due dates, and responsible parties. **The Technology Leadership Budget**™ will produce a detailed three-year budget specific to your firm's needs, vision, and expectations.	**The Kolbe Team Success Program**™ helps you diagnose your organization's productivity problems and offer prescriptions for success. This seminar allows your teams to have an interactive format in which to explore the ways different instinctive strengths play off each other. Results of this informative seminar forecast individual stress as well as the probability of team success.	**The Boomer Technology Circles**™ are exclusive groups of firms that join together to examine current issues and share common concerns about management and technology challenges they are facing today. **The Firm Summit**™ is an opportunity to have your firm's annual management retreat facilitated by Boomer Consulting. We leverage over 20 years of experience working with CPA firms to help you make the most of this valuable time.

The Circle meetings are designed to meet a number of objectives, such as issues that Boomer regards as "hot topics" in the accounting industry, information sharing among clients through breakout sessions and participant-led presentations, accountability through the 90-day game plan, progress reports, and planning future meetings.

The focal point of the meetings is information sharing among the Circle members. During the breakout sessions and member-led presentations, members share the most pressing issues in their firms and the solutions they are pursuing. Breakout sessions have only five-to-seven participants and provide an intimate setting for knowledge transfer. The member-led presentations are assigned to members at the previous meeting and cover industry topics agreed upon by the members.

BCI employees play the role of facilitators during the conference, only presenting information to clients for two out of the twelve hours of meeting time. This practice helps to keep clients abreast of the major issues facing the accounting industry today and provides BCI employees with some "face time" during the meetings.

Accountability is achieved by using a 90-day game plan and progress reports. At the end of each meeting, each participant fills out a 90-day game plan form that includes short-term goals during the next three months. These plans are shared among participants in the breakout sessions. At the beginning of the subsequent meeting, each participant also fills out a progress report that lets the members reflect on those goals that have been accomplished and those that require additional work. The progress reports also are shared among participants during the breakout sessions. This process creates accountability for goals and adds an element of peer pressure.

Finally, the Circles also involve the members in the planning process for the next meeting. BCI facilitates the suggestions and ultimate decisions for the next meeting's agenda, but the ideas and decisions ultimately are provided by the Circle's members. This process also helps to ensure that content is fresh and relevant because it comes straight from the members who work directly in the industry.

RELATIONSHIPS AND IMAGE

BCI develops long-term relationships with its clients by positioning itself as a coach to accounting firms and assuring that the content of the Circle meetings is timely and relevant. Social events are built into each meeting to strengthen relationships: Breakfast is served each day before the meetings begin, and an optional cocktail hour and dinner provide two additional opportunities for members to interact. These activities provide clients with an opportunity to have one-on-one discussions with Boomer Consulting employees.

Special care also is taken to ensure that all elements of the Circles promote an image of prestige and exclusivity. Meetings are held at The Fairmont Kansas City at the Plaza, one of the finest hotels in Kansas City, and most members also stay at the hotel. Exclusivity is achieved by giving Circle members access to a special section of the Boomer website www.boomer.com and to a variety of tools not available to non-Circle clients.

Questions

1. How does the Boomer Technology Circle illustrate the concept of the bidirectional service supply relationship?
2. How has Boomer Consulting, Inc., made the client a coproducer in the service delivery process?
3. How is the concept of "leverage" achieved by Boomer Consulting?
4. Can the Boomer Technology Circles be applied to other industries? What are some of the risks in pursuing this strategy?

Evolution of B2C E-Commerce in Japan[18] CASE 9.2

THE JAPANESE *KONBINI* DISTRIBUTION SYSTEM

In the United States, most convenience stores serve a carmobile society so they have gasoline pumps in addition to their shelved items. In Japan, *konbinis* are located everywhere, and it seems as if you cannot go two blocks without running into one of the country's major convenience store chains. These ubiquitous 24-hour retailers have become trendy substitutes for larger supermarkets, and they are an important part of everyday life in Japan.

Konbinis number more than 50,000, and they have an advanced distribution network that is the target of a new alternative for distributing merchandise and receiving payment for items ordered through the Internet. The largest of the convenience store chains is retailing giant Ito-Yokado's, with about 8,000 7-Eleven stores.

The continuing economic recession has reduced consumer spending, resulting in a market saturation of convenience stores. Competition among the *konbini* chains is fierce because market areas are limited and each chain is selling similar products. The chains have turned to technology to expand sales and are installing online terminals that offer customers the chance to shop for goods and services one would not expect a convenience store to sell. This new offering improves customer service and wins business not only from rival chains but also from other retailers.

Because sales are made online, the terminals overcome one of the barriers to increasing convenience store sales—the lack of merchandising space and the cost of holding inventory. The average *konbini* store has a floor area of fewer than 1,000 square feet, but it markets about 2,800 items. An online terminal allows the store to add about 1,000 items with no extra stock on hand because items are delivered at a later date and need only temporary storage space. This system, unlike that in the United States, requires no home delivery expense because the customer picks up the purchase. Consolidating order delivery and using the existing transportation network result in significant savings.

What began as a *solution* to the problem of lack of store space and a way to diversify the merchandise and services offered by the store resulted in a new e-commerce revolution once the *konbinis* added websites. The sheer number of stores and existing distribution network became a natural delivery system for goods ordered over the web. This innovation removed the barriers that restricted full-scale development of e-commerce in Japan (i.e., low credit card usage, lack of alternative access to the Internet, and a lack of flexibility in delivery hours).

THE INTERNET SHOPPING EXPERIENCE

Shoppers can visit the *konbini*'s website or the website of a participating online store by accessing the Internet from their homes or by using the multimedia online terminal at the store. These in-store Internet kiosks also provide a way of ordering merchandise that is not currently in stock at the store. After choosing the merchandise, buyers who are reluctant to provide their credit card information online can select "Pay at a 7-Eleven store" as their payment method.

After selecting the *konbini* payment method, the customer prints a purchase slip containing a bar code. The customer then takes the purchase slip to the nearest *konbini* store, where it will be scanned and cash payment accepted. An online shopper who does not have a printer can still use the service by giving his or her assigned unique purchase slip number to a store clerk. Actual products are delivered to the store a few days later for customer pickup. Large items or perishable goods, such as flowers, are delivered to the customer's home.

FIGURE 9.7
Online Transaction Flows

Source: Reprinted with permission from James A. Fitzsimmons and Jorge Okada, "Evolution of B2C E-Commerce in Japan," in *International Journal of Business Performance Management* 4, no. 2, (2003), Fig. 4.

top image: ©Ingram Publishing RF; bottom image: ©ClassicStock/Alamy Stock Photo

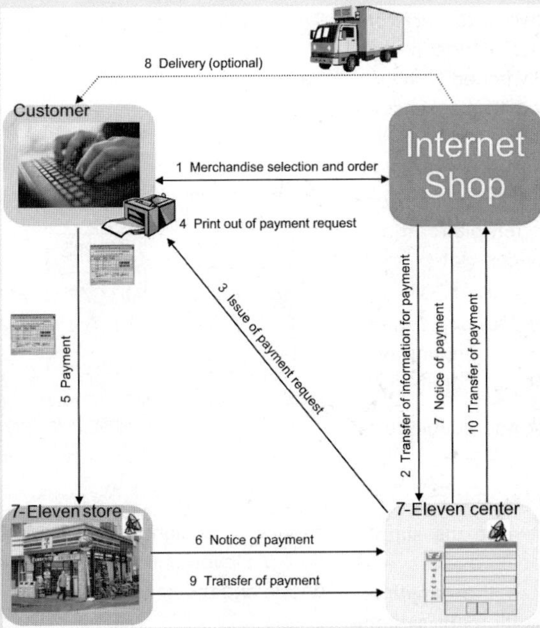

TABLE 9.8
Advantages of Online Sales

Customers	*Konbinis*	Other E-Tailers
• Free access to the Internet from the store's online terminal	• Diversification of products offered without holding inventory	• Easy to implement a secure, reliable, low-cost payment system
• Easy order pickup	• Increased number of customers and frequency of visits	• Economy of using centralized distribution centers
• Convenient payment method any time, any day	• New source of revenue from payment commissions	• Partner with a well-known convenience store chain
• Multiple payment methods, including cash		

Digital products such as software and music can be downloaded immediately from a multimedia terminal in the store. The terminal system also includes a digital printer for instant delivery of purchased pictures or photos taken with a built-in digital camera. A MiniDisc drive and MemoryStick slot allow customers to buy favorite songs and receive them immediately. The machine also includes a scanner and a smart card reader/writer. Figure 9.7 diagrams the system's flow of transactions and Table 9.8 outlines the advantages of such a system for the customers, *konbinis,* and other e-tailers.

M-COMMERCE DEVELOPMENT

In Japan, salaried workers and students have to spend long hours in a train to commute to their places of work and schools. The Japanese people take advantage of their free time to read the newspaper, check their daily schedules, or simply listen to music on their portable MP3 players.

Introduction of new wireless devices has created a new panorama inside trains. People are replacing the traditional newspaper, which is hard to read in a crowded space, with miniature wireless phones that can display news and provide access to the Internet. Today, it's common to see commuters' heads pointed down actively reading their phone.

Mobile phones have pushed past their fixed-line predecessors as the preferred mode of communication in Japan because fees have come down and the Internet offers many online services for cell phones. The number of mobile phone subscribers in Japan is outnumbering those using fixed-line phones rapidly.

The wireless phenomenon has opened a huge mobile e-commerce market in Japan based on four key elements:

1. *High penetration rate of Internet-enabled wireless cellular phones.* The booming popularity of Internet-capable mobile phones has fueled a rapid growth of Internet use in Japan.

2. *Implementation of a packet data network to facilitate economic delivery of interactive services.* iMode mobile phone service operates over a packet-switched network, which means that customers pay only for the data transmitted, regardless of the connection time.
3. *Equal opportunities for content providers that spur innovation and drive third-party advertising that builds buzz about the platform.* iMode adopted an open platform and ensured that consumers' preferred services got primary placement.
4. *An adequate environment and time available for browsing the Internet using handheld devices.* Train commuting provides a perfect environment for using mobile e-commerce.

Among these key elements, only the last one is unique to the Japanese experience.

FIGURE 9.8 Direct Code Product Selection Using Cellular Phone

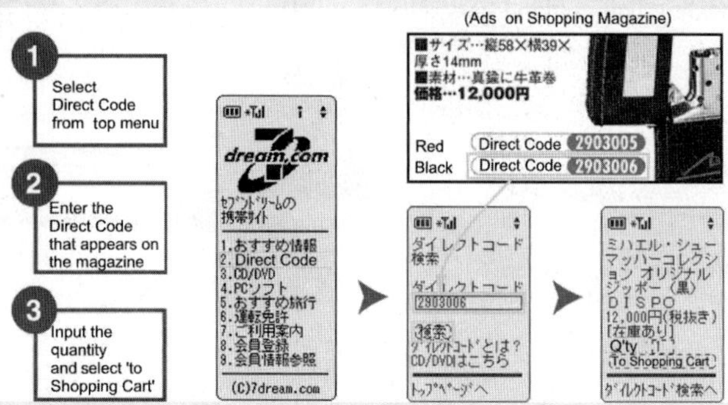

Source: Reprinted with permission from James A. Fitzsimmons and Jorge Okada, "Evolution of B2C E-Commerce in Japan," in *International Journal of Business Performance Management* 4, no. 2 (2003), Fig. 7

THE MARRIAGE OF *"KONBINI* AND MOBILE"

The *konbini* m-commerce concept goes beyond the simple mobility of Internet access devices like cell phones and computer tablets. The concept incorporates the "anytime, everywhere" notion of a distribution and settlement system by linking the convenience store network with cell phones, other mobile devices, and the Internet. This service enables consumers to place an order for merchandise from a cell phone inside a train and pick it up at a convenience store on their way home.

A customer uses his or her cellular phone to order a product using a "direct code" number. Free catalogs present goods for sale and a direct code for each item. The transaction to purchase a Zippo lighter is illustrated in Figure 9.8. The advertisement in the shopping magazine shows the direct code for a black Zippo lighter as 2903006. This direct code is entered on a 7-Eleven shopping cart screen displayed on the cellular phone and the item is picked up later at the store.

Questions

1. What features of the 7-Eleven Japan distribution system illustrate the concept of the bidirectional service supply relationship?
2. Does the 7-Eleven Japan distribution system exhibit scalability economies?
3. How does the 7-Eleven example of B2C e-commerce in Japan illustrate the impact of culture on service system design?
4. Will the 7-Eleven "*Konbini* and mobile" system be adopted in the United States?

Mortgage Service Game[19] CASE 9.3

Securing a mortgage often is a time-consuming and frustrating experience for a homebuyer. The process involves multiple stages with many handoffs to independent organizations providing specialized services (e.g., property survey and title search). The mortgage service game is a computer simulation of the mortgage service process in which the human player will control the decisions of one entity and the computer will make decisions for the other actors. This game is used to explore the dynamics of a serial service process.

Figure 9.9 depicts a block diagram of the mortgage supply chain. Each mortgage application passes through four stages as shown on the right-hand side of the figure: *Credit Check* (employment confirmation and review of credit history), *Survey* (establish property boundary, note easements, and applicable zoning laws), *Appraisal* (establish value of property using comparables), and *Title Search* (ensure the property is uncontested and without liens). Because all of the stages are modeled in a similar fashion, only one stage, the survey stage, will be described as an example of each stage's processing.

Note that the middle column of the block diagram contains a sequence of backlog boxes (queues of work-in-process) representing the movement of applications through the process to completion. For example, after each application is checked for the credit worthiness (Credit Check), the application moves from the inventory of applications waiting for credit check (Credit Check Backlog) to join the backlog of surveys (Survey Backlog). Each week, based on the backlog of surveys—which is the only information available to the player controlling the survey stage of the system when using a decentralized strategy—the player sets the target capacity of the system by deciding to hire or fire employees: in this case, surveyors. However, it takes time to find, interview, and hire or, conversely, to give notice and fire employees; so the *actual* Survey Capacity will lag the *Target Survey Capacity* by an average of one month. Those surveyors currently in the employ of the survey company will then carry out as many surveys as they can during the following week. On the block diagram this is shown as a "bow tie" representing a valve controlling the flow of applications between survey backlog and appraisal backlog. Thus, as each application's survey is completed (Survey), the application will then leave the Survey Backlog to join the next backlog downstream—in this case, the Appraisal Backlog.

FIGURE 9.9
Block Diagram of Mortgage Service Game

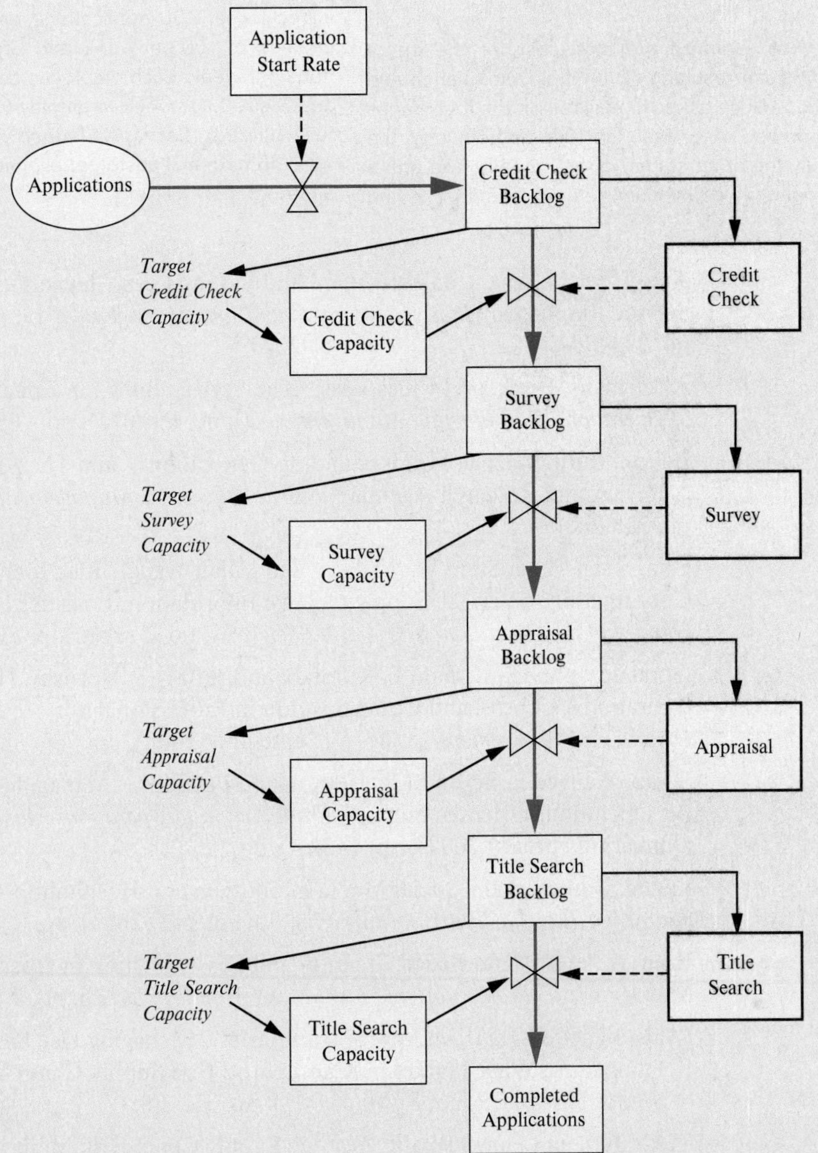

Although, the purpose of this process is to eliminate applications that are too risky, we will assume that each application ultimately is approved. This is a reasonable assumption because, despite the fact that a random survival rate for each stage does indeed complicate management of the service chain, the primary dynamic control problems derive from other sources. In particular, the largest problem arises because a separate company generally manages each stage of the process. Each of these companies controls its own individual capacity, but it usually sees only its own backlog when making its decisions, not the global new-application rate or the backlog of other stages. This situation creates a phenomenon similar to the bullwhip effect observed in physical goods supply chains, albeit here the "inventories" are strictly backlogs of work-in-process. As in any service there is no way to stockpile finished-goods inventory in advance as a buffer against fluctuating demand. Rather, each stage must manage its backlog entirely by managing its capacity, that is, the number of workers it employs. Because each employee has a productivity rate of four applications per day, the completion rate per day of applications at any stage is constrained to the minimum of the capacity as measured by the number of employees or backlog plus any inflow from the previous stage.

At the beginning of each week, each stage (company) can change its target capacity by deciding to hire or lay off employees. However, it takes time to advertise, interview, and hire employees; so the rate of capacity change is not achieved all at once but over several days. This translates into an average lag for hiring (or firing employees) of 20 days or four weeks. If the player makes another change before the original adjustment is reached, the old target will be discarded, and capacity will begin to adjust the following day from its current value advancing toward the new target.

GOAL

The objective is to minimize the total cost for the entire mortgage supply chain resulting from employee salaries and service delays. You will be asked to play one of the four stages (Credit Check, Survey, Appraisal, or Title Search) and the computer will play the other stages in the process. The entire supply chain begins in equilibrium with each stage having a backlog of 200 applications, arrival rate of 100 per week, capacity of 100 per week, and target capacity of 100 applications per week. Each employee costs $2,000 to hire or lay off and $1,000 per week to employ (or $50 per application when fully utilized). Each backlogged application costs $100 per week in potential customer alienation. The game is played for a period of 50 weeks.

Selected Bibliography

Akcay, Yalcin, Anant Balakrishnan, and Susan H. Xu. "Dynamic Assignment of Flexible Service Resources." *Production and Operations Management* 19, no. 3 (May–June 2010), pp. 279–304.

Akkermans, Henk, and Chris Voss. "The Service Bullwhip Effect." *International Journal of Operations & Production Management* 33, no. 6 (2013), pp. 765–88.

Bolton, Ruth N., et al. "Understanding Generation Y and Their Use of Social Media: A Review and Research Agenda." *Journal of Service Management* 24, no. 3 (2013), pp. 245–67.

Choi, Tsan-Ming, Stein W. Wallace, and Yulan Wang. "Risk Management and Coordination in Service Supply Chains: Information, Logistics and Outsourcing." *Journal of the Operational Research Society* 67, no. 2 (2016), pp. 159–64.

Goodale, John C., Donald F. Kuratko, and Jeffrey S. Hornsby. "Influence Factors for Operational Control and Compensation in Professional Service Firms." *Journal of Operations Management* 26, no. 5 (September 2008), pp. 669–88.

Hopp, Wallace J., Seyed M.R. Iravani, and Fang Liu. "Managing White-Collar Work: An Operations-Oriented Survey." *Production and Operations Management* 18, no. 1 (January–February 2009), pp. 1–32.

Leung, Daniel, et al. "Social Media in Tourism and Hospitality: A Literature Review." *Journal of Travel & Tourism Marketing* 30, no. 1–2 (2013), pp. 3–22.

Roth, A., et al. "Knowledge Creation and Dissemination in Operations and Supply Chain Management." *Production and Operations Management* 25, no. 9 (2016), pp. 1473–88.

Ryals, Lynette J., and Andrew S. Humphries. "Managing Key Business-to-Business Relationships: What Marketing Can Learn From Supply Chain Management." *Journal of Service Research* 9, no. 4 (May 2007), pp. 312–26.

Vilko, Jyri, and Paavo Ritala. "Service Supply Chain Risk Management." *Operations and Supply Chain Management* 7, no. 3 (2014), pp. 139–40.

Wang, Yulan, et al. "Service Supply Chain Management: A Review of Operational Models." *European Journal of Operational Research* 247, no. 3 (2015), pp. 685–98.

Xia, Yu, et al. "Competition and Market Segmentation of the Call Center Service Supply Chain." *European Journal of Operational Research* 247, no. 2 (2015), pp. 504–14.

Xue, Mei, and Joy M. Field. "Service Coproduction with Information Stickiness and Incomplete Contacts: Implications for Consulting Services Design." *Production and Operations Management* 17, no. 3 (May–June 2008), pp. 357–72.

Endnotes

1. Tom Davis, "Effective Supply Chain Management," *Sloan Management Review* 34, no. 4 (Summer 1993), pp. 42–43.
2. From Scott E. Sampson, "Customer–Supplier Duality and Bidirectional Supply Chains in Service Organizations," *International Journal of Service Industry Management* 11, no. 4 (2000), pp. 348–64.
3. http://www.youtube.com/watch?v=0eUeL3n7fDs.
4. http://www.usatoday.com/money/economy/story/2012-05-14/socialmedia-economy-companies/55029088/1.
5. Christopher Elliott, "5 Businesses That Will Live (or Die) by Social Media," *CBS MoneyWatch,* August 25, 2011.

6. Amy Kristy, "5 Ways to Use Social Media in the Service Industry," OnMark Solutions. (http://www.onmarksolutions.com/), June 23, 2011.
7. Becky Yerak, "Insurance Industry Entering Age of Innovation," *Chicago Tribune,* December 4, 2011.
8. Ron Callari, "Social Media Service for Hospitality Industry Shows Early Results," *InventorSpot.com,* 2011.
9. Community e-book, "How to Create a Social Media Strategy for the Financial Services Industry," *radian6.com,* December 2011.
10. http://www.usatoday.com/money/economy/story/2012-05-14/socialmedia-economy-companies/55029088/1.
11. http://www.socialnomics.net.
12. Prepared by Tom Leuschen under the supervision of Professor James A. Fitzsimmons.
13. From James Brian Quinn, Philip Anderson, and Sydney Finkelstein, "Managing Professional Intellect: Making the Most of the Best," *Harvard Business Review,* March–April 1996, pp. 71–80.
14. E. M. Rasiel, *The McKinsey Way: Using the Techniques of the World's Top Strategic Consultants to Help You and Your Business* (New York: McGraw-Hill, 1999).
15. J. Prosek, *Army of Entrepreneurs: Create an Engaged and Empowered Workforce for Exceptional Business Growth,* AMACOM, 2011, pp. 50–52.
16. R. Hayes, G. Pisano, D. Upton, and S. Wheelwright, *Operations Strategy and Technology: Pursuing the Competitive Edge* (New York: John Wiley, 2004), pp. 119–38.
17. Prepared by Eric Baur, Jim Boomer, Chad Turner, and Matt Wallace under the supervision of Professor James A. Fitzsimmons.
18. Shane Stiles, "Konbini Commerce–Japanese Convenience Stores and E-commerce," July 7, 2000, http://www.gate39.com/business/konbinicommerce.html, January 2001.
19. From Edward G. Anderson and Douglas J. Morrice, "A Simulation Game for Service-Oriented Supply Chain Management: Does Information Sharing Help Managers with Service Capacity Decisions?" *Journal of Production and Operations Management* 9, no. 1 (2000), pp. 40–55.

Chapter 10

Globalization of Services

Learning Objectives

After completing this chapter, you should be able to:

1. Identify and differentiate the four domestic growth and expansion strategies.
2. Discuss the nature of franchising from the points of view of the franchiser and the franchisee.
3. Differentiate between the three generic international strategies.
4. Discuss the three factors to be considered in planning transnational operations.
5. Discuss the five C's that must be balanced in a borderless world.
6. Identify and differentiate the five global service strategies.

In early October 2001, on the first Muslim holy day after American warplanes began the bombing campaign in Afghanistan, thousands of protesters spilled out onto the streets of Karachi, Pakistan.[1] Armed with sticks and bats, intermittently chanting "Death to America," they made their way through the streets smashing windows and setting fires to a bus and several cars along the way. The mob's objective was the U.S. Consulate. But police barricades and tear gas turned them back, so they went looking for the next-best option–Colonel Sanders.

It didn't matter to the demonstrators that the nearby KFC was owned locally. The red, white, and blue logo was justification enough. The owners tried to cover the KFC signs in an attempt to protect their investment, but their effort was futile and the protesters set fire to the restaurant before being dispersed by police.

YUM! Brands, owners of quick service restaurants KFC, Pizza Hut, and Taco Bell, is committed to international growth and has been going global in a big way with stores located in more than 80 countries, including Japan, Australia, Mexico, Malaysia, Saudi Arabia, and throughout Europe. In China, where KFC has more than 500 restaurants, an average of ten new stores are opened each month.

Like most successful global companies, YUM! Brands believes its business is local. As a practical matter, an overseas restaurant must adapt its menu to local tastes. KFC, for example, sells teriyaki crispy strips in Japan, stresses gravy in northern England, offers fresh rice with soy sauce in Thailand, makes a potato-and-onion croquette in Holland, and in China the chicken is spicier the farther inland you travel.

YUM! Brands' success abroad followed the proven franchise model of allowing local franchise operators flexibility while maintaining quality control and a central marketing message. YUM! Brands closes down franchisees that do not meet the company's standards and introduces new products into the market, going beyond the old "chicken-in-a-bucket" concept. In skeptical France, Holland, and Germany, YUM! Brands first established corporate-owned restaurants to demonstrate success and entice new franchisees to join.

Chapter Preview

This chapter begins with a look at service growth and expansion in the context of multisite and multiservice expansion strategies. Using these dimensions, we put services into four classifications: focused service, focused network, clustered service, and diversified network.

Franchising can be an effective multisite expansion strategy for a well-defined service concept. We will explore benefits to the franchisee and responsibilities of the franchiser in an organizational arrangement held together by a contract.

Because our world has become "borderless," service expansion no longer can end with development of the domestic market alone. Expansion overseas presents unique challenges, however, such as the cultural transferability of the service and discriminatory practices of foreign governments to protect their own domestic services from competition.

Domestic Growth and Expansion Strategies

The expectation of an entrepreneurial innovation is initial acceptance of the service concept followed by increasing customer demand. The need to expand a successful innovative service often is thrust on the owner by the pressure of market potential and the desire to protect the service concept from competitors through building barriers to entry. To understand better the various ways in which a firm can expand its concept, consider Figure 10.1, which shows the fundamental expansion strategies that are available to service firms. We shall explore each of these strategies in turn with a discussion of the risks involved and the implications for management.

Focused Service

Typically, a service innovation begins at a single location with an initial service concept. This initial service concept usually is a well-defined vision focused on delivering a new and unique service. For example, Fred Smith's vision for Federal Express was use of Memphis, Tennessee, as a single hub-and-spoke network to guarantee overnight delivery of packages.

Success leads to increased demand, which requires capacity expansion at the site. Typically, the facility is expanded and personnel are added.

The successful firm also will attract competition and need to build a preferred position among as many customers as possible in the local market area. Adding peripheral services is one approach to penetrating the market or holding market share against the competition. Examples of peripheral services for a restaurant include a salad bar or drive-through window. The core service for a successful restaurant, however, usually is excellent cuisine.

Risks that are associated with a single service location include being captive to the future economic growth of that area and being vulnerable to competition that can move in and capture market share. Management and control of the enterprise, however, are much simpler than in any of the other growth strategies.

FIGURE 10.1
Multisite and Multiservice Expansion Strategies

	Single Service	Multiservice
Single Location	*Focused service:* • Dental practice • Retail store • Family restaurant	*Clustered service:* • Stanford University • Mayo Clinic • USAA Insurance
Multisite	*Focused network:* • Federal Express • McDonald's • Red Roof Inns	*Diversified network:* • NationsBank • American Express • Accenture

Many examples of successful focused services exist. Consider fine restaurants in particular, such as Chez Panisse in Berkeley or Antoine's in New Orleans. A *focused service* often is limited to a single site because of talented personnel, such as an award-winning chef or a nationally recognized heart surgeon. If the site is a key element of the service, such as a sheltered cove for a marina, it might not be duplicated easily elsewhere.

Focused Network

A service firm that must be readily accessible to customers (e.g., a fast-food restaurant) must consider adding sites to achieve significant growth. For firms such as McDonald's, a *focused network* allows management to maintain control through franchising, which ensures consistency of service across all locations. For services such as Federal Express and other transportation or communications firms, the existence of a network is required merely to enable the service to function. Also, an entrepreneurial firm that has a successful, well-defined service concept and wants to reach a mass market can prevent imitation from competitors by capturing premium locations in different geographic areas.

The service concept must be well focused, however, so it is easy to replicate with rigorous control of service quality and costs. Frequently, the "cookie-cutter" concept of replicating service units is employed in facility construction, operating manuals, and personnel training. Franchising often is used to achieve the objective of rapid growth, using investment capital from franchisees that have the motivation to be independent operators. A more complete discussion of franchising is found later in this chapter.

For a single site, the founder is physically present to manage the firm's resources, market the service, train personnel, and ensure the integrity of the service concept. Especially in the beginning, expansion can occur on an incremental basis. Initially, as the number of locations grows, managerial control slowly shifts from being informal to being formal so that the owner can control operations effectively even though he or she is not physically present at the additional sites.

Managing a network of service locations requires different management skills, however, and it involves the challenges of using sophisticated communications and control. Above all, the service concept must be rationalized and communicated to unit managers and staff, who then must execute the service consistently on a daily basis. Much planning must precede a multisite expansion, such as preparing training and operations manuals, branding the concept, and launching a national marketing effort.

Service growth using the multisite strategy is very attractive because of its ability to reach the mass market quickly, but the risks of overexpansion and loss of control have resulted in many failures. Even so, the miles of "franchise rows" that are found in almost every city attest to the success of delivering a focused service through a multisite network.

Finally, having multiple sites in different geographic locations reduces the financial risk to the firm from severe, localized economic downturns. A longitudinal study of occupancy at La Quinta Motor Inns dramatically illustrates the benefit of geographic risk containment. Founded in Texas, La Quinta Motor Inns became a major presence in the state, with inns in all of the major Texas cities by 1980. During the oil and gas boom that followed, La Quinta began an expansion strategy of opening inns in the oil-producing states of Colorado, Louisiana, Oklahoma, and Wyoming. When the oil and gas boom ended in the mid-1980s, the occupancy of many of the new inns, and even some in Texas, plummeted. A financial disaster for the firm was avoided, however, because other La Quinta inns that were not associated with the oil and gas industry continued to prosper.[2]

Clustered Service

Service firms with large fixed facilities often decide to grow by diversifying the service they offer. For example, during the 1970s, many small colleges expanded into four-year regional universities to accommodate the increasing demand for a university degree.

Another example is United Services Automobile Association (USAA), which originally was founded to provide automobile insurance for military officers by direct mail. The company now serves the entire military community. Headquartered in San Antonio, Texas, USAA now is a major employer, and the physical facility is situated in a campuslike setting of 281 acres and has five regional offices. Today, the services offered by USAA have been expanded to include banking, mutual funds, auto and homeowners' insurance, life and health insurance, financial planning, travel services, and a buying service. Large medical complexes such as the Mayo Clinic, M.D. Anderson, and Massachusetts General Hospital are examples of classic multiservice, single-site facilities, or *clustered service*. All these examples share the common feature that their service market is not defined by their location. For some, such as medical centers and colleges, customers are willing to travel to the service location and spend considerable time at the facility (even years in the case of college students). For others, such as USAA, travel is unnecessary, because business is conducted without the need for physical interaction with a customer.

A major risk of service diversification is potential loss of focus and neglect of the core service. For example, a ski resort can decide to use idle facilities during the summer by attracting conference business; however, the accommodations, food, and beverage facilities that are suitable for skiers might be inadequate for hosting such meetings. One saving grace in this situation is that at least the different market segments are separated by the seasons. Facility management becomes extremely complex when an attempt is made to serve more than one market segment concurrently. For example, hotels serving both tourists and business customers might have difficulty satisfying both markets.

To avoid losing focus, a strategy of "concentric diversification" has been advocated.[3] Concentric diversification limits expansion to services with synergistic logic around the core service. The evolution of the convenience store is an excellent example. Beginning with a limited selection of convenience items that could be purchased in a hurry, these stores have added self-serve gasoline, an automatic car wash, and self-serve microwave lunches. Concentric diversification creates economies of scope, because the additional services require only marginal increases in variable costs (e.g., no additional cashier is needed).

Diversified Network

Service firms that grow through acquisition often find themselves combining both the multisite and the multiservice strategies. Several years ago, United Airlines acquired hotels and car-rental agencies in the belief that sufficient synergy existed through use of its Apollo reservation system to direct the traveling customer to its several businesses. Anticipated revenues never materialized, however, so United sold off the peripheral services and returned to its core airline business. Managing a *diversified network* is a very complex task, as United Airlines and many other firms have learned.

Success more often is realized when the services are offered under one brand name that establishes a broad marketing image. American Express has been particularly successful managing a global service network that offers financial and travel services with real synergy.

Franchising

Franchising is an alternative to internally generated expansion for a firm seeking to develop a focused network of geographically dispersed units. Franchising allows the firm to expand rapidly with minimal capital requirements by selling the business concept to prospective owner-operators bound by a contractual agreement. Incorporation of conformance quality into the service concept is the hallmark of the franchising agreement. The franchiser guarantees a consistent service, because the concept is standardized

What city is this? Franchising has been criticized for homogenizing the American landscape. ©David Barber/PhotoEdit

in design, operation, and pricing. Just as they make no distinction between products of the same brand, customers expect identical service from any franchise outlet. All outlets benefit from this consistency in service, because customers develop a brand loyalty that is not bound by geography.

The Nature of Franchising

The International Franchise Association defines franchising as a system by which a firm (i.e., the franchiser) grants to others (i.e., the franchisees) the right and license (i.e., the franchise) to sell a product or service and, possibly, use the business system developed by the firm.

The franchisee owns the business through payment of a franchise fee and purchase of the facility and equipment, and he or she assumes responsibility for all normal operating activities, including hiring employees, making daily decisions, and determining local advertising. The initial investment will vary depending on capital requirements. For example, to open a McDonald's franchise, requires a total investment of $1 to $2.2 million, with liquid capital available of $750,000 and a franchise fee of $45,000. The service franchisee usually is granted an exclusive right or license to deliver the service in a specific market region to protect the franchisee against dilution of sales from other franchisees of the same brand. For example, Hardee's, a fast-food restaurant, agrees not to license another Hardee's franchisee within 1½ miles of existing locations.

The franchiser retains the right to dictate conditions. Standard operating procedures must be followed. Materials must be purchased from either the franchiser or an approved supplier. No deviation from the product line is permitted, training sessions must be attended, and continuing royalty fees (e.g., 4 percent of gross sales for Wendy's) must be paid.

Benefits to the Franchisee

As a franchisee, the owner relinquishes some personal independence and control in return for a relationship based on the expectation of greater gains through group membership. The franchisee is given the opportunity to own a small business that carries a lower-than-normal risk of failure because of the identification with an established service brand. Membership in the franchiser organization also includes many additional benefits.

Management Training

Before opening a new outlet, many franchisers provide an extensive training program. For example, McDonald's franchisees must spend two weeks at Hamburger University in suburban Chicago learning the McDonald's way of food preparation and customer service. This training accomplishes two objectives. First, the franchisee becomes prepared to operate a business profitably; second, McDonald's ensures that its procedures will be followed to guarantee consistency across units. Subsequent training often is offered online or by traveling consultants.

Brand Name

The franchisee gains immediate customer recognition from the nationally known and advertised brand name. The result is more immediate increased customer draw; thus, the break-even point is reached sooner than in a traditional new-business venture.

National Advertising

Although the franchisee usually must contribute a specified percentage of gross sales to the franchiser for national advertising, the results benefit all operations. Further, for businesses such as fast-food restaurants and motels in particular, a significant proportion of sales derives from customers arriving from outside the immediate geographic region.

Acquisition of a Proven Business

Traditionally, independent owners face a high rate of failure, which a franchisee can expect to avoid. The franchiser has a track record of selecting appropriate sites, operating a reliable accounting system, and, most important, delivering a service concept that already is accepted by the public.

Economies of Scale

As a member of the franchiser network, the franchisee benefits from centralized purchasing and savings on the cost of materials and equipment that are unavailable to an independent owner.

Issues for the Franchiser

Franchising relies heavily on the motivation of investor-owners, which allows the firm to grow without the cost of developing key managers. Of course, the process of screening potential franchisees must go beyond the minimum requirement of simply having the necessary capital. For example, Benihana of Tokyo found that many early franchisees were unqualified to manage an authentic Japanese-theme restaurant.

Other issues include decisions on the degree of franchisee autonomy, the nature of the franchise contract, and a process for conflict resolution.

Franchisee Autonomy

A franchisee's autonomy is the amount of freedom that is permitted in the operation of the unit. The degree of autonomy is a function of the extent of operations programming dictated in the franchise contract and of the success of "branding" the national advertising achieves.

The extent of operations programming is important to guarantee compliance with uniform standards of quality and service throughout the entire chain. If some franchisees were allowed to operate at substandard levels, the image of the entire chain would suffer. A highly programmed operation might include:

1. Franchiser specifications such as day-to-day operating procedures, site selection, facility design, accounting system, supplies used and their sources, pricing, and menu items for the restaurant.
2. Frequent inspections of the facility.
3. The right to repurchase the outlet for noncompliance.

Branding reinforces operations programming by establishing rather clear customer expectations from which it is difficult for the individual franchisee to deviate. In addition, successful branding should lead to a greater profit potential, reduced risk, and a more sought-after investment opportunity.

Franchise Contract

Control and power tend to concentrate in the hands of the franchiser, and this raises questions concerning the relationship between franchiser and franchisee as well as the misuse of power. The franchise contract is the vehicle for providing this relationship on a continuing basis. Very often, these contracts include specific obligations on the part of the franchisee but are ambiguous regarding the responsibilities of the franchiser, and, often, no attention is given to the rights of the franchisee. For example, litigation has arisen from contract stipulations regarding establishment of the resale value of the franchise and binding agreements requiring the purchase of supplies from the franchiser.

The objective in writing franchise contracts should be to avoid future litigation that might prevent a cooperative relationship from developing. Franchise contracts should be prepared to protect both parties and preserve the competitive strength of the entire franchise organization.

Conflict Resolution

An intelligent and fair franchise contract is the most effective means to reduce potential conflict. Conflict frequently arises, however, over the following issues because of differing objectives of the franchiser and franchisee:

1. How should fees be established and profits distributed?
2. When should franchisee facilities be upgraded, and how are the costs to be shared?
3. How far should the franchiser go in saturating a single market area with outlets?

The franchise system is a superorganization requiring interorganizational management. Thus, a critical task of the franchiser is the development of policy and procedures to handle conflict before it becomes divisive and impairs the entire system.

Globalization of Services

Because its customers increasingly wanted to send packages to Europe and Asia, Federal Express decided in 1988 to duplicate its service overseas resulting in a first-ever quarterly operating loss for the company in 1991. Unfortunately, Federal Express arrived well after the competition DHL and TNT, which, having imitated the Federal Express concept in the late 1970s, had been providing express service to this region for about a decade. Also, Federal Express was unprepared for the government regulations and bureaucratic red tape that are used to protect established firms. For example, it took three years to get permission from Japan to make direct flights from the Memphis hub to Tokyo, a key link in the overseas system. Just days before that service was to begin, however, Federal Express was notified that no packages weighing more than 70 pounds could pass through Tokyo; this was a provision to protect local transport businesses.

The company's obsession with tight central control also contributed to the problems. Until recently, all shipping bills were printed in English, and the cutoff time for package pickups was 5 PM, as is the practice in the United States. The Spanish, however, typically work until 8 PM after a lengthy midday break. Federal Express now is relaxing its go-it-alone, centralized-control method of business that has been successful in the United States. Pickup times, weight standards, and technology now will vary from country to country, and joint ventures with local firms are being sought to handle deliveries and marketing.[4]

Another issue is the frequent lack of supporting infrastructure, something we take for granted in the United States, in some foreign countries. For example, the opening of the first McDonald's in Moscow required substantial supplier development. Management not only had to build a commissary to prepare all products for the restaurant but also had to show farmers how to plant and harvest the crops that were needed (e.g., potatoes and lettuce).

Despite all of these challenges, the search for growth can be found most easily overseas. Consider the countries in the top ten in Gross Domestic Product (GDP) shown in Figure 10.2. Note that Purchasing Power Parity (PPP) adjusts for the differences in wages and prices among countries. The conclusion is that new customers will be found in the emerging economies.

Generic International Strategies

Bartlett and Ghoshal developed the general framework shown in Figure 10.3 to classify international strategies under various conditions.[5] The appropriate strategy will depend on the strength of two forces, global integration and local responsiveness. The force toward global integration refers to factors such as the presence of economies of scale or opportunities to exploit certain assets or competitive advantages globally. The force toward local responsiveness reflects the need for service customization to adapt to local needs or

FIGURE 10.2
The Top 10 Countries by GDP (PPP), 2014

Source: http://statisticstimes.com/economy/world-gdp-ranking-ppp.php

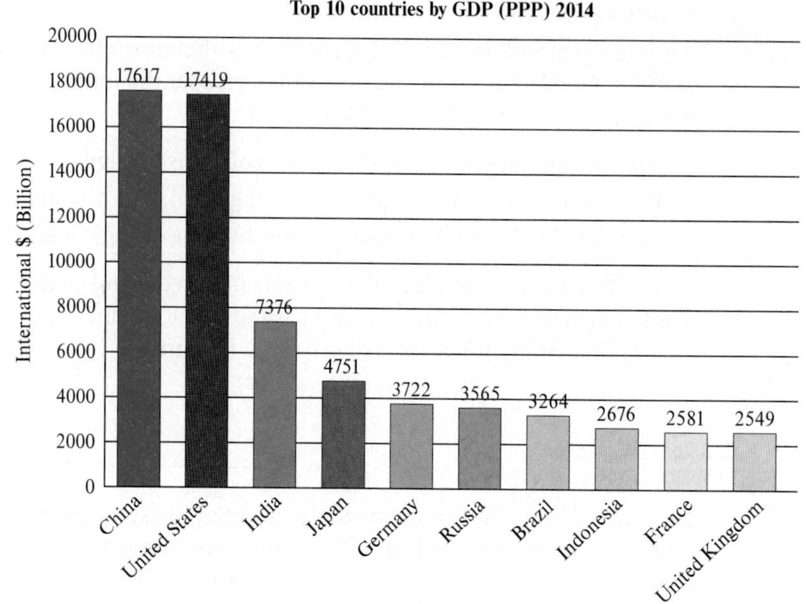

FIGURE 10.3
Generic International Strategies

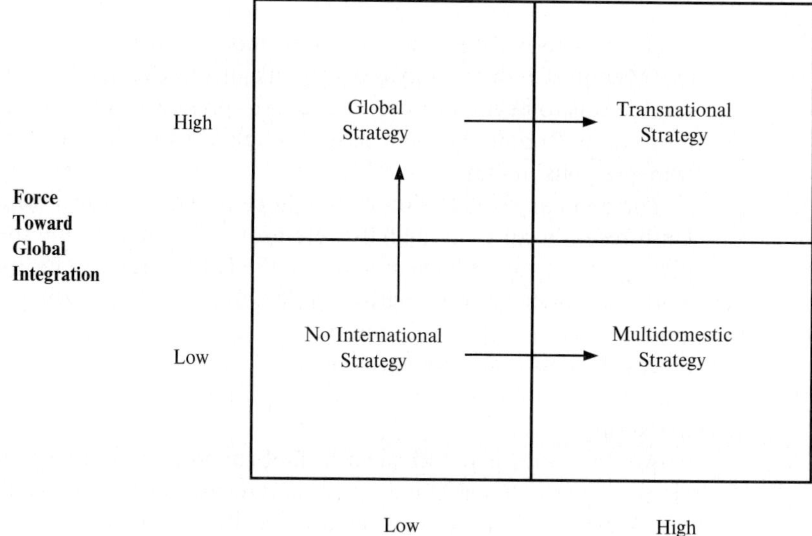

culture, including host government control. Figure 10.3 suggests that service firms in the lower-left quadrant will have little interest in an international strategy, while others will need to decide upon which direction to take in the international market.

Global Strategy

For the global strategy the world is seen as one large market that can be approached in a homogeneous way or at least integrated across countries. Firms with a strong brand and special identity such as Ikea, the international Swedish furniture, housewares, and accessories retailer, or flag carriers such as Singapore Airlines, follow this strategy. Citibank has positioned itself as a global retail bank that allows its customers to do their banking anyway, anywhere, and anytime.

Multidomestic Strategy

Professional service firms such as the law firm Fulbright and Jaworski, the consulting firm Booz Allen Hamilton, and the publisher McGraw-Hill often follow the multidomestic strategy. Overseas offices form a confederation of autonomous units serving the needs in the local country and they are staffed and managed by local nationals.

Transnational Strategy

A transnational strategy is adopted when there are benefits from leveraging certain corporate assets such as research and specialized expertise but the service delivery must be adapted to local needs. Toys "R" Us, in contrast to Ikea, gives local managers great latitude to address local toy tastes, but within a formula store layout and centralized procurement. Some companies such as McDonald's are moving away from the global strategy position toward the transnational strategy by altering, for example, menus to appeal to local tastes and customs (e.g., a vegetarian sandwich in India and beer in Germany).

The Nature of the Borderless World[6]

Kenichi Ohmae, who has written extensively on strategic management, argues that we now live in a borderless world, where customers worldwide are aware of the best products and services and expect to purchase them with no concern over their national origin. In his strategic view, all firms compete in an interlinked world economy, and to be effective, they must balance the five C's of strategic planning: *c*ustomers, *c*ompetitors, *c*ompany, *c*urrency, and *c*ountry.

Customers

When people vote with their pocketbooks, they are interested in quality, price, design, value, and personal appeal. Brand labels such as the "golden arches" are spreading all over the world, and news of excellence is hard to suppress. The availability of information, particularly in the industrialized "Triad" markets of North America, Europe, and Asia, has empowered customers and stimulated competition.

Competitors

Nothing stays proprietary for long. Equipment and software vendors supply their products and services to a wide range of customers, and the result is rapid dispersion of the technology available to all firms. Two factors, time and being the first mover, now have become more critical as elements of strategy. Further, a single firm cannot be on the cutting edge of all technologies. Thus, operating globally means operating with partners, a lesson that Federal Express has learned.

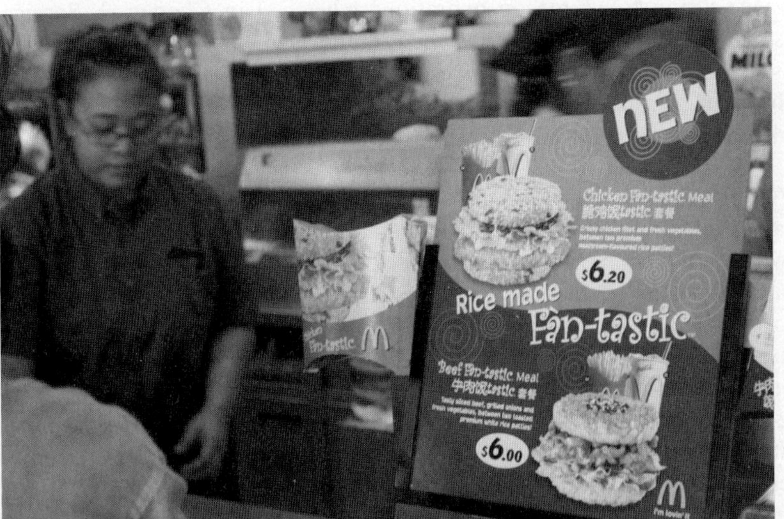

When a successful business in one country expands to another country, it often modifies some features of the service package to accommodate the local culture. ©McGraw-Hill Education/Christopher Kerrigan, photographer

Company

Automation during the recent past has moved firms from a variable-cost to a fixed-cost environment. Management focus thus has changed from boosting profits by reducing material and labor costs to increasing sales to cover fixed costs. This is particularly true for many service firms (e.g., airlines and communications businesses), which to a large extent are fixed-cost activities with huge investments in facilities and equipment. The search for a larger market has driven these firms toward globalization.

The nature of a firm's corporate culture, however, can determine how effectively its service will travel overseas. The domestic success of Federal Express was built on a go-it-alone attitude, on rewards for nonunion employees who propose cost-cutting ideas, and on direct access to the CEO, Fred Smith, with any complaints. In contrast, UPS, which works with a union labor force and strict work standards, has moved overseas with fewer problems.

Currency

Global companies have tried to neutralize their exposure to fluctuating currency exchange rates by matching costs to revenues and becoming strong in all regions of the Triad so that if one region is negative, it may be offset by others that are positive. Companies also have employed international finance techniques such as hedging and options. Thus, to become currency-neutral, a firm is forced into global expansion.

Country

Having a strong presence in all Triad regions provides additional strategic benefits beyond currency considerations. First, as noted, exposure to economic downturns in one region might be offset by operations in other economies. Second, selling in your competitor's domestic market neutralizes that competitor's option to employ a strategy of using excessive profits earned in a protected domestic market for expansion overseas. For example, U.S. pharmaceuticals offer drugs at inflated prices domestically and then sell the same drug in Canada at a steep discount.

Only truly global companies, however, can achieve "global localization" (a term coined by Akio Morita of Sony) and, thereby, be accepted as a local company while maintaining the benefits of worldwide operations. To reach this level, a firm must become close to the customers in the foreign country and accommodate their unique service needs. For fast-food restaurants, discovering the drinking and eating habits of the host country is critical for success; thus, instead of expecting the Germans to enjoy a Big Mac with a Coke, McDonald's added beer to the menu. Permitting local management to modify the service within limits to accommodate local tastes should be encouraged, even at the risk of introducing some inconsistency across locations. An extreme example is Mr. Donut Japan, which changed everything about its product and service except the logo.

Planning Transnational Operations

The strategic service vision for domestic operations advanced in Chapter 2, Service Strategy, requires modification to account for the cultural elements that will influence operations success overseas. In Table 10.1, new questions are proposed to internationalize the elements of the strategic service vision. Three questions in particular—cultural transferability, labor market norms, and host-government policy—will be addressed in depth.

Cultural Transferability

Perhaps the greatest dilemma for service globalization is the need to balance global standardization with local customization. Commercial banking would seem to be culturally neutral, because financial needs and associated business transactions are relatively homogeneous worldwide. The Middle East is an exception, however. The Muslim faith does not allow interest charges on loans, so banks must adapt by creating service charges that include, but do not mention, interest costs. Customer services also are faced with the obvious language barrier and behavioral customs that might affect the service delivery (e.g., midday siesta in Spain).

In food service, however, the desire often is to emulate the cultural experience of a foreign land. The success of Benihana of Tokyo in the United States results partly from creating the illusion of a Japanese dining experience while still serving familiar food. Likewise, for many non-Americans, eating at McDonald's and drinking a Coke is an opportunity to experience something "American." In contrast, Benetton, an Italian clothier and retail company, strives for a universal, nonnational image.

TABLE 10.1 International Elements of the Strategic Service Vision

Service Delivery System	Operating Strategy	Service Concept	Target Market Segments
Available technology? Infrastructure? Utility service?	Appropriate managerial practice? Participative? Autocratic?	What are customer expectations? Perception of value? Service ethic?	What are the market segments? Domestic? Multinational? Tourist?
Labor market norms and customs?	Labor market institutions? Government regulations? Unions?	Service encounter? Language? Acceptance of self-serve?	What are important cultural differences? Language? Life style? Disposable income?
Space availability?			
Interaction with suppliers?			
Educating customers?	Host government policies?	What are the usage patterns?	What are the workforce demographics? Skills? Age distribution? Attitudes? Work ethic?
	Language? Front office? Back office?	Cultural transferability?	

Labor Market Norms

Labor market norms and customs extend beyond language differences. Geert Hofstede conducted an extensive survey of work-related values across some 50 countries, capturing differences across five dimensions.[7]

- *Power Distance Index (PDI)* focuses on the degree of equality, or inequality, between people in the country's society. A *high* power distance ranking indicates that inequalities of power and wealth have been allowed to grow within the society. These societies are more likely to follow a caste system that does not allow significant upward mobility of its citizens. A *low* power distance ranking indicates the society de-emphasizes the differences between citizen's power and wealth. In these societies equality and opportunity for everyone are stressed.
- *Individualism (IDV)* focuses on the degree the society reinforces individual or collective achievement and interpersonal relationships. A *high* individualism ranking indicates that individuality and individual rights are paramount within the society. Individuals in these societies might tend to form a larger number of looser relationships. A *low* individualism ranking typifies societies of a more collectivist nature with close ties between individuals. These cultures reinforce extended families and collectives where everyone takes responsibility for fellow members of their group.
- *Masculinity (MAS)* focuses on the degree the society reinforces, or does not reinforce, the traditional masculine work role model of male achievement, control, and power. A *high* masculinity ranking indicates the country experiences a high degree of gender differentiation. In these cultures, males dominate a significant portion of the society and power structure, with females being controlled by male domination. A *low* masculinity ranking indicates the country has a low level of differentiation and discrimination between genders. In these cultures, females are treated equally to males in all aspects of the society.
- *Uncertainty Avoidance Index (UAI)* focuses on the level of tolerance for uncertainty and ambiguity within the society (i.e., unstructured situations). A *high* uncertainty avoidance ranking indicates the country has a low tolerance for uncertainty and ambiguity. This creates a rule-oriented society that institutes laws, rules, regulations, and controls in order to reduce the amount of uncertainty. A *low* uncertainty avoidance ranking

indicates the country has less concern about ambiguity and uncertainty and has more tolerance for a variety of opinions. This is reflected in a society that is less rule-oriented, more readily accepts change, and takes more and greater risks.

- *Long-Term Orientation (LTO)* focuses on the degree the society embraces, or does not embrace long-term devotion to traditional, forward thinking values. *High* long-term orientation ranking indicates the country subscribes to the values of long-term commitments and respect for tradition. This is thought to support a strong work ethic where long-term rewards are expected as a result of today's hard work. However, business might take longer to develop in this society, particularly for an "outsider." A *low* long-term orientation ranking indicates the country does not reinforce the concept of long-term, traditional orientation. In this culture, change can occur more rapidly as long-term traditions and commitments do not become impediments to change.

Assuming that worker norms are the same worldwide is a mistake. Disney, for example, was surprised with the lack of local worker acceptance of foreign business practices when it opened its theme park outside Paris. Local French employees resisted playing the Disney character roles and maintaining strict hygiene standards because they considered the practices to be a restriction of their individualism. The problem of ignoring local norms extends to customers as well. For example, alcoholic drinks are not served at Disney parks in the United States and Japan, so wine was not offered at meals in France, where the custom of having wine with meals is a source of national pride.

Host-Government Policy

Host governments play a significant role in restricting the growth of service globalization. This includes, but is not limited to, making it difficult to repatriate funds (i.e., take profits out of the host country). Discrimination has taken a number of creative forms, such as banning the sale of insurance by foreign firms, giving preferential treatment to local shippers, placing restrictions on the international flow of information, and creating delays in the processing of licensing agreements. Restricting foreign airlines' landing rights and the ability to pick up passengers at an intermediate stop (i.e., other than a port of entry) protects national carriers.

Nations might perceive both an economic and a cultural threat in the import of unrestricted foreign services. Information-based services are a particular target, as governments create regulations on international banking, bans on private ownership of satellite dishes (e.g., China and Saudi Arabia), and restrictions on full access to the Internet. Labor-intensive services, however, often are welcomed because they create local employment opportunities.

Global Service Strategies[8]

Firms considering a global reach must pay attention to selecting the appropriate global competitive strategy for their service. The service company that responds to heightened global competition will look very different from firms with only a domestic focus. Globally focused firms will have a flexible delivery system, a brand recognized for quality, and a diverse workforce.

Five basic globalization strategies can be identified: (1) multicountry expansion, (2) importing customers, (3) following your customers, (4) service offshoring, and (5) beating the clock. These strategies are not all mutually exclusive, however. One can think of a number of ways to combine strategies (e.g., combining multicountry expansion with beating the clock).

Table 10.2 shows how each globalization strategy is affected by the globalization factors faced by multinational service firms. Using this table, managers can consider how these factors affect the implementation of various candidate strategies and their likelihood of

TABLE 10.2 Considerations in Selecting a Global Service Strategy

Source: Adapted from Curtis P. McLaughlin and James A. Fitzsimmons, "Strategies for Globalizing Service Operations," *International Journal of Service Industry Management* 7, no. 4, 1996, pp. 45–59.

	Global Service Strategies				
Globalization Factors	**Multicountry Expansion**	**Importing Customers**	**Following Your Customers**	**Service Offshoring**	**Beating the Clock**
Customization	Usually a standard service	Strategic opportunity	Re-prototype locally	Quality and coordination	More need for reliability and coordination
Complexity	Usually routine	Strategic opportunity	Modify operations	Opportunity for focus	Time compression
Information intensity	Satellite network	On-site advantage	Move experienced managers	Training investments	Exploit opportunity
Cultural adaptation	Modify service	Accommodate foreign guests	Could be necessary to achieve scale	Cultural understanding	Common language necessary
Customer contact	Train local workers	Develop foreign language and cultural sensitivity skills	Develop foreign customers	Specialize in back-office service components	Provide extended hours of service
Labor intensity	Reduce labor costs	Increased labor costs	Hire local personnel	Reduced labor costs	Reduced labor costs
Other	Government restrictions	Logistics management	Inadequate infrastructure	Home office employee morale	Capital investments

success for a specific business in a target country or region. Table 10.2 also summarizes key opportunities and potential problems that each globalization factor contributes to each global service strategy. The service strategy and management implications for service globalization are discussed, beginning with the multicountry expansion strategy.

Multicountry Expansion

Multisite expansion commonly has been accomplished using franchising to attract investors and a "cookie-cutter" approach to clone the service rapidly in multiple locations. This expansion strategy is necessary when the service market is defined by the need for customers to travel physically to the service facility. Exporting a successful service to another country without modification, however, can capitalize on selling "a country's cultural experience," as illustrated by the success of McDonald's in Europe, and especially by its experience in Moscow. Cultural adaptation often requires some modification of the service concept, however, as seen in the availability of beer in German McDonald's.

Many strategic issues are involved in moving a service operation out and around the world, or *multicountry expansion*. Duplicating a service worldwide is best accomplished when routine services are involved, such as one experiences at Starbucks. The customer-contact or front-office operations require sensitivity to the local culture, however. The best approach would appear to be hiring and training locals to handle that part of the process in consultation with those who know the approaches that have been successful in other countries.

With the exception of professional services, customization and complexity are not important issues considering the routine nature of many multisite consumer services (e.g., fast food). Information intensity is not an important consideration either, but managing a global network of service sites might require communications by satellite.

Cultural adaptation, however, is a major issue in service design. Should it be centralized or managed country by country? These questions were addressed by Kentucky Fried Chicken, as noted by the following quote explaining the situation faced by overseas managers.[9]

> The country managers were like Roman governors sent to govern distant provinces with nothing more than an exhortation to maintain Rome's imperial power and reputation. Few had any operating expertise, they were offered little staff support and the only attention paid to operations was Colonel Sanders' personal efforts to maintain the quality of his original product. Each country manager was on his own to make a success of his venture, and most had to learn the business from scratch.

Unfortunately, the corporate staff seemed to have had little to offer, except to try making the foreign operation conform to the U.S. template. After all, the raison d'être of franchising collapses in the face of local cultural adaptation. The country managers were well aware, however, that the cookie-cutter approach also would not work.

Importing Customers

For the multiservice single-site strategy to be successful internationally, customers must be willing to travel a long distance and stay for an extended time, or telecommunications must be substituted for physical travel. Many services such as prestigious colleges and universities, medical centers (e.g., Mayo Clinic), and tourist attractions (e.g., Disney World) meet these stipulations. Because of a unique tourist attraction at a particular location (e.g., Mt. Crested Butte in Colorado), a service evolves that is focused on that attraction, such as catering to skiers in the winter and mountain bikers in the summer. Rather than exporting the service as in a multisite strategy, the multiservice strategy involves *importing customers*.

A service that decides to retain its location and attract customers from around the world will be faced with developing the foreign-language skill and cultural sensitivity of its customer-contact employees. A company might have to pay more to get those skills. The unique features of the location (e.g., tourist attraction or reputation of service personnel) will dictate the selection of this strategy. Differentiation will occur through customization and complexity of the service, and transportation infrastructure and logistics management will be challenging to accommodate visitors. For example, at one time the Cook Islands in the South Pacific was served by air from Los Angeles by direct flight every day except Thursday and Sunday.

Following Your Customers

Many service companies open offices overseas not to serve the local markets but to follow their corporate clients overseas and continue to serve them. Attracting local business might require modifications in the service package, however, as well as employment of people who are familiar with local business practices.

To implement the strategy to *follow your customers*, one of the largest business-travel agencies has formed partnerships in almost every area of the world. Its corporate customers want their people served adequately wherever they go. Our global "age of terrorism" has spawned several businesses that issue travel advisories and extricate clients who are stranded in the midst of a dangerous situation, such as a civil or military uprising or a natural disaster.

Just as law firms expanded into multiple cities to align themselves with their corporate accounts, service companies are pushed to operate in the same countries as their clients. The truly global company wants and demands truly global service from its travel agents, auditors, consultants, and others.

The weakness of this strategy for a company already committed to overseas operations is that it ignores the vast markets represented by the rapidly growing middle classes of many countries. Companies that continue to serve these populations, consequently, are free to grow without competition until they reach sufficient quality and scale to become a threat internationally.

Usually, the sales volume that is available from visitors or expatriates in a foreign country is small. This leaves the service manager with interesting choices–should I design my service to follow my customers and their needs, design it to adapt to the local culture, or make a compromise between the two and hope to straddle them both successfully? Everything that operations managers know about services would seem to argue against the likelihood of a successful straddle. Therefore, managers have interesting focus and scale issues to contend with in terms of whether to serve expatriates and visitors or cater to local customers. Where expatriate markets are small and the local market requires considerable adaptation, partnering with local organizations seems to be an attractive alternative. Even when a new service prototype is not needed for the front office, it may be necessary to adapt back-office operations to the local environment and bring in experienced and flexible managers to make the transplantation work in the face of local infrastructure and social system complexities.

Service Offshoring

Service offshoring is a class of outsourcing that is distinguished by the foreign location of the outsourced provider. Consequently, offshoring can be considered a global service strategy. Some service firms can save labor costs by sending back-office operations via the Internet to overseas locations and focus on customer contact activities locally. For example, a discount brokerage can have the routine market transaction activities and customer account maintenance performed overseas, but retain the customized professional advising activities domestically. The flight of U.S. call centers to India is an example of remote customer service conducted from abroad that takes advantage of the population's English language skills. However, some quality problems have arisen when poorly trained employees on a night shift in India (to match the U.S. working day) have voice contact with customers. Corporate customer complaints at Dell Computer led to moving some call center work back to the United States.

Although the labor cost savings is an attractive incentive to offshore back-office activities, there are investment costs to be considered in training, instilling a cultural understanding, and addressing adverse employee morale factors within the offshoring company.

The offshoring practice will continue because many countries have large pools of unemployed and underemployed English-speaking educated persons. Many of these people have high levels of technical training, especially those who have quantitative skills and can adapt to higher levels of service. Some of the current market segments for service offshoring include customer service, financial analysis, income tax preparation, payment services, software development, and research and development.

Beating the Clock

Beating the clock describes the competitive advantages gained from the fact that one can bypass the constraints of the clock and domestic time zones, including time-based domestic work rules and regulations. Companies in the United States long have known that combining the demand from multiple time zones could improve the productivity of reservation clerks and telemarketers. Symantec, a leader in cybersecurity, provides technical support to its more easterly U.S. customers by transferring their early morning telephone inquiries to a support center in Ireland. The advantage is derived from supplying service to East Coast customers at hours when the California office would be closed. Being able to give 24-hour service despite local work norms or government regulations on market closings has helped to produce the true globalization of securities markets.

Projects can be expedited by taking advantage of coordinated activities around the globe. For example, a North Carolina bank is having its loan record systems expanded and reprogrammed by an Indian firm. Indian personnel in the United States communicate daily with programmers in India via satellite. The bank management is delighted because the work goes quickly as workers at the Indian site do programming for one-half of the clock and workers at the North Carolina site do testing and debugging during the other half.

Service Benchmark

SMALL WORLD AND OTHER MYTHS

In just a few hours we can be on a far-off island or another continent and we are struck by how small our world is. Even for companies doing business in other countries, the world is small when we consider the time it takes to travel and the far less time that it takes to communicate via computers and telecommunications.

When we consider the human and cultural aspects of doing business in diverse countries, however, we easily can believe the Earth is expanding along with the universe. The differences between cultures sometime seem insurmountable. Until recently in former eastern bloc countries, for example, goods were in short supply and those who sold them had the upper hand. Customers felt subservient to those who dished out the attitude along with the goods. Today shelves are stocked as never before, but servers and customers alike have trouble with the concept of "the customer is always right." A smiling server is suspect, and customers are not always patient with a server who is struggling with new ways of doing business.

In other cases, differences have been accommodated, oftentimes to the benefit and amusement of the differing cultures. McDonald's is sometimes credited with bringing a higher level of restroom cleanliness to an overseas community—sort of a "potty purity" ambassador.

The advantages from time compression of the software development process are not likely to go unnoticed in a number of settings. Time-based competition is a widely accepted strategy in manufacturing. In the real-time world of services, there is every reason to expect new innovations to use the speed of light to beat the clock around the world and gain a competitive advantage.

Managers should look at their service processes to find ways in which electronic means can be used to beat the clock. Once these are identified, managers can develop either offensive or defensive strategies. This analysis should include consideration of the potential impact of time-zone shifts on marketing, operations, or human resource aspects of the service. Can such shifts (1) result in economies of operation, (2) provide better access for foreign and domestic customers, (3) support time-based competition in operations, or (4) add to the creativity available in the process without slowing it down? Defensive strategies would involve forming strategic alliances in other time zones. Offensive activities might involve moving to or modifying operations in nondomestic time zones to tap new markets or improve existing ones to beat the competition by beating the clock.

The need for greater reliability and coordination among locations and time zones might require substantial additional investments in training, methods of operation, and telecommunications. Telecommunications certainly will be necessary to make the shift in location transparent to the customer and to realize the full value from the time advantage.

Summary

A successful service innovation can grow in two fundamental ways: (1) duplication of the service in different geographic locations with a multisite strategy of becoming a "focused network" or (2) incorporation of different services at the original site using a multiservice strategy, thereby becoming a "clustered service." Although it is not necessarily a desirable objective, some mature service firms combine both strategies and become a "diversified network."

Franchising has become the most common method to implement a multisite strategy in a very rapid manner, using capital that is furnished by investor-owners. Franchising is attractive to prospective entrepreneurs because of the many advantages of buying into a proven concept, but most important, the risk of failure is diminished.

We now live in a "borderless world," with information on products and services available to customers worldwide. For many services, a global presence no longer is an option but a necessity if they wish to continue to serve their customers. Overseas expansion has its risks and challenges depending on the cultural transferability of the service, network development in a foreign land, and government discrimination against foreign services.

Key Terms and Definitions

Beating the clock using service locations around the globe to achieve 24-hour service availability. *p. 293*
Clustered service a situation in which many services are offered at a single location (e.g., a hospital). *p. 282*
Diversified network a situation in which many services are offered at multiple locations (e.g., branch banks). *p. 282*
Focused network a single service offered at multiple sites, often by use of franchising (e.g., a motel chain). *p. 281*
Focused service a single service offered at a single location (e.g., a family restaurant). *p. 281*
Follow your customers a concept involving expansion overseas to service existing customers who already have established multinational operations. *p. 292*
Franchising a method of duplicating a service concept by attracting investors who become owner-operators bound by a contractual agreement to offer the service in a consistent manner. *p. 282*
Importing customers an approach to growth that attracts customers to an existing site rather than building sites overseas. *p. 292*
Multicountry expansion a growth strategy in which a service is replicated in more than one country using a franchising formula with little adaptation to the local culture. *p. 291*
Service offshoring sending back-office activities overseas to gain labor cost savings. *p. 293*

Topics for Discussion

1. Recall that service operations can be classified as processing people, goods, or information. What challenges are faced in each category when globalization is undertaken?
2. Chili's, a U.S.-based restaurant chain that offers Mexican-inspired foods, has its largest establishment in Monterrey, Mexico. Why is Chili's so successful in Monterrey?
3. What is the inherent conflict in a franchising arrangement?
4. What explains the continuing trade surplus in services for the United States?

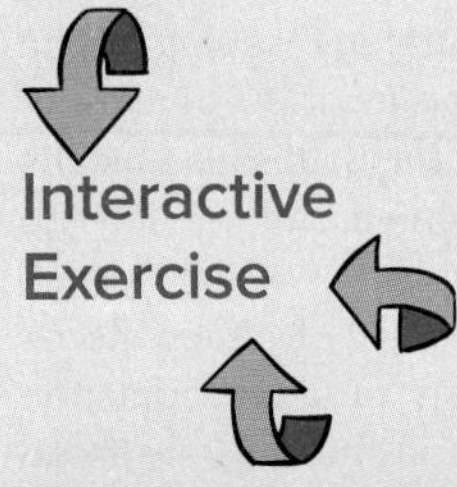

Interactive Exercise

The class is broken into small groups with at least one international student in each group, if possible. Based on overseas travel, have the group report on features of day-to-day living that they have found different from home and worth emulating.

Goodwill Industries of Central Texas[10] CASE 10.1

"Every time you donate to Goodwill, you give someone the power to change his or her life by getting a job . . . Who knew the shirt you wore last year could turn into a job for someone?" —*Helping!* magazine, a publication of Goodwill Industries International Inc., Winter 1998

COMPANY BACKGROUND

Goodwill Industries of Central Texas (GICT) is a nonprofit organization that is independently run and operated, but is affiliated with Goodwill Industries International Inc. (GIII), an organization that helps individual Goodwills with resource issues, national marketing campaigns, executive search information, and federal legislative lobbying. Currently, there are 164 Goodwills in North America and 13 Goodwill-affiliated organizations throughout other parts of the world—each focused on the same mission.

DONATIONS TO DOLLARS

Goodwill Industries operates primarily through the generosity of people and businesses in the local community. The Donated Goods department generates the greatest source of its revenue. The organization relies heavily on donations of used clothing, housewares, electronics, sporting goods, and any other sellable items in order to generate the revenue necessary to provide its services. Figure 10.4 displays actual 2009 revenue by source, a distribution typical of the past several years.

THE CHALLENGE AHEAD

Executive management recognizes the emergence of an increasingly competitive marketplace in the thrift arena. This fact is forcing the organization to change the way it does business. Recently there has been increasing pressure for the stores to perform better and better each year despite much

FIGURE 10.4
2009 Sources of Revenue

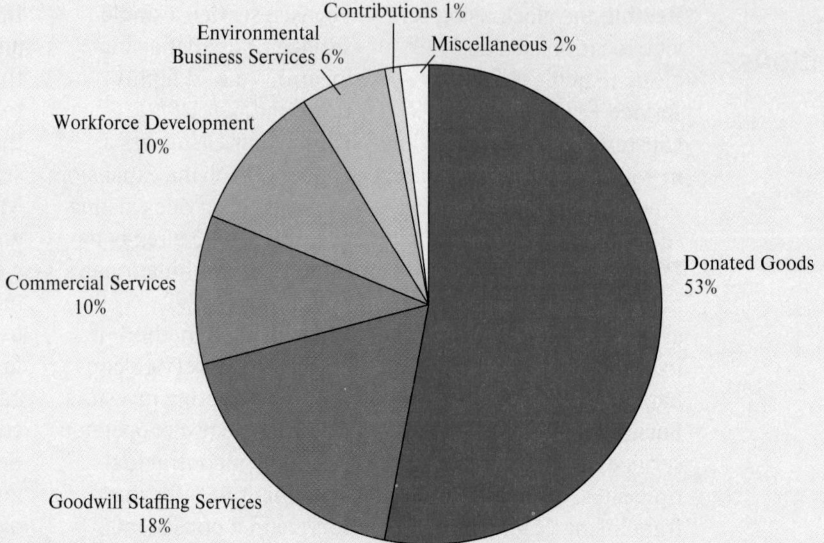

stiffer competition for employees and donations. As a result, some retail locations failed to meet store revenue goals. To compound the problem, Goodwill experienced periods of high employee turnover in the 1990s. The mission of Goodwill is to help people find meaningful employment, but when a person is hired as an employee of Retail Operations, the organization tries to retain that person to help create a stable and highly qualified workforce.

THE COMPETITION

Goodwill is faced with competition on two fronts—competition for donations and competition for the sale of those donations. Until several years ago, Goodwill Industries had little competition for its primary raw material—donated used goods. People donated to Goodwill because there was no other outlet except the trash pile. The Salvation Army emerged as a competitor, but for a long time the Salvation Army and Goodwill were the only shows in town. That began to change, however, with the emergence and popularity of consignment stores and mom-and-pop thrift stores. People began to have more choices as to where to donate or sell their used items. These small operations not only eat up potential donations, but also they increase the competition for sales as well. The thrift dollar has become much more competitive in the 2010s. For example, for-profit thrift stores, such as Thrift Town, actively solicit used goods from the same population as Goodwill.

Despite the increase in local competition, however, the retail operations of GICT has grown significantly since 2002. The organization had 22 retail stores, 8 bookstores with attended donation centers, and 3 attended donation dropoff sites in 2011. A newly purchased large building now serves as a resource center for the consolidation of two warehouses, offices, job-training classroom, meeting rooms for other non-profits and community activities, a conference room, and retail space. Three more stores were expected to open before the end of the year. The company has an explicit strategy to expand its operations by opening and operating new locations throughout the 15-county territory for which it is responsible.

WHAT HAS SUSTAINED GROWTH?

Goodwill has developed a unique strategy for competing in the broader local retail market. The company chooses not to compete head-to-head with other retailers for the traditional holiday (i.e., year-end holiday season) spending dollar. Instead, it creates a niche for itself by marketing Halloween costumes and decorations. Stores are decorated in Halloween themes and employees are encouraged to come to work in costumes. About 45 percent of the annual advertising budget is geared toward Halloween promotions. This strategy seems to be working, because October accounts for almost 30 percent of retail revenue for the year. On the other hand, this also means that a bad financial Halloween could mean a bad year for the organization.

Goodwill Industries has relied on its ability to open stores in high-traffic locations that are close to the population that donates to their stores and shops in them. There is no formal process for searching for new locations. The decision is left up to the management of the retail operations after visiting potential locations. Goodwill even has built a store from the ground up in a new suburban community development. This was a significant shift from a long-standing philosophy of leasing or buying properties that had a history of being productive.

Goodwill has stayed relatively healthy during the recent global, national, and local economic crises because it has diversified its operations. In addition to its long-standing resale and job training services, it now has Goodwill Staffing Services that provides employees for governmental agencies and private businesses, Goodwill Commercial Services to supply workers for jobs such as custodians and landscapers, Goodwill Computer Works that refurbishes and sells used computing-related equipment, and book and other specialty sales.

Finally, Goodwill polished its image with the public by trying to look more like a department store than like a thrift shop. The stores purchased new fixtures and spruced up the exteriors with new signs and paint. Great care is taken to ensure that dressing rooms are cleaned regularly and that donation drop-off sites look appealing and clean. The transportation department at one time painted its trucks with the Goodwill logo and the phrase "those jeans you donated just got someone a job."

CUSTOMER ISSUES

A frequent criticism from the public is the difficulty they have in donating to the organization. At one time Goodwill offered a donation pickup service but stopped doing it because of too much difficulty coordinating pickups at homes. The organization also is concerned with the amount of "trash" that the home pickup workers had to deal with. Now donors must transport their items to the nearest donation site.

Another area of customer concern is Goodwill's retail policy of "all sales are final." Customers complain when they purchase an item that works during testing at a store but fails to operate at home. The "all sales final" policy means that it is impossible to get a refund, but the manager is empowered to offer a store exchange. These exchanges occur rarely. Part of the reason for the policy is that it is difficult to prove that the items being returned were previously purchased from Goodwill. The organization provides a 7-day return period for online purchases under specific circumstances such as items that have been substantially misrepresented or damaged during shipping.

Questions

1. Who are Goodwill's customers and how have their demographics changed over time?
2. How should the introduction of for-profit thrifts affect Goodwill's decisions about the role of customer service?
3. How can Goodwill differentiate itself from the competition?
4. Visit http://shopgoodwill.com/ where Goodwill auctions items of special interest and discuss why this online store has great profit potential.

FedEx: Tiger International Acquisition[11] CASE 10.2

What has become one of America's great success stories began operations almost two decades ago in Memphis, Tennessee. At that time, those who knew of Fred Smith's idea did not realize that his small company was about to revolutionize the air-cargo industry.

In 1972, the Civil Aeronautics Board ruled that operators flying aircraft with an "all-up" weight of less than 75,000 pounds could be classified as an "air taxi" and would not be required to obtain a certificate of "public convenience and necessity" to operate. This made it possible for Federal Express (FedEx) to penetrate the heavily entrenched air-freight industry. FedEx ordered a fleet of 33 Dassault Falcon fan-jets in 1972 and commenced operations a year later. On April 17, 1973, the company delivered 18 packages, becoming the first to offer nationwide overnight delivery.

One of FedEx's fundamental principles was use of the hub-and-spoke system, in which all packages were flown to Memphis first, sorted during the night, and then shipped to their destinations the following morning. This system allowed FedEx to serve a large number of cities with a minimum number of aircraft. It also provided tight control and efficiency of ground operations and soon became increasingly important as package-tracking systems were installed.

During the first two years of operations, FedEx lost money, but revenues surpassed the $5 billion mark in fiscal year 1989, partly because of the acquisition of Tiger International.

As Table 10.3 shows, FedEx began global expansion in 1984, when it purchased Gelco International. FedEx followed that expansion with its first scheduled flight to Europe in 1985, and it established a European headquarters in Brussels, Belgium, that same year.

Domestic operations were expanded as well. In 1986, regional hubs were established in Oakland, California, and in Newark, New Jersey. In 1987, a sorting facility was opened in Indianapolis, and Honolulu was chosen for the Far East headquarters. That same year, FedEx was granted the rights to a small-cargo route to Japan, and the following year the company was making regularly scheduled flights to Asia.

International expansion did not result in immediate international success, however. In Asia, its planes were flying at half their capacity because of treaty restrictions, and a lack of back-up planes in its South American operations jeopardized guaranteed delivery when regular aircraft were grounded. Even worse, many managers of the companies acquired in Europe had quit.

As a solution to these international bottlenecks, FedEx made a dramatic move in December 1988, announcing plans to purchase Tiger International, the parent company of Flying Tigers, the world's largest heavy-cargo airline. The purchase price was about $880 million.

This action catapulted FedEx to the forefront of the international cargo market, giving it landing rights in 21 additional countries; however, the addition of Tigers was not without challenges. For example, the leveraged acquisition more than doubled FedEx's long-term debt, to approximately $2 billion. Moreover, FedEx had bought into the business of delivering heavy cargo, much of which was not sent overnight, which represented a significant departure from FedEx's traditional market niche. One of the largest dilemmas facing FedEx following the merger was how to integrate the two workforces.

MAJOR PLAYERS IN THE DOMESTIC AIR-CARGO INDUSTRY

Federal Express is the nation's largest overnight carrier, with more than 40 percent of the domestic market. United Parcel Service (UPS), DHL (an international carrier based in Brussels), and a few other carriers account for the remaining market share. FedEx had revenues of $3.9 billion and a net income of $188 million in 1988. FedEx had lost approximately $74 million on its international business since 1985, however, prompting

TABLE 10.3 **Federal Express Corporation and Flying Tiger Timeline**

1973	Began service with Falcon fan-jets to 25 cities from Memphis in April.
1977	Air-cargo industry deregulated.
1978	Purchased its first Boeing 727 and became a publicly held corporation.
1980	Took delivery of first McDonnell Douglas DC10 and implemented computerized tracking system.
1981	Introduced Overnight Letter, a lower-cost document service. Opened greatly expanded Superhub in Memphis.
1982	Shortened overnight delivery commitment to 10:30 AM in all major markets.
1983	Opened first Business Service Center. Became first company to achieve annual revenues of $1 billion in ten years.
1984	Purchased Gelco International and made first scheduled trans-Atlantic flight to Europe. Established European headquarters in Brussels.
1986	Enhanced tracking and informational capabilities with introduction of SuperTracker. Acquired Lex Wilkinson Ltd. of United Kingdom and Cansica of Canada.
1987	Acquired Indianapolis hub. Was granted exclusive small-cargo route to Japan.
1988	Scheduled first trans-Pacific flight to Japan. Acquired nine offshore transportation companies.
	Announced plan to purchase Tiger International.
1989	Completed purchase of Tiger International and merged Flying Tigers into system, becoming the world's largest full-service all-cargo airline.

the carrier to purchase Tiger International. That acquisition, which gained U.S. government approval on January 31, 1989, gave FedEx a strong entry position into heavy cargo as well as access to 21 additional countries.

Price wars, which began with UPS's entry into the overnight business, have decreased FedEx's revenues per package by 15 percent since 1984. Another setback to FedEx was its $350 million loss on Zapmail, which it dropped in 1986. A document transmission service that relayed information via satellite, Zapmail was quickly made obsolete by facsimile machines.

FedEx does offer its customers several other benefits not matched by its competitors, however. For example, it offers a 1-hour "on-call" pickup service, and through use of its database information system, COSMOS, FedEx guarantees that it can locate any package in its possession within 30 minutes. FedEx has found that this type of customer security helps to ensure continued growth.

THE NATURE OF THE COMPETITION

The air-cargo industry has undergone a series of mergers resulting from price wars that rocked the industry. Also, marketing alliances have been formed between domestic and foreign carriers to take advantage of international trade and to create new routes and services (e.g., package tracking).

When UPS entered the overnight-package market in 1982, competition rose substantially, starting the series of price wars that have hurt all air-cargo players. FedEx's average revenue per package declined by 30.3 percent between 1983 and 1988.

Fortunately, it appears that the price-cutting strategy might have run its course. When UPS, which created the price wars, announced another price cut in October 1988, its competitors refused to follow, and in January 1993, UPS announced its first price increase in almost six years, a 5 percent increase in charges for next-day service. Several factors such as continued overcapacity, low switching costs, and high exit barriers, however, will continue to make the air-cargo industry extremely competitive.

CONCLUSIONS ON THE AIR-CARGO ENVIRONMENT

Although the situation might be improving, intraindustry competition and rivalry remain the main deterrent to the air-cargo industry. With overcapacity in the industry, firms, desperate to fill planes, continue to realize declining yields on the packages they ship.

Moreover, passenger airlines reentered the air-cargo market with increased vigor, which also does not help the capacity situation. All of these factors are leading current players to consolidate their operations in hope of achieving increased economies of scale.

Technology is acting as both friend and foe of the air-cargo industry. Facsimile machines have carved a large niche from the overnight-document segment; on the other hand, improved databases are enabling companies to provide their clients with another valuable service: improved tracking information on the status of important shipments.

Until now, the large number of shippers has enabled buyers to enjoy low rates, but because of their wide dispersion, buyers are not able to control the air-cargo companies effectively. Likewise, air-cargo companies continue to have an advantage over their suppliers. The ability to purchase older planes keeps firms less dependent on aircraft manufacturers, and a large, unskilled labor pool helps to keep hub labor costs down. A lack of available airport facilities, however, presents a serious problem to the commercial air-freight industry. Not only is the lack of landing slots a problem in the United States, but acquiring government-controlled access to crowded international hubs can present a formidable challenge.

WORLDWIDE DISTRIBUTION

As the globe continues to shrink and economies grow more interdependent, customers are demanding new services to facilitate revamped production processes. One of the most publicized is the just-in-time (JIT) system that many U.S. firms have borrowed from their Japanese competitors. JIT systems argue for elimination of the traditional inventory stockpiles common to manufacturing, including the raw material, work-in-process, and finished-goods inventories. Without question, such a scheme relies on having the right part at the right place at the right time.

Air express has been able to play a reliable role in delivering these needed materials on time. FedEx and its competitors have succeeded in contracting with manufacturers to supply the needed logistical expertise to support its JIT framework. Essentially, the planes have become flying warehouses. As this area grows, the Tiger addition to FedEx should reap large yields with its ability to handle the heavier shipments that are associated with international manufacturing. For example, an increasing amount of parts made in Asia are being shipped to the United States for final assembly.

POWERSHIP

To facilitate further penetration into a customer's business, FedEx developed Powership, which is a program that locates terminals on a client's premises and, thus, enables FedEx to stay abreast of the firm's needs. In simplifying the daily shipping process, an automated program tracks shipments, provides pricing information, and prints invoices. Such a device helps to eliminate the administrative need of reconciling manifests with invoices.

At FedEx, customer automation is expected to play an increasingly significant role. The company has kept up with the explosive growth of technology and now offers several ancillary resources such as its Compatible Solutions Program, Developer Resource Center, FedEx Ship Manager Software, and FedEx Mobile. By tying technological innovations with reliable on-time delivery, FedEx is achieving its goal of getting closer to the customer.

CORPORATE CULTURE

Many believe that FedEx could not have grown to its current magnitude had it been forced to deal with the added pressure of negotiating with a unionized workforce. FedEx has never employed organized labor, although attempts at unionization have been made. In 1976, the International Association of Machinists and Aerospace Workers tried to organize the company's mechanics, who rejected the offer. Likewise, FedEx's pilots rejected an offer by the Airline Pilots Association during that same period. In 1978, the Teamsters attempted to organize the hub sorters but could not get enough signatures for a vote.

Despite an admirable human resource track record, the outlook for FedEx to continue its past performance is hazy. Because of the Tiger International acquisition, FedEx had to merge the unionized Flying Tigers workforce with its own union-free environment. Previously, the willingness of FedEx workers to go above and beyond in performing their duties had given the company a marked advantage over UPS, the nation's largest employer of United Brotherhood of Teamsters members. As the FedEx–Tiger merger progressed, however, many questions remained to be answered.

ACQUISITION OF TIGER INTERNATIONAL

In December 1988, FedEx announced its intent to purchase Flying Tigers, and in early 1989, more than 40 years of air-cargo experience were merged with FedEx. Besides giving FedEx entry into an additional 21 nations, the Tigers merger possessed several other advantages for the aggressive company. Almost overnight, FedEx became owner of the world's largest full-service, all-cargo airline, nearly three times the size of its nearest competitor. Because FedEx could use this large fleet on its newly acquired routes, it no longer would be forced into the position of contracting out to other freight carriers in markets not served previously.

The addition of heavy freight to the FedEx service mix was viewed as a boost to its traditional express package–delivery business. The merger fit in neatly with the company's plans to focus on the higher-margin box business while shifting away from document service. During the preceding two years, box shipments had increased by 53 percent, generating as much as 80 percent of revenues and an estimated 90 percent of profits.

On the downside, as noted earlier, the $2 billion debt that was incurred by the merger and the capital intensiveness of the heavy-cargo business made the company more vulnerable to economic swings. Although the merger meshed well into its plans, FedEx still was a newcomer to the heavy-cargo market.

Another hurdle was that many premerger Flying Tigers customers were competitors that used Tigers to reach markets where they, like FedEx, had no service or could not establish service.

Finally, FedEx had to integrate the 6,500 unionized Tigers workers into a union-free company. Although Flying Tigers was founded with much the same type of entrepreneurial spirit that was cherished at Federal Express, the carrier had seen its workforce become members of organized labor early in its existence.

At the time of the merger, the Tigers union ties were severed. FedEx promised to find positions for all employees, but critics felt that the union background of Tigers workers would dilute the corporate culture at Federal Express. Whether FedEx could continue its success story appeared to hinge on its ability to impart its way of life to the Tigers workers, not vice versa.

Questions

1. Describe the growth strategy of Federal Express. How did this strategy differ from those of its competitors?
2. What risks were involved in the acquisition of Tiger International?
3. In addition to the question of merging FedEx and Flying Tigers pilots, what other problems could have been anticipated in accomplishing this acquisition?
4. Suggest a plan of action that Fred Smith could have used to address the potential acquisition problems given in your answer to the previous question.

Selected Bibliography

Aharoni, Yair, ed. *Coalitions and Competition (Routledge Revivals): The Globalization of Professional Business Services.* London: Routledge, 2014.

Hahn, Eugene D., and Kraiwinee Bunyaratavej. "Services Cultural Alignment in Offshoring: The Impact of Cultural Dimensions on Offshoring Location Choices." *Journal of Operations Management* 28, no. 3 (May 2010), pp. 186–93.

——, ——. "Offshoring of Information-based Services: Structural Breaks in Industry Life Cycles." *Service Science* 3, no. 3 (Fall 2011), pp. 329–55.

Karmarkar, Uday. "OM Forum–The Service and Information Economy: Research Opportunities." *Manufacturing & Service Operations Management* 17, no. 2 (2015), pp. 136–41.

McIvor, Ronan. "How the Transaction Cost and Resource-Based Theories of the Firm Inform Outsourcing Evaluation." *Journal of Operations Management* 27, no. 1 (January 2009), pp. 45–63.

Robbins, Thomas R., and Terry P. Harrison. "New Project Staffing for Outsourced Call Centers with Global Service Level Agreements." *Service Science* 3, no. 1 (Spring 2011), pp. 41–66.

Tate, Wendy L., Lisa M. Ellram, and Stephen W. Brown. "Offshore Outsourcing of Services: A Stakeholder Perspective." *Journal of Service Research* 12, no. 1 (August 2009), pp. 56–72.

Youngdahl, William, Kannan Ramaswamy, and Rohit Verma (eds.). "Special Issue: Offshoring of Service and Knowledge Work." *Journal of Operations Management* 26, no. 2 (March 2008), pp. 135–336.

Endnotes

1. From Brian O'Keefe, "The New Future: Global Brands," *Fortune,* November 26, 2001. http://www.fortune.com/indexw.jhtml?channel=artcol.jhtml&doc_id=205047.
2. S. E. Kimes and J. A. Fitzsimmons, "Selecting Profitable Hotel Sites at La Quinta Motor Inns," *Interfaces* 20, no. 2 (March 1990) pp. 12–20.
3. M. Carman and Eric Langeard, "Growth Strategies for Service Firms," *Strategic Management Journal* 1, no. 1 (January–March 1980), p. 19.
4. From Daniel Pearl, "Federal Express Finds Its Pioneering Formula Falls Flat Overseas," *The Wall Street Journal,* April 15, 1991, p. 1.
5. From Christopher A. Bartlett and Sumantra Ghoshal, *Managing Across Borders: The Transnational Solution,* 2nd ed. (Boston: Harvard Business School Press, 1998).
6. From Kenichi Ohmae, *The Borderless World* (New York: Harper Business 1990), p. 19.
7. From Geert Hofstede, "Cultural Dimensions," on ITIM Creating Cultural Dimensions website, http://www.geert-hofstede.com, June 30, 2004.
8. From Curtis P. McLaughlin and James A. Fitzsimmons, "Strategies for Globalizing Service Operations," *International Journal of Service Industry Management* 7, no. 4 (1996), pp. 45–59.
9. Kentucky Fried Chicken (Japan) Limited, case no. 9-387-043, Harvard Business School, Boston, 1993, p. 1.
10. Prepared by Steve Callahan, Cindy Gage, and Kathleen Woodhouse under the supervision of Professor James A. Fitzsimmons.
11. Prepared by Garland Wilkinson under the supervision of Professor James A. Fitzsimmons.

Chapter 11

Managing Capacity and Demand

Learning Objectives

After completing this chapter, you should be able to:

1. Describe the strategies for matching capacity and demand for services.
2. Determine the overbooking strategy for a service that minimizes expected loss.
3. Use a linear programming model to prepare a weekly workshift schedule with two consecutive days off for each employee.
4. Prepare a work schedule for part-time employees.
5. Explain what yield management is, when its use is appropriate, and how it can be accomplished using the critical fractile criterion.

After fixed capacity investment decisions have been made (e.g., number of hotel rooms to be built or aircraft to be purchased), the hotel beds must be filled or the airline seats sold to make the daily operations profitable. The subject of this chapter is the challenge that is faced by managers of matching service capacity with customer demand on a daily basis in a dynamic environment.

Service capacity is a perishable commodity. For example, a plane flying with empty seats has lost forever the revenue opportunity of carrying those additional passengers. American Airlines was the first in its industry to address this problem and to realize the potential of using what now is called *yield management*, which was discussed briefly in Chapter 2, Service Strategy, and will be addressed in more detail here. Use of information technology to support yield management was not lost on Mr. Donald Burr, CEO of People Express, whose failing airline was bought by Texas Air in 1986. He has remarked that he was killed by a computer chip.

Unlike products that are stored in warehouses for future consumption, a service is an intangible personal experience that cannot be transferred from one person to another. Instead, a service is produced and consumed simultaneously. Whenever demand for a service falls short of the capacity to serve, the results are idle servers and facilities. Further, the variability in service demand is quite pronounced, and, in fact, our culture and habits contribute to these fluctuations. For example, most of us eat our meals at the same hours and take our vacations in July and August, and studies of hospitals indicate low utilization in the summer and fall months. These natural variations in service demand create periods of idle service at some times and of consumer waiting at others.

Chapter Preview

We begin with a discussion of two generic strategies: level capacity and chase demand. For the level capacity strategy, we introduce marketing-oriented strategies such as price incentives that can smooth customer demand to utilize better the fixed capacity. For the chase demand strategy, we consider operations-oriented strategies such as workshift scheduling to vary capacity to match the changing levels of customer demand. In conclusion, a hybrid strategy called yield management is explored that uses sophisticated real-time information systems to maximize revenue.

Generic Strategies of Level Capacity or Chase Demand

There are two generic strategies for capacity management: level capacity and chase demand. Table 11.1 illustrates the trade-offs between these two strategies. Utilities practice a pure form of *level capacity* because power stations are expensive and customers expect uninterrupted service. The pure form of *chase demand* is best illustrated by call centers that schedule the number of telephone agents according to expected hourly demand. Most services, however, are able to accommodate a hybrid strategy. For example, facility capacity in hotel beds is fixed but staffing can vary according to seasonal demand. The next two sections address the strategies shown in Figure 11.1 for demand management when a level capacity is being maintained and strategies for capacity management when a chase demand is being pursued.

Strategies for Managing Demand

Customer-Induced Variability[1]

The variability in customer arrival rates is a well-known challenge for service managers attempting to match capacity with demand. However, Frances Frei describes five sources of customer-induced variability in service operations. The common *arrival variability* results in either idle servers or waiting customers because independent decisions of customers seeking service are not evenly spaced in time. The level of customer knowledge, physical ability, and skill creates *capability variability* because some customers can perform tasks easily while others require hand-holding. *Request variability* results from the unique demands of customers that create uneven service times; for example, a bank customer who wants to purchase a CD and another customer who wants to cash a check. When customers are expected to perform a role in a service interaction (e.g., return a shopping cart to its corral), the level of commitment results in *effort variability.* Finally, the expectation of what it means to be treated well varies among customers and results in *subjective preference variability.* For example, one diner might appreciate the warmth of a waiter's first name introduction while another resents the presumption of intimacy. Personal preferences introduce an unpredictability that makes it difficult to serve a broad base of customers uniformly.

Strategies for managing customer-induced variability fall into two categories: accommodation and reduction. The accommodation strategy favors customer experience over operational efficiency. The reduction strategy favors operational simplicity over service

TABLE 11.1
Level Capacity and Chase Demand Trade-offs

Strategic Dimension	Level Capacity	Chase Demand
Customer waiting	Generally low	Moderate
Employee utilization	Moderate	High
Labor-skill level	High	Low
Labor turnover	Low	High
Training required per employee	High	Low
Working conditions	Pleasant	Hectic
Supervision required	Low	High
Forecasting	Long-run	Short-run

FIGURE 11.1
Strategies for Matching Capacity of and Demand for Services

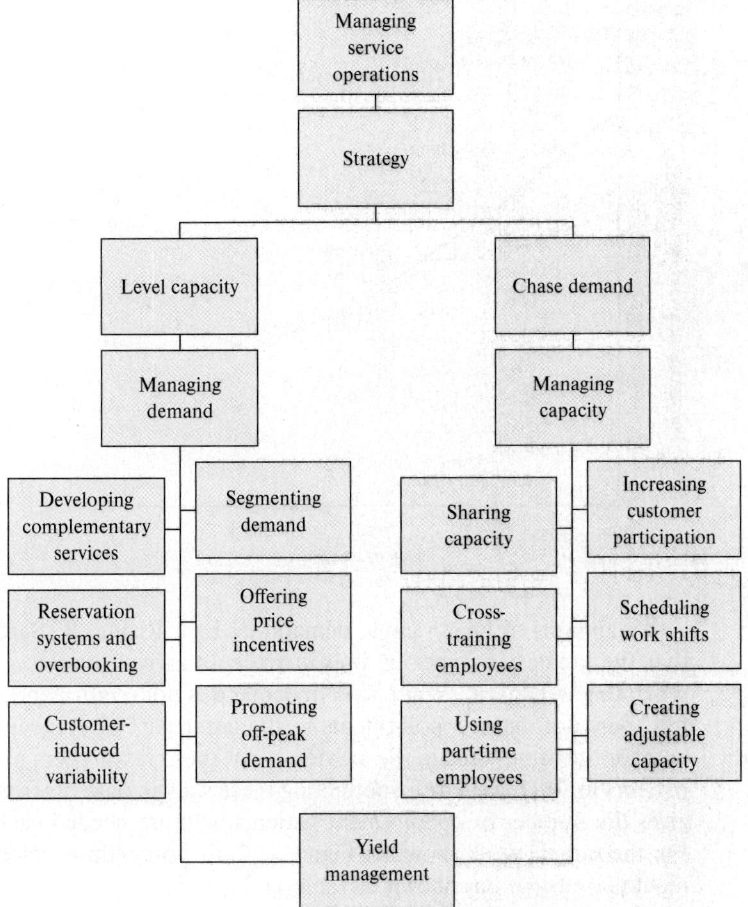

experience. Creative hybrid strategies that give customers a choice could accomplish operational simplicity without compromising service experience (e.g., airlines can offer self-service check-in and an option of curbside check-in). Example strategies to manage customer-induced variability are outlined in Table 11.2.

Segmenting Demand

Demand for a service seldom derives from a homogeneous source. For example, airlines differentiate between weekday business travelers and weekend pleasure travelers. Demand often is grouped into random arrivals and planned arrivals. For example, a drive-in bank can expect visits from its commercial account holders on a regular, daily basis and at approximately the same time; it also can expect visits from its personal account holders on a random basis.

TABLE 11.2
Strategies for Managing Customer-Induced Variability

Type of Variability	Accommodation	Reduction
Arrival	Provide generous staffing	Require reservations
Capability	Adapt to customer skill levels	Target customers based on capability
Request	Cross-train employees	Limit service breadth
Effort	Do work for customers	Reward increased effort
Subjective preference	Diagnose expectations and adapt	Persuade customers to adjust expectations

FIGURE 11.2
Effect of Smoothing Physician Visits

Source: E. J. Rising, R. Baron, and B. Averill, "A Systems Analysis of a University Health-Service Outpatient Clinic." Reprinted with permission from *Operations Research* 21, no. 5, September–October 1973, p. 1035, Operations Research Society of America. No further reproduction permitted without the consent of the copyright owner.

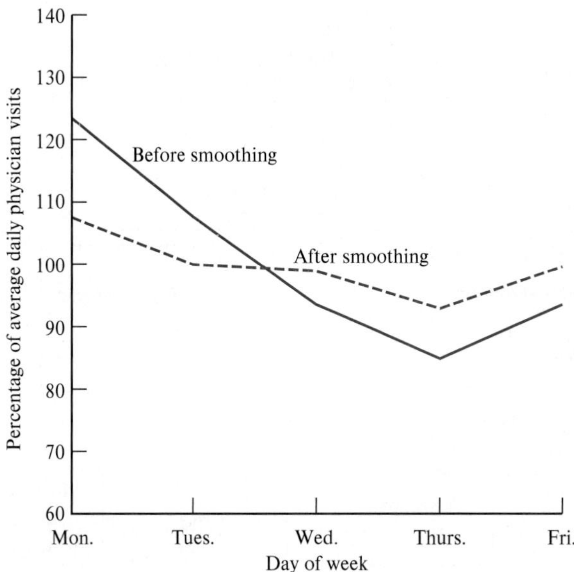

An analysis of health clinic demand by E. J. Rising, R. Baron, and B. Averill showed that the greatest number of walk-in patients arrived on Monday and fewer during the remaining weekdays.[2] While walk-in demand is not controllable, appointments are. Therefore, why not make appointments in the latter part of the week to level demand? Using data for the same week in the previous year, these researchers noted the number of walk-in patients for each weekday. Subtracting these walk-in patients from daily physician capacity gives the number of appointment patients who are needed each day to smooth demand. For the sample week shown in Figure 11.2, this procedure yielded the number of appointment periods per day shown in Table 11.3.

The daily smoothing of demand was refined further by scheduling appointments at appropriate times during the day. After a two-month shakedown period, smoothing demand yielded the following benefits:

1. The number of patients seen increased by 13.4 percent.
2. This increase in patient demand was met, even though 5.1 percent fewer physician hours were scheduled.
3. The overall time physicians spent with patients increased 5.0 percent because of the increased number of appointments.
4. The average waiting time for patients remained the same.
5. A team of sociologists concluded that physician morale increased.

Offering Price Incentives

There are many examples of differential pricing. Consider the following:

1. Matinee or reduced prices before 6 PM at movie theaters.
2. Off-season hotel rates at resort locations.
3. Peak-load pricing by utility companies.

TABLE 11.3
Smoothing Demand by Appointment Scheduling

Day	Appointments
Monday	84
Tuesday	89
Wednesday	124
Thursday	129
Friday	114

TABLE 11.4
Suggested Discriminatory Fee Schedule

Experience Type	Days and Weeks of Camping Season	Number of Days	Daily Fee
1	Saturdays and Sundays of weeks 10 to 15, plus Dominion Day and civic holidays	14	$6.00
2	Saturdays and Sundays of weeks 3 to 9 and 15 to 19, plus Victoria Day	23	2.50
3	Fridays of weeks 3 to 15, plus all other days of weeks 9 to 15 that are not in experience type 1 or 2	43	0.50
4	Rest of camping season	78	Free

Differential pricing has been suggested for campsites to encourage better use of this scarce resource. For example, J. C. Nautiyal and R. L. Chowdhary developed a discriminatory pricing system to ensure that Ontario Provincial Parks camping fees accurately reflect the marginal benefit of the last campsite on any given day.[3]

They identified four different camping experiences on the basis of days and weeks of the camping season. Table 11.4 contains a schedule of daily fees by experience type.

These experience groupings were made on the basis of total daily occupancy in the park under the assumption that occupancy is directly affected by available leisure time and climate. Campers in each experience group were interviewed to determine their travel costs. The marginal visitor was assumed to be the camper who incurred the highest cost in coming to the recreation site. This information was used to develop a demand curve for each experience type and, given the available number of campsites, the campsite fee was determined by means of these demand curves. Table 11.5 compares revenues generated under the existing system with those estimated when using discriminatory fees. Note that under the proposal, more campers are attracted, but with a corresponding reduction in total revenue. During the 78 days of free camping, however, a savings in labor cost is possible, because no ranger is needed to collect fees at the campsite. Even so, for the arrangement to work effectively in altering demand, it must be well advertised and include an advance booking system for campsites.

Note the projected increase in demand for experience type 3 because of the substantially reduced fee. The result of off-peak pricing is to tap a latent demand for campsites instead of redistributing peak demand to off-peak times. Thus, discriminatory pricing fills in the valleys (i.e., periods of low demand) instead of leveling off the peaks. The result is better overall utilization of a scarce resource and, for a private sector firm, the potential for increased profit (assuming that fees cover variable costs). Private firms, however, also would want to avoid directing high-paying customers to low-rate schedules. For example, airlines discourage the business traveler from using discount fares through restrictions such as requiring passengers to remain at their destination over a weekend.

Promoting Off-Peak Demand

Creative use of off-peak capacity results from seeking different sources of demand. One example is use of a resort hotel during the off-season as a retreat location for business

TABLE 11.5
Comparison of Existing Revenue and Projected Revenue from Discriminatory Pricing

Experience Type	Existing Fee of $2.50		Discriminatory Fee	
	Campsites Occupied	Revenue	Campsites Occupied (est.)	Revenue
1	5,891	$14,727	5,000	$30,000
2	8,978	22,445	8,500	21,250
3	6,129	15,322	15,500	7,750
4	4,979	12,447	—	—
Total	25,977	$64,941	29,000	$59,000

or professional groups. Another is a mountain ski resort that becomes a staging area for backpacking during the summer.

The strategy of promoting off-peak demand can be used to discourage overtaxing the facility at other times. A department store's appeal to "shop early and avoid the Christmas rush" as well as a supermarket's offer of double coupons on Wednesdays are examples.

Developing Complementary Services

Restaurants have discovered the benefits of complementary services by adding a bar. Diverting waiting customers into the lounge during busy periods can be profitable for the restaurant as well as soothing to anxious consumers. Movie theaters traditionally have sold popcorn and soft drinks, but now they also include video games in their lobbies. These examples illustrate complementary services being offered to occupy waiting consumers.

The concept of holistic medicine, which combines traditional medical attention with nutritional and psychiatric care, is a further example. Developing complementary services is a natural way to expand one's market, and it is particularly attractive if the new demands for service are contracyclical and result in a more uniform aggregate demand (i.e., when the new service demand is high, the original service demand is low). This explains why nearly all heating contractors also perform air-conditioning services.

Reservation Systems and Overbooking

Taking reservations presells the potential service. As reservations are made, additional demand is deflected to other time slots at the same facility or to other facilities within the same organization. Hotel chains with national reservation systems regularly book customers in nearby hotels owned by their chain when the customer's first choice is not available.

Reservations also benefit consumers by reducing waiting and guaranteeing service availability. Problems do arise, however, when customers fail to honor their reservations. (These customers are referred to as *no-shows.*) Usually, customers are not held financially liable for missing their reservations. This can lead to undesirable behavior, such as when passengers make several flight reservations to cover contingencies. This was a common practice of business passengers who did not know exactly when they would be able to depart; with multiple reservations, they would be assured of a flight out as soon as they were able to leave. All unused reservations result in empty seats, however, unless the airline is notified of the cancellations in advance. To control no-shows among discount flyers, airlines now issue nonrefundable tickets and hotels require cancellation before 6 PM of the day of arrival or a one night stay is charged to their credit cards.

Faced with flying empty seats because of the no-shows, airlines adopted a strategy of *overbooking*. By accepting reservations for more than the available seats, airlines hedge against significant numbers of no-shows; however, the airlines risk turning away passengers with reservations if they overbook too many seats. Because of overbooking abuses, the U.S. Federal Aviation Administration instituted regulations requiring airlines to reimburse overbooked passengers and to find them space on the next available flight. Similarly, many hotels place their overbooked guests in a nearby hotel of equal quality at no expense to the guests. A good overbooking strategy should minimize the expected opportunity cost of idle service capacity as well as the expected cost of turning away reservations. Thus, adopting an overbooking strategy requires training front-office personnel (e.g., front-desk clerks at a hotel) to handle graciously guests whose reservations cannot be honored. At a minimum, a courtesy van should be available to transport the customer to a competitor's hotel after making arrangements for an equivalent room. Consider the overbooking analysis for Surfside Hotel in Example 11.1.

Example 11.1 Surfside Hotel

During the past tourist season, Surfside Hotel did not achieve very high occupancy despite a reservation system that was designed to keep the hotel fully booked. Apparently, prospective guests were making reservations that, for one reason or another, they failed to honor. A review of front-desk records during the current peak period, when the hotel was fully booked, revealed the record of no-shows given in Table 11.6.

TABLE 11.6
Surfside Hotel No-Show Experience

No-shows *d*	Probability *P(d)*	Reservations Overbooked *x*	Cumulative Probability *P(d < x)*
0	.07	0	0
1	.19	1	.07
2	.22	2	.26
3	.16	3	.48
4	.12	4	.64
5	.10	5	.76
6	.07	6	.86
7	.04	7	.93
8	.02	8	.97
9	.01	9	.99

A room that remains vacant because of a no-show results in an opportunity loss of the $40 room contribution. The expected number of no-shows is calculated from Table 11.6 as

$$0(.07) + 1(.19) + 2(.22) + \cdots + 8(.02) + 9(.01) = 3.04$$

This yields an expected opportunity loss of 3.04 × $40, or $121.60, per night. To avoid some of this loss, management is considering an overbooking policy; however, if a guest holding a reservation is turned away owing to overbooking, then other costs are incurred. Surfside has made arrangements with a nearby hotel to pay for the rooms of guests whom it cannot accommodate. Further, a penalty is associated with the loss of customer goodwill and the impact this has on future business. Management estimates this total loss to be approximately $100 per guest "walked" (a term used by the hotel industry). A good overbooking strategy should strike a balance between the opportunity cost of a vacant room and the cost of not honoring a reservation; the best overbooking strategy should minimize the expected cost in the long run.

Table 11.7 displays the loss that is associated with each possible overbooking alternative. Note that no costs are incurred along the diagonal of the table, because in each case, the number of reservations that were overbooked exactly matched the no-shows for that day (e.g., if 4 reservations were overbooked and 4 guests failed to arrive, then every guest who did arrive would be accommodated and, further, the hotel is fully occupied, which is a win–win situation). The values above the diagonal are determined by moving across each row and increasing the cost by a multiple of $100 for each reservation that could not be honored,

TABLE 11.7 **Overbooking Loss Table**

		Reservations Overbooked									
No-shows	Probability	0	1	2	3	4	5	6	7	8	9
0	.07	0	100	200	300	400	500	600	700	800	900
1	.19	40	0	100	200	300	400	500	600	700	800
2	.22	80	40	0	100	200	300	400	500	600	700
3	.16	120	80	40	0	100	200	300	400	500	600
4	.12	160	120	80	40	0	100	200	300	400	500
5	.10	200	160	120	80	40	0	100	200	300	400
6	.07	240	200	160	120	80	40	0	100	200	300
7	.04	280	240	200	160	120	80	40	0	100	200
8	.02	320	280	240	200	160	120	80	40	0	100
9	.01	360	320	280	240	200	160	120	80	40	0
Expected loss ($)	—	121.60	91.40	87.80	115.00	164.60	231.00	311.40	401.60	497.40	560.00

because fewer no-shows occurred than anticipated. For example, consider the first row, which is associated with zero no-shows occurring, and note that a \$100 loss is associated with overbooking by one reservation. The values below the diagonal are shown as increasing by multiples of \$40 as we move down each column, because more no-shows occurred than expected, which resulted in vacant rooms for the night. For example, consider the first column that is associated with not implementing an overbooking strategy, and note the increasing cost implications of trusting guests to honor their reservations.

For each overbooking reservation strategy, the expected loss is calculated by multiplying the loss for each no-show possibility by its probability of occurrence and then adding the products. For example, the expected loss of overbooking by two reservations is calculated by multiplying the probabilities in column 2 (i.e., Probability) by the losses in column 5 (i.e., 2 Reservations Overbooked) as follows:

$$.07(\$200) + .19(\$100) + .22(\$0) + .16(\$40) + .12(\$80) + .10(\$120)$$
$$+ .07(\$160) + .04(\$200) + .02(\$240) + .01(\$280) = \$87.80$$

Table 11.7 indicates that a policy of overbooking by two rooms will minimize the expected loss in the long run. If this policy is adopted, we can realize an average gain of \$33.80 per night from overbooking. That is the difference in the expected loss of not overbooking of \$121.60 and the expected loss from overbooking by two rooms of \$87.80. This substantial amount explains why overbooking is a popular strategy for capacity-constrained service firms such as airlines and hotels.

In Chapter 15, Managing Service Inventory, the *critical fractile* criterion is derived for perishable goods, which we apply to our inventory of rooms:

$$P(d < x) \leq \frac{C_u}{C_u + C_o} \tag{1}$$

where

x = the number of rooms overbooked

d = the number of no-shows based on past experience

C_u = the \$40 room contribution that is lost when a reservation is not honored (i.e., the number of no-shows is *under*estimated)

C_o = the \$100 opportunity loss associated with not having a room available for an overbooked guest (i.e., the number of no-shows is *over*estimated)

This critical probability, which is based on marginal analysis, also can be used to identify the best overbooking strategy. Thus, the number of rooms overbooked should just cover the cumulative probability of no-shows and no more, as calculated below:

$$P(d < x) \leq \frac{\$40}{\$40 + \$100} \leq 0.286$$

From Table 11.6, a strategy of overbooking by two rooms satisfies the critical fractile criterion, because the cumulative probability $P(d < x) = 0.26$ and, thus, confirms the earlier decision based on minimizing the expected overbooking loss.

Strategies for Managing Capacity

Defining Service Capacity

Service capacity is defined in terms of an achievable level of output per unit of time (e.g., transactions per day for a *busy* bank teller). Notice that for service providers our measure of capacity is based on a busy employee and *not* on observed output that must always be less than capacity as discussed in Chapter 12, Managing Waiting Lines. However, service capacity also can be defined in terms of the supporting facility, such as number of hotel beds or available seat miles at the system level for airlines. For airlines, we see that capacity can be limited by several factors such as available labor by skill classification

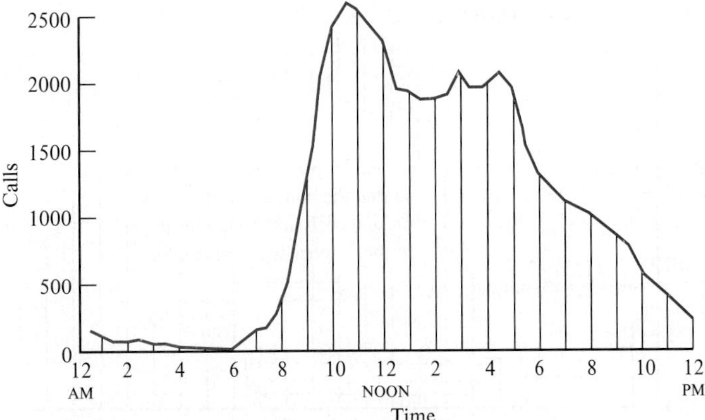

FIGURE 11.3
Daily Demand for Telephone Operators

Source: E. S. Buffa, M. J. Cosgrove, and B. J. Luce, "An Integrated Work Shift Scheduling System," *Decision Sciences* 7, no. 4, October 1976, p. 622. Reprinted with permission from Decision Sciences Institute, Georgia State University.

(pilots, cabin crew, ground crew, and maintenance personnel), equipment (number and type of aircraft), and availability of gates. This airline example also illustrates a common service operations challenge of deploying capacity to different locations appropriately.

For many services, demand cannot be smoothed very effectively. Consider, for example, demand at a call center as shown in Figure 11.3. These data are the half-hourly call rates during a typical 24-hour day. We see that the peak volume (2,500 calls) occurs at 10:30 AM and the minimum volume (20 calls) occurs at 5:30 AM. The peak-to-valley variation is 125 to 1. No inducements are likely to change this demand pattern substantially; therefore, control must come from adjusting service capacity to match demand. Several strategies can be used to achieve this goal.

Daily Workshift Scheduling

By scheduling workshifts carefully during the day, the profile of service capacity can be made to approximate demand. Workshift scheduling is an important staffing problem for many service organizations that face cyclical demand, such as telephone companies, hospitals, banks, and police departments.

The general approach begins with a forecast of demand by hour, which is converted to hourly service staffing requirements. The time interval could be less than an hour; for example, 15-minute intervals are used by fast-food restaurants to schedule work during meal periods. Next, a schedule of tours, or shifts, is developed to match the staffing requirements profile as closely as possible. Finally, specific service personnel are assigned to tours, or shifts. The telephone-operator staffing problem illustrated in Example 11.2 will be used to demonstrate the analysis required in the four step schedule building process.

Example 11.2 Marin County 911 Response

Step 1. Forecast Demand

Daily demand is forecast in half-hour intervals, as shown in Figure 11.3, and must account for both weekday and weekend variations as well as seasonal adjustments. The Saturday and Sunday call load was found to be approximately 55 percent of the typical weekday load. Summer months were found to be generally lower in demand. Special high-demand days, such as Mother's Day and Christmas, were taken into account.

Step 2. Convert to Operator Requirements

A profile of half-hour operator requirements is developed on the basis of the forecast daily demand and call distribution. The agreed service level requires that 89 percent of the time, an incoming call must be answered within 10 seconds. The half-hour operator requirements are determined using a conventional queuing model (found in Chapter 13, Capacity Planning and Queuing Models) to ensure that the service level is achieved for each half hour.[4] The result is a topline profile of operators required by the half hour, as shown in Figure 11.4.

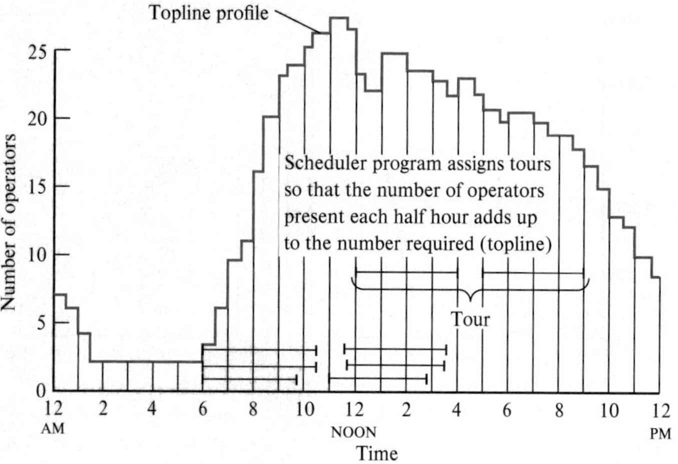

FIGURE 11.4
Profile of Operator Requirements and Tour Assignments

Source: E. S. Buffa, M. J. Cosgrove, and B. J. Luce, "An Integrated Work Shift Scheduling System," *Decision Sciences* 7, no. 4, October 1976, p. 626. Reprinted with permission from Decision Sciences Institute, Georgia State University.

Step 3. Schedule Shifts

Tours, representing various start and end times of work, need to be assigned so that they aggregate to the topline profile, shown in Figure 11.4. Each tour consists of two working sessions separated by a rest pause or meal period (e.g., 9 AM–1 PM, lunch break, 2 PM–6 PM). The set of possible tours is defined by state and federal laws, union agreements, and company policy. A heuristic computer program prepared especially for this problem chooses tours from the permissible set such that the absolute difference between operator requirements and operators assigned is minimized when summed over all "*n*" half-hour periods. If R_i is the number of operators required in period *i* and W_i is the number of operators assigned in period *i*, then the objective can be stated as follows:

$$\text{Minimize} \quad \sum_{i=1}^{n} |R_i - W_i| \tag{2}$$

The schedule-building process is shown schematically in Figure 11.5. At each iteration, one tour at a time is selected from all possible tours. The tour selected at each step is the one that best meets the criterion stated in equation (2). Because this procedure favors shorter tours, the different shift lengths are weighted in the calculation to avoid this bias. The result is a list of tours required to meet the forecast demand, as well as a schedule of lunch and rest periods during those tours.

Step 4. Assign Operators to Shifts

Given the set of tours required, the assignment of operators to these tours is complicated because of the 24-hour, 7-days-per-week operation. Questions of equity arise regarding the timing of days off and the assignment of overtime work, which involves extra pay. Furthermore,

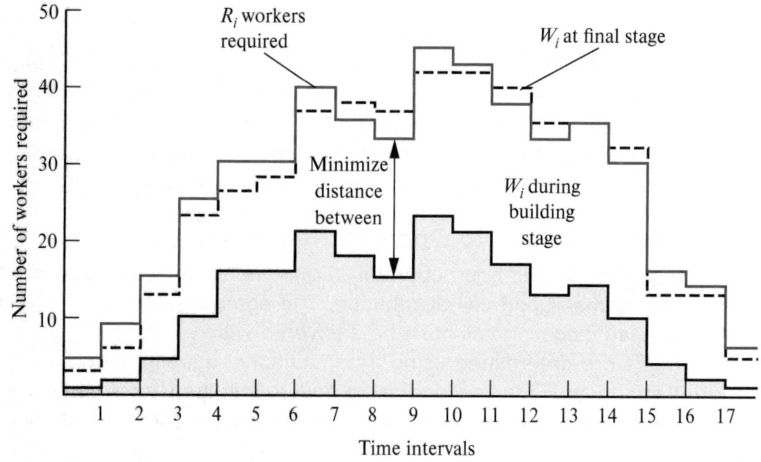

FIGURE 11.5
The Schedule-Building Process

Source: E. S. Buffa, M. J. Cosgrove, and B. J. Luce, "An Integrated Work Shift Scheduling System," *Decision Sciences* 7, no. 4, October 1976, p. 622. Reprinted with permission from Decision Sciences Institute, Georgia State University.

when work schedules repeatedly conflict with other priorities such as child care and medical appointments, the result can be poor morale, absenteeism, and attrition. A popular approach to this challenge is the use of a web-based shift bidding system. Such a system empowers operators to bid directly on the specific tour they desire through online auctions using bonus points, seniority, and rank. Bonus points can be awarded based upon criteria such as operator's performance, completion of previous undesirable tours, or failure to obtain requested tours in the past year. The use of clearly defined criteria results in perceptions of fairness and satisfaction from engaging in the scheduling process.

Weekly Workshift Scheduling with Days-Off Constraint

As noted, developing tours to match the profile of daily demand is only part of the problem. Many public services such as police, fire protection, and emergency hospital care must be available 24 hours a day, every day of the week. For these organizations, a typical employee works 5 days a week with 2 consecutive days off each week, but not necessarily Saturday and Sunday. Management is interested in developing work schedules and meeting the varying employee requirements for weekdays and weekends with the smallest number of staff members possible.

This problem can be formulated as an integer linear programming (ILP) model. To begin, the desired staffing levels are determined for each day in the week. The problem then becomes one of determining the minimum number of employees required for assignment to each of seven possible tours. Each tour consists of 5 days on and 2 consecutive days off; each will begin on a different day of the week and last for 5 consecutive working days. Consider the following general formulation of this problem as an ILP model.

Variable definitions:

x_i = number of employees assigned to tour *i,* where day *i* begins 2 consecutive days off (e.g., employees assigned to tour 1 have Sunday and Monday off)

b_j = desired staffing level for day *j*

Objective function:

$$\text{Minimize} \quad x_1 + x_2 + x_3 + x_4 + x_5 + x_6 + x_7$$

Constraints:

$$\begin{aligned}
&\text{Sunday} && x_2 + x_3 + x_4 + x_5 + x_6 \geq b_1 \\
&\text{Monday} && x_3 + x_4 + x_5 + x_6 + x_7 \geq b_2 \\
&\text{Tuesday} && x_1 + x_4 + x_5 + x_6 + x_7 \geq b_3 \\
&\text{Wednesday} && x_1 + x_2 + x_5 + x_6 + x_7 \geq b_4 \\
&\text{Thursday} && x_1 + x_2 + x_3 + x_6 + x_7 \geq b_5 \\
&\text{Friday} && x_1 + x_2 + x_3 + x_4 + x_7 \geq b_6 \\
&\text{Saturday} && x_1 + x_2 + x_3 + x_4 + x_5 \geq b_7
\end{aligned}$$

$$x_i \geq 0 \text{ and integer}$$

Example 11.3 Hospital Emergency Room

The emergency room is operated on a 24-hour, 7-days-per-week schedule. The day is divided into three eight-hour shifts. The total number of nurses required during the day shift is

Day	Su	M	Tu	W	Th	F	Sa
Nurses	3	6	5	6	5	5	5

TABLE 11.8
Weekly Nurse Staffing Schedule, x = Workday

Nurse	Su	M	Tu	W	Th	F	Sa
A	. . .	. . .	x	x	x	x	x
B	x	. . .	. . .	x	x	x	x
C	x	x	. . .	. . .	x	x	x
D	x	x	. . .	. . .	x	x	x
E	x	x	x	x	. . .	. . .	x
F	x	x	x	x	. . .	. . .	x
G	x	x	x	x	. . .	. . .	x
H	. . .	x	x	x	x	x	. . .
Total	6	6	5	6	5	5	7
Required	3	6	5	6	5	5	5
Excess	3	0	0	0	0	0	2

The emergency room director is interested in developing a workforce schedule that will minimize the number of nurses required to staff the facility. Nurses work 5 days a week and are entitled to 2 consecutive days off each week.

The ILP model above is formulated with the appropriate right-hand-side constraint values (i.e., $b_1 = 3$, $b_2 = 6, \ldots, b_6 = 5$, $b_7 = 5$), and the solution yields the following results: $x_1 = 1$, $x_2 = 1$, $x_3 = 2$, $x_4 = 0$, $x_5 = 3$, $x_6 = 0$, $x_7 = 1$. This means we have one tour with Sunday and Monday off, one tour with Monday and Tuesday off, two tours with Tuesday and Wednesday off, three tours with Thursday and Friday off, and one tour with Saturday and Sunday off. The corresponding staffing schedule is shown in Table 11.8 with excess staff occurring only on Sunday and Saturday.

These scheduling problems typically result in multiple optimal solutions. For example, in this case, the solution $x_1 = 1$, $x_2 = 1$, $x_3 = 1$, $x_4 = 1$, $x_5 = 1$, $x_6 = 1$, $x_7 = 2$ is feasible and also requires eight nurses. Why might this second solution be preferred to the schedule shown in Table 11.8?

Increasing Customer Participation

The strategy of increasing customer participation is illustrated best by the fast-food restaurants that have eliminated personnel who serve food and clear tables. The customer (now a coproducer) not only places the order directly from a limited menu but also clears the table after the meal. Naturally, the customer expects faster service and less-expensive meals to compensate for this help; however, the service provider benefits in many subtle ways. Of course, there are fewer personnel to supervise and to pay, but more important, the customer as a coproducer provides labor just at the moment it is required. Thus, capacity to serve varies more directly with demand rather than being fixed.

For example, consider the need for passenger cooperation to achieve a timely aircraft boarding. Turning aircraft around at a gate between flights has become a science–just like a pit stop at NASCAR. Boarding delays result in failure to meet departure times that then can cascade throughout the airline network. Studying the orchestrated teamwork performed by NASCAR pit crews, airlines experimented with different ways to sequence boarding passengers. The most common boarding method is rear-to-front, in order to keep congestion away from entering passengers. United tried "outside-in" boarding, which boards window seats prior to aisle seats but later abandoned the idea. Delta Airlines uses "zones" where a smart system combines rows into different zones. More recently airlines have started boarding passengers without carry-on bags first, a reward for checking bags that avoids the delay of schlepping bags into overhead bins. On the other hand, Southwest Airlines never has assigned seats and claims that its boarding process is superior to the other assigned-seat methods.

Creating Adjustable Capacity

A portion of capacity can be made variable through design. Airlines routinely move the partition between first class and coach to meet the changing mix of passengers. An innovative restaurant, Benihana of Tokyo, arranged its floor plan to accommodate eating areas serving two tables of eight diners each. Chefs are assigned to each area, and they prepare the meal at the table in a theatrical manner, with flashing knives and animated movements. Thus, the restaurant can adjust its capacity effectively by having only the number of chefs on duty that is needed.

Capacity at peak periods can be expanded by the effective use of slack times. Performing supportive tasks during slower periods of demand allows employees to concentrate on essential tasks during rush periods. This strategy requires some cross-training of employees to allow performance of noncustomer-contact tasks during slow-demand periods. For example, servers at a restaurant can wrap silverware in napkins or clean the premises when demand is low; thus, they are free of these tasks during the rush period.

Sharing Capacity

A service delivery system often requires a large investment in equipment and facilities. During periods of underutilization, it might be possible to find other uses for this capacity. Airlines have cooperated in this manner for years. At small airports, airlines share the same gates, ramps, baggage-handling equipment, and ground personnel. It also is common for some airlines to lease their aircraft to others during the off-season; the lease agreement includes painting on the appropriate insignia and refurbishing the interior.

Cross-Training Employees

Some service systems are made up of several operations. When one operation is busy, another operation sometimes might be idle. Cross-training employees to perform tasks in several operations creates flexible capacity to meet localized peaks in demand.

The gains from cross-training employees can be seen at supermarkets. When queues develop at the cash registers, the manager calls on stockers to operate registers until the surge is over. Likewise, during slow periods, some of the cashiers are busy stocking shelves. This approach also can help to build an esprit de corps and give employees relief from monotony. In fast-food restaurants, cross-trained employees create capacity flexibility, because tasks can be reassigned to fewer employees during slow periods (temporarily enlarging the job) and become more specialized during busy periods (division of labor).

Using Part-Time Employees

When peaks of activity are persistent and predictable, such as at mealtimes in restaurants or paydays in banks, part-time help can supplement regular employees. If the required skills and training are minimal, then a ready part-time labor pool is available from high school and college students as well as others who are interested in supplementing their primary source of income.

Another source of part-time help is off-duty personnel who are placed on standby. Airlines and hospitals often pay their personnel some nominal fee to restrict their activities and be ready for work if they are needed. As shown in Example 11.4, scheduling part-time employees is a three-step process.

Example 11.4 Scheduling Part-Time Tellers at Meridian Drive-In Bank[5]

Drive-in banks experience predictable variations in activity on different days of the week. Figure 11.6 shows the teller requirements for a typical week based on customer demand variations. This bank usually employed enough tellers to meet peak demands on Friday; however, the policy created considerable idle teller time on the low-demand days, particularly Tuesday and Thursday. To reduce teller costs, management decided to employ part-time tellers and to reduce the full-time staff to a level that just meets the demand for Tuesday. Further, to provide

FIGURE 11.6
Teller Requirements

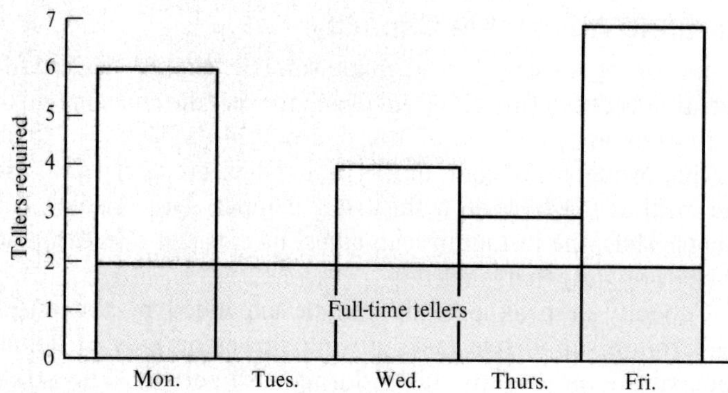

equity in hours worked, it was decided that a part-time teller should work at least 2, but no more than 3, days in a week.

A primary objective of scheduling part-time workers is to meet the requirements with the minimum number of teller-days. A secondary objective is to have a minimum number of part-time tellers. Minimizing the number of part-time tellers is illustrated here, but the same procedure can be used for scheduling part-time employees in many other services.

Step 1: Determine the Minimum Number of Part-Time Tellers Needed

Figure 11.6 shows that with two full-time tellers, 12 teller-days remain to be covered during the week. Using 3-day schedules, we see that five tellers on Friday determines the feasible minimum in this case.

Step 2: Develop a Decreasing-Demand Histogram

From Figure 11.6, note the daily part-time teller requirements. Re-sequence the days in order of decreasing demand, as shown in Figure 11.7.

Step 3: Assign Tellers to the Histogram

Starting with the first part-time teller, assign that individual in Figure 11.7 to the first block on Friday, the second teller to block two, and so forth until all five part-time tellers are assigned. Repeat the sequence with Monday, and carry over the remaining tellers into Wednesday. Table 11.9 summarizes the resulting part-time work schedule, which consists of two 3-day work assignments for Tellers 1 and 2 and three 2-day work assignments for Tellers 3, 4, and 5.

FIGURE 11.7
Histogram of Decreasing Part-Time Teller Demand

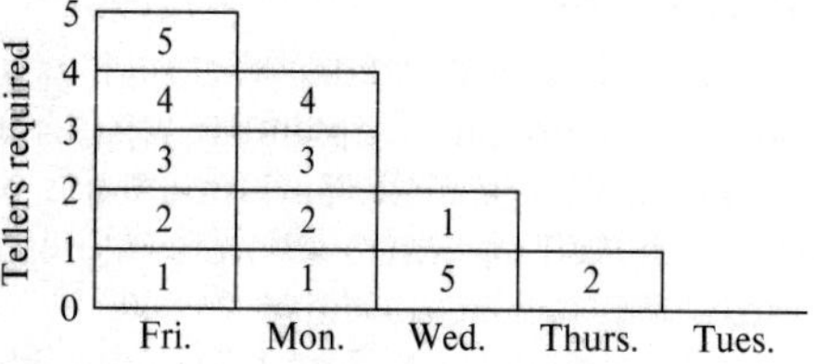

TABLE 11.9
Part-Time Work Schedule

Source: V.A. Mabert and A.R. Raedels, "The Detail Scheduling of a Part-Time Work Force: A Case Study of Teller Staffing," *Decision Sciences* 8, no. 1 (January 1977), pp. 109–20.

Teller	Mon.	Tues.	Wed.	Thurs.	Fri.
1	X	. . .	X	. . .	X
2	X	. . .	. . .	X	X
3, 4	X	. . .	. . .	. . .	X
5	. . .	. . .	X	. . .	X

Yield Management[6]

Since deregulation permitted airlines to set their own prices, a new approach to revenue maximization–called *yield management*–has emerged. Yield management is a comprehensive system that incorporates many of the strategies discussed earlier in this chapter (e.g., using reservation systems, overbooking, and segmenting demand).

Because of the perishable nature of airline seats (i.e., once a flight has departed, the potential revenue from an empty seat is lost forever), offering a discount on fares to fill the aircraft became attractive. Selling all seats at a discount, however, would preclude the possibility of selling some at full price. Yield management attempts to allocate the fixed capacity of seats on a flight to match the potential demand in various market segments (e.g., business, coach, tourist, and senior) in the most profitable manner. Although airlines were the first to develop yield management, other capacity-constrained service industries (e.g., hotels, rental-car firms, and cruise lines) also are adopting this practice.

The economic motivation behind yield management is captured in Figure 11.8, an illustration of pricing a coach seat on a cross-country flight. Figure 11.8a illustrates the traditional fixed price relationship between a downward sloping demand curve and

FIGURE 11.8
Airline Pricing for a Coach Seat on a Cross-Country Flight

a. Traditional Fixed Price

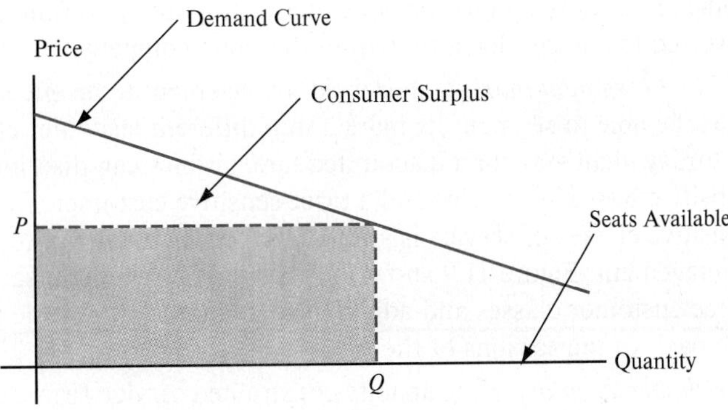

Total Revenue = PQ

b. Multiple Pricing Using Yield Management

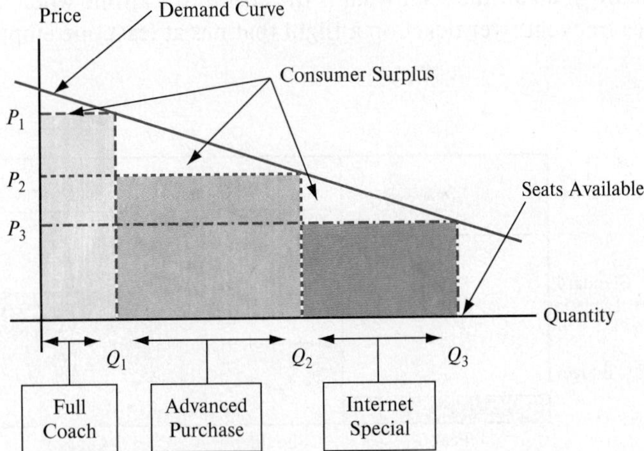

Total Revenue = $P_1Q_1 + (Q_2 - Q_1)P_2 + (Q_3 - Q_2)P_3$

quantity sold. Provided Q is less than or equal to the seats available, the total revenue for the flight is P (price) × Q (quantity of seats sold) = PQ. The typical result is empty seats and a large consumer surplus (many passengers willing to spend considerably more for the flight than the fixed price).

Figure 11.8b shows the same demand curve with different prices for three segmented markets: P_1 for full coach, P_2 for advanced purchase, and P_3 for Internet special. A small number of passengers are willing to pay a premium for "full coach" because the ticket can be purchased at anytime and is fully refundable. Advanced purchase tickets must be purchased 14 days in advance and are not refundable. Internet special is a nonrefundable e-ticket available on the airline website whenever the flight is not expected to be fully booked (i.e., an opportunity to sell excess seats at a discount). For yield management the total revenue is the sum of (price) × (quantity) for passengers in each segment: $P_1Q_1 + (Q_2 - Q_1)P_2 + (Q_3 - Q_2)P_3$. The result explains why passengers find few empty seats in today's market. Furthermore, consumer surplus has been significantly reduced yielding higher total revenue for the airlines.

Yield management is most appropriate for service firms that exhibit the following characteristics:

Relatively fixed capacity. Service firms with a substantial investment in facilities (e.g., hotels and airlines) can be considered as being capacity-constrained. Once all the seats on a flight are sold, further demand can be met only by booking passengers on a later flight. Motel chains with multiple inns in the same city, however, have some capacity flexibility, because guests attempting to find a room at one site can be diverted to another location within the same company.

Ability to segment markets. For yield management to be effective, the service firm must be able to segment its market into different customer classes. By requiring a Saturday-night stay for a discounted fare, airlines can discriminate between a time-sensitive business traveler and a price-sensitive customer. Developing various price-sensitive classes of service is a major marketing challenge for a firm using yield management. Figure 11.9 shows how a resort hotel might segment its market into three customer classes and adjust the allocation of available rooms to each class on the basis of the seasons of the year.

Perishable inventory. For capacity-constrained service firms, each room or seat is referred to as a *unit* of inventory to be sold (actually, to be rented). As noted for the airlines, revenue from an unsold seat is lost forever. Airlines attempt to minimize this spoiled inventory by encouraging standby passengers. Given this time-perishable nature of an airline seat, what is the cost to the airline when a passenger is awarded a free frequent flyer ticket on a flight that has at least one empty seat?

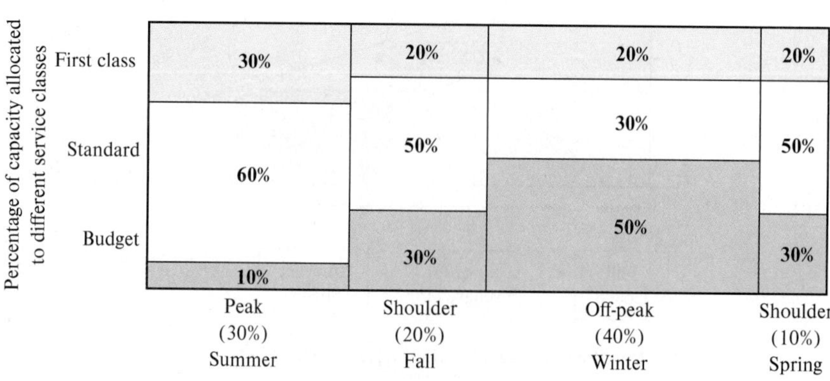

FIGURE 11.9
Seasonal Allocation of Rooms by Service Class for a Resort Hotel

Source: Adapted from Christopher H. Lovelock, "Strategies for Managing Demand in Capacity-Constrained Service Organizations," *Service Industries Journal* 4, no. 3, November 1984, p. 23.

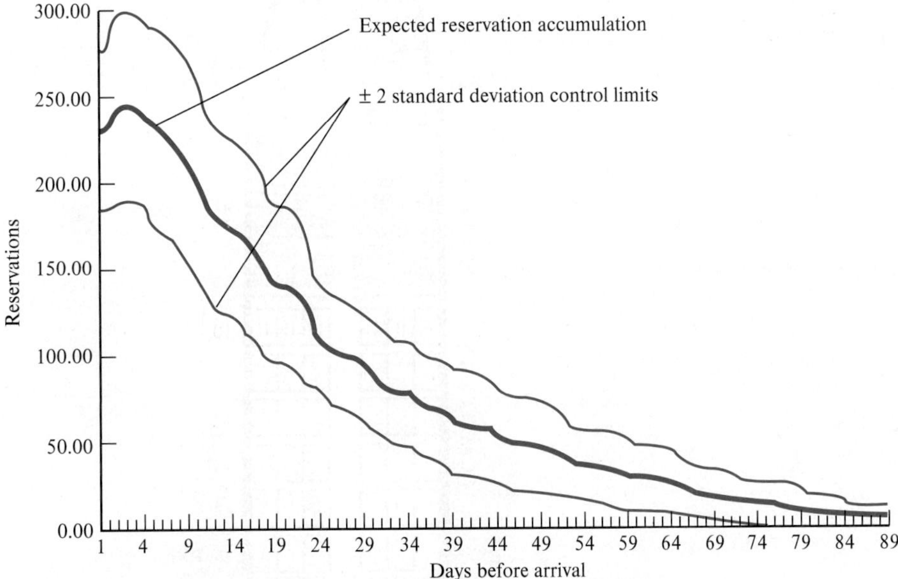

FIGURE 11.10
Demand Control Chart for a Hotel

Source: Adapted from Sheryl E. Kimes, "Yield Management: A Tool for Capacity-Constrained Service Firms," *Journal of Operations Management* 8, no. 4, October 1989, p. 359. Reprinted with permission, The American Production and Inventory Society.

Product sold in advance. Reservation systems are adopted by service firms to sell capacity in advance of use; however, managers are faced with the uncertainty of whether to accept an early reservation at a discount price or to wait and hope to sell the inventory unit to a higher-paying customer. In Figure 11.10, a demand control chart (recall quality-control charts from Chapter 6, Service Quality) is drawn for a hotel on the basis of past bookings for a particular day of the week and season of the year. Because some variation in demand is expected, an acceptable range (in this case, ±2 standard deviations) is drawn around the expected reservation accumulation curve. If demand is higher than expected, budget-rate classes are closed and only reservations at standard rates accepted. If the accumulation of reservations falls below the acceptable range, then reservations for rooms at budget rates are accepted.

Fluctuating demand. Using demand forecasting, yield management allows managers to increase utilization during periods of slow demand and to increase revenue during periods of high demand. By controlling the availability of budget rates, managers can maximize total revenue for the constrained service. Yield management is implemented in real time by opening and/or closing reserved sections–even on an hourly basis if desired.

Low marginal sales costs and high marginal capacity change costs. The cost of selling an additional unit of inventory must be low, such as the negligible cost of a snack for an airline passenger. The marginal cost of capacity additions is large, however, because of the necessary lumpy facility investment (i.e., a hotel addition must be at least an increment of 100 rooms).

Example 11.5 Blackjack Airline

During the recent economic slump, Blackjack Airline discovered that airplanes on its Los Angeles–to–Las Vegas route have been flying with more empty seats than usual. To stimulate demand, it has decided to offer a special, nonrefundable, 14-day advance-purchase "gamblers fare" for only $49 one-way based on a round-trip ticket. The regular full-fare coach ticket costs $69 one-way. The Boeing 737 used by Blackjack, as shown in Figure 11.11, has a capacity of 95 passengers in coach, and management wants to limit the number of seats that are sold at the discount fare in order to sell full-fare tickets to passengers who have not made advance travel plans. Considering recent experience, the demand for full-fare tickets appears to have a normal distribution, with a mean of 60 and a standard deviation of 15.

FIGURE 11.11
The Boeing 737 Cabin

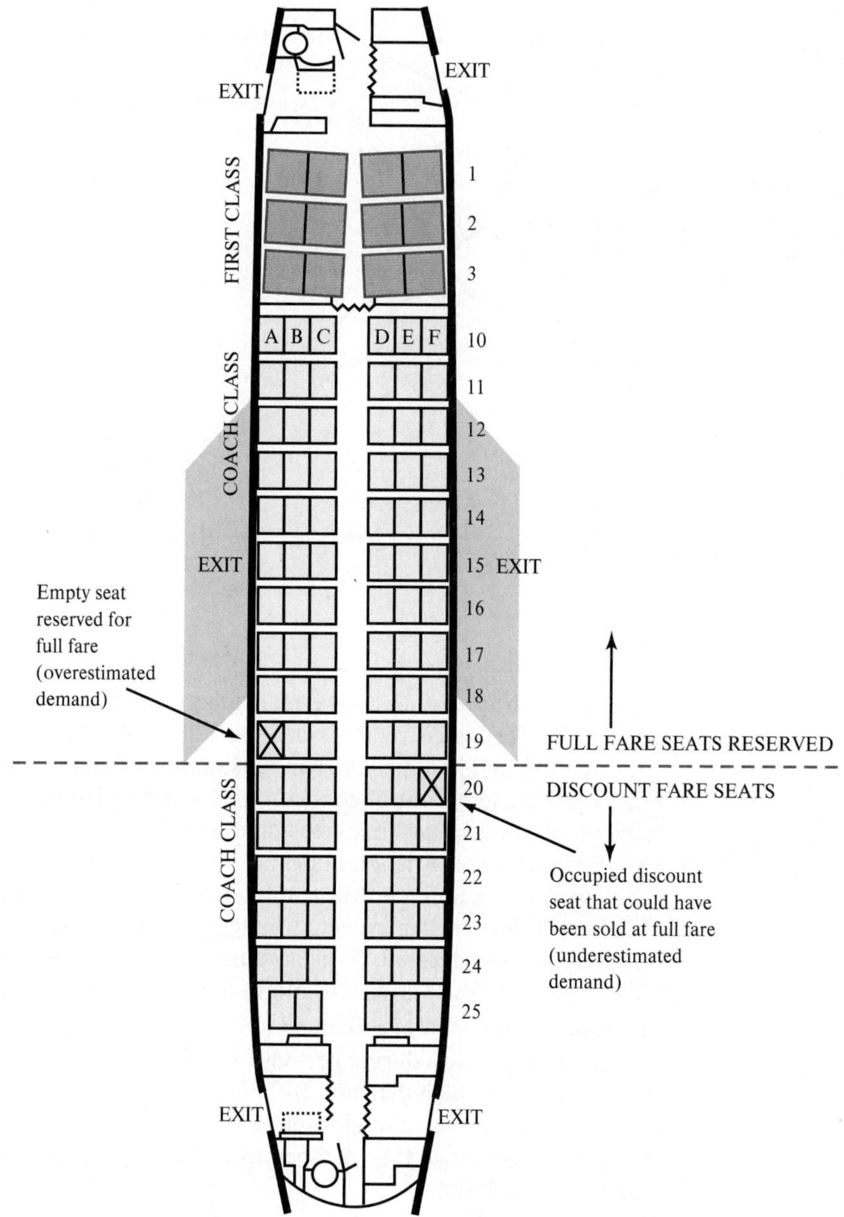

The yield management problem can be analyzed with the critical fractile model used earlier in the chapter [equation (1)] for analyzing the overbooking problem.

$$P(d < x) \leq \frac{C_u}{C_u + C_o}$$

where

x = seats reserved for full-fare passengers

d = demand for full-fare tickets

C_u = lost revenue associated with reserving too few seats at full fare (underestimated demand). The lost opportunity is the difference between the fares (\$69 − \$49 = \$20) because we assume that the nonshopper passenger, willing to pay full fare, purchased a seat at the discount price.

C_o = cost of reserving one too many seats for sale at full fare (overestimated demand). We assume that the empty full-fare seat could have been sold at the discount price of \$49.

FIGURE 11.12
Critical Fractile for Blackjack Airline

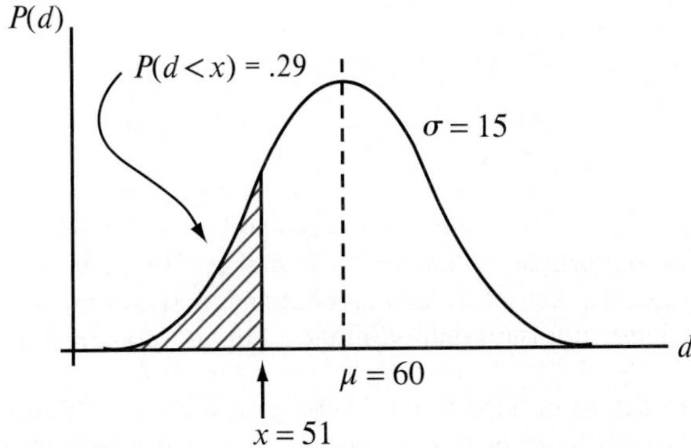

The critical fractile value $P(d < x) = \$20/(\$20 + \$49) = 0.29$ (see Figure 11.12). From Appendix A, Areas of a Standard Normal Distribution, the z value for a cumulative probability of 0.29 in the left tail is −0.55. Thus, the number of full-fare seats to reserve is found as follows:

$$\begin{aligned}\text{Reserved full-fare seats} &= \mu + z\sigma \\ &= 60 + (-0.55)(15) \\ &= 51\end{aligned}$$

Yield Management Applications

The following discussion provides a sampling of how yield management is used by other companies that face high fixed costs/low variable costs, spoilage, and temporary demand imbalances to accomplish the same goals that airline pricing and yield management systems achieve.

Holiday Inn Rate Optimization (HIRO)[7]

The hotel industry is similar to the airline industry, because hotels have extremely high costs invested in real estate and maintenance, temporary capacity, and demand imbalances. Imbalances such as varying peak and low seasons, spoilage, and rooms not rented out for a night all represent lost revenue opportunities. Holiday Inn has recognized these classic management problems and uses both demand and capacity management to maximize revenues.

To achieve Holiday Inn's corporate objectives of ensuring that maximum occupancy and revenue are realized in each hotel and that guests, franchises, and internal staff are experiencing the highest level of customer satisfaction, Holiday Inn installed its Holiday Inn Rate Optimization system (HIRO). The goal of maximizing occupancy and revenue means renting as many rooms as possible for the best price that the market will bear. With more than 500,000 rooms in the equation, a yield management optimization system could increase revenue tremendously.

HIRO, which is similar to American Airlines' SABRE, uses historical and current booking behavior to analyze room requests for each hotel. The yield management optimization equation includes seasonal occupancy patterns, local events, weekly cycles, and current trends to develop a hurdle price (i.e., the lowest point at which rooms should be booked at that particular hotel). The system predicts full occupancy at hotels and "filters out" discounted requests. HIRO even uses overbooking to account for cancellations and no-shows. As with any yield management system in the service industry, HIRO helps the hotel manager balance the ability to charge full price for a room and still maintain satisfaction from Holiday Inn's loyal customer base.

Ryder's RyderFirst[8]

Ryder must manage the same logistical problems that are faced by any transportation company, and the shipping and trucking industry can use yield management to maximize

Service Benchmark

PAY UP FRONT AND TAKE YOUR CHANCES

Looking for some adventure in your life? Try shopping an opaque website such as Priceline.com or Hotwire.com where you can book reservations for a dream holiday at a resort or a flight to an exotic location for a bargain rate. The keyword here is *opaque,* which translates into "make a nonrefundable payment up front and take what you get sight unseen." Of course, you do have an opportunity to set some parameters for your adventure, such as an ultimate destination, a quality rating for accommodations, and sometimes a particular area of a city, before you commit your hard-earned money, but you don't know what you actually get until it's too late.

If a hotel, an airline, or an auto-rental company have unsold rooms, seats, or vehicles, they lose money. Opaque Internet sites represent an opportunity for such businesses to get some return from those available resources (or on their excess capacity) without incurring the wrath of customers who pay the customary rates.

revenue very effectively. Again, we see the classic business problem of high fixed costs/low variable costs with an expansive fleet of trucks, temporary capacity, and demand imbalances resulting from the seasonality of shipping (i.e., holidays and other peak inventory stocking periods), the threat of spoilage, and valuable unused capacity.

With the help of the American Airlines Decision Technology Group (AADT), Ryder implemented a yield management, pricing, and logistics system that helps it react quickly to competition and take advantage of the price elasticities of its different customer segments. The yield management system allows Ryder to move its truck capacity from areas of surplus to areas of demand by modeling the historical utilization patterns in each market.

Restaurant Catering Software[9]

Yield management techniques are being incorporated into software for use in the restaurant catering industry to ensure efficient utilization of expensive kitchens. Yield management software alerts operators to the potential for increased off-premise or catering bookings during anticipated low in-store demand days, thus enhancing overall profitability. Computer modeling also includes the manipulation of prices based on demand fluctuations. For example, a restaurant might reduce its menu item prices to increase customer count and overall revenue. Similarly, in peak demand periods, item prices may be raised to increase the average check revenue. Yield management helps to smooth the fluctuating demand patterns in the catering industry by anticipating when temporary demand and capacity imbalances will occur.

Amtrak[10]

As far back as 1988, Amtrak introduced a pricing and yield management system identical to that of airlines. This yield management system utilizes a tiered-fare structure, overbooking, discount allocation, and traffic management to maximize yields and capacity utilization. Like the airlines, Amtrak uses the yield management market information to decide what routes to enter and how much capacity is necessary to satisfy demand. Amtrak's flexible capacity allows it to make last-minute capacity adjustments much more easily than in the airline industry by attaching and detaching different classes of rail cars.

Summary

The inherent variability of demand creates a challenge for managers trying to make the best use of service capacity. The problem can be approached from two generic strategies: level capacity and chase demand.

With level capacity strategy the focus is on smoothing demand to permit fuller utilization of a fixed service capacity. Various alternatives for managing demand are available, such as segmenting demand, offering price incentives, promoting off-peak use, and developing complementary services and reservation systems.

With a chase demand strategy the focus is on opportunities to adjust capacity to match changes in demand levels. Many alternatives have been proposed to adjust service capacity including workshift scheduling, using part-time employees, cross-training employees, increasing customer coproduction, and sharing capacity with other firms.

A mixed, or hybrid, strategy is best illustrated by the use of yield management that maximizes revenue through price discrimination and capacity allocation in real-time.

Key Terms and Definitions

Chase demand a strategy of adjusting capacity to match demand fluctuations. *p. 302*

Critical fractile the cumulative probability of demand formed by the ratio of the cost of *under*estimating demand divided by the sum of the costs of *under*estimating demand and *over*estimating demand. *p. 308*

Level capacity a strategy of holding capacity fixed allowing for underutilization and some customer waiting. *p. 302*

Overbooking taking reservations in excess of available capacity in anticipation of customer no-shows. *p. 306*

Yield management a comprehensive system to maximize revenue for capacity-constrained services using reservation systems, overbooking, and partitioning demand. *p. 301*

Topics for Discussion

1. What organizational problems can arise from the use of part-time employees?
2. How can computer-based reservation systems increase service capacity utilization?
3. Illustrate how a particular service has implemented strategies for managing both demand and capacity successfully.
4. What possible dangers are associated with developing complementary services?
5. Will the widespread use of yield management eventually erode the concept of fixed prices for any service?
6. Go to http://en.wikipedia.org/wiki/Yield_management and discuss the ethical issues associated with yield management.

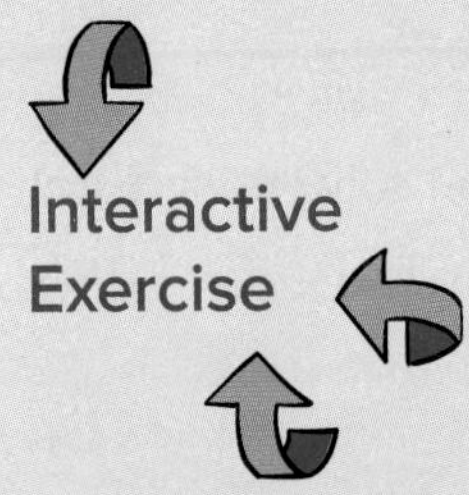

Interactive Exercise

Recall the incident on April 9, 2017, when United Airlines had a passenger dragged from his seat on an overbooked flight. See the news item for further details at: *https://www.nytimes.com/2017/04/10/business/united-flight-passenger-dragged.html.* How could this situation have been handled differently?

Solved Problems

1. Overbooking Problem

Problem Statement

A family-run inn is considering the use of overbooking, because the frequency of no-shows listed below has left many rooms vacant during the past summer season. An empty room represents an opportunity cost of $69, which is the average room rate. Accommodating an overbooked guest is expensive, however, because the nearby resort rooms average $119 and the inn must pay the difference. What would be the expected gain per night from overbooking?

No-shows	0	1	2	3
Frequency	4	3	2	1

Solution

First, create an overbooking loss table using $69 as the cost of an empty room and $119 – $69 = $50 as the cost of "walking" a guest.

No-shows	Probability	Reservations Overbooked 0	1	2	3
0	.4	0	50	100	150
1	.3	69	0	50	100
2	.2	138	69	0	50
3	.1	207	138	69	0
Expected loss		$69.00	$47.60	$61.90	$100.00

Second, calculate the expected loss by multiplying each overbooking column by the corresponding probability of no-shows and then adding each term. For 0 reservations overbooked, this yields

$$(0)(.4) + (69)(.3) + (138)(.2) + 4\,(207)(.1) = 69$$

Looking across the expected-loss row, we find that overbooking by one reservation will minimize the expected loss and result in an expected nightly gain from overbooking of $69.00 – $47.60 = $21.40.

2. Weekly Workshift Scheduling

Problem Statement

The telephone reservation department for a major car-rental firm has the daily shift requirements for operators below:

Day	Su	M	Tu	W	Th	F	Sa
Operators	4	8	8	7	7	6	5

Prepare a weekly workshift schedule with two consecutive days off.

Solution

Formulate the problem as an integer linear programming model, and solve using Excel Solver.

Objective function:

$$\text{Minimize} \quad x_1 + x_2 + x_3 + x_4 + x_5 + x_6 + x_7$$

Constraints:

$$\begin{aligned}
&\text{Sunday} && x_2 + x_3 + x_4 + x_5 + x_6 \geq 4\\
&\text{Monday} && x_3 + x_4 + x_5 + x_6 + x_7 \geq 8\\
&\text{Tuesday} && x_1 + x_4 + x_5 + x_6 + x_7 \geq 8\\
&\text{Wednesday} && x_1 + x_2 + x_5 + x_6 + x_7 \geq 7\\
&\text{Thursday} && x_1 + x_2 + x_3 + x_6 + x_7 \geq 7\\
&\text{Friday} && x_1 + x_2 + x_3 + x_4 + x_7 \geq 6\\
&\text{Saturday} && x_1 + x_2 + x_3 + x_4 + x_5 \geq 5\\
& && x_i \geq 0 \text{ and integer}
\end{aligned}$$

Using Excel Solver yields the following: $x_1 = 2$, $x_2 = 0$, $x_3 = 0$, $x_4 = 0$, $x_5 = 3$, $x_6 = 1$, $x_7 = 4$.

The corresponding weekly workshift schedule is

	Schedule Matrix, x = Workday						
Operator	**Su**	**M**	**Tu**	**W**	**Th**	**F**	**Sa**
A	...	...	x	x	x	x	x
B	...	...	x	x	x	x	x
C	x	x	x	x	...	...	x
D	x	x	x	x	...	...	x
E	x	x	x	x	...	...	x
F	x	x	x	x	x	...	...
G	...	x	x	x	x	x	...
H	...	x	x	x	x	x	...
I	...	x	x	x	x	x	...
J	...	x	x	x	x	x	...
Total	4	8	10	10	7	6	5
Required	4	8	8	7	7	6	5
Excess	0	0	2	3	0	0	0

3. Yield Management

Problem Statement

A ski resort is planning a year-end promotion by offering a weekend special for $159 per person based on double occupancy. The high season rate for these rooms, which includes lift tickets, normally is $299. Management wants to hold some rooms for late arrivals who are willing to pay the high season rate. If the weekend demand for skiers, willing to pay the high season rate, is a normal distribution with a mean of 50 and a standard deviation of 10, how many rooms should be set aside for full-paying skiers?

Solution

Using equation (1), we can determine the critical fractile as follows:

$$P(d < x) \leq \frac{C_u}{C_u + C_o} = \frac{140}{(140)(159)} \leq 0.468$$

Where:

C_u = lost revenue associated with setting aside too few rooms (underestimated demand). Opportunity loss is the difference in rates ($299 – $159 = $140).

C_o = cost of reserving one too many rooms (overestimated demand). Assume vacant room would have been sold for special rate of $159.

Turning to areas of a standard normal distribution in Appendix A, the z value for a cumulative probability of 0.468 is −0.08. Thus, the number of rooms to protect for full-paying skiers is

$$\begin{aligned} \mu + z\sigma &= 50 + (-0.08)(10) \\ &= 49 \text{ rooms} \end{aligned}$$

Exercises

11.1. An outpatient clinic has kept a record of walk-in patients during the past year. The table below shows the expected number of walk-ins by day of the week:

Day	Mon.	Tues.	Wed.	Thurs.	Fri.
Walk-ins	50	30	40	35	40

The clinic has a staff of five physicians, and each can examine 15 patients a day on average.

a. What is the maximum number of appointments that should be scheduled for each day if it is desirable to smooth out the demand for the week?

b. Why would you recommend against scheduling appointments at their maximum level?

c. If most walk-ins arrive in the morning, when should the appointments be made to avoid excessive waiting?

11.2. Reconsider Example 11.1 (Surfside Hotel), because rising costs now have resulted in a $100 opportunity loss from a no-show. Assume that the no-show experience has not significantly changed and that the resulting loss when a guest is overbooked still is $100. Should Surfside revise its no-show policy?

11.3. A commuter airline overbooks all of its flights by one passenger (i.e., the ticket agent will take seven reservations for an airplane that has only six seats). The no-show experience for the past 20 days is shown below:

No-shows	0	1	2	3	4
Frequency	6	5	4	3	2

Using the critical fractile $P(d < x) \leq C_u/(C_u + C_o)$, find the maximum implied overbooking opportunity loss C_o if the revenue C_u from a passenger is $20.

11.4. Crazy Joe operates a canoe rental service on the Gualala River. He currently leases 15 canoes from a dealer in a nearby city at a cost of $10 per day. On weekends, when the water is high, he picks up the canoes and drives to a launching point on the river, where he rents canoes to white-water enthusiasts for $30 per day. Lately, canoeists have complained about the unavailability of canoes, so Crazy Joe has recorded the demand for canoes and found the experience below for the past 20 days:

Daily demand	10	11	12	13	14	15	16	17	18	19	20
Frequency	1	1	2	2	2	3	3	2	2	1	1

Recommend an appropriate number of canoes to lease.

11.5. An airline serving Denver's International Airport and Steamboat Springs, Colorado, is considering overbooking its flights to avoid flying with empty seats. For example, the ticket agent is thinking of taking seven reservations for an airplane that has only six seats. During the past month, the no-show experience has been

No-shows	0	1	2	3	4
Percentage	30	25	20	15	10

The operating costs associated with each flight are pilot, $150; first officer, $100; fuel, $30; and landing fee, $20.

What would be your recommendation for overbooking if a one-way ticket sells for $80 and the cost of not honoring a reservation is a free lift ticket worth $50 plus a seat on the next flight? What is the expected profit per flight for your overbooking choice?

11.6. Reconsider Example 11.2 (Hospital Emergency Room) to determine if additional nurses will be required to staff the revised daily shift requirements shown below:

Day	Sun.	Mon.	Tues.	Wed.	Thurs.	Fri.	Sat.
Nurses	3	6	5	6	6	6	5

Develop a weekly workshift schedule providing 2 consecutive days off per week for each nurse. Formulate the problem as an integer linear programming model to minimize the number of nurses needed, and solve using Excel Solver. If more nurses are required than the existing staff of eight, suggest an alternative to hiring full-time nurses.

11.7. The sheriff has been asked by the county commissioners to increase weekend patrols in the lake region during the summer months. The sheriff has proposed the following weekly schedule, shifting deputies from weekday assignments to weekends:

Day	Sun.	Mon.	Tues.	Wed.	Thurs.	Fri.	Sat.
Assignments	6	4	4	4	5	5	6

Develop a weekly workshift schedule of duty tours, providing 2 consecutive days off per week for each officer. Formulate the problem as an integer linear programming model to minimize the number of officers needed, and solve using Excel Solver.

11.8. Reconsider Example 11.5 (Blackjack Airline). After initial success with the Los Angeles-to-Las Vegas route, Blackjack Airline's demand for full-fare tickets has increased to an average of 75, with the standard deviation remaining at 15. Consequently, Blackjack has decided to raise all ticket prices by $10. Under these new conditions, how many full-fare seats should Blackjack reserve?

11.9. Town and Country has experienced a substantial increase in business volume because of recent fare wars between the major air carriers. Town and Country operates a single office at a major international airport, with a fleet of 60 compact and 30 midsize cars. Recent developments have prompted management to rethink the company's reservation policy. The table below contains data on the rental experience of Town and Country:

Car	Rental Rate	Discount Rate	Daily Demand	Standard Deviation
Compact	$30	$20	50	15
Midsize	$40	$30	30	10

The daily demand appears to follow a normal distribution; however, it has been observed that midsize-car customers do not choose to rent a compact when no midsize car is available. The discount rate is available to persons who are willing to reserve a car at least 14 days in advance and agree to pick up that car within 2 hours after their flight arrives. Otherwise, a nonrefundable deposit against their credit card will be forfeited. The current reservation policy is that 40 compact cars are held for customers who are willing to pay the full rate and 25 midsize cars are held for full rate-paying customers.

a. Using yield management, determine the optimal number of compact and midsize cars to be held for customers paying the full rate.
b. Given your optimal reservation policy determined here, would you consider a fleet expansion?

River City National Bank — CASE 11.1

River City National Bank has been in business for 10 years and is a fast-growing community bank. Its president, Gary Miller, took over his position 5 years ago in an effort to get the bank on its feet. He is one of the youngest bank presidents in the southwest, and his energy and enthusiasm explain his rapid advancement. Mr. Miller has been the key factor behind the bank's increased status and maintenance of high standards. One reason for this is that the customers come first in Mr. Miller's eyes; to him, one of the bank's main objectives is to serve its customers better.

The main bank lobby has one commercial teller and three paying-and-receiving teller booths. The lobby is designed to have room for long lines should they occur. Attached to the main bank are six drive-in lanes (one is commercial only) and one walk-up window to the side of the drive-in. Because of the bank's rapid growth, the drive-in lanes and lobby have been overcrowded constantly, although the bank has some of the longest hours in town. The lobby is open from 9 AM until 2 PM, Monday through Saturday, and reopens from 4 to 6 PM on Friday. The drive-in is open from 7 AM until midnight, Monday through Friday, and on Saturday from 7 AM. until 7 PM. Several old and good customers have complained, however. They did not like the long wait in line and also felt that the tellers were becoming quite surly.

This was very disheartening to Mr. Miller, despite the cause of the problem being the increased business. Thus, it was with his strong recommendation that the board of directors finally approved the building of a remote drive-in bank just down the street. As Figure 11.13 shows, this new drive-in can be approached from two directions and has four lanes on either side. The first lane on either side is commercial only, and the last lane on each side has been built but is not yet operational. Hours for this facility are 7 AM to 7 PM, Monday through Saturday.

The bank employs both full-time and part-time tellers. The lobby tellers and the morning tellers (7 AM to 2 PM) are considered to be full-time employees, whereas the drive-in tellers on the afternoon shift (2 PM to 7 PM) and the night-owl shift (7 PM to midnight) are considered to be part-time. The tellers perform normal banking services: cashing checks, receiving deposits, verifying deposit balances, selling money orders and traveler's checks, and cashing government savings bonds.

At present, overcrowding for the most part has been eliminated. The hardest challenge to resolving the situation was making customers aware of the new facility. After six months, tellers at the remote drive-in still hear customers say, "I didn't realize ya'll were over here. I'm going to start coming here more often!"

Now, instead of facing an overcrowding situation, the bank is finding problems with fluctuating demand. River City National rarely experienced this problem until the extra capacity of tellers and drive-in lanes was added in the new remote facility.

Two full- and four part-time tellers are employed at the remote drive-in Monday through Friday. Scheduling on Saturdays is no problem, because all six tellers take turns rotating, with most working every other Saturday. On paydays and Fridays, the lanes at the remote drive-in have cars lined up out to the street. A high demand for money and service from the bank is the main reason for this dilemma, but certainly not the only one. Many customers are not ready when they get to the bank. They need a pen or a deposit slip, or they do not have their check filled out or endorsed yet. Of course, this creates idle time for the tellers. There also are other problems with customers that take time, such as explaining that their accounts are overdrawn and their payroll checks therefore must be deposited instead of cashed. In addition, there usually is a handful of noncustomers who are trying to cash payroll or personal checks. These people can become quite obstinate and take up a lot of time when they find that their checks cannot be cashed. Transactions take 30 seconds on average; transaction times range from 10 seconds for a straight deposit to 90 seconds for cashing a bond to about 3 minutes for making out traveler's checks. (The latter occurs very rarely.)

Compared with the peak banking days, the rest of the week is very quiet. The main bank stays busy but is not crowded. On the other hand, business at the remote drive-in is unusually slow. Mr. Miller's drive-in supervisor, Ms. Shang-ling Chen, studied the number of transactions that tellers at the remote facility made on the average. The figures for a typical month are shown in Table 11.10.

Once again, customers are complaining. When tellers at the remote drive-in close out at 7 PM on Fridays, they are always turning people away while they are in the process of balancing. These customers have asked Mr. Miller to keep the new drive-in open at least until 9 PM on Friday. The tellers are very much against the idea, but the board of directors is beginning to favor it. Mr. Miller wants to keep his customers happy but feels there must be some other way to resolve the situation. Therefore, he calls in Ms. Chen and requests that she look into the problem and make some recommendations for a solution.

Assignment

As Ms. Chen's top aide, you are assigned the task of analyzing the situation and recommending a solution. This is your opportunity to serve your company and community as well as to make yourself "look good" and earn points toward your raise and promotion.

FIGURE 11.13
Layout of Remote Drive-In

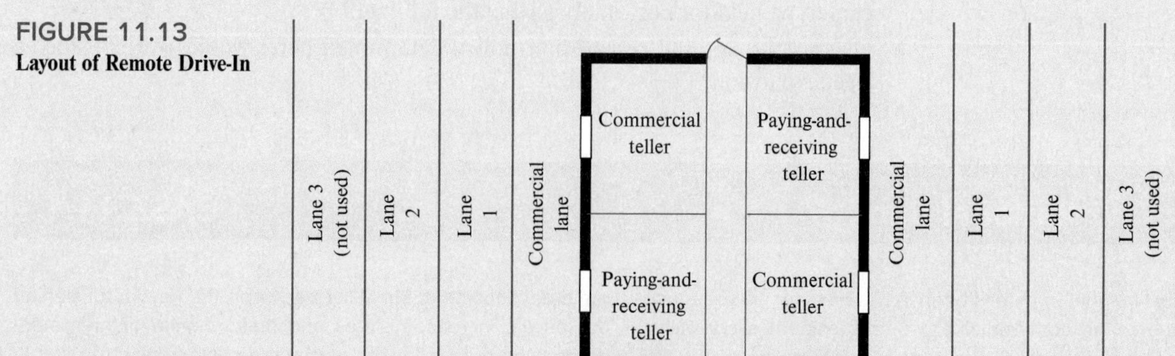

TABLE 11.10 **Transactions for Typical Month at Remote Drive-In**

	First Week		Second Week	
Day of Week	**Morning Shift**	**Afternoon Shift**	**Morning Shift**	**Afternoon Shift**
Monday	. . .	. . .	175	133
Tuesday	. . .	. . .	120	85
Wednesday	200	195	122	115
Thursday	156	113	111	100
Friday	223*	210	236*	225
Saturday	142	127	103	98
	Third Week		**Fourth Week**	
Day of Week	**Morning Shift**	**Afternoon Shift**	**Morning Shift**	**Afternoon Shift**
Monday	149	120	182	171
Tuesday	136	77	159	137
Wednesday	182	186	143	103
Thursday	172	152	118	99
Friday	215*	230	206*	197
Saturday	147	150	170	156
	Fifth Week			
Day of Week	**Morning Shift**	**Afternoon Shift**		
Monday	169	111		
Tuesday	112	89		
Wednesday	92	95		
Thursday	147	163		
Friday	259*	298		

*Most of these transactions occurred after 10 AM.

Gateway International Airport[11] CASE 11.2

Gateway International Airport (GIA) has experienced substantial growth in both commercial and general aviation operations during the past several years. (An *operation* is a landing or takeoff.) Because of the initiation of new commercial service at the airport, which is scheduled for several months in the future, the Federal Aviation Administration (FAA) has concluded that the increased operations and associated change in the hourly distribution of takeoffs and landings will require an entirely new work schedule for the current air traffic control (ATC) staff. The FAA feels that GIA might need to hire additional ATC personnel, because the present staff of five probably will not be enough to handle the expected demand.

After examining the various service plans that each commercial airline submitted for the next 6-month period, the FAA developed an average hourly demand forecast of total operations (Figure 11.14) and a weekly forecast of variation from the average daily demand (Figure 11.15). An assistant to the manager for operations has been delegated the task of developing workforce requirements and schedules for the ATC staff to maintain an adequate level of operational safety with a minimum of excess ATC "capacity."

The various constraints are:

1. Each controller will work a continuous, 8-hour shift (ignoring any lunch break), which always will begin at the start of an hour at any time during the day (i.e., any and all shifts begin at X:00), and the controller must have at least 16 hours off before resuming duty.
2. Each controller will work exactly 5 days per week.
3. Each controller is entitled to 2 consecutive days off, with any consecutive pair of days being eligible.
4. FAA guidelines will govern GIA's workforce requirements so that the ratio of total operations to the number of available controllers in any hourly period cannot exceed 16.

Questions

1. Assume that you are the assistant to the manager for operations at the FAA. Use the techniques of workshift scheduling to analyze the total workforce requirements and days-off schedule. For the primary analysis, assume that
   a. Operator requirements will be based on a shift profile of demand (i.e., 8 hours).

FIGURE 11.14
Average Hourly Demand for Operations

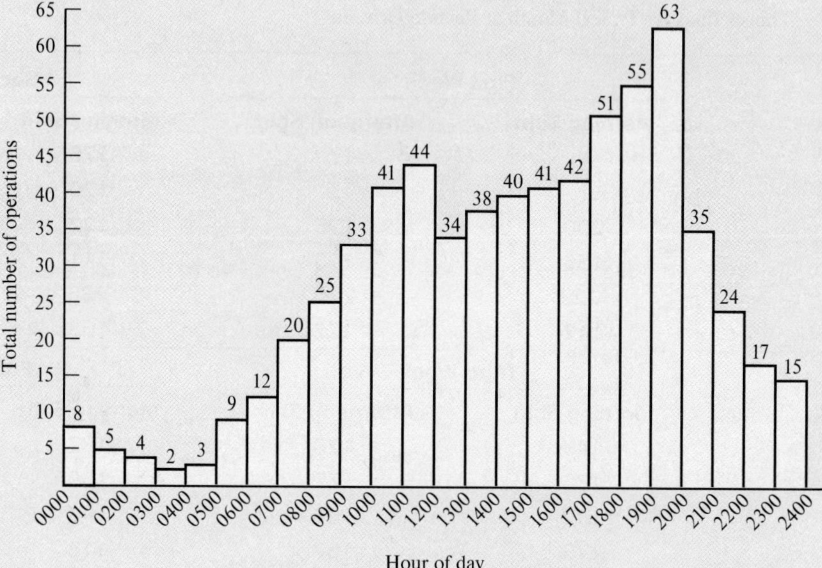

FIGURE 11.15
Daily Demand Variation from Average

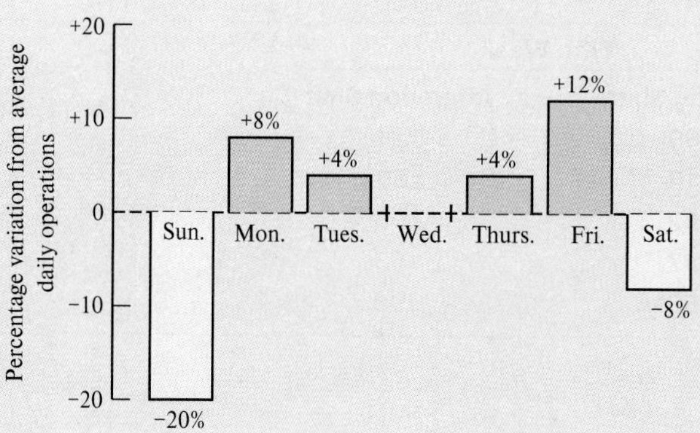

b. There will be exactly three separate shifts each day, with no overlapping of shifts.

c. The distribution of hourly demand in Figure 11.14 is constant for each day of the week, but the levels of hourly demand vary during the week as shown in Figure 11.15.

2. On the basis of your primary analysis, discuss the potential implications for workforce requirements and days-off scheduling if assumptions a and b above are relaxed so that the analysis can be based on hourly demand without the constraints of a preset number of shifts and no overlapping of shifts. In other words, discuss the effects of analyzing hourly demand requirements on the basis of each ATC position essentially having its own shift, which can overlap with any other ATC shift to meet that demand.

3. Do you feel this would result in a larger or smaller degree of difficulty in meeting the four general constraints? Why?

4. What additional suggestions can you make to the manager of operations to minimize the workforce requirements level and days-off scheduling difficulty?

The Yield Management Analyst[12] — CASE 11.3

On the morning of November 10, 2002, Jon Thomas, market analyst for the Mexico leisure markets, canceled more than 300 seats "illegally" reserved on two flights to Acapulco. All of the seats on Jon's Acapulco flights were booked by the same sales representative under a corporate name, Uniden Corporation. Jon could tell that the sales representative reserved space one passenger at a time using the relevant available fare; some seats were reserved at round-trip fares of more than $2,000 per person. By using a special corporate name field, the sales representative used a common gaming technique to suspend auto-cancellation and instant purchase payment programs that are required for all individual bookings by SABRE (semi-automated business research environment), American Airlines' (AA's) customer reservation system. Jon felt justified in canceling this space, because he previously had denied the group-space request and the sales representative subsequently violated established rules regarding the reservation of space for large groups.

No more than 24 hours after Jon canceled the Uniden Corporation's space, he received an irate phone call from Patty Dial, the Dallas–Fort Worth area regional sales manager. Uniden, a local Fort Worth–based company, needed more than 300 seats to Acapulco for its annual sales incentive trip. Jon faces the conflict of whether to accept or deny large groups each day, and he realizes that his market judgment is all part of managing yield for each flight. The Uniden group issue escalated to higher levels of management when Uniden, a major corporate customer for AA, found out that space promised by AA's sales representative had been canceled. With the customer relations issue in mind, Jon entered a negotiation process with Patty to reallocate space.

Normal group reservation procedure requires the sales representative to send an electronic message to the yield management analyst to request a block of space on a flight. The yield management analyst's prerogative is to approve the request and block space for the group or to deny that request. The yield management analyst uses a variety of decision support systems based on historical market activity to make this decision. From the sales representatives' perspectives, capturing this group is a clear victory, because it drives market share through increased sales volume for their regions. From the yield manager's perspective, filling the plane with one group at the same fare on a peak-period flight is a wasted opportunity to use excess demand and the market's limited capacity to maximize revenue per passenger. Unfortunately, sales representatives can fool SABRE into accepting group reservations without the yield manager's approval. As in Jon's case, a sales representative can book seats in blocks of fewer than 10 passengers, set up a corporate name field in the reservation that suspends all auto-cancellation programs, establish a sales contract, and negotiate a special off-tariff price for the group regardless of the fares listed in each reservation.

Conflicting corporate objectives for sales representatives and yield managers is a major source of frustration for a yield management analyst. AA's sales representatives establish monthly revenue and passenger goals to meet progressively higher market share objectives. Sales representatives maintain relationships with large corporate clients and travel agencies, and they implement volume- and revenue-based discount programs for large corporate accounts and travel agencies. AA's yield management analyst attempts to maximize aircraft utilization (revenue per passenger and load factor at the same time) to improve overall market revenue. The yield management analyst has very little contact with the end customer and uses decision support systems to manipulate pricing and inventory allocation programs. The sales representative's goal is stimulation of sales, while the yield management analyst's goal is sales optimization. Jon and Patty's conflict highlights a situation in which yield management and sales objectives come in direct conflict and the system breaks down.

Yield management is an ideal operating strategy for companies that face temporary imbalances between capacity and demand, spoilage (i.e., a product that must be used immediately), and high fixed costs/low variable costs. Yield management enables companies to maximize use of constrained productive capacity with a discriminating eye on product yield. Each day, Jon faces the decision of whether to fill a plane early with lower fares or to save space for higher-revenue passengers.

YIELD MANAGEMENT IN THE AIRLINE INDUSTRY

Passenger demand often outpaces capacity during peak seasons, days, or other times, as in Jon's Acapulco market. In essence, airlines face temporary imbalances between capacity and demand on a daily basis. In the situation that Jon faces, only Aeromexico, Mexicana, and AA have direct flights to Mexico from Dallas. During low-season periods, it is difficult to fill these planes, whereas in high season, there is more demand than the total market capacity can handle. Clearly, AA faces high fixed costs and low variable costs, because adding one more passenger to a flight costs very little compared with the fixed costs of providing and maintaining the scheduled aircraft service. Finally, once the airplane pulls away from the gate, all of the empty seats can never be sold, and this results in spoilage. When faced with excess demand and limited capacity, the yield management analyst may "choose" what traffic is most desirable to optimize the total revenue on each flight. The different levels of yield management sophistication between airlines is the source of a competitive advantage in some highly competitive markets.

From mid-November through the end of May, Jon's Mexico leisure market enters its peak season and provides an excellent opportunity for textbook yield management strategies. During the time that this case covers, AA has a total of nine daily round-trip flights to Acapulco, Cancun, and Puerto Vallarta. Jon is in charge of setting all the fares connecting Mexico with the rest of the world as well as managing the inventory control. Each origin–destination market, such as Dallas–Cancun, has more than 30 fares to maintain. In general, all airlines use price discrimination and yield management to maximize revenue. By maintaining a tiered-fare structure, the yield management analyst can force passengers to pay higher prices in times of greater demand.

Jon helps AA to maintain a tiered, market-based fare structure that leverages the price sensitivities and flexibility of its business and leisure customer segments. Fare rules and prices are differentiated based on the time and date of the flight, origin of the passenger, and historical demand patterns in that market. Table 11.11 outlines the different behavior of the two passenger segments.

Facing spoilage, high fixed costs/low variable costs, and temporary demand imbalances, airlines use *both* demand and capacity management to maximize revenue. Airlines use three yield management tools to maximize revenue and sell the "right" fares to the "right" passengers: "overbooking, discount allocation, and traffic management."[13] To execute price discrimination with a tiered-fare structure, the airplane capacity is divided into different sections, regardless of where the passenger sits (unless the passenger is in business or first class). The yield management analyst spreads the available fares over the sections (i.e., discount allocation) and uses overbooking and traffic management strategies to maximize revenue.

Taking passenger reservations beyond the true capacity of the airplane to ensure a full flight is referred to as *overbooking*. This strategy, based on seasonally adjusted historical data, accounts for expected no-shows, last-minute cancellations,

TABLE 11.11
Behavior of Airline Passenger Segments

Leisure Passenger	Business Passenger
Price-sensitive	Price-insensitive
Advance booking	Last minute booking
Flexible day and time	Inflexible on day and time
Long trips	Short trips
Discretionary travel	Time-dependent travel
Consults travel agents	Frequent flyer and knows destination
Travels over weekends	Weekday travel only
Seasonal travel	Less seasonal
Little loyalty	Loyalty based on frequent flyer credit

and missed connections. Overbooking generates a tremendous amount of incremental revenue for the airline, and it provides airline travelers with greater choice. More flights and fares are made available to a greater number of passengers. In Jon's Mexico leisure markets, levels of overbooking average approximately 25 percent more than capacity and can reach as high as 50 percent. The overbooking level typically starts off high 6 months before departure of a flight and slowly declines as bookings turn over, then restricts excess sales, and forces "selling up" during periods closer to departure.

Discount allocation works together with traffic management to spread the tiered-fare structure over the different inventory sections of a plane. Discount allocation attempts to save seats for higher-valued, last-minute business customers who are willing to pay more than the discounted price. AA's Boeing 737, which is the aircraft used in Jon's Mexico markets, holds 100 passengers: 12 in first class and 88 in coach. On a typical flight, Jon may have two or three separate fares for first-class passengers and 25 different fares for coach passengers. AA's traffic management or indexing system automatically spreads Jon's fares over the plane's inventory sections to provide more inventory for higher-paying and less inventory for lower-paying passengers when faced with excess demand. Traffic management or AA's indexing system also values long-haul, higher-paying passengers more than short-haul passengers, and it provides increased inventory availability for the higher fares.

Overbooking and discount allocation levels are set differently based on historical demand patterns for the particular flight's departure time, day of week, days until departure, and season of departure. The levels change daily for each flight in AA's expansive system based on fluctuating demand. Jon is responsible for overriding system decisions and implementing different and new discount allocation and traffic management strategies to improve the average revenue per passenger and the load factor of his market. Specifically, Jon decides what fares to file for each passenger group, what restrictions to apply to each fare, how many seats to save between higher- and lower-valued fares, increased availability for longer-haul and high-demand markets, and inventory restriction for lower-valued fares.

SABRE opens flights for sale more than 300 days before departure. Maintaining yield in a volatile market, such as Jon's Mexico leisure markets, adds increased uncertainty because of the large fluctuation and less predictable nature of the historical demand patterns. Jon's Mexico leisure markets are especially unpredictable, because frequent yet dispersed group movements distort decision support system inventory projections, average demand, overbooking levels, and discounted seat allocation.

Assignment

Read the following instructions for the Yield Management Game. Your instructor will provide passenger data and a tally sheet for a class exercise on "game day."

Yield Management Game and Instructions

The yield management game illustrates the trade-off between overbooking (selling more than capacity) and spoilage (having idle capacity), with the objective of maximizing revenue when faced with excess demand in the form of various revenues per passenger and different passenger volumes. This particular game focuses on airline capacity management, but is applicable to all fixed capacity services (e.g., hotels and cruise ships).

When allocating seats to prospective passengers, the yield management analyst confronts a problem of maximizing total revenue for each flight. This includes capturing the ideal mix of discount and premium passengers at full capacity utilization without overselling too many customers. The objective of revenue maximization is simple (fill the airplane with the highest paying passengers), but uncertainty makes it a challenge.

Specifically, historical booking trends in the airline industry indicate that the more flexible discount or leisure traveler makes reservations far in advance of departure, while the inflexible premium or business traveler waits until the last minute, often walking up to the plane at the time of departure. To capitalize on this passenger behavior, the airlines have exercised price discrimination to differentiate the passengers with advance purchase, time-of-day, and duration of stay requirements. While price discrimination helps the airline to manage its capacity constrained resource, it does not address how many seats to sell each customer segment—business or leisure passengers.

To further complicate the yield management analyst's task of maximizing total revenue, last minute cancellations, passengers missing connections (misconnect), and no-shows threaten to "spoil" (empty seats) seats and lose potential revenue. You will be using the strategies of *discount allocation* and *overbooking* to address this problem.

Discount allocation is necessary because a plane can be filled long before departure with discount passengers—clearly not a revenue maximizing strategy. Therefore, the yield management analyst attempts to "save" seats for the last-minute premium demand by allocating only a certain amount of seats to early-booking leisure passengers. While overbooking helps overcome spoilage, it opens the possibility for oversales. The yield management analyst attempts to weigh the cost of an oversale against the cost of "spoiling" seats or losing potential revenue from an additional sale. The analyst prefers to oversell the flight up to the point where the oversale cost equals the additional revenue of adding a passenger.

In this game, you will act as the yield management analyst in charge of a pseudo-flight. Based on the historical booking pattern for your flight, leisure passenger demand, typically large groups, appears as far out as 100 days before departure up until 14 days before departure. Business passenger demand enters the market closer to departure at approximately nine days prior to departure up until the time of departure. Other historical market statistics for your plane show that the average misconnect, no-show, and cancellation rate for this peak season flight is 20 percent and the average revenue per passenger is $400.

Both oversales and spoilage cost the airline revenue: oversales are a direct expense, while spoilage is lost potential revenue. The higher the number of oversales, the more money gate agents must pay to get passengers off the plane. Your objective is to maximize total revenue generated on this flight.

GAME FACTS

Airplane Capacity: 100 seats

Historical Market Information:

Average no-show, misconnect, and cancellation rate: 20 percent

Average revenue per passenger: $400

Spoilage penalty: $200 for each empty seat

Oversale penalty:

1–5 oversales	$200 per passenger
6–10	$500
10–15	$800
16+	$1,000

Game Phases

The game will be played in three phases reflecting the different time periods prior to departure. *Phase I* is total passenger demand received outside of 13 days prior to departure. *Phase II* is total passenger demand between 13 days prior to departure and the day of departure. Historical market trends suggest that large groups and families make reservations during Phase I, while individuals and business passengers make reservations during Phase II. *Phase III* shows you the number of passengers who actually show up for the flight and their resulting revenue contribution.

Objective: Maximize Total Revenue!

Sequoia Airlines — CASE 11.4

Sequoia Airlines is a well-established regional airline serving California, Nevada, Arizona, and Utah. Sequoia competes against much larger carriers in this regional market, and its management feels that the price, frequency of flight service, ability to meet schedules, baggage handling, and image projected by its flight attendants are the most important marketing factors that airline passengers consider when deciding to use a particular carrier.

In each of these areas, Sequoia is attaining its desired objectives. Maintaining its flight-attendant staff at desired levels has been difficult in the past, however, and many times, it has had to ask flight attendants to work overtime because of worker shortages. This has resulted in excessive personnel costs and some morale problems among the attendants. One reason for these worker shortages is a higher-than-industry-average turnover rate resulting from experienced attendants being hired away by other airlines. This is not due entirely to morale problems; that cause seems to become important only during seasonal peak-demand periods, when shortages are particularly bad. By interviewing the existing personnel, Sequoia has discovered that competing regional carriers (whose training programs are not as highly developed) have been hiring away from Sequoia a significant proportion of its staff by offering slightly higher direct salaries, attractive indirect benefit packages, and guarantees of a minimum number of flying hours in off-peak demand periods.

As a beginning, Sequoia's management has asked for a 6-month hiring and training analysis of the flight attendant staff requirements beginning next month (July). An investigation of the operations schedule indicates that 14,000 attendant-hours are needed in July, 16,000 in August, 13,000 in September, 12,000 in October, 18,000 in November, and 20,000 in December. Sequoia's training program for new personnel requires an entire month of classroom preparation before they are assigned to regular flight service. As junior flight attendants, they remain on probationary status for 1 additional month. Periodically, there is some personnel movement from the working flight attendant staff to the staff that supervises the training of new employees. Figure 11.16 shows the relationships and percentages of interstaff movements.

When no personnel shortages occur, each junior flight attendant normally works an average of 140 hours per month and is paid a salary of $1,050 during the probationary period. During the training period, each new employee is paid $750. Experienced flight attendants receive an average salary of $1,400 per month and work an average of 125 hours per month. Each instructor receives a salary of $1,500 per month.

The poorly kept secret of Sequoia's personalized training program is that the number of trainees is limited to no more than five per instructor. Instructors not needed in a particular month (i.e., surplus) serve as flight attendants. To ensure a high level of quality in flight service, Sequoia requires that

FIGURE 11.16
Sequoia Airlines Flight-Attendant Flows

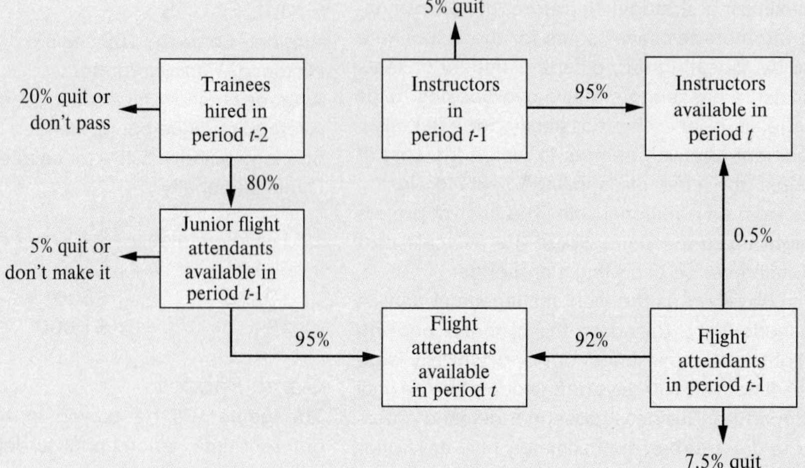

the proportion of junior flight attendant hours not exceed 25 percent of any month's total (i.e., junior plus experienced) attendant hours.

In May, Sequoia hired 10 new employees to enter the training program, and this month, it hired 10 more. At the beginning of June, there were 120 experienced flight attendants and six instructors on Sequoia's staff.

Let T_t = number of trainees hired at the beginning of period t, with $t = 1, 2, 3, 4, 5, 6$

J_t = number of junior flight attendants available at the beginning of period t, with $t = 1, 2, 3, 4, 5, 6$

F_t = number of experienced flight attendants available at the beginning of period t, with $t = 1, 2, 3, 4, 5, 6$

I_t = number of instructors available at the beginning of period t, with $t = 1, 2, 3, 4, 5, 6$

S_t = number of surplus instructors available as flight attendants at the beginning of period t, with $t = 1, 2, 3, 4, 5, 6$

Questions

1. For the forecast period (i.e., July–December), determine the number of new trainees who must be hired at the beginning of each month so that total personnel costs for the flight-attendant staff and training program are minimized. Formulate the problem as an LP model and solve.
2. How would you deal with noninteger results?
3. Discuss how you would use the LP model to make your hiring decision for the next six months.

Selected Bibliography

Alderighi, Marco, Marcella Nicolini, and Claudio A. Piga. "Combined Effects of Capacity and Time on Fares: Insights from the Yield Management of a Low-Cost Airline." *Review of Economics and Statistics* 97, no. 4 (2015), pp. 900–15.

Best, T. J., et al. "Managing Hospital Inpatient Bed Capacity Through Partitioning Care into Focused Wings." *Manufacturing & Service Operations Management* 17, no. 2 (2015), pp. 157–76.

Chevalier, Philippe, and Jean-Christophe Van den Schrieck. "Optimizing the Staffing and Routing of Small-Size Hierarchical Call Centers." *Production and Operations Management* 17, no. 3 (May–June 2008), pp. 306–19.

Dobson, Gregory, Sameer Hasia, and Edieal J. Pinker. "Reserving Capacity for Urgent Patients in Primary Care." *Production and Operations Management* 20, no. 3 (May–June 2011), pp. 456–73.

Helm, Jonathan E., Shervin Ahmad Beygi, and Mark P. Van Oyen. "Design and Analysis of Hospital Admission Control for Operational Effectiveness." *Production and Operations Management* 20, no. 3 (May–June 2011), pp. 359–74.

Jerath, Kinshuk, Anuj Kumar, and Serguei Netessine. "An Information Stock Model of Customer Behavior in Multichannel Customer Support Services." *Manufacturing & Service Operations Management* 17, no. 3 (2015), pp. 368–83.

Mei, Hu, and Zehui Zhan. "An Analysis of Customer Room Choice Model and Revenue Management Practices in the Hotel Industry." *International Journal of Hospitality Management* 33 (2013), pp. 178–83.

Ormeic, E. Lerzan, and O. Zeynep Aksin. "Revenue Management through Dynamic Cross Selling in Call Centers." *Production and Operations Management* 19, no. 6 (November-December 2010), pp. 742-56.

Queenan, Carrie Crystal, et al. "A Comparison of Unconstraining Methods to Improve Revenue Management Systems." *Production and Operations Management* 16, no. 6 (November-December 2007), pp. 729-46.

Ramdas, Kamalini, Jonathan Williams, and Marc Lipson. "Can Financial Markets Inform Operational Improvement Efforts? Evidence from the Airline Industry." *Manufacturing & Service Operations Management* 15, no. 3 (2013), pp. 405-22.

Thompson, Gary M. "Labor Scheduling, Part 1: Forecasting Demand." *Cornell Hotel and Restaurant Administration Quarterly* (October 1998), pp. 22-31.

——. "Labor Scheduling, Part 2: Knowing How Many On-Duty Employees to Schedule." *Cornell Hotel and Restaurant Administration Quarterly* (December 1998), pp. 26-37.

——. "Labor Scheduling, Part 3: Developing a Workforce Schedule." *Cornell Hotel and Restaurant Administration Quarterly* (February 1999), pp. 86-96.

——. "Labor Scheduling, Part 4: Controlling Workforce Schedules in Real-Time." *Cornell Hotel and Restaurant Administration Quarterly* (June 1999), pp. 86-96.

——, and Robert J. Kwortnik, Jr. "Pooling Restaurant Reservations to Increase Service Efficiency." *Journal of Service Research* 10, no. 4 (May 2008), pp. 335-46.

Veeraraghavan, Senthil, and Ramnath Vaidyanathan. "Measuring Seat Value in Stadiums and Theaters." *Production and Operations Management* 21, no. 1 (January-February 2012), pp. 49-68.

Xia, Cathy H., and Parijat Dube. "Dynamic Pricing in e-Services under Demand Uncertainty." *Production and Operations Management* 16, no. 6 (November-December 2007), pp. 701-12.

Endnotes

1. Frances X. Frei, "Breaking the Trade-Off Between Efficiency and Service," *Harvard Business Review* 84, no. 11 (November 2006), pp. 92-101.
2. E. J. Rising, R. Baron, and B. Averill, "A Systems Analysis of a University Health-Service Outpatient Clinic," *Operations Research* 21, no. 5 (September 1973), pp. 1030-47.
3. J. C. Nautiyal and R. L. Chowdhary, "A Suggested Basis for Pricing Campsites: Demand Estimation in an Ontario Park," *Journal of Leisure Research* 7, no. 2 (1975), pp. 95-107.
4. The *M/M/c* queuing model as described in Chapter 13 is used. This model permits the calculation of probabilities for having a telephone caller wait for different numbers of operators.
5. From V. A. Mabert and A. R. Raedels, "The Detail Scheduling of a Part-Time Work Force: A Case Study of Teller Staffing," *Decision Sciences* 8, no. 1 (January 1977), pp. 109-20.
6. From Sheryl E. Kimes, "Yield Management: A Tool for Capacity-Constrained Service Firms," *Journal of Operations Management* 8, no. 4 (October 1989), pp. 348-63.
7. Lenny Leibmann, "Holiday Inn Maximizes Profitability with a Complex Network Infrastructure," *LAN Magazine* 10, no. 6 (June 1995), p. 123.
8. "On the Road to Rebound," *Information Week,* September 3, 1991, p. 32.
9. Michael Kasavana, "Catering Software: Problems for Off-Premise Bookings Can Greatly Increase Operational Efficiency," *Restaurant Business* 90, no. 13 (September 1, 1991), p. 90.
10. "Travel Advisory: Amtrak Adopts Fare System of Airlines," *The New York Times,* December 4, 1989, Section 3, p. 3.
11. Prepared by James H. Vance under the supervision of Professor James A. Fitzsimmons.
12. Adapted with permission from Kevin Baker and Robert B. Freund, "The Yield Management Analyst," University of Texas at Austin, 1994.
13. Quoted from Barbara Amster, former vice president of the American Airlines Pricing and Yield Management Department.

Chapter 12

Managing Waiting Lines

Learning Objectives

After completing this chapter, you should be able to:

1. Describe the economics of waiting lines using examples.
2. Describe how queues form.
3. Describe the psychology behind Maister's two "laws of service."
4. Apply strategies to address the four attributes of waiting.
5. Describe the essential features of a queuing system.
6. Describe the relationship between a negative exponential distribution of time between arrivals and a Poisson distribution of arrival rates.

On June 14, 1972, the United States of America Bank (of Chicago) launched an anniversary sale. The commodity on sale was money, and each of the first 35 persons could "buy" a $100 bill for $80 in cash. Those farther down the queue could each obtain similar but declining bonuses: the next 50 could gain $10 each; 75, $4 each; 100, $2 each; and the following 100, $1 each. Each of the next 100 persons could get a $2 bill for $1.60 and, finally, 800 (subsequently, it seems, expanded to 1,800) persons could gain $0.50 each. The expected waiting time in such an unusual event was unpredictable; on the other hand, it was easy to assess the money value of the commodity being distributed.

First in line were four brothers aged 16, 17, 19, and 24. Because the smallest was 6′2″, their priority was assured. "I figured," said Carl, the youngest brother, "that we spent 17 hours to make a $20 profit. That's about $1.29 an hour."

"You can make better than that washing dishes," added another of the brothers. Had they been better informed they could have waited less time. The 35th person to join the line arrived around midnight, had to wait just 9 hours, and was the last to earn $20–$2.22 per hour. To confirm her right, she made a list of all those ahead of her in the line.

"Why am I here?" she asked. "Well, that $20 is the same as a day's pay to me. And I don't even have to declare it on my income tax. It's a gift, isn't it?"[1]

The experience described above demonstrates that those in line considered their waiting time as the cost of securing a "free" good. Today it is not uncommon to wait 15 seconds for an advertisement to finish before reading an online *New York Times* article. While waiting can have a number of economic interpretations, its true cost is always difficult to determine. For this reason, the trade-off between the cost of waiting and the cost of providing service seldom is made explicit, yet service providers must consider the physical, behavioral, and economic aspects of the consumer waiting experience in their decision making.

Chapter Preview

Our understanding of waiting lines begins with a discussion of the economic considerations from both a provider and customer perspective followed by a discussion of how queues form. We shall discover that the perception of waiting often is more important to the customer than the actual time spent waiting, suggesting that innovative ways should be found to reduce the negative aspects of waiting. Finally, the essential features of a queuing system are described and queuing terminology is defined.

The Economics of Waiting

The economic cost of waiting can be viewed from two perspectives. For a firm, the cost of keeping an employee (i.e., an internal customer) waiting can be measured by unproductive wages. For external customers, the cost of waiting is the forgone alternative use of that time. Added to this are the costs of boredom, anxiety, and other psychological distresses.

In a competitive market, excessive waiting—or even the expectation of long waits—can lead to lost sales. How often have you driven by a filling station, observed many cars lined up at the pumps, and then decided not to stop? One strategy to avoid lost sales is to conceal the queue from arriving customers. In the case of restaurants, this often is achieved by diverting people into the bar, a tactic that frequently results in increased sales. Amusement parks such as Disneyland require people to pay for their tickets outside the park, where they are unable to observe the waiting lines inside. Casinos "snake" the waiting line for nightclub acts through the slot-machine area both to hide its true length and to foster impulsive gambling.

The consumer can be considered a resource with the potential to participate in the service process. For example, a patient who is waiting for a doctor can be asked to complete a medical history record and thereby save valuable physician time (i.e., service capacity). The waiting period also can be used to educate the person about good health habits, which can be achieved by making health publications or YouTube videos available. As another example, restaurants are quite innovative in their approaches to engaging the customer directly in providing the service. After giving your order to a waiter in many restaurants, you are asked to go to the salad bar and prepare your own salad, which you eat while the cook prepares your meal.

Consumer waiting may be viewed as a contribution to productivity by permitting greater utilization of limited capacity. The situation of customers waiting in line for a service is analogous to the work-in-process inventory for a manufacturing firm. The service firm actually is inventorying customers to increase the overall efficiency of the process. In service systems, higher utilization of facilities is purchased at the price of customer waiting. Prominent examples can be found in public services such as post offices, medical clinics, and welfare offices, where high utilization is achieved with long queues.

Queuing Systems

A *queue* is a line of waiting customers who require service from one or more servers. The queue need not be a physical line of individuals in front of a server, however. A person being placed on "hold" by a telephone operator is an example of a virtual queue. Servers typically are considered to be individual stations where customers receive service. The stereotypical queue—people waiting in a formal line for service—as seen at the check-out counters of a supermarket may be what comes to mind but other queuing systems are used. Consider the following variations:

1. Servers need not be limited to serving one customer at a time. Transportation systems such as buses, airplanes, and elevators are bulk services.
2. The consumer need not always travel to the service facility; in some systems, the server actually comes to the consumer. This approach is illustrated by urban services such as fire and police protection as well as by ambulance service.

What is the economic cost to society of airport screening? ©Digital Vision/ Getty Images RF

3. The service may consist of stages of queues in a series or of a more complex network of queues. For example, consider the haunted-house attraction at amusement parks like Disneyland, where queues are staged in sequence so that visitors can be processed in batches and entertained during the waiting periods (e.g., first outside on the walk, then in the vestibule, and finally on the ride itself).

In any service system, a queue forms whenever current demand exceeds the existing capacity to serve. This occurs when servers are so busy that arriving consumers cannot receive immediate service. Such a situation is bound to happen in any system for which arrivals occur at varying times and service times also vary.

Waiting is part of everyone's life, and it can involve an incredible amount of time. For example, a typical day might include waiting at several stoplights, waiting for someone to answer the telephone, waiting for your meal to be served, waiting for the elevator, waiting to be checked out at the supermarket—the list goes on and on.

Strategies for Managing Customer Waiting

Burger King Restaurants began by offering flame-broiled hamburgers and snakes. Customers, of course, enjoyed the hamburgers more than the snakes. The snakes in this case were of the "get-in-line-and-wait" kind . . . and wait and wait. Burger King hardly was unique in this respect—most managers in those days gave little thought to the impact of customer waiting. Businesses and customers merely accepted waiting in line for service as a necessary fact of life. As competitive pressures grew in the service world, however, service businesses began to see that managing their waiting lines effectively might give them an edge in their respective markets. One of the first researchers to investigate the human aspects of waiting and ways to manage the waiting experience was David H. Maister.

The Psychology of Waiting

The first strategy of managing waiting lines is to consider the psychological impact of waiting for a service, either in person or in a virtual queue online or on the phone. If waiting is such an integral and ordinary part of our lives, why does it cause us so much grief? Maister offers some interesting perspectives on this subject.

He suggests two "Laws of Service."[2] The first deals with the customer's expectations versus his or her perceptions. If a customer receives better service than he or she expects, then the customer departs a happy, satisfied person, and the service might benefit from a Facebook effect (i.e., the happy customer will tell friends about the good service). Note, however, that the trickle-down effect can work both ways: A service can earn a bad reputation in the same manner (and create more interesting stories for the customer to pass along).

Maister's second law states that it is hard to play "catch-up ball." By this, he means that first impressions can influence the rest of the service experience; thus, a service that requires its customers to wait would be advised to make that period a pleasant experience. To do the "impossible"–to make waiting at least tolerable and, at best, pleasant and productive–a competitive service management must consider many aspects of the psychology of waiting and come up with creative ways of soothing the savage customers.

That Old Empty Feeling

Just as "nature abhors a vacuum," people dislike "empty time." Empty, or unoccupied, time feels awful and keeps us from other productive activities. Empty time frequently is physically uncomfortable–it makes us feel powerless and at the mercy of servers, whom we might perceive as uncaring about us, and, perhaps worst of all, seems to last forever. The second strategy of managing customer waiting challenges the service organization to fill this time in a positive way. Often, merely providing comfortable chairs or a fresh coat of paint to cheer up the environment will fill the void. Furnishings in a waiting area can affect indirectly the perception of waiting. The fixed-bench seating in bus and rail terminals discourages conversation. The light, movable table-and-chair arrangement of a European sidewalk café brings people together and provides opportunities for socializing. In another situation, a music recording may be enough to occupy a telephone caller who is waiting on hold and, at the same time, reassure the caller that he or she has not been disconnected. An enlightened alternative, used by some firms, is to put the burden on them to call you back when a contact number is requested.

Another method to fill time that is widely noted in the literature is that of installing mirrors near elevators. Hotels, for example, record fewer complaints about excessive waits for elevators that are surrounded by mirrors. The mirrors allow people to occupy their time by checking their grooming and surreptitiously observing others who are waiting. Services often can make waiting times productive as well as pleasurable. Instead of treating the telephone caller mentioned above to the strains of Mozart or Madonna, the service can air some commercials. Such a practice involves risk, however, because some people resent being subjected to this tactic when they are being held captive. At Romano's Macaroni Grill, diners waiting for a table can stay in the entry area and watch a chef prepare meals, which certainly stimulates appetites. No need to play "catch-up ball" here. Each diner reaches the table happily anticipating an agreeable experience rather than sourly grumbling, "It's about time!"

Services that consist of several stages, such as one might find at a diagnostic clinic, can conceal waiting by asking people to walk between successive stages. There are innumerable other ways to fill time: reading matter, television monitors, live entertainment, posters, artwork, toys to occupy children, and cookies and pots of coffee. The diversions are limited only by management's imagination and desire to serve the customer effectively.

A Foot in the Door

As noted above, some diversions merely fill time so that waiting doesn't seem so long, and others also can provide the service organization with some ancillary benefits. Happy customers are more likely than unhappy customers to be profitable customers. The third strategy of managing customer waiting is to give customers the feeling that they are not, in fact, waiting.

Maister points out that "service-related" diversions themselves, such as handing out menus to waiting diners or medical history forms (and paper cups) to waiting patients, "convey a sense that service has started." One's level of anxiety subsides considerably once service has started. In fact, people generally can tolerate longer waits, within reason, if they feel service has begun better than they can tolerate such waits if service has not even started. Another view is that customers become dissatisfied more quickly with an initial wait than with subsequent waits after the service has begun.

The Light at the End of the Tunnel

The fourth strategy for managing customer waiting involves relieving the customer's anxiety about how long the wait will be. Many anxieties are at work before service begins. Have I been forgotten? Did you get my order? This line doesn't seem to be moving; will I ever get served? If I run to the restroom, will I lose my turn? When will the plumber get here? Will the plumber get here at all? Whether rational or not, these anxieties might be the single biggest factor influencing the waiting customer.

Managers must recognize these anxieties and develop strategies to alleviate them. In some cases, this might be a simple matter of having an employee acknowledge the customer's presence. At other times, telling the customer how long he or she will have to wait is sufficient reassurance that the wait at some point will end. Signs can serve this purpose as well. As you approach the Port Aransas, Texas, ferry landing, for example, you see signs posted along the road noting the number of minutes you have left to wait if you are stopped in line at that point.

Consider another example of queue management at Burger King Restaurants, which eventually tamed its snakes. As we noted, the business originally used a "conventional" lineup that required customers to arrange themselves in single file behind a single cash register, where orders were taken. Assemblers prepared the orders and presented them to customers at the far end of the counter.

Dissatisfaction with the slowness of the single-line arrangement led Burger King to try the "hospitality" line-up, in which cash registers are evenly spaced along the counter and customers select a line (in effect betting on which of several will move the fastest). Some customers enjoy the challenge of choosing the best line, but others are disappointed, especially when they choose the wrong line.

In this arrangement, the cashier who takes an order also assembles the order. Although the hospitality line-up proved to be very flexible in meeting peak-period demand, it was more labor-intensive than the conventional line-up. Consequently, Burger King made yet another change, this time to a "multiconventional" line-up, which is a hybrid of both earlier systems. The restaurant returned to a single line, but a new cash register allowed up to six orders to be recorded at the same time. Assemblers, rather than cash register employees, prepare the orders and distribute them at the end of the counter. Returning to a single line guaranteed fairness, because all customers were served in the order of their arrivals. In addition, customers had enough time to make their meal selections without slowing the entire order-taking process.

Burger King's concern with reducing customer waiting time represented a trend toward providing faster service. In many cases, speed of delivery is viewed as a competitive advantage in the marketplace. For example, many hotels today will total your bill and slide it under your room door during the last night of your stay, thereby achieving "zero waiting time" at the check-out counter.

When appropriate, scheduling appointments is another strategy to reduce waiting time, but it is not foolproof. Unforeseen events might interfere, or prior appointments might require more time than expected. If the appointed time comes and goes, the anxiety of not knowing how long the wait will be sets in—along with some measure of irritation at the "insult" of being stood up. A simple explanation and apology for the delays, however, usually will go a long way in reestablishing goodwill.

Excuse Me, but I Was Next

Uncertain and unexplained waits create their own anxieties and, as noted above, occasionally some resentment in customers. The moment a customer sees a later arrival being served first, however, anxiety about how long the wait will be is transformed into anger about the unfairness of it all. This can lead to a testy—if not explosive—situation, and the service provider is just as likely as the usurper to be the target of the anger. The fifth strategy of managing customer waiting addresses the issue of fairness in the delivery process.

A simple way to avoid violations of the first-come, first-served (FCFS) queuing policy is the take-a-number arrangement. For example, customers entering a pastry shop take a number from a dispenser and wait for it to be called. The number currently being served may be displayed so that the new customer can see how long the wait will be. With this simple measure, management has relieved the customer's anxiety over the length of the wait—and the possibility of being treated unfairly. As an ancillary benefit, it also encourages "impulse buying" through allowing the customer to wander about the shop instead of needing to protect a place in line. As equitable as it is, however, this system is not totally free from producing anxiety; it does require the customer to stay alert for the numbers being called or risk losing his or her place in line.

Another simple way to foster FCFS service when there are multiple servers is use of a single queue. Banks, post offices, and airline check-in counters commonly employ this technique. A customer who enters one of these facilities joins the back of the line; the first person in line is served by the next available server. Anxiety is relieved, because there is no fear that later arrivals will "slip" ahead of their rightful place.[3] Often, customers who have been "guaranteed" their place in this way will relax and enjoy a few pleasantries with others in the line. Note that such camaraderie also occupies the customer's empty time and makes the waiting time seem shorter. Queue configurations are examined in more detail later in this chapter.

Not all services lend themselves to such a straightforward prioritization, however. Police service is one example; for obvious reasons, an officer on the way to a call about a "noisy dog next door" will change priorities when told to respond to a "robbery in progress." In this case, the dispatcher can ameliorate the "noisy dog" caller's wait anxiety by explaining the department's response policy and providing the caller with a reasonable expectation of when an officer will arrive.

Other services might wish to give preferential treatment to special customers. Consider the express check-in for "high rollers" at Las Vegas hotels, or advanced boarding for first-class passengers at the gate. Keep in mind, however, that such special "perks" also can engender irritation among the unfavored who are standing in long lines nearby. A management sensitive to the concerns of all its customers will take measures to avoid an image of obvious discrimination. In the example just mentioned, one solution might be to "conceal" the preferential treatment by locating it in an area (e.g., first-class lounge) that is separate from the regular service line.

Essential Features of Queuing Systems

Fluctuations in demand for service are difficult to cope with because the consumption and production of services occur simultaneously. Customers typically arrive at random and place immediate demands on the available service. If service capacity is fully utilized at the time of his or her arrival, then the customer is expected to wait patiently in line. Varying arrival rates and service time requirements result in the formation of queues

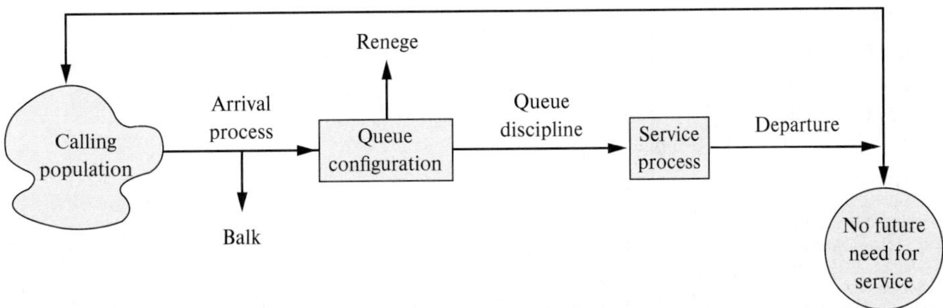

FIGURE 12.1
Queuing System Schematic

(i.e., lines of customers waiting their turn for service). The management of queues is a continuing challenge for service managers.

Figure 12.1 depicts the essential features of queuing systems. These are (1) calling population, (2) arrival process, (3) queue configuration, (4) queue discipline, and (5) service process.

Services obtain customers from a *calling population*. The rate at which they arrive is determined by the *arrival process.* If servers are idle, then the customer is attended immediately; otherwise, the customer is diverted to a queue, which can have various configurations. At this point, some customers may *balk* when confronted with a long or slow-moving waiting line and seek service elsewhere. Other customers, after joining the queue, might consider the delay to be intolerable, and so they *renege*, which means that they leave the line before service is rendered. When a server does become available, a customer then is selected from the queue and service begins. The policy governing the selection is known as the *queue discipline*. The service facility can consist of no servers (i.e., self-service), one or more servers, or complex arrangements of servers in series or in parallel. After the service has been rendered, the customer departs the facility. At that time, the customer either might rejoin the calling population for future return or exit with no intention of returning.

We now discuss in more detail each of these five essential features of queuing systems.

Calling Population

The calling population need not be homogeneous; it might consist of several subpopulations. For example, arrivals at an outpatient clinic can be divided into walk-in patients, patients with appointments, and emergency patients. Each class of patient places different demands on services, but more important, the waiting expectations of each will differ significantly.

In some queuing systems, the source of calls might be limited to a finite number of people. For example, consider the demands on an office copier by a staff of three secretaries. In this case, the probability of future arrivals depends on the number of persons who currently are in the system seeking service. For instance, the probability of a future arrival becomes zero once the third secretary joins the copier queue. Unless the population is quite small, however, an assumption of independent arrivals or infinite population usually suffices. Figure 12.2 shows a classification of the calling population.

FIGURE 12.2
Classification of Calling Population

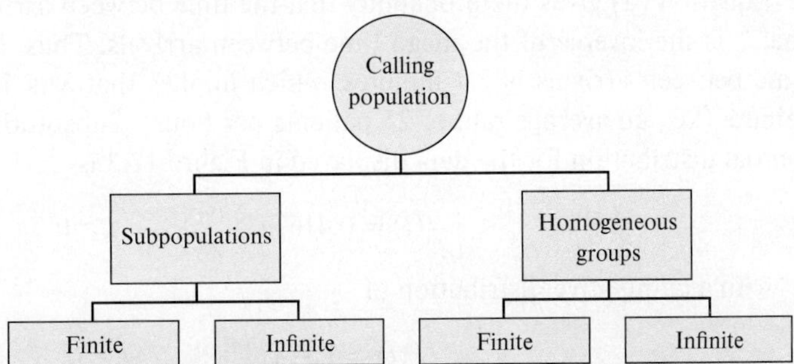

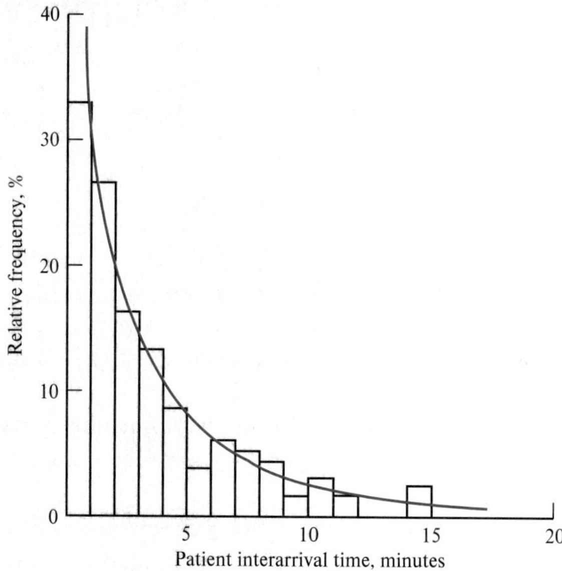

FIGURE 12.3
Distribution of Patient Interarrival Times for a University Health Clinic

Source: E. J. Rising, R. Baron, and B. Averill, "A Systems Analysis of a University Health-Service Outpatient Clinic." Reprinted with permission from *Operations Research* 21, no. 5, September-October 1973, p. 1038, Operations Society of America. No further reproduction permitted without the consent of the copyrighted owner.

Arrival Process

Any analysis of a service system must begin with a complete understanding of the temporal and spatial distribution of the demand for that service. Typically, data are collected by recording the actual times of arrivals. These data then are used to calculate interarrival times. Many empirical studies indicate that the distribution of interarrival times will be exponential, and the shape of the curve in Figure 12.3 is typical of the *exponential distribution*. Note the high frequency at the origin and the long tail that tapers off to the right. The exponential distribution also can be recognized by noting that both the mean and the standard deviation are theoretically equal ($\mu = 2.4$ and $\sigma = 2.6$ for Figure 12.3).

The exponential distribution has a continuous probability density function of the form

$$f(t) = \lambda e^{-\lambda t} \qquad t \geq 0 \tag{1}$$

where λ = average arrival rate within a given interval of time (e.g., minutes, hours, days)

t = time between arrivals

e = base of natural logarithms (2.718 . . .)

mean = $1/\lambda$

variance = $1/\lambda^2$

The cumulative distribution function is

$$F(t) = 1 - e^{-\lambda t} \qquad t \geq 0 \tag{2}$$

Equation (2) gives the probability that the time between arrivals will be t or less. Note that λ is the inverse of the mean time between arrivals. Thus, for Figure 12.3, the mean time between arrivals is 2.4 minutes, which implies that λ is $1/2.4 = 0.4167$ arrival per minute (i.e., an average rate of 25 patients per hour). Substituting 0.4167 for λ, the exponential distribution for the data displayed in Figure 12.3 is

$$f(t) = 0.4167e^{-0.4167t} \qquad t \geq 0$$

with a cumulative distribution of

$$F(t) = 1 - e^{-0.4167t} \qquad t \geq 0$$

The cumulative distribution above can be used to find the probability that if a patient has already arrived, another will arrive in the next 5 minutes. We simply substitute 5 for *t*, and so

$$F(5) = 1 - e^{-0.4167(5)}$$
$$= 1 - 0.124$$
$$= 0.876$$

Thus, there is an 87.6 percent chance that another patient will arrive in the next 5 minute interval. Test this phenomenon the next time you are waiting in a physician's office.

Another distribution, known as the *Poisson distribution*, has a unique relationship to the exponential distribution. The Poisson distribution is a discrete probability function of the form

$$f(n) = \frac{(\lambda t)^n e^{-\lambda t}}{n!} \qquad n = 0, 1, 2, 3 \ldots \tag{3}$$

where λ = average arrival rate within a given interval of time (e.g., minutes, hours, days)

t = number of time periods of interest (usually $t = 1$)

n = number of arrivals (0, 1, 2, . . .)

e = base of natural logarithms (2.718. . .)

mean = λt

variance = λt

The Poisson distribution gives the probability of n arrivals during the time interval t. For the data of Figure 12.3, substituting for $\lambda = 25$ and $t = 1$, an equivalent description of the arrival process is

$$f(n) = \frac{[(25)(1)]^n e^{-(25)(1)}}{n!} \qquad n = 0, 1, 2, 3, \ldots$$

This gives the probability of 0, 1, 2, . . . patients arriving during any 1-hour interval. Note that we have taken the option of converting $\lambda = 0.4167$ arrival per minute to $\lambda = 25$ arrivals per hour. This function can be used to calculate the interesting probability that no patients will arrive during a 1-hour interval by substituting 0 for n as shown below:

$$f(0) = \frac{[(25)(1)]^0 e^{-(25)(1)}}{0!} = e^{-25} = 1.4 \times 10^{-11}, \text{ a very small probability}$$

Figure 12.4 shows the relationship between the Poisson distribution (i.e., arrivals per hour) and the exponential distribution (i.e., minutes between arrivals). As can be seen, they represent alternative views of the same process. Thus, an exponential distribution of interarrival times with a mean of 2.4 minutes is equivalent to a Poisson distribution of the number of arrivals per hour with a mean of 25 (i.e., 60/2.4).

Service demand data often are collected automatically (e.g., by trip wires on highways), and the number of arrivals over a period of time is divided by the number of time intervals

FIGURE 12.4
Poisson and Exponential Equivalence

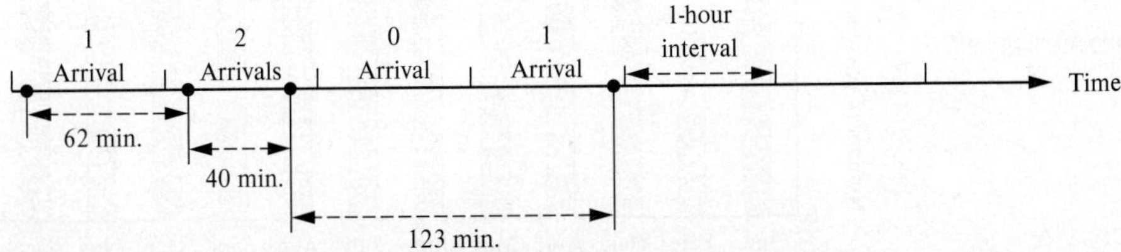

to arrive at an average rate per unit of time. The demand rate during the unit of time should be stationary with respect to time (i.e., lambda [λ] is a constant); otherwise, the underlying fluctuations in demand rate as a function of time will not be accounted for. This dynamic feature of demand is illustrated in Figure 12.5 for hours in a day, in Figure 12.6 for days of the week, and in Figure 12.7 for months of the year. Figure 12.8 presents a classification of arrival processes.

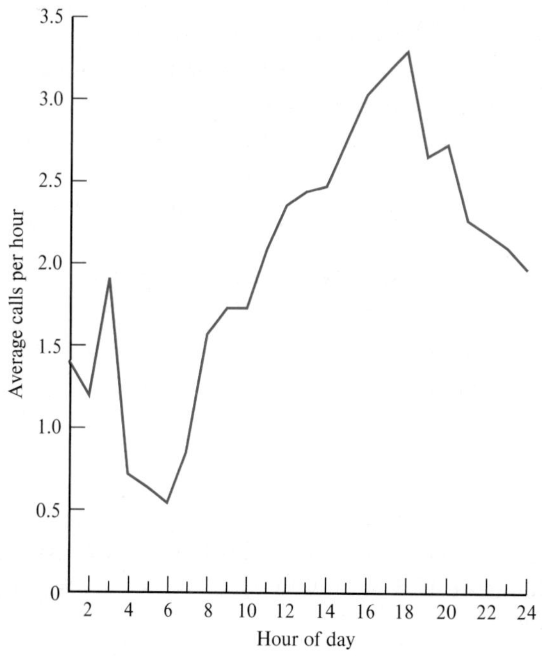

FIGURE 12.5
Ambulance Calls by Hour of Day

Source: James A. Fitzsimmons, "The Use of Spectral Analysis to Validate Planning Models," *Socio-Economic Planning* 8, no. 3, June 1974, p. 127. Copyright © 1974, Pergamon Press Ltd.

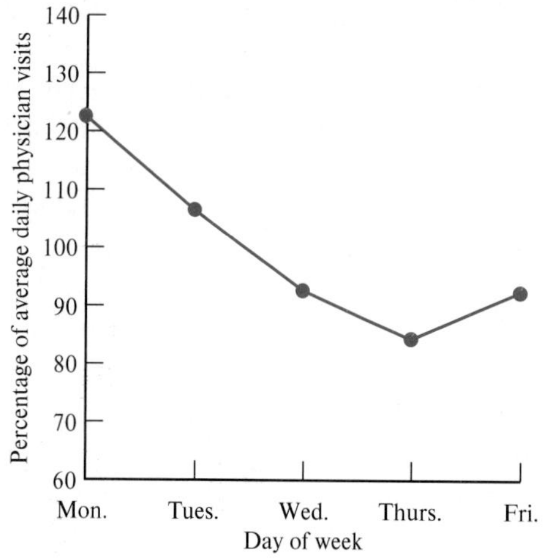

FIGURE 12.6
Patient Arrivals at Health Clinic by Day of Week

E. J. Rising, R. Baron, and B. Averill, "A Systems Analysis of a University Health-Service Outpatient Clinic." Reprinted with permission from *Operations Research* 21, no. 5, September–October 1973, p. 1035, Operations Society of America. No further reproduction permitted without the consent of the copyrighted owner.

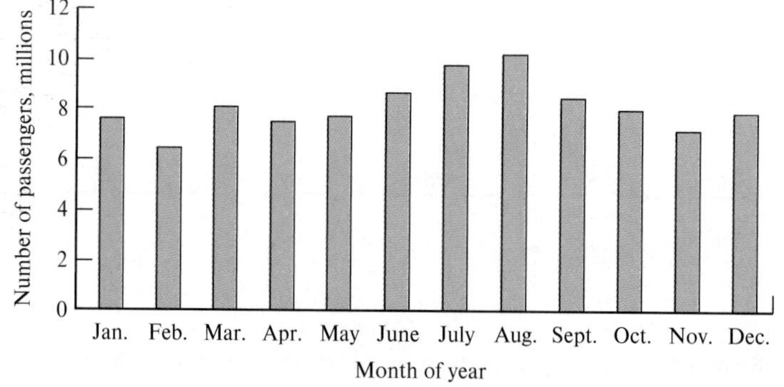

FIGURE 12.7
Airline Passenger Travel between U.S. and the World, 1994

Source: http://www.bts.gov/oai/international/table1.txt.

FIGURE 12.8
Classification of Arrival Process

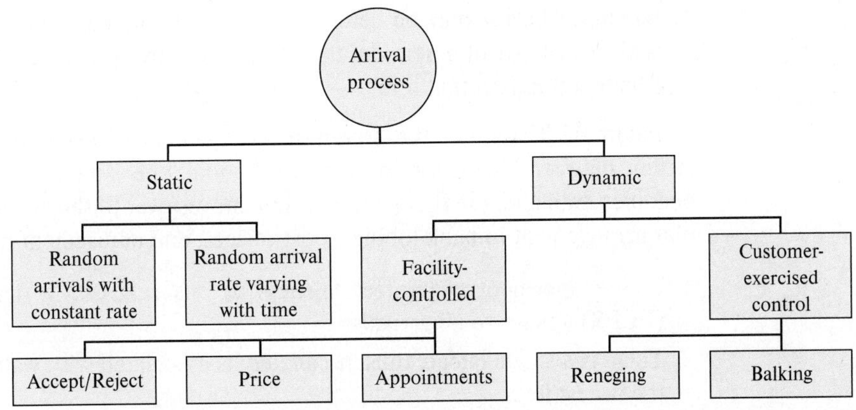

Our discussion has focused on the frequency of demand as a function of time, but the spatial distribution of demand also might vary. This is particularly true of emergency ambulance demand in an urban area, which has a spatial shift in demand resulting from the temporary movements of population from residential areas to commercial and industrial areas during working hours.

Queue Configuration

Queue configuration refers to the number of queues, their locations, their spatial requirements, and their effects on customer behavior. Figure 12.9 illustrates three alternative waiting configurations for a service, such as a bank, a post office, or a bakery, where multiple servers are available.

For the multiple-queue alternative shown in Figure 12.9*a*, the arriving customer must decide which queue to join. The decision need not be irrevocable, however, because one can switch to the end of another line. This line-switching activity is called *jockeying*. In any event, watching the line next to you moving faster than your own is a source of aggravation, but the multiple-queue configuration does have the following advantages:

1. The service provided can be differentiated. The use of express lanes in supermarkets is an example. Shoppers with small demands on service can be isolated and processed quickly, thereby avoiding long waits for little service.
2. Division of labor is possible. For example, drive-in banks assign the more experienced teller to the commercial lane.
3. The customer has the option of selecting a particular server of preference.

FIGURE 12.9
Alternative Waiting-Area Configurations

Multiple Queues

(*a*)

Take a Number

3 4 2 8 6 10 12 7 11 9 5

(*c*)

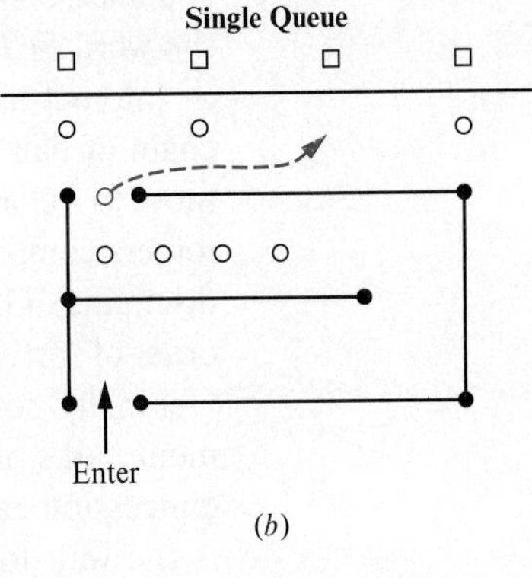

(*b*)

4. Balking behavior may be deterred. When arriving customers see a long, single queue snaked in front of a service, they often interpret this as evidence of a long wait and decide not to join that line.

Figure 12.9*b* depicts the common arrangement of brass posts with red velvet ropes strung between them, forcing arrivals to join one sinuous queue. Whenever a server becomes available, the first person in line moves over to the service counter. This is a popular arrangement in bank lobbies, post offices, and amusement parks. Its advantages are:

1. The arrangement guarantees fairness by ensuring that a first-come, first-served rule (FCFS) applies to all arrivals.
2. There is a single queue; thus, no anxiety is associated with waiting to see if one selected the fastest line.
3. With only one entrance at the rear of the queue, the problem of cutting-in is resolved and reneging made difficult.
4. Privacy is enhanced because the transaction is conducted with no one standing immediately behind the person being served.
5. This arrangement is more efficient in terms of reducing the average time that customers spend waiting in line.

Figure 12.9*c* illustrates a variation on the single queue in which the arriving customer takes a number to indicate his or her place in line. When using such numbers to indicate positions in a queue, there is no need for a formal line. Customers are free to wander about, strike up a conversation, relax in a chair, or pursue some other diversion. Unfortunately, as noted earlier, customers must remain alert to hear their numbers being called or risk missing their turns for service. Bakeries make subtle use of the "take-a-number" system to increase impulse sales. Customers who are given the chance to browse among the tantalizing pastries often find that they purchase more than just the loaf of fresh bread for which they came.

The virtual queue is perhaps the most frustrating of all because there is no visible indication of your position in line. When placed on hold while trying to reach a business, a caller is reluctant to hang up because the call might be answered momentarily but is also frustrated by losing productive use of this waiting time. Some call centers have addressed this problem by periodically reporting the caller's position in line.

If the waiting area is inadequate to accommodate all customers desiring service, then they are turned away. This condition is referred to as a *finite queue.* Restaurants with limited parking might experience this problem to a certain extent. A public parking garage is a classic example because, once the last stall is taken, future arrivals are rejected with the word *FULL* until a car is retrieved.

Internet technology is playing a new role in queue configuration. Great Clips, a national chain of hair stylists, allows online check-in using its website or an app, so customers can move to a chair immediately upon arrival. Unaware of the online check-in option, regular customers complained about customers cutting ahead of them (a violation of the FCFS queue discipline). Great Clips then installed a monitor showing already checked-in customers in the order of "arrival"–online or physical. That alleviated some anxiety of the regular customers.

Finally, concealment of the waiting line itself can deter customers from balking. Amusement parks often process waiting customers by stages. The first stage is a line outside the concession entrance, the second is the wait in an inside vestibule area, and the final stage is the wait for an empty vehicle to convey a party through the attraction. Figure 12.10 shows a classification of queue configurations.

Queue Discipline

The queue discipline is a policy established by management to select the next customer from the queue for service. The most popular service discipline is the first-come,

FIGURE 12.10
Classification of Queue Configurations

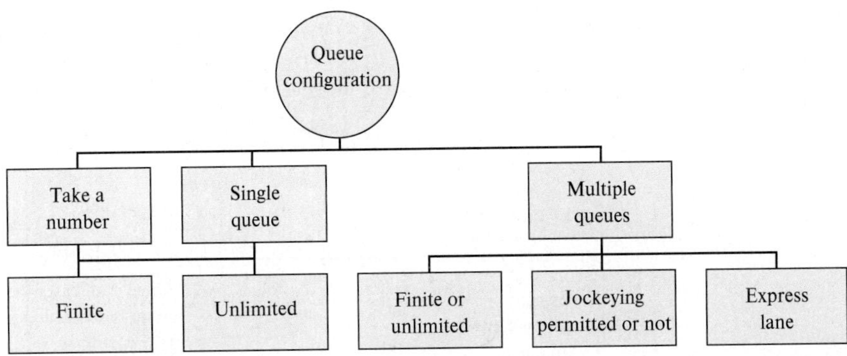

first-served (FCFS) rule. This represents an egalitarian approach to serving waiting customers, because all customers are treated alike. The rule is considered to be static because no information other than position in line is used to identify the next customer for service.

Dynamic queue disciplines are based on some attribute of the customer or status of the waiting line. For example, consider that a professor who has a queue of students outside his or her door during office hours might select the next student based on a probable short activity time (e.g., turn in a paper). This shortest-processing-time (SPT) rule has the property of minimizing the average time that customers spend in the system (i.e., both waiting and being served). This rule is seldom used in its pure form, however, because customers who require long service times would continually be pushed to the back of the queue for more recent arrivals requiring shorter times.

A more sophisticated dynamic queue discipline is the $c\mu$ priority rule where "c" is a linear delay cost rate and "μ" is the rate of customers served per unit time. This priority rule has the social optimization objective of maximizing the sum of benefits for customer plus provider. The rule assigns priority to customers in increasing order of their $c\mu$ index (i.e., high cost and short service time moves one to the front of the queue). Note how this addresses the shortcoming of the SPT rule by combining the cost of delay with the service processing time $1/\mu$. This priority rule is ideal for servicing customers within the same organization because the value of c is easily determined.

Typically, arrivals are placed in priority classes on the basis of some attribute, and the FCFS rule is used within each class. An example is the express check-out counter at supermarkets, where orders of 10 or fewer items are processed. This allows large stores to segment their customers and, thereby, compete with the neighborhood convenience stores that provide prompt service.

In a medical setting, the procedure known as *triage* is used to give priority to those who would benefit most from immediate treatment. The most responsive queue discipline is the preemptive priority rule. Under this rule, the service currently in process for a person is interrupted to serve a newly arrived customer with higher priority. This rule usually is reserved for emergency services, such as fire or ambulance service. An ambulance that is on the way to a hospital to pick up a patient for routine transfer will interrupt this mission to respond to a suspected cardiac-arrest call.

Creative dynamic queue disciplines take advantage of the status of the queue. Consider the concept of round-robin service as used by a dentist with multiple examination rooms. For example, a patient is given a local anesthetic before a tooth extraction. While the anesthetic takes effect, the dentist moves to another patient who requires x-rays. Thus, customers share the service provider by alternating between waiting and being served. When the number of customers in the queue becomes large, the option of using the SPT rule within a FCFS discipline might be acceptable in a socially agreeable queue. Note that for multiple queues, when jockeying is permitted, the FCFS rule cannot be guaranteed. Figure 12.11 shows a classification of queue disciplines.

FIGURE 12.11
Classification of Queue Discipline

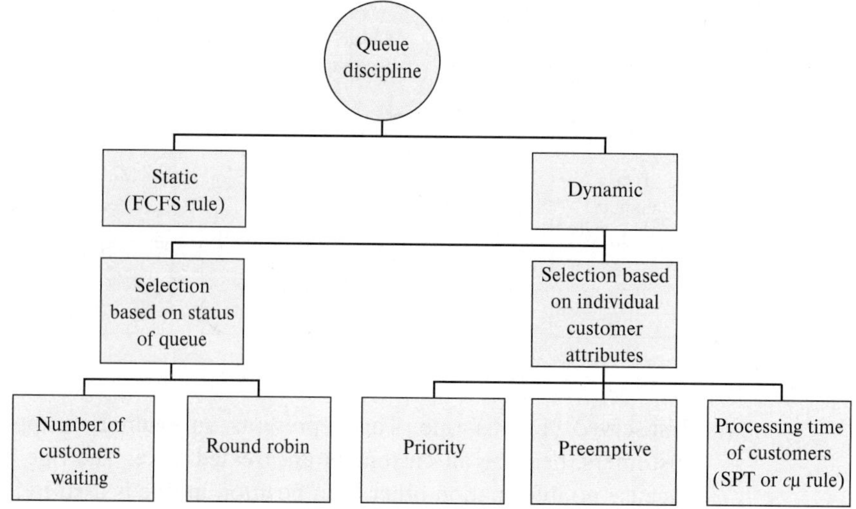

One particularly demanding type of queue with which most people are familiar is the Transportation Security Administration (TSA) screening process at airports. In an effort to ameliorate this frustrating and aggravating process (one passenger in early 2012 made the national news when he stripped down—completely—to pass through the security check!), the TSA is partnered with U.S. airlines to develop the "Pre✓™" system (also known as Trusted Traveler Program) to expedite screening for selected groups of passengers.[4] TSA's Pre✓™ is a prescreening initiative that makes risk assessments of passengers who voluntarily participate prior to their arrival at the airport checkpoint. The volunteers are U.S. citizens who are members of existing Customs and Border Protection (CBP) Trusted Traveler programs, including Global Entry, NEXUS, and SENTRI, as well as eligible airline frequent flyers. If TSA determines a passenger is eligible for expedited screening, the passenger can enter his or her Known Traveler Number (KTN) in an airline's data base. The boarding pass then will display the TSA Pre✓™ symbol so the passenger can be screened in the expedited precheck line (which sometimes is faster than the general TSA screening lines). Passengers in the precheck line are "excused" from removing items such as shoes, liquids, laptops, light jackets, and belts. A recent ruling allows passengers aged 75 and older to keep on their shoes even when they go through the general security check . . . a positive perk of aging!

Recently, TSA has come under severe criticism for taking too long for security screening, and airlines as well as airports have tried different methods to reduce congestion. One such method is the 5-bin loading that Delta Airlines together with TSA tried out in selected airports in summer of 2016. In the 5-bin system, five passengers start loading five separate bins with their personal belongings simultaneously on a stationary table. The bins are pushed to the conveyor belt leading to the X-ray unit in the order in which they are loaded. This way, one slow passenger will not keep the line from moving. Also, bins are circulated in an internal *Kanban*-like conveyor belt so that no passenger will have to wait for a bin.

Municipalities as well as individuals must deal with queuing challenges. Anyone who faces a daily commute to work, school, or other destination recognizes the benefits that an efficient rapid-transit system can offer. But how can such a system be operated efficiently?

The U.S. Federal Transit Administration (FTA) works continuously to find ways to improve public transportation systems by addressing traffic congestion, urban sprawl, central city decline, and air pollution. Some well-known concepts include high-occupancy vehicle (HOV) lanes, dedicated bus lanes, regulated entry to and exit from highways, and offline ticketing to facilitate faster boarding of public conveyances.

Recently, however, technology is playing a big role in efficient operations of bus services by managing waiting lines and traffic controls better.[5] Such systems reduce delays in bus service owing to excessive waits at intersection signals. In one system, a program algorithm and transponder or other electronic communication capability allows a bus approaching a traffic signal to extend the green light, or to advance a red light to green, and proceed through the intersection without stopping. In this case, the bus driver determines when signal priority is needed to maintain the bus schedule. In another system, a bus system equipped with an automatic vehicle location (AVL) system transmits a signal to an operations center, where a computerized system determines if a bus is running on or behind schedule. If the bus is behind schedule, the priority system adjusts the operation of traffic signals along the bus's route strategically so that the bus can make up time while minimizing traffic disruptions for other motorists.

Another strategy that can be used on streets with dedicated bus lanes gives a bus a "queue jump" by adding a signal phase that advances the green light for the bus lane prior to the green light for the other traffic lanes.

Service Process

The distribution of service times, arrangement of servers, management policies, and server behavior all contribute to service performance. Figure 12.12 contains histograms of several service time distributions in an outpatient clinic with $\bar{x} = 1/\mu$. As the figure shows, the distribution of service times can be of any form. Conceivably, the service time could be a constant, such as the time to process a car through an automated car wash; however, when the service is brief and simple to perform (e.g., preparing orders at a fast-food restaurant, collecting tolls at a bridge, or checking out items at a supermarket), the distribution of service times frequently is exponential (see Figure 12.3). The histogram for second-service times, Figure 12.12*c*, most closely approximates an exponential distribution. The second-service times represent those brief encounters in which, for example, the physician prescribes a medication or goes over your test results

FIGURE 12.12
Histograms of Outpatient-Clinic Service Times

Source: E. J. Rising, R. Baron, and B. Averill, "A Systems Analysis of a University Health-Service Outpatient Clinic." Reprinted with permission from *Operations Research* 21, no. 5, September–October 1973, p. 1039, Operations Society of America. No further reproduction permitted without the consent of the copyrighted owner.

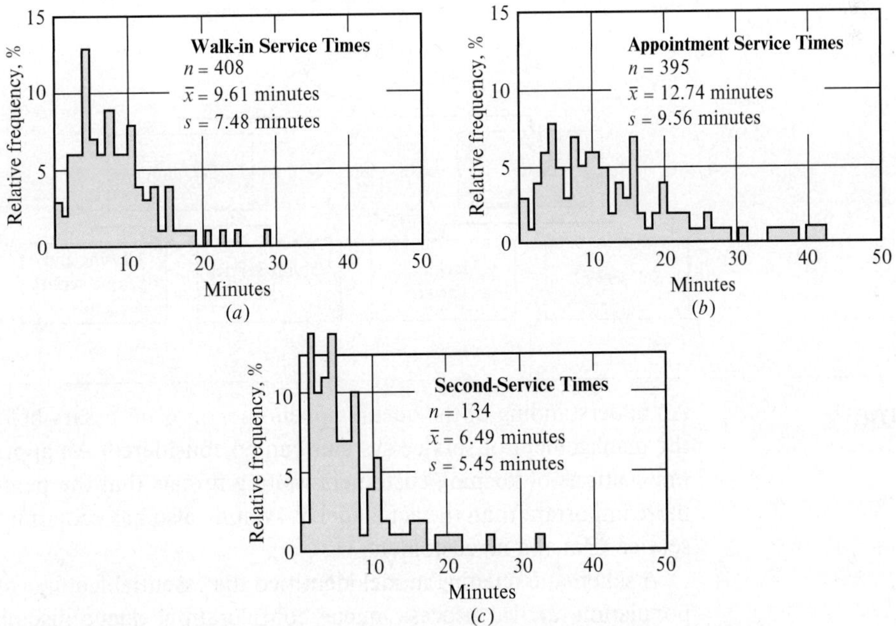

TABLE 12.1
Service Facility Arrangements

Service Facility	Server Arrangement
Parking lot	Self-service
Cafeteria	Servers in series
Toll booths	Servers in parallel
Supermarket	Self-serve, first stage; parallel servers, second stage
Hospital	Services in parallel and series, not all used by each patient

with you. The distribution of service times is a reflection of the variations in customer needs and server performances.

Table 12.1 illustrates the variety of service facility arrangements that are possible. With servers in parallel, management gains flexibility in meeting the variations in demand for service. Management can vary the service capacity effectively by opening and closing service lines to meet changes in demand. At a bank, additional teller windows are opened when the length of queues becomes excessive. Cross-training employees also adds to this flexibility. For example, at supermarkets, stockers often are used as cashiers when lines become long at the check-out counters. A final advantage of parallel servers is that they provide redundancy in case of equipment failures.

The behavior of service personnel toward customers is critical to the success of the organization. Under the pressure of long waiting lines, a server may speed up and spend less time with each customer; unfortunately, a gracious and leisurely manner then becomes curt and impersonal. Sustained pressure to hurry can increase the rate of customer processing, but it also sacrifices quality. This behavior on the part of a pressured server also can have a detrimental effect on other servers in the system. For example, a busy 911 telephone operator might dispatch yet another patrol car before properly screening the call for its critical nature; in this situation, the operator should have spent more time than usual to ensure that the limited resources of patrol cars were being dispatched to the most critical cases. Service processes are classified in Figure 12.13.

FIGURE 12.13
Classification of Service Processes

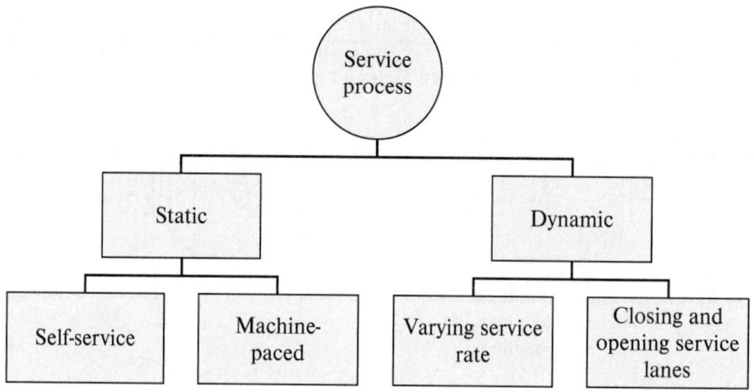

Summary

An understanding of the queuing phenomenon is necessary before creative approaches to the management of service systems can be considered. An appreciation of the behavioral implications of keeping customers waiting reveals that the perception of waiting often is more important than the actual delay. Waiting also has economic implications for both the service firm and its customers.

A schematic queuing model identified the essential features of queuing systems: calling population, arrival process, queue configuration, queue discipline, and service process. An understanding of each feature provides insights and identifies management options for improving customer service.

Service Benchmark

THE MAGIC OF DISNEY MAKES QUEUES DISAPPEAR

Time goes slowly when you're in line, but guests at Disney theme parks have the alternative of joining a virtual queue. In 1999, Disney instituted "FastPass," a computerized ticketing system that allows customers to make reservations for popular rides and avoid waiting in long lines. To get a FastPass, the customer inserts a regular admission ticket into a designated slot in a kiosk, and a computer prints out a ticket with a designated one-hour time window for later in the day. When the designated time window arrives, the customer can walk into the attraction without waiting. Customers can use the time that would otherwise be wasted in waiting lines at restaurants, gift stores, or less-popular rides. Such customers get more pleasure during their visit, and Disney gets more money! FastPass requires no additional fee, but restrictions apply including a limit on the number of FastPasses allowed at any given time.

In 2012, Disney began testing FastPass+, which allows guests to make reservations for ride times before they begin their vacations. Guests staying at Disney resorts are contacted by e-mail and given an opportunity to prepare a FastPass+ itinerary for their day at the park. FastPass+ guests are supplied with RFID-equipped wristbands that just need to be swiped near the reserved attraction to gain admittance.

Disney has realized unexpected benefits of FastPass, such as leveling demand by filling slow periods with FastPass reservations and anticipating future ride demand so extra capacity can be added when needed (e.g., adding an extra car to the Magic Mountain ride).

Key Terms and Definitions

Balk occurs when an arriving customer sees a long queue and decides not to seek service. *p. 341*

Calling population source of service customers from a market area. *p. 341*

Exponential distribution the continuous distribution that describes the time between arrivals or service times. *p. 342*

Jockeying the practice of customers in a multiple-queue system leaving one queue to join another. *p. 345*

Poisson distribution the discrete distribution that describes random arrivals or departures from a busy server per time interval (e.g., hour). *p. 343*

Queue discipline a rule for selecting the next customer in line to be served (e.g., FCFS). *p. 341*

Reneging occurs when a customer in queue departs before obtaining service. *p. 341*

Topics for Discussion

1. Suggest some strategies for controlling the variability in service times.
2. Suggest diversions that could make waiting less painful.
3. Select a bad and a good waiting experience, and contrast the situations with respect to the aesthetics of the surroundings, diversions, people waiting, and attitude of servers.
4. Suggest ways that service management can influence the arrival times of customers.
5. When the line becomes long at some fast-food restaurants, an employee will walk along the line taking orders. What are the benefits of this policy?

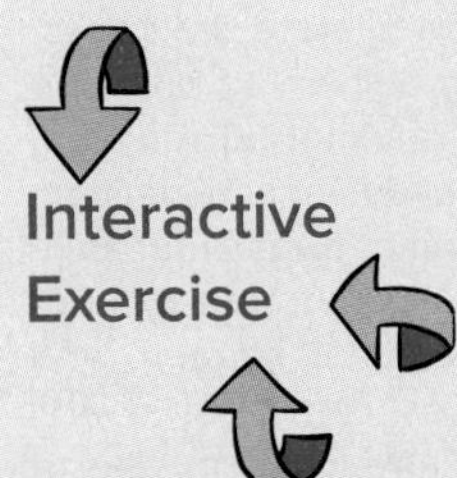

Interactive Exercise

The class breaks into small groups with at least one international student in each group, if possible. Based on overseas travel, each group reports on observations of waiting behavior from a cultural perspective.

Solved Problem

Problem Statement

A fast-food restaurant is interested in studying its arrival of customers. During the busy lunch period they have observed an average of 20 customers arriving per hour Poisson distributed.

a. If a customer has just entered the store, what is the probability of another arrival in the next 10 minutes?

b. What is the probability of two customers arriving in a five minute window?

Solution

a. We use equation (2) with a $\lambda = 20/60 = 1/3$ arrival per minute because our focus is on the next $t = 10$-minute time interval.

$$F(t) = 1 - e^{-\lambda t} = 1 - e^{-(1/3)(10)} = 0.96 \text{ almost a certainty}$$

b. We use equation (3) with $\lambda = 20/60 = 1/3$ arrival per minute because our focus is on the next $t = 5$-minute time interval.

$$f(n) = \frac{\lambda t^n e^{-\lambda t}}{n!} = \frac{[(1/3)(5)]^2 e^{-(1/3)(5)}}{2!} = 0.26$$

Exercises

12.1. You show up early in the morning to buy tickets for a concert but you find a long line and are told that the average time between arrivals has been about 15 minutes.

a. What is the chance you will lose your place in line, if just after arriving, you leave for 5 minutes to use the restroom?

b. What is the probability that zero, one, or two arrivals will come during your five minute rest break?

12.2 Create a Poisson histogram in the range from zero to nine arrivals per hour for a distribution with mean of 4 arrivals per hour. Is your distribution symmetrical about the mean?

12.3 Using equation (2) prepare the cumulative exponential distribution for the patient interarrival times shown in Figure 12.3 with a mean of 0.4167 arrivals per minute. Plot your distribution over a range of zero to ten minutes in increments of one minute. What is the upper limit of your distribution?

Thrifty Car Rental — CASE 12.1

Thrifty Car Rental (now part of Hertz) began as a regional business in the southwest, but it now has more than 470 locations across the country and almost 600 international locations. About 80 percent of its U.S. locations are at airports, and the rest are based in communities. About 75 percent of the vehicles in its fleet get 26 mpg or better. The company serves both tourist and business customers.

The service counter where customers are processed by Thrifty's personnel has a simple design. In the "old days," it varied only in the number of cubbyholes that kept various forms within easy reach of the servers. Today, the cubbies and forms have given way to computer terminals for more streamlined service. The number of servers varies with the size of the local market and the level of demand at specific times. In smaller markets, Thrifty might need three people at one time behind the counter, but in the largest markets, this number could be as high as eight when demand is heaviest. Usually, these peak-demand times reflect the airport's inbound-outbound flight schedule; as they occur, one or more attendants can deal exclusively with clients who have made prior arrangements to pick up a vehicle or with those who are returning vehicles. When this situation exists, these attendants hang appropriate messages above their chosen stations to indicate their special service functions to clientele. Because the speed of customer service is an important factor in maintaining Thrifty's competitive edge, management and service personnel have worked very hard to ensure that each client is processed without unnecessary delay.

Another important factor in Thrifty's competitive stance is the ability to turn incoming vehicles around and quickly prepare them for new clients. The following steps are necessary to process a vehicle from incoming delivery to outgoing delivery: (1) confirmation of odometer reading, (2) refueling and confirmation of fuel charge, (3) visual damage inspection, (4) priority assessment, (5) interior cleaning, (6) maintenance assessment, (7) maintenance and check-out, (8) exterior cleaning and polishing, (9) refueling and lot storage, and (10) delivery to customer.

When a client returns a vehicle to any location, one of Thrifty's crew will confirm the odometer reading, drive about 200 meters to the service lot, and confirm any fuel charge necessary to refill the car's tank. In some cases, the crew member might be able to process all of this information on a hand-held computer, and the customer can be on her or his way without having to queue up in the office. In less streamlined locations, the crew member will relay the information to all attendants immediately so that the client can complete payment inside and be released as soon as possible. Technology in some locations allows a customer to get a receipt from the intake attendant where the car is parked, rather than go inside the office to "check out." If the crew member notices any interior or exterior damage to the vehicle, the attendant will notify the manager on duty; the client then must clarify his or her responsibility and will be delayed until the situation is resolved. After the damage-inspection step, the fleet supervisor assigns a priority status to incoming cars on the basis of the company's known (i.e., certain) demand and reserve policy (for walk-up clients): high-priority treatment for cars that are needed within the next six-hour period, and normal treatment for everything else.

After the vehicle's interior is cleaned thoroughly and sprayed with a mild air freshener, a mechanic examines the vehicle's maintenance record, gives the vehicle a test drive, and notes on a form any maintenance actions he or she deems necessary. Thrifty has certain policies covering periodic normal maintenance, such as oil and filter changes, tire rotation and balancing, lubrication, coolant replacement, and engine tune ups. Major special maintenance actions, such as brake repair, transmission repair or adjustment, or air-conditioning and heating repair, are performed as needed.

Typically, a garage in Thrifty's system has a standard side-by-side, three-bay design: two bays always are used for normal maintenance, and the third is used for either normal or special maintenance. About 20 percent of the time is spent on special maintenance in this third bay. In general, Thrifty uses a team of five mechanics for its garages: one master mechanic (who is the garage manager), two journeymen mechanics, and two apprentices. The apprentices who are responsible for all normal maintenance tasks except the engine tune-up are stationed to service every vehicle in each outside bay, and alternate on vehicles in the middle bay. The journeyman mechanics are responsible for all other maintenance, and they also alternate on servicing vehicles in the middle bay.

After servicing, the vehicle is moved outside to the car wash area, and a team of two people washes, rinses, and buffs the exterior to ensure a good appearance. Because part of the rinse cycle contains a wax-type liquid compound, the vehicle usually does not require a time-consuming wax job. From this point, the vehicle's fuel tank again is topped off, and the vehicle is placed in the lot for storage.

ASSIGNMENT

On the basis of your experience and the description of Thrifty's operations, describe the five essential features of the queuing systems at the customer counter, the garage, and the car wash.

Eye'll Be Seeing You[6] — CASE 12.2

Mrs. F arrives 15 minutes early for a 1:30 PM appointment with her Austin, Texas, ophthalmologist, Dr. X. The waiting room is empty and all of the prior names on the sign-in sheet are crossed out. The receptionist looks up but does not acknowledge her presence. Mrs. F, unaware of the drama about to unfold, happily anticipates that she might not have to wait long beyond her scheduled time and settles into a chair to read the book she has brought with her. Large windows completely surround three sides of the waiting room. The receptionist sits behind a large opening in the remaining wall. Attractive artwork decorates the available wall space, and trailing plants rest on a shelf above the receptionist's opening. This is an appealing, comfortable waiting room.

At 1:25 PM, another patient, Jack, arrives. Mrs. F knows his name must be Jack, because the receptionist addresses him by first name and the two share some light-hearted pleasantries. Jack takes a seat and starts looking through a magazine.

At 1:40 PM, a very agitated woman enters and approaches the receptionist. She explains that she is very sorry she missed her 1 o'clock appointment and asks if it would be possible for Dr. X to see her anyway. The receptionist replies very coldly, "You're wrong. Your appointment was for 11."

"But I have 1 o'clock written down!" responds the patient, whose agitation now has changed to distress.

"Well, you're wrong."

"Oh dear, is there any way I can be worked in?" pleads the patient.

"We'll see. Sit down."

Mrs. F and her two "companions" wait until 1:50 PM, when staff person number 2 (SP2) opens the door between the waiting room and the hallway leading to the various treatment areas. She summons Jack, and they laugh together as she leads him to the back. Mrs. F thinks to herself, "I was here first, but maybe he just arrived late for an earlier appointment," then goes back to her book. Five minutes later, Ms. SP2 appears at the door and summons the distressed patient. At this point, Mrs. F walks to the back area (she's a long-time patient and knows the territory), seeks out Ms. SP2, and says, "I wonder if I've been forgotten. I was here before those two people who have just been taken in ahead of me."

Ms. SP2 replies very brusquely, "Your file's been pulled. Go sit down."

Once again occupying an empty waiting room, Mrs. F returns to her reading. At 2:15 PM (no patient has yet emerged from a treatment area), Ms. SP2 finally summons Mrs. F and takes her to room 1, where she uses two instruments to make some preliminary measurements of Mrs. F's eyes. This is standard procedure in Dr. X's practice. Also standard is measuring the patient's present eyeglass prescription on a third instrument in room 1. Mrs. F extends her eyeglasses to Ms. SP2, but Ms. SP2 brushes past her and says curtly, "This way." Mrs. F then is led to a seat in the "dilating area," although no drops have been put in her eyes to start dilation.

The light in the dilating area is dimmed to protect dilating eyes, but Mrs. F is able to continue reading her book. No one else is seated in the dilating area. At 2:45 PM, Ms. SP2 reappears, says, "this way" (a woman of very few words, our Ms. SP2), and marches off to examining room 3. "Wait here," she commands, leaving Mrs. F to seat herself in the darkened room.

Mrs. F can hear Dr. X and Jack laughing in the next examining room. At 2:55 PM, she hears the two men say good-bye and leave the room. Mrs. F expects Dr. X to enter her room shortly. At 3:15 PM, however, when he still has not appeared, she walks forward and interrupts Ms. SP2, the receptionist, the bookkeeper, and Ms. SP3, who are socializing. "Excuse me, but have I been forgotten?" she asks. Ms. SP2 turns her head from her companions and replies, "No, he's in the line. Go sit down."

Mrs. F wonders what that means but returns to her assigned place. She is here, after all, for a particular visual problem, not just for a routine check-up.

All good things, however, including Mrs. F's patience and endurance of abusive treatment, eventually end. At 4:00 PM, Mrs. F does some marching of her own—to the front desk, where she announces to the assembled Mss. SP1 through SP4 that she has been waiting since 1:30 PM, that she has been sitting in the back for 2½ hours, and that not once during that time has one member of the staff come to let her know what the problem is, how much longer she can expect to wait, or, indeed, that she has not been forgotten. She adds that she will wait no longer, and she feels forced to seek the services of a physician who chooses to deliver health care. There are several patients seated in the waiting room at the time.

There is an epilogue to this case. Mrs. F went directly home and wrote the following letter to Dr. X informing him of the treatment she had (not) received at his office and stating that she and her family would seek care elsewhere:

_____

_____

January 5, 2005

_____, M.D.

Austin, Texas

Dear Dr. _____:

It is with very real regret that I am transferring our eye care to another physician, and I want you to know the reason for my decision.

It is 4:22 PM, and I have just returned home from a 1:30 PM appointment with(out) you. The appointment was made because I had received an adverse report from Seton Hospital's recent home vision test. I was kept waiting in the dilation area and in examining room 3 for more than two-and-one-half hours, during which time not one single member of your staff gave me any explanation for the delay or assured me I had not been forgotten. When I finally asked if I were forgotten, I was treated with a very bad attitude ("how dare I even ask!") and still was given no reason for the delay or any estimate of how much longer I would have to wait. Consequently, I left without seeing you.

As I stated above, I make this change with very real regret, because I value your expertise and the treatment you personally have given the four of us during these past many years. But I will not tolerate the callous treatment of your staff.

Sincerely yours,

Mrs. _____

Questions

1. In this chapter, we referred to Maister's First and Second Laws of Service. How do they relate to this case?
2. What features of a good waiting process are evident in Dr. X's practice? List the shortcomings that you see.
3. Do you think that Mrs. F is typical of most people waiting for a service? How so? How not?
4. If Dr. X were concerned with keeping the F family as patients, how could he have responded to Mrs. F's letter? Write a letter on Dr. X's behalf to Mrs. F.
5. How could Dr. X prevent such incidents in the future?
6. List constructive ways in which customers can respond when services fall seriously short of their requirements or expectations.

Field Study — CASE 12.3

Go forth armed with clipboard and stopwatch and study an actual waiting experience (e.g., post office, fast-food restaurant, retail bank). Begin with a sketch of the layout noting the queue configuration. Describe the characteristics of the calling population and the queue discipline in use. For the arrival process, take a large enough sample of the time in minutes between arrivals to determine if the distribution between arrivals is distributed exponentially (or arrivals per hour are Poisson distributed). Collect a sample of the service times to determine if they are distributed exponentially.

Selected Bibliography

Buell, Ryan W., and Michael I. Norton. "The Labor Illusion: How Operational Transparency Increases Perceived Value." *Management Science* 57 (September 2011), pp. 1564–79.

Cayirli, Tugba, Emre Veral, and Harry Rosen. "Assessment of Patient Classification in Appointment System Design." *Production and Operations Management* 17, no. 3 (May–June 2008), pp. 338–53.

Chambers, Chester, and Panagiotis Kouvelis. "Modeling and Managing the Percentage of Satisfied Customers in Hidden and Revealed Waiting Line Systems." *Production and Operations Management* 15, no. 1 (Spring 2006), pp. 103–16.

Gillam, G., et al. "Line, Line, Everywhere a Line: Cultural Considerations for Waiting-Line Managers." *Business Horizons* 57, no. 4 (2014), pp. 533–39.

Ibrahim, Rouba, and Ward Whitt. "Real-Time Delay Estimation Based on Delay History in Many-Server Service Systems with Time-Varying Arrivals." *Production and Operations Management* 20, no. 5 (September–October 2011), pp. 654–67.

Lakshmi, C., and Sivakumar Appa Iyer. "Application of Queuing Theory in Healthcare: A Literature Review." *Operations Research for Health Care* 2, no. 1 (2013), pp. 25–39.

Perry, Jonathan, et al. "Fastpass: A Centralized Zero-Queue Datacenter Network." *ACM SIGCOMM Computer Communication Review* 44, no. 4 (2014).

Salzaruo, Peter A., Kurt M. Bretthauer, Murray J. Cote, and Kenneth L. Schultz. "The Impact of Variability and Patient Information on Health Care System Performance." *Production and Operations Management* 20, no. 6 (November–December 2011), pp. 848–59.

Voorhees, Clay M., et al. "It Depends: Moderating the Relationships Among Perceived Waiting Time, Anger, and Regret." *Journal of Service Research* 12, no. 2 (November 2009), pp. 138–55.

Whiting, Anita, and Naveen Donthu. "Managing Voice-to-Voice Encounters: Reducing the Agony of Being Put on Hold." *Journal of Service Research* 8, no. 3 (February 2006), pp. 234–44.

Wu, Tim. *The Attention Merchants: The Epic Scramble to Get Inside Our Heads.* New York: Knopf, 2016

Xu, Kuang, and Carri W. Chan. "Using Future Information to Reduce Waiting Times in the Emergency Department via Diversion." *Manufacturing & Service Operations Management* 18.3 (2016): 314–31.

Endnotes

1. Yoram Barzel, "A Theory of Rationing by Waiting," *Journal of Law and Economics* 17, no. 1 (April 1974), p. 74.
2. Adapted from David H. Maister, "The Psychology of Waiting Lines." In J. A. Czepiel, M. R. Solomon, and C. F. Surprenant (eds.), *The Service Encounter.* Lexington, Mass.: Lexington Press, 1985, chap. 8, pp. 113–23.
3. For a discussion of slips and skips, see Richard C. Larson, "Perspectives on Queues: Social Justice and the Psychology of Queuing," *Operations Research* 35, no. 6 (November–December 1987), pp. 895–905.
4. http://www.tsa.gov/what-we-do/escreening.shtm.
5. http://www.fta.gov./4390.html.
6. This case, sad to say, is true in its entirety. The names of the physician and his staff have been omitted, not to protect them but because this kind of treatment of patients is so pervasive in the American health care system that it serves no purpose to identify them. We offer the case for two reasons: first, because it is very instructive regarding important material in this chapter, and second, because it points out that customers and providers must work together in our evolving service society. Service providers must be sensitive to the needs of customers and customers must demand and reward good service.

Chapter 13

Capacity Planning and Queuing Models

Learning Objectives

After completing this chapter, you should be able to:

1. Discuss the strategic role of capacity planning.
2. Describe a queuing model using the *A/B/C* notation.
3. Use queuing models to calculate system performance measures.
4. Describe the relationships between queuing system characteristics.
5. Use queuing models and various decision criteria for capacity planning.

The capacity planning decision involves a trade-off between the cost of providing a service and the cost or inconvenience of customer waiting. The cost of service capacity is determined by the number of servers on duty, whereas customer inconvenience is measured by waiting time. Figure 13.1 illustrates this trade-off, assuming that a monetary cost can be attributed to waiting. Increasing service capacity typically results in lower waiting costs and higher service costs. If the combined cost to the firm constitutes our planning criterion, then an optimal service capacity minimizes these service-versus-waiting costs.

Xerox Corporation faced precisely this dilemma when it introduced the Model 9200 Duplicating System.[1] The company's existing service and maintenance operation, which consisted of individual technical representatives serving individual territories, no longer was able to provide the level of service that gave the company its decisive competitive advantage. Compromising the level of service meant that customers would have to wait, which would translate in this case into lost revenue for the customer (and, indirectly, for Xerox). Consequently, Xerox performed a queuing analysis to determine the best way to resolve its dilemma. Initial constraints, primarily involving human factors such as some

FIGURE 13.1
Economic Trade-Off in Capacity Planning

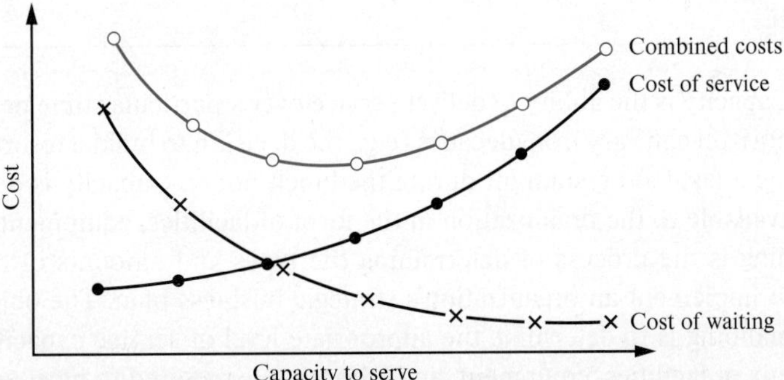

loss of autonomy by the technical representatives and perceptions by the customer of less "personal" attention, led the company to consider establishing miniteams of service people who could provide faster service for more customers.

The cost to the Xerox customer was straightforward, because the Model 9200 was being used to replace a printer's previous offset system. Thus, a Xerox machine that was "down" meant lost income. The problem Xerox faced at this point was to determine the appropriate number of members to assign to each team. The company used queuing analysis to minimize both the customer waiting cost and the Xerox service cost, and arrived at an optimum result of three representatives per team. The monetary cost of delaying a customer usually is more difficult to calculate than in this example and sometimes it is impossible to determine. In a hospital, the cost of keeping a surgical team waiting for a pathologist's report could be the combined salaries of the team members plus the operating room cost. The cost of keeping a patient waiting in the reception room for a physician, however, is not easily calculated because circumstances affect the customer's perception of waiting.

The trade-off between customer waiting and service capacity can be seen daily. For example, an emergency ambulance seldom is busy more than 30 percent of the time. Such low utilization is required in exchange for the ability to provide assistance on a moment's notice. Excess ambulance capacity is necessary, because the implicit cost of waiting for this particular service is exorbitant in terms of human lives. The usual scene at a post office, however, is lines of impatient people waiting for service. Here, a judgment has been made that the implicit cost of waiting is not critical—and certainly not life-threatening—and, in addition, customers have few alternatives. Another result of this strategy is harried postal employees, who might not be able to provide the best possible service under the pressure of demanding customers!

Chapter Preview

The chapter begins with a discussion of the strategic role of capacity planning for service firms. The lack of control over customer demands for service and the presence of the customer in the process complicate capacity planning. For services, it is necessary to predict the degree of customer waiting associated with different levels of capacity. This chapter presents a number of analytical queuing models for use in making these waiting time predictions. The models are analytical and equations have been derived for each case. Given a minimal amount of data—in particular, the mean arrival rate and the mean service rate—the equations can generate characteristics of the system, such as the average time a customer should expect to wait. From these calculations, capacity planning decisions, such as determining the size of a parking lot, can be made, using different criteria. In addition, the queuing models help explain the queuing phenomenon. The models, for example, can predict the results of adding servers to a multiple-server system, as shown in the Xerox case, or they can show the effect of reducing service time variation on waiting time.

Capacity Planning

Capacity is the ability to deliver service over a particular time period. For services, the time horizon can vary from decades (e.g., the decision to build a resort hotel) to hours (e.g., staffing a fast-food restaurant during the lunch hour). Capacity is determined by the resources available to the organization in the form of facilities, equipment, and labor. Capacity planning is the process of determining the types and amounts of resources that are required to implement an organization's strategic business plan. The objective of strategic capacity planning is to determine the appropriate level of service capacity by specifying the proper mix of facilities, equipment, and labor that is required to meet anticipated demand.

Capacity planning is a challenge for service firms because of the open system nature of service operations and, thus, the inability to create a steady flow of activity to use capacity fully. For service systems, idle capacity (e.g., service providers waiting for customers) always is a reality. As noted in Chapter 12, Managing Waiting Lines, customer arrivals can fluctuate from one minute to the next (e.g., a call center) and the time customers spend being served also varies (e.g., diners at a gourmet restaurant). Because of the inability of services to control the demands placed upon them, capacity usually is measured in terms of inputs (e.g., number of hotel rooms) rather than outputs (e.g., guest nights).

The capacity decision is complicated further because customers are participants in the service process and the level of congestion has an impact on the quality of the service experience. The recent increase in customer complaints about flying experiences is related directly to the success of airlines in filling their planes to capacity (e.g., consider your anxiety while hoping no one will sit in the center seat next to you). On the other hand, however, people seek out the excitement of a crowded nightclub.

Strategic Role of Capacity Decisions

Capacity decisions in services have strategic importance based on the time horizon in question. The decision to build a luxury hotel in a city can be a preemptive strike against a competitor, because the market demand for guests is so limited that only one hotel can survive. This occurs because capacity of fixed facilities comes in economically feasible sizes (e.g., a 500-room luxury hotel versus a 100-room budget motel). Thus, if a luxury hotel can be feasible with a 60 percent average occupancy, a market of 300 guest nights will support only one hotel. For this reason we seldom find both a Ritz Carlton and a Four Seasons hotel in midsized cities.

Failure to plan for short-term capacity needs, such as staffing for the lunch hour, can generate customers for the competition. This is true particularly when customers can gauge the expected waiting time by observing the length of the queue and then renege or balk, seeking service elsewhere.

Significant and irreversible financial investment (e.g., building a hotel) results from a capacity decision that must be balanced against the costs of lost sales if capacity is inadequate or against operating losses if demand does not reach expectations. Because physical capacity (i.e., facilities and equipment) is added in discrete units (e.g., adding another aircraft to a fleet), the ability to match capacity with demand is fruitless and a strategy of building ahead of demand often is taken to avoid losing customers. Communication providers such as AT&T, which first supported the iPhone, learned that a successful marketing campaign can lead to hostile customers if capacity is not in place to handle the growing demand. To illustrate a common mistake, Example 13.1 shows an inappropriate approach to planning service capacity by ignoring the queuing phenomenon found in service operations.

Example 13.1 Capacity Planning for Cookies and Cream—Naive Approach

An enterprising student is considering opening a "Cookies and Ice Cream" shop in space that has become available in a food court. Observations of traffic during the lunch hour suggest a potential peak demand of 50 customers, each ordering on average one ice cream sundae, six baked-to-order cookies, and a 12-ounce self-serve soft drink and spending 20 minutes at a table.

A cookie sheet can accommodate a dozen cookies and baking time is 10 minutes. One server requires on average 6 minutes to take an order, mix a batch of cookies, make change, prepare the sundae, and assemble the order. Capacity requirements are determined by calculating the units of facility, equipment, and labor needed to accommodate the anticipated peak demand.

Facility requirements include the seats necessary to accommodate diners. We will use a relationship called "Little's Law," discussed later in the chapter, to calculate the seats required. Little's Law states that the average number of customers in a system (L) is equal to the arrival rate (λ) times the average waiting time (W) or $L = \lambda W$. With 50 customers arriving during the peak hour and each staying approximately 20 minutes, or one-third of an hour, we need (50)(20/60) = 16.7 chairs.

Equipment requirements include the calculation of the number of cookie sheets needed. This is determined by dividing the total number of cookies ordered for the hour by the capability of one cookie sheet that is used for only 10 minutes per batch (i.e., reused 6 times per hour). Assume that orders can be combined to fill a sheet.

$$\text{Number of cookie sheets needed} = \frac{\text{(50 customers/hour)(6 cookies/order)}}{\text{(12 cookies/sheet)(6 cycles/hour)}} = 4.17$$

Labor requirement is focused on calculating the number of servers required. As in the equipment calculations, we divide the total minutes of server time demanded for the hour by one unit of service capability (i.e., 60 minutes available for the hour).

$$\text{Number of servers needed} = \frac{\text{(50 customers/hour)(6 minutes each)}}{\text{(60 minutes/hour)}} = 5.0$$

Caution needs to be exercised in implementing the results of such a naive capacity planning exercise. Excess capacity is required in a service system because variability in customer arrivals and service times is the expectation and creates idle capacity that is lost. As we shall see in the queuing model section, the capacity to serve must *exceed* the arrival rate to avoid out-of-control waiting lines. Because the calculations for capacity needs are based on averages, the results represent an infeasible solution to our capacity requirements. Our capacity planning analysis of Cookies and Cream will be revisited in Example 13.6 with a more sophisticated queuing analysis after our discussion of queuing models.

Analytical Queuing Models

Many different queuing models exist. A popular system classifies parallel-server queuing models using the following notation in which three features are identified: *A/B/C*. *A* represents the distribution of time between arrivals, *B* the distribution of service times, and *C* the number of parallel servers (e.g., cashiers at a supermarket). The descriptive symbols used for the arrival and service distributions include

M = exponential interarrival or service time distribution (or the equivalent Poisson distribution of arrival or service rate)

D = deterministic or constant interarrival or service time

E_k = Erlang distribution with shape parameter k (if $k = 1$, then Erlang is equivalent to exponential; if $k = \infty$, then Erlang is equivalent to deterministic)

G = general distribution with mean and variance (e.g., normal, uniform, or any empirical distribution)

Thus, *M/M/*1 designates a single-server queuing model with Poisson arrival rate and exponential service time distribution. The *A/B/C* notation will be used here to define the class to which a queuing model belongs. Further considerations that are particular to the model in question, such as if the queue length is *finite* because of little space (e.g., a parking lot) or a small number of potential customers (e.g., an office cafeteria), will be noted. Figure 13.2 classifies the six analytical queuing models that we will study in this chapter according to these features using the *A/B/C* notation. Each queuing model (e.g., *M/M/*1) also is given a roman numeral (e.g., I, II, III) to designate a set of equations for that model. These equations are repeated in Appendix D, Equations for Selected Queuing Models.

A final consideration involves the concepts of *transient state* and *steady state*. In a transient state, the values of the operating characteristics of a system depend on time. In a steady state, the system characteristics are independent of time, and the system is considered to be in statistical equilibrium. Because of their dependence on initial

FIGURE 13.2 **Classification of Queuing Models**

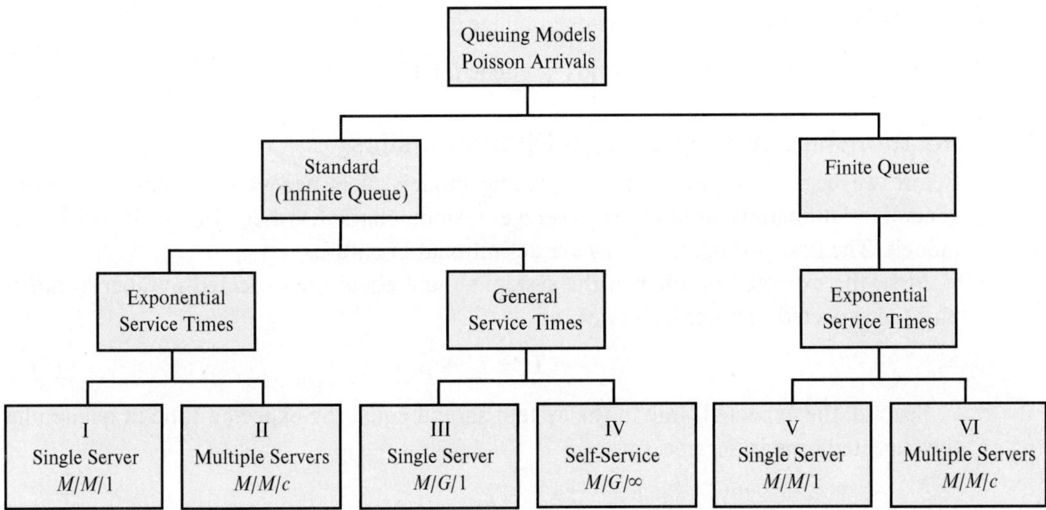

conditions, system characteristics usually are transient during the early stages of operation. For example, compare the initial conditions for a department store at opening time on a normal business day and on an end-of-year-sale day, when crowds overwhelm the clerks. The number in queue initially will be quite large, but given a long enough period of time, the system eventually will settle down. Once normal conditions have been reached, a statistical equilibrium is achieved in which the number in queue assumes a distribution that is independent of the starting condition. All the queuing model equations found in Appendix D assume that a steady state has been reached. Most service systems operate in a dynamic environment, with arrival rates sometimes changing every hour; thus, a steady state seldom is achieved. However, steady-state models can provide useful system performance projections for long-range capacity planning decisions.

For each queuing model, the assumptions underlying its derivation are noted. The usefulness of an analytical model for a particular situation is limited by these assumptions. If the assumptions are invalid for a particular application (e.g., Poisson arrival rate does not apply), then one typically resorts to a computer simulation (see the end-of-chapter supplement, Computer Simulation).

Applications of these queuing models to decision-making situations use the equations found in Appendix D. The symbols used in these models and their definitions are

n = number of customers in the system

λ = [lambda] mean arrival rate (e.g., customer arrivals per hour)

μ = [mu] mean service rate per busy server (e.g., service capacity in customers per hour)

ρ = [rho](λ/μ) mean number of customers in service

N = maximum number of customers allowed in the system

c = number of servers

P_n = probability of exactly n customers in the system

L_s = mean number of customers in the system

L_q = mean number of customers in queue

L_b = mean number of customers in queue for a busy system

W_s = mean time customer spends in the system

W_q = mean time customer spends in queue

W_b = mean time customer spends in queue for a busy system

Relationships among System Characteristics

Before we begin our discussion of queuing models, it is necessary to point out some general relationships among the average system characteristics that exist across all models. The first two relationships are definitional in nature.

First, the expected number in the system should equal the expected number in queue plus the expected number in service, or

$$L_s = L_q + \rho \tag{1}$$

Second, the expected time in the system should equal the expected time in queue plus the expected time in service, or

$$W_s = W_q + \frac{1}{\mu} \tag{2}$$

where $1/\mu$ is the reciprocal of the service rate.

Further, the following relationship exists between the expected number in the system and the expected time in the system:

$$W_s = \frac{1}{\lambda} L_s \tag{3}$$

This relationship, referred to as Little's Law, when restated as $L = \lambda W$, also holds true for the expected number in queue and the expected waiting time:[2]

$$W_q = \frac{1}{\lambda} L_q \tag{4}$$

The characteristics for a busy system are conditional values that are based on the probability that the system is busy, or $P(n \geq c)$. Thus, the expected number in queue for a busy system simply is the expected number under all system states divided by the probability of the system being busy, or

$$L_b = \frac{L_q}{P(n \geq c)} \tag{5}$$

Similarly, the expected waiting time in queue for a busy system is

$$W_b = \frac{W_q}{P(n \geq c)} \tag{6}$$

When equations (1) and (6) are applied for systems with a finite queue, an effective arrival rate must be used for λ. For a system with a finite queue, the effective arrival rate is $\lambda(1 - P_N)$.

These relationships are very useful because they permit derivation of all the average characteristics of a system from the knowledge of one characteristic obtained by analysis or by the collection of data on actual system performance (e.g., the average wait time of customers in queue–Wq).

Standard *M/M/*1 Model

Every queuing model requires specific assumptions regarding the queuing system features (i.e., calling population, arrival process, queue configuration, queue discipline, and service process). The application of any queuing model, therefore, should include validation with respect to these assumptions. The derivation of the standard *M/M/*1 model requires the following set of assumptions about the queuing system:

1. *Calling population.* An infinite or very large population of callers arriving. The callers are independent of each other and not influenced by the queuing system (e.g., no appointments or reservations allowed).
2. *Arrival process.* Negative exponential distribution of interarrival times or Poisson distribution of arrival rate.
3. *Queue configuration.* Single waiting line with no restrictions on length and no balking or reneging.
4. *Queue discipline.* First-come, first-served (FCFS).
5. *Service process.* One server with negative exponential distribution of service times.

Figure 13.3 presents a schematic for the *M/M/*1 queuing model that shows the single server as a circle within a square, which denotes a customer in service. The Poisson arrival rate has a mean of λ, and an arrow indicates that future customers join the end of the queue. The mean service rate of μ is shown with an arrow below the server. The illustration has three customers in queue (L_q) and four customers in the system (L_s). Keep this schematic in mind as we explore applications of the formulas for the single-server queuing system.

The selected equations found in Appendix D can be used to calculate performance characteristics on the basis of only the mean arrival rate λ and the mean service rate per server μ. These equations clearly indicate why the mean service rate μ for a single-server model must be greater than the mean arrival rate λ (i.e., capacity must *exceed* demand). If this condition were not true and μ was equal to λ, the mean values for the operating characteristics would be undefined, because all the equations for mean values have the denominator ($\mu - \lambda$). Theoretically, the system would never reach a steady state with the queue growing to infinity.

Example 13.2 Boat Ramp

Lake Travis has one launching ramp near the dam for people who trailer their small boats to the recreational site. A study of cars arriving with boats in tow indicates a Poisson distribution with a mean rate of $\lambda = 6$ boats per hour during the morning launch. A test of the data collected on launch times suggests that an exponential distribution with a mean of 6 minutes per boat (equivalent service rate $\mu = 10$ boats launched per hour) is a good fit. If the other assumptions for an *M/M/*1 model apply (i.e., infinite calling population, no queue length restrictions, no balking or reneging, and FCFS queue discipline), then the equations found in Appendix D (and repeated here) can be used to calculate the system characteristics.

(Note: $\rho = \lambda/\mu = 6/10 = 0.6$.)

Probability that the system is busy and an arriving customer waits (i.e., $k = 1$):

$$P(n \geq k) = \rho^k = \rho^1 = 0.6^1 = 0.6 \tag{I.2}$$

Probability of finding the ramp idle:

$$P_0 = 1 - \rho = 0.4 \tag{I.1}$$

Mean number of boats in the system:

$$L_s = \frac{\lambda}{\mu - \lambda} = \frac{6}{10 - 6} = 1.5 \text{ boats} \tag{I.4}$$

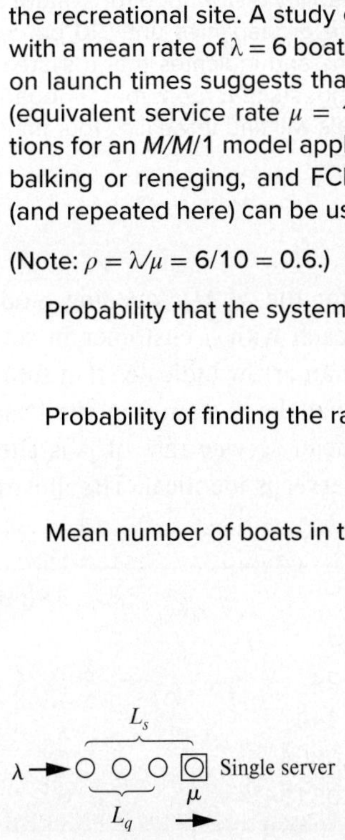

FIGURE 13.3
M/M/1 Queue Configuration

L_s

λ → ○ ○ ○ ▣ Single server

L_q μ →

Mean number of boats in queue:

$$L_q = \frac{\rho\lambda}{\mu - \lambda} = \frac{(0.6)(6)}{10 - 6} = 0.9 \text{ boat} \quad \textbf{(I.5)}$$

Mean time in the system:

$$W_s = \frac{1}{\mu - \lambda} = \frac{1}{10 - 6} = 0.25 \text{ hour (15min.)} \quad \textbf{(I.7)}$$

Mean time in queue:

$$W_q = \frac{\rho}{\mu - \lambda} = \frac{0.6}{10 - 6} = 0.15 \text{ hour (9min.)} \quad \textbf{(I.8)}$$

From our calculations, we find that the boat ramp is busy 60 percent of the time. Thus, arrivals can expect immediate access to the ramp without delay 40 percent of the time (i.e., when the ramp is idle). The calculations are internally consistent, because the mean time in the system (W_s) of 15 minutes is the sum of the mean time in queue (W_q) of 9 minutes and the mean service time of 6 minutes. Arrivals can expect to find the number in the system (L_s) to be 1.5 boats and the expected number in queue (L_q) to be 0.9 boat. The expected number of boats in queue plus the expected number being launched should sum to the expected number of boats in the system. The expected number of boats being launched is not 1.0, but instead is the probability of a busy system multiplied by one server or $\rho(1) = 0.6$ boat. Adding 0.6 boat on average in the process of being launched and 0.9 boat on average in queue, we get the expected 1.5 boats in the system.

Note that the number of customers in the system, *n,* is a random variable with a probability distribution given by equation (I.3), which is found in Appendix D and repeated here with $(1 - \rho)$ substituted for P_0

$$P_n = (1 - \rho)\rho^n \quad \textbf{(I.3)}$$

The number of customers in the system also can be used to identify system states. For example, when $n = 0$, the system is idle. When $n = 1$, the server is busy but no queue exists; when $n = 2$, the server is busy and a queue of 1 has formed. The probability distribution for *n* can be very useful in determining the proper size of a waiting area.

For the boat ramp example, determine the number of parking spaces needed to ensure that 90 percent of the time, a person arriving at the boat ramp will find a space to park while waiting to launch. Repeatedly using the probability distribution for system states for increasing values of *n,* we accumulate the system-state probabilities until 90 percent assurance is exceeded. Table 13.1 contains these calculations and indicates that a system state of $n = 4$ or less will occur 92 percent of the time. This suggests that room for four boat trailers should be provided because 92 percent of the time arrivals will find three (i.e., four minus the one being served) or fewer people waiting in queue to launch.

Standard *M/M/c* Model

Figure 13.4 presents a schematic for the *M/M/c* queuing model that shows "*c*" servers in parallel (using the • symbol), each with a customer in service. The Poisson arrival rate with a mean of λ is shown and an arrow indicates that future customers join a single queue. A dashed arrow indicates that the customer at the head of the queue will move to the first available server. The mean service rate of μ is shown with an arrow below the server and signifies that each server is identical. The illustration is shown with three

TABLE 13.1
Determining Required Number of Parking Spaces

n	P_n	P(number of customers $\leq n$)
0	$(0.4)(0.6)^0 = 0.4$	0.4
1	$(0.4)(0.6)^1 = 0.24$	0.64
2	$(0.4)(0.6)^2 = 0.144$	0.784
3	$(0.4)(0.6)^3 = 0.0864$	0.8704
4	$(0.4)(0.6)^4 = 0.05184$	0.92224

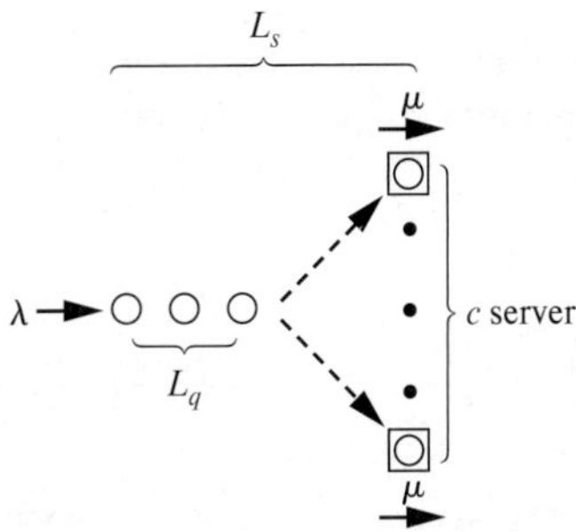

FIGURE 13.4
***M/M/c* Queue Configuration**

customers in queue (L_q) and five customers in the system (L_s) assuming two servers. Keep this schematic in mind as we explore applications of the formulas for the single queue, multiple server queuing system.

The assumptions for the standard *M/M/c* model are the same as those for the standard *M/M*/1 model, with the stipulation that service rates across channels be independent and equal (i.e., all servers are considered to be identical). As before, $\rho = \lambda/\mu$; however, ρ (mean number of customers being served) now must be less than *c,* the number of servers, for steady-state results to occur. If we define the system utilization factor as $\lambda/c\mu$, then for any steady-state system, the utilization factor must range between 0 and 1. Figure 13.5 illustrates the characteristic curves for L_s as a function of the utilization factor and *c,* the number of parallel servers. These curves graphically demonstrate the excessive congestion that occurs as one attempts to gain full utilization of service capacity.

The curves also can be used to demonstrate the disproportional gain that occurs when congestion is reduced by adding parallel servers. For example, consider a single server system ($c = 1$) with a utilization factor of 0.8. From Figure 13.5, the value of L_s is 4. By adding another identical server, a two-channel system is created, and the utilization factor is reduced by one-half to 0.4. Figure 13.5 gives $L_s \approx 1$, and a 400 percent reduction in congestion is achieved just by doubling the number of servers.

Now, instead of creating a two-channel system, double the service rate of the single-server system and, thus, reduce the utilization factor to 0.4. Figure 13.5 gives $L_s \approx 0.67$ for this superserver system; however, this additional gain in reducing L_s is obtained at the cost of increasing the expected number in queue (from $L_q = 0.15$ to 0.27), as seen in Table 13.2. This is not surprising, because a single-server system would require more people to wait in line. In a multiple-server system of equal capacity, more people are able to be in service; thus, fewer wait in line. Therefore, the decision to use one superserver or the equivalent

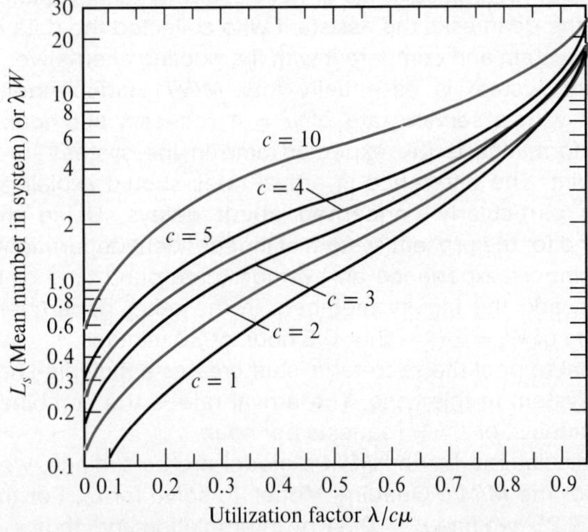

FIGURE 13.5
M/M/c Model Curves for L_s

TABLE 13.2
Effects of Doubling Service Capacity

System Characteristic	Single-Server Baseline System	Two-Server System	Single-Superserver System
ρ	0.8	0.8	0.4
$(\lambda/c\mu)$*	0.8	0.4	0.4
L_s	4.0	0.95	0.67
L_q	3.2	0.15	0.27

*Utilization factor.

capacity with several servers in parallel depends on whether to focus on waiting time in queue or time in the system.

As noted in Chapter 11, Managing Capacity and Demand, a concern for reducing the waiting time in queue usually is advisable, particularly if people must wait in line physically. Further, once service begins, the customer's attitude toward time changes, because now the customer is the center of attention. However, in the early days of mainframe computers an entire university community was served by one central computer because short turnaround time (i.e., time in the system) and computational power were of primary importance.

Consolidating the entire service capacity into a single superserver is one approach to achieving economies of scale in services. Another is the concept of pooling services, which is accomplished by gathering together independent servers at one central location to form a single service facility with multiple servers.

Example 13.3 The Secretarial Pool

A small business school has assigned a secretary to each of its four departments: accounting, finance, marketing, and management. Each secretary prepares class materials and correspondence only for her or his own departmental faculty. The dean has received complaints from the faculty, however, and particularly from the accounting faculty, about delays in getting work accomplished. The dean assigns an assistant to collect data on arrival rates and service times. After analyzing these data, the assistant reports that secretarial work arrives with a Poisson distribution at an average rate of $\lambda = 2$ requests per hour for all departments except accounting, which has an average rate of $\lambda = 3$ requests per hour. The average time to complete a piece of work is 15 minutes regardless of its source, and the service times are distributed exponentially.

Because of budget limitations, no additional secretaries can be hired. The dean believes, however, that service could be improved if all the secretaries were pooled and instructed to receive work from the entire business school faculty. All work requests would be received at one central location and processed on a first-come, first-served basis by the first secretary who became available, regardless of his or her departmental affiliation. Before proposing the plan to the faculty, the dean asks the assistant who collected the data to analyze the performance of the existing system and compare it with the pooling alternative.

The present system is essentially four *M/M/*1 independent, single-channel queuing systems, each with a service rate of $\mu = 4$ requests per hour. The appropriate measure of system performance is the expected time in the system—or turnaround time, from the faculty viewpoint. The difference in arrival rates should explain why the accounting faculty members are particularly concerned about delays. Using the *M/M/*1 equation $W_s = 1/(\mu - \lambda)$, we find for the present system of independent departmental secretaries that accounting faculty members experience an average turnaround time of $W_s = 1/(4 - 3) = 1.0$ hour, or 60 minutes, and the faculty members in the other departments experience an average turnaround time of $W_s = 1/(4 - 2) = 0.5$ hour, or 30 minutes.

The proposal to pool the secretarial staff creates a multiple-channel, single-queue system, or an *M/M/*4 system in this case. The arrival rate is the combined arrivals (2 + 2 + 2 + 3) from all departments, or $\lambda = 9$ requests per hour.

Because calculations for the *M/M/c* model are so tedious, we typically use Appendix C, Values of *Lq* for the *M/M/c* Queuing Model, to solve for L_q. For this problem, in which $c = 4$ and $\rho = 9/4 = 2.25$ we find $L_q = 0.31$ by interpolation and, thus, $L_s = L_q + \rho = 2.56$.

Using equation (5)

$$W_s = \frac{L_s}{\lambda} = \frac{2.56}{9} = 0.28 \text{ hour, or } 17 \text{ minutes}$$

The substantial reduction in expected turnaround time from 30 minutes (60 minutes for the accounting faculty) to 17 minutes should easily win faculty approval.

The benefits from pooling are achieved through better utilization of idle secretaries. Under the departmental system, four independent queues existed, which allowed situations to develop in which a secretary in one department could be burdened with a long waiting line of work whereas a secretary in another department was idle. If a waiting request could be transferred to the idle secretary, then it would be processed immediately. Switching to a single queue avoids the utilization problem by not allowing a secretary to become idle until the waiting line of requests is empty.

The success of pooling service resources comes from realizing that congestion results from variation in the rate of arrivals and service times. If a total systems perspective of the process is taken, temporary idleness at one location can be used to reduce congestion at another that has been caused by a temporary surge in demand or time-consuming requests. Further, server idleness that can be put to use, but is not, represents lost service capacity and results in a deterioration of service quality as measured by customer waiting. The concept of pooling need not apply only to servers who are at different locations. The common practice in banks and post offices of having customers form a single queue rather than line up in front of the individual windows represents an application of the pooling concept. Theoretically, the average waiting time is reduced from that of multiple queues; however, the single long line may give arriving customers the impression of long waits. This is the reason McDonald's gave for abandoning the idea: it was feared that customers would balk if they were to see a long line.

Pooling service resources at one location should be undertaken with some caution if customers must travel to that facility. In this case, the expected travel time to the facility should be included with the expected waiting time in queue when the proposal is evaluated. For emergency services, dispersing servers throughout the service area generally is preferred to assigning all services to one central location. An emergency ambulance system is a particularly good example of this need for physically dispersed servers to minimize response time.

*M/G/*1 Model

For the *M/G/*1 model, any general service time distribution with mean $E(t)$ and variance $V(t)$ may be used. The condition that ρ be less than 1 still applies for the steady state, where ρ now equals $\lambda E(t)$. Except for the generality of the service time distribution, all of the assumptions for the standard *M/M/*1 model apply. Unfortunately, an equation does not exist for determining the system-state probabilities; however, the list of equations in Appendix D does contain equations for L_s, L_q, W_s, and W_q. Equation (III.2) is repeated here, because the appearance of the service time variance term $V(t)$ provides some interesting insights:

$$L_q = \frac{\rho^2 + \lambda^2 V(t)}{2(1-\rho)} \qquad \text{(III.2)}$$

Clearly, the expected number of customers waiting for service relates directly to the variability of service times. This suggests that customer waiting can be reduced by controlling the variability in service times. For example, the limited menu of fast-food restaurants contributes to their success, because such reduction in the variety of offered meals allows for standardization of service.

Recall that the variance of the exponential distribution is $1/\mu^2$, and note that substituting this value for $V(t)$ in equation (III.2) yields $L_q = \rho^2/(1-\rho)$, which is equivalent to equation (I.5) for the standard *M/M/*1 model. Now consider the *M/D/*1 model, with a deterministic service time and zero variance. Again, according to equation (III.2), when $V(t) = 0$, then $L_q = \rho^2/[2(1-\rho)]$. Thus, one-half of the congestion measured by

L_q is explained by the variation in service times. This implies that the variability in time between arrivals accounts for the remaining congestion. Thus, considerable potential exists for reducing congestion simply by using appointments or reservations to control the variability in arrivals. Congestion in a queuing system is caused equally by variability in service times and interarrival times; therefore, strategies for controlling congestion should address both sources.

General Self-Service $M/G/\infty$ Model

If a multiple-server system has an infinite number of servers or arrivals serve themselves, then no arriving customer must wait for service. This, of course, describes exactly the concept that has made the modern supermarket so popular. At least during the shopping portion (excluding checkout), customers do not experience waiting. The number of customers in the process of shopping does vary because of random arrivals and differing service times, and the probability distribution of the number of customers in the system can be calculated by means of equation (IV.1), which is repeated here.

Note that this distribution for P_n in fact is Poisson, with the mean, or L_s, being equal to ρ. Further, this model is not restricted to an exponential distribution of service times.

$$P_n = \frac{e^{-p}}{n!}\rho^n \quad \text{where} \quad L_s = \rho \tag{IV.1}$$

This model also is useful as an approximation to describe circumstances in which waiting might occur only rarely (e.g., emergency ambulance services). Using the Poisson distribution of the number of customers in the system, we can calculate the number of servers that is required to ensure that the probability of someone waiting is quite small.

Example 13.4 Supermarket

The typical supermarket can be viewed as two queuing systems in tandem. The arriving customer secures a shopping cart and proceeds to serve himself or herself by picking items from the shelves. On completing this task, the shopper joins a single queue (a new idea to reduce waiting caused by multiple queues) behind the checkout registers. The checker tallies the bill, makes change, and sacks the groceries; thereupon the shopper exits the store.

With Poisson-distributed arrivals, departures from a queuing system also are Poisson-distributed, allowing the supermarket system to be analyzed as two independent systems in series. The first is a self-service shopping, or $M/M/\infty$, system, and the second (at the cash registers) is an $M/M/c$ system. Observation of customer behavior indicates that arrivals are Poisson-distributed, with a rate of 30 per hour, and that shopping is completed in 20 minutes on the average, with exponential distribution. Shoppers then join the single queue behind the three checkout registers and wait until a register becomes available. The checkout process requires 5 minutes on average, with exponential distribution.

For the shopping experience, the $M/M/\infty$ model applies, with $\rho = 30/3$, resulting in $L_s = 10$ customers on the average being engaged in the shopping activity. To study the checkout system, we use Appendix C with $c = 3$ and $\rho = 30/12 = 2.5$, and find that $L_q = 3.5$. The average number of customers in the checkout area is $L_s = L_q + \rho = 6$ customers. Together, we find on average a total of 16 shoppers in the store. The expected time that a customer spends in the supermarket is 20 minutes shopping plus 12 minutes (i.e., $L_s/\lambda = 6/30 = 0.2$ hour) checking out, for a total of 32 minutes.

Finite-Queue $M/M/1$ Model

A modification of the standard $M/M/1$ model can be made by introducing a restriction on the number of customers allowed in the system. Let N represent the maximum number of customers allowed; thus, if a customer arrives and finds N customers already are in the system, then the arrival departs without seeking service. An example of this type of *finite queue* is a telephone exchange in which callers are put on hold until all the trunk lines are in use; then, any further callers receive a busy signal. Except for this one characteristic of finite capacity, all of the assumptions of the standard $M/M/1$ model still hold. Note that the traffic intensity ρ now can exceed unity. Further, P_N represents the probability of not joining the system, and λP_N is the expected number of customers who are lost.

This particular model is very useful in estimating lost sales to be expected from an inadequate waiting area or excessive queue length. In the boat ramp Example 13.2, assume that the waiting area can accommodate only two boat trailers; thus, $N = 3$ for the system. Using equations (V.1) and (V.3) found in Appendix D and repeated here, we can calculate the probabilities of 0, 1, 2, and 3 customers being in the system when $N = 3$ and $\rho = 0.6$:

$$P_0 = \frac{1-\rho}{1-\rho^{N+1}} \quad \text{for } \lambda \neq \mu \tag{V.1}$$

$$P_n = P_0\rho^n \quad \text{for } n \leq N \tag{V.3}$$

n	Calculation	P_n
0	$\frac{1-0.6}{1-0.6^4}(0.6)^0$	0.46
1	$(0.46)(0.6)^1$	0.27
2	$(0.46)(0.6)^2$	0.17
3	$(0.46)(0.6)^3$	0.10
		1.00

Note that this distribution totals 1.00, which indicates that we have accounted for all possible system states. System state $n = 3$ occurs 10 percent of the time. Recall with an arrival rate of 6 people per hour, 0.6 person per hour (6×0.10) will find inadequate waiting space and look elsewhere for a launching site. Using equation (V.4), which is repeated here, we can calculate the expected number in the system (L_s) to be 0.9. This figure is much smaller than that in the unlimited-queue case ($L_s = 1.5$), because on average, only 90 percent of the arrivals are processed.

$$\begin{aligned} L_s &= \frac{\rho}{1-\rho} - \frac{(N+1)\rho^{N+1}}{1-\rho^{N+1}} \quad \text{for } \lambda \neq \mu \qquad \text{(V.4)} \\ &= \frac{0.6}{1-0.6} - \frac{4(0.6)^4}{1-(0.6)^4} \\ &= 1.5 - 0.6 \\ &= 0.9 \end{aligned}$$

Finite-Queue *M/M/c* Model

This finite-queue $M/M/c$ model is similar to the finite-queue $M/M/1$ model, with the exception that N, the maximum number in the system, must be equal to or greater than c, the number of servers. An arriving customer is rejected if the number in the system equals N or the length of the queue is $N - c$. All other assumptions for the standard $M/M/c$ model hold, except that ρ now can exceed c. Because excess customers are rejected, the system can reach a steady state even when the capacity is inadequate to meet the total demand (i.e., $\lambda \geq c\mu$).

An interesting variation on this model is the no-queue situation, which occurs when no possibility exists for a customer to wait—because a waiting area is not provided. This situation can be modeled as a finite-queue system with $N = c$. A parking lot is an illustration of this no-queue situation. If we consider each parking space as a server, then when the parking lot is completely full, an opportunity for further service no longer exists and future arrivals must be rejected. If c equals the number of parking spaces, then the parking lot system can be modeled as a no-queue variation of the finite-queue $M/M/c$ model.

Capacity Planning Criteria

Queuing theory indicates that, in the long run, capacity to serve must exceed the demand. If this criterion is not met, at least one of the following adjustments must occur:

1. Excessive waiting by customers will result in some reneging (i.e., a customer leaves the queue before being served) and, thus, in some reduction of demand.
2. Excessive waiting, if known or observed by potential customers, will cause them to reconsider their need for service and, thus, will reduce demand.
3. Under the pressure of long waiting lines, servers may speed up, spending less time with each customer, and, thus, increase service capacity. A gracious and leisurely manner, however, now becomes curt and impersonal.
4. Sustained pressure to hurry might result in eliminating time-consuming features and performing the bare minimum and, thus, service capacity is increased.

These uncontrolled situations result from inadequate service capacity, which can be avoided through rational capacity planning.

Several approaches to capacity planning are explored on the basis of different criteria for evaluating service system performance. Determining the desired level of service capacity implies a trade-off between the cost of service and the cost of customer waiting, as suggested by Figure 13.1. Thus, capacity analysis will utilize the queuing models to predict customer waiting for various levels of service.

Average Customer Waiting Time

The criterion of average customer waiting time for capacity planning is appropriate in several circumstances. For example, a restaurant owner might wish to promote liquor sales in the bar and, therefore, stipulates that customers be kept waiting 5 minutes on average for a table. It has been suggested that because the face of a watch typically is divided into 5-minute increments, people who are waiting in line might not realize how long they have been waiting until at least 5 minutes have passed. Therefore, in designing a drive-in bank facility, it might be advisable to have customers wait no more than 5 minutes on average for service. In these cases, use of the standard $M/M/c$ model would be appropriate to identify the service capacity in terms of the number of servers that would guarantee the desired expected customer waiting time.

Example 13.5 Drive-in Bank

Excessive congestion is a problem during the weekday noon hour at a downtown drive-in bank facility. Bank officials fear customers might take their accounts elsewhere unless service is improved. A study of customer arrivals during the noon hour indicates an average arrival rate of 30 per hour, with Poisson distribution. Banking transactions take 3 minutes on average, with exponential distribution. Because of the layout of the drive-in facility, arriving customers must select one of three lanes for service. Once a customer is in a lane, it is impossible for him or her to renege or jockey between lanes because of separating medians. Assuming that arriving customers select lanes at random, we can treat the system as parallel, independent, single-channel queuing systems with the arrival rate divided evenly among the tellers. If the bank officers agree to a criterion that customers should wait no more than 5 minutes on average,

TABLE 13.3
Expected Time in Queue for Bank Teller Alternatives

Number of Tellers	λ per Teller	μ	W_b, min.
3	10	20	6
4	7.5	20	4.8

how many drive-in tellers are required? Because we are concerned only with customers who actually wait, equation (I.9), which is repeated here, is appropriate:

$$W_b = \frac{1}{\mu - \lambda} \tag{I.9}$$

For the current three-teller system, arrivals per teller are $\lambda = 30/3 = 10$ per hour. Thus, $W_b = 1/(20 - 10) = 0.1$ hour, or 6 minutes. Table 13.3 indicates that one additional teller is required to meet the service criterion.

Example 13.6 Capacity Planning for Cookies and Cream—Queuing Analysis

In the naive capacity planning for Example 13.1, we used averages to determine that a need existed for 16.7 chairs, 4.17 cookie sheets, and 5 servers. We pointed out that these values would be inadequate because of the nature of services that require capacity in excess of expected demand. Suppose our criterion for acceptable service is an expected customer waiting time in queue of one minute (i.e., $W_Q = 1/60$ hour) for each resource (i.e., chairs, cookie sheets, and servers). Using Little's Law, a one-minute wait time given an arrival rate of $\lambda = 50$ per hour translates into $L_Q = \lambda W_Q = 50/60 = 0.833$. Table 13.4 contains the queuing analysis using Appendix C to find the value for L_Q where possible (i.e., $\rho < 8$) for cookie sheets and servers, and in the case of determining the number of chairs, reverting to the tedious equations for the *M/M/c* model found in Appendix D.

As the queuing analysis indicates, we need many more resources than the naive analysis indicated. This becomes obvious when we realize that the naive analysis was only an exercise in determining the value for $\rho = \lambda/\mu$. But for queuing systems to be feasible, the number of servers must exceed the value of ρ.

Probability of Excessive Waiting

For public services that have difficulty identifying the economic cost of waiting, a service level often is specified. This service level is stated in a manner such that *P* or more percent of all customers should experience a delay of fewer than *T* time units. For example, a federal guideline states that the response time for 95 percent of all ambulance calls should be less than 10 minutes for urban and less than 30 minutes for rural systems. The Public Utilities Commission gives a similar performance criterion for telephone service, directing that telephone service must be provided at a resource level such that 89 percent of the time, an incoming call can be answered within 10 seconds. A probability distribution of delays is required to identify service levels that will meet these probabilities

TABLE 13.4
Queuing Analysis for Cookies and Creams

Resource	μ in Customers/Hour	$\rho = 50/\mu$	Number Required for $L_Q < 0.833$
Chairs	$\frac{60 \text{ min./hr.}}{20 \text{ min./customer}} = 3$	16.7	22*
Cookie sheets	$\frac{(60 \text{ min./hr.})(12 \text{ cookies})}{(10 \text{ min./customer})(6 \text{ cookies})} = 12$	4.17	6
Servers	$\frac{60 \text{ min./lhr.}}{6 \text{ min./customer}} = 10$	5.0	7

*$L_Q = 0.582$ using equations (II.1), (II.4), and (II.5) from Appendix D.

of not exceeding a certain excessive delay, and equations for these delay probabilities are available for the standard $M/M/c$ model. For the case when no delay is desired ($T = 0$), equation (II.3) can be used to find a value for c such that the probability of immediate service is at least P percent.

Example 13.7 Self-Serve Gas Station

A retail gasoline distributor plans to construct a credit/debit-only self-service filling station on vacant property leading into a new housing development. On the basis of the traffic in that area, the distributor forecasts a demand of 24 cars on average per hour. Time studies that have been conducted at other sites reveal an average self-service time of 5 minutes for a driver to fill the tank, pay, and drive away. The service times are distributed exponentially, and past experience justifies assuming an arrival rate with a Poisson distribution. The distributor believes that the success of self-service stations results from competitive gasoline prices and the customers' desires for fast service. Therefore, the distributor would like to install enough pumps to guarantee that arriving customers will find a free pump at least 95 percent of the time. We use equation (II.3) to calculate the probability that a customer waits for various values of c, and results for up to six pumps are summarized in Table 13.5. When $c = 6$, the $P(n \geq c)$ reaches a value of 0.02 and, thus, meets the criterion that fewer than 5 percent of arriving customers have to wait. This result suggests that six pumps should be installed.

Minimizing the Sum of Customer Waiting Costs and Service Costs

If both customers and servers are members of the same organization, then the costs of providing service and employee waiting are equally important to the organization's effectiveness. This situation arises, for example, when organizations rely on a captive service, such as a secretarial pool or a photocopying facility. In these cases, the cost of employees' waiting time is equal at least to their average salary, and in fact, this cost could be considerably more if all of the implications of waiting, such as the frustration of not completing a task or the effect of delays on others in the organization, are assessed.

The economic trade-off depicted in Figure 13.1 best describes this situation in which the capacity to serve can be increased by adding servers. As servers are added, the cost of service increases, but this cost is offset by a corresponding decrease in the cost of waiting. Adding both costs results in a convex total-cost curve for the organization that identifies a service capacity with minimum combined costs. The queuing models are used to predict the expected waiting time of employees for different levels of capacity, and the values are substituted in the total-cost function here.

Assuming linear cost functions for service and waiting and comparing alternatives based on steady-state performance, we calculate the total cost per unit of time (hour) as

$$\text{Total cost per hour} = \text{Hourly cost of service} + \text{Hourly waiting cost}$$

$$\begin{aligned} TC &= C_s C + C_w \lambda W_s \\ &= C_s C + C_w L_s \text{ (from Little's Law)} \end{aligned} \quad (7)$$

where

C = number of servers

C_s = hourly cost per server

C_w = hourly cost of waiting customer

TABLE 13.5 Probability of Finding All Gas Pumps in Use

c	P_0	$P(n \geq c)$
3	0.11	0.44
4	0.13	0.27
5	0.134	0.06
6	0.135	0.02

For equation (7), waiting is defined as time in the system; however, if waiting in queue is more appropriate, then L_q is substituted for L_s. In situations in which service is self-service, such as using a copying or a fax machine, waiting in queue might be justified.

Example 13.8
Workstation Rental

The director of a large engineering staff is considering the rental of several workstations that will permit the staff to analyze structural design problems. On the basis of a survey of the staff, the director finds that the department will generate, on average, eight requests per hour for structural analysis, and the engineers estimate that the average analysis will require 15 minutes. A workstation that is adequate for these needs rents for $10 per hour. When the average salary of the engineering staff is considered, the cost of keeping an engineer idle is $30 per hour. For a "quick and dirty" analysis, the director assumes that requests for service are Poisson distributed and that user times are exponentially distributed. Further, the engineering staff is large enough to assume an infinite calling population. Using the standard *M/M/c* model with $\rho = 8/4 = 2$ and Appendix C to calculate L_q, the director obtains the results shown in Table 13.6.

Note that L_q is used instead of L_s in the calculations, because the engineer is productive while using the workstation. The results indicate that four workstations will minimize the combined costs of rent for the workstations and salary for the waiting engineers.

Our assumption of waiting costs being linear with time, as shown in equation (7), is suspect because, as the delay increases, a larger percentage of customers become dissatisfied and vocal, possibly creating a mass exodus. First, the longer the wait, the more irritated customers become and the greater the probability that they will take their future business elsewhere. In addition, they will tell friends and relatives of their bad experiences, which also will affect future sales. Finally, the loss of an immediate sale is small compared with the future stream of lost revenues when a customer is lost forever. In practice, however, the linear assumption usually is made because of the difficulty of determining a customer waiting cost function.

Probability of Sales Lost Because of Inadequate Waiting Area

This planning criterion concerns capacity of the waiting area rather than capacity to serve. An inadequate waiting area can cause potential customers to balk and seek service elsewhere. This problem is of particular concern where arriving customers can see the waiting area, such as the parking lot at a restaurant or the driveway at a drive-in bank. Analysis of these systems uses the finite-queue *M/M/c* model to estimate the number of balking customers.

If N is the maximum number of customers allowed in the system, then P_N is the probability of a customer arriving and finding the system to be full. Thus, P_N represents the probability of sales lost because of an inadequate waiting area, and λP_N represents the expected number of sales lost per unit of time. The cost of sales lost because of an inadequate waiting area now can be compared with the possible investment in additional space.

Example 13.9
Downtown Parking Lot

A parking lot is a multiple-server queuing system without a queue; that is, the lot can be considered a service system in which each parking space is a server. After the lot is full, subsequent arrivals are rejected, because the system has no provision for a queue. Thus, a parking lot is a finite-queuing system with a queue capacity of zero, because $N = c$.

TABLE 13.6
Total Cost of Workstation Rental Alternatives

c	L_q	$C_s c$	$C_w L_q$	TC
3	0.88	$30	$26.4	$56.4
4	0.17	40	5.1	45.1
5	0.04	50	1.2	51.2
6	0.01	60	0.3	60.3

Service Benchmark

DON'T GUESSTIMATE, SIMULATE!

Simulation is more than computer models used to study queuing systems. True, simulation is very useful for exploring and testing "what-if" scenarios to improve service operations. Telecom giant AT&T uses simulation in very different ways, however.

The company used a highly customized business simulation from BTS to facilitate its AT&T Strategy Execution Initiative.[3] Some of the objectives of the initiative were to enhance cross-functional and business unit collaboration, tackle real-world business issues, create stronger networks among employees, and energize the company's workforce. This simulation involved competition among four teams of employees who first proposed and evaluated various capabilities such as cross-selling and opening a web capability, then explored a variety of cross-business initiatives, and finally considered implementation of their proposals and the effect of their proposals on employee engagement and customer satisfaction.

AT&T also uses "hands-on" simulation as part of its Disaster Recovery Network.[4] Employees engage in quarterly disaster-exercise simulations at many locations in the United States, the United Kingdom, and Germany. Some of these simulations involve recovery operations, wireless emergency communications, special operations (Hazmat response), customer/agency outreach, incident management, and technology/disaster implementation. During an actual simulation drill, employees work in teams to deploy equipment from different warehouses and assemble the equipment. The equipment then is set up in large trailers and replicates exactly the infrastructure that has been damaged by human-made disasters or natural disasters. AT&T's effort to improve its emergency response capability constantly is especially important in an age when the daily lives of people and businesses are so dependent on the rapid flow of information.

With this model in mind, an enterprising student notes the availability of a vacant lot in the central business district. The student learns from a real estate agent that the owner is willing to rent the property as a parking lot for $50 a day until a buyer is found. After making some observations of traffic in the area, the student finds that approximately 10 cars per hour have difficulty finding space in the parking garage of the department store across the street from the vacant lot. The garage attendant reports that customers spend approximately 1 hour shopping in the store. To calculate the feasibility of this venture, the student assumes that arrivals are Poisson distributed and that shopping times are exponentially distributed. The student is interested in what potential business is lost because the lot has room for only 6 cars.

This parking lot can be considered an *M/M/c* finite-queuing system with no provision for a queue. Therefore, equations for the finite-queue *M/M/c* model are calculated with $c = N$. Substituting for $c = N$ in equations (VI.1), (VI.2), (VI.4), and (VI.7) yields the following results for the *no-queue case* (i.e., $LQ = WQ = 0$). No other equations are applicable.

$$P_0 = \frac{1}{\sum_{i=0}^{N} \frac{\rho^i}{i!}} \tag{8}$$

$$P_n = \frac{\rho^n}{n!} P_0 \tag{9}$$

$$L_s = \rho(1 - P_N) \tag{10}$$

$$W_s = \frac{1}{\mu} \tag{11}$$

With $\lambda = 10$, $N = 6$, and $\mu = 1$, we calculate $P_0 = 0.000349$ using equation (8) and calculate $P_6 = 0.48$ using equation (9). Thus, of the 10 arriving customers per hour, approximately one-half ($10 \times 0.48 = 4.8$) find the lot full. Therefore, this lot with a capacity of 6 cars serves approximately one-half the demand.

Summary

When their assumptions are met, analytical queuing models can help service system managers to evaluate possible alternative courses of action by predicting waiting time statistics. The models also provide insights that help to explain such queuing phenomena as pooling, the effect of finite queues on realized demand, the nonproportional effects of adding servers on waiting time, and the importance of controlling demand as seen by reducing service time variance. The approach to capacity planning depends on the criterion of system performance being used. Further, queuing models are useful in the analysis because of their ability to predict system performance. If the queuing model assumptions are not met or the system is too complex, however, then computer simulation modeling as addressed in the chapter supplement is required.

Key Terms and Definitions

***A/B/C* classification of queuing models** where *A* stands for the arrival distribution, *B* for the service time distribution, and *C* for the number of servers in a parallel-server queuing system. *p. 360*

Finite queue a queue that is limited physically (e.g., a limited number of parking spaces). *p. 368*

Steady state the condition of a system when distribution of its characteristics, such as the number of customers in the queue, becomes stationary regarding time (i.e., the system has moved out of an initial transient state and reached statistical equilibrium). *p. 360*

Transient state (warm-up period) is the condition of a system when operating characteristics are dependent on time. *p. 360*

Topics for Discussion

1. Discuss how one can determine the economic cost of keeping customers waiting.
2. Example 13.1 presented a naive capacity planning exercise and was criticized for using averages. Recall the concept of a "bottleneck" from Chapter 5, Supporting Facility and Process Flows, and suggest other reservations about this planning exercise.
3. For a queuing system with a finite queue, the arrival rate can exceed the capacity to serve. Use an example to explain how this is possible.
4. What are some disadvantages associated with the concept of pooling service resources?
5. Discuss how the $M/G/\infty$ model could be used to determine the number of emergency medical vehicles required to serve a community.

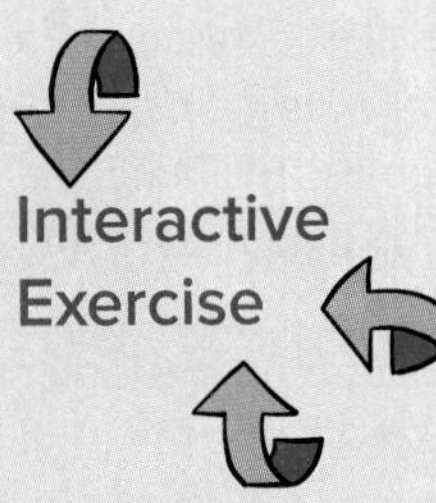

Interactive Exercise

With Microsoft Office Visio resident on your computer, download the free Process Simulator from http://www.promodel/products/ProcessSimulator/. In the Demo panel select "Medical Clinic" and follow instructions to simulate scenarios. Have the class explain by process flow analysis why the "Urine Batch=2" scenario performed the best in terms of average time in system and the "Additional Nurse" scenario showed no improvement over the "Baseline" for the same criterion.

Solved Problems

1. Calculating System Characteristics

Problem Statement

Sunset Airlines is reviewing its check-in procedures in anticipation of its "two for the price of one" fare promotion. Presently, a single clerk spends an average of 3 minutes per passenger checking luggage and issuing boarding passes. Service times have a negative exponential distribution, and passenger arrivals are Poisson distributed, with an anticipated mean of 15 per hour during flight operations.

a. What is the probability that an arriving passenger will be served immediately without waiting?

Solution

Note that we have an *M/M/*1 system with $\lambda = 15$ per hour and $\mu = 60/3 = 20$ per hour. Using equation (I.1):

$$P(\text{system idle}) = P_0 = 1 - \rho$$
$$= 1 - (15/20)$$
$$= 0.25$$

b. The area immediately in front of the Sunset counter can accommodate only three passengers, including the one being served. What percentage of time will this area be inadequate for waiting passengers?

Solution

Using equation (I.2):

$$P\,(\textit{inadequate waiting space}) = P(n \geq 4) = \rho^4 = (15/20)^4 = 0.316$$

Thus, the waiting area is inadequate 32 percent of the time.

c. Anticipating an increase in demand, Sunset has decided to add another clerk when passengers begin to experience an average wait time in queue of 17 minutes. Because arrival rates are monitored at the check-in counter, determine what arrival rate per hour would indicate the need for another clerk.

Solution

Set equation (I.8) equal to 17/60 hour, substitute $\mu = 20$, and solve for λ:

$$W_q = \frac{\rho}{\mu - \lambda} = \frac{\lambda}{20}\left[\frac{1}{20 - \lambda}\right] = \frac{\lambda}{400 - 20\lambda} = \frac{17}{60}$$

Therefore, $\lambda = 17$ per hour.

2. Capacity Planning

Problem Statement

The average arrival rate of customers has reached 20 per hour, and Sunset Airlines must increase the capacity of its check-in system with the addition of one clerk. Based on a customer survey, $15 per hour is considered to be the opportunity cost of waiting in queue. Clerks are paid $10 per hour and still process a passenger in 3 minutes. Evaluate the following check-in system alternatives to find the least expensive arrangement using total hourly costs of clerks and customers waiting in queue.

a. Consider a multiple-queue configuration with separate waiting lines and no customer jockeying. Assuming demand is divided equally among the two clerks, what is the total hourly cost of this arrangement?

Solution

Treat each line as independent *M/M/*1 queues, with total system cost being twice the single-line cost. Calculate the value for L_q using equation (I.5) and substitute in equation (7) to determine the line cost:

$$L_q = \frac{\rho\lambda}{\mu - \lambda}$$
$$= \frac{10}{20}\left[\frac{10}{20 - 10}\right]$$
$$= 0.5$$

Therefore, total system cost = 2[10 + 15(0.5)] = \$35 per hour.

b. Consider adding one self-serve automatic ticketing machine (ATM) with a constant service time of 3 minutes to help the single clerk. Assume demand is divided equally between the single live clerk and the ATM. What is the total hourly cost of this arrangement if the ATM operating costs are negligible?

Solution

Treat each line as independent, with one being an $M/M/1$ as in part a, with $L_q = 0.5$, and the other being an $M/D/1$ (constant service of ATM). First, calculate the L_q for the ATM line using equation (III.2) with $V(t) = 0$:

$$L_q = \frac{\rho^2 + \lambda^2 V(t)}{2(1-\rho)}$$

$$= \frac{0.5^2 + 10^2(0)}{2(1-0.5)}$$

$$= 0.25$$

Therefore, total system cost = single clerk + ATM = 10 + 15(0.5) + 0 + 15(0.25) = \$21.25 per hour.

c. Consider a single-queue arrangement with two live tellers. What is the total hourly cost of this arrangement?

Solution

From Appendix C, with $c = 2$ and $\rho = 20/20 = 1$, we find $L_q = 0.333$, so the total system cost = 10(2) + 15(0.333) = \$25 per hour.

Exercises

13.1 A general-purpose auto-repair garage has one mechanic who specializes in muffler installations. Customers seeking service arrive at an average rate of 2 per hour, with a Poisson distribution. The average time to install a muffler is 20 minutes, with negative exponential distribution.

a. On arrival at the garage, how many customers should one expect to find in the system?

b. The management is interested in adding another mechanic when the customer's average time in the system exceeds 90 minutes. If business continues to increase, at what arrival rate per hour will an additional mechanic be needed?

13.2 A business school is considering replacing its copy machine with a faster model. Past records show that the average student arrival rate is 24 per hour, Poisson distributed, and that the service times are distributed exponentially. The selection committee has been instructed to consider only machines that will yield an average turnaround time (i.e., expected time in the system) of 5 minutes or less. What is the smallest processing rate per hour that can be considered?

13.3 The Lower Colorado River Authority (LCRA) has been studying congestion at the boat-launching ramp near Mansfield Dam. On weekends, the arrival rate averages 5 boaters per hour, Poisson distributed. The average time to launch or retrieve a boat is 10 minutes, with negative exponential distribution. Assume that only one boat can be launched or retrieved at a time.

a. The LCRA plans to add another ramp when the average turnaround time (i.e., time in the system) exceeds 90 minutes. At what average arrival rate per hour should the LCRA begin to consider adding another ramp?

b. If there were room to park only 2 boats at the top of the ramp in preparation for launching, how often would an arrival find insufficient parking space?

13.4 On average, 4 customers per hour use the public telephone in the sheriff's detention area, and this use has a Poisson distribution. The length of a phone call varies according to a negative exponential distribution, with a mean of 5 minutes. The sheriff will install a second telephone booth when an arrival can expect to wait 3 minutes or longer for the phone.

a. By how much must the arrival rate per hour increase to justify a second telephone booth?

b. Suppose the criterion for justifying a second booth is changed to the following: install a second booth when the probability of having to wait at all exceeds 0.6. Under this criterion, by how much must the arrival rate per hour increase to justify a second booth?

13.5. A company has a central document-copying service. Arrivals are assumed to follow the Poisson probability distribution, with a mean rate of 15 per hour. Service times are assumed to follow the exponential distribution. With the present copying equipment, the average service time is 3 minutes. A new machine is available that will have a mean service time of 2 minutes. The average wage of the people who bring the documents to be copied is $8 an hour.

a. If the new machine can be rented for $10 per hour more than the old machine, should the company rent the new machine? Consider lost productive time of employees as time spent waiting in queue only because the copying machine is a self-serve device.

b. For the old copying machine, what is the probability when a person arrives that he or she will encounter people already waiting in line for service? (Be careful to identify properly the number of customers who might be present for this situation to arise.)

c. Suppose the new copying machine is rented. How many chairs should be provided for those waiting in line if we are satisfied when there will be enough chairs at least 90 percent of the time?

13.6. Sea Dock, a private firm, operates an unloading facility in the Gulf of Mexico for supertankers delivering crude oil for refineries in the Port Arthur area of Texas. Records show that, on average, 2 tankers arrive per day, with a Poisson distribution. Supertankers are unloaded one at a time on a first-come, first-served (FCFS) basis. Unloading requires approximately 8 hours of a 24-hour working day, and unloading times have a negative exponential distribution.

a. Sea Dock has provided mooring space for 3 tankers. Is this sufficient to meet the U.S. Coast Guard requirement that at least 19 of 20 arrivals should find mooring space available?

b. Sea Dock can increase its unloading capacity to a rate of 4 ships per day through additional labor at a cost of $480 per day. Considering the $1,000-per-day demurrage fee charged to Sea Dock for keeping a supertanker idle (this includes unloading time as well as time spent waiting in queue), should management consider this expansion opportunity?

13.7. Last National Bank is concerned about the level of service at its single drive-in window. A study of customer arrivals during the window's busy period revealed that, on average, 20 customers per hour arrive, with a Poisson distribution, and they are given FCFS service, requiring an average of 2 minutes, with service times having a negative exponential distribution.

a. What is the expected number of customers waiting in queue?

b. If Last National were using an automated teller machine with a constant service time of 2 minutes, what would be the expected number of drive-in customers in the system?

c. There is space in the drive for 3 cars (including the one being served). What is the probability of traffic on the street being blocked by cars waiting to turn into the bank driveway?

d. Last National is considering adding tellers at the current drive-in facility. It has decided on \$5 per hour as the imputed cost of customer waiting time in the system. The hourly cost of a teller is \$10. The average arrival rate of customers has reached 30 per hour. On the basis of the total hourly cost of tellers and customer waiting, how many tellers do you recommend? Assume that with use of pneumatic tubes, tellers can serve customers as though there were a single queue.

13.8. Green Valley Airport has been in operation for several years and is beginning to experience flight congestion. A study of airport operations revealed that planes arrive at an average rate of 12 per hour, with a Poisson distribution. On the single runway, a plane can land and be cleared every 4 minutes on average, and service times have a negative exponential distribution. Planes are processed on an FCFS basis, with takeoffs occurring between landings. Planes waiting to land are asked to circle the airport.

a. What is the expected number of airplanes circling the airport, waiting in queue for clearance to land?

b. A new ground-approach radar system approved by the Federal Aviation Administration is being considered as a means of reducing congestion. Under this system, planes can be processed at a constant rate of 15 per hour (i.e., the variance is zero). What would be the expected number of airplanes circling the airport, waiting in queue for clearance to land, if this system were to be used?

c. Assume that the cost of keeping an airplane in the air is approximately \$70 per hour. If the cost of the proposed radar system were \$100 per hour, would you recommend its adoption?

13.91. Community Bank is planning to expand its drive-in facility. Observations of the existing single-teller window reveal that customers arrive at an average rate of 10 per hour, with a Poisson distribution, and that they are given FCFS service, with an average transaction time of 5 minutes. Transaction times have a negative exponential distribution. Community Bank has decided to add another teller and to install four remote stations with pneumatic tubes running from the stations to the tellers, who are located in a glassed-in building. The cost of keeping a customer waiting in the system is represented as a \$5-per-hour loss of goodwill. The hourly cost of a teller is \$10.

a. Assume that each teller is assigned two stations exclusively, that demand is divided equally among the stations, and that no customer jockeying is permitted. What is the average number of customers waiting in the entire system?

b. If, instead, both tellers work all the stations and the customer waiting the longest is served by the next available teller, what is the average number of customers in the system?

c. What hourly savings are achieved by pooling the tellers?

13.10. Consider a one-pump gas station that satisfies the assumptions for the $M/M/1$ model. It is estimated that, on average, customers arrive to buy gas when their tanks are one-eighth full. The mean time to service a customer is 4 minutes, and the arrival rate is 6 customers per hour.

a. Determine the expected length of the queue and the expected time in the system.

b. Suppose that customers perceive a gas shortage (when there is none) and respond by changing the fill-up criterion to more than one-eighth full on average. Assuming that changes in λ are inversely proportional to changes in the fill-up criterion, compare results when the fill-up criterion is one-quarter full with the results in part a.

c. Making the same assumption as in part b, compare the results obtained if the fill-up criterion is one-half full. Do we have the makings of a behaviorally induced gasoline panic?

d. It is reasonable to assume that the time to service a customer will decrease as the fill-up criterion increases. Under "normal" conditions, it takes, on average, 2 minutes to pump the gasoline and 2 minutes to clean the windshield, check the oil, and collect the money. Rework parts b and c if the time to pump the gasoline changes proportionally to changes in the fill-up criterion.

Houston Port Authority — CASE 13.1

The Houston Port Authority has engaged you as a consultant to advise it on possible changes in the handling of wheat exports. At present, a crew of dockworkers using conventional belt conveyors unloads hopper cars containing wheat into cargo ships bound overseas. The crew is known to take an average of 30 minutes to unload a car. The crew is paid a total wage of $50 per hour. Hopper car arrivals have averaged 12 per 8-hour shift. The railroad assesses a demurrage charge from time of arrival to release at a rate of $15 per hour on rolling stock not in service. Partially unloaded cars from one shift are first in line for the following shift.

A chi-square "goodness-of-fit" analysis of arrival rates for the past months indicates a Poisson distribution. Data on unloading times for this period can be assumed to follow a negative exponential distribution.

Because of excessive demurrage charges, adding another work crew has been proposed. A visit to the work area indicates that both crews will be unable to work together on the same car because of congestion; however, two cars can be unloaded simultaneously with one crew per car.

During your deliberations, the industrial engineering staff reports that a pneumatic handling system has become available. This system can transfer wheat from cars to cargo ships at a constant rate of three cars per hour, 24 hours per day, with the assistance of a skilled operator earning $15 per hour. Such a system would cost $400,000 installed. The Port Authority uses a 10 percent discount rate for capital improvement projects. The port is in operation 24 hours per day, 365 days per year. For this analysis, assume a 10-year planning horizon, and prepare a recommendation for the Port Authority.

Freedom Express — CASE 13.2

Freedom Express (FreeEx), affectionately known as the Filibuster Fly, is a small commuter airline based in Washington, DC, that serves the U.S. East Coast. It runs nonstop flights between several cities and Reagan National Airport (DCA).

DCA frequently is congested, and at such times, planes are required to fly in a "stack" over the field. In other words, planes in the process of landing and those waiting for permission to land are deployed above the field.

FreeEx management is interested in determining how long its planes will have to wait so that an adequate amount of fuel can be loaded before departure from the outlying city to cover both the intercity flying time and the time in the stack. Excess fuel represents an unnecessary cost, however, because it reduces the payload capacity. Equally important is the present cost of aviation fuel, $2.80 per gallon, and an average consumption rate of 20 gallons per minute.

The rate of arrival for all planes at DCA varies by the hour. The arrival rate and time in the stack are greatest each weekday between 4 and 5 PM, and so FreeEx selected this time period for an initial study.

The study indicated that the mean arrival rate is 20 planes per hour, or one every 3 minutes. The variance about this mean, resulting from flight cancellations as well as charter and private flights, is characterized by a Poisson distribution.

During clear weather, the DCA control tower can land 1 plane per minute, or 60 planes per hour. Landings cannot exceed this rate in the interest of air safety. When the weather is bad, the landing rate is 30 per hour. Both good and bad-weather landing rates are mean rates with a Poisson distribution. FreeEx's flights are short enough that management usually can tell before takeoff in an outlying city whether or not the rate of landings in DCA will be reduced because of weather considerations.

When a plane runs short of fuel while in the stack, it is given priority to land out of order. DCA rules, however, make clear that the airport will not tolerate abuse of this consideration. Therefore, FreeEx ensures that its planes carry enough fuel so that it will take advantage of the policy no more than 1 time in 20.

Questions

1. During periods of bad weather, as compared with periods of clear weather, how many additional gallons of fuel on average should FreeEx expect its planes to consume because of airport congestion?
2. Given FreeEx's policy of ensuring that its planes do not run out of fuel more than 1 in 20 times while waiting to land, how many reserve gallons (i.e., gallons over and above expected usage) should be provided for clear-weather flights? For bad-weather flights?
3. During bad weather, FreeEx has the option of instructing the Washington air controller to place its planes in a holding pattern from which planes are directed to land either

at Reagan National or at Dulles International, whichever becomes available first. Assume that the Dulles landing rate in bad weather also is 30 per hour, Poisson distributed, and that the combined arrival rate for both airports is 40 per hour. If FreeEx must pay $200 per flight to charter a bus to transport its passengers from Dulles to Reagan National, should it exercise the option of permitting its aircraft to land at Dulles during bad weather? Assume that if the option is used, FreeEx's aircraft will be diverted to Dulles about one-half the time.

Renaissance Clinic (A) — CASE 13.3

Renaissance Clinic is a hospital dedicated to the health care of women. It is located in the hill country surrounding Austin, Texas, and offers an environment that is unique in the city. At the time of a visit, a patient of Dr. Margaret Thompson's practice is directed by the receptionist either to a nurse clinician or to Dr. Thompson. On some occasions, a patient might see both the nurse and the doctor. In the Renaissance Clinic (B) case (see the Computer Simulation later in this chapter), we used a computer simulation model to determine resource allocation.

For this case, we want to apply queuing theory to Dr. Thompson's practice. The data in Table 13.7 were collected over several days of typical activity and the histograms indicate that arrival rates and service rates fit a Poisson distribution. Figure 13.6 shows the flow of patients during routine office visits.

Assignments

1. Assume the waiting lines at the receptionist, the nurse clinician, and the doctor are managed independently with an FCFS priority. Using queuing formulas and the assumption that patients exiting from an activity follow a Poisson distribution, estimate the following statistics:
   a. Average waiting time in each of the queues (i.e., receptionist, nurse clinician, and physician).
   b. Average time in the entire system for each of the three patient paths.
   c. Overall average time in the system (i.e., expected time for an arriving patient).
   d. Average idle time in minutes per hour of work for the receptionist, the nurse clinician, and the doctor.
2. What are the key assumptions involved in your analysis above? Discuss the appropriateness of each in this situation.
3. What would be the impact on the above calculations of adding a second doctor to the clinic and sharing the doctor queue between them on a "first MD available" basis?
4. The clinic is considering adopting a queue priority system that is determined by the time of entry into the system at the receptionist. How might patients waiting for the doctor react to this policy?

TABLE 13.7
Arrival and Service Rates at Renaissance Clinic

Model Parameter	Description	Expectations
λ	Arrival rate of patients	30 per hour
p_1	Fraction of patients who go to nurse clinician	2/3
p_2	Fraction of nurse clinician patients who also see physician	0.15
μ_R	Service rate of receptionist	40 per hour
μ_N	Service rate of nurse clinician	30 per hour
μ_P	Service rate of physician	15 per hour

FIGURE 13.6
Patient Flow at Renaissance Clinic

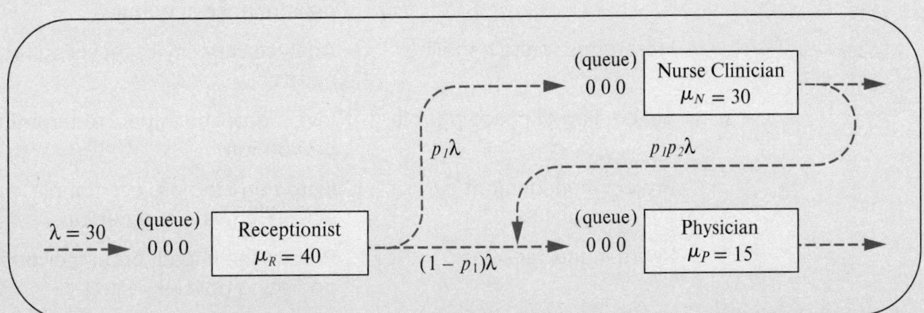

Chapter 13 Supplement

Computer Simulation

Computer simulation provides management an experimental laboratory in which to study a model of a real system and to determine how the system might respond to changes in policies, resource levels, or customer demand. A system, for our purposes, is defined as a combination of elements that interact to accomplish an objective. Systems simulation can be used to answer "what-if" questions about existing or proposed systems. For example, what if another teller is added in a bank lobby? What if some tellers handle only depositors? What if an ATM is placed outside the lobby? The response of the system to these changes can be "observed" over an extended period by means of a simulation. Without having to change the real system, a simulation model generates estimates of system performance, such as average customer waiting time, for each scenario of interest. An animated simulation running on a personal computer allows decision makers to view the activity of the system (e.g., flow of customers) in accelerated time.

Service delivery systems are both dynamic and stochastic in their nature. A *dynamic* system is one that is influenced by actions over time. The queue behavior at an airline terminal, for example, is subject to arrival of passengers that vary by time of day (i.e., early morning versus midday). *Stochastic* refers to the underlying probabilistic nature of a system with events occurring at random from a probability distribution. Recall that the Poisson distribution of customer arrivals is a random process, because the arrival of any future customer is unpredictable even though the average number of arrivals during an hour may be known. Table 13.8 shows examples of simulation applications in services.

Systems Simulation

Basically, computer simulation is a tool for evaluating ideas. The process of developing a systems simulation is a substantial undertaking that has been made easier with the availability of modeling software such as ServiceModel, to be discussed later. The experimental nature of systems simulation is shown in Figure 13.7.

TABLE 13.8
Examples of Simulation Applications in Services

Application	Simulation Objective
Staffing bank tellers	Consider the waiting time of customers when determining the number of tellers to staff a workshift
Emergency ambulance location	Analyze the response time implications of location options
Hospital–patient flows	Develop procedures to manage patient flows and resource utilization
Order processing	Analyze order processing procedures to support just-in-time shipments
Aircraft maintenance	Determine the impact on downtime of preventive maintenance schedules
Hazardous waste handling	Analyze capacity of recycling facilities and transportation needs
Scheduling of police patrols	Investigate the impact of targeting crime areas on crime prevention
Project management	Determine the project completion time distribution when activity times are uncertain
Recreational facilities	Predict the impact upon facilities under different operating policies

FIGURE 13.7
The Process of System Simulation

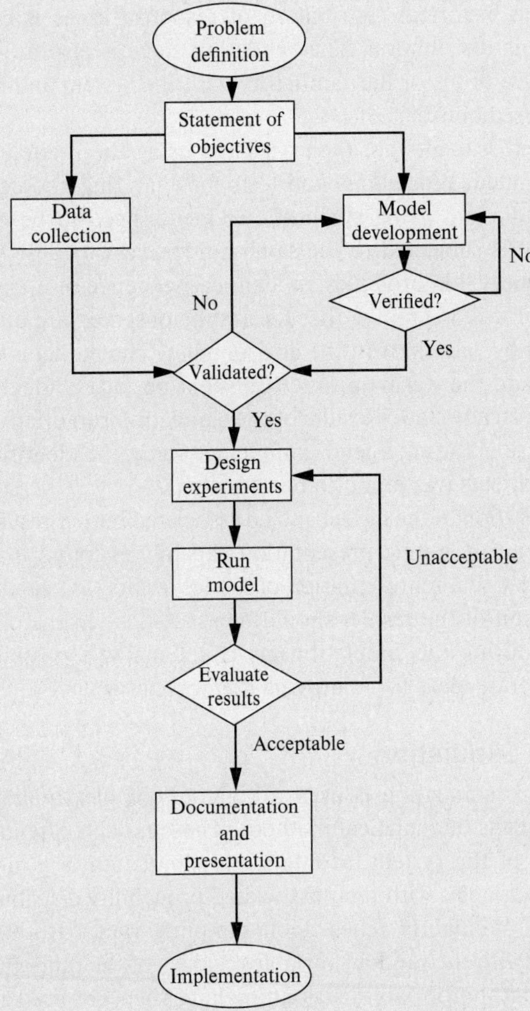

Simulation Methodology

Developing an accurate and concise problem definition is important because this activity involves the client in the process and facilitates implementation of the results. The statement of objectives follows naturally and provides a framework for the scope of the model and system performance measures.

Data collection and model development often are accomplished concurrently to save time. For ongoing systems, historical data such as the distribution of customer arrivals might be available or the data can be collected on-site. For systems that do not yet exist, data, of course, are not available, but other data might be available from similar systems. The model development begins with a conceptual abstraction of the system, perhaps in the form of a process flowchart. As event processing and relationships between events are defined, the conceptual model becomes a logic model.

After a preliminary model has been developed, it is checked or *verified* to ascertain that it works in the way intended. Verification is accomplished by running the model step by step to be sure that the intended logic is being followed. Another method is to perform a few hand calculations to see if they agree with the computer output. Most complex models will require some "debugging" to fix shortcomings in the logic.

Validation makes sure the model reflects the operations of the real system under study in sufficient detail to address the problem. Data collected on the real system are compared with results generated by the model. In the validation of an emergency ambulance model, for example, the historical distribution of response times is compared to the model's prediction of this distribution. The validation stage is also an excellent time to involve the client because of his or her familiarity with the system and the need to be convinced of the model's credibility.

Simulation experiments are then designed using the preliminary ideas about alternatives to be evaluated. Procedures and tests for analyzing and comparing alternatives are formulated. Studies involving stochastic elements need to be controlled to ensure that each experiment is subjected to the same randomness by designating a common stream of random numbers that produces an identical sequence of events. This control of inputs to the simulation will guarantee that the results observed are due to the "treatment" and not confounded by variations in the environment. The model is run for a certain number of replications and the warm-up time (transient period) is identified before statistics are recorded during steady state. Results of the simulation run often suggest additional experiments. In the case of the emergency ambulance study, the identification of which hospitals would receive patients was found to be important.

Each configuration of the model and its associated output results should be documented for future reference. Graphic presentation capabilities found in simulation software produce an effective visual representation of model results that can be self-explanatory.

Implementation of the results should be assured when the client is involved from the beginning and during the simulation process. Finally, a postmortem of the simulation study could generate ideas for improving the next project.

Monte Carlo Simulation

Typically, systems simulation is used to analyze complex models that cannot be solved practically by means of analytical methods. These models often are stochastic to account for the realities of the system. Monte Carlo simulation is a method that enables us to model random variables with their associated probability distributions.

Monte Carlo simulation relies upon sampling values from the probability distributions associated with the random variables. Values of the random variables are selected at random from the appropriate distributions and then are used in the simulation. These random variables are generated repetitively during the simulation to imitate the behavior of the variables.

There are several methods that can be used to select observations of random variables from their probability distributions, but all are based on the use of random numbers. A *random number* (*RN*) is a special random variable that is uniformly distributed between 0 and 1. This means that all values in the interval [0, 1] have equal likelihood of being selected.

Computer-based simulations actually use *pseudo-random* numbers. These are values that behave like random numbers, although they are generated using a mathematical function. While pseudo-random numbers are not truly random, they have the appearance of being random. Pseudo-random numbers have the advantage of not requiring large amounts of file space in the computer. More important, they permit the exact replication of experimental conditions by allowing the same stream of numbers to be realized from a "seed" value. Table 13.9 gives a sample of some pseudo-random numbers generated by the Excel function RAND( ) that returns a uniform distributed *RN* between 0-1.

Generating Random Variables

How are random numbers used to obtain observations of random variables? First we need to realize that random variables can be either *discrete* (e.g., number of customers arriving during an hour) or *continuous* (e.g., the time a customer spends being served). The process of generating observations in both cases makes use of the unique feature of any random variable–its cumulative distribution always sums to 1.0.

TABLE 13.9
Uniformly Distributed Random Numbers [0, 1]

0.65481	0.32533	0.60527	0.73407
0.90124	0.04805	0.59466	0.41994
0.74350	0.68953	0.45973	0.25298
0.09893	0.02529	0.46670	0.20539
0.61196	0.99970	0.82512	0.61427
0.15474	0.74717	0.12472	0.58021
0.94557	0.10805	0.29529	0.19255
0.42481	0.77602	0.39333	0.33440
0.23523	0.32135	0.20106	0.57546
0.04493	0.45753	0.42941	0.21615

Discrete Random Variable

Consider the distribution of airline passengers waiting to board a rental car shuttle shown in the first column of Table 13.10. The third column of Table 13.10 contains the cumulative distribution of passengers, which is determined by the successive summing of the probabilities from top to bottom [e.g., $F(2) = p(1) + p(2) = 0.02 + 0.03 = 0.05$]. The cumulative distribution gives the likelihood that the number of passengers is fewer than or equal to the specific value. The probabilities must range from 0 to 1. Recall that the random number *RN* is uniformly distributed in the interval [0, 1]. This relationship between the cumulative distribution and *RN* is the basis for generating observations of random variables.

Now we can make some observations of passengers boarding the shuttle by using the cumulative distribution and the random numbers. This approach for generating observations of random variables, known as the *inverse transformation method,* is straightforward:

1. Select any random number *RN* from Table 13.9.
2. Equate the cumulative distribution to the random number. In Table 13.10, for example, use the last column to find the interval within which *RN* lies.
3. Read across to the first column for the number of passengers boarding that equates the cumulative distribution to the random number. This value is the observation used in the simulation.

As an example, begin in the upper-left corner of Table 13.9 and select the first random number as $RN = 0.65481$. Using Table 13.10, note that our *RN* falls into the range $[0.50 \le RN < 0.70]$ and that this range is associated with 5 passengers. The process is illustrated graphically in Figure 13.8 where the cumulative distribution is displayed by a bar graph. Note that the portion of each bar exposed to the vertical axis is equal to the probability of the associated random variable. To make another observation, we move down the column in Table 13.9 to the next random number $RN = 0.90124$. Reading across Table 13.10

TABLE 13.10
Probability Distribution of Passengers and Random-Number Assignment

Passengers x	Probability $p(x)$	Cumulative Distribution $F(x)$	Random-Number Assignment
1	0.02	0.02	$0.00 \le RN < 0.02$
2	0.03	0.05	$0.02 \le RN < 0.05$
3	0.15	0.20	$0.05 \le RN < 0.20$
4	0.30	0.50	$0.20 \le RN < 0.50$
5	0.20	0.70	$0.50 \le RN < 0.70$
6	0.15	0.85	$0.70 \le RN < 0.85$
7	0.08	0.93	$0.85 \le RN < 0.93$
8	0.05	0.98	$0.93 \le RN < 0.98$
9	0.02	1.00	$0.98 \le RN < 1.00$

FIGURE 13.8 **Cumulative Distribution of Passengers**

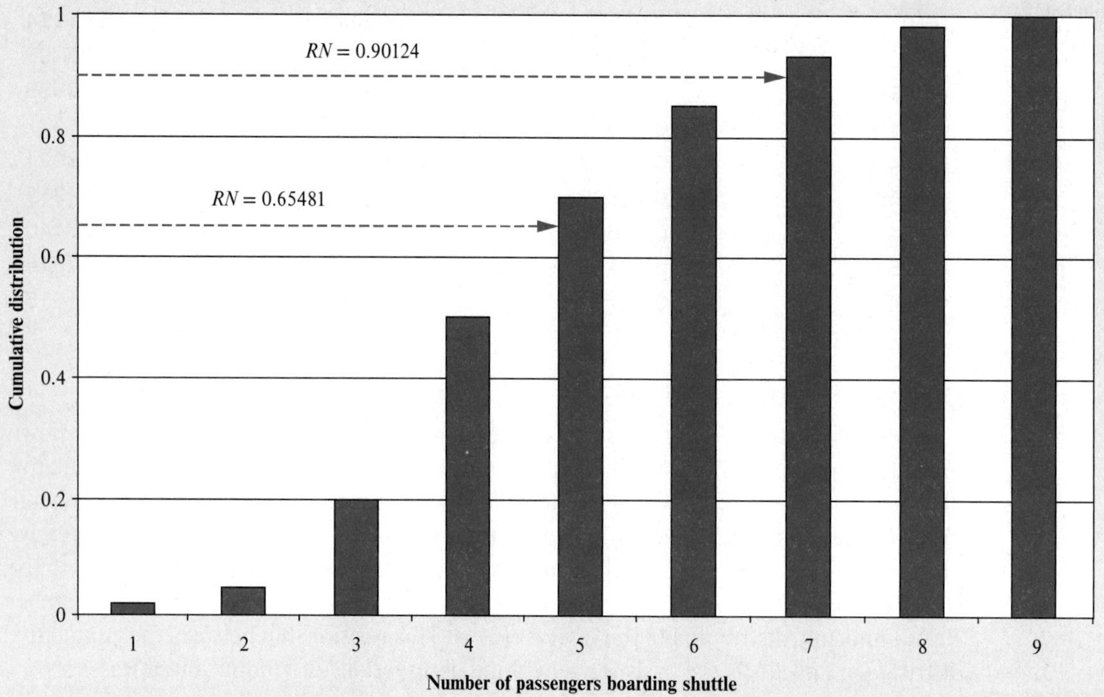

from the *RN* assignment range [0.85 ≤ *RN* < 0.93] we find 7 boarding passengers as the second observation. If we repeat this process many times, 2 percent of the observations of service time will be 1 passenger, 3 percent will be 2 passengers, and so on, mimicking the actual distribution.

Continuous Random Variable

The approach for selecting random variables from continuous distributions will equate *RN* to the cumulative distribution function and solve for the random variable value. We illustrate this approach for three common continuous random variable distributions: uniform, negative exponential, and normal.

1. *Uniform Distribution* For a random variable uniformly distributed between values a and $b(b > a)$, the function that returns a value x given *RN* is

$$x = a + RN(b - a) \tag{12}$$

Assume, for example, that the distribution of shuttle travel time from remote parking to the airport terminal is uniform over the range of 10 to 20 minutes. For this case, our random variable function is

$$x = 10 + RN(20 - 10)$$

2. *Negative Exponential Distribution* Recall from Chapter 12, Managing Waiting Lines, that the cumulative distribution for the negative exponential distribution is given by equation (2) as

$$F(x) = 1 - e^{-\lambda x}$$

Set $RN = F(x) = 1 - e^{-\lambda x}$ and solve to get $e^{-\lambda x} = 1 - RN$. Taking logs to the base e and solving for x, we obtain the following function that returns a negative exponentially distributed random variable x given an *RN*:

$$x = \frac{1}{\lambda}\log_e(1 - RN) \quad \text{or, more simply,} \quad x = -\frac{1}{\lambda}\log_e RN \tag{13}$$

Assume, for example, that the distribution of customer arrivals at the shuttle stop is Poisson with a mean of 15 arrivals per hour. If we are interested in generating the time between arrivals, the negative exponential distribution is appropriate. Thus, the time between arrivals measured in hours is obtained from the random variable function:

$$x = -\frac{1}{15}\log_e RN$$

3. *Normal Distribution* Because the normal distribution does not have a closed form expression for the cumulative distribution, we use a property of the Central Limit Theorem to devise a method for generating a standard normal deviate z with $\mu = 0$ and $\sigma^2 = 1$. We begin with two considerations. First, recall from the Central Limit Theorem that the distribution of means from any source has a normal distribution. Second, the random number RN is uniformly distributed between 0 and 1. For a uniform distribution between the values of a and b, the mean and variance are

$$\mu = a + \frac{(b-a)}{2} \qquad \text{and} \qquad \sigma^2 = \frac{(b-a)^2}{12}$$

Thus, the random number RN has $\mu = 1/2$ and $\sigma^2 = 1/12$. To generate a standard normal deviate z with mean 0 and variance of 1, therefore, we simply add together 12 RNs and subtract 6, as shown below:

$$\frac{x-\mu}{\sigma} = \sum_{i=1}^{12} RN_i - 6 \quad \text{or}$$

$$x = \mu + \sigma\left[\sum_{i=1}^{12} RN_i - 6\right] \tag{14}$$

Suppose, for example, that the travel times for our shuttle have a normal distribution with mean of 15 minutes and standard deviation of 2 minutes. Then the random variable function is

$$x = 15 + 2\left[\sum_{i=1}^{12} RN_i - 6\right]$$

Discrete-Event Simulation

A discrete-event simulation is driven by events that occur at certain points in time such as the arrival of a customer or completion of a service. When an event occurs, the state of the system changes. A customer arrival increases the number of customers in the system, for example, while a customer departure (i.e., service completion) reduces the number in the system. The computer maintains a timing device known as the simulation clock, which advances with each event taking place. After each event occurs, descriptors of the state of the system are recorded.

Figure 13.9 shows the flowchart of a discrete-event simulation for an airline ticket counter. First, the arrival time of the next customer is generated based upon an interarrival time distribution using the inverse transformation method. The simulation clock that begins at time 0 is set equal to the next chronological event time. If the next event is an arrival, then the consumer either will enter service or wait in line, depending upon the status of the server. If the next event is a departure (i.e., service completion), then either another consumer will enter service or the server will become idle, depending on the status of the waiting line. The state of the system is updated in response to the event, and the clock time is compared with a prespecified maximum time. If the clock time is greater than or equal to the maximum time, then summary statistics describing the system are calculated and printed, and the simulation is stopped. Otherwise, the clock moves to the next event time.

FIGURE 13.9 **Flowchart of Airline Ticket Counter Discrete-Event Simulation**

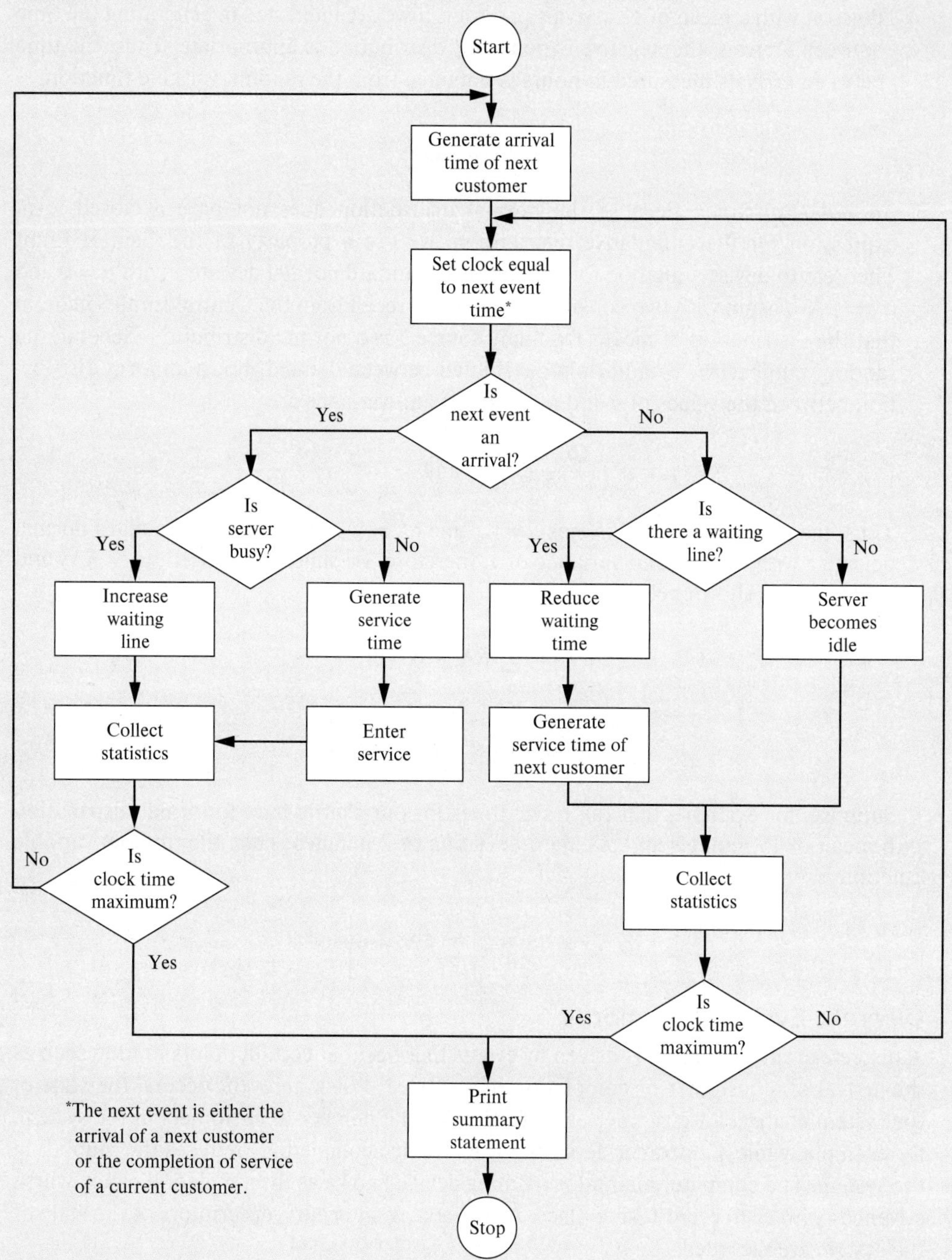

*The next event is either the arrival of a next customer or the completion of service of a current customer.

Example 13.10 Airline Ticket Counter Simulation

A discrete-event simulation will be used to observe the activities at an airline ticket counter. The system has a single ticket agent and customers are served on a first-come, first-served basis. In this simulation we are concerned with the number of customers waiting, their waiting time, and the status of the ticket agent (i.e., busy or idle).

Table 13.11 gives the service times and interarrival times (i.e., time between arrivals) of the first 10 customers. The service times and interarrival times were generated from appropriate probability distributions using the inverse transformation method.

The simulation clock begins at time 0. Table 13.12 gives the times that each customer arrives, enters service, and departs service. For example, the first customer arrives at time 5, immediately enters service, and departs at time 9. Customer 4, however, arrives at time 18 and

TABLE 13.11
Interarrival Times and Service Times for First 10 Customers

Customer	Interarrival Time, Min.	Service Time, Min.
1	5	4
2	4	3
3	4	6
4	5	4
5	3	2
6	4	5
7	5	4
8	5	6
9	4	4
10	3	5

TABLE 13.12
Simulation of First 10 Customers (Time in Minutes)

Customer	Arrival Time	Time Service Begins	Time Service Ends	Time in Line	Time in System	Time Agent Idle
1	5	5	9	0	4	5
2	9	9	12	0	3	0
3	13	13	19	0	6	1
4	18	19	23	1	5	0
5	21	23	25	2	4	0
6	25	25	30	0	5	0
7	30	30	34	0	4	0
8	35	35	41	0	6	1
9	39	41	45	2	6	0
10	42	45	50	3	8	0

finds the server busy. This customer enters service at time 19 and departs at time 23. The total time waiting in line for the 10 customers is 8 minutes. This gives an average waiting time of 0.8 minute per customer. We see that the ticket agent was idle for a total of 7 minutes out of the 50-minute simulation, or 14 percent idleness.

Process Simulator by ProModel[5]

Process Simulator installs as a plug-in to Microsoft Office Visio® to run simulation models inside Visio process flowcharts, value stream maps, and facility layouts for analysis (e.g., what-if scenarios), capacity planning (e.g., measure effect on customer waiting times from adding additional servers), or to conduct basic process improvement studies. A free trial edition is available at http://www.promodel.com/products/ProcessSimulator/, and a tutorial at http://www.promodel.com/services/refreshercourse/.

Example 13.10 Automobile Driver's License Office Revisited

Recall Example 5.2 in Chapter 5, Supporting Facility and Process Flows, where we developed a flow diagram of six activities and identified the bottleneck activity as activity 3 "check for violations and restrictions." This static (e.g., fixed cycle times) approach to workflow analysis does not account for the effect of variation in cycle times on system performance. Queuing theory tells us that variations in customer arrival times and variation in service times lead to customer queues and/or idle resources. Data from Table 5.2 is repeated below with distributions assigned to each cycle time. For our example application of Process Simulator, a variety of distributions have been selected:

- E(15) represents an exponential distribution with mean of 15
- U(30,5) represents a uniform distribution with mean 30 and half-range of 5
- N(60,5) represents a normal distribution with mean 60 and standard deviation 5
- T(30,40,50) represents a triangular distribution with mode 40, min 30, and max 50
- Photographing the applicant takes a constant time of 20
- ER(30,2) represents an Erlang distribution with mean 30 and shape parameter 2

The screenshot in Figure 13.10 shows the process flow diagram for the license renewal process using the customer entity figure available from the left side of the screen. The empty arrow from the Customer avatar to Review Application (first activity) is the arrival process generator with properties set to E(60) to stress test our model because arrivals will average one per minute. Each activity has properties set to the appropriate activity time distribution from Table 13.13. Note PROCESS SIMULATOR at the top of the screen. This pull-down menu shows "Simulation Properties" where the warm-up time, run-length, and number of replications for the simulation exercise are set. This simulation has values of 1 hour, 40 hours, and 10 replications

The simulation report is shown in Figure 13.11. Notice the bar chart of activity states showing solid for percent operation and striped for percent idle. This chart clearly shows "Check for Violations" as the bottleneck activity with operations for 84 percent of the time. Also, note the average customer time in the system is 2,240 seconds which means that on average the customer only spends approximately 9 percent (195/2240) of his/her time being served.

FIGURE 13.10 Screenshot of License Renewal Process Flow Diagram

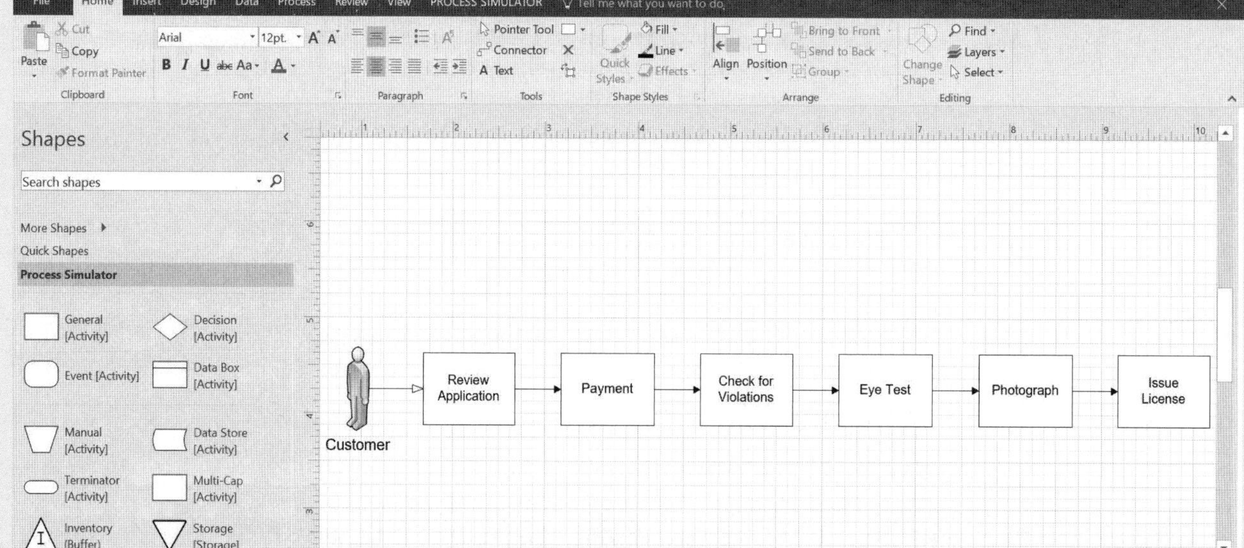

TABLE 13.13
License Renewal Activity Time Distributions

Activity	Description	Cycle Time, Sec.	Distribution
1	Review Application	15	E(15)
2	Payment	30	U(30,5)
3	Check for Violations	60	N(60,5)
4	Eye Test	0	T(30,40,50)
5	Photograph	20	20
6	Issue License	30	ER(30,2)

FIGURE 13.11 **Screenshot of License Renewal Process Simulator Report**

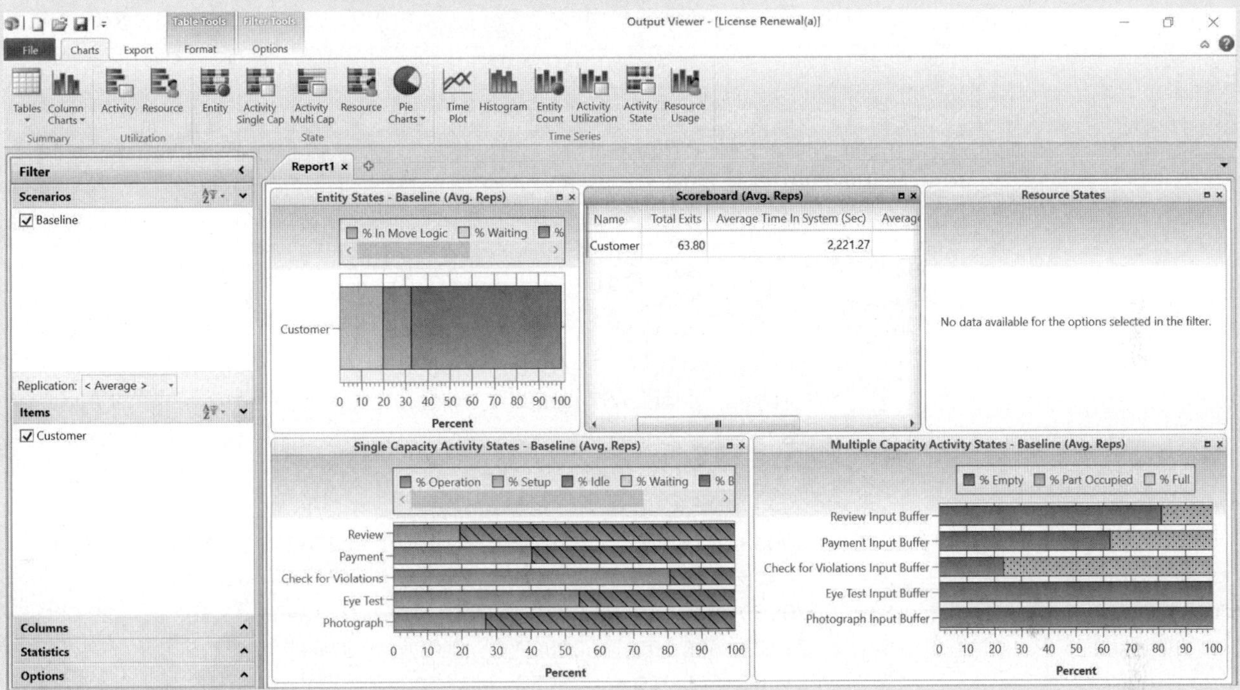

Solved Problems

1. Monte Carlo Simulation

Problem Statement

A textbook publishing company is considering the release of three books next year. Because of a cash flow problem, the company is interested in predicting the expected revenue and its range from sales of these books. Using the Monte Carlo method, simulate 10 realizations of the first year's sales experience.

Book	Expected Sales in First Year	Selling Price
A	200	$25
B	1,000	10
C	3,000	5

Deviation from Expected Sales, %	Probability
80	0.1
90	0.2
100	0.4
110	0.2
120	0.1

Solution

Step 1: Prepare a cumulative distribution for sales deviations and random number assignment table.

Sales Deviation, %	Probability	Cumulative Probability	Random Number Assignment
80	.1	.1	$0 \leq RN < .1$
90	.2	.3	$.1 \leq RN < .3$
100	.4	.7	$.3 \leq RN < .7$
110	.2	.9	$.7 \leq RN < .9$
120	.1	1.0	$.9 \leq RN < 1.0$

Step 2: Prepare a Monte Carlo simulation table with *RN* selected from Appendix B, Uniformly Distributed Random Numbers [0, 1], beginning at the top of the first column and working down in sequence.

Sales Revenue Realization	*RN*	Book A $5,000 Expected	*RN*	Book B $10,000 Expected	*RN*	Book C $15,000 Expected	Total Sales Revenue $
1	.06785	4,000	.81075	11,000	.98544	18,000	33,000
2	.31479	5,000	.12484	9,000	.23882	13,500	27,500
3	.23897	4,500	.40374	10,000	.73622	16,500	31,000
4	.36952	5,000	.14510	9,000	.12719	13,500	27,500
5	.99407	6,000	.32694	10,000	.42780	15,000	31,000
6	.00633	4,000	.38490	10,000	.22363	13,500	27,500
7	.54105	5,000	.31786	10,000	.47556	15,000	30,000
8	.70850	5,500	.64791	10,000	.21424	13,500	29,000
9	.77524	5,500	.39867	10,000	.87641	16,500	32,000
10	.51653	5,000	.75057	11,000	.88287	16,500	32,500

The expected sales revenue is $30,100, with a range of $27,500 to $33,000.

2. Discrete-Event Simulation

Problem Statement

Dr. Swift, a veterinarian, has the following appointment schedule for Saturday morning:

Patient	Appointment Time	Expected Duration, Min.
A	9:00	10
B	9:15	20
C	9:30	30
D	10:00	10
E	10:15	30
F	10:45	20
G	11:00	10
H	11:15	30

His receptionist has researched past records and determined the following distributions:

Arrival Time	Frequency	Appointment Duration, % of Expected Time	Frequency
20 min. early	10	80	5
10 min. early	20	90	25
Just on time	50	100	30
10 min. late	10	110	25
Not show up (NS)	10	120	15
	100		100

Two days ago, Dr. Swift received a telegram from New York advising him that his mother is seriously ill. He is scheduled to fly east at 2 PM Saturday. In order to get to the airport on time, he knows that he must leave the office by noon. Develop a discrete event simulation model to assist Dr. Swift in determining the probability of completing his morning appointments in time to make the flight. Test the model with the simulation of one Saturday's experience.

Solution

Step 1: Prepare a simulation flowchart.

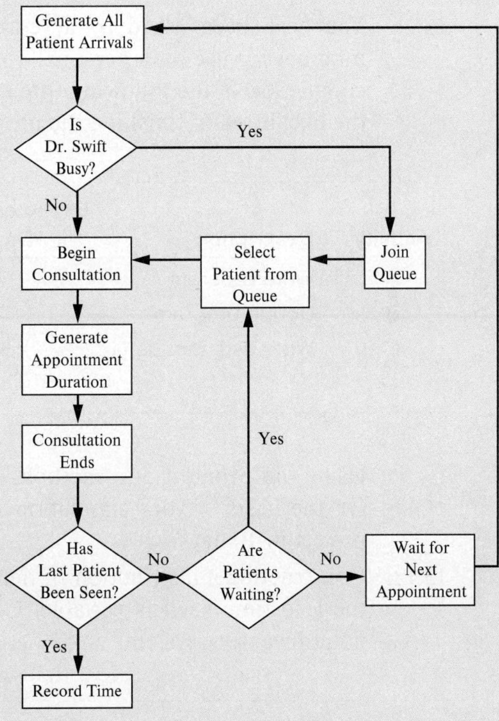

Step 2: Prepare random number assignment tables.

Patient Arrival	Cumulative Probability	*RN* Assignment	Appointment Duration %	Cumulative Probability	*RN* Assignment
−20	.1	$.0 \leq RN < .1$	80	.05	$.00 \leq RN < .05$
−10	.3	$.1 \leq RN < .3$	90	.30	$.05 \leq RN < .30$
On time	.8	$.3 \leq RN < .8$	100	.60	$.30 \leq RN < .60$
+10	.9	$.8 \leq RN < .9$	110	.85	$.60 \leq RN < .85$
NS	1.0	$.9 \leq RN < 1.0$	120	1.00	$.85 \leq RN < 1.0$

Step 3: Prepare realization table and conduct simulation.

Patient Arrival	*RN*	Arrival Time	*RN*	Appointment Duration	Time Begins	Time Ends
A	.06785	8:40	.73622	11	8:40	8:51
B	.81075	9:25	.36952	20	9:25	9:45
C	.98544	NS	.14510	27	—	—
D	.31479	10:00	.12719	9	10:00	10:09
E	.12484	10:05	.99407	36	10:09	10:45
F	.23882	10:35	.32694	20	10:45	11:05
G	.23897	10:50	.42780	10	11:05	11:15
H	.40374	11:15	.00633	24	11:15	11:39

For this realization of the Saturday morning, Dr. Swift can leave the office at 11:39. Many more replications, however, would be needed to obtain a distribution of office departures in order to assess the probability of leaving by noon.

Exercises

13.11. You have been asked by a retail association to develop an inventory control program for use on a personal computer. The program development requires the completion of the following three activities in sequence. You are concerned about the likelihood of finishing the project in the promised 10 days.

Activity	Description	Expected Time, Days	Deviation from Expected Time, Days	Probability
A	Write program	5	+2	0.1
B	Debug program	2	+1	0.2
C	Write user manual	3	0	0.3
			−1	0.4

Using the Monte Carlo method, simulate 10 program development experiences. On the basis of your simulation results, what is the probability of finishing the project in 10 days?

13.12. Constructing a distribution of demand during reorder lead time is complicated if the lead time itself is variable. Consider the following distribution for a reorder point inventory system.

Daily Demand	
Demand	**Probability**
0	0.1
1	0.2
2	0.3
3	0.4

Lead Time	
Days	**Probability**
1	0.1
2	0.5
3	0.4

a. What is the range of possible demands during the variable lead time?

b. Using the Monte Carlo method and random numbers from Appendix B, simulate 10 demands during lead time that could be used to form a histogram.

13.13. The Dell Factory Outlet has the following daily demand distribution for laptop computer carrying cases.

Demand	Probability
0	.1
1	.2
2	.3
3	.25
4	.15
5 or more	0

Simulate 5 days of retail sales using the following inventory policy. If the ending inventory of cases is 0 or 1, order enough units such that the starting inventory on the next day will be 5 cases. Ordered units arrive the next morning and are stocked before the store opens for business. If a stock-out occurs, the sale is lost.

The cost structure is as follows:

Storage cost = \$0.10/unit/day

Shortage cost = \$5/unit

Order cost = \$3/order

Fill in the following simulation table using the random numbers provided.

Day	Starting Inventory	Random Number	Daily Demand	Ending Inventory	Storage Cost	Shortage Cost	Order Cost	Total Daily Cost
1	4	.153						
2		.379						
3		.821						
4		.962						
5		.731						

13.14. The Coast Guard maintains a lighted buoy in the harbor entrance to warn ships of a dangerous reef. The flashing beacon contains two high-intensity quartz halogen bulbs. The supplier has provided the following data on bulb life:

Life, Months	Probability
1	0.05
2	0.15
3	0.20
4	0.30
5	0.20
6	0.10

The estimated cost of dispatching a motor launch with a crew to the buoy to remove and replace the weatherproof cover over the bulbs is \$50, and the bulbs cost \$10 each. The time involved in replacing a bulb is negligible. Coast Guard regulations require that both bulbs work all the time.

a. Develop a Monte Carlo simulation model that will help the Coast Guard to decide between the following replacement policies: (1) Replace only the bulb that burns out or (2) replace both bulbs when one burns out.

b. Simulate five years of activity using random numbers from Appendix B. Discuss some questions of experimental design that this problem poses.

c. Can you think of other bulb replacement policies to test?

13.15. The project network for building a garage is shown in Figure 13.12 with activity times and their deviations found in Table 13.14.

a. Develop a Monte Carlo simulation model that can be used to generate a distribution of project completion times (longest path from node 1 to 8).

b. Simulate 5 project completion experiences using random numbers from Appendix B. What is the expected project duration time?

13.16. Consider the travel network shown in Figure 13.13 in which the probabilities of selecting a route from each node are shown in parentheses.

a. Develop a Monte Carlo simulation model to determine the expected trip time from node 1 to node 7.

b. Simulate 10 trips and calculate the expected trip time.

FIGURE 13.12
Project Network for Building a Garage

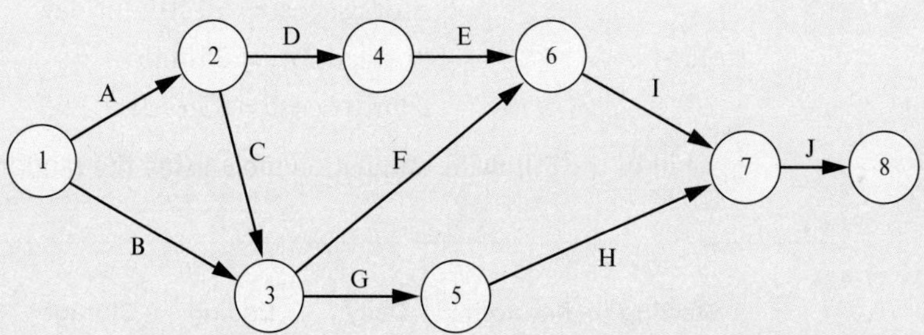

TABLE 13.14
Expected Times and Deviations

Activity	Expected Time, Days	Deviation from Expected Time, Days	Probability
A	3	+2	0.2
B	5	+1	0.3
C	2	0	0.4
D	4	−1	0.1
E	3		
F	4		
G	2		
H	4		
I	3		
J	2		

FIGURE 13.13
Travel Network

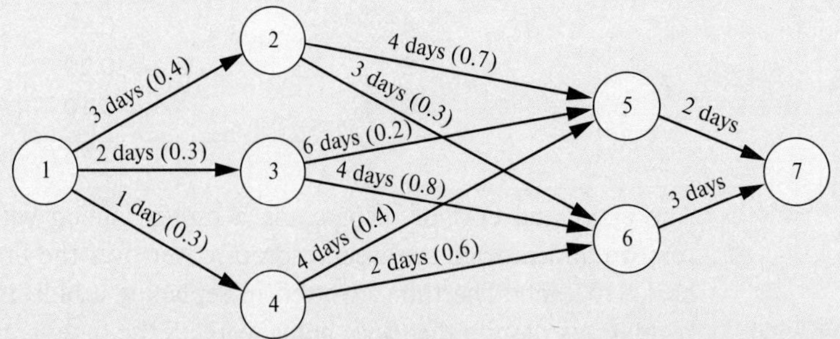

13.17. The number of fires occurring during a 24-hour day follows a Poisson distribution with a mean of 4 fires per day as shown in the accompanying table. In examining past records, the fire chief finds that 75 percent of all fires require only one truck and the amount of time required to extinguish a fire is normally distributed with a mean of 3 hours and a standard deviation of 0.5 hour. The other 25 percent of reported fires required 2 trucks and the time to put them out is normally distributed with a mean of 4 hours and a standard deviation of 1 hour. Assume the district has 10 trucks and use a simulation sample of 10 days to determine the average daily utilization of trucks.

Fires per Day	0	1	2	3	4	5	6	7	8	9
Probability	.02	.07	.15	.20	.20	.16	.10	.06	.03	.01

13.18. Electronic Car Group (ECG), a firm specializing in the diagnosis of automobile engine problems, is planning to open a new service center with two diagnostic bays. Based on the experience at other ECG facilities, it has been found that the diagnostic service time is a uniform distribution between 40 and 60 minutes. Based on its historical experience and the demographics of the new location, ECG believes the average time between customer arrivals will be 60 minutes with a negative exponential distribution. Simulate eight hours (480 minutes) of operations with a two-bay facility, recording the waiting time of customers. ECG expects customers will wait while their cars are being diagnosed and plans to promote an unconditional guarantee that customers who wait more than 60 minutes will receive a gift certificate. From your simulation, how many gift certificates do you expect to give out per day?

Drivers License Renewal — CASE 13.4

Let us revisit the Automobile Driver's License Office Example 5.2 and model the proposed process improvement shown as Figure 5.6 (b). Recall that the improvement consisted of combining activities 1 and 4 (Review Application and Eye Test) to create two parallel activities each followed by activity 3 (Check for Violations) with activities 2, 5, and 6 completing the flow process. Use the activity time distributions in Table 13.15 and an arrival distribution with exponential distribution with mean of 30 seconds.

Assignments

1. Using Process Simulator, draw the process flow diagram and assign the distributions from Table 13.15 as properties for each activity. Assign the empty arrival arrow property an E(30) distribution and split the arrivals between the first two parallel activities "Review Applications/ Eye Test."
2. Run the simulation using a one hour warm-up, 40 hour run length, and replicate 10 times.
3. Does the simulation report show another activity that now could be a bottleneck?

TABLE 13.15
License Renewal Activity Time Distributions

Activity	Description	Cycle Time, Sec.	Distribution
1,4	Review Application/Eye Test	55	T(40,55,70)
3	Check for Violations	60	N(60,5)
2	Payment	30	U(30,5)
5	Photograph	20	20
6	Issue License	30	ER(30,2)

Renaissance Clinic (B) — CASE 13.5

On a hillside in Rollingwood, a community just southwest of Austin, Texas, the Renaissance Clinic provides dedicated obstetric and gynecological services. The medical treatment at this facility is wrapped in an exclusive-feeling physical environment that is distinctly unique in Austin. The practice of Dr. Margaret Thompson is one of supporting care within an efficient and friendly facility. Attention to the ambiance is reflected in a brightly colored interior that makes patients feel better just entering. A relaxed atmosphere prevails in the birthing rooms that are large enough to hold several family members in a homelike atmosphere of wood floors and quilts on the beds. The practice is intimate—only a receptionist and a nurse clinician assist Dr. Thompson. The receptionist has been trained to screen patients and directs them either to the nurse clinician's waiting area or to Dr. Thompson's waiting area. Some patients, following a preliminary examination by the nurse clinician, will be asked to join the queue to see Dr. Thompson. Figure 13.14 shows the flow of patients during routine office visits. The arrival rate per hour was found to be Poisson distributed [E(interarrival time in minutes)], and the service times in minutes were uniformly distributed [U(range)] for the receptionist and normally distributed [N(μ, σ)] for the nurse and physician. The data in Table 13.16 were collected over several days of typical activity.

Assignments

1. Model this system using Process Simulator to determine the utilization of each resource (receptionist, nurse clinician, and physician) and the average time in the system for an arriving patient.
2. If you could hire one more person to augment the staff, what position would be your choice (receptionist, nurse clinician, or physician)? How have the clinic performance measures changed after hiring one more person?
3. What further advice would you give Dr. Thompson on the operation of her clinic?

FIGURE 13.14 **Flow of Patients for Routine Office Visits**

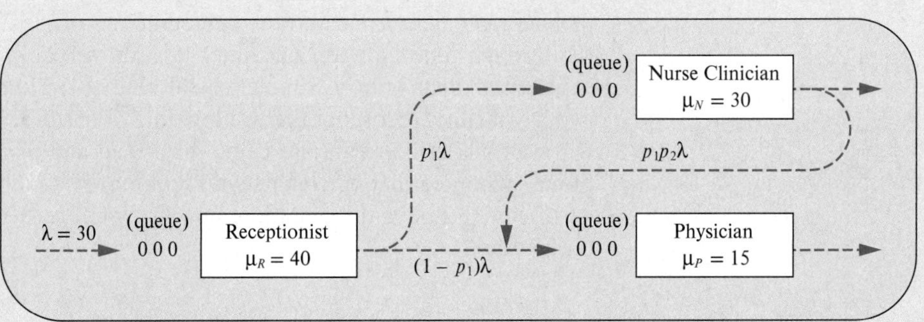

TABLE 13.16 **Processing Data at Renaissance Clinic**

Model Parameter	Description	Expectations
λ	Arrival rate of patients	30 per hour or E(2)
p_1	Fraction of patients who go to nurse clinician	2/3
p_2	Fraction of nurse clinician patients who also see physician	0.15
μ_R	Service rate of receptionist	40 per hour or U(1,2)
μ_N	Service rate of nurse clinician	30 per hour or N(2,1)
μ_P	Service rate of physician	15 per hour or N(4,2)

Selected Bibliography

Bordoloi, Sanjeev K., and Keith Beach. "Improving Operational Efficiency in an Inner-city Emergency Department." *Health Services Management Research* 20, no. 2 (2007), pp. 105–12.

Bretthauer, Kurt M., H. Sebastian Heese, Hubert Pun, and Edwin Coe. "Blocking in Healthcare Operations: A New Heuristic and an Application." *Production and Operations Management* 20, no. 3 (May–June), pp. 375–91.

Chan, Wyean, Ger Koole, and Pierre L'Ecuyer. "Dynamic Call Center Routing Policies Using Call Waiting and Agent Idle Times." *Manufacturing & Service Operations Management* 16, no. 4 (2014), pp. 544–60.

De Lange, Robert, Ilya Samoilovich, and Bo van der Rhee. "Virtual Queuing at Airport Security Lanes." *European Journal of Operational Research* 225, no. 1 (2013), pp. 153–65.

Gans, N., Shen, et al. "Parametric Forecasting and Stochastic Programming Models for Call Center Workforce Scheduling." *Manufacturing & Service Operations Management* 17, no. 4 (2015), pp. 571–88.

Koole, Ger. *Call Center Optimization.* Amsterdam: MG Books, 2013.

Kulkarni, Vidyadhar G., et al. "Optimal Allocation of Effort to Software Maintenance: A Queuing Theory Approach." *Production and Operations Management* 18, no. 5 (September–October 2009), pp. 506–15.

van Dijk, Nico M., and Erik van der Sluis. "To Pool or Not to Pool in Call Centers." *Production and Operations Management* 17, no. 3 (May–June 2008), pp. 296–305.

Yang, M., et al. "Improving Voting Systems through Service Operations Management." *Production and Operations Management* 23, no. 7 (2014), pp. 1083–97.

Endnotes

1. W. H. Bleuel, "Management Science's Impact on Service Strategy," *Interfaces* 6, no. 1 (November 1975), part 2, pp. 4–12.
2. J. D. C. Little, "A Proof of the Queuing Formula: $L = \lambda W$," *Operations Research* 9, no. 3 (May–June 1961), pp. 383–87. Also W. S. Jewell, "A Simple Proof of $L = \lambda W$," *Operations Research* 15, no. 6 (November–December 1967), pp. 1109–116; S. Stidham, Jr., "A Last Word on $L = \lambda W$," *Operations Research* 22, no. 2 (March–April 1974), pp. 417–21.
3. http://www.bts.com/news-insights/video-gallery-details.aspx?vid=9fc26ea0-9617-4928-a0dc-88a9aea82805, March 5, 2012.
4. http://www.att.com/gen/press-room?pid=22547&cdvn=news&newsarticleid=33999; http://www.att.com/gen/corporate-citizenship?pid=17918, May, 11, 2012; http://www.corp.att.com/ndr, May, 11, 2012; http://www.corp.att.com/ndr/deployment1.html, May 11, 2012; http://www.corp.att.com/ndr/exercises.html, May 11, 2012.
5. From R. E. Bateman, R. G. Bowden, T. J. Gogg, C. R. Harrell, and J. R. A. Mott, *System Improvement Using Simulation,* 5th ed. Orem, Utah: PROMODEL Corporation, 1997.

Part 4

Quantitative Models for Service Management

The final chapters introduce quantitative models that have important applications in service operations. First, we focus on the use of exponential smoothing models to forecast expected demand for services, which can vary by month, day, and hour. A variety of inventory management models are developed in the next chapter, and applications of RFID to services are discussed. We conclude the text with the topic of project management, which is an important management skill in any environment, but particularly in the management of consulting engagements.

Chapter 14

Forecasting Demand for Services

Learning Objectives

After completing this chapter, you should be able to:

1. Recommend the appropriate forecasting model for a given situation.
2. Conduct a Delphi forecasting exercise.
3. Describe the features of exponential smoothing that make it an attractive model for time series forecasting.
4. Conduct time series forecasting using the exponential smoothing model with trend and seasonal adjustments.

When hungry folks go to a fast-food restaurant, they expect to get their food fast, but they don't want a burger that's been acquiring a tan under a warming light for 10 minutes. So how can an operator of such a restaurant know when and how many burgers to cook at a given time? Hyper-Active Technologies (now part of The Acrelec Group) has an answer. The company offers fast-food restaurants a way to give kitchen workers a heads-up on what orders to expect by using rooftop cameras to monitor traffic entering the parking lot and drive-thru. Using historical data, predictions are made based on type of vehicle (e.g., a minivan signals many mouths to feed) and occupants (e.g., teenagers or adults) to determine order preference (i.e., burger with fries or chicken sandwich). The kitchen worker can use this information to prepare food in advance of the actual order so that it will be ready just in time for a customer.

Suppose, for example, during a McDonald's Big Mac promotion, five cars accumulate in the drive-thru during a six-minute period. We know, based on historical data, there is a 100 percent chance that someone will order a Big Mac within the next three minutes. In the fast-food business it's not enough to know that you sell 120 burgers during the lunch hour on weekdays. Managers must know during which 20-minute-window the kitchen needs to prepare food in anticipation of demand. If they underestimate, lines begin to form and service morphs into slow food; overestimating results in profits lost from wasted food. Early results of this recognition software have shown waste to be cut in half and wait times at the drive-thru reduced by 25 to 40 seconds–an eternity in the fast-food industry.[1]

Chapter Preview

The chapter begins with an overview of forecasting methods and the criteria for selecting a method. We begin our discussion with subjective models that are used at the initial planning stage for a project or marketing campaign when a long-term horizon is being considered. The Delphi technique is illustrated with an application to government policy planning for nuclear power. Causal models use regression analysis to form a linear relationship between independent variables and a dependent variable of interest. The selection of a site for a day care center is used to illustrate causal modeling when forecasting geographic demand.

The discussion of time series models begins with the common N-period moving average. A more sophisticated time series model, called *exponential smoothing,* is introduced with the capability to accommodate trends and seasonal data.

The Choice of Forecasting Method

Forecasting techniques allow us to translate the multitude of information available from databases into strategies that can give a service a competitive advantage. The particular techniques we will describe are classified into three basic models: subjective, causal, and time series. We note, however, that whereas some services may use only one or another of these models, others will use two or more depending on the application. For example, a fast-food restaurant might be interested in using a time series model to forecast the daily demand for menu items. The demand for hospital services, however, has both temporal and spatial characteristics, which will require the use of both time series and causal models. On occasion, service firms can use subjective models to assess the future impact of changing demographics, such as the aging of the general population. Overall, as we move from subjective to causal to time series models, the forecast time horizon becomes shorter. The models, their characteristics, and their possible applications are shown in Table 14.1.

Subjective Models

Most forecasting techniques, such as time series and causal models, are based on data whose pattern is relatively stable over time, so we can expect to make reasonably useful forecasts. In some cases, however, we might have few or no data with which to work, or we might have data that exhibit patterns and relationships only over the short run and, therefore, are not useful for long-range forecasts.

When we lack sufficient or appropriate data, we must resort to forecast methods that are subjective or qualitative in nature. These include the Delphi method, cross-impact analysis, and historical analogy.

TABLE 14.1 **Characteristics of Forecasting Methods**

Method	Data Required	Relative Cost	Forecast Horizon	Application
Subjective models:				
Delphi method	Survey results	High	Long term	Technological forecasting
Cross-impact analysis	Correlations between events	High	Long term	Technological forecasting
Historical analogy	Several years of data for a similar situation	High	Medium to long term	Life cycle demand projection
Causal models:				
Regression	All past data for all variables	Moderate	Medium term	Demand forecasting
Econometric	All past data for all variables	Moderate to high	Medium to long term	Economic conditions
Time series models:				
Moving average	*N* most recent observations	Very low	Short term	Demand forecasting
Exponential smoothing	Previous smoothed value and most recent observation	Very low	Short term	Demand forecasting

Delphi Method

Developed at the Rand Corporation by Olaf Helmer, the *Delphi method* is based on expert opinion. In its simplest form, persons with expertise in a given area are asked questions, and these individuals are not permitted to interact with each other. Typically, the participants are asked to make numerical estimates. For example, they might be asked to predict the highest Dow Jones average for the coming year.

The test administrator tabulates the results into quartiles and supplies these findings to the experts, who then are asked to reconsider their answers in light of the new information. Additionally, those whose opinions fall in the two outside quartiles are asked to justify their opinions. All the information from this round of questioning is tabulated and once again returned to the participants. On this occasion, each participant who remains outside the middle two quartiles (i.e., the interquartile range) might be asked to provide an argument as to why he or she believes those at the opposite extreme are incorrect.

The process might continue through several more iterations, with the intent of eventually having the experts arrive at a consensus that can be used for future planning. This method is very labor-intensive and requires input from persons with expert knowledge. Obviously, Delphi is a very expensive, time-consuming method and is practical only for long-term forecasting.

Example 14.1 Nuclear Power Delphi Study

An example of the Delphi method can be seen in a study of the nuclear power industry.[2] Ninety-eight persons agreed to participate in this study. These people occupied key upper-level positions with architect-engineering firms, reactor manufacturers, and utility companies in the industrial sector concerned with nuclear power as well as with state regulatory agencies, state energy commissions, congressional staffs, and nuclear regulatory agencies in the public sector.

The round 1 questionnaire contained 37 questions, 11 concerning the past evolution of the nuclear industry and 26 concerning the future. These questions were to be answered on a seven-point Likert scale, ranging from "strongly agree" to "uncertain" to "strongly disagree," as shown below:

It is desirable that utilities be permitted to integrate capital investment costs more aggressively into rate structures.

___	___	___	___	___	___	___	___
No jdgmt.	Strongly disagr.	Disagr.	Disagr. somewh.	Uncert.	Agree somewh.	Agree	Strongly agree

The questionnaire also asked for open-ended comments.

For round 2 of this study, the administrator provided a comprehensive summary of the first-round responses to the 11 questions concerning the past and a summary of the open-ended comments concerning the future. The number of responses to the question above are noted below, with the median (*M*) and interquartile range (designated by the vertical bars) shown below the responses:

	1	6	5	6	15	35	8
No jdgmt.	Strongly disagr.	Disagr.	Disagr. somewh.	Uncert.	Agree somewh.	Agree	Strongly agree
			|…………	…………	…………	M ….|	

The 11 questions concerning the past were dropped from the round 2 questionnaire, and 11 new questions prompted by the open-ended comments from round 1 were added. The participants were invited to "defend" their positions with supporting comments if their opinions fell outside the interquartile range.

For round 3, which was the final round in this study, the administrator once again supplied the participants with feedback, this time from round 2, and invited the participants to "vote" again on the same questions. The following illustration of the resulting median and interquartile range after each round of voting demonstrates how the opinions shifted and finally arrived at a consensus for this particular question:

	1	6	5	6	15	35	8
No jdgmt.	Strongly disagr.	Disagr.	Disagr. somewh.	Uncert.	Agree somewh.	Agree	Strongly agree
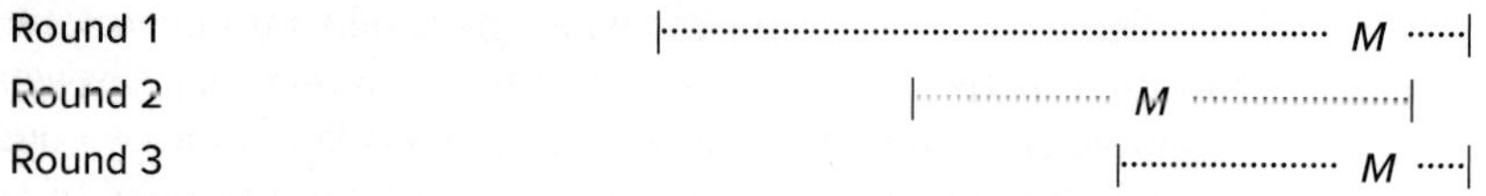 Round 1			|········	········	········	M ·····|	
Round 2				|········	M ········	·····|	
Round 3					|········	M ·····|	

As noted, some of the questions asked for assessments of where the industry has been and where it stands today. Other questions not only asked the experts where they thought it should be headed but also to address issues such as resource allocation and the political realities affecting the future of nuclear power. As shown, the Delphi method is a useful tool in addressing situations for which quantifiable data are not available.

Cross-Impact Analysis

Cross-impact analysis assumes that some future event is related to the occurrence of an earlier event. As in the Delphi method, a panel of experts studies a set of correlations between events presented in a matrix. These correlations form the basis for estimating the likelihood of a future event occurring.

For example, consider a forecast that assumes $5-per-gallon gasoline prices by 2020 (event A) and the corresponding doubling of ridership on mass transit by 2030 (event B). By initial consensus, it might be determined that given A, the conditional probability of B is .7, and that given B, the conditional probability of A is .6. These probabilities are shown in the matrix below:

	Probability of Event	
Given event	A	B
A	—	.7
B	**.6**	—

Assume that the forecasted unconditional probability for doubling mass transit ridership by 2030 is 1.0 and that the forecasted unconditional probability of $5 per gallon for gasoline by 2020 is .8. These new values are statistically inconsistent with the values in the matrix. The inconsistencies would be pointed out to the experts on the panel, who then would revise their estimates in a series of iterations. As with the Delphi method, an experienced administrator is needed to arrive at a satisfactory conditional probability matrix that can be used for generating a forecast.

Historical Analogy

Historical analogy assumes that the introduction and growth pattern of a new service will mimic the pattern of a similar concept for which data are available. Historical analogy frequently is used to forecast the market penetration or life cycle of a new service. The concept of a product life cycle as used in marketing involves stages, such as introduction, growth, maturity, and decline.

A famous use of historical analogy was the prediction of the market penetration by color television based on the experience with black-and-white television only a few years earlier. Of course, the appropriate analogy is not always so obvious. For example, growth in the demand for housekeeping services could follow the growth curve for child-care services. Because the pattern of previous data can have many interpretations and the analogy can be questioned, the credibility of any forecast using this method often is suspect. The acceptance of historical analogy forecasts depends on making a convincing analogy.

Causal Models

Short-term forecasts can be made fairly easily when we are presented with uncomplicated data. On occasion, however, a competitive service organization must deal with a wealth of statistical information, some of which might be relevant to making profitable forecasts and some of which might be extraneous. In these situations, it also is more likely that the forecasts must be made for the next year–or for the next decade–rather than just for the next day, week, or month. Obviously, a long-term forecast has the potential of spelling success or devastation for the organization. Therefore, we need a way of separating out the critical information and processing it to help us make an appropriate forecast.

Causal models make assumptions that are similar to those of time series models (which we will consider later): that the data follow an identifiable pattern over time and that an identifiable relationship exists between the information we wish to forecast and other factors. These models range from very simple ones, in which the forecast is based on a technique called *regression analysis,* to those known as *econometric models,* which use a system of equations.

Regression Models

A regression model is a relationship between the factor being forecasted, which is designated as the *dependent variable* (or Y), and the factors that determine the value of Y, which are designated as the *independent variables* or (X_i). If there are n independent variables, then the relationship between the dependent variable Y and the independent variables X_i is expressed as

$$Y = a_0 + a_1X_1 + a_2X_2 + \cdots + a_nX_n \tag{1}$$

The values a_0, a_1, a_2, . . . , a_n are coefficients that are determined by the computer program being used. If calculations are done by hand, values are determined by using regression equations found in elementary statistics texts.

Example 14.2 Locating a Day Care Center

The quality of service facility location analysis rests on an accurate assessment of geographic demand for the service (i.e., demand by geographic area). The assessment requires the selection both of some geographic unit that partitions the service area (e.g., census tract or ZIP code) and some method for predicting demand from each of these partitions (e.g., retailers asking customers for their ZIP code).

To demonstrate the process of assessing geographic demand, consider the challenge of locating a day care center. The target population consists of families with children younger than five years and at least one employable adult. A census tract is selected as the geographic unit because demographic data on the residents are readily available in digital form from the U.S. Census Bureau. The dependent variable Y_i is the percentage of families from census tract i in need of day care. Statistical analysis using readily available software such as SAS results in the following regression model:

$$Y_i = 0.58\,X_{1i} + 0.43\,X_{2i} + 0.85\,X_{3i}$$

where

Y_i = percentage of families from census tract i in need of day care

X_{1i} = percentage of families in census track i with children under five years old

X_{2i} = percentage of families in census track i with a single female head of household

X_{3i} = percentage of families in census track i with both parents working

The percentage, Y_i, estimated for each census track, then is multiplied by both the number of families in the census track and the average number of children younger than five years per family. The result is the estimate for the number of children that require day care service from each census track (i.e., geographic demand for day care).

Development of a regression model requires an extensive data collection effort to meet the needs of the individual organization, which often involves considerable time and expense. The model also requires expertise in the selection of independent and dependent variables to ensure a relationship that has a logical and meaningful interpretation. For these reasons, regression models are appropriate for making medium- and long-term forecasts.

Econometric Models

Econometric models are versions of regression models that involve a system of equations. The equations are related to each other, and the coefficients are determined as in the simpler regression models. An econometric model consists of a set of simultaneous equations expressing a dependent variable in terms of several different independent variables. Econometric models require extensive data collection and sophisticated analysis to create; thus, they generally are used for long-range forecasts.

Time Series Models

Time series models are applicable for making short-term forecasts when the values of observations occur in an identifiable pattern over time. These models range from the simple *N-period moving average* model to the more sophisticated and useful *exponential smoothing* models.

Exponential smoothing models are particularly useful because they can be adapted to track the components of a forecast (i.e., average, trend, and seasonality). The average is an estimate of the underlying mean of a random variable (e.g., customer demand), trend is either an increasing or decreasing increment in each period, and seasonality is a recurring cycle such as daily demand at a restaurant or annual demand at a tourist resort. Note that each of these components is stochastic in nature and the underlying value can change over time (e.g., trend could switch from positive to negative). Using exponential smoothing, each component is tracked and the results are combined to obtain a forecast. We begin our study of time series models with the simple *N*-period moving average.

N-Period Moving Average

Sometimes, observations that are made over a period of time appear to have a random pattern; consequently, we do not feel confident in basing forecasts on them. Consider the data in Table 14.2 for a 100-room hotel in a college town. We have decided to forecast only Saturday occupancy because the demand for each day of the week is influenced by different forces. For example, on weekdays, demand is generated by business travelers, but weekend guests often are people on vacation or visiting friends.

Selection of the forecasting period is an important consideration and should be based on the nature of the demand and the ability to use that information. For example, fast-food restaurants forecast demand by the hour of the day.

The hotel owner has noted increased occupancy for the past two Saturdays and wishes to prepare for the coming weekend (i.e., September 12), perhaps by discontinuing the practice of offering discount rates. Do the higher occupancy figures indicate a change in

TABLE 14.2
Saturday Occupancy at a 100-Room Hotel

Saturday	Period	Occupancy	Three-Period Moving Average	Forecast
Aug. 1	1	79		
8	2	84		
15	3	83	82	
22	4	81	83	82
29	5	98	87	83
Sept. 5	6	100	93	87
12	7			93

the underlying average occupancy? To answer this question, we need a way of taking out the "noise" of occasional blips in the pattern so that we do not overreact to a change that is random rather than permanent and significant.

The N-period moving-average method can be used in this simple example to smooth out random variations and produce a reliable estimate of the underlying average occupancy. The method calculates a moving average MA_t for period t on the basis of selecting N of the most recent actual observations A_t, as shown in equation (2):

$$MA_t = \frac{A_t + A_{t-1} + A_{t-2} + \cdots A_{t-N+1}}{N} \tag{2}$$

If we select N equal to 3, then we cannot begin our calculation until period 3 (i.e., August 15), at which time we add the occupancy figures for the three most recent Saturdays (i.e., August 1, 8, and 15) and divide the sum by 3 to arrive at a three-period moving average of $[(83 + 84 + 79)/3] = 82$. We use this value to forecast occupancy for the following Saturday (i.e., August 22). The moving-average forecast has smoothed out the random fluctuations to track better the average occupancy, which then is used to forecast the next period. Each three-period *moving-average forecast* thus involves simply adding the three most recent occupancy values and dividing by 3. For example, to arrive at the moving average for August 22, we drop the value for August 1, add the value for August 22, and recalculate the average, getting 83. Continuing this iterative process for the remaining data, we see how the moving-average occupancy of approximately 82 percent for Saturdays in August has increased recently, reflecting the near-capacity occupancy of the past two weekends. If the local college football team, after playing two consecutive home games, is scheduled for an away game on September 12, how confident are you in forecasting next Saturday's occupancy at 93 percent?

Although our N-period moving average has identified a change in the underlying average occupancy, this method is slow to react because old data are given the same weight (i.e., $1/N$) as new data in calculating the averages. More recent data might be better indicators of change; therefore, we might wish to assign more weight to recent observations. Rather than arbitrarily assigning weights to our moving-average data to fix this shortcoming, we instead will use a more sophisticated forecasting method that systematically ages the data. Our next topic, exponential smoothing, also can accommodate trends and seasonality in the data.

Simple Exponential Smoothing

Simple exponential smoothing is the time series method most frequently used for demand forecasting. Simple exponential smoothing also "smooths out" blips in the data, but its power over the N-period moving average is threefold: (1) old data never are dropped or lost, (2) older data are given progressively less weight, and (3) the calculation is simple and requires only the most recent data.

Simple exponential smoothing is based on the concept of feeding back the *forecast error* to correct the previous smoothed value. In equation (3) below, S_t is the smoothed value for period t, A_t is the actual observed value for period t, and α is a smoothing constant that usually is assigned a value between 0.1 and 0.5.

$$S_t = S_{t-1} + \alpha(A_t - S_{t-1}) \tag{3}$$

The term $(A_t - S_{t-1})$ represents the forecast error because it is the difference between the actual observation and the smoothed value that was calculated in the prior period. A fraction α of this forecast error is added to the previous smoothed value to obtain the new smoothed value S_t. Note how self-correcting this method is when you consider that forecast errors can be either positive or negative.

Our moving-average analysis of the occupancy data in Table 14.2 indicated an actual increase in average occupancy over the two most recent Saturdays. These same occupancy data are repeated in Table 14.3, with the actual value for each period (A_t) shown in the third column. Using simple exponential smoothing, we will demonstrate again that a significant change in the mean occupancy has occurred.

Because we must start somewhere, let the first observed, or actual, value A_t in a series of data equal the first smoothed value S_t. Therefore, as Table 14.3 shows, S_1 for August 1 equals A_1 for August 1, or 79.00. The smoothed value for August 8 (S_2) then can be derived from the actual value for August 8 (A_2) and the previous smoothed value for August 1 (S_1) according to equation (3). We have selected an α equal to 0.5 because, as will be shown later, this results in a forecast that is similar to the one obtained using a three-period moving average. For August 8:

$$
\begin{aligned}
S_2 &= S_1 + \alpha(A_2 - S_1) \\
&= 79.00 + 0.5(84 - 79.00) \\
&= 81.50
\end{aligned}
$$

Similar calculations then are made to determine the smoothed values (S_3, S_4, S_5, S_6) for successive periods.

Simple exponential smoothing assumes that the pattern of data is distributed about a constant mean. Thus, the smoothed value calculated in period t is used as the forecast for period $(t + 1)$ rounded to an integer, as shown below:

$$F_{t+1} = S_t \tag{4}$$

Our best estimate for August 15 occupancy will be 81.50, the most recent smoothed value at the end of August 8. Note that the forecast error (84 – 79) was a positive 5 (i.e., we underestimated demand by 5), and that one-half of this error was added to the previous smoothed value to increase the new estimate of average occupancy. This concept of error feedback to correct an earlier estimate is an idea borrowed from control theory.

The smoothed values shown in Table 14.3 were calculated using an α value of 0.5. As noted, however, if we wish to make the smoothed values less responsive to the latest data, we can assign a smaller value to α. Figure 14.1 demonstrates graphically how an α of 0.1 and of 0.5 smooth the curve of the actual values. We can see easily in this figure that the smoothed curve, particularly with an α of 0.5, has reduced the extremes (i.e., the dips and peak) and responded to the increased occupancy in the last two Saturdays. Therefore, basing forecasts on smoothed data helps to prevent overreacting to the extremes in the actual observed values.

Equation (3) can be rewritten as follows:

$$S_t = \alpha(A_t) + (1 - \alpha)S_{t-1} \tag{5}$$

The basis for the name "exponential smoothing" can be observed in the weights that are given past data in equation (5). We see that A_t is given a weight α in determining S_t, and we easily can show by substitution that A_{t-1} is given a weight α(1 – α). In general, actual value A_{t-n} is given a weight $\alpha(1 - \alpha)^n$, as Figure 14.2 shows by graphing the exponential decay

TABLE 14.3 Simple Exponential Smoothing: Saturday Hotel Occupancy (α = 0.5)

Saturday	Period	Actual Occupancy	Smoothed Value	Forecast	Error	Absolute Error	Squared Error	Percent Error
	t	A_t	S_t	F_t	$A_t - F_t$	$\lvert A_t - F_t\rvert$	$(A_t - F_t)^2$	$\frac{\lvert A_t - F_t\rvert}{A_t}$
Aug. 1	1	79	79.00					
8	2	84	81.50	79	5	5	25	6
15	3	83	82.25	82	1	1	1	1
22	4	81	81.63	82	−1	1	1	1
29	5	98	89.81	82	16	16	256	16
Sept. 5	6	100	94.91	90	10	10	100	10
				Total	31	33	383	34
				Forecast Error	CFE 31	MAD 6.6	MSE 76.6	MAPE 6.8

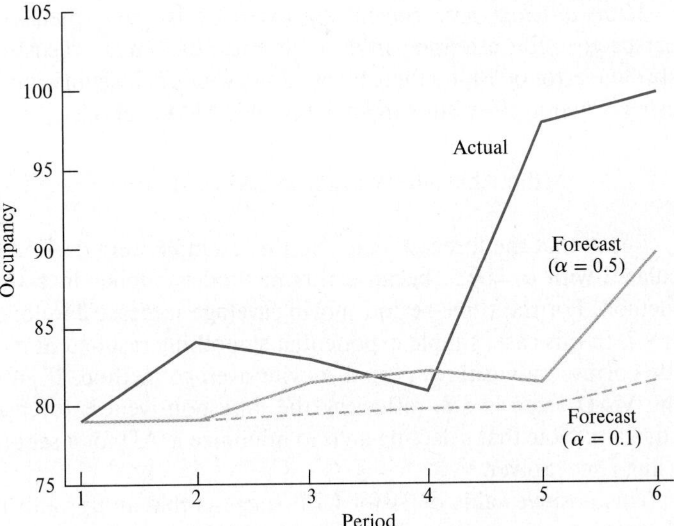

FIGURE 14.1
Simple Exponential Smoothing: Saturday Hotel Occupancy ($\alpha = 0.1$ and $\alpha = 0.5$)

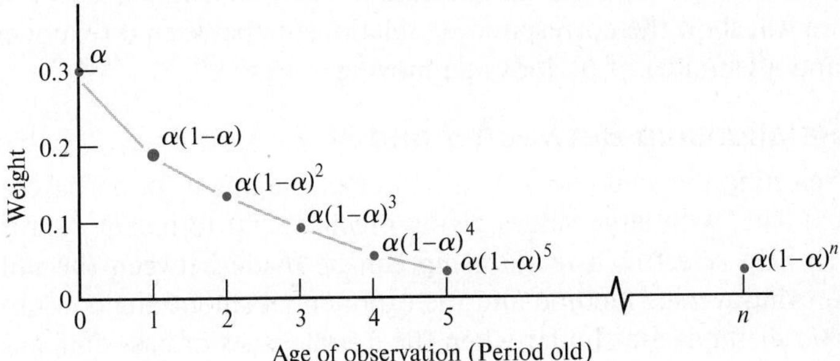

FIGURE 14.2
Distribution of Weight Given Past Data in Exponential Smoothing ($\alpha = 0.3$)

of weights given a series of observations over time. Note that older observations never disappear entirely from the calculation of S_t as they would when the N-period moving average is used, but they do assume progressively decreasing importance.

Forecast Error

Although it is obvious in Figure 14.1 that the forecast curves have smoothed out the peaks and valleys of the actual data, albeit with some lag, how do we measure the accuracy of forecasts?

First, we should expect an unbiased forecast with respect to its tracking of the actual mean for the data. Thus, the sum of the forecast errors should tend toward zero, taking into account both positive and negative differences. If it does, then we should look for underlying trends or seasonality and account for them explicitly. We use equation (6) and the results shown in Table 14.3 to calculate the *cumulative forecast error* (CFE) to be 31.

$$\text{Cumulative Forcast Error (CFE)} = \sum_{t=1}^{n}(A_t - F_t) \tag{6}$$

The most commonly used measure of forecast error is *mean absolute deviation* (MAD) calculated using equation (7). In Table 14.3, the mean absolute deviation is 6.6. We will continue to use MAD, which gives equal weight to each error, as our measure of forecast error throughout the remainder of the chapter.

$$\text{Mean Absolute Deviation (MAD)} = \frac{1}{n}\sum_{t=1}^{n}|A_t - F_t| \tag{7}$$

If large errors are particularly serious, squaring the error will give them more weight. The *mean squared error* (MSE) for the results in Table 14.3 is calculated using equation (8) and results in a value of 76.6, which reflects the large errors in periods 5 and 6.

$$\text{Mean Square Error (MSE)} = \frac{1}{n}\sum_{t=1}^{n}(A_t - F_t)^2 \tag{8}$$

Mean absolute percentage error (MAPE) is used when errors need to be put into perspective. For example, an absolute error of 2 in a forecast of 10 is huge relative to an absolute error of 2 for a forecast of 1,000, which is insignificant. For the data in Table 14.3, using equation (9) results in an acceptable MAPE of 6.8.

$$\text{Mean Absolute Percentage Error (MAPE)} = \frac{1}{n}\sum_{t=1}^{n}\frac{|A_t - F_t|}{A_t}(100) \qquad (9)$$

Recall that the forecast values in this example were derived from smoothed values calculated with $\alpha = 0.5$, because this method is similar to a three-period moving-average method. For the three-period moving-average forecast developed earlier, the MAD value is 9.7. In this case, simple exponential smoothing resulted in more accurate forecasts than the corresponding three-period moving-average method. If an α of 0.1 is used, however, the MAD value is 8.8, reflecting the unresponsiveness to change of a small smoothing constant. Note that selecting an α to minimize MAD for a set of data can be accomplished using Excel Solver.

This positive value of 31 for CFE suggests that an upward trend exists in the data and that our simple exponential smoothing forecasts are falling short of actual hotel occupancy. Thus, we must incorporate a trend adjustment into our forecast. First, however, we will show the corresponding relationship between α (exponential smoothing constant) and N (number of periods in a moving average).

Relationship Between α and N

Selecting the value for α is a matter of judgment, often based on the pattern of historical data, with large values giving much weight to recent data in anticipation of changes. To help select α, a relationship can be made between the number of periods N in the moving-average method and the exponential smoothing constant α. If we assume that the two methods are similar when the average ages of past data are equal, then the following relationship results:

Moving average:

$$\begin{aligned}\text{Average age} &= \frac{(0 + 1 + 2 + \cdots + N - 1)}{N}\\ &= \frac{(N-1)(N/2)}{N}\\ &= \frac{N-1}{2}\end{aligned}$$

Exponential smoothing:

$$\begin{aligned}\text{Average age} &= 0(\alpha) + 1(\alpha)(1-\alpha) + 2(\alpha)(1-\alpha)^2 + \cdots\\ &= \frac{(1-\alpha)}{\alpha}\end{aligned}$$

The average age for exponential smoothing is a geometric series with the sum equal to

$$\frac{ar}{(1-r)^2} \qquad \text{for } a = \alpha \qquad \text{and} \qquad r = 1 - \alpha$$

When the average ages for exponential smoothing and moving average are equated, the result is

$$\alpha = \frac{2}{(N+1)} \qquad \text{or} \qquad N = \frac{(2-\alpha)}{\alpha}$$

Using this relationship results in the following sample values for equating α and N:

α	0.05	0.1	0.2	0.3	0.4	0.5	0.667
N	39	19	9	5.7	4	3	2

As shown, the usual assignment of a smoothing value between 0.1 and 0.5 is reasonable when compared with the number of periods in an equivalent moving-average forecast. The particular value assigned to α is a trade-off between overreacting to random fluctuations about a constant mean and detecting a change in the mean value. Higher values of α are more responsive to change because of the greater weight that is given to recent data. In practice, the value of α often is selected on the basis of minimizing the forecast error as measured by the mean absolute deviation (MAD).

Exponential Smoothing with Trend Adjustment

The *trend* in a set of data is the average rate at which the observed values change from one period to the next over time. The changes created by the trend can be treated using an extension of simple exponential smoothing.

Table 14.4 follows the experience of a new commuter airline during its first eight weeks of business. The average weekly load factors (i.e., percentages of seats sold) show a steady increase, from approximately 30 percent for week 1 to approximately 70 percent for week 8. In this example, the smoothed value S_t is calculated using equation (10), which is equation (5) modified by the addition of a trend value T_{t-1} to the previous smoothed value S_{t-1} to account for the weekly rate of increase in the load factor.

$$S_t = \alpha(A_t) + (1 - \alpha)(S_{t-1} + T_{t-1}) \tag{10}$$

To incorporate a trend adjustment in our calculation, we will use β as a smoothing constant. This constant usually is assigned a value between 0.1 and 0.5 and can be the same as, or different from, α. The trend for a given period t is defined by $(S_t - S_{t-1})$, the rate of change in smoothed value from one period to the next (i.e., the slope of the demand curve). The smoothed trend T_t then is calculated at period t using equation (11), which is a modification of the basic exponential smoothing equation–equation (5)–with the observed trend $(S_t - S_{t-1})$ used in place of A_t.

$$T_t = \beta(S_t - S_{t-1}) + (1 - \beta)T_{t-1} \tag{11}$$

To anticipate cash flows during the business startup period, the commuter airline owners are interested in forecasting future weekly load factors. After observing the first two weeks of activity, you are asked to provide a forecast for week 3. The smoothed values, trend figures, and forecasts in Table 14.4 are calculated in a stepwise manner. For the first observation in a series, week 1 in this instance, the smoothed value S_1 is equal to the actual value A_1, and the trend T_1 is set equal to 0.00. The forecast for week 2 is calculated using equation (12). In this case, $F_2 = 31 + 0.00 = 31$ rounded to an integer.

$$F_{t+1} = S_t + T_t \tag{12}$$

TABLE 14.4
Exponential Smoothing with Trend Adjustment: Commuter Airline Load Factor ($\alpha = 0.5$, $\beta = 0.3$)

Week	Actual Load Factor	Smoothed Value	Smoothed Trend	Forecast	Forecast Error
t	A_t	S_t	T_t	F_t	$\lvert A_t - F_t\rvert$
1	31	31.00	0.00		
2	40	35.50	1.35	31	9
3	43	39.93	2.27	37	6
4	52	47.10	3.74	42	10
5	49	49.92	3.47	51	2
6	64	58.69	5.06	53	11
7	58	60.88	4.20	64	6
8	68	66.54	4.63	65	3
					MAD 6.7

To compute the smoothed values for week 2 and a forecast for week 3, we will use $\alpha = 0.5$ and $\beta = 0.3$. First, the smoothed value S_2 for week 2 is calculated using equation (6):

$$S_2 = (0.5)(40) + (1 - 0.5)(31 + 0.00)$$
$$= 35.50$$

Now, we calculate the trend for week 2 with equation (7):

$$T_2 = (0.3)(35.50 - 31.00) + (1 - 0.3)0.00$$
$$= 1.35$$

The final step is to make a forecast for week 3 according to equation (8):

$$F_3 = 35.5 + 1.35 = 36.85 \cong 37$$

When the actual data for the following weeks are received, similar calculations can be made for the smoothed value, the trend, the forecast, and the forecast error. For all of the forecasts shown in Table 14.4, the MAD is 6.7.

The sum of the forecast error values (both positive and negative) is a measure of forecast bias. For this example $\Sigma(A_t - F_t) = 9 + 6 + 10 - 2 + 11 - 6 + 3 = 31$. The sum of the forecast errors for an unbiased forecast should approach zero (i.e., the positive and negative errors cancel out each other).

In Figure 14.3, the actual load factors are plotted against the forecasts. Note, that even with trend adjustment the forecast has lagged actual except for weeks 5 and 7.

Exponential Smoothing with Seasonal Adjustment

To account for seasonal effects on a set of data, we can use another extension of simple exponential smoothing. In simplest terms, we first remove the seasonality from the data and then smooth those data as we already have learned; finally, we put the seasonality back in to determine a forecast.

We will apply this seasonal adjustment to the data in Table 14.5, which reports the number of passengers per month taking a ferry to a resort island in the Caribbean for the years 2019 and 2020. In general, we denote a cycle L as the length of one season. L may be any length of time, even the 24 hours of a day, but frequently, as in this case, it is 12 months. Note that we must have actual data for at least one full season before we can begin smoothing and forecasting calculations.

A *seasonality index* I_t is used to deseasonalize the data in a given cycle L. Initially, I_t is estimated by calculating a ratio of the actual value for period t, A_t, divided by the average value $\overline{A}$ for all periods in cycle L as shown in equation (13):

$$I_t = \frac{A_t}{\overline{A}} \tag{13}$$

where $\overline{A} = (A_1 + A_2 + \ldots A_L)/L$

In our passenger ferry example, $\overline{A} = 1.971.83$ (average passengers per month for 2019), and by substituting this value into equation (13), we can calculate the index I_t for each

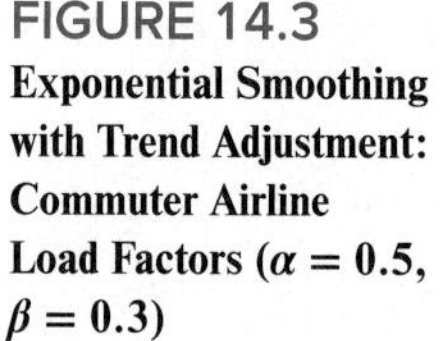

FIGURE 14.3
Exponential Smoothing with Trend Adjustment: Commuter Airline Load Factors ($\alpha = 0.5$, $\beta = 0.3$)

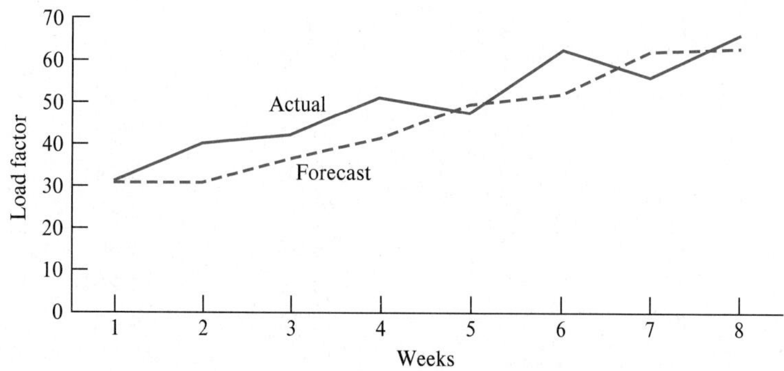

TABLE 14.5
Exponential Smoothing with Seasonal Adjustment: Ferry Passengers Taken to a Resort Island ($\alpha = 0.2$, $\gamma = 0.3$)

Period	t	Actual Passengers A_t	Smoothed Value S_t	Index I_t	Fore-cast F_t	Forecast Error $\lvert A_t - F_t \rvert$
2019						
January	1	1,651	—	0.837	—	
February	2	1,305	—	0.662	—	
March	3	1,617	—	0.820	—	
April	4	1,721	—	0.873	—	
May	5	2,015	—	1.022	—	
June	6	2,297	—	1.165	—	
July	7	2,606	—	1.322	—	
August	8	2,687	—	1.363	—	
September	9	2,292	—	1.162	—	
October	10	1,981	—	1.005	—	
November	11	1,696	—	0.860	—	
December	12	1,794	1,794.00	0.910	—	
2020						
January	13	1,806	1,866.74	0.876	—	—
February	14	1,731	2,016.35	0.721	1,236	495
March	15	1,733	2,035.76	0.829	1,653	80
April	16	1,904	2,064.81	0.888	1,777	127
May	17	2,036	2,050.28	1.013	2,110	74
June	18	2,560	2,079.71	1.185	2,389	171
July	19	2,679	2,069.06	1.314	2,749	70
August	20	2,821	2,069.19	1.363	2,820	1
September	21	2,359	2,061.38	1.157	2,404	45
October	22	2,160	2,078.95	1.015	2,072	88
November	23	1,802	2,082.23	0.862	1,788	14
December	24	1,853	2,073.04	0.905	1,895	42
						MAD 110

period in the first season of 12 periods. The resulting indices for the months of 2019, which are shown in column 5 of Table 14.5, then are used to deseasonalize the data for the corresponding months in 2020 according to equation (14), which is a minor modification of our basic exponential smoothing equation–equation (5)–with A_t adjusted to account for seasonality using index I_{t-L}.

$$S_t = \alpha \frac{A_t}{I_{t-L}} + (1 - \alpha)S_{t-1} \tag{14}$$

For this example, data for the 12 months in 2019 are used to give initial estimates of the seasonality indices. Therefore, we cannot begin to calculate new smoothed data until period 13 (i.e., January 2020). To begin the process, we assume that S_{12} equals A_{12}, as shown in Table 14.5 with a value of 1,794.00. The smoothed value for January 2020 now can be calculated using equation (14), with $I_{t-L} = 0.837$ (i.e., the index I_t of 12 months ago for January 2019) and $\alpha = 0.2$:

$$S_{13} = (0.2)\frac{1{,}806}{0.837} + (1 - 0.2)1{,}794.00$$
$$= 1{,}866.74$$

The forecast for February (period $t + 1$) then is made by seasonalizing the smoothed value for January according to the following formula:

$$F_{t+1} = (S_t)(I_{t-L+1}) \tag{15}$$

Note that the seasonalizing factor I_{t-L+1} in this case is the index I_t for February 2019. Therefore, our forecast for February 2020 is

$$F_{14} = (1{,}866.74)(0.662)$$
$$= 1{,}235.78 \cong 1236$$

If the seasonality indices are stable, forecasts that are based on only one cycle, L, will be reliable. If, however, the indices are not stable, they can be adjusted, or smoothed, as new data become available. After calculating the smoothed value S_t for an actual value A_t at the most recent period t, we can denote a new observation for a seasonality index at period t as (A_t/S_t). To apply the concept of exponential smoothing to the index, we use a new constant γ, which usually is assigned a value between 0.1 and 0.5. The smoothed estimate of the seasonality index then is calculated from the following formula:

$$I_t = \gamma\frac{A_t}{S_t} + (1-\gamma)I_{t-L} \tag{16}$$

Now, we can continue the calculations for 2020 in Table 14.5 by using equation (16) to update the seasonality indices for each month for future use. Remember, however, that in actual practice, smoothed values, indices, and forecasts for each period (i.e., month) in this new season of L periods would be calculated on a month-to-month basis as the most recent actual values became available. Here, according to equation (16), the new smoothed seasonality index for January 2020, I_{13}, using $\gamma = 0.3$ is

$$I_{13} = 0.3\frac{1{,}806}{1{,}866.74} + (1-0.3)0.867 = 0.876$$

The MAD for February through December 2020 is 110, which indicates a very good fit of forecasts to actual data that exhibit a definite seasonality. Is it possible, however, to make even more accurate forecasts?

Exponential Smoothing with Trend and Seasonal Adjustments

The answer to the earlier question–Is it possible to make even more accurate forecasts? –is yes (sometimes). In some cases, adjusting only for trend or seasonality will provide the current best estimate of the average; in other cases, the forecast can be improved by considering all factors together. We can include *both* trend and seasonal adjustments in exponential smoothing by weighting a *base* smoothed value with trend and seasonal indices to forecast the following period. The appropriate equations are

$$S_t = \alpha\frac{A_t}{I_{t-L}} + (1-\alpha)(S_{t-1} + T_{t-1}) \tag{17}$$

$$T_t = \beta(S_t - S_{t-1}) + (1-\beta)T_{t-1} \tag{18}$$

$$I_t = \gamma\frac{A_t}{S_t} + (1-\gamma)I_{t-L} \tag{19}$$

$$F_{t+1} = (S_t + T_t)I_{t-L+1} \tag{20}$$

The values in Table 14.6 shown in bold are the result of Excel formulas. Table 14.7 contains the formulas for February 2020 shown on line 20 of Table 14.6. These formulas are automatically repeated for lines 21 through 30 using the copy command in Excel. Note the use of $B$1, $B$2, and $B$3 to freeze the cell reference to the smoothing parameters (alpha, beta, gamma) when the formulas are copied. This feature allows one to change these parameters and recalculate the forecasts to find the values for α, β, and γ that

TABLE 14.6 Exponential Smoothing with Seasonal and Trend Adjustments: Excel Spreadsheet Illustration Ferry Passengers Taken to a Resort Island (*alpha* = 0.2 , *beta* = 0.2, *gamma* = 0.3)

	A	B	C	D	E	F	G	H
1	*alpha*	0.2						
2	*beta*	0.2						
3	*gamma*	0.3						
4			Actual	Smoothed	Trend	Index	Forecast	Error
5	Period	t	A_t	S_t	T_t	I_t	F_t	$\|A_t - F_t\|$
6				2019–2020				
7	January	1	1,651			0.837		
8	February	2	1,305			0.662		
9	March	3	1,617			0.820		
10	April	4	1,721			0.873		
11	May	5	2,015			1.022		
12	June	6	2,297			1.165		
13	July	7	2,606			1.322		
14	August	8	2,687			1.363		
15	September	9	2,292			1.162		
16	October	10	1,981			1.005		
17	November	11	1,696			0.860		
18	December	12	1,794	1,794.00	0.00	0.910		
19	January	13	1,806	**1,866.74**	**14.55**	**0.876**		
20	February	14	1,731	**2,027.99**	**43.89**	**0.719**	**1,245**	**486**
21	March	15	1,733	**2,080.19**	**45.55**	**0.824**	**1,699**	**34**
22	April	16	1,904	**2,136.79**	**47.76**	**0.878**	**1,856**	**48**
23	May	17	2,036	**2,146.07**	**40.07**	**1.000**	**2,233**	**197**
24	June	18	2,560	**2,188.39**	**40.52**	**1.166**	**2,547**	**13**
25	July	19	2,679	**2,188.42**	**32.42**	**1.293**	**2,947**	**268**
26	August	20	2,821	**2,190.61**	**26.37**	**1.340**	**3,027**	**206**
27	September	21	2,359	**2,179.61**	**18.90**	**1.138**	**2,576**	**217**
28	October	22	2,160	**2,188.66**	**16.93**	**1.000**	**2,210**	**50**
29	November	23	1,802	**2,183.54**	**12.52**	**0.850**	**1,897**	**95**
30	December	24	1,853	**2,164.10**	**6.13**	**0.894**	**1,998**	**145**
31								
32							MAD	160

TABLE 14.7 February 2020 Excel Formulas Found in Table 14.6

Cell	Value	Formula	Excel Representation
D20	2027.99	(17)	=C20/F8 *$B$1+ (1 – $B$1)*(D19 + E19)
E20	43.89	(18)	=$B$2*(D20 – D19) + (1 – $B$2)*E19
F20	0.719	(19)	=$B$3*C20/D20 + (1 – $B$1)*F8
G20	1245	(20)	=(D19 – E19)*F8
H20	486	—	=ABS(G20 – C20)

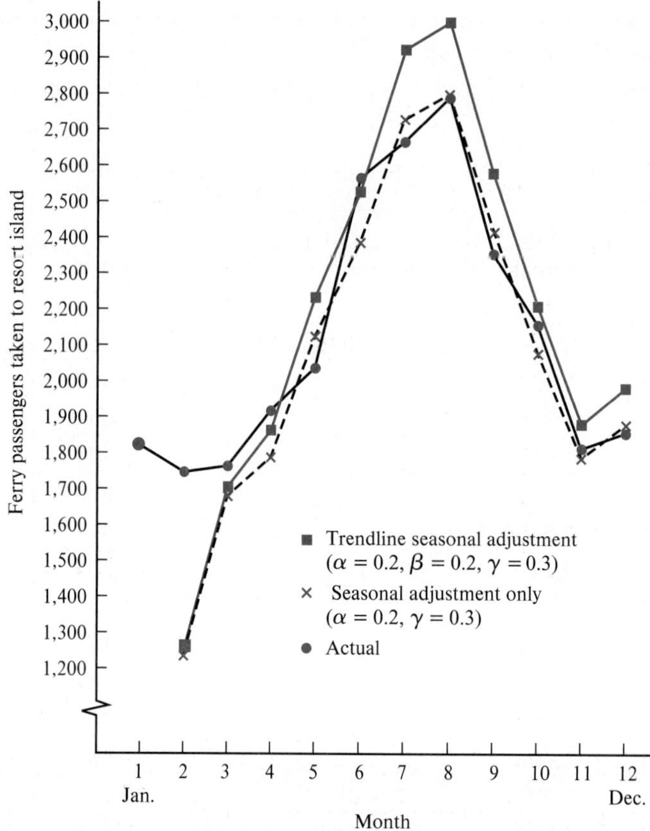

FIGURE 14.4
Exponential Smoothing with Seasonal Adjustment

minimize MAD. The resulting MAD of 160 tells us that, in this case, we have not gained any improvement in our forecast by adding a trend adjustment to the seasonal adjustment used in Table 14.5. Figure 14.4 demonstrates graphically the results of treating the actual data with a seasonal adjustment only, and with both seasonal and trend adjustments.

Summary of Exponential Smoothing

Exponential smoothing is a relatively easy and straightforward way to make short-term forecasts. This forecasting process has many attributes, including:

- All past data are considered in the smoothing process.
- Recent data are assigned more weight than older data.
- Only the most recent data are required to update a forecast.
- The model is easy to implement on a personal computer using spreadsheet software.
- Smoothing constants allow us to alter the rate at which the model responds to changes in the underlying pattern in the data.

Summary

Decisions to embark on a new service concept often require subjective judgments about the future needs of customers. Subjective models like the Delphi method allow a panel of experts to defend their positions concerning the future and, through a number of iterations, these experts approach a consensus. Regression models have found application in service location analysis because of the need to account for several independent variables that contribute to demand generation. We ended our discussion of forecasting with an examination of time series models. Although the moving-average method is straightforward, we discovered that exponential smoothing has many superior qualities and has found wide acceptance in practice. Accounting for trends and seasonality is an important feature in forecasting service demand and is accommodated easily by means of exponential smoothing.

Service Benchmark

GOOGLING THE FUTURE

Marketing professionals have a new tool in Google Trends, an index of searches for a particular word updated daily. This information can be a leading indicator of future consumer buying behavior because it captures the search effort prior to purchase. Take, for example, the words Ford and vehicle and the corresponding Ford light-vehicle sales for the years 2004–2008.

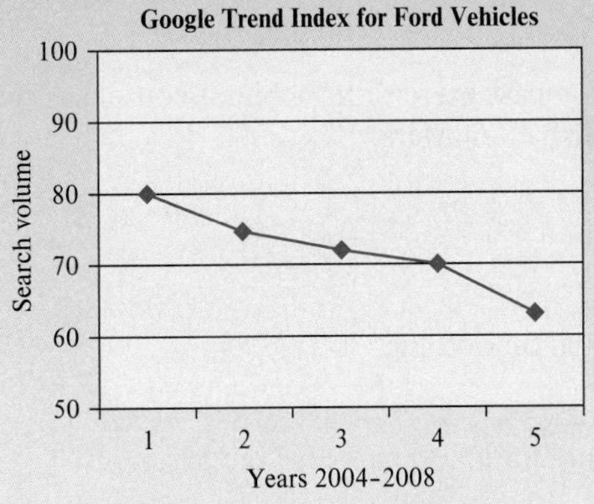

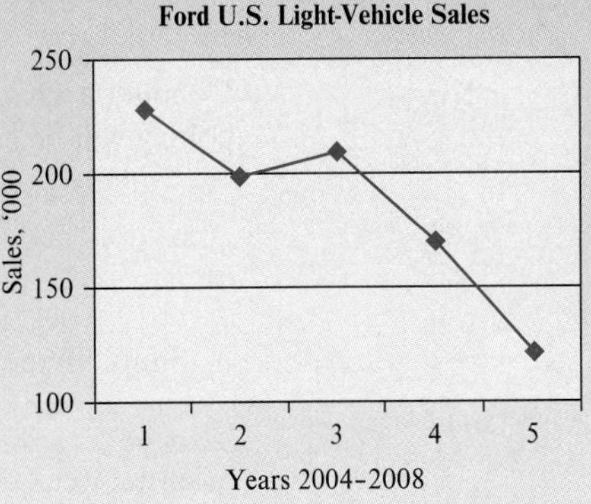

The power of Google Trends has been used by country tourist bureaus. For example, a high volume of searches for Hong Kong by people in the United States, Britain, and Australia is related to future tourist visits.

Source: Reported in "Googling the Future," *The Economist,* April 18, 2009, p. 82.

Key Terms and Definitions

Cross-impact analysis a technological forecasting method that assumes some future event is related to an earlier event with an estimated probability. *p. 406*

Cumulative forecast error (CFE) is the sum of forecast errors that should approach zero for an unbiased forecast. *p. 411*

Delphi method a technological forecasting method that uses a group of experts to arrive at a consensus about the future. *p. 405*

Exponential smoothing a time series forecast based on the concept of adjusting a previous forecast by feeding back a percentage of the forecast error. *p. 408*

Forecast error the difference between the actual observation and the forecasted value. *p. 409*

Mean absolute deviation (MAD) a measure of forecasting accuracy calculated as the average absolute forecast error. *p. 411*

Mean absolute percentage error (MAPE) puts the forecast error in perspective. *p. 412*

Mean squared error (MSE) gives large errors more weight in the measure of forecast accuracy. *p. 411*

Moving-average forecast a simple time series forecast formed by adding together the most recent data and dividing by the number of observations. *p. 409*

Topics for Discussion

1. What characteristics of service organizations make forecast accuracy important?
2. For each of the three forecasting methods (i.e., time series, causal, and subjective), what costs are associated with the development and use of the forecast model? What costs are associated with forecast error?
3. The number of customers at a bank likely will vary by the hour of the day and by the day of the month. What are the implications of this for choosing a forecasting model?

4. Suggest a number of independent variables for a regression model to predict the potential sales volume of a given location for a retail store (e.g., a video rental store).
5. Why is the *N*-period moving-average model still in common use if the simple exponential smoothing model has superior qualities?
6. What changes in α, β, and γ would you recommend to improve the performance of the trendline seasonal adjustment forecast shown in Figure 14.4?

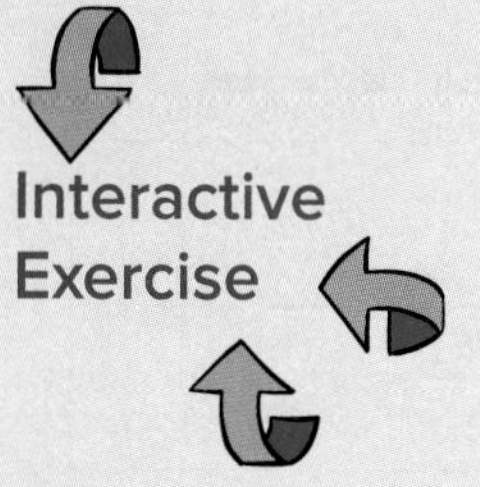

Interactive Exercise

Conduct a Delphi forecast exercise to obtain a consensus on the decade when a human colony will be established on Mars.

Solved Problems

1. Simple Exponential Smoothing

Problem Statement

The first-week demand for a new barbecue burger is

Day	Demand, Burgers
Monday	22
Tuesday	27
Wednesday	38
Thursday	32
Friday	34

What is the forecast demand for next Monday using a smoothing constant $\alpha = 0.3$?

Solution

Using equation (5) with $\alpha = 0.3$ yields the simple exponential smoothing model $S_t = 0.3(A_t) + 0.7(S_{t-1})$ with $F_{t+1} = S_t$. The calculations are shown in the worktable below.

Day	Period t	Actual A_t	Smoothed S_t	Forecast F_t	Error $\lvert A_t - F_t \rvert$
Mon.	1	22	22	—	—
Tues.	2	27	23.5	22	5
Wed.	3	38	27.85	24	14
Thurs.	4	32	29.095	28	4
Fri.	5	34	30.5665	29	5
Mon.				31	MAD = 7.0

2. Exponential Smoothing with Trend

Problem Statement

Recalculate the forecast for next Monday using a trend adjustment with $\beta = 0.2$. Using the MAD measure, compare the quality of this trend-adjusted forecast with the simple exponential smoothing in Problem 1.

Solution

Using equations (6), (7), and (8) with $\alpha = 0.3$ and $\beta = 0.2$, we formulate an exponential smoothing model with trend adjustment. Application of this model is shown in the following worktable.

$$S_t = 0.3(A_t) + 0.7(S_{t-1} + T_{t-1})$$

$$T_t = 0.2(S_t - S_{t-1}) + 0.8(T_{t-1})$$

$$F_{t+1} = S_t + T_t$$

Day	Period t	Actual A_t	Smoothed S_t	Trend T_t	Forecast F_t	Error $\|A_t - F_t\|$
Mon.	1	22	22	0	—	—
Tues.	2	27	23.5	0.3	22	5
Wed.	3	38	28.06	1.15	23.8 ≅ 24	14
Thurs.	4	32	30.047	1.3174	29.21 ≅ 29	3
Fri.	5	34	31.55508	1.355536	31.3644 ≅ 31	3
Mon.					32.9106 ≅ 33	MAD = 6.25

3. Exponential Smoothing with Seasonal Adjustment

Problem Statement

Given the data below from the second week, there appears to be a cycle during the week peaking on Wednesday. Recalculate the forecast for Monday of the following week using a seasonal adjustment with $\gamma = 0.3$.

Day	Demand, Burgers
Monday	25
Tuesday	31
Wednesday	42
Thursday	34
Friday	32

Solution

Using equations (13), (14), (15), and (16) with $\alpha = 0.3$ and $\gamma = 0.2$ yields the following exponential smoothing model with seasonal adjustment.

$$I_t = \frac{A_t}{A}$$

$$S_t = 0.3\frac{A_t}{I_{t-L}} + 0.7(S_{t-1})$$

$$F_{t+1} = (S_t)(I_{t-L+1})$$

$$I_t = 0.2\frac{A_t}{S_t} + 0.8(I_{t-L})$$

First, the average value $\overline{A}$ for the first week is calculated for use in formula (9).

$$\overline{A} = (22 + 27 + 38 + 32 + 34)/5 = 30.6$$

Second, using equation (9), the initial seasonality indexes are calculated as shown in the worktable below for the first week:

Day	Period t	Actual A_t	Smoothed S_t	Index I_t
Mon.	1	22	—	0.72
Tues.	2	27	—	0.88
Wed.	3	38	—	1.24
Thurs.	4	32	—	1.05
Fri.	5	34	34	1.11

Third, the smoothed values, updated seasonal index, and forecast are made using equations (14), (15), and (16) as shown in the worktable below:

Day	Period t	Actual A_t	Smoothed S_t	Index I_t	Forecast F_t	Error $\|A_t - F_t\|$
Mon.	6	25	34.217	0.74	—	—
Tues.	7	31	34.520	0.88	30.11 = 30	1
Wed.	8	42	34.325	1.24	42.80 = 43	1
Thurs.	9	34	33.742	1.04	36.04 = 36	2
Fri.	10	32	32.268	1.09	37.45 = 37	5
Mon.	11				23.88 = 24	MAD = 2.25

Exercises

14.1. In September, there were 1,035 checking-account customers at a neighborhood bank. The forecast for September, which was made in August, was for 1,065 checking-account customers. Use an α of 0.1 to update the forecast for October.

14.2. During the noon hour this past Wednesday at a fast-food restaurant, 72 hamburgers were sold. The smoothed value calculated the week before was 67. Update the forecast for next Wednesday using simple exponential smoothing and an α of 0.1.

14.3. For the data in Exercise 14.2, update the fast-food restaurant forecast if a trend value of 1.4 was calculated for the previous week. Use a β of 0.3 to update the trend for this week, and determine the forecast for next Wednesday using exponential smoothing with trend adjustment.

14.4. The demand for a certain drug in a hospital has been increasing. For the past six months, the following demand has been observed:

Month	Demand, Units
January	15
February	18
March	22
April	23
May	27
June	26

Use a three-month moving average to make a forecast for July.

14.5. For the data in Exercise 14.4, use an α of 0.1 to make a forecast for July.

14.6. For the data in Exercise 14.4, use an α of 0.1 and a β of 0.2 to make a forecast for July and August. Calculate the MAD for your January through June forecasts.

14.7. Prepare a spreadsheet model for the Saturday hotel occupancy data in Table 14.3, and recalculate the forecasts using an α of 0.3. What is the new MAD?

14.8. Prepare a spreadsheet model for the commuter airline's weekly load factor data in Table 14.4, and recalculate the forecasts using an α of 0.2 and a β of 0.2. Have you improved on the original MAD?

14.9. Prepare a spreadsheet model for the ferry passenger data in Table 14.5, and recalculate the forecasts using an α of 0.3 and a γ of 0.2. Has this change in the smoothing constants improved the MAD?

14.10. Prepare a spreadsheet model for the ferry passenger data in Table 14.6, and recalculate the forecasts using an α of 0.3, a β of 0.1, and a γ of 0.2. Has this change in the smoothing constants improved the MAD?

Oak Hollow Medical Evaluation Center[3] — CASE 14.1

Oak Hollow Medical Evaluation Center is a nonprofit agency offering multidisciplinary diagnostic services to study children with disabilities or developmental delays. The center can test each patient for physical, psychological, or social problems. Fees for services are based on an ability-to-pay schedule.

The evaluation center exists in a highly competitive environment. Many public-spirited organizations are competing for shrinking funds, and many groups such as private physicians, private and school psychologists, and social service organizations also are "competing" for the same patients. As a result of this situation, the center finds itself in an increasingly vulnerable financial position.

Mr. Abel, the director of the center, is becoming increasingly concerned with the center's ability to attract adequate funding and serve community needs. Mr. Abel now must develop an accurate estimate of the future patient load, staffing requirements, and operating expenses as part of his effort to attract funding. To this end, the director has approached an operations management professor at the local university for assistance in preparing a patient, staffing, and budget forecast for the coming year. The professor has asked you to aid her in this project. Tables 14.8 through 14.11 give you some pertinent information.

Assignments

1. Given the information available and your knowledge of different forecasting techniques, recommend a specific forecasting technique for this study. Consider the advantages and disadvantages of your preferred technique, and identify what additional information, if any, Mr. Abel would need.
2. Develop forecasts for patient, staffing, and budget levels for next year.

TABLE 14.8 Annual Number of Patient Tests Performed*

Test	2018	2019	2020	2021	2022
Physical exam	390	468	509	490	582
Speech and hearing screening	102	124	180	148	204
Psychological testing	168	312	376	386	437
Social-worker interview	106	188	184	222	244

*All entering patients are given a physical examination. Patients then are scheduled for additional testing deemed appropriate.

TABLE 14.9 Annual Expenses

Area	2018	2019	2020	2021	2022
Physical and neurological exams	$18,200	$24,960	$ 32,760	$ 31,500	$ 41,600
Speech and hearing tests	2,040	2,074	3,960	3,950	4,850
Psychological testing	6,720	12,480	16,450	16,870	20,202
Social-worker interview	3,320	3,948	4,416	5,550	7,592
Subtotal	$30,280	$43,462	$ 57,586	$ 57,870	$ 74,244
Other expenses	46,559	48,887	51,820	55,447	59,883
Total	$76,839	$92,349	$109,406	$113,317	$134,127

TABLE 14.10 Monthly Patient Demand, September 2021–December 2022

	Physical Exam	Speech and Hearing Tests	Psychological Testing	Social-Worker Interview
		2021		
September	54	16	42	24
October	67	21	54	31
November	74	22	48	33
December	29	9	23	13

TABLE 14.10 (Continued)

	Physical Exam	Speech and Hearing Tests	Psychological Testing	Social-Worker Interview
		2022		
January	58	20	44	24
February	52	18	39	22
March	47	16	35	20
April	41	14	31	17
May	35	12	26	15
June	29	10	22	12
July	23	8	17	10
August	29	10	22	12
September	65	24	48	27
October	81	29	61	34
November	87	31	66	37
December	35	12	26	14

TABLE 14.11 Current Staffing Levels*

Physicians	2 part-time, 18 hours per week
Speech and hearing clinician	1 part-time, 20 hours per week
Psychologists	1 full-time, 38 hours per week
	1 part-time, 16 hours per week
Social worker	1 full-time, 40 hours per week

*The Oak Hollow Medical Evaluation Center operates on a 50-week year.

Gnomial Functions, Inc.[4] CASE 14.2

Gnomial Functions, Inc. (GFI), is a medium-sized consulting firm in San Francisco that specializes in developing various forecasts of product demand, sales, consumption, or other information for its clients. To a lesser degree, it also has developed ongoing models for internal use by its clients. When contacted by a potential client, GFI usually establishes a basic work agreement with the firm's top management that sets out the general goals of the end product, primary contact personnel in both firms, and an outline of the project's overall scope (including any necessary time constraints for intermediate and final completion and a rough price estimate for the contract). Following this step, a team of GFI personnel is assembled to determine the most appropriate forecasting technique and develop a more detailed work program to be used as the basis for final contract negotiations. This team, which can vary in size according to the scope of the project and the client's needs, will perform the tasks that are established by the work program in conjunction with any personnel from the client firm who would be included in the team.

Recently, GFI was contacted by a rapidly growing regional firm that manufactures, sells, and installs active solar water-heating equipment for commercial and residential applications. DynaSol Industries has seen its sales increase by more than 200 percent during the past 18 months, and it wishes to obtain a reliable estimate of its sales during the next 18 months. The company management expects that sales should increase substantially because of competing energy costs, tax-credit availability, and fundamental shifts in the attitudes of the regional population toward so-called exotic solar systems. The company also faces increasing competition within this burgeoning market. This situation requires major strategic decisions concerning the company's future. When GFI was contacted, DynaSol almost had reached the manufacturing capacity of its present facility, and if it wishes to continue growing with the market, it must expand either by relocating to a new facility entirely or by developing a second manufacturing location. Each involves certain known costs, and each has its advantages and disadvantages. The major unknown factors as far as management is concerned are growth of the overall market for this type of product and how large a market share the company would be able to capture.

Table 14.12 contains the preliminary information available to GFI on DynaSol's past sales.

Assignments

1. Given the information available and your knowledge of different forecasting techniques, develop a recommendation for utilizing a specific forecasting technique in the

subsequent study. The final contract negotiations are pending, and so it is essential that you account for the advantages and disadvantages of your preferred technique as they would apply to the problem at hand and point out any additional information you would like to have.

2. Assume that you are a member of DynaSol's small marketing department and that the contract negotiations with GFI have fallen through irrevocably. The company's top management has decided to use your expertise to develop a forecast for the next six months (and, perhaps, for the six-month period following that one as well), because it must have some information on which to base a decision about expanding its operations. Develop such a forecast, and for the benefit of top management, note any reservations or qualifications you feel are vital to its understanding and use of the information.

TABLE 14.12
DynaSol Monthly Sales for Period September 2018–February 2020

Month	DynaSol Industries Sales, Units	Sales	Regional Market Sales, Units	Sales
		2018		
September	24	$ 44,736	223	$ 396,048
October	28	52,192	228	404,928
November	31	59,517	230	408,480
December	32	61,437	231	422,564
		2019		
January	30	57,998	229	418,905
February	35	67,197	235	429,881
March	39	78,621	240	439,027
April	40	80,637	265	484,759
May	43	86,684	281	529,449
June	47	94,748	298	561,479
July	51	110,009	314	680,332
August	54	116,480	354	747,596
September	59	127,265	389	809,095
October	62	137,748	421	931,401
November	67	148,857	466	1,001,356
December	69	153,300	501	1,057,320
		2020		
January	74	161,121	529	1,057,320
February	79	172,007	573	1,145,264

Selected Bibliography

Armstrong, J. Scott, ed. *Principles of Forecasting: A Handbook for Researchers and Practitioners.* Nowell, MA: Kluwer, 2001.

Ferreira, Kris Johnson, Bin Hong Alex Lee, and David Simchi-Levi. "Analytics for an Online Retailer: Demand Forecasting and Price Optimization." *Manufacturing & Service Operations Management* 18, no. 1 (2015), pp. 69-88.

Ma, Y., et al. "The Bullwhip Effect on Product Orders and Inventory: A Perspective of Demand Forecasting Techniques." *International Journal of Production Research* 51, no. 1 (2013), pp. 281–302.

Mishra, Birendra K., Srinivasan Raghunathan, and Xiaohang Yue. "Demand Forecast Sharing in Supply Chains." *Production and Operations Management* 18, no. 2 (March–April 2009), pp. 152–66.

Oliva, Rogelio, and Noel Watson. "Managing Functional Biases in Organizational Forecasts: A Case Study of Consensus Forecasting in Supply Chain Planning." *Production and Operations Management* 18, no. 2 (March–April 2009), pp. 138–51.

Ramo, Simon, and Ronald Sugar. *Strategic Business Forecasting: A Structured Approach to Shaping the Future of Your Business.* New York: McGraw-Hill, 2009.

van der Laan, E., et al. "Demand Forecasting and Order Planning for Humanitarian Logistics: An Empirical Assessment." *Journal of Operations Management* 45 (2016), pp. 114–22.

Endnotes

1. Charles Sheehan, "Business Hungry for Speed Adds Recognition Technology," *Austin American-Statesman,* September 8, 2004, p. C3.
2. C. H. Davis and J. A. Fitzsimmons, "The Future of Nuclear Power in the United States," *Technological Forecasting and Social Change* 40, no. 2 (September 1991), pp. 151–64.
3. Prepared by Frank Krafka under the supervision of Professor James A. Fitzsimmons.
4. Prepared by Frank Krafka under the supervision of Professor James A. Fitzsimmons.

Chapter 15

Managing Service Inventory

Learning Objectives

After completing this chapter, you should be able to:

1. Discuss the role of information technology in the management of inventory.
2. Describe the function, characteristics, and costs of an inventory system.
3. Determine the order quantity for various inventory applications.
4. Determine the reorder point and safety stock for inventory systems with uncertain demand.
5. Design a continuous or periodic review inventory-control system.
6. Conduct an ABC analysis of inventory items.
7. Use either expected value or incremental analysis to determine the order quantity for the single-period inventory model.
8. Describe the rationale behind the retail discounting model.

All agree that well-stocked shelves make happy customers, but do well-stocked shelves make retailers happy as well? Consider a pharmacy with a shelf-full of a particular prescription medicine. If all of that medicine does not sell quickly, the pharmacy might have a shelf-full of medication that has passed its expiration date and no longer can be sold. The obvious dilemma is to match "stores-on-hand" to demand. The pharmacy certainly does not want to turn away sick customers because it is out of the requested medicine; on the other hand, it also does not want to incur the losses that result from an inventory of out-of-date medicine.

In the "old" days, inventory management required workers to monitor sales and stock-on-hand, then to mail or phone orders for new supplies when it "seemed" to be advisable. This system frequently resulted in excess inventories or stockouts (i.e., the empty-shelf syndrome). Information management, however, has transformed inventory management into a process that allows the service to meet customer demands without incurring the expense of excess inventory. Use of computer-based information systems in inventory management represents one of the earliest and most successful applications of information technology. All of us are familiar with the bar codes, as shown in Figure 15.1, that are found on nearly every inventory item purchased in retail stores. The bar code supplies information that allows management to track where inventory is located and how fast it is moving. For example, most supermarkets use computerized inventory systems to maintain records of inventory balances automatically based on *point-of-sale (POS)* scanning of the bar codes on items. When stock levels are depleted (or reach a predetermined reorder point), a purchase order to a preapproved vendor is initiated automatically using *electronic data interchange (EDI)*. When the order is received, the inventory balance is adjusted accordingly. Such use of information technology saves costs by avoiding paperwork, facilitating

FIGURE 15.1
Bar Code Applications

Bar code printed on a 20 ounce can of Hunt's Big John's Beans 'n Fixin's

Bar code stapled to an eight foot length of 1" × 2" pine stock

cash management, and creating a system that responds quickly to inventory needs among suppliers, service providers, and customers.

Tracking SKUs (stock keeping units) with bar codes in a retail store is very effective when handling individual items. However, keeping track of a pallet as it moves through

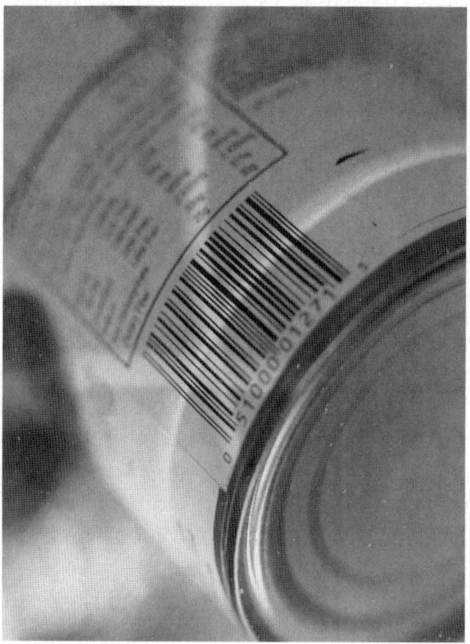

As items are scanned, the bar code identifies the price and records the new inventory level. Replenishment orders are triggered automatically when the inventory level falls below a predetermined point. ©Nick Koudis/Getty Images RF

the supply chain from ship container to a truck, is unloaded at a warehouse, and finally is loaded onto another truck for delivery to a retail store is facilitated using RFID (radio frequency identification). RFID is a concept in which a small radio device is imbedded on the pallet and transmits information identifying its contents automatically as the pallet moves down a conveyor. Many opportunities exist for application of RFID in services, such as medical bracelets for patients in hospitals.

Chapter Preview

Managing the facilitating goods component of a service package involves cost tradeoffs, customer service, and information systems. This chapter begins with a discussion of the role of inventory in services, its characteristics, and costs. A fundamental inventory management question concerns what quantity to order. Order quantity models are developed for various inventory applications.

When to place an order (called a *reorder point*) is another inventory management question. This decision is complicated when services are faced with uncertain demand and, thus, safety stocks to protect against stockouts are needed. The continuous review system and the periodic review system are computer information systems for implementing these decisions. Design parameters for each of these systems are developed with illustrations. The ABC classification of inventory items is used to identify which computer inventory system to install.

The chapter concludes with a discussion of two special inventory situations. For perishable goods, a model is developed to identify the optimal order quantity to balance the opportunity cost of underestimating demand with the lost investment in inventory resulting from overestimating demand. Finally, a retail discounting model is proposed to determine the discount price for items that are not selling to generate cash to buy more popular goods.

Inventory Theory

Inventory theory covers several aspects of the inventory of goods and supplies, including the role that inventory plays in the operation of a service, the characteristics of various inventory systems, and the costs that are involved in maintaining inventories.

Role of Inventory in Services

Inventories serve a variety of functions in service organizations, such as decoupling the stages in the distribution cycle, accommodating a heavy seasonal demand, and maintaining a supply of materials as a hedge against anticipated increases in their cost. We will look at these and other functions in more detail later; first, we will examine the inventory distribution system.

Decoupling inventories. Consider the physical goods distribution system depicted in Figure 15.2. Two types of flow exist within the system. One is the flow of information beginning with the customer and proceeding back to the original source(s) of the goods or service, and the other is the actual movement of goods–in this case, from the producer to the customer–by way of inventory reserves at each stage of the system.

Following the diagram, we see that the customer makes a demand, and for the purposes of our analysis, we will consider this demand to be a random variable with an associated probability distribution. When, for example, demand for a box of cereal occurs at a

FIGURE 15.2
Physical Goods Distribution System

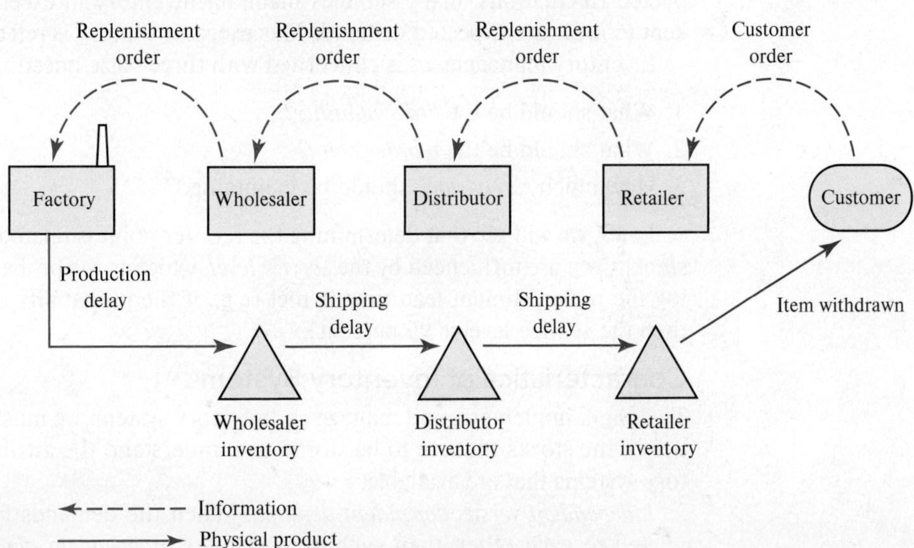

grocery retailer, the item is withdrawn from the available stock (either on the shelf or in the retailer's inventory). As the demand continues, the stock must be replenished, and an order is placed with the distributor. From the time the order is made until it is received, however, the available stock continues to decline. This interval is called the *replenishment lead time,* and it can vary from a day to a week or even more. The lead time also can vary from one order period to another. This flow of information originating with the customer's demand is directed in turn along the distribution channel to the producer.

If we follow the movement of the item itself, we see that it makes its way through the distribution channel with stops at the various inventory sites where it is held in readiness for the next leg of its journey to the customer. Each of these inventory stages serves as a buffer, allowing each organization in the interdependent system to operate somewhat independently and without interruption. Here, we can see the *decoupling function* of inventory systems. The retailer, distributor, wholesaler, and factory are stages in the system, and a stockout at any stage would have immediate and drastic consequences for the others. Inventories, however, decouple these stages and help to avoid expensive interruptions of service.

Seasonal inventories. Some services involve significant seasonal demands. Consider toy stores and the year-end holidays, camping-gear retailers and summer vacation time, or garden-supply stores and spring planting time. Services that experience such cyclical high-demand times might accumulate large inventories in advance of the high-demand season to accommodate their customers.

Speculative inventories. A service that anticipates a significant increase in the cost of a good in which it deals might find it more economical to accumulate and maintain a large inventory at present prices rather than to replenish its supplies after the increase. The strategy of maintaining a speculative inventory is known as *forward buying.* The reverse of this strategy occurred in the spring of 1996, when U.S. oil companies anticipated the reentry of Iraq into the international petroleum market, which would decrease the market value of the resource. These companies did not want to have huge reserves of "pre-Iraq" expensive oil when the world price dropped; therefore, they allowed their reserves (i.e., their inventory) to decline drastically–*forward hedging!*

Cyclical inventories. The term *cyclical inventory* refers to normal variations in the level of inventories. In other words, the level of stock in inventory is at its highest just after an order is received, and it declines to its lowest point just before a new order is received.

In-transit inventories. The term *in-transit inventories* is used for stock that has been ordered but has not yet arrived.

Safety stocks. An effective service maintains an inventory of stock that will meet expected demand. Services operate in a dynamic environment, however, which means that uncertainties in replenishment lead time and demand always exist. To deal with such unexpected fluctuations, many services maintain inventory in excess of the inventory that is kept to meet the expected demand. This excess inventory is referred to as *safety stock.*

Inventory management is concerned with three basic questions:

1. What should be the *order quantity*?
2. What should be the *reorder point*?
3. How much *safety stock* should be maintained?

Later, we will see that determining the reorder point is related to determining the safety stock. Both are influenced by the *service level,* which is the probability that all demand during the replenishment lead time is met (e.g., if the probability of a stockout is 5 percent, then the service level is 95 percent).

Characteristics of Inventory Systems

To design, implement, and manage an inventory system, we must consider the characteristics of the stocks that are to be stored and understand the attributes of the various inventory systems that are available.

Independent versus dependent demand. When the demands for different items are not related to each other, then each item exhibits *independent demand.* An example of this situation is a neighborhood grocery store's stock of goods that is depleted based upon random consumption by customers. Independent demand is described as a probability distribution with forecasts based on historical data. Service examples include seats sold on a particular flight or room sales for a business hotel.

In other cases, the demand for one inventory item is related to the demand for another; for example, the daily demand for ketchup packets at a McDonald's restaurant is dependent on the number of French fry orders. This type of demand is called *dependent demand* because demand is derived from sales of another product. The operation of a bakery provides a more complex example. For every pastry item, a bill of material (or recipe in this case) determines exactly the number of eggs and the amount of other ingredients such as sugar, flour, and yeast that will be necessary to complete a particular size order. Managing dependent demand items must also consider the procurement lead time to ensure their timely arrival in support of the final product (e.g., deliver McDonald's ketchup packets once each week).

Type of customer demand. When evaluating the type of demand, we first look for any trends, cycles, or seasonality. Has demand been increasing steadily during the observation period without significant drops, or do we see a monthly cycle in which demand begins high and then tapers off by the end of the month? As noted earlier, demand can be seasonal, also.

Planning time horizon. Management must consider whether it will stock an inventory of a particular item indefinitely or if the need for the item is temporary. For example, a hospital always will need tanks of oxygen, but a sports clothing retailer will not need an endless supply of Olympic sweatshirts.

Replenishment lead time. The replenishment lead time has an obvious impact on inventory needs. If we expect a relatively long time between placing an order and receiving it, we must carry a larger inventory than if we anticipate a short lead time, especially when critical items are involved. If lead time is stochastic with an associated probability distribution, we can use this information to determine our inventory needs during the lead time.

Constraints and relevant inventory costs. Some constraints are straightforward. For example, available storage space determines the maximum amount of goods that can be stored, and the "shelf life" of a good likewise might limit the number of perishable items that can be held in inventory. Other constraints are more complex, such as the costs of maintaining an inventory, and there are other obvious costs such as the capital expenditures for the storage facility, be it a warehouse or a walk-in refrigerator. Items held in inventory also represent a capital expenditure (i.e., they represent an opportunity cost of capital). Other costs include those of personnel and the maintenance required to manage the inventory as well as "incidentals" such as insurance and taxes on the inventoried assets. Yet another cost to consider is that of overcoming existing constraints (e.g., what would it cost to expand the size of the warehouse or refrigerator?).

Relevant Costs of an Inventory System

The performance of an inventory system usually is gauged by its average annual cost. Relevant costs to be considered include holding costs, ordering costs, stockout costs, and the purchase cost of the items. Table 15.1 provides a detailed listing of the sources of these costs. The inventory holding cost is the cost that varies directly with the number of items held in stock. The opportunity cost associated with capital tied up in inventory is a major component of the holding cost. Other components are insurance cost, obsolescence cost, deterioration cost, and direct handling cost. The ordering cost is the cost that varies directly with the number of orders that are placed. Order preparation, transportation, receiving, and inspection on arrival are major contributors to the ordering cost of purchases from suppliers. The stockout cost varies directly with the number of units out of stock, and this cost includes the margin on a lost sale and the potential loss of future sales. The purchase cost of the item can be a function of the order size when quantity discounts are offered by the supplier.

TABLE 15.1
Inventory Management Costs

Ordering costs
- Preparing specifications for items to be purchased
- Locating or identifying potential suppliers and soliciting bids
- Evaluating bids and selecting suppliers
- Negotiating prices
- Preparing purchase orders
- Issuing or transmitting purchase orders to outside suppliers
- Following up to ensure that purchase orders are received by suppliers

Receiving and inspection costs
- Transportation, shipping, and pickup
- Preparing and handling records of receipts and other paperwork
- Examining packages for visible damage
- Unpacking items
- Counting or weighing items to ensure that the correct amount has been delivered
- Withdrawing samples and transmitting them to inspection and testing organizations
- Inspecting or testing items to ensure that they conform to purchase specifications
- Transferring items into storage areas

Holding or carrying costs
- Interest charges on money invested in inventories
- Opportunity cost of capital tied up in inventory items, warehouses, and other parts of the inventory system
- Taxes and insurance
- Moving items into and out of inventory stores and keeping records of the movements
- Theft or pilferage
- Providing security systems for protecting inventories
- Breakage, damage, and spoilage
- Obsolescence of parts and disposal of out-of-date materials
- Depreciation
- Storage space and facilities (size is usually based upon maximum inventories rather than average)
- Providing controlled environments of temperature, humidity, dust, etc.
- Managing (tasks such as supervising stores personnel, taking physical inventory periodically, verifying and correcting records, etc.)

Shortage costs
- Lost sales and profits
- Customer dissatisfaction and ill-will; lost customers
- Penalties for late delivery or nondelivery
- Expediting orders to replenish exhausted stock

In the following section, we will develop models that determine the appropriate size of the order quantity based on minimizing the total annual cost of the inventory system.

Order Quantity Models

Many different models have been developed to answer the question: How much do we order? All these models use relevant inventory costs as the criteria for gauging performance; however, each is based on a particular inventory situation that is best described by a plot of inventory level versus time. Figure 15.3 shows the actual stock record (i.e., inventory behavior) during a year for an item at an auto parts store. As shown, the demand rate can be considered to be approximately constant; thus, replenishment orders (40 units in this case) can be placed to arrive when units on hand approach zero but still are sufficient to avoid a stockout.

The inventory stock behavior over time is modeled to account for the costs both of holding and of ordering inventory over a typical year. Using calculus, the functional form

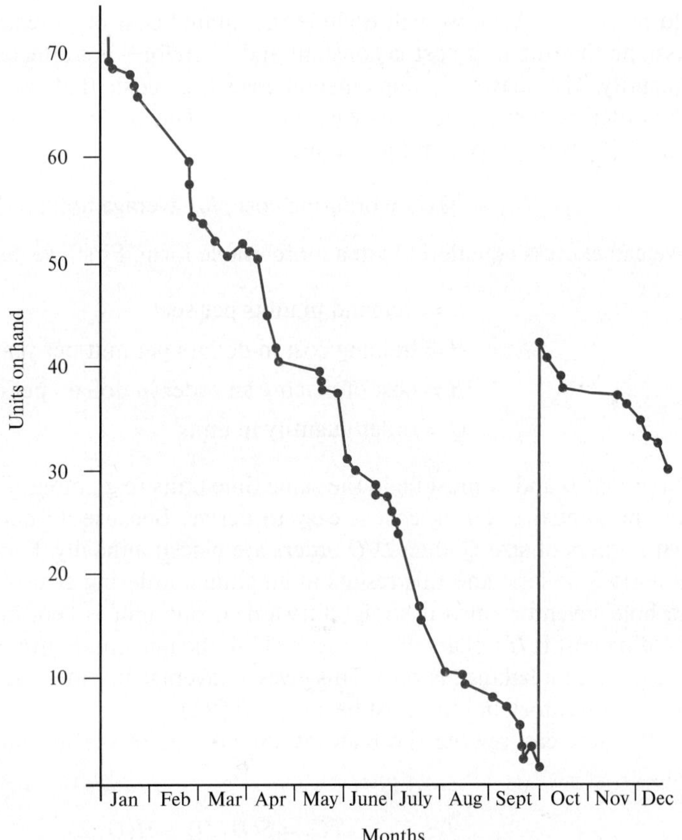

FIGURE 15.3
Actual Stock Record for an Auto Part

of the inventory costs is differentiated to arrive at an optimal value for the order quantity, which is referred to as Q^*. The best-known inventory model is a simple equation to determine an economic order quantity for purchased lots.

Economic Order Quantity

The simple *economic order quantity (EOQ)* model, which assumes a constant rate of demand and no stockouts, is a surprisingly accurate model for retail grocery items such as sugar, flour, and other staples. In this situation, demand appears to be constant, because a large number of customers make periodic purchases in small amounts and stockouts of these necessities are not permitted. Figure 15.4 depicts the inventory balances over time for this simple system, with a cycle being repeated every Q/D fraction (i.e., order quantity/annual demand) of a year. For example, if Q is 100 units and the annual demand D is 1,200, then the cycle will be repeated each month. We want to determine Q^*, the quantity that minimizes relevant costs. There are no costs associated with stockouts because they

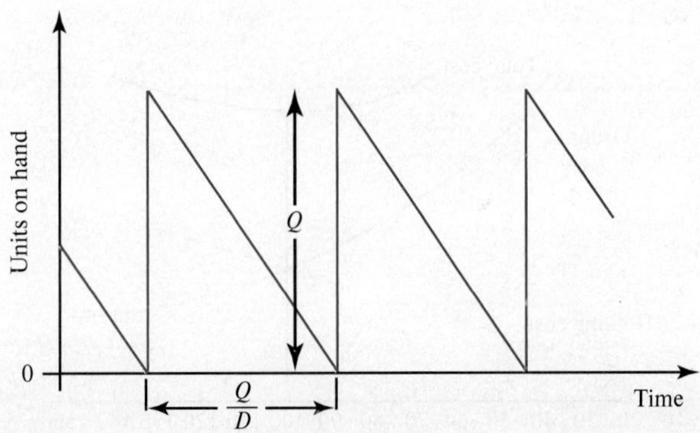

FIGURE 15.4
Inventory Levels for *EOQ* Model

do not occur. Also, we will exclude the annual cost of purchasing the item because we assume that the unit cost is constant and, therefore, not affected by the size of the order quantity. This leaves two incremental costs (i.e., costs that vary with the order quantity): the ordering cost and inventory holding cost. The *total cost purchase lot* (TC_p) function for an *EOQ* inventory system for one year is

$$TC_p = \text{ordering cost } plus \text{ average holding cost} \tag{1}$$

We can express equation (1) in a more usable form. First, we define some notation:

D = demand in units per year
H = holding cost in dollars per unit per year
S = cost of placing an order in dollars per order
Q = order quantity in units

Note that D and H must be in the same time units (e.g., months, years).

The annual ordering cost is easy to derive. Because all demand D must be satisfied with orders of size Q, then D/Q orders are placed annually. Each time an order is placed, it costs S dollars, and this results in an annual ordering cost of $S(D/Q)$. The annual cost to hold inventory also is straightforward. If one unit is kept in inventory for 1 year, the holding cost is H dollars. From Figure 15.4, the maximum inventory balance is Q, whereas the minimum balance is zero. This gives an average inventory level of $Q/2$ units. Thus, the annual inventory holding cost becomes $H(Q/2)$.

We now can rewrite the relevant annual cost of the inventory system with purchase lots as

$$TC_p = S(D/Q) + H(Q/2) \tag{2}$$

As Figure 15.5 shows, both the holding cost and the ordering cost change with different values of Q, and the total cost curve is shaped as a shallow bowl. Thus, there is a unique value of Q that gives a minimum total annual cost for the inventory system. This value, of course, is the *EOQ*; however, other nearby values of Q are only slightly more costly.

There are several ways to determine *EOQ*. For example, we can take the derivative of equation (2) with respect to Q, set the derivative equal to zero, and solve for *EOQ*.[1] There is another, easier way to solve for *EOQ*, however. Observe that the minimum of TC_p occurs where the ordering cost equals the inventory holding cost. Therefore, we can equate the two costs and solve for *EOQ*.

$$\begin{aligned} S(D/Q) &= H(Q/2) \\ Q^2 &= 2DS/H \\ EOQ &= \sqrt{\frac{2DS}{H}} \end{aligned} \tag{3}$$

FIGURE 15.5
Relevant Annual Costs for *EOQ* Model

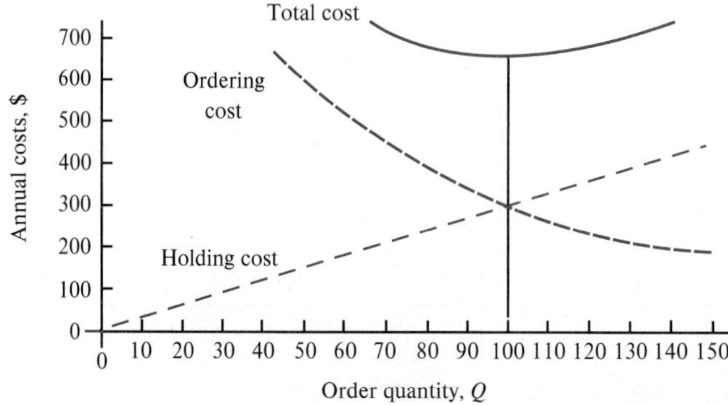

TABLE 15.2
Tabulation of Inventory Costs

Order Quantity Q	Order Cost, \$30	Inventory Holding Cost, \$6	Total Cost TC_p
70	428.57	210.00	638.57
80	375.00	240.00	615.00
90	333.33	270.00	603.33
100	300.00	300.00	600.00
110	272.73	330.00	602.73
120	250.00	360.00	610.00
130	230.77	390.00	620.77

Example 15.1 Rocky Mountain Power—*EOQ*

Rocky Mountain Power (RMP) maintains an inventory of spare parts that is valued at nearly \$8 million. This inventory is composed of thousands of different stock-keeping units (SKUs) used for power generation and utility line maintenance, and the inventory balances are updated on a computerized information system.

Glass insulators (i.e., SKU 1341) have a relatively stable usage rate, averaging 1,000 items per year. RMP purchases these insulators from the manufacturer at a cost of \$20 per unit delivered to the Denver warehouse. An order for replenishment is placed whenever the inventory balance reaches a predetermined reorder point. The cost that is associated with placing an order is estimated to be \$30. This includes the cost of order processing, receiving, and distribution to outlying substations.

An estimate of the annual inventory holding cost for SKU 1341 is \$6 per unit. This holding cost represents a 30 percent opportunity cost of capital. SKU 1341 is essential, and RMP must avoid depleting its stock of this item. We want to determine the replenishment order size for SKU 1341 that minimizes the relevant inventory costs.

From the problem description, we know the following:

$$D = 1{,}000 \text{ units per year}$$
$$S = \$30 \text{ per order}$$
$$H = \$6 \text{ per unit per year}$$

We can substitute values of Q into equation (2) to see what happens to the total annual cost. From Table 15.2, we see that as Q increases from 70 units, TC_p decreases, until it reaches a minimum at \$600. From this point on, TC_p increases. When plotted in Figure 15.5, these values demonstrate the bowl-shaped total annual cost curve. Of course, we can calculate the *EOQ* directly by using equation (3), which gives

$$EOQ = \sqrt{\frac{2DS}{H}}$$

$$EOQ = \sqrt{\frac{2(1{,}000)(30)}{6}} = 100 \text{ units}$$

The annual relevant cost when $Q^* = 100$ units, as shown in Table 15.2, is \$600 equally divided between ordering cost and holding cost. Nearby values of Q could be considered as being more appropriate, however. For example, an order of 120 units (10 boxes of a dozen each) has a TC_p exceeding the *EOQ* by only \$10 per year.

Inventory Model with Quantity Discounts

Suppliers have their own interest in the size of the order quantity. Production runs cost money to set up and often result in an economical batch size. For example, the time and effort that are necessary to make a batch of four dozen chocolate chip cookies is not much more than for baking a batch of one dozen. Similarly, manufacturing firms have an interest in encouraging customers to buy in full batch sizes. Further, savings in transportation costs are available to shippers who require a full truckload instead of a less-than-full truckload. Offering a per-unit price discount to customers who order in large quantities permits the savings in manufacture and transportation to be shared between both parties. Very often, the price break occurs at an order quantity much larger than the customer's *EOQ*. Thus, a trade-off occurs between a savings on the cost of purchasing the inventory and the expense of holding a larger-than-desired quantity. To study this trade-off, we must recognize that the price of the item now is a variable and must be included in the total annual cost function. Thus, our TC_p equation (2) is modified by adding the purchase cost, and this new equation is called *total cost with quantity discounts* (TC_{qd}).

$$\text{Total cost} = \text{Purchase cost} + \text{Ordering cost} + \text{Holding cost}$$

$$TC_{qd} = CD + S(D/Q) + I(CQ/2) \tag{4}$$

where C = unit cost of item in dollars
I = annual inventory holding cost as a percentage (expressed as a decimal) of the cost of the item (note: $IC = H$)

To demonstrate the trade-off analysis in the evaluation of a quantity discount offer, we return to the Rocky Mountain Power example.

Example 15.2 Rocky Mountain Power—Quantity Discount Problem

The supplier of the glass insulators, SKU 1341, is negotiating with RMP to place replenishment order quantities in lots greater than the current 100-unit size. The following quantity discount schedule has been proposed:

Order Quantity	Unit Price
1–239	$20.00
240–599	19.50
≥600	18.75

How should RMP respond? Because the price of the item now varies with the order quantity, the appropriate inventory cost model now becomes equation (4). The value for the holding cost percentage is determined using the relationship $IC = H$ and solving for $I = H/C = 6/20 = .30$. How does one proceed, however, to use equation (4) to determine the order quantity that minimizes the total annual inventory cost, which now includes the purchase cost as well as the ordering and holding costs? Figure 15.6 illustrates one option, which is plotting the total cost

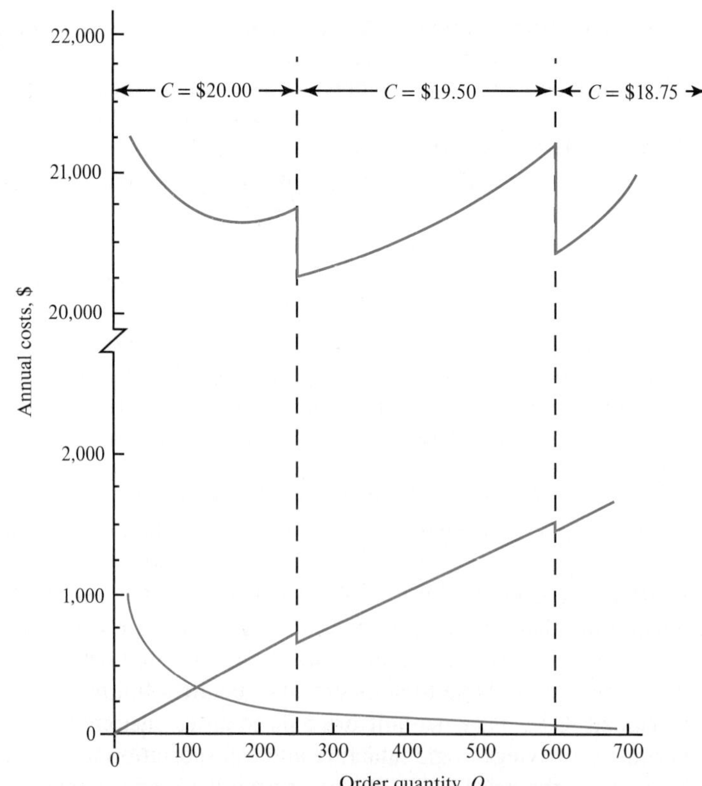

FIGURE 15.6
Annual Costs for the Quantity Discount Model

as a function of order quantity and noting the lowest point of the resulting *discontinuous* curve (in this case, at the price break of 240 units).

We can arrive at this same conclusion, however, using the following analytical steps:

1. Compute *EOQ* for the *lowest* price per unit, substituting $IC = H$ in equation (3):

$$EOQ = \sqrt{\frac{2DS}{IC}}$$

$$EOQ = \sqrt{\frac{2(1{,}000)(30)}{(0.30)(18.75)}}$$

$$= 103, \text{ but the price of \$18.75 is appropriate only for } EOQ \geq 600.$$

2. If the *EOQ* falls outside the appropriate price range (as occurred in the last paragraph), then we recalculate *EOQ* for the next lowest price and proceed until the *EOQ* is found in the appropriate price range. Therefore, we recalculate the *EOQ* for a price of \$19.50 (i.e., substitute 19.50 for C) and obtain a revised *EOQ* of 101. This result is not useful, however, because the *EOQ* of 101 is outside the appropriate range of 240 to 599 for a unit price of \$19.50. Next, we calculate the *EOQ* with $C = \$20$ and obtain a value of 100, which is appropriate because it falls within the range of 1 to 239 for a unit price of \$20. The table below summarizes the series of calculations we make to arrive at an appropriate *EOQ:*

Order Quantity	Unit Price	*EOQ*
≥600	\$18.75	103
240–599	19.50	101
1–239	20.00	100 (appropriate *EOQ*)

3. Calculate TC_{qd} using equation (4) for the *EOQ* found in step 2 and compare with TC_{qd} when substituting for the Q's that just obtain all higher price discounts (the discontinuity points in the TC_{qd} function as shown in Figure 15.6). Select the Q that minimizes TC_{qd}.

$$\begin{aligned}
TC_{qd}\,(EOQ = 100) &= 20(1{,}000) + 30(1{,}000)/100 + 0.30(20)(100)/2 \\
(C = 20) & \\
&= 20{,}000 + 300 + 300 \\
&= 20{,}600 \\
TC_{qd}\,(Q = 240) &= 19.50(1{,}000) + 30(1{,}000)/240 + 0.30(19.50)(240)/2 \\
(C = 19.50) & \\
&= 19{,}500 + 125 + 702 \\
&= 20{,}327 \\
TC_{qd}(Q = 600) &= 18.75(1{,}000) + 30(1{,}000)/600 + 0.30(18.75)(600)/2 \\
(C = 18.75) & \\
&= 18{,}750 + 50 + 1{,}687.5 \\
&= 20{,}487.5
\end{aligned}$$

Total annual costs are minimized with an order quantity of 240 units.

Inventory Model with Planned Shortages

When customers are willing to tolerate stockouts, an inventory system with planned shortages is possible. For example, a tire store might not stock all sizes of high-performance tires, knowing that a customer is willing to wait a day or two if the particular tire is out of stock. For this strategy to be acceptable to customers, however, the promised delivery date must be adhered to, and it must be within a reasonable length of time. Otherwise, customers would fault the retailer for being unreliable.

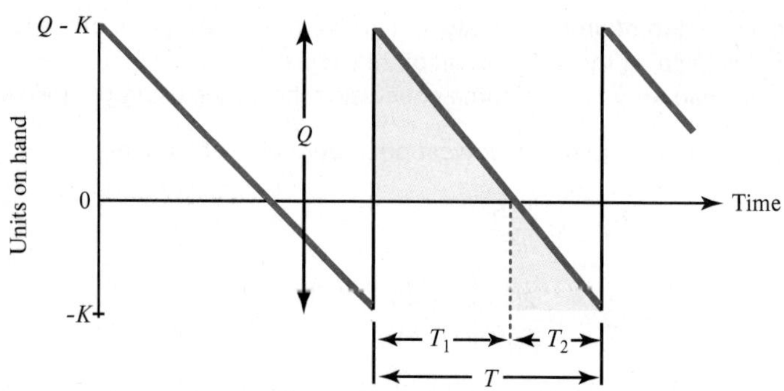

FIGURE 15.7
Inventory Levels for the Planned Shortages Model

Using electronic data interchange (EDI) and predictable delivery from suppliers, a strategy of minimal inventory stocking can be implemented. The benefits of such a system are captured by the trade-off between the cost of holding inventory and the cost that is associated with a stockout that can be *backordered.* An item is considered to be backordered when a customer is willing to wait for delivery; thus, the sale is not lost. Some subjective cost should be associated with customer inconvenience, however. Software manufacturers have taken this tolerance of stockouts to the extreme by creating "vaporware," which is software that is planned but not yet available. Such a company advertises this software to gauge the level of demand; however, excessive use of this strategy risks the credibility of the firm in the mind of customers. For retailers, this strategy can attract customers when the inventory cost savings are passed along as everyday low prices.

Figure 15.7 illustrates the idealized behavior of a planned shortage inventory system assuming a constant rate of demand and customers who will wait until the next order quantity Q is received to satisfy backorders that have accumulated to a maximum of K units. A new total inventory cost equation, which is called *total costs with backorders* (TC_b), now is required:

$$TC_b = \text{ordering cost } \textit{plus} \text{ holding cost } \textit{plus} \text{ backorder cost}$$

$$= S\frac{D}{Q} + H\frac{(Q-K)^2}{2Q} + B\frac{K^2}{2Q} \qquad (5)$$

where K = number of stockouts backordered when order quantity arrives
B = backorder cost in dollars per unit per year

Using the similar-triangles argument from geometry (i.e., the sides and heights of right triangles are proportional) and noting that inventory is held physically only for a fraction of the inventory cycle, the expression for average inventory can be derived as follows:

$$\text{Average inventory held during the inventory cycle} = \left(\frac{Q-K}{2}\right)\left(\frac{T_1}{T}\right)$$

but, by similar triangles, $T_1/T = (Q - K)/Q$ and, by substitution, we obtain $(Q - K)^2/2Q$.

In a similar manner, we can derive the expression for average backorders as follows:

$$\text{Average number of backorders held during the inventory cycle} = \left(\frac{K}{2}\right)\left(\frac{T_2}{T}\right)$$

but, by similar triangles, $T_2/T = K/Q$ and, by substitution, we obtain $K^2/2Q$.

Because the total inventory cost expression shown in equation (5) contains two decision variables, Q and K, we must take partial derivatives and solve for each variable to obtain the following values for order quantity and size of backorders:[2]

TABLE 15.3
Values for Q^* and K^* as a Function of Backorder Cost

B	Q^*	K^*	Inventory Levels
$B \rightarrow \infty$	$\sqrt{\frac{2DS}{H}}$	0	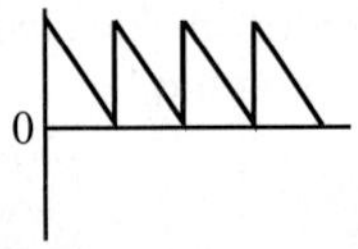 0
$0 < B < \infty$	$\sqrt{\frac{2DS}{H}\left(\frac{H+B}{B}\right)}$	$Q^*\left[\frac{H}{H+B}\right]$	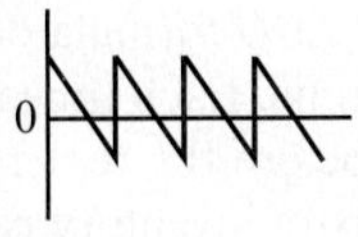 0
$B \rightarrow 0$	Undefined	Q^*	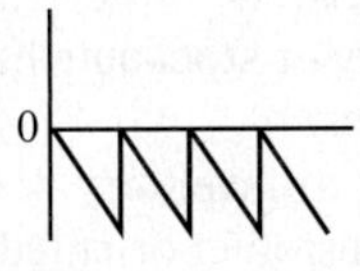 0

$$Q^* = \sqrt{\frac{2DS}{H}\left(\frac{H+B}{B}\right)} \tag{6}$$

$$K^* = Q^*\left(\frac{H}{H+B}\right) \tag{7}$$

The planned shortages model and the resulting equations (6) and (7) provide considerable insight into inventory systems when the backorder cost B is permitted to take on values from 0 to ∞ as shown in Table 15.3. Substituting ∞ for B in equation (6) reduces the equation to the classic *EOQ* equation (3). Thus, when a business uses the classic *EOQ*, the implication is that backorder cost is infinitely large and no stockout should occur. Because the cost of a backorder has a finite value, however, using the *EOQ* equation results in an inventory system that is more costly than necessary.

Letting the backorder cost decrease to zero results in an undefined value for *EOQ* because we have division by zero. However, inventory models that fit this situation do exist. For example, consider patients waiting for heart transplants. Because the donors cannot be inventoried, we have a queue or inventory of recipients in backorder status who are waiting for an available donor.

Example 15.3 Rocky Mountain Power—Planned Shortages Problem

Assume that the cost of a backorder for the glass insulator is the price of a $50 overnight FedEx package. Using equations (6) and (7), calculate a new order quantity and maximum backorder accumulation. Has a savings in total annual costs been realized compared with the classic *EOQ* approach?

$$Q^* = \sqrt{\frac{2DS}{H}\left(\frac{H+B}{B}\right)} = \sqrt{\frac{2(1{,}000)(30)}{6}\left(\frac{6+50}{50}\right)} = 106$$

$$K^* = Q^*\left(\frac{H}{H+B}\right) = 106\left(\frac{6}{6+50}\right) = 11$$

$$TC_b = S\frac{D}{Q} + H\frac{(Q-K)^2}{2Q} + B\frac{K^2}{2Q}$$

$$= 30\frac{1{,}000}{106} + 6\frac{(106-11)^2}{2(106)} + 50\frac{11^2}{2(106)}$$

$$= 283 + 255 + 29 = 567$$

Recall that the TC_p for the EOQ of 100 was \$600, a value \$33 in excess of the TC_b calculated above. Thus, using the simple EOQ model can be costly because of the implied assumption that stockouts cannot occur. Note that on an annual basis, both ordering and holding costs have been reduced significantly below the \$300 value for the EOQ model at the small cost of \$29 for backordering.

Inventory Management under Uncertainty

The simple *EOQ* formula does not consider uncertainties in demand rate or in replenishment lead time. Each time an order is placed, these uncertainties pose a risk of stockouts occurring before the replenishment order arrives. To reduce the risk of stockouts during this time, extra inventory can be held in excess of expected demand during the lead time. A trade-off exists between the cost of investing in and holding excess inventory and the cost of stockouts, however. In any event, except by good luck, either some stock remains in inventory or stockouts have occurred and the shelves are bare when the replenishment order arrives.

The key to inventory management under uncertainty is the concept of a *service level.* This is a customer-oriented term and is defined as the percentage of demand occurring during the lead time that can be satisfied from inventory. Some analytical approaches for determining the optimal service level have been suggested, but in practice, selecting a service level is a policy decision. Consider, for example, a convenience store. Depending on competition and the patience of customers, cold beer might require a 99 percent service level, but a 95 percent service level might be appropriate for fresh bread.

The service level is used to determine a *reorder point (ROP),* which is the level of inventory on hand when a replenishment order is initiated. The reorder point is set to achieve a prespecified service level. This, of course, requires information on the frequency distribution of demand during the replenishment lead time (LT). When we set the reorder point, we also are determining the *safety stock* level (SS), which is the excess inventory that is held during the reorder lead time to achieve the desired service level. The reorder point equals the safety stock level plus the *average demand during the lead time* (d_L). That is,

$$ROP = SS + d_L \tag{8}$$

The demand during lead time distribution now can be described in the following general manner, where the daily demand has a mean μ and standard deviation σ:

$$d_L = \mu(LT) \tag{9}$$

$$\sigma_L = \sigma\sqrt{LT} \tag{10}$$

The Central Limit Theorem allows us to assume that the demand during lead time distribution has a normal distribution no matter what the daily demand distribution is. The safety stock now can be calculated using the following equation, where z_r is the standard normal deviate for r percent service level:

$$SS = z_r\sigma\sqrt{LT} \tag{11}$$

Figure 15.8 illustrates the concept of establishing a demand during lead time distribution for the case in which daily demand has a mean of 3 and standard deviation of 1.5 and the lead time is 4 days. Note that the ROP is the stock level that is on hand when an order is placed and, thus, should be sufficient to satisfy r percent of demand during the lead time. We assume that daily demand is an independent variable. The independence assumption permits the summation of individual daily demand means and variances to arrive at a total demand during the lead time, which has a normal distribution based on the Central Limit Theorem.

FIGURE 15.8
Demand During Lead Time

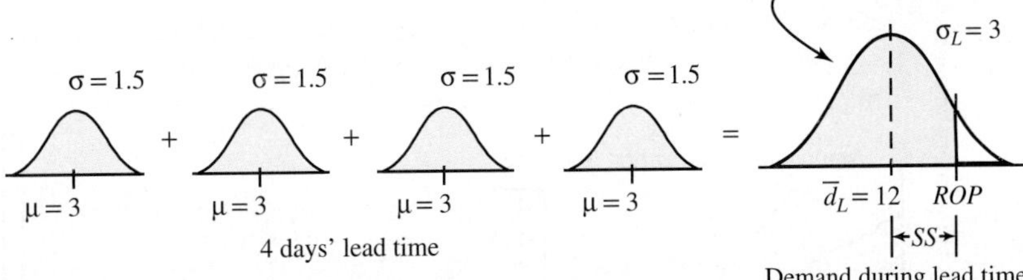

Example 15.4 Rocky Mountain Power—Reorder Point

Recall inventory item SKU 1341, the glass insulator. RMP's computerized information system has tracked the daily demand rate for this item. Daily demand appears to be distributed normally with mean $\mu = 3$ and standard deviation $\sigma = 1.5$. The replenishment lead time has been a constant 4 days. Because SKU 1341 is an important item for utility line maintenance, it is company policy to achieve a 95 percent service level for such items. What reorder point and safety stock should be recommended?

Using equations (9) and (10), the demand during lead time for RMP becomes

$$d_L = \mu(LT) = 3(4) = 12$$

$$\sigma_L = \sigma\sqrt{LT} = 1.5\sqrt{4} = 3$$

Then, we turn to the Standard Normal Distribution in Appendix A, Areas of Standard Normal Distribution, to find that $z = 1.645$ leaves 5 percent in one tail to guarantee a 95 percent service level. The safety stock that is required to ensure the desired service level is calculated using equation (11):

$$\begin{aligned} SS &= z_r\sigma\sqrt{LT} \\ &= (1.645)(1.5)\sqrt{4} \\ &= 5 \end{aligned}$$

Using equation (8), we find the reorder point for RMP to be

$$\begin{aligned} ROP &= SS + d_L \\ &= 5 + 12 \\ &= 17 \end{aligned}$$

Inventory Control Systems

Many different inventory control systems are used in actual practice. They differ in the methods for determining the order quantity and when a replenishment order should be made. We shall restrict our discussion here to two of the most common inventory control systems: the continuous review system (Q, r), and the periodic review system (i.e., order-up-to). In all inventory control systems, two questions must be answered: (1) When should an order be placed? and (2) What size is the order quantity? Because inventory control systems face uncertainty in demand, we will find that when one of these questions is answered using a fixed value, the answer to the other must accommodate the uncertainty in demand.

Continuous Review System

Figure 15.9 depicts inventory balances for the continuous review system. The inventory level decreases in a variable fashion because of uncertainty in demand until it reaches a predetermined trigger level, the reorder point *ROP.* When the inventory balance reaches the *ROP,* an order for replenishment is placed with the vendor. For this inventory system, the order quantity *EOQ* is fixed (i.e., *EOQ* units always are ordered each time an order is placed). An example of this "two bin" system is the Hallmark greeting card stand that has

FIGURE 15.9 **Continuous Review System (*Q, r*)**

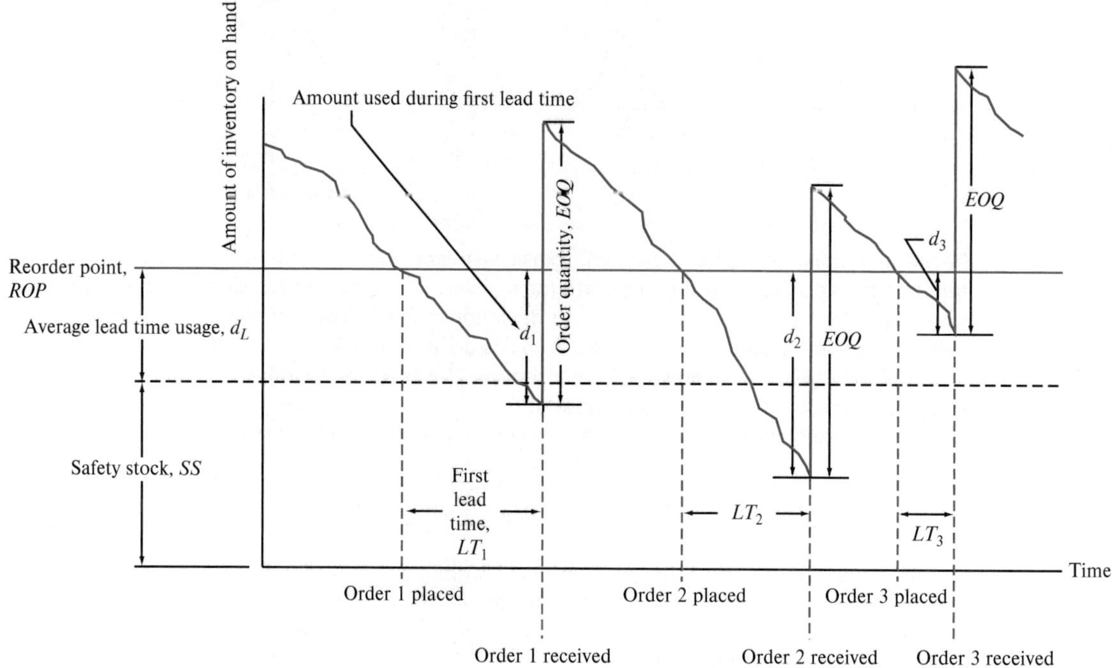

a reorder card, containing the stock number, placed near the back of the card display to remind the retailer to reorder the item before the remaining cards are sold.

From the time the reorder point is reached until the replenishment is received, the inventory level continues to decline. Generally, there will be some inventory remaining just before the replenishment is received. The average inventory balance just when the replenishment arrives is the safety stock level *SS*. This inventory is maintained to protect against stockouts that might result from unusually high levels of demand and/or longer-than-expected replenishment lead time. On occasion, however, a stockout does occur. For this system, unsatisfied demand during the lead time period is backordered until the replenishment order is received, in which case the backordered items are set aside and the remaining part of the *EOQ* placed in stock.

Note that for the continuous review system, the order quantity is fixed, but the cycle time between orders varies. A computerized information system using bar codes for each SKU can track inventory balances continuously to indicate when the reorder point is reached. Retailers like Walmart use *point-of-sale (POS)* cash registers to record up-to-the-minute status of stock levels, with an end-of-day report on all items that have reached their reorder points. In many cases, the purchase order is generated automatically by the computer and sent to the vendor or, in the case of Walmart, to its distribution center for the next shipment.

The parameter equations for the continuous review system are

$$EOQ = \sqrt{\frac{2DS}{H}}$$

$$ROP = SS + \mu(LT)$$

$$SS = z_r\sigma\sqrt{LT}$$

Periodic Review System

Figure 15.10 depicts inventory balances for the periodic review system. Orders for replenishment are placed after a fixed review period *RP* has elapsed. The order quantity varies

FIGURE 15.10 **Periodic Review System (Order-Up-To)**

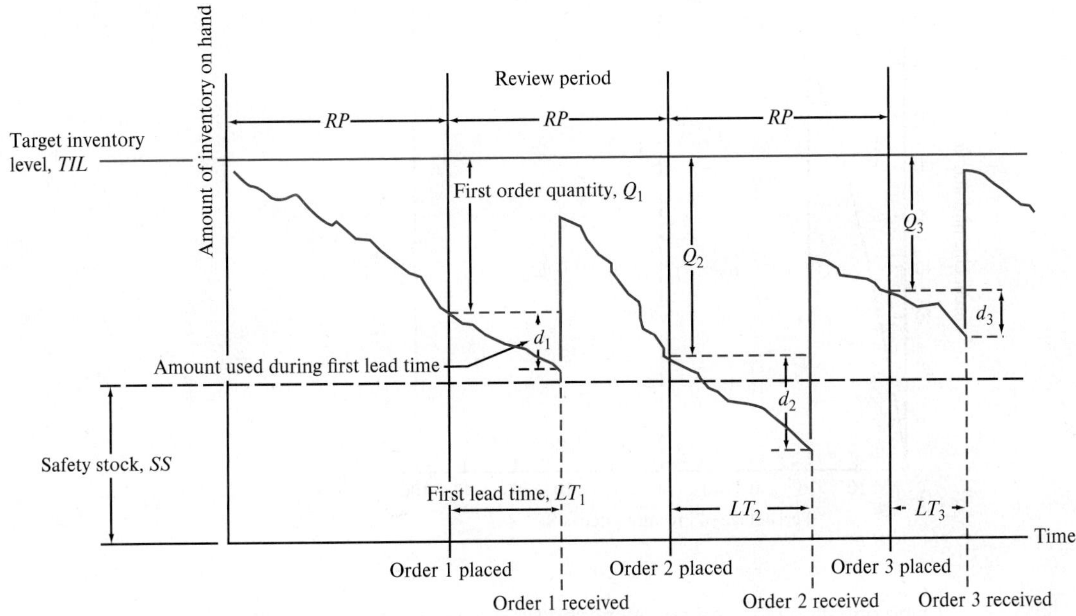

and is calculated to be that needed to bring the total inventory (i.e., on-hand plus on-order) up to some predetermined target inventory level *TIL*. Note that occasional back-orders can occur with the continuous review system. With the periodic review system, the order quantity varies in response to the demand rate, whereas the cycle time between orders is fixed.

To determine the fixed-review period, first calculate an *EOQ;* then divide the resulting value by the average daily demand to arrive at an expected cycle time. The resulting review period thus balances the holding and ordering costs to achieve a minimum total incremental cost for the system.

The periodic review system generally is used when orders for many different SKUs are consolidated for replenishment for a distributor or regional warehouse that resupplies on a periodic basis (e.g., restocking a convenience store once a week).

The parameter equations for the periodic review system are noted below, where the daily demand has a mean of μ and a standard deviation of σ. Note that exposure to a stockout for the periodic review system is the review period plus the lead time (i.e., $RP + LT$) instead of just the lead time (LT) as in the continuous review system. Thus, carrying extra inventory is the cost that is paid for lack of continuous information on the inventory status.

$$RP = EOQ / \mu \tag{12}$$

$$TIL = SS + \mu(RP + LT) \tag{13}$$

$$SS = z_r \sigma \sqrt{RP + LT} \tag{14}$$

Example 15.5 Rocky Mountain Power—Periodic Review System

Recall from Example 15.4 that for inventory item SKU 1341, the glass insulator, daily demand is distributed normally, with mean $\mu = 3$ and standard deviation $\sigma = 1.5$. In Example 15.1, the *EOQ* was calculated to be 100 units. The replenishment lead time has been a constant 4 days. Again, because SKU 1341 is an important item for utility line maintenance, it is company policy to achieve a 95 percent service level for such items. If a periodic review system is selected to control glass insulator inventory, what are the recommended review period, target inventory level, and safety stock?

FIGURE 15.11
ABC Classification of Inventory Items

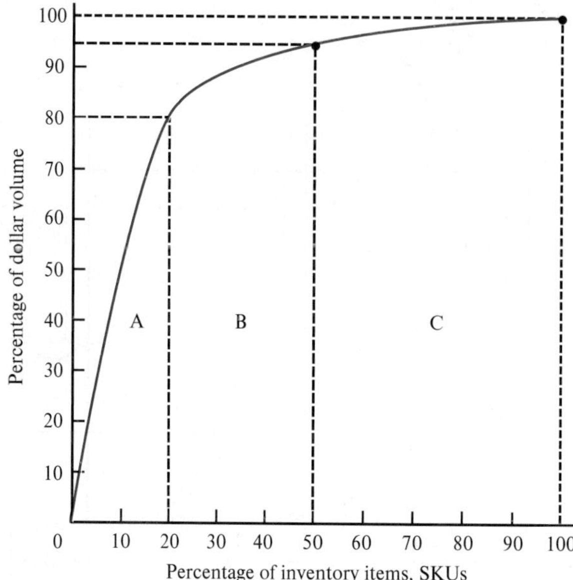

Using equation (12), the review period $RP = 100/3 = 33$ days, or approximately once each month. The safety stock is calculated using equation (14):

$$SS = z_r \sigma \sqrt{RP + LT} = (1.645)(1.5)\sqrt{33 + 4} = 15$$

The target inventory level is determined using equation (13):

$$TIL = SS + \mu(RP + LT) = 15 + 3(33 + 4) = 126$$

Thus, once every month the inventory of SKU 1341 on hand is noted with an order placed for an amount that is equal to the difference between that inventory and the target level of 126 units.

The ABCs of Inventory Control

Usually, a few inventory items or SKUs account for most of the inventory value as measured by dollar volume (i.e., demand multiplied by item cost). Thus, we must pay close attention to these few items that control most of the inventory value. The 80–20 rule, observed by Vilfredo Pareto, is useful for inventory classification. The ABC classification system, shown graphically in Figure 15.11, often is used to organize SKUs into three groups depending on their value. The A class typically contains about 20 percent of inventory items but accounts for 80 percent of dollar volume. These significant items need close attention. At the other extreme are the insignificant class C items, which usually represent 50 percent of inventory items but account for only about 5 percent of the dollar volume. In the middle is class B, which represents 30 percent of items and 15 percent of the dollar volume. Before an inventory control system is decided on, an ABC classification usually is undertaken. Selecting the appropriate inventory control system should be based on the significance of the inventory items.

Table 15.4 shows inventory items for a discount electronics store arranged in order of decreasing dollar volume to achieve an ABC classification. In this case, two items (i.e., computers and home theaters) comprise 20 percent of SKUs and account for 74 percent of the total dollar volume. These are the few costly A items that require special managerial attention, because they represent a significant sales opportunity loss if they are out of stock. Intensive computer monitoring of inventory levels as found in the continuous review system should be used for these items.

As is common, 50 percent of the items account for a small percentage of the dollar volume inventory value (in this case, 10 percent). These are the inexpensive C items and

TABLE 15.4 Inventory Items Listed in Descending Order of Dollar Volume

Inventory Item	Unit Cost ($)	Monthly Sales (Units)	Dollar Volume ($)	Percent of Dollar Volume	Percent of SKUs	Class
Home theaters	5,000	30	150,000	74	20	A
Computers	2,500	30	75,000			
Television sets	400	60	24,000			
Refrigerators	1,000	15	15,000	16	30	B
Displays	250	40	10,000			
Speakers	150	60	9,000			
Cameras	200	40	8,000			
Software	50	100	5,000	10	50	C
Thumb drives	5	1,000	5,000			
CDs	10	400	4,000			
Totals			305,000	100	100	

can be managed in a more casual fashion, because a stockout does not represent a serious loss of revenue. For these items, a periodic review system might be used. The review period can be relatively long as well, which results in infrequent orders for large quantities of low-value items.

The three B items are not costly enough to require special management attention, but they are not so cheap that they can be overstocked. Either a continuous review or a periodic review system could be used to manage these items. Today, however, bar coding and sophisticated POS (point-of-sale) systems can reduce the cost of monitoring inventory levels to the point that a continuous review inventory system is feasible for all items.

Radio Frequency Identification

Radio frequency identification (RFID) is an automatic identification method that relies on storing data and retrieving the data remotely using devices called RFID tags or transponders. The tag consists of an integrated circuit on a silicon chip with an antenna. A reader emits a radio signal to activate the tag; read the stored data; and, in some cases, write data as well. For monitoring inventory in supply chains, the tags are attached to shipping pallets, but they could be incorporated into a product or implanted in an animal or human being. RFID technology is similar to bar codes, but it conveys much more information and does not require line-of-sight reading.

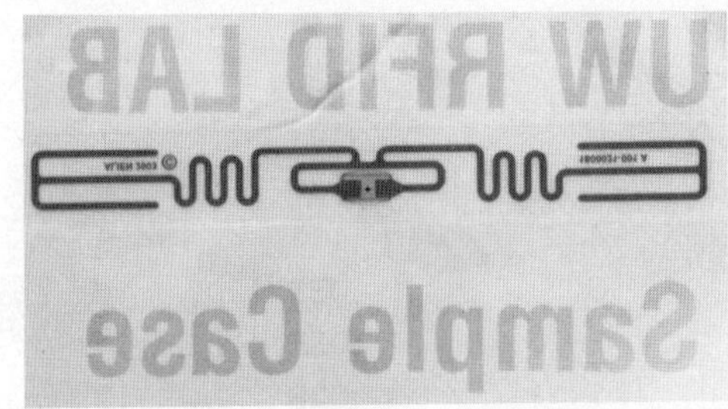

RFID chip from backside of a label used at a University of Wisconsin–Madison engineering research lab, August 12, 2005. ©Andy Manis/AP Images

Today, airlines, for example, use barcode readers on baggage conveyors, but the readers miss a high percentage of the tagged luggage. A handheld scanner works better but slows loading. Because a passive RFID tag can be read up to a few meters, bags could be identified as they pass a baggage-conveyor reader, and luggage then can be sorted and routed to the correct flight automatically. The Australian air carrier Qantas now uses RFID tags and readers in its national operations and has plans to extend the capability worldwide. In 2016, the cost of a roll of 1,000 tags ranged from $142 to $718 for 5,000, and readers ranged from $49 to $5,000, depending upon capabilities.

RFID tags currently are used in several other service industry applications:

- *Passports.* The first RFID passport was issued by Malaysia in 1998.
- *Transport payments.* RFID passes were introduced in Paris in 1995 and now are used by travelers throughout Europe.
- *Human implants.* Nightclubs in Barcelona and Rotterdam use an implanted chip to identify their VIP customers, who then use it to pay for drinks.
- *Libraries.* RFID is replacing barcodes on library items.
- *Patient identification.* Implanted RFID tags help hospitals to avoid mistakes.

Single-Period Model for Perishable Goods

Businesses sometimes accumulate an inventory in anticipation of future sales that will occur during a short period of time, after which the unsold items are drastically reduced in value. Retail examples include fresh pastries and seasonal items like swimsuits. Given some data on past sales experience, the question to answer is how much to stock? If too small, the order quantity results in the possibility of lost sales. If the order quantity is too large, however, unsold stock represents a lost investment that might have minimal salvage value. This inventory decision is referred to as the classic "news vendor problem" because day old newspapers are next to worthless.

A bakery must decide each morning how many boxes, each containing one dozen donuts, to prepare. Unsold donuts will be sold the following day at a discount. We begin with some notation and then proceed to solve the problem using two different approaches—expected value analysis and marginal analysis.

D = boxes of donuts demanded

Q = boxes of donuts stocked

P = selling price of one box of donuts, $10

C = cost of one box of donuts, $4

S = salvage value of one box of donuts, $2

D	Frequency	*p(D)*	*Q*	*P(D < Q)*
2	1	.028	2	.000
3	2	.055	3	.028
4	3	.083	4	.083
5	4	.111	5	.166
6	5	.139	6	.277
7	6	.167	7	.416
8	5	.139	8	.583
9	4	.111	9	.722
10	3	.083	10	.838
11	2	.055	11	.916
12	1	.028	12	.971

Expected Value Analysis

A payoff table shown in Table 15.5 is constructed to account for the financial result of each combination of actual boxes of donuts demanded and stock level selected (for convenience, we will limit Q to values between 6 and 10). Using the probability of boxes of donuts demanded, an expected profit will be calculated for each column of the payoff

TABLE 15.5
Payoff Table

		Stock Q				
p(D)	*D*	6	7	8	9	10
.028	2	4	2	0	−2	−4
.055	3	12	10	8	6	4
.083	4	20	18	16	14	12
.111	5	28	26	24	22	20
.139	6	36	34	32	30	28
.167	7	36	42	40	38	36
.139	8	36	42	48	46	44
.111	9	36	42	48	54	52
.083	10	36	42	48	54	60
.055	11	36	42	48	54	60
.028	12	36	42	48	54	60
Expected profit:		$31.54	$34.43	$35.77	$35.99	$35.33

table (i.e., stock level Q). The stock level that yields the maximum expected profit will best balance the opportunity cost of lost sales and cost of investment in unsold donuts. The payoff table is best constructed beginning with the upper left-hand cell. For cell ($D = 2$, $Q = 6$), we have the following financial result:

Sales:	2($10)	=	$20
Salvage:	(6 – 2)($2)	=	8
Total revenue:			$28
Less cost:	6($4)	=	−24
Profit:			$ 4

Note that as one moves across the rows, the profit decreases by $(S - C) = 2 - 4 = -\$2$, because one more unsold box of donuts must be salvaged. As one moves down the columns, the profit increases by $(P - S) = 10 - 2 = \$8$, because one more unit is sold avoiding one unit being salvaged. This increase in profit continues until the diagonal, where $D = Q$ is reached, after which the profit remains the same as all available stock is sold and additional demand is not being satisfied.

The expected profit for each stock level Q from 6 to 10 is calculated and shown at the bottom of the table below. Expected profit for $Q = 6$ is calculated by multiplying the probability of demand $p(D)$ in the first column by each payoff in column three under $Q = 6$:

$$\text{Expected profit (for } Q = 6) =$$
$$.0284(4) + .055(12) + .083(20) + \ldots + .055(36) + .028(36) = \$31.54$$

For this example, a stock of nine boxes of donuts ($Q^* = 9$) will maximize expected profit at $35.99 per period.

Marginal Analysis

Another approach to the classic news vendor problem uses an economic principle called *marginal analysis.* The argument is that the vendor should continue increasing the stock (size of Q) until the expected revenue on the last unit stocked just exceeds the expected loss on the last sale. From this principle, we can derive a very useful probability called the *critical fractile:*

FIGURE 15.12
Critical Fractile

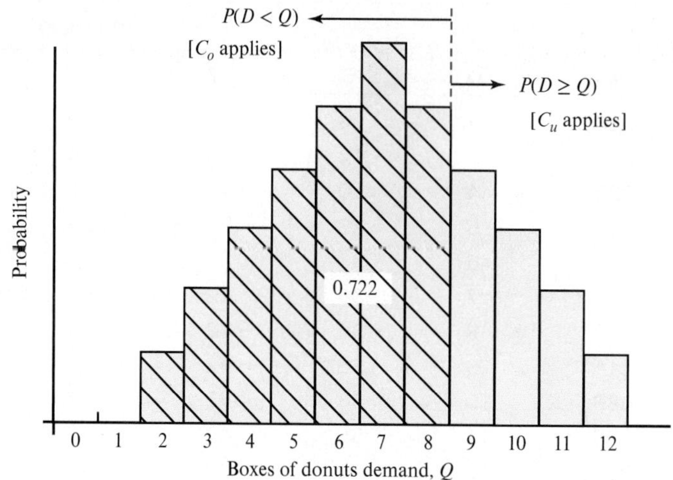

$$E(\text{revenue on last sale}) \geq E(\text{loss on last sale})$$

$$P(\text{revenue})(\text{unit revenue}) \geq P(\text{loss})(\text{unit loss})$$

$$P(D \geq Q)C_u \geq P(D < Q)C_o$$

$$[1 - P(D < Q)]C_u \geq P(D < Q)C_o$$

$$P(D < Q) \geq \frac{C_u}{C_u + C_o} \tag{15}$$

where

C_u = unit contribution from sale, $P - C = \$6$ (opportunity cost of *under*estimating demand)

C_o = unit loss from not selling, $C - S = \$2$ (cost of *over*estimating demand)

$P(D < Q)$ = probability of not selling all donuts stocked

$P(D \geq Q)$ = probability of selling all donuts stocked

Using equation (15), we find $P(D< Q) \leq 6/(6 + 2) \leq .75$. Thus, stock $Q = 9$, because as Figure 15.12 shows, the boxes of donuts demand from 2 through 8 sums to a cumulative probability of 0.722. Looking back at the expected profit line in the payoff table, we find confirmation of the marginal analysis principle. Each time we increase Q, beginning with a value of 6 in our abbreviated table, there is a corresponding increase in profit up to the value of 9, after which profit decreases with the 10th unit, creating an expected loss of $0.66.

Retail Discounting Model

Even with the best planning, attempting to anticipate customer demand has its risks. The sleeveless shirt that seemed to be such a great fashion statement at the Las Vegas trade show just did not catch on in Peoria. Such "dogs" end up on the shelf for months, collecting dust and depriving the retailer of shelf space for displaying new items that might sell faster. Discounting them means a loss of some profit margin, and besides, what should be an appropriate discount? In any event, the retailer surely never would sell them below cost. This dilemma can be resolved by determining the break-even discount price that will clear the inventory of "dogs" in short order and, thus, generate capital to invest in good stock that will turn rapidly. In retailing, profit is a function of mark-up multiplied by turnover. The following terms will be used for determining the discount price:

S = current selling price

D = discount price

P = profit margin on cost (the percent mark-up as a decimal)

Y = average number of years to sell entire stock of "dogs" at current price (total number of years to clear stock divided by 2)

N = *inventory turns*, the number of times good stock turns over during the year

The break-even discount price will be found by equating the loss per item to the gain from investing the revenue that is obtained in good stock:

$$\text{Loss per item} = \text{Gain from revenue}$$

$$S - D = D(PNY)$$

Thus, the discount price is

$$D = \frac{S}{(1 + PNY)} \tag{16}$$

Example 15.6 Sportstown

The Titanium Princess Terminator tennis racket has not been selling well, perhaps because of its poor weight distribution. The racket is well made, however, and retails at $29.95 with a 40 percent mark-up on cost. Only one sale was made last year, and there were 10 rackets remaining in stock. More popular rackets were selling at a rate of 25 per year.

The percent mark-up on cost as a decimal is $P = 0.40$, with a selling price $S = \$29.95$. With current sales of one per year, the average number of years to clear the stock of 10 rackets is $Y = 10/2 = 5$. If these "dogs" were good rackets, then $25/10 = 2.5$ lots would sell per year; thus, $N = 2.5$. Using equation (16), the discount price is

$$D = \frac{29.95}{[1 + (0.40)(2.5)(5)]}$$

$$= \frac{29.95}{6}$$

$$= \$4.99$$

Thus, the 10 tennis rackets should be discounted immediately to sell at a price of $4.99 each. Note that we will take an opportunity loss of ($S - D$) = ($29.95 – $4.99) = $24.96 per item; however, the $4.99 will be placed immediately in fast-moving stock. The $4.99 will be marked up by 40 percent and, thus, return $2.00 each time a good racket is sold, (0.40)($4.99). Good stock, however, turns over 2.5 times a year, compared with a "dog" that sells one item per year and, thus, makes 2.5($2.00) = $5.00 a year. Because it will take 5 years on average to clear out the "dogs," the total revenue gain from reinvestment of profits is 5($5.00) = $25.00.

In other words, we can either hold the "dogs" and eventually sell all of them at $29.95, or we can sell them all immediately at $4.99, put the money (i.e., $50.00) into good stock, and regain our losses in 5 years. Note that the discount price results in a break-even in which no money is made, and we need not discount to that extreme low level. Because the wholesale price was $29.95/1.4 = $21.39, we might wish to discount the rackets initially to a price of $19.95. If the rackets sell quickly, we will make money even though the selling price is below cost, because the money tied up in inventory now is moving.

This extreme discount of $4.99 could be avoided by turning over the stale inventory of 10 tennis rackets to a third party. Slow-moving merchandise is typically discarded in the following ways: returned to the manufacturer or distributor, liquidated to companies

Service Benchmark

YOUR BAG IS TAGGED

Qantas Airlines is using radio frequency identification (RFID) at all of its Australian airports to automate baggage handling. The system, called Q Bag Tag, features a luggage tag with a passive RFID inlay that enables self-service baggage drops. The Q Bag Tag can store flight information for up to four connecting flights and can be reused for an unlimited number of future flights. After obtaining a boarding pass and attaching a Q Bag Tag to his or her luggage, the passenger places the bag on a weight-scale conveyor belt, which then weighs the luggage while an RFID reader records the tag's unique ID number. The system then activates the Q Bag Tag and programs the flight and final destination data directly onto the Q Bag Tag's RFID chip. The bag continues its journey into the baggage handling area, where it is routed and screened by means of RFID readers. The benefits include improved accuracy of luggage handling and reduced passenger processing time at the gate. A huge challenge was to overcome the problem of reading only the bag on the scale conveyor and not nearby bags of other waiting passengers.

Source: http://www.rfidjournal.com/article/view/896.

(e.g., Overstock.com) that resells the items in an online retail market, or sold to salvage companies that process the metals (e.g., aluminum tennis frame) and other components of value. In the negotiation with the third party, the discount calculated using equation (16) represents your reserve price (i.e., the least you would be willing to sell each item). If negotiation fails, a donation of the rackets to a local high school tennis team would be considered a deduction when filing income taxes.

Summary

Inventory management can influence significantly the success of an organization. For some organizations, the extent to which their objectives are achieved is affected by the inventory system they adopt. Good inventory management is characterized by concern for inventory holding costs, inventory ordering costs, shortage costs, and the purchase price of the items. Further, the lead time for replenishment and the appropriate service level should be considered.

Because of the widespread use of bar coding and RFID chips, keeping track of inventory using computers is common practice. This simplifies the manipulations of large amounts of data relevant to inventory decisions.

Key Terms and Definitions

Backorder a demand that is not satisfied immediately because of a stockout but is satisfied later because the customer is willing to wait until the replenishment order arrives to take delivery. *p. 438*

Critical fractile the cumulative probability that demand will be less than the stock level that guarantees that marginal revenue just exceeds the marginal cost of the last item stocked. *p. 447*

Dependent demand the need for an item in inventory that is directly related to another item. *p. 431*

Economic order quantity *(EOQ)* the reorder quantity that minimizes the total incremental cost of holding inventory and the cost of ordering replenishments. *p. 433*

Electronic data interchange *(EDI)* a computerized exchange of data between organizations that eliminates paper-based documents. *p. 428*

Independent demand the need for different items in inventory that are not related to each other. *p. 430*

Inventory turns the number of times an inventory stock is sold per year, calculated by dividing annual demand by the average inventory held. *p. 449*

Point-of-sale *(POS)* online linking of sales transactions, using computerized cash registers, bar-code scanners, or credit-card readers, to a central computer allowing immediate updating of sales, inventory, and pricing information. *p. 442*

Radio frequency identification *(RFID)* an automatic identification that relies on near field radio transmission of data. *p. 445*

Reorder point *(ROP)* level of inventory both on hand and on order when a reorder of a fixed quantity is made. *p. 440*

Replenishment lead time the time, usually in days, from an order being placed with a vendor to the delivery being made. *p. 430*

Safety stock inventory held in excess of expected demand during lead time to satisfy a desired service level. *p. 440*

Service level the probability that demand will be satisfied during replenishment lead time. *p. 440*

Topics for Discussion

1. Discuss the functions of inventory for different organizations in the supply chain (i.e., manufacturing, suppliers, distributors, and retailers).
2. How would one find values for inventory management costs?
3. Compare and contrast a continuous review inventory system with a periodic review inventory system.
4. Discuss how information technology can help to create a competitive advantage through inventory management.
5. How valid are the assumptions for the simple *EOQ* model?
6. How is a service level determined for most inventory items?
7. Service capacity (e.g., seats on an aircraft) has characteristics similar to inventories. What inventory model would apply?
8. Identify dependent and independent demand for an airline and a hospital.

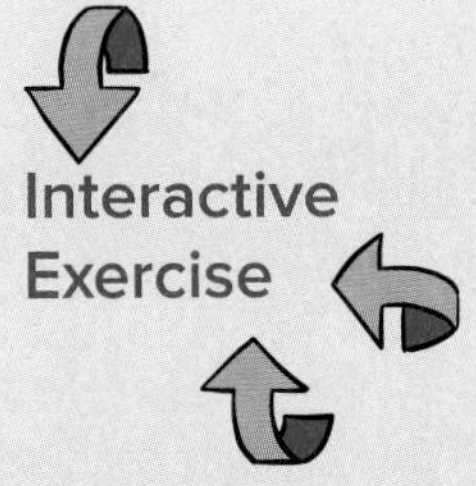

Interactive Exercise

The class engages in an estimation of the cost of a 12-ounce serving of Coke in various situations (e.g., supermarket, convenience store, fast-food restaurant, sit-down restaurant, and ballpark). Explain why each venue has a different cost.

Solved Problems

1. Continuous Review (Q, r) System

Problem Statement

A resort hotel is planning to install a computerized inventory system to manage the complementary guest toilet items such as soap and shampoo. The daily usage rate for bars of soap appears to be distributed normally, with mean $\mu = 16$ and standard deviation $\sigma = 3$. Once an order is placed, it takes a full week before delivery is made. The effort to place an order and receive the shipment is approximately one hour's time for a staff person who is paid \$10 per hour. The opportunity cost of capital is 20 percent per year. A bar of soap is valued at approximately \$0.25. The hotel is concerned about stockouts of such a basic item and, thus, desires a 94 percent service level. Recommend an order quantity (Q) and reorder point (r) for a continuous review system.

Solution

First, calculate the value of Q using equation (3) for the parameters below:

$$D = (16)(365) = 5{,}840 \text{ per year}$$

$$S = 10$$

$$H = IC = (0.20)(0.25) = 0.05$$

$$EOQ = \sqrt{\frac{2DS}{H}} = \sqrt{\frac{2(5{,}840)(10)}{0.05}} = 1{,}528.4 \cong 1{,}500$$

Second, determine the demand during lead-time distribution using equations (9) and (10):

$$d_L = \mu(LT) = (16)(7) = 112$$

$$\sigma_L = \sigma\sqrt{LT} = 3\sqrt{7} = 7.94 \cong 8$$

Third, calculate the safety stock using equation (11), and find the z value in Appendix A with .06 probability in one tail:

$$SS = z_r \sigma \sqrt{LT} = (1.555)(8) = 12.44 \cong 13 \text{(round up to be conservative)}$$

Finally, the reorder point is the sum of the safety stock and the mean demand during lead-time:

$$ROP = SS + d_L = 13 + 112 = 125$$

2. Periodic Review (Order-Up-To) System

Problem Statement

The resort hotel manager was not interested in continuously monitoring the usage of complementary toilet items, which he felt were better classified as low-value C items. Thus, he requested that a periodic review system be used. Recommend a review period and target inventory level for a system with a 94 percent service level.

Solution

First, calculate the review period using equation (12) based on the *EOQ* from problem 1:

$$RP = EOQ/\mu = 1{,}500/16 = 93.75 \text{ days (or every 3 months)}$$

Second, calculate the safety stock using equation (14):

$$SS = z_r \sigma \sqrt{RT + LT} = (1.555)(3)\sqrt{94 + 7} = 46.9 \cong 47 \text{ units}$$

Finally, calculate the target inventory level using equation (13):

$$TIL = SS + \mu(RP + LT) = 47\ (16)(94 + 7) = 1{,}663 \text{ units}$$

3. Perishable Goods

Problem Statement

A commuter airline prides itself on customer service, with features such as providing its morning passengers with a copy of *The Wall Street Journal.* The paper costs $1.50 per issue on subscription. The newsstand price is $2.50. What size subscription should be ordered if a small plane with only six seats has experienced the demand distribution below:

Passengers	2	3	4	5	6
Probability	.1	.2	.2	.3	.2

Solution

First, prepare a $P(D < Q)$ distribution as shown:

Q	2	3	4	5	6
P(D < Q)	0	.1	.3	.5	.8

Second, identify the cost of underestimating demand as $C_u = \$2.50$, the cost of buying a newsstand paper for the passenger without one.

Third, identify the cost of overestimating demand as $C_o = \$1.50$, the cost of a paper not used.

Finally, using equation (15), we determine the critical fractile $P(D < Q) \leq C_u/(C_u + C_o) \leq 2.5/(2.5 + 1.5) \leq 0.625$. Thus, buy a five-paper subscription to *The Wall Street Journal.*

Exercises

15.1. Annual demand for the notebook binders that Ted's Stationery Shop sells is 10,000 units. Ted operates his business on a 200-workday year. The unit cost of a binder is \$2, and the cost of placing an order with his supplier is \$0.40. The cost of carrying a binder in stock for one year is 10 percent of its value

a. What should the *EOQ* be?

b. How many orders are placed per year?

c. How many working days elapse between reorders?

15.2. Deep Six Seafood, a restaurant that is open 360 days a year, specializes in fresh Maine lobsters at a cost of \$10 each. Air freight charges have increased significantly, and it now costs Deep Six \$48 to place an order. Because the lobsters are shipped live in a saltwater tub, the order cost is not affected by order sizes. The cost to keep a lobster alive until needed runs about \$0.02 per day. The demand for lobsters during the 1-day lead time is as follows:

Lead-Time Demand	Probability
0	.05
1	.10
2	.20
3	.30
4	.20
5	.10
6	.05

a. Deep Six would like to reconsider its order size. What would you recommend as an *EOQ*?

b. The Maine distributor is willing to give Deep Six a \$0.50 discount on each lobster if orders are placed in lots of 360 each. Should Deep Six accept this offer?

c. If Deep Six insists on maintaining a safety stock of 2 lobsters, what is the service level?

15.3. Dutch Farms imports cheese by the case from Holland for distribution to its Texas retail outlets. During the year (360 days), Dutch Farms sells 1,080 cases of cheese. Because of spoilage, Dutch Farms estimates that it costs the firm \$6 per year to store a case of cheese. The cost to place an order runs about \$10. The desired service level is 98 percent. The demand for cheese during the 1-day lead time is shown below.

Lead-Time Demand (Cases)	Probability
0	.02
1	.08
2	.20
3	.40
4	.20
5	.08
6	.02

a. Calculate the *EOQ* for Dutch Farms.

b. How many cases should Dutch Farms hold as safety stock against stockouts?

c. Dutch Farms owns a refrigerated warehouse with a capacity of 500 cubic feet. If each case of cheese requires 10 cubic feet and must be refrigerated, how much per year could Dutch Farms afford to spend on renting additional space?

15.4. The local distributor for Macho Heavy Beer is reconsidering its inventory policy now that only kegs will be sold. The sales forecast for next year (200 days) is 600 kegs. The cost to store a keg of Macho in a refrigerated warehouse is approximately $3 per year. Placing an order with the factory costs about $4. The demand for Macho during the 1-day lead time is

Lead-Time Demand (Kegs)	Probability
0	.03
1	.12
2	.20
3	.30
4	.20
5	.12
6	.03

a. Recommend an *EOQ* for Macho Heavy Beer.

b. If orders are placed in carload lots of 200 kegs, the brewery is willing to give the local distributor a $0.25 discount on the wholesale price of each keg. Based on analysis of total variable inventory costs, is this offer attractive?

c. What is the recommended safety stock if Macho decides on an 85 percent service level?

15.5. Books-to-Go, Inc., has a recurring problem of clearing its shelves of hardcover books when the publisher releases the paperback edition. These books take up shelf space, and the sales are slow. More important, however, they tie up capital with which to buy new bestsellers. Typically, hardcover bestsellers initially retail for $39.95 and have sales of approximately 30 per month during the introductory period. When the paperback becomes available, hardcover sales plummet to approximately 3 per month. The markup on bestsellers is 50 percent of cost.

a. If the paperback version sells for $12.95 and 15 hardbacks are in stock, recommend a discount price for the hardcover version.

b. Explain why the discount price is not influenced by the number of hardcovers in stock.

15.6. Spanish Interiors imports ceramic floor tiles from Mexico with various patterns in anticipation of contractor needs. These tiles usually are ordered a year before delivery, and the production run for each tile pattern requires a separate setup. Therefore, the orders must be large to defray the setup cost. Because orders are made far in advance of customer needs, the company must guess what the contractors will like and order patterns in anticipation of these demands. Occasionally, tile patterns fall out of favor, and Spanish Interiors is stuck with slow-moving stock. The markup is 30 percent of the tile cost, and the inventory usually turns over about three times per year. There are two slow-moving tile patterns in stock that management estimates will take 2 years each to clear. The sunburst pattern currently retails for $0.70 per square and the saguaro cactus pattern for $1.05 per square. Calculate the lowest discount price for each pattern that will clear the stock quickly.

15.7. Monthly demand for an inventory item is a normally distributed random variable with a mean of 20 units and a variance of 4. Demand follows this distribution every month, 12 months a year. When inventory reaches a predetermined level, an order for replenishment is placed. The fixed ordering cost is $60 per order. The items cost $4 per unit, and the annual inventory holding cost is 25 percent of the average value of the inventory. The replenishment lead time is exactly 4 months.

a. Determine the *EOQ*.

b. Assume that a 10 percent "all units" discount will be given if the order quantity is greater than or equal to 100 units. What order quantity would you recommend with this offer?

c. Determine the necessary reorder point and safety stock to achieve a 90 percent service level.

15.8. The daily demand for an item is distributed normally, with a mean of 5 and a variance of 2. The cost to place an order is $10, and the carrying charge per day is estimated at 10 percent of the inventory value. The supplier has offered the following purchase plan:

$$\text{Cost per unit} = \begin{cases} \$15 \text{ if} & Q < 10 \\ \$14 \text{ if} & 10 \leq Q < 50 \\ \$12 \text{ if} & Q \geq 50 \end{cases}$$

a. Recommend an optimal order quantity that will minimize the total inventory costs of ordering and holding plus the purchase cost of the units. Although it is not necessary, you can assume 360 days a year.

b. Determine the reorder point and safety stock that will achieve a 95 percent service level given a constant 2-day delivery lead time. Assume daily demand is an independent variable.

15.9. River City Cement Co. maintains an inventory of lime that is purchased from a local supplier. River City uses an average of 200,000 pounds of lime annually in its manufacturing operations (assume 50 operating weeks per year). The lime is purchased from the supplier at a cost of $0.10 per pound. The inventory holding cost is 30 percent of the average value of the inventory, and the cost of placing an order for replenishment is estimated to be $12 per order.

a. Assume that River City orders 10,000 pounds of lime every time it places an order for replenishment. What is the average annual cost of maintaining the inventory?

b. Determine the *EOQ*. If the forecast of annual demand is 10 percent less than actual, how much "extra" is River City paying annually because of an inaccurate forecast of demand (note that this means actual demand for lime averages 220,000 pounds)?

c. Assume that the supplier offers River City a 10 percent "all units" discount if the order quantity is 13,000 pounds or more. Also, assume that annual demand for lime averages 200,000 pounds. What is the best order quantity?

15.10. A popular item stocked by the Fair Deal Department Store has an annual demand of 600 units. The cost to purchase these units from the supplier is $20 per unit and $12 to prepare the purchase order. The annual inventory holding cost is 20 percent of the purchase cost. The manager tries to maintain the probability of stockout at 5 percent or less. Lead time demand is uniform, between 30 and 70 (i.e., the probability of lead time is $1/41 = .0244$ for demand $= 30, 31, \ldots, 70$).

a. Calculate the *EOQ*.

b. Calculate the reorder point.

c. Calculate the safety stock.

d. If we purchase 80 units or more, the unit purchase cost is reduced to $19. Calculate the *EOQ* for this quantity discount case.

15.11. The Supermart Store is about to place an order for Valentine's Day candy. The candy can be bought for $1.40 per box, and it is sold for $2.90 per box up to Valentine's Day. After Valentine's Day, any remaining boxes are sold for $1.00 each. All surplus candy can be sold at this reduced price. Demand at the regular retail price is a random variable with the following discrete probability distribution:

Demand (Boxes)	Probability
8	.15
9	.15
10	.30
11	.30
12	.10

a. Determine the expected demand for boxes of candy at the regular retail price.

b. Determine the optimal number of boxes to stock using the critical fractile approach.

c. What is the expected profit for your order in part b?

15.12. Suppose the XYZ Company, which has an annual demand of 12,000 units per year, order cost of $25, and annual holding cost per unit of $0.50, decides to operate with a planned shortage inventory policy with the backorder cost estimated as $5 per unit per year.

a. Determine the *EOQ*.

b. Determine the maximum number of backorders.

c. Determine the maximum inventory level.

d. Determine the cycle time in workdays (assume 250 workdays per year).

e. Determine the total inventory cost per year.

15.13. The A & M Hobby Shop carries a line of radio-controlled model racing cars. Demand for these cars is assumed to be a constant rate of 40 cars per month. The cars cost $60 each, and ordering costs are approximately $15 per order regardless of the order size. Inventory carrying costs are 20 percent annually.

a. Determine the *EOQ* and total annual costs under the assumption that no back orders are permitted.

b. Using a $45-per-unit-per-year backorder cost, determine the minimum cost inventory policy and total annual cost.

c. What is the maximum number of days a customer would have to wait for a backorder under the policy in part b? Assume the hobby shop is open for business 300 days per year.

d. Would you recommend a no-backorder or a backorder inventory policy for this product? Explain.

e. If the lead time is 6 days, what is the reorder point in terms of on-hand inventory for both the no-backorder and the backorder inventory policies?

15.14. The J & B Card Shop sells calendars with different coral reef pictures shown for each month. The once-a-year order for each year's calendar arrives in September. From past experience, the September-to-July demand for these calendars can be approximated by a normal distribution with mean of 500 and standard deviation of 120. The calendars cost $1.50 each, and J & B sells them for $3 each.

a. If J & B throws out all unsold calendars at the end of July (i.e., salvage value is zero), how many calendars should be ordered?

b. If J & B reduces the calendar price to $1 at the end of July and can sell all surplus calendars at this price, how many calendars should be ordered?

15.15. The Gilbert Air Conditioning Company is considering purchase of a special shipment of portable air conditioners from China. Each unit will cost Gilbert $80 and be sold for $125. Gilbert does not want to carry over surplus air conditioners to the following year. Thus, all surplus units will be sold to a wholesaler who has agreed to take them for $50 per unit. Given the probability distribution for air conditioners shown below, recommend an order quantity and the anticipated profit using expected value analysis:

Demand	Estimated Probability
0	.30
1	.35
2	.20
3	.10
4	.05

15.16. To limit dependence on imported oil, the Four Corners Power Company has decided to cover a fixed part of the regional demand for electricity by using coal. The annual demand for coal is estimated to be 500,000 tons, which are used uniformly throughout the year. The coal can be strip-mined near the power-generating plant and delivered with a setup requiring 2 days for a cost of $2,000 per mining run. Holding coal in inventory costs approximately $3.00 per ton per year.

a. Determine the economic order quantity for coal assuming 250 workdays per year.

b. Assume the daily demand for coal is distributed normally, with mean of 2,000 tons and standard deviation of 500 tons. What quantity should be set as safety stock to guarantee a 99 percent service level?

c. If the coal were mined in quantities of 50,000 tons per order, a savings of $0.01 per ton could be passed along to the power company. Should Four Corners Power Company reconsider its coal production quantity as calculated in part a?

d. What would be the basis for determining the cost of a coal stockout for Four Corners Power Company?

15.17. A wholesaler encounters a constant demand of 200 cases of one brand and box size of soap flakes per week from his retail accounts. He obtains the soap flakes from the manufacturer at $10 per case after paying the transportation costs. The average cost of each order placed is $5, and he computes his inventory carrying charges as 20 percent of the average inventory value on hand over a 1-year period.

a. Compute the *EOQ* for this product.

b. Assuming a constant lead time of 5 days for this product, what is the minimum reorder point that will allow the wholesaler to provide 100 percent customer service? Assume 5 operating days per week.

c. Determine the wholesaler's total cost per year for this product.

d. The manufacturer offers the wholesaler a quantity discount of $1 per case for purchasing in quantities of 400 cases or more. Should the wholesaler take advantage of this quantity discount?

15.18. Leapyear Tire is interested in carrying insufficient numbers of budget tires deliberately. If a customer finds a budget tire is not available, a salesperson will try to sell a more expensive substitute tire, but if this strategy fails, the customer is placed on a waiting list and notified when the next order arrives from the distributor. Leapyear Tire wishes to design an ordering system that will allow backorders to accumulate to a number approximately one-tenth the size of the replenishment order quantity at the time the delivery arrives from the distributor. The cost to hold a tire in stock for a year is $2 and the cost to place an order with the distributor is $9.

a. What is the implied cost of backordering a customer?

b. What would be the recommended order quantity for a 195HR14 tire with an annual demand of 1,000?

A.D. Small Consulting CASE 15.1

A.D. Small, Inc., provides management consulting services from its offices located in more than 300 cities in the United States and abroad. The company recruits its staff from top graduates of recognized MBA programs. Upon joining A.D. Small, a recruit attends an intensive two-month training program at the Boston headquarters, and upon successful completion of the training program is assigned to a consulting team in a field office.

To make sure that the training program covers new management concepts and techniques, A.D. Small retains internationally recognized professors from the Harvard Business School and MIT's Sloan School of Management to conduct the program. The professors are paid a fixed retainer for their services so that the cost of providing the training program, exclusive of salaries paid to recruits while attending the program, does not depend upon the number of recruits who participate. Faculty salaries and other expenses for the training program amount to a total of approximately $850,000.

Because personnel in a consulting capacity tend to be uncommonly well qualified and to develop many contacts with organizations through the consulting process, A.D. Small's staff members experience many lucrative opportunities to accept permanent positions with client firms. To maintain harmonious relationships with its clients, A.D. Small cannot vigorously discourage the pirating of its staff. As a result, A.D. Small must obtain about 180 new recruits per year to replace departing staff members. Departing staff members leave A.D. Small at an essentially uniform rate throughout the year. The attrition rate is approximately 3.5 persons per week.

Thornton McDougall, director of human resources at A.D. Small, was discussing personnel problems with Lou Carlson, president. "Lou, I've been playing with some figures, and it looks like we should rethink our training program. As you know we need about 180 new people each year and have fallen into the habit of bringing in 180 new recruits each June for our annual training program. However, on graduation day we have 180 more people on the payroll than we actually need, each earning about $90,000 per year. During the year, of course, positions will become available for these new people due to the normal attrition process, but until the positions open we are carrying a surplus of a very expensive commodity. It might be prudent to conduct more than one training program each year with smaller enrollments. That way we could cut down on the period between the time that an individual is put on the payroll and the time that the person is actually needed."

Lou Carlson responded, "Thornton, that is an interesting idea. It seems to me that there are two fundamental issues that must be addressed. The first issue is how often we should conduct a training program. The second issue is how many people should be enrolled in each session. Also, we must recognize our obligations to our clients. We must make sure that we will always have enough trained people on hand to service our accounts. The one thing that we cannot afford is a shortage of qualified staff."

Assignments

Use inventory models to address Lou Carlson's questions. Support your recommendations with cost justification.

Last Resort Restaurant[3] CASE 15.2

The Last Resort Restaurant is famous for its special pastry cream dessert. The dessert is made of layers of pastry and cream filling flavored with coffee liqueur and topped with a delicate vanilla icing and shaved dark chocolate. The dessert, called Sweet Revenge, is based on the recipe of Thomas Quinn, a famous chef who served in the British army in Belgium during the Napoleonic Wars.

Unfortunately, because of the delicate fresh dairy ingredients, Sweet Revenge must be served on the day it is made. This presents a problem for the owner, because he has to instruct the chef on how many Sweet Revenges to prepare each day. The owner and great-grandson, Martin Quinn, determined that the contribution to fixed costs and profit from each serving of Sweet Revenge is $2.95. This is based on a menu price of $3.95 minus a cost of $1.00 to produce.

Quinn believes that stocking out of Sweet Revenge hurts the reputation of the restaurant. While he feels that it might be difficult to prove, he thinks that stocking out of the dessert might be acceptable to 80 percent of the customers. He also believes that 20 percent of the people would be seriously upset by the situation. He estimates that one-half of these persons would be upset enough not to come back to the Last Resort for some period. The loss of business from this group would be roughly $20 per each disappointed person. The other one-half of the disappointed group would decide never to come back. The present value of lost future business for this group is estimated to be $100 per each disappointed person.

Mr. Quinn collected data on how many Sweet Revenges were ordered each day for a representative period shown in Table 15.6. He feels there is no seasonal or daily trend for the demand.

Questions

1. Assuming that the cost of stockout is the lost contribution of one dessert, how many portions of Sweet Revenge should the chef prepare each weekday?
2. Based on Martin Quinn's estimate of other stockout costs, how many servings should the chef prepare?
3. If, historically, desserts were prepared to cover 95 percent of demand, what was the implied stockout cost?

TABLE 15.6
Weekday Demand for Sweet Revenge

Monday	Tuesday	Wednesday	Thursday	Friday
250	275	260	300	290
235	250	295	310	360
240	275	286	236	294
289	315	340	256	311

Elysian Cycles[4] CASE 15.3

Located in a major southwestern U.S. city, Elysian Cycles (EC) is a wholesale distributor of bicycles and bicycle parts. Its primary retail outlets are located in eight cities within a 400-mile radius of the distribution center. These retail outlets generally depend on receiving orders for additional stock within two days after notifying the distribution center (if the stock is available). The company's management feels this is a valuable marketing tool that aids its survival in a highly competitive industry.

EC distributes a wide variety of finished bicycles, but all are based on five different frame designs, each of which is available in several sizes. Table 15.7 gives a breakdown of product options that are available to the retail outlets.

EC receives these different styles from a single manufacturer overseas, and shipments can take as long as four weeks from the time an order is made by telephone or Internet. Including the costs of communication, paperwork, and customs clearance, EC estimates that it incurs a cost of $65 each time an order is placed. The cost per bicycle is roughly 60 percent of the suggested list price for any of the styles available.

Demand for these bicycles is somewhat seasonal in nature, being heavier in spring and early summer and tapering off through fall and winter (except for a heavy surge in the six weeks before Christmas). A breakdown of the previous year's business with the retail outlets usually forms the basis for EC's yearly operations plan. A growth factor (either positive or negative) is used to refine further the demand estimate by reflecting the upcoming yearly market. By developing a yearly plan and updating it when appropriate, EC can establish a reasonable basis for obtaining any necessary financing from the bank. Last year's monthly demand for the different bicycle styles that EC distributes is shown in Table 15.8.

Because of the increasing popularity of bicycles for recreational purposes and for supplanting some automobile usage, EC believes that its market might grow by as much as 25 percent in the upcoming year. There have been years when the full amount of expected growth did not materialize, however,

TABLE 15.7
Prices and Options of Available Bicycles

Frame Style	Available Sizes, in.	Number of Gears	Suggested List Price
A	16, 20, 24	10	$ 99.95
B	16, 20, 24	15	124.95
C	16, 20, 24, 26	15	169.95
D	20, 24, 26	15	219.95
E	20, 24, 26	21	349.95

TABLE 15.8
Monthly Bicycle Demand

	Frame Style					
Month	A	B	C	D	E	Total
January	0	3	5	2	0	10
February	2	8	10	3	1	24
March	4	15	21	12	2	54
April	4	35	40	21	3	103
May	3	43	65	37	3	151
June	3	27	41	18	2	91
July	2	13	26	11	1	53
August	1	10	16	9	1	37
September	1	9	11	7	1	29
October	1	8	10	7	2	28
November	2	15	19	12	3	51
December	3	30	33	19	4	89
Total	26	216	297	158	23	720

so EC has decided to base its plan on a more conservative 15 percent growth factor to allow for variations in consumer buying habits and to ensure that it is not overstocked excessively if the expected market does not occur. Holding costs that are associated with inventory of any bicycle style are estimated to be about 0.75 percent of the unit cost of a bicycle per month.

Assignments

Develop an inventory control plan for EC to use as the basis for its upcoming annual plan. Justify your reason for choosing a particular type (or combination of types) of inventory system(s). For your particular plan, specify the safety stock requirement if EC institutes a policy of maintaining a 95 percent service level.

Selected Bibliography

Alptekinoglu, A., A. Banerjee, A. Paul, and N. Jain. "Inventory Pooling to Deliver Differentiated Service." *Manufacturing & Service Operations Management* 15, no. 1 (2013), pp. 33–44.

Camdereli, Almua Z., and Jayashankar M. Swaminathan. "Misplaced Inventory and Radio-Frequency Identification (RFID) Technology: Information and Coordination." *Production and Operations Management* 19, no. 1 (January–February 2010), pp. 1–18.

Craig, Nathan C., and Ananth Raman. "Improving Store Liquidation." *Manufacturing & Service Operations Management* 18, no. 1 (2015), pp. 89–103.

Dutta, Amitava, Hau L. Lee, and Seungjin Whang. "RFID and Operations Management: Technology, Value, and Incentives." *Production and Operations Management* 16, no. 5 (September–October 2007), pp. 646–55.

Gallego, Guillermo, Robert Phillips, and Ozge Sahin. "Strategic Management of Distressed Inventory." *Production and Operations Management* 17, no. 4 (July–August 2008), pp. 402–15.

Gavirnenni, Srinagesh, and Alice M. Isen. "Anatomy of a Newsvendor Decision: Observations from a Verbal Protocol Analysis." *Production and Operations Management* 19, no. 4 (July–August 2010), pp. 453–62.

Mogre, Riccardo, Rajit Gadh, and Arunabh Chattopadhyay. "Using Survey Data to Design a RFID Centric Service System for Hospitals." *Service Science* 1, no. 3 (Fall 2009), pp. 189–207.

Nair, Suresh K., and Richard G. Anderson. "A Specialized Inventory Problem in Banks: Optimizing Retail Sweeps." *Production and Operations Management* 17, no. 3 (May–June 2008), pp. 285–95.

Natarajan, Karthik V., and Jayashankar M. Swaminathan. "Inventory Management in Humanitarian Operations: Impact of Amount, Schedule, and Uncertainty in Funding." *Manufacturing & Service Operations Management* 16, no. 4 (2014), pp. 595–603.

Ovchinnikov, Anton, and Joseph M. Milner. "Revenue Management with End-of-Period Discounts in the Presence of Customer Learning." *Production and Operations Management* 21, no. 1 (January–February 2012), pp. 69–84.

Qi, Lian, Zuo-Jun Max Shen, and Lawrence V. Snyder. "A Continuous-Review Inventory Model with Disruptions at Both Supplier and Retailer." *Production and Operations Management* 18, no. 5 (September–October 2009), pp. 516–32.

Teunter, Ruud H., M. Zied Babai, and Aris A. Syntetos. "ABC Classification: Service Levels and Inventory Costs." *Production and Operations Management* 19, no. 3 (May–June 2010), pp. 343–52.

Endnotes

1. $dTCp/dQ = -DS/Q^2 + H/2 = 0$, thus $Q^2 = 2DS/H$ and $Q^* = \sqrt{2DS/H}$.
2. Taking the partial derivative of equation (5) with respect to K yields $-2H(Q - K)/2Q + 2BK/2Q$, which is set = 0 and solved for $K^* = Q[H/(H + B)]$. Note that $Q - K = Q\,[B/(H + B)]$ and substituting for K in (5) yields a $TC_b = DS/Q + H[BQ/(H + B)]^2/2\,Q + B[HQ/(H + B)]^2/2Q$. Taking the partial derivative with respect to Q yields $-\,DS/Q^2 + HB^2/2(H + B)^2 + BH^2/2(H + B)^2$, which is set = 0 and solved for $Q^* = \sqrt{2DS(H + B)/HB}$.
3. Adapted from Earl Sasser, R. Paul Olsen, and D. Daryl Wyckoff, *Management of Service Operations* (Boston: Allyn and Bacon, 1978), pp. 102–3.
4. Prepared by James H. Vance under the supervision of Professor James A. Fitzsimmons.

Chapter 16

Managing Service Projects

Learning Objectives

After completing this chapter, you should be able to:

1. Describe the nature of project management.
2. Illustrate the use of a Gantt chart and discuss its limitations.
3. Construct a project network.
4. Perform critical path analysis on a project network.
5. Allocate limited resources to a project.
6. Crash activities to reduce the project completion time.
7. Analyze a project with uncertain activity times to determine the project completion distribution.
8. Monitor a project for time, cost, and schedule variance using an earned value chart.
9. Discuss reasons why projects fail to meet performance, time, and cost objectives.

Projects can vary widely in their complexity, resource requirements, time needed for completion, and risk. Consider, for example, projects that might be undertaken by a passenger airline: opening a new route, overhauling an aircraft, implementing a new marketing strategy, installing a new reservation system, integrating a new fleet of aircraft into an existing system, and changing in-flight service. In this age of time-based competition, successful project management can bring new services to the marketplace sooner, thereby preempting rivals and capturing market share. For example, in the construction industry, Lehrer McGovern Bovis became famous for its construction management services by achieving significant time savings when it used an overlapping phased design-construction process in which the foundation was poured before the final drawings were completed.

The risks that are inherent in a project can threaten the survival of a company. For example, failure to complete a project on time can bankrupt a small construction firm when the contract includes a penalty cost for delay. The potential risks and rewards associated with a project are factors that enter into building a project team, selecting a project leader, and developing a strategy for successful completion of the project.

Chapter Preview

The chapter begins with an overview of the nature of projects and the challenges facing the project manager. Project planning begins with a work breakdown schedule and formation of a project team. Traditional bar-chart methods for project scheduling are then presented and discussed. We also introduce the concept of a project network and describe and illustrate methods of analysis. Microsoft Project is used to illustrate the ease and power of project management software. Project planning issues, such as dealing with resource constraints, activity crashing, and uncertainty, are explored. Techniques for monitoring projects to achieve objectives for time, cost, and performance conclude the chapter.

The Nature of Project Management

Characteristics of Projects

A *project* can be thought of as the allocation of resources directed toward a specific objective following a planned, organized approach. Project management involves planning, scheduling, and controlling project activities to achieve timely project completion within budget and meeting performance expectations. Project management is a challenge because the three objectives (cost, time, and performance) are in conflict. More time could enhance performance or quality, for example, but a contractual due date would be sacrificed and costs would exceed budget.

All projects have the following characteristics in common:

1. *Purpose.* The project is usually a one-time activity with clear objectives. An exception, for example, would include the periodic maintenance that airlines perform on their aircraft.
2. *Life cycle.* Each project follows a life cycle of tasks that include project conception, selection of the project to pursue, planning, scheduling, monitoring, control of project activities, and, finally, project termination.
3. *Interdependencies.* Projects involve many activities that must be performed in a specified sequence. The sequence generally is dictated by technological or strategic considerations. For large-scale projects, such as Boeing's development of the 787 aircraft, many partners require extensive coordination.
4. *Uniqueness.* Usually each project has novel features that require customized managerial attention. Many project elements, however, are common and learning can be transferred.
5. *Conflict.* Many stakeholders (e.g., client, parent organization, project team, partners, and functional areas) have conflicting objectives. Thus, projects involve a substantial commitment of resources and management attention during the life of the project.

Project Management Process

Organizations initiate projects for a variety of reasons, such as constructing a new facility, introducing a new service, or performing a consulting engagement. All of these reasons are catalysts that lead to the inception of a project. The management functions of planning, scheduling, and controlling are actively pursued from project conception to termination.

Planning

A project begins with a clearly defined statement of work and objectives agreed upon by all parties. This statement is a written description of the objectives, and it contains a tentative schedule that specifies start and completion dates and a proposed budget. The project scope is divided and subdivided into work packages. An aid to planning is the development of a *work breakdown structure (WBS),* which is a hierarchical tree or indented outline of the tasks required to achieve the objective. A WBS begins with the end objective and successively subdivides work into manageable components such as tasks, subtasks, and work elements. Consider the WBS shown in Figure 16.1, the project of moving a hospital across town to a new location. The project (or program if it is multiyear) is defined as "move the hospital." One task is "move patients." A subtask is "arrange for ambulance transportation." A work element is "prepare patients for the move." The detailed project definition provided by the WBS helps to identify the skills and responsibilities that are necessary to achieve the project goals, and it also provides a framework for budgeting.

FIGURE 16.1
Work Breakdown Structure

1.0 Move the hospital (Project)
  1.1 Move patients (Task)
    1.1.1 Arrange for ambulance (Subtask)
      1.1.1.1 Prepare patients for the move (Work element)
      1.1.1.2 Box patients' personal effects (Work element)
  1.2 Move furniture (Task)
    1.2.1 Contract with moving company (Subtask)
•
•
•

Scheduling

Scheduling begins with time and cost estimates for each work element or activity and a determination of the precedence relationships between activities. A project network diagram is prepared to provide a visual picture of the project schedule. Project management then is used to determine the start and finish dates for each activity in the project. Allocation of resources to specific activities also is planned at this time, a process that can influence the project duration and cost.

Controlling

The final project schedule becomes the basis upon which the project is implemented and monitored for progress against intermediate completion steps (called milestones). Expenditures against the budget also can be tracked using the project schedule. Controlling is concerned with making sure that all aspects of project implementation are carried out according to both time and budget. If some goals are not met, the schedule and plan are revised as necessary to ensure that project objectives are achieved.

Selecting the Project Manager

Managing a project requires special skills because the objectives of time, cost, and performance are conflicting. The following attributes of candidates should be considered:

- *Credibility*–the technical and administrative experience.
- *Sensitivity*–political and interpersonal conflict-resolution skills.
- *Ability to handle stress*–ability to manage multiple objectives within an uncertain environment.
- *Leadership*–ability to communicate goal attainment with integrity and enthusiasm.

Building the Project Team

Time is required to build personal relationships that result in accepting differences, being open to disagreement, and enjoying participation in activities together. In projects, people who never have worked together often are assigned to the same team. This group of individuals must develop into an effective team to achieve the project objective. Four sequential stages of team development usually are followed: forming, storming, norming, and performing.

Forming

Forming is the phase when team members get acquainted, similar to the early "courting" phase of a relationship. Team members usually have positive expectations and are eager to get started but are unsure of their roles in the team. Feelings characteristic of this stage include excitement, anticipation, suspicion, anxiety, and hesitancy. The project manager needs to provide direction and structure. During orientation sessions, the project objective, scope of work, schedule, and team operating procedures must be communicated clearly. Discussing the team's make-up and pointing out complementary skills and expertise will help to resolve anxiety about roles to be played by the members. To ensure buy-in, it is important to involve the team in developing the project plans.

Storming

In this stage, work begins in earnest and reality sets in, although it does not necessarily match expectations. Team members become dissatisfied with both project constraints and dependence on the direction and authority of the project manager. Conflict emerges, tension increases, and morale is low during this stage. The storming stage is characterized by feelings of frustration, anger, and hostility. The project manager needs to achieve agreement on methods for handling and resolving conflict. This is the time for the project manager to provide an understanding and supportive environment. Dissatisfaction and conflict must be addressed to avoid future dysfunctional behavior.

Norming

After passing through the storming stage, project team cohesion begins to develop and the operating environment is accepted. Control and decision making are transferred from the project manager to the project team. A feeling of camaraderie emerges as trust develops and team members share information and confide in one another. Personal friendships might develop that reach beyond the work environment. The project manager takes on a supportive role and recognizes the progress made by the team. Work performance and productivity accelerate during this phase.

Performing

In the final stage, the team is highly committed and eager to achieve the project objectives. Confidence is high and a sense of unity and pride in team accomplishments emerges. The team feels fully empowered, and members frequently collaborate to solve problems and help with implementation. During this stage, the project manager fully delegates responsibility and authority to the team but monitors its progress with respect to performance, budget, and schedule. If actual progress falls behind, the project manager facilitates and supports the development and implementation of corrective action. Finally, the project manager is in a position to mentor and support the professional development of people working on the project.

Principles of Effective Project Management

General guidelines have evolved from experience in managing projects. Some principles to keep in mind include the following:

1. Direct people individually and as a team.
2. Reinforce the excitement of the project.
3. Keep everyone informed.
4. Build agreements that vitalize team members (i.e., manage healthy conflict).
5. Empower yourself and team members.
6. Encourage risk taking and creativity.

The importance of projects has attracted much attention in recent times and has yielded techniques to help managers. Our discussion begins with Gantt charts and concludes with personal computer software used to analyze projects that are modeled as networks.

Techniques for Project Management

Gantt Project Charts

Developed by Henry Gantt in 1916, a *Gantt chart* is used to determine the timing of individual activities in a project. This chart plots a time line for each activity against a calendar. Gantt charts are a useful tool for portraying visually the schedule of activities and monitoring the progress of a project against its plan.

The first step in using a Gantt chart is to break down the project into discrete activities. "Discrete" means that each activity has a distinct beginning and end. After the project has been decomposed into its activities, the sequence of those activities is determined. This task is easier said than done, however. Usually, there are several possible strategies for carrying out a project, and it might not be obvious which one is best. The skill of the project manager, along with the input of other people interested in the project, ultimately determine the sequence that is adopted. A Gantt chart also requires time estimates for each activity. The durations of the activities are assumed to be deterministic and known, which means that we presume to know exactly how long each activity will take. Of course, this is not realistic, but it does provide estimates that are helpful for managing a project.

Example 16.1 Servicing a Boeing 747

A Gantt chart can be used to schedule a periodic or repetitive project, because the sequence of activities is well understood and past experience has determined how long each activity takes. Consider the required activities in a routine, 50-minute layover of a Boeing 747 passenger aircraft. Figure 16.2 is a Gantt chart that displays each activity with a horizontal bar indicating its duration in minutes and the scheduled beginning and ending times. Many activities, such as galley servicing, can be accomplished concurrently with others, because the corresponding horizontal bars overlap each other and, thus, are scheduled to be performed during the same time period. For lavatory servicing, however, the aft, center, and forward sections are serviced in sequence, not concurrently. This chart can be used to determine the labor and equipment resources that are required to complete the project on time. Once under way, activities that fall behind schedule can be noted by drawing a vertical line representing the current time and noting which activities have not finished as scheduled and, consequently, need attention to get back on schedule and finish the project in 50 minutes.

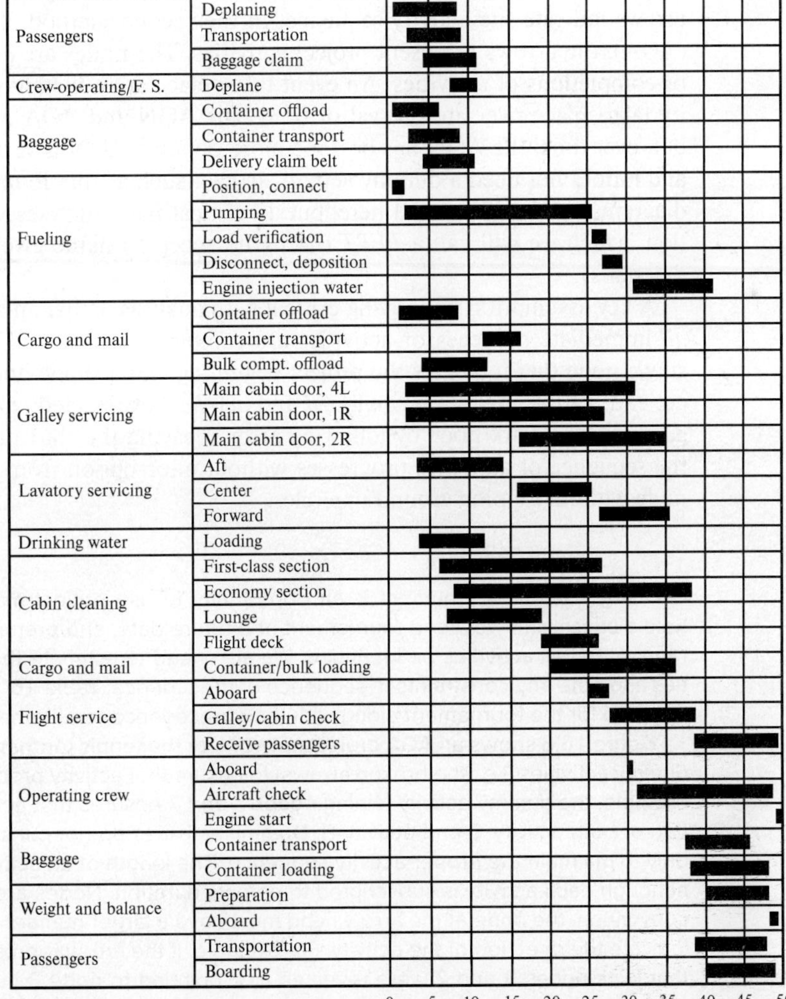

FIGURE 16.2
Gantt Chart Schedule of Service Activities for a Boeing 747

A Critique of Gantt Charts

Gantt charts have several appealing features that account for their continued acceptance. They are visual, easy to construct, and easy to understand. More important, however, they result in forced planning. To construct a chart, the project manager is compelled to think in detail about activity scheduling and resource requirements.

Despite their appealing features, Gantt charts are inadequate for large-scale, complex projects. In particular, they do not show clearly the interdependence of activities. For example, in Figure 16.2, galley servicing that uses the main cabin door 2R is delayed, because access to this door is blocked by cargo and mail operations. Consequently, it is difficult to evaluate the effects of changes in project implementation that can result from activity delays or changes in sequence. These charts also do not give any indication about the relative importance of individual activities in completing the project on schedule (i.e., which activities can be delayed without delaying the entire project). Therefore, because the relative importance of individual activities is the basis for allocating resources and managerial attention, Gantt charts are too ineffective and cumbersome to use with large, complicated projects. Consequently, network-based techniques were developed specifically to overcome the deficiencies of Gantt charts.

Constructing a Project Network

A network consists of a set of circles called nodes and also a set of arrows. The arrows connect the nodes to give a visual presentation of the sequence of activities. In one method, known as *activity on node* (AON), the nodes represent project activities, whereas the arrows indicate the activity sequence. In the second method, known as *activity on arrow* (AOA), the arrows represent project activities. The nodes are *events,* which are the starts or completions of activities. An event takes place at an instant of time, whereas an activity takes place over an interval of time. The AON and AOA methods are equally good, but, over time, the AON has become more popular. AON is very straightforward to draw, and it does not need a dummy activity artifact such as that found in AOA diagrams. Both diagrams will be illustrated here, but all critical path analyses will use the AON convention, which we will call a *PERT chart* (the accepted name given to project management diagrams).

A key assumption underlying critical path analysis is that an activity cannot begin until *all* immediate predecessor activities are completed. Also, a PERT chart generally has a single node that indicates the project beginning and a single node that indicates the project end. PERT charts are *connected* and *acyclic.* "Connected" means that it is possible to get to any network node by following arrows leaving the start node. "Acyclic" means that the sequence of activities progresses without interruption from the start node to the end node without looping around in circles.

Example 16.2 Tennis Tournament—Project Network

Planning a tennis tournament is an opportunity to use project management. The goal is to hold a successful weekend tournament at a future date, and preparations for the tournament require that all activities be identified. We also need to estimate the durations of these activities and note any constraints in sequence or precedence. Table 16.1 lists the activities that are required for the tournament along with their precedence requirements and durations.

Figure 16.3 shows an AOA project network for the tennis tournament. Note the use of three dummy activities (i.e., the broken arrows) to ensure that activity precedence is not violated. For example, the dummy activity joining nodes 3 and 7 ensures that activity F follows the completion of both activity C and activity B. Dummy activities do not consume time but are included only to maintain the proper activity sequence. The length of an activity arrow has no meaning, although each activity is subscripted to note its duration. Nodes are numbered according to a convention: the node at the arrow head must have a larger number than the node at the tail to indicate the direction of the activity. For example, if the arrow representing the dummy activity that joins nodes 3 and 7 were reversed (i.e., pointing to node 3 instead of node 7), then the precedence interpretation would change (i.e., activity D would follow activity B, which is not correct). Preparing an AOA network requires much care and is prone to errors.

TABLE 16.1
Tennis Tournament Activities

Activity Description	Code	Immediate Predecessor	Estimated Duration (Days)
Negotiate for location	A	—	2
Contact seeded players	B	—	8
Plan promotion	C	A	3
Locate officials	D	C	2
Send RSVP invitations	E	C	10
Sign player contracts	F	B,C	4
Purchase balls and trophies	G	D	4
Negotiate catering	H	E,F	1
Prepare location	I	E,G	3
Tournament	J	H,I	2

Figure 16.4 is a PERT chart (AON network) of the same tennis tournament project. In this case, arrows represent the sequence of activities, and nodes represent the activities themselves. Preparing a PERT chart is a simple matter of drawing nodes in approximate sequence from beginning to end and joining the nodes with arrows in the appropriate direction. Sometimes a start or finish node is added, as in the tennis tournament example. Note that the AOA and AON networks describe the same sequence of activities.

Critical Path Method

The *critical path method (CPM)* is an approach to determine the start and finish dates for individual activities in a project. A result of this method is the identification of a *critical path,* or unbroken chain of activities from the start to the end of the project. A delay in the starting time of any critical path activity results in a delay in the project completion time. Because of their importance for completing the project, *critical activities* receive top priority in the allocation of resources and managerial effort. In the spirit of *management by exception,* the critical activities are the exceptions that need close scrutiny.

CPM involves some simple calculations, and Table 16.2 lists the notations that are used in this analysis. Note that we have not indicated how the expected activity duration t is determined. In many cases, these values are assumed to be deterministic (i.e., constants) and are based on expert judgment and past experience. In other cases, the expected durations are assumed to be the arithmetic means of known probability distributions. We shall discuss the deterministic case first and treat probability distributions later.

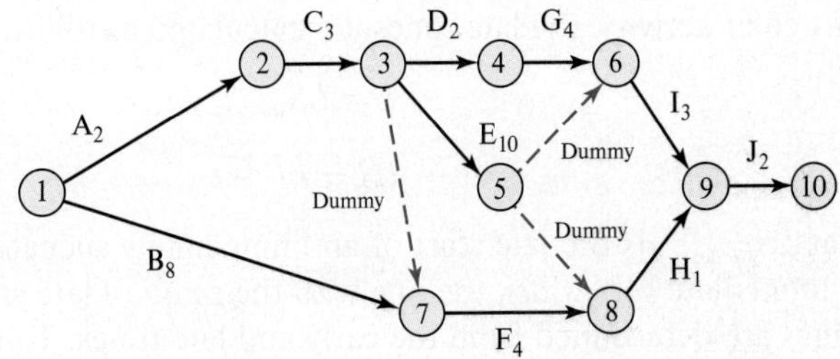

FIGURE 16.3
AOA Network for Tennis Tournament

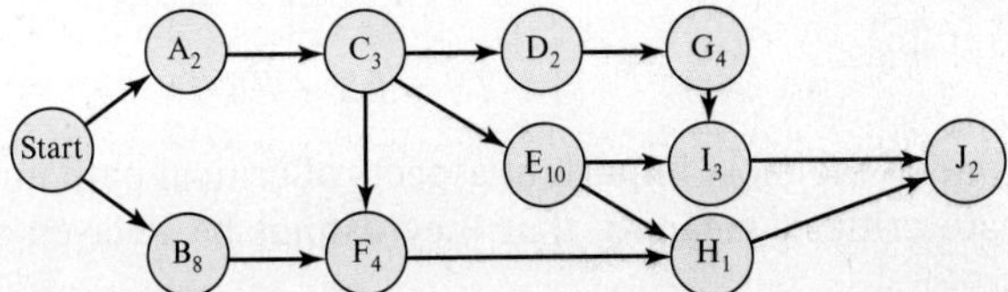

FIGURE 16.4
PERT Chart (AON Network) for Tennis Tournament

TABLE 16.2
Notation for Critical Path Method

Item	Symbol	Definition
Expected activity duration	t	The expected duration of an activity
Early start	ES	The earliest time an activity can begin if all previous activities are begun at their earliest times
Early finish	EF	The earliest time an activity can be completed if it is started at its early start time
Late start	LS	The latest time an activity can begin without delaying the completion of the project
Late finish	LF	The latest time an activity can be completed if it is started at its latest start time
Total slack	TS	The amount of time an activity can be delayed without delaying the completion of the project

CPM involves calculating early times (ES and EF), late times (LS and LF), and a slack time (TS). Early times are calculated for each activity beginning with the first activity and moving successively forward through the network to the final activity. Thus, the early times (ES and EF) are calculated by a *forward pass* through the project. The early start for the first activity is set equal to zero, and the early times for a particular activity are calculated as

$$ES = EF_{predecessor} \tag{1}$$

$$EF = ES + t \tag{2}$$

Note that $EF_{predecessor}$ is the early finish of an immediately preceding activity and that t is the duration of the activity under consideration. When there are several immediate *predecessors*, the one with the *largest* early finish time is used. The early finish for the last activity is the early finish for the project as a whole.

Late times (LS and LF) are calculated for each activity, beginning with the last activity in the network and moving successively backward through the network to the first activity. The late times thus are calculated by a *backward pass* through the project. By convention, the late finish for the last activity is set equal to the early finish (i.e., $LF = EF$). If a project completion date is known, then this date can be used as the late finish for the last activity. For any particular activity, the late times are calculated as follows:

$$LF = LS_{successor} \tag{3}$$

$$LS = LF - t \tag{4}$$

Note that $LS_{successor}$ is the late start of an immediately succeeding activity. When there are several immediate *successors*, the one with the *smallest* late start is used.

Slack times are determined from the early and late times. Total slack (TS) for an activity can be calculated in either of two equivalent ways:

$$TS = LF - EF \quad \text{or} \tag{5}$$

$$TS = LS - ES \tag{6}$$

Slack is one of the most important aspects of critical path analysis. Activities that have zero slack are critical, meaning that they cannot be delayed without also delaying the project completion time. When displayed on a Gantt chart, the set of critical activities always forms a complete and unbroken path from the initial node to the completion node of the network. Such a path is referred to as the *critical path;* in terms of duration time, this is the longest path in the network. A project network has *at least* one critical path, and it could have two or more.

Example 16.3 Tennis Tournament—Critical Path Analysis

The PERT chart of the tennis tournament is shown in Figure 16.5. Each node is labeled with the activity code, and the duration is a subscript. Next to each node is a cross to be filled in with the activity schedule times, which are calculated as shown below (note that t represents the activity time):

$$TS = LS - ES$$

$$\begin{array}{c|c} ES = EF_{predecessor} & EF = ES + t \\ \hline LS = LF - t & LF = LS_{successor} \end{array}$$

Early times are calculated beginning with the "start" node (i.e., forward pass) and are recorded in the top row of the cross for each activity, after which we see that the project will take 20 days to complete (i.e., *EF* for the last activity). Note that we need to be especially careful to select the predecessor with the *largest EF* as the time for the *ES* of the activity in question, which occurs when more than one arrow comes into a node (i.e., activities E and F converge on node H). Because no single activity begins the project, an artificial activity or "start" node is created with a duration of zero. Using this convention, we have a single "start" and a single "finish" node for the project. (Artificial "finish" nodes are used when a project does not have a single concluding activity.)

Figure 16.6 shows the completed critical path analysis. Note that per convention, the late finish for the last activity is set equal to 20 days. This value is the starting point for calculating late times (i.e., backward pass), which are entered into the bottom row of the cross for each activity. Again, we must use caution to select the successor with the *smallest LS* as the time for the *LF* of the activity in question, which occurs when more than one arrow departs from a node (i.e., activities D, E, and F following node C).

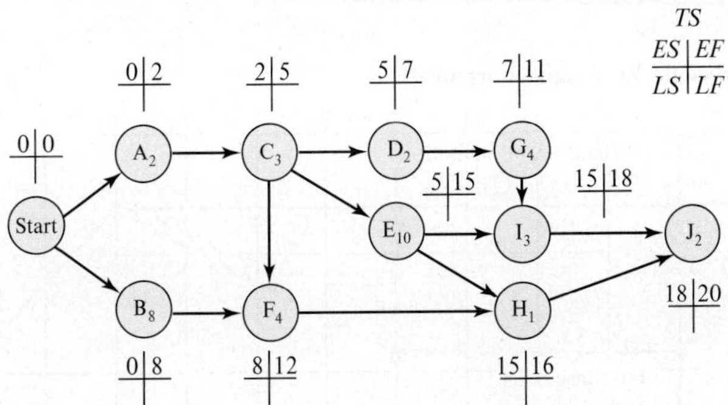

FIGURE 16.5
PERT Chart for Tennis Tournament with Early Time Calculations

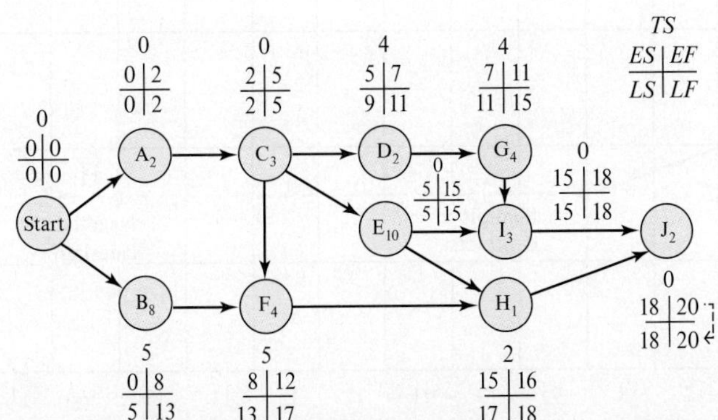

FIGURE 16.6
Completed Critical Path Analysis for Tennis Tournament

The critical activities have zero slack, which is easily seen as the difference between *ES* and *LS* or between *EF* and *LF;* thus, these activities have no scheduling flexibility. The critical path is defined by the critical activities A-C-E-I-J. As shown in Figure 16.7, the critical path represents the unbroken line of activities from beginning to end of the project. Any delay in activities on this path will delay the completion of the project beyond the 20 days.

Figure 16.7 is a modified activity-on-arrow PERT chart (recall Figure 16.3), without dummy arrows, on which each activity is plotted with an arrow equal to its duration in days and scheduled to begin at its early start date. The dotted lines following activities G, F, and H represent slack on noncritical paths. This figure provides a visual picture of a project schedule. For example, activity G has 4 days of total slack. The start of this activity can be delayed, or its duration may take longer than expected, up to a total of 4 days without affecting the project completion time. Note that the 5 days of total slack for activities B and F include the 2 days of total slack of activity H. Thus, if used to its maximum limit, total slack for an activity can drive a following activity to become critical. For example, if the start of activity F were delayed 5 days until the beginning of day 14, then activity H must be accomplished on day 18 with no slack available. Activity F could be delayed 3 days, however, without affecting the *ES* of the following activity (i.e., H). The length of the dotted lines immediately following activities F, G, and H represent what is called *free slack,* because these delays have no effect on the early start of following activities.

Microsoft Project Analysis

The tennis tournament also can be analyzed using the software program Microsoft Project. Data are entered using the Gantt chart format shown in Figure 16.8, with a calendar noting the dates and days in the week. Each activity's duration and precedence relationship are entered, creating an early start schedule after the last activity has been entered. Note the critical activities are bars that begin immediately after each other and, together, add up to the 20-day project duration, including weekend days (i.e., Saturday and Sunday).

A Microsoft Project PERT chart is shown in Figure 16.9. The critical path is shown with bold boxes and heavy arrows. Corresponding to the Gantt chart, the scheduled start (i.e., beginning of day) and scheduled finish (i.e., end of day) dates are noted for each

FIGURE 16.7 **PERT Early Start Schedule for Tennis Tournament**

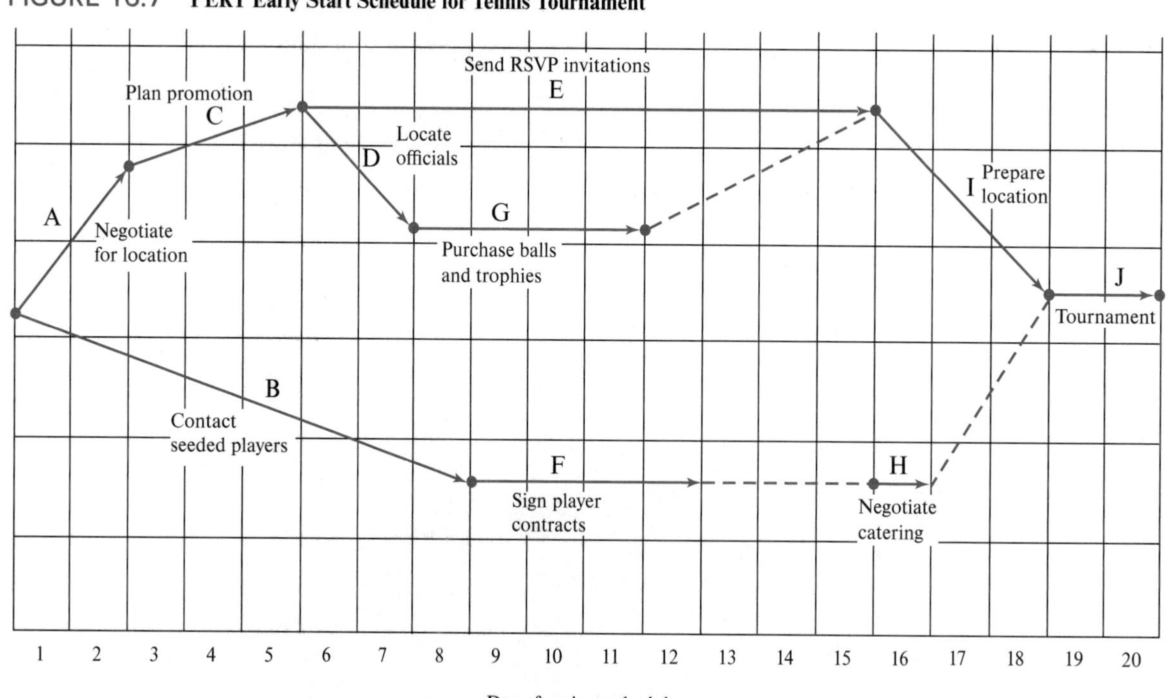

FIGURE 16.8 Microsoft Project Gantt Chart

ID	Task Name	Duration	
1	Negotiate for locations	2 days	Jim
2	Contract seeded players	8 days	Sanjeev
3	Plan promotion	3 days	Mona
4	Locate officials	2 days	Jim
5	Send RSVP invitations	10 days	Mona
6	Sign player contracts	4 days	Sanjeev
7	Purchase balls & trophies	4 days	Jim
8	Negotiate catering	1 day	Jim
9	Prepare location	3 days	Sanjeev
10	Tournament	2 days	Jim

'13: M T W T F S | Jun 16, '13: S M T W T F S | Jun 23, '13: S M T W T F S | Jun 30, '13: S M

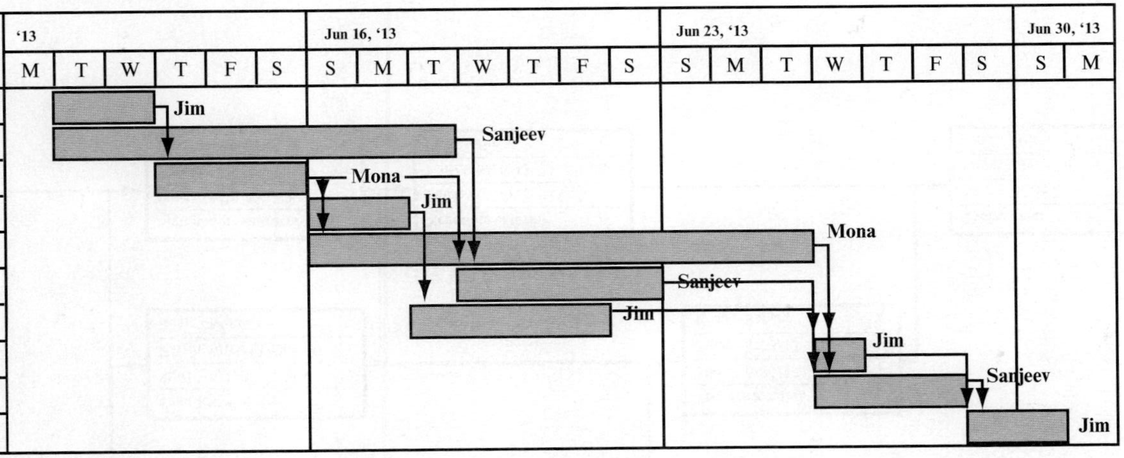

FIGURE 16.9 **Microsoft Project PERT Chart**

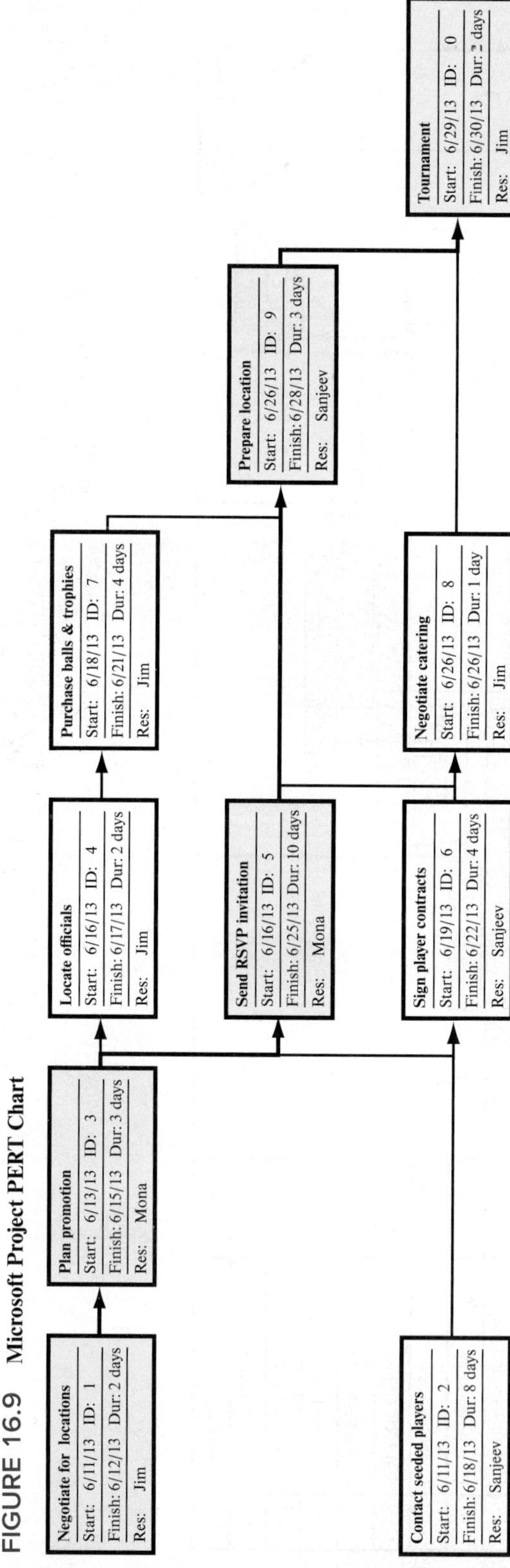
Negotiate for locations
Start: 6/11/13 ID: 1
Finish: 6/12/13 Dur: 2 days
Res: Jim
Contact seeded players
Start: 6/11/13 ID: 2
Finish: 6/18/13 Dur: 8 days
Res: Sanjeev
Plan promotion
Start: 6/13/13 ID: 3
Finish: 6/15/13 Dur: 3 days
Res: Mona
Locate officials
Start: 6/16/13 ID: 4
Finish: 6/17/13 Dur: 2 days
Res: Jim
Send RSVP invitation
Start: 6/16/13 ID: 5
Finish: 6/25/13 Dur: 10 days
Res: Mona
Sign player contracts
Start: 6/19/13 ID: 6
Finish: 6/22/13 Dur: 4 days
Res: Sanjeev
Purchase balls & trophies
Start: 6/18/13 ID: 7
Finish: 6/21/13 Dur: 4 days
Res: Jim
Negotiate catering
Start: 6/26/13 ID: 8
Finish: 6/26/13 Dur: 1 day
Res: Jim
Prepare location
Start: 6/26/13 ID: 9
Finish: 6/28/13 Dur: 3 days
Res: Sanjeev
Tournament
Start: 6/29/13 ID: 0
Finish: 6/30/13 Dur: 2 days
Res: Jim

activity and the activity ID number. The days of duration for each activity also are noted. For example, the first activity, "Negotiate for locations," which requires 2 days to accomplish, begins at the start of day 6/11/13 and finishes at the end of day 6/12/13.

Of what value is the information provided by critical path analysis? First, we know which activities likely will determine the project completion time if everything goes according to plan. We have identified the activities that cannot be delayed and, consequently, require more intense managerial attention. We also have identified noncritical activities that have some scheduling flexibility and can be used to advantage (e.g., the 4 slack days needed to purchase balls and trophies can be used to shop for bargains). Related to this, of course, is the allocation of resources. For example, workers might be shifted from activities with slack time to critical activities to reduce the risk of a project overrun or to make up for delays.

Resource Constraints

To this point in our analysis of project networks, we have assumed (although not explicitly) that resources are available to perform many activities concurrently. As shown in Figure 16.9, our PERT chart reveals three paths in parallel, with only the longest being critical and, thus, determining the project completion time. For example, while RSVP invitations are being extended (i.e., the critical path activity), balls and trophies are being purchased and player contracts are being signed. During this time period, if each task requires one person to perform it, then at least three people would be required to support our entire project schedule. In addition to workers, resource constraints also could include equipment availability (e.g., construction crane), shared facility (e.g., laboratory), and specialists (e.g., computer programmers). Ignoring the effect of resource constraints can result in a project schedule being infeasible; thus, the expected project completion date would be unattainable.

Returning to the tennis tournament example, an early start Gantt chart is shown in Figure 16.10. An early start schedule is created simply by starting each activity at its early start time (i.e., every line is drawn as far left as possible). In Figure 16.10, the critical path activities are drawn with a heavy line, indicating that the scheduling of these activities cannot be changed if we wish to complete the project in 20 days. The noncritical path activities (i.e., those with slack) are drawn with a light line, indicating that flexibility exists in their schedules. Assuming that one person is required to perform each activity, we have added a "Personnel Required" row at the bottom to indicate the staffing levels for each day in the project. As shown, the scheduled use of resources varies greatly, from one person during the last 4 days to 3 people during the 6th through 11th days.

Using the scheduling flexibility of the noncritical activities, the resource-leveled schedule shown in Figure 16.11 can be created. Note that all the noncritical activities except B have delayed start dates, with activities F and H starting on their late start dates. If only two persons are available to arrange this tournament, however, then the project duration must be extended by 1 day, because our leveled schedule shows that three persons are required on day 14. As might be expected, resource constraints result in stretching out the completion time of a project.

Activity Crashing

Construction projects often are undertaken with target completion dates that are important to the client. For example, consider the construction of a student dormitory at a university. If the project is not ready for occupancy by the last week of August, then a serious disruption would occur. At one university, students were housed temporarily in local hotels at the contractor's expense. For this reason, construction contracts often contain clauses to reward early project completion or to penalize a project overrun.

FIGURE 16.10 **Early Start Gantt Chart**

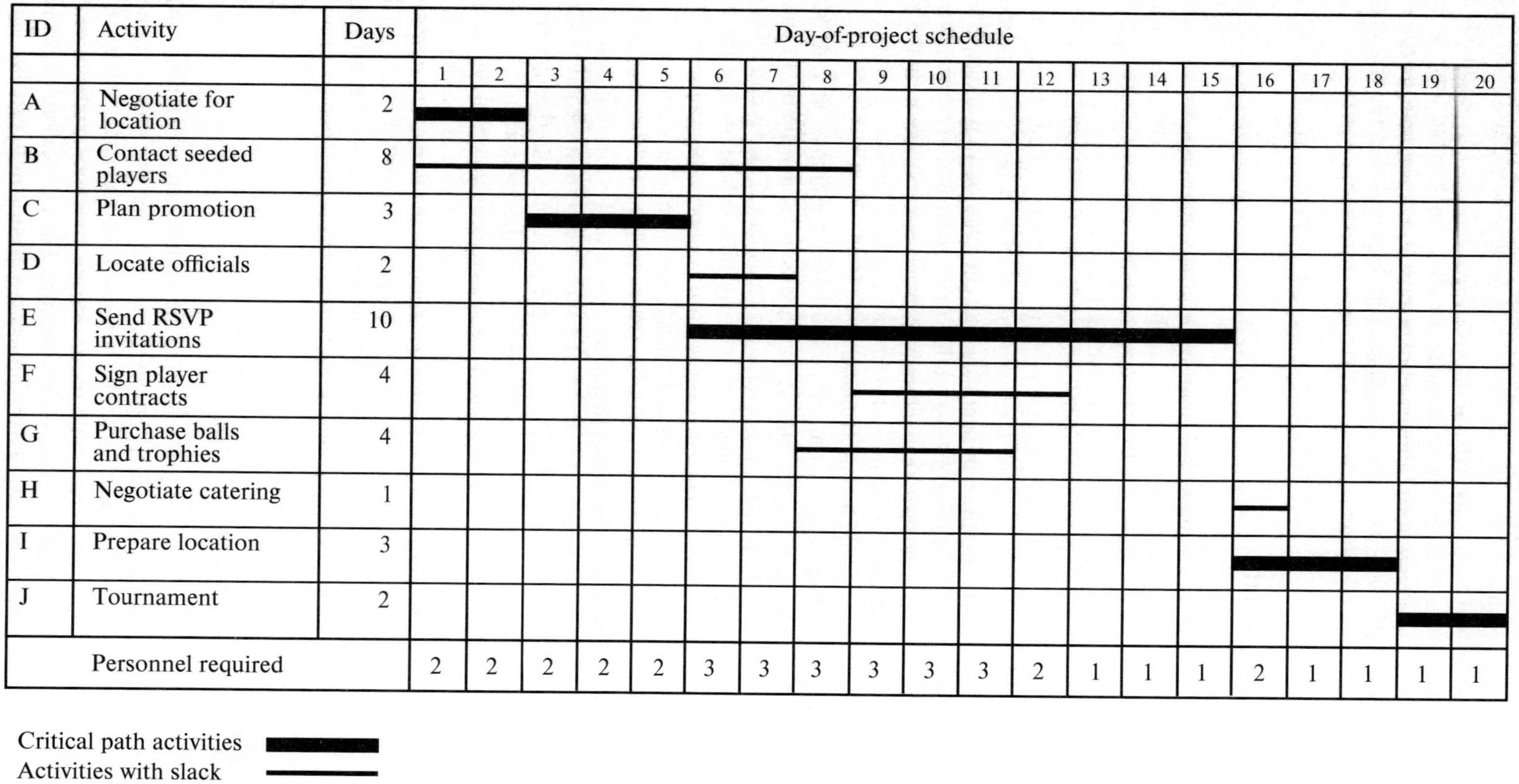

ID	Activity	Days	Day-of-project schedule																			
			1	2	3	4	5	6	7	8	9	10	11	12	13	14	15	16	17	18	19	20
A	Negotiate for location	2																				
B	Contact seeded players	8																				
C	Plan promotion	3																				
D	Locate officials	2																				
E	Send RSVP invitations	10																				
F	Sign player contracts	4																				
G	Purchase balls and trophies	4																				
H	Negotiate catering	1																				
I	Prepare location	3																				
J	Tournament	2																				
	Personnel required		2	2	2	2	2	3	3	3	3	3	3	2	1	1	1	2	1	1	1	1

Critical path activities
Activities with slack

FIGURE 16.11 **Resource-Leveled Schedule**

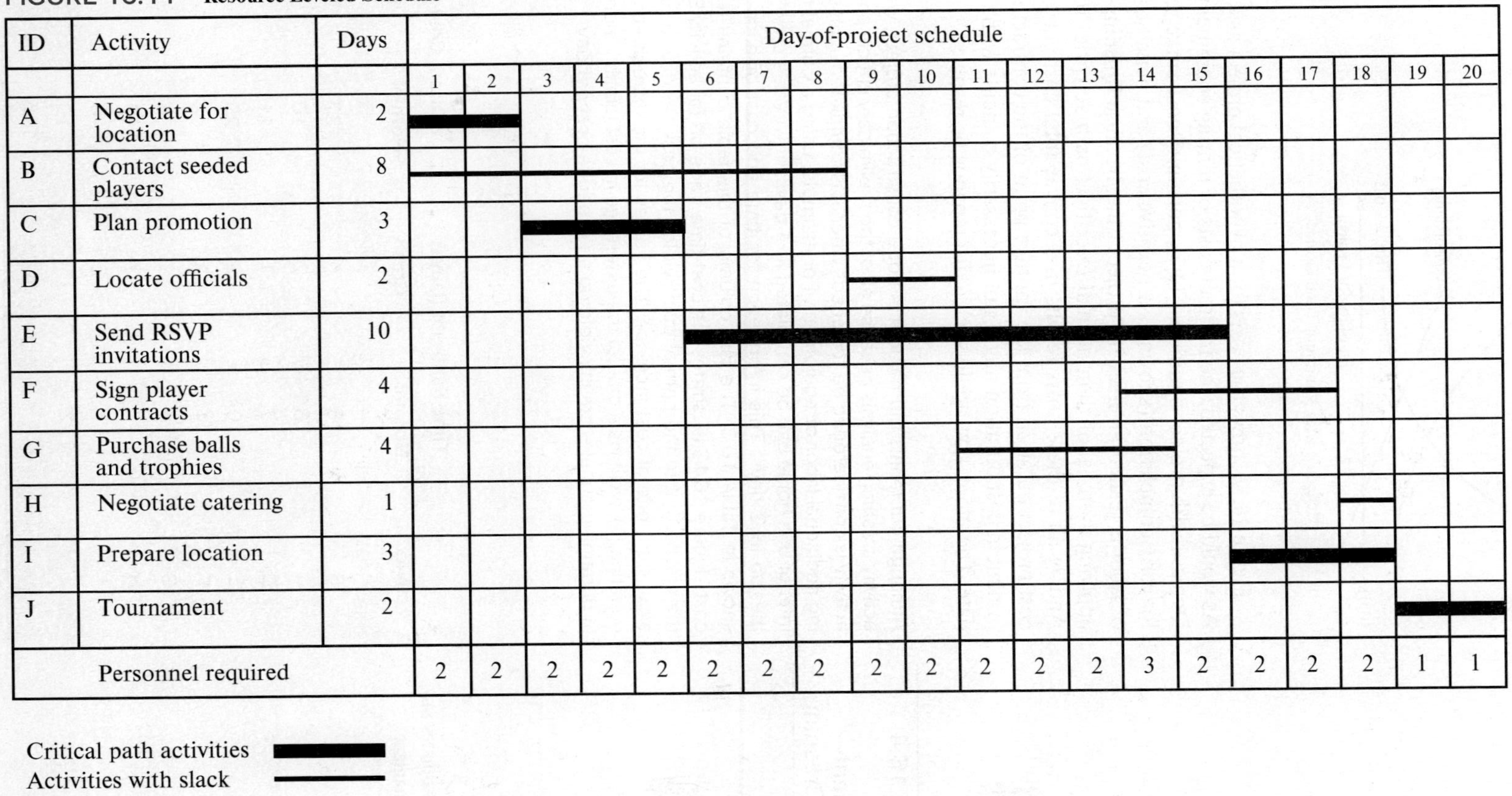

ID	Activity	Days	Day-of-project schedule																			
			1	2	3	4	5	6	7	8	9	10	11	12	13	14	15	16	17	18	19	20
A	Negotiate for location	2																				
B	Contact seeded players	8																				
C	Plan promotion	3																				
D	Locate officials	2																				
E	Send RSVP invitations	10																				
F	Sign player contracts	4																				
G	Purchase balls and trophies	4																				
H	Negotiate catering	1																				
I	Prepare location	3																				
J	Tournament	2																				
	Personnel required		2	2	2	2	2	2	2	2	2	2	2	2	2	3	2	2	2	2	1	1

Critical path activities

Activities with slack

FIGURE 16.12
Costs for Hypothetical Project

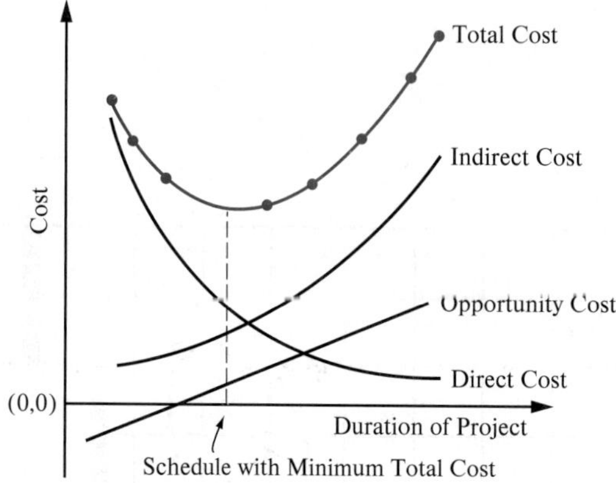

Figure 16.12 shows the costs for a hypothetical project as a function of project duration. As would be expected, the indirect costs of renting equipment, supervision, and insurance increase with project duration. The opportunity cost curve reflects the contractual bonus for early completion (shown as a negative cost) and penalties for overrun. The direct cost of labor is related inversely to project time, because finishing a project in a hurry requires applying more labor than normal to critical path activities to speed up their completion. Adding all of these costs results in a convex total cost curve that identifies a minimum-cost project duration from the vantage point of the contractor. Note that the contractor's minimum cost duration might not necessarily coincide with the client's target completion date. Therefore, how could such a discrepancy be resolved?

Example 16.4 Tennis Tournament—Activity Crashing

Although our tennis tournament is not a construction project, we will use it for illustrating the activity crashing analysis because all of the preliminary critical path analysis has been done. An activity is considered to be "crashed" when it is completed in less time than is normal by applying additional labor or equipment. For example, using a normal two-person painting crew, the interior of a home can be completed in 4 days; however, a crew of four painters could "crash" the job in 2 days. This information for time and cost of each tennis tournament activity is shown in Table 16.3. The last column of this table contains a calculation called "expedite-cost." Figure 16.13 illustrates the cost-time trade-off for activity E. The slope of the line joining the crash point to the normal point yields the cost per day to expedite the activity assuming a constant rate of cost increase. The values for the expedite-cost slope are calculated using equation (7), which is a ratio of the difference in cost (crash − normal) divided by the difference in duration (normal − crash), yielding an expedite-cost per day.

$$S = \frac{C^* - C}{D - D^*} \tag{7}$$

TABLE 16.3
Cost-Time Estimates for Tennis Tournament

	Time Estimate (Days)		Direct Cost ($)		
Activity	**Normal**	**Crash**	**Normal**	**Crash**	**Expedite-Cost Slope ($/Day)**
A	2	1	5	15	10
B	8	6	22	30	4
C	3	2	10	13	3
D	2	1	11	17	6
E	10	6	20	40	5
F	4	3	8	15	7
G	4	3	9	10	1
H	1	1	10	10	—
I	3	2	8	10	2
J	2	1	12	20	8
			115		

FIGURE 16.13
Activity Cost-Time Trade-Off

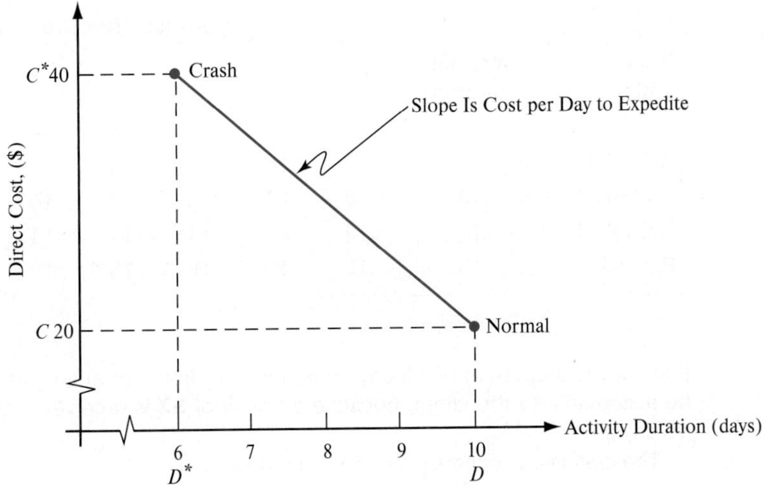

where

C = activity cost (* for crash cost)

D = activity duration (* for crash duration)

In performing the complete analysis that results in a total cost determination for various project durations, schedules for indirect costs and opportunity costs are required. Table 16.4 shows the indirect cost schedule, ranging from \$45 to \$13, and the opportunity costs, ranging from \$8 to – \$8. The analysis begins with the first row showing the normal project duration and costs (the direct cost of 115 came from Table 16.3). The project duration is incrementally reduced 1 day at a time by crashing an activity on the critical path. Using the expedite-cost as a guide, the critical activity with the least expedite-cost is selected (e.g., for the critical path A-C-E-I-J, we find from Table 16.3 that activity I costs only \$2 to crash 1 day).

Table 16.5 is used to keep track of changes in *all* project paths as we reduce the time of activities on the critical path(s). Note that we have given activity I an asterisk, because it cannot be crashed further (i.e., only 1 day was available) and, thus, is no longer a candidate for crashing. In Table 16.5 under the I* column, we have the revised path durations for the project and find that path A-C-E-I-J, with a duration of 19 days, remains the only critical path. We next turn to activity C to crash for 1 day, followed by crashing activity E for 3 straight days until we create two critical paths of 15 days' duration. With both path A-C-E-I-J and path B-F-H-J being critical, any reduction in project duration must reduce the duration of each path simultaneously. Candidates include selecting activity E on one path and B on the other, at a combined cost of \$9, or selecting activity J, which is common to both paths, at a cost of \$8. As seen in Table 16.5, further crashing involves multiple critical paths. Once the project duration reaches 12 days, it cannot be reduced further in duration, because critical path A-C-E-I-J now contains all activities with an asterisk (i.e., no candidates remain to be crashed). From Table 16.4, however, we see

TABLE 16.4
Total Cost Calculations

Project Duration	Activity Crashed	Direct Cost \$	Indirect Cost \$	Opportunity Cost \$	Total Cost \$
20	Normal	115	45	8	168
19	I*	117	41	6	164
18	C*	120	37	4	161
17	E	125	33	2	160
16	E	130	29	0	159
15	E	135	25	−2	158
14	J*	143	21	−4	160
13	E*,B	152	17	−6	163
12	A*,B*	166	13	−8	171

TABLE 16.5
Project Path Durations Following Crashing

Project Paths	Normal Duration	Duration after Crashing Activity							
		I*	C*	E	E	E	J*	E*,B	A*,B*
A-C-D-G-I-J	16	15	14	14	14	14	13	13	12
A-C-E-I-J	20	19	18	17	16	15	14	13	12
A-C-E-H-J	18	18	17	16	15	14	13	12	11
A-C-F-H-J	12	12	11	11	11	11	10	10	9
B-F-H-J	15	15	15	15	15	15	14	13	12

that a project duration of 15 days reaches a minimum total cost of $158. This duration would be acceptable to the client, because a bonus of $2 is received if the project is completed in 15 days.

The crashing procedure can be summarized as

1. Calculate the expedite-cost for each activity using equation (7).
2. List all the paths in the project network and their normal duration.
3. Crash by 1 day the least costly (i.e., minimum expedite-cost) activity on the critical path or the least costly combination of activities on common critical paths. Record the cost of the crashed schedule.
4. Update the duration for each path in the project network.
5. If an activity has reached its crash time, note with an asterisk and do not consider it as a further candidate.
6. If a critical path contains activities that are noted with an asterisk, STOP; otherwise, GO to 3.

Incorporating Uncertainty in Activity Times

In Example 16.4, we assumed that activity duration t was a constant. For many situations, however, this assumption is not practical because of the uncertainties involved in carrying out the activities. These durations generally are random variables that have associated probability distributions. Therefore, we do not know in advance the exact durations of all activities; consequently, we cannot determine the exact completion time of the project.

Estimating Activity Duration Distributions

To this point in our analysis, we have assumed that activity durations are known with certainty. However, for projects requiring creativity and experimentation (e.g., staging a Broadway play) or construction projects in adverse locations (e.g., the Alaska crude-oil pipeline), activity durations are random variables. Figure 16.14 shows a typical Beta distribution that is commonly used to describe the duration of uncertain activities. This

FIGURE 16.14
Beta Distribution of Activity Duration

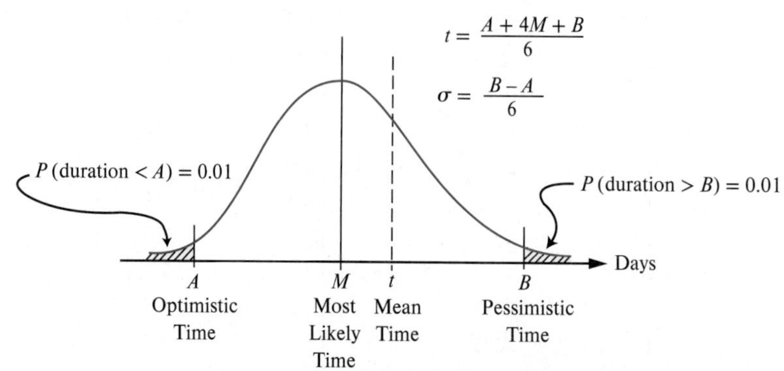

distribution captures the "skewness" in the distribution of activity duration that is likely to have a mean that is greater than the mode. Further, the Beta distribution can be approximated by simple formulas that require only three critical time estimates:

1. *Optimistic time* (A). This is the duration of an activity if no complications or problems occur. As a rule of thumb, there should be about a 1 percent chance of the actual duration being less than A.
2. *Most likely time* (M). This is the duration that is most likely to occur. In statistical terms, M is the modal value.
3. *Pessimistic time* (B). This is the duration of an activity if extraordinary problems arise. As a rule of thumb, there should be about a 1 percent chance of the actual duration ever exceeding B.

Using these three time estimates, the following equations can be used to calculate the mean and the variance of each activity distribution. The equation for the mean is a weighted average, with the modal value being given a weight of four:

$$t = (A + 4M + B)/6 \tag{8}$$

Recall that our definitions of optimistic and pessimistic times stipulate that 98 percent of the distribution should be contained within the range $A - B$. Thus, the standard deviation formula assumes that the optimistic time A and the pessimistic time B are six standard deviations apart.

$$\sigma = (B - A)/6 \tag{9}$$

The activity variance, which we will use in calculating the project completion time distribution, becomes

$$\sigma^2 = (B - A)^2/36 \tag{10}$$

Project Completion Time Distribution

Because each activity has a distribution, the project itself will have a completion time distribution that is based on the path of longest duration. The steps involved in the analysis are

1. For every activity, obtain estimates of A, M, and B.
2. Use equation (8) to calculate the expected activity durations, and perform critical path analysis using the expected activity durations t.
3. The expected project completion time T is assumed to be the sum of the expected durations of activities on the critical path.
4. The variance of project completion time σ_T^2 is assumed to be the sum of the variances of activities on the critical path. These variances are calculated by means of equation (10).
5. The project completion time is assumed to be distributed normally.[1]
6. Probabilities regarding project completion time can be determined from standard normal tables. (See Appendix A, Areas of a Standard Normal Distribution.)

Example 16.5 Tennis Tournament—Project Completion Time Distribution

We revisit the tennis tournament project once again, but now we assume that the activity durations are uncertain and obtain the three time estimates as recorded in Table 16.6. Because the tennis facility is booked for other matches, you are asked to find the probability of finishing the tournament within 24 days of initiating negotiations (i.e., of completing the entire project).

The variances and expected activity durations are calculated by means of equations (8) and (10) and are given in Table 16.6. Note that the expected activity durations are identical to the values that were used in the critical path analysis performed in Example 16.3. Thus, the critical path A-C-E-I-J, which was identified earlier in Figure 16.6, will be the focus of our determination of the project completion time distribution.

TABLE 16.6
Variances and Expected Activity Durations

Activity	Time Estimates *A*	*M*	*B*	Variance, σ^2	Expected Duration, *t*
A	1	2	3	4/36	2
B	5	8	11	36/36	8
C	2	3	4	4/36	3
D	1	2	3	4/36	2
E	6	9	18	144/36	10
F	2	4	6	16/36	4
G	1	3	11	100/36	4
H	1	1	1	0	1
I	2	2	8	36/36	3
J	2	2	2	0	2

We expect the sum of activity durations on this path to take 20 days and, thus, this path determines the expected project completion time *T*. The variance of project completion time is calculated by summing the variances that are associated with the critical activities. This yields

$$\sigma_T^2 = 4/36 + 4/36 + 144/36 + 36/36 + 0 = 188/36 = 5.2$$

We now can use *T* and σ_T^2 to determine the probability of finishing the project within 24 days. The *Z* value for the standard normal deviate is calculated using equation (11):

$$Z = \frac{X - \mu}{\sigma} \tag{11}$$

Thus, for the tennis tournament:

$$Z = \frac{X - \mu}{\sigma} = \frac{24 - T}{\sigma_T} = \frac{24 - 20}{\sqrt{5.2}} = 1.75$$

From the standard normal table with $Z = 1.75$, we find the probability of completing the project within 24 days to be approximately 0.96. Figure 16.15 shows the normal distribution of the project completion time with a 0.04 probability of exceeding 24 days' duration.

A Critique of the Project Completion Time Analysis

The key assumption underlying our analysis leading to a project completion time distribution is that the critical path as calculated from expected activity durations actually will be the true critical path. This is a critical assumption because it suggests that we know the critical path before all of the uncertain activities have been completed. In reality, the critical path itself is a random variable that is not known for certain until the project is completed. We know that the duration of the critical path is uncertain and has a probability distribution associated with it; likewise, the durations of other paths are uncertain. Consequently, it is possible for a path with an expected duration of less than the critical path to become the realized critical path because activities on this path have taken much longer than expected. The net effect is that a path not identified as being critical could determine project completion. Thus, estimates of expected completion time and variance of completion time for the project are biased when they are based only on the single critical path.

FIGURE 16.15
Project Completion Time Distribution

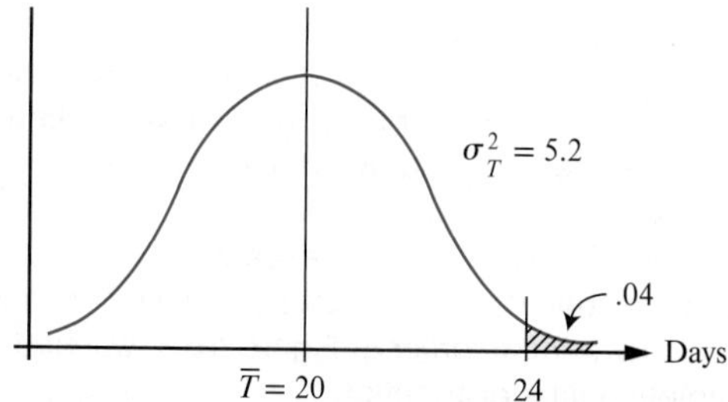

For the variance, the bias can be either on the high or the low side, but the expected project completion time is always biased optimistically. That is, the true expected completion time always is greater than or equal to the estimate.

A simple guideline can assist in giving a feel for the accuracy of these estimates: if the expected duration of the critical path is much longer than that of any other path, then the estimates likely will be good. In this case, the critical path very likely will determine the actual project completion time. If the project network contains noncritical paths with very little total slack time, however, these paths might affect project completion time. This situation is called *merge node bias.* That is, the project completion node has several paths coming into it, any one of which could be the critical path that determines the project completion time. In our analysis, only the most likely path is assumed to be critical; thus, our project completion time distribution is biased optimistically because other near critical paths are ignored. Example 16.6 illustrates the effect on the probability of completing a project when a near-critical path contains an activity with a large variance.

Example 16.6 Tennis Tournament—Merge Node Bias

A few days into the project, we discover that the purchase of balls and a trophy (i.e., activity G) might take longer than expected, with revised estimates of $A = 2$, $M = 3$, and $B = 28$. What effect does this have on the probability of completing the project in 24 days?

First, we recalculate the expected duration and variance of activity G using equations (8) and (10) and find that $t = 7$ and $\sigma^2 = 676/36$. Recall from Figure 16.7 that activity G initially had a 4-day expected duration and total slack of 4 days. Thus, with a revised duration of 7 days, activity G still is noncritical, with a $TS = 1$. The large variance of activity G, however, will have an impact on the likelihood of this path A-C-D-G-I-J becoming critical. A completion time distribution can be determined for this near-critical path in the following manner:

Near-Critical Path	t	σ^2
A	2	4/36
C	3	4/36
D	2	4/36
G	7	676/36
I	3	36/36
J	2	0
	$T = 19$	$\sigma_T^2 = 724/36 = 20$

We now can use T and σ_T^2 of the near-critical path to determine the probability of finishing the project within 24 days. The Z value for the standard normal deviate is calculated using equation (11):

$$Z = \frac{X - \mu}{\sigma} = \frac{24 - T}{\sigma_T} = \frac{24 - 19}{\sqrt{20}} = 1.12$$

Referring to the standard normal table with $Z = 1.12$, we find that the probability of completing the project within 24 days is approximately 0.87. The completion time distribution for this near-critical path is shown in Figure 16.16. Thus, a near-critical path with a high variance activity should not be ignored, because, in fact, such a path can become critical and delay the project completion time. Computer simulation (see Chapter 13 Supplement) is an approach to determine the project completion time distribution more accurately.

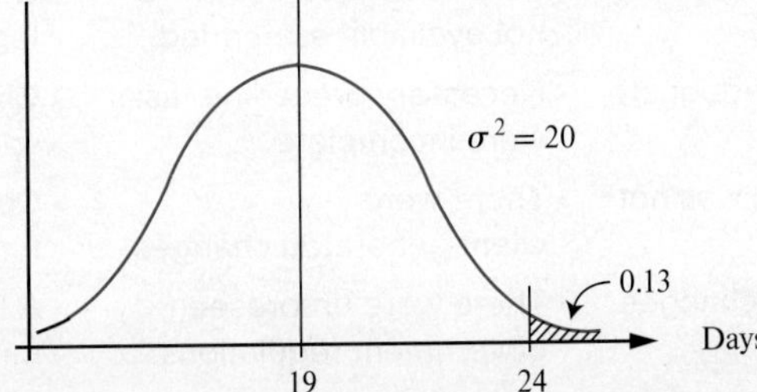

FIGURE 16.16
Near-Critical Path Completion Time Distribution

Problems with Implementing Critical Path Analysis

The mechanics of critical path analysis make the use of network models appear to be deceptively simple. After all, the calculations are straightforward. Network analysis does not resolve all the problems inherent in project management, however. Two major concerns are developing the project network and eliciting time estimates for activities.

The project network indicates the sequence in which activities are to be performed. For most projects, several different strategies can be adopted. The technological factors along with the influences of people who are concerned with the project generally determine which strategy is selected. As the project is implemented, the project network is subject to review and possible revision, which might be needed because some activities get off schedule or resources might not be available when needed.

Reviewing and revising the project network can be very time-consuming. The individuals involved with the project must be consulted about anticipated changes. The process of reviewing and revising the project network is an ongoing process that is made easier with the use of computer software.

The second concern in using network models is eliciting time estimates for activities. Obviously, poor estimates impact the accuracy of project planning. Resident experts often are sought out for their experience in past projects. Good time estimates are difficult to obtain, however, because people disagree and consensus might be difficult to achieve.

Another problem is that of bias introduced into estimates of activity durations. For example, an individual actually might expect to carry out an activity in 8 days but gives an estimate of 10 days. Thus, the individual provides a few days' leeway by padding the estimate. To avoid these problems, a database of actual times on past projects could be developed to provide time estimates for common activities. For example, painting the walls of a room could be estimated based on the time per square foot from past experience.

Monitoring Projects

Dealing with uncertainty is the hallmark of project management. The original plans and expectations are seldom realized, because projects often are pioneering endeavors. Monitoring progress against plans is an important activity for the project manager because early detection of problems can lead to corrections in time to avoid failure. Table 16.7 contains examples of unexpected problems in the areas of cost, time, and performance.

TABLE 16.7
Sources of Unexpected Problems

Cost	Time	Performance
• Difficulties require more resources	• There were delays owing to technical difficulties	• Unexpected technical problems arise
• Scope of work increases	• Initial time estimates were optimistic	• Insufficient resources are available
• Initial bids or estimates were too low	• Task sequencing was incorrect	• Insurmountable technical difficulties occur
• Reporting was poor or untimely	• Required resources were not available as needed	• Quality or reliability problems occur
• Budgeting was inadequate	• Necessary preceding tasks were incomplete	• Client requires changes in specifications
• Corrective control was not exercised in time	• There were client-generated changes	• Complications arise with functional areas
• There were price changes of inputs	• There were unforeseen government regulations	• A technological breakthrough occurs

Earned Value Chart

Project management tools, such as the project network diagram, are designed to be visual in nature, because they can communicate project status to clients and team members quickly. The earned value chart shown in Figure 16.17 is an effective method of visualizing the project status regarding the objectives of time and costs. The solid line represents the scheduled cost expenditures (i.e., baseline) as a function of time. The dashed actual cost line in this example is drawn above the planned cost expenditure line to illustrate a project that is exceeding cost estimates for work accomplished. The bold solid line below the budgeted cost expenditure line represents the value of work completed.

Three sources of variance are shown on the earned value chart: time, cost, and schedule. Because this project is running over budget and behind schedule, all three variances are negative. Note that negative variances indicate problems that need immediate attention. When using project management software like Microsoft Project to monitor project progress, the earned value report is generated automatically. The variances are defined as

Time variance = STWP − ATWP

STWP = Scheduled time for work performed

ATWP = Actual time used for work performed

Cost variance = BCWP − ACWP

BCWP = Budgeted cost for work performed

ACWP = Actual cost of work performed

Schedule variance = BCWP − BCWS

BCWP = Budgeted cost of work performed

BCWS = Budgeted cost of work scheduled to be performed to date

Project Termination

Some projects are not successful and termination can occur in several ways. Upon completion of a project, however, the preparation of a project history report can become a learning document for improvement in managing future projects. Methods of project termination include

Extinction: Successfully completed or killed.

Addition: Successful project becomes institutionalized as part of parent organization.

Integration: Successful project is dismantled and distributed throughout parent organization.

Starvation: Slow death by budget cuts.

FIGURE 16.17
Earned Value Chart

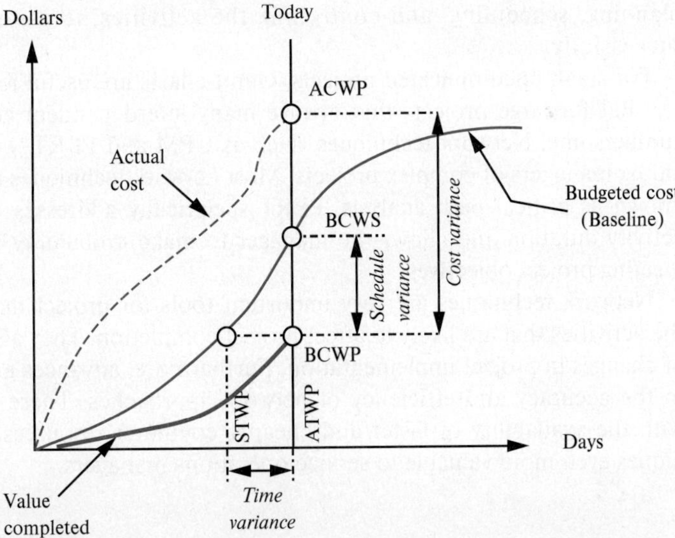

Service Benchmark

THE HOUSE THAT WARREN BUILT

Do you believe a four-bedroom house could be built in four hours? Warren Jack thought so, so he went to work with ProChain (ProChain Solutions, Inc.) and Microsoft Project software to make it happen. Habitat for Humanity sponsored the project.

The ProChain software was used in an iterative fashion to develop a final plan for the tasks and order of the tasks, given the available labor. During this planning phase, the critical path time was kept below three hours, excluding buffer time.

Predictably, glitches occurred. The bathroom was scheduled to be completed in 30 minutes but took 90 minutes. A second glitch occurred when a preassembled wiring loom for the ceiling was inserted through the trusses wrong end first. The misdirection was not discovered until the gable end sheathing was fastened into place, precluding removal of the loom. Solving this problem also took extra time, but ProChain had allowed time buffers that compensated for the possibility of overruns.

In the end, the house that Warren built was ready for its new family in 3 hours, 44 minutes, and 59 seconds, a new record for Habitat for Humanity.

[**Note:** To learn more about inserting time buffers in a project plan read Eliyahu M. Goldratt, *Critical Chain,* cited in the Selected Bibliography.]

Project History Report

The project history report documents the project experience and provides opportunities to learn from mistakes and success. A history report should include

Project performance: Comparison of proposal with termination evaluation.
Administrative performance: Comments on effective and ineffective practices.
Organizational structure: How good was it?
Project and administrative teams: Confidential assessment of team members.
Techniques of project management: Seek recommendations for improvement.

Summary

Managers of organizations typically are immersed in the detailed operations of ongoing projects. They also are responsible for generating new projects. The vitality of an organization can be seen in the way projects are conceived and carried out. For dynamic organizations, project management has important dimensions that involve planning, scheduling, and controlling the activities necessary to carry out a project successfully.

For small uncomplicated projects, Gantt charts are useful for assisting project managers. But for large projects that involve many interdependent activities, Gantt charts are cumbersome. Network techniques, such as CPM and PERT, were developed as tools for aiding managers of complex projects. Most network techniques use a similar methodology known as critical path analysis. PERT specifically addresses the problem of uncertain activity duration and allows the manager to make probability statements with regard to meeting project objectives.

Network techniques are very important tools for project management. They indicate the activities that are likely to affect project completion. They also facilitate the evaluation of changes in project implementation. Furthermore, advances are being made with regard to the accuracy and efficiency of network approaches. These advances, in conjunction with the availability of faster and cheaper computer resources, will make network techniques even more valuable to service operations managers.

Key Terms and Definitions

Critical activities activities on the critical path that, if delayed, would result in the delay of the project as a whole. *p. 467*
Critical path the sequence of activities in a project that has the longest duration, thus defining the project completion time. *p. 467*
Critical path method (CPM) the process for determining the start and finish dates for individual activities, thus creating the *critical path* for the project. *p. 467*
Gantt chart a graphical representation of the project schedule containing horizontal bars for each activity with the length of the bars corresponding to the duration of the activity. *p. 465*
PERT chart a graphical representation of the relationship between activities using arrows to show precedence and nodes for activity descriptions. *p. 466*
Predecessor an activity that must precede another activity. *p. 468*
Project a collection of related activities or steps that are performed in a specified sequence for the purpose of meeting a defined, nonroutine goal. *p. 462*
Successor an activity that follows another activity. *p. 468*
Work breakdown structure (WBS) a family-tree subdivision of the effort that is required to achieve the project objective. *p. 462*

Topics for Discussion

1. Give an example that demonstrates the trade-off inherent in projects among cost, time, and performance.
2. Illustrate the four stages of team building from your own experience.
3. Are Gantt charts still viable project management tools? Explain.
4. Explain why the PERT estimate of expected project duration is always optimistic. Can we get any feel for the magnitude of the bias?
5. Discuss the differences among time variance, cost variance, and schedule variance.
6. Conduct a Google search on "project finance" and find employment opportunities in project finance. What is the role of finance in projects?

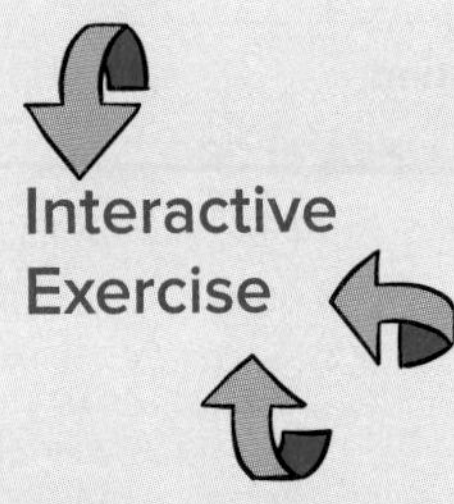

Interactive Exercise

Prepare a work breakdown structure (WBS) for a homecoming dance.

Solved Problems

1. Critical Path Analysis

Problem Statement

You have been asked to head a special project team at McDonald's to bring out a new breakfast item called the McWaffle. You have prepared the network diagram below showing the necessary activities with their expected times in days. Calculate the scheduling times *ES, LS, EF,* and *LF,* and slack time *TS* for each activity. What are the critical path and project duration?

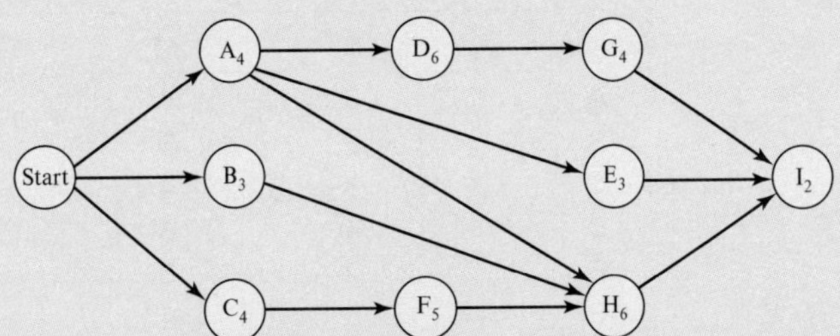

Solution

		Forward Pass		Backward Pass		
Activity	**Time**	***ES***	***EF***	***LF***	***LS***	***TS* = *LS* − *ES***
A	4	0	4	5	1	1
B	3	0	3	9	6	6
C	4	0	4	4	0	0
D	6	4	10	11	5	1
E	3	4	7	15	12	8
F	5	4	9	9	4	0
G	4	10	14	15	11	1
H	6	9	15	15	9	0
I	2	15	17	17	15	0

The critical path activities are C, F, H, and I, because $TS = 0$ in each case. The project duration is 17 days, the sum of the critical path activity times.

2. Activity Crashing

Problem Statement

For the network above, assume that an activity's daily expedite-cost in dollars per day is equal to the activity's time (e.g., the cost to reduce the activity time of H by one day is $6). Further, assume that each activity can be crashed only 1 day. What activities should be crashed to reduce the project duration by 3 days at least cost?

Solution

In the following table the circled numbers represent the project duration, starting with 17 days. After activity C is crashed, two paths become critical; thus, two activities must be crashed (one on each path) to achieve a 14-day project duration.

		Activities Crashed		
Project Path	**Normal Time**	**I**	**C**	**F&A or F&G**
A-D-G-I	16	15	(15)	(14)
A-E-I	9	8	8	8 or 7
A-H-I	12	11	11	11 or 10
B-H-I	11	10	10	10
C-F-H-I	(17)	(16)	(15)	(14)

3. Incorporating Uncertainty in Activity Times

Problem Statement

Assume the McWaffle project above contained some uncertain activity times as shown below. Calculate the mean and variance of all activities, and determine the probability of completing the project within 20 days without crashing any activities.

Solution

First, calculate the mean and variance for each activity using equations (8) and (10):

Activity	*A*	*M*	*B*	Mean	Variance
A	3	4	5	4	4/36
B	3	3	3	3	0
C	3	4	5	4	4/36
D	4	6	8	6	16/36
E	2	3	4	3	4/36
F	2	4	12	5	100/36
G	3	4	5	4	4/36
H	4	5	12	6	64/36
I	2	2	2	2	0

Second, determine the critical path. This calculation yields activity means that are identical to those of the original problem statement. Thus, the critical path is C-F-H-I, with an expected time of $T = 17$ days. The variance of the project completion time is the sum of the critical activity variances. This yields $\sigma_T^2 = 4/36 + 100/36 + 64/36 + 0 = 168/36 = 4.67$. Using equation (11), we calculate the Z value for a project completion within 20 days:

$$Z = \frac{X - \mu}{\sigma} = \frac{20 - T}{\sigma_T} = \frac{20 - 17}{\sqrt{4.67}} = 1.39$$

Using Appendix A, Areas of a Standard Normal Distribution, we find a probability of $0.5 + 0.4177 = 0.9177$, or approximately a 92 percent chance of competing the project within 20 days.

Exercises

16.1. An electric utility is planning its annual project of shutting down one of its steam boilers for maintenance and repair. An analysis of this project has identified the following principal activities and their expected times and relationships.

Activity	Time, Days	Immediate Predecessor
A	4	—
B	3	—
C	4	—
D	6	A
E	3	A
F	5	C
G	4	D
H	6	A,B,F
I	2	E,G,H

a. Prepare a project network diagram.
b. Calculate the scheduling times and total slack for each activity.
c. List the critical path activities and project duration.
d. Assuming that one worker is required for each activity, prepare a resource-leveled schedule. What is the maximum number of workers required to finish the project on time?

16.2. A consulting firm is planning a reengineering project for a client. The following activities and time estimates have been identified:

Activity	Time, Days	Immediate Predecessor
A	1	—
B	2	—
C	2	—
D	2	A,B
E	4	A,C
F	1	C
G	4	D
H	8	G,E,F

a. Draw a project network diagram.

b. Calculate the scheduling times and total slack for each activity.

c. List the critical path activities and project duration.

d. Assuming that one worker is required for each activity, prepare a resource-leveled schedule. What is the maximum number of workers required to finish the project on time?

16.3. Slippery Rock College is planning a basketball tournament The following information has been collected on each activity in the project:

Activity	Time, Days	Immediate Predecessor	Description
A	3	—	Select teams
B	5	A	Mail out invitations
C	10	—	Arrange accommodations
D	3	B,C	Plan promotion
E	5	B,C	Print tickets
F	10	E	Sell tickets
G	8	C	Complete arrangements
H	3	G	Develop schedules
I	2	D,H	Practice
J	3	F,I	Conduct tournament

a. Draw a network diagram of this project, and label the activities and events.

b. Calculate the total slack and scheduling times for all activities. What is the critical path?

c. When should team selection begin if the tournament is scheduled to start on the morning of December 27? (Include Saturday and Sunday as working days.)

16.4. A simple network consisting of four activities has the following network diagram:

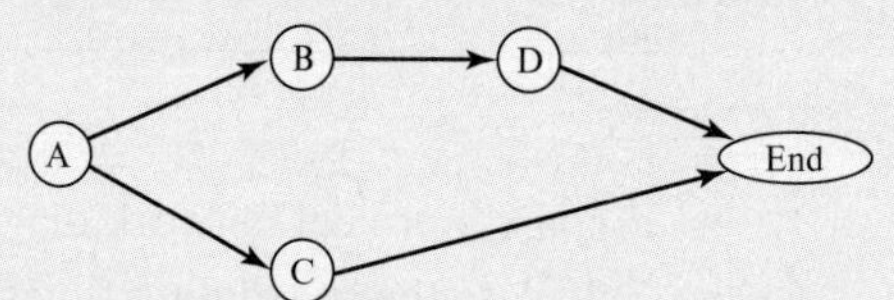

The cost/time relationships for the activities are shown in the table below:

Activity	Minimum Time, Weeks	Maximum Time, Weeks	Cost/Time Relationship ($1,000)
A	5	10	100 – (3 × activity time)
B	5	10	100 – (2 × activity time)
C	10	30	100 – (2 × activity time)
D	10	15	100 – (5 × activity time)

For example, if completed in 5 weeks, activity A would require $85,000, and if completed in 10 weeks, it would require $70,000.

a. What is the minimum cost of completing this project in 20 weeks?

b. If the desired completion date is 33 weeks and the profit markup is 20 percent above cost, what should be the bid price for this project?

16.5. The following project network and table provide the normal times and costs as well as the crash times and costs for the activities required to complete a project. Crash the completion time to the minimum level.

Activity	Normal Time, Weeks	Cost	Crash Time, Weeks	Cost
A	4	$2,500	2	$6,000
B	5	4,000	4	5,000
C	2	3,000	1	5,000
D	2	2,000	1	3,000
E	6	3,000	4	4,000
F	3	2,000	1	5,000
G	1	2,000	1	2,000

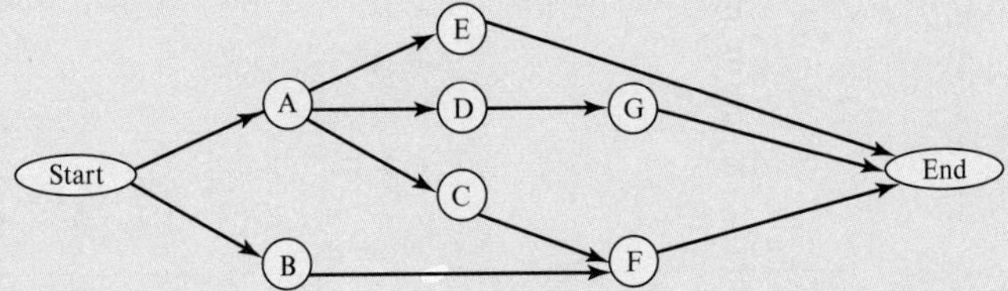

16.6. A construction firm has been commissioned to renew a portion of the Alaska crude-oil pipeline that has fallen into a state of disrepair. The project activities with the estimated times and their relationships are shown below:

Activity	Code	Time, Days	Immediate Predecessor
Assemble crew for job	A	10	—
Build inventory with old line	B	28	—
Measure and sketch old line	C	2	A
Develop materials list	D	1	C
Erect scaffolding	E	2	D
Procure pipe	F	30	D
Procure valves	G	45	D
Deactivate old line	H	1	B,D
Remove old line	I	6	E,H
Prefabricate new line	J	5	F
Place valves	K	1	E,G,H
Place new pipe	L	6	I,J
Weld pipe	M	2	L
Connect valves	N	1	K,M
Insulate	O	4	K,M
Pressure test	P	1	N
Remove scaffolding	Q	1	N,O
Clean up	R	1	P,Q

a. Prepare a project network.
b. List the critical path activities and the expected project duration.
c. Determine the scheduling times and total slack for all activities.
d. In the contract, a bonus of $100,000 per day will be paid for each day the project is completed earlier than its expected duration. Evaluate the following alternatives to shorten the project duration and then make a recommendation:
   1. Crash activity B by 4 days at a cost of $100,000.
   2. Crash activity G by 1 day at a cost of $50,000.
   3. Crash activity O by 2 days at a cost of $150,000.
   4. Crash activity O by 2 days by drawing resources from activity N, thereby extending the time of N by 2 days.

16.7. The following activities have been identified by a consulting firm that is developing an information system for an insurance firm to make a transition to a "paperless" organization:

		Activity Duration, Months		
Activity	**Immediate Predecessor**	**Optimistic**	**Most Likely**	**Pessimistic**
A	—	4	6	8
B	—	1	2	3
C	A	4	4	4
D	A	4	5	6
E	B	7	10	16
F	B	8	9	10
G	C	2	2	2
H	D,E,G	2	3	7
I	F	1	3	11

a. Draw the project network showing the activities with their expected times.
b. What is the critical path and the expected duration of the project?
c. What is the probability of completing the project within 2 years?

16.8. The following activities are required for completing a project:

		Activity Duration, Days		
Activity	**Immediate Predecessor**	**Optimistic**	**Most Likely**	**Pessimistic**
A	—	3	6	15
B	—	2	5	14
C	A	6	12	30
D	A	2	5	8
E	C	5	11	17
F	D	3	6	15
G	B	3	9	27
H	E,F	1	4	7
I	G	4	19	28
J	H,I	1	1	1

a. Draw a network diagram of this project showing the activities and their expected duration times.
b. What is the critical path and the expected completion time of the project?
c. What is the probability of completing the project in 41 days or less?

16.9. The project network and table below show the expected number of weeks to complete a series of activities and the corresponding variances:

Activity	**Expected Duration, Weeks**	**Variance, Weeks**
A	5	1
B	10	2
C	4	1
D	7	1
E	6	2
F	8	1
G	4	2
H	3	1
I	5	1
J	7	2
K	8	3

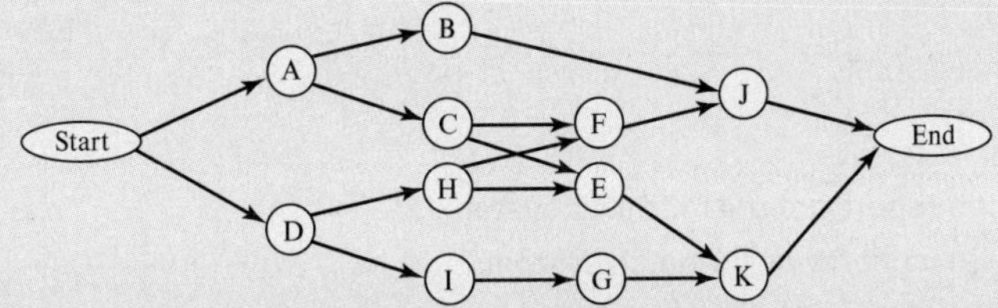

a. Determine the critical path and the earliest expected completion time.

b. What is the probability of completing the project in 24 weeks or less?

16.10. You have been asked to plan the following covert operation for the AIC:

Activity	Immediate Predecessor	Activity Duration, Days		
		Optimistic	Most Likely	Pessimistic
A	—	1	2	3
B	A	3	3	3
C	B	4	6	8
D	A	2	8	8
E	A	6	9	12
F	D,C	4	7	10
G	D	10	10	16
H	D,E	4	5	6
I	F,G,H	2	2	2

a. Draw a network diagram for this project.

b. Calculate the expected time and variance for each activity.

c. Determine the critical path and the expected project completion time.

d. What is the probability of the project taking more than 25 days to complete?

Info-Systems, Inc. — CASE 16.1

Info-Systems is a rapidly growing firm that specializes in information systems consulting. In the past, its projects have been relatively short term and did not require extensive project scheduling or close management surveillance. Recently, however, Info-Systems was awarded a contract to develop and implement an enterprise resource planning (ERP) system for a manufacturing firm.

During the initial proposal study, Info-Systems determined that the manufacturing firm's current hardware configuration was inadequate to meet its long-term needs, and new general hardware specifications were developed. Therefore, as part of its assignment, Info-Systems is to perform a vendor evaluation and selection for this new hardware. The initial study also proposed that the system would comprise a combination of batch and online processing and estimated a minimum of 1 year for completion.

Info-Systems plans to divide the project into four major areas involving the activities to support: (1) hardware selection and installation, (2) batch processing development, (3) online processing development, and (4) conversion from the old system to the new one. Further, it feels the use of a project management system would be very beneficial in providing a more definitive estimate of the probable project completion, in controlling the project once it is under way, and in assigning personnel to the project at the appropriate times. Therefore, Info-Systems has assigned several of its senior staff to develop a detailed task list, which is presented below:

Tasks		Work Duration, Days	Immediate Predecessor
A.	Evaluate and select hardware.	30	—
B.	Develop batch processing system requirements (e.g., data definition, transaction volume).	60	—
C.	Develop online processing requirements (e.g., volume response times).	40	—
D.	Define specific hardware requirements; order and receive.	100	A,B,C

(continued)

(continued)

Tasks		Work Duration, Days	Immediate Predecessor
E.	Design report layouts for batch system.	30	B
F.	Design input forms for batch system.	20	E
G.	Design screen layouts for online system.	25	C
H.	Design file layouts.	20	F,G
I.	Prepare program specifications for *daily* batch cycle.	30	H
J.	Prepare program specifications for *weekly* batch cycle.	20	H
K.	Prepare program specifications for *monthly* batch cycle.	15	H
L.	Prepare program specifications for online processing.	20	H
M.	Install and test new hardware.	15	D
N.	Code programs for *daily* batch cycle.	20	I
O.	Code programs for *weekly* batch cycle.	15	J
P.	Code programs for *monthly* batch cycle.	10	K
Q.	Code programs for online cycle.	18	L
R.	Document batch system.	35	I,J,K
S.	Document online system.	25	L
T.	Test *daily* cycle.	20	M,N
U.	Test *weekly* cycle.	15	M,O
V.	Test *monthly* cycle.	12	M,P
W.	Test online processing.	15	M,Q
X.	Test total system.	20	T,U,V,W
Y.	Design conversion requirements, programs, and files.	30	H
Z.	Prepare conversion programs.	20	Y
AA.	Test conversion programs.	15	Z
BB.	Run actual conversion.	3	X,AA
CC.	Operate system in parallel and train users.	60	R,S,BB
DD.	Gain user acceptance.	5	CC
EE.	Implement production system.	5	DD

Questions

1. Using Microsoft Project, prepare a network and identify the critical path activities, the expected project duration, and scheduling times for all activities.
2. The elapsed time for delivery of the hardware is estimated at 90 days. Would the project completion time be affected if delivery of the hardware were delayed by 30 days? Would the critical path change?
3. Using the original network and critical path, what strategies could management consider to complete the project on time if activity B were delayed by several weeks?

Whittier County Hospital — CASE 16.2

After 50 years at its present location, Whittier County Hospital is preparing to move into a new building sometime in the near future, when construction and outfitting are completed. The hospital's board of directors has appointed a special management committee to control the entire procedure, including coordination with outside agencies as well as internal departments. As a first step in its mission, the committee wishes to develop a base of information that will be used to (1) establish an initial sketch plan for proceeding through the detailed planning and moving phases and (2) provide a fundamental management and scheduling tool for day-to-day operations during the transition period.

The management staff believes that a PERT analysis of a sketch plan would be very helpful to the committee's understanding of the moving process, so it begins to develop a network of activities and duration estimates for the task. After consultation with the general contractor at the building site, it is estimated that completion of construction and checking the newly installed equipment likely will take 50 more days, with 40 and 60 days being the optimistic and pessimistic estimates, respectively. At this point the structure will be vacated by the contractor and turned over to the board.

Before this occurs, however, a detailed plan of action for each hospital department must be drawn up for approval by the Move Committee (as it is formally known). The staff estimates this will take at least 10 days, perhaps as many as 20 days, and most likely 15 days to develop and secure approval.

Once the detailed plan has received an initial go-ahead, the staff will have a number of activities to perform before a trial run and subsequent evaluation of the plan are made:

1. Develop and distribute an information newsletter to all hospital employees outlining the general procedures, with specific procedures attached for each department; it is estimated that this will take at least 3, probably 4, and at most, 7 days.
2. Develop information and generate media coverage for the upcoming events; this is estimated to take at least (and probably) 2 days, and 3 days at most.
3. Negotiate with local EMS and private ambulance services for transferring the patients; this is estimated to take at least 10, probably 14, and at most, 20 days.
4. Negotiate with professional moving companies for transferring equipment, records, and supplies; this is estimated to take at least 4, probably 5, and at most, 8 days.
5. Coordinate the procedures with, and determine the responsibilities of, the local police and fire departments; this is estimated to take at least 3, probably 5, and at most, 10 days.
6. Coordinate the admissions and exchange procedures during the transition period with other hospitals in the surrounding area; this is estimated to take at least 2, probably 3, and at most, 5 days.

Once the construction and equipment checkouts are completed, the new facility must be cleaned thoroughly by hospital staff before the actual move so that it will conform to the required levels for such institutions. Also, after the contractor vacates the premises, the employees can be oriented to the layout and workings of the new building. Because this orientation process is very important, the management staff wants to ensure that it begins after the newsletter is distributed and that it is completed before the trial run of the move. The staff estimates that cleaning and orientation can occur at the same time without problems. Cleaning will take at least 2, probably 3, and at most, 5 days; the employee orientation will take at least 4, probably 5, and at most, 7 days.

Although the actual trial run will take only 1 day, the entire activity, including evaluation, is estimated to need at least (and most likely) 3 days, with 5 days at most if serious problems are encountered. Once this step is finished, coordination of final plans and schedules with the patient and equipment carriers, local agencies, and area hospitals should take 2 days (3 at most). Finally, the completed schedules and procedures will be discussed in each department throughout the hospital on the day before moving day, and this discussion is expected to run the entire day because of the normal work schedules and tasks that all employees will be maintaining.

For the moving day, the staff has broken the entire process into seven different activities for the sketch plan:

	Activity Duration, Days		
Activity	**Optimistic**	**Most Likely**	**Pessimistic**
Administration, accounting, and business office	0.25	0.5	1.0
Library and medical/personnel records	0.25	0.5	0.75
Laboratory and purchasing/stores	0.3	0.8	1.0
Housekeeping and food services	0.5	0.75	1.3
Other equipment and supplies that must move same day as patients	0.8	1.0	1.2
Move patients	0.4	1.0	1.0
Noncritical equipment and supplies moved after patients	1.0	2.0	2.5

The staff members feel confident that basic operations will be fully under way at the new location once the first six activities are complete, and this is the critical goal established by the hospital's board of directors. The new location, of course, will not be fully operational until the remaining, noncritical equipment and supplies are moved.

Questions

1. Assume that you are part of the management staff whose task is to develop this sketch plan. Using Microsoft Project, develop the PERT network as outlined above, identify the critical path, and determine the expected time to reach basic operational status at the new facility.
2. The board of directors has said that it would like to try to move on a Sunday to minimize interference with weekday traffic. If there are Sundays that fall 46, 53, 60, 67, and 74 days from now, determine the probability (using a normal distribution) of reaching basic operational status at the new location on the two Sundays that are closest to the expected time you calculated previously.
3. Briefly assess the potential problems you see in applying critical path analysis to the sketch plan for moving Whittier County Hospital.

Selected Bibliography

Bendoly, Elliot, and Morgan Swink. "Moderating Effects of Information Access on Project Management Behavior, Performance and Perceptions." *Journal of Operations Management* 25, no. 3 (April 2007), pp. 604–22.

Brassard, Michael, and Diane Ritter. *The Memory Jogger II.* Methuen, MA: GOAL/QPC, 1994.

Browning, Tyson R. "On the Alignment of the Purposes and Views of Process Models in Project Management." *Journal of Operations Management* 28, no. 4 (July 2010), pp. 316–32.

Gattiker, Thomas F., and Craig R. Carter. "Understanding Project Champions' Ability to Gain Intra-Organizational Commitment for Environmental Projects." *Journal of Operations Management* 28, no. 1 (Jan 2010), pp. 72–85.

Gawande, Atul, *The Checklist Manifesto: How to Get Things Right.* New York: Metropolitan Books, 2009.

Goldratt, Eliyahu M. *Critical Chain.* Great Barrington, MA: North River Press, 1997.

Harris, James L. "Key Foundations of Successful Project Planning and Management." *Project Planning & Management: A Guide for Nurses and Interprofessional Teams* (2015): 1.

Hill, Gerard M. *The complete project management office handbook*. CRC Press, 2013.

Phillips, Joseph. *PMP, Project Management Professional (Certification Study Guides).* McGraw-Hill Osborne Media, 2013.

Verma, Devesh, Anant Mishra, and Kingshuk K. Sinha. "The Development and Application of a Process Model for R&D Project Management in a High Tech Firm: A Field Study." *Journal of Operations Management* 29, no. 5 (July 2011), pp. 462–76.

Endnote

1. This assumption is based on the Central Limit Theorem from statistics, which states that the sum of many independent random variables is a random variable that tends to be distributed normally. In this case, the project completion time is the sum of the individual durations of activities on the critical path.

Appendix 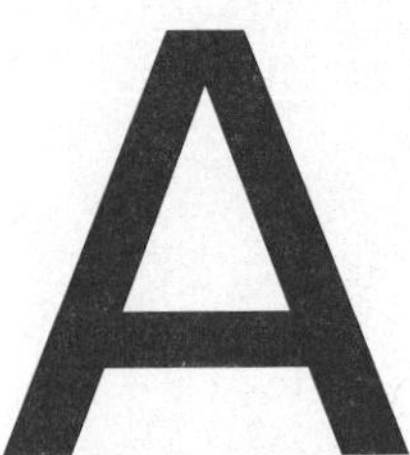

Areas of Standard Normal Distribution[1]

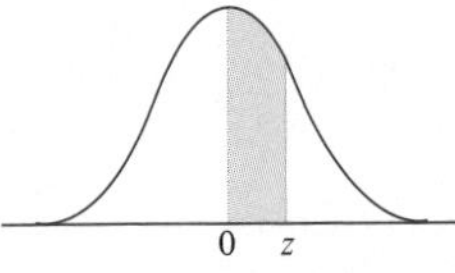

An entry in the table is the area under the curve that is between $z = 0$ and a positive value of z. The area in the tail is found by subtracting the table entry from 0.5. Areas for negative values of z are obtained by symmetry. For example, the area in the right tail for a positive z of 1.65 is $(0.5 - 0.4505) = 0.0495$.

z	0.00	0.01	0.02	0.03	0.04	0.05	0.06	0.07	0.08	0.09
0.0	0.0000	0.0040	0.0080	0.0120	0.0160	0.0199	0.0239	0.0279	0.0319	0.0359
0.1	0.0398	0.0438	0.0478	0.0517	0.0557	0.0596	0.0636	0.0675	0.0714	0.0753
0.2	0.0793	0.0832	0.0871	0.0910	0.0948	0.0987	0.1026	0.1064	0.1103	0.1141
0.3	0.1179	0.1217	0.1255	0.1293	0.1331	0.1368	0.1406	0.1443	0.1480	0.1517
0.4	0.1554	0.1591	0.1628	0.1664	0.1700	0.1736	0.1772	0.1808	0.1844	0.1879
0.5	0.1915	0.1950	0.1985	0.2019	0.2054	0.2088	0.2123	0.2157	0.2190	0.2224
0.6	0.2257	0.2291	0.2324	0.2357	0.2389	0.2422	0.2454	0.2486	0.2517	0.2549
0.7	0.2580	0.2611	0.2642	0.2673	0.2703	0.2734	0.2764	0.2794	0.2823	0.2852
0.8	0.2881	0.2910	0.2939	0.2967	0.2995	0.3023	0.3051	0.3078	0.3106	0.3133
0.9	0.3159	0.3186	0.3212	0.3238	0.3264	0.3289	0.3315	0.3340	0.3365	0.3389
1.0	0.3413	0.3438	0.3461	0.3485	0.3508	0.3531	0.3554	0.3577	0.3599	0.3621
1.1	0.3643	0.3665	0.3686	0.3708	0.3729	0.3749	0.3770	0.3790	0.3810	0.3830
1.2	0.3849	0.3869	0.3888	0.3907	0.3925	0.3944	0.3962	0.3980	0.3997	0.4015
1.3	0.4032	0.4049	0.4066	0.4082	0.4099	0.4115	0.4131	0.4147	0.4162	0.4177
1.4	0.4192	0.4207	0.4222	0.4236	0.4251	0.4265	0.4279	0.4292	0.4306	0.4319
1.5	0.4332	0.4345	0.4357	0.4370	0.4382	0.4394	0.4406	0.4418	0.4429	0.4441
1.6	0.4452	0.4463	0.4474	0.4484	0.4495	0.4505	0.4515	0.4525	0.4535	0.4545
1.7	0.4554	0.4564	0.4573	0.4582	0.4591	0.4599	0.4608	0.4616	0.4625	0.4633
1.8	0.4641	0.4649	0.4656	0.4664	0.4671	0.4678	0.4686	0.4693	0.4699	0.4706
1.9	0.4713	0.4719	0.4726	0.4732	0.4738	0.4744	0.4750	0.4756	0.4761	0.4767
2.0	0.4772	0.4778	0.4783	0.4788	0.4793	0.4798	0.4803	0.4808	0.4812	0.4817
2.1	0.4821	0.4826	0.4830	0.4834	0.4838	0.4842	0.4846	0.4850	0.4854	0.4857
2.2	0.4861	0.4864	0.4868	0.4871	0.4875	0.4878	0.4881	0.4884	0.4887	0.4890
2.3	0.4893	0.4896	0.4898	0.4901	0.4904	0.4906	0.4909	0.4911	0.4913	0.4916
2.4	0.4918	0.4920	0.4922	0.4925	0.4927	0.4929	0.4931	0.4932	0.4934	0.4936
2.5	0.4938	0.4940	0.4941	0.4943	0.4945	0.4946	0.4948	0.4949	0.4951	0.4952
2.6	0.4953	0.4955	0.4956	0.4957	0.4959	0.4960	0.4961	0.4962	0.4963	0.4964
2.7	0.4965	0.4966	0.4967	0.4968	0.4969	0.4970	0.4971	0.4972	0.4973	0.4974
2.8	0.4974	0.4975	0.4976	0.4977	0.4977	0.4978	0.4979	0.4979	0.4980	0.4981
2.9	0.4981	0.4982	0.4982	0.4983	0.4984	0.4984	0.4985	0.4985	0.4986	0.4986
3.0	0.4987	0.4987	0.4987	0.4988	0.4988	0.4989	0.4989	0.4989	0.4990	0.4990

[1] Using Microsoft Excel, these probabilities are generated with the equation NORMS DIST (z) – 0.5.

Appendix 

Uniformly Distributed Random Numbers [0, 1]

0.06785	0.39867	0.90588	0.17801
0.81075	0.87641	0.67964	0.43877
0.98544	0.51653	0.44093	0.79428
0.31479	0.75057	0.28248	0.26863
0.12484	0.88287	0.78805	0.00907
0.23882	0.82137	0.51759	0.24723
0.23897	0.93060	0.94078	0.44676
0.40374	0.57000	0.33415	0.90000
0.73622	0.85896	0.36825	0.31500
0.36952	0.39367	0.09426	0.79517
0.14510	0.05047	0.01535	0.46997
0.12719	0.35159	0.55903	0.01268
0.99407	0.53816	0.64881	0.64309
0.32694	0.57237	0.74242	0.68045
0.42780	0.54704	0.63281	0.92243
0.00633	0.87197	0.90597	0.95629
0.38490	0.27804	0.06567	0.49591
0.22363	0.96354	0.25298	0.88459
0.54105	0.62235	0.93190	0.66122
0.31786	0.84724	0.04084	0.98260
0.47556	0.38855	0.52135	0.34085
0.70850	0.55051	0.86505	0.21192
0.64791	0.89438	0.83997	0.00898
0.21424	0.34592	0.77920	0.16675
0.77524	0.41976	0.08429	0.71506

Appendix C

Values of L_q for the *M/M/c* Queuing Model

ρ	c = 1	c = 2	c = 3	c = 4	c = 5	c = 6	c = 7	c = 8
0.15	0.026	0.001						
0.20	0.050	0.002						
0.25	0.083	0.004						
0.30	0.129	0.007						
0.35	0.188	0.011						
0.40	0.267	0.017						
0.45	0.368	0.024	0.002					
0.50	0.500	0.033	0.003					
0.55	0.672	0.045	0.004					
0.60	0.900	0.059	0.006					
0.65	1.207	0.077	0.008					
0.70	1.633	0.098	0.011					
0.75	2.250	0.123	0.015					
0.80	3.200	0.152	0.019					
0.85	4.817	0.187	0.024	0.003				
0.90	8.100	0.229	0.030	0.004				
0.95	18.050	0.277	0.037	0.005				
1.0		0.333	0.045	0.007				
1.1		0.477	0.066	0.011				
1.2		0.675	0.094	0.016	0.003			
1.3		0.951	0.130	0.023	0.004			
1.4		1.345	0.177	0.032	0.006			
1.5		1.929	0.237	0.045	0.009			
1.6		2.844	0.313	0.060	0.012			
1.7		4.426	0.409	0.080	0.017			
1.8		7.674	0.532	0.105	0.023			
1.9		17.587	0.688	0.136	0.030	0.007		
2.0			0.889	0.174	0.040	0.009		
2.1			1.149	0.220	0.052	0.012		
2.2			1.491	0.277	0.066	0.016		
2.3			1.951	0.346	0.084	0.021		
2.4			2.589	0.431	0.105	0.027	0.007	
2.5			3.511	0.533	0.130	0.034	0.009	
2.6			4.933	0.658	0.161	0.043	0.011	
2.7			7.354	0.811	0.198	0.053	0.014	

(*continued*)

ρ	c = 1	c = 2	c = 3	c = 4	c = 5	c = 6	c = 7	c = 8
2.8			12.273	1.000	0.241	0.066	0.018	
2.9			27.193	1.234	0.293	0.081	0.023	
3.0				1.528	0.354	0.099	0.028	0.008
3.1				1.902	0.427	0.120	0.035	0.010
3.2				2.386	0.513	0.145	0.043	0.012
3.3				3.027	0.615	0.174	0.052	0.015
3.4				3.906	0.737	0.209	0.063	0.019
3.5				5.165	0.882	0.248	0.076	0.023
3.6				7.090	1.055	0.295	0.091	0.028
3.7				10.347	1.265	0.349	0.109	0.034
3.8				16.937	1.519	0.412	0.129	0.041
3.9				36.859	1.830	0.485	0.153	0.050
4.0					2.216	0.570	0.180	0.059
4.1					2.703	0.668	0.212	0.070
4.2					3.327	0.784	0.248	0.083
4.3					4.149	0.919	0.289	0.097
4.4					5.268	1.078	0.337	0.114
4.5					6.862	1.265	0.391	0.133
4.6					9.289	1.487	0.453	0.156
4.7					13.382	1.752	0.525	0.181
4.8					21.641	2.071	0.607	0.209
4.9					46.566	2.459	0.702	0.242
5.0						2.938	0.810	0.279
5.1						3.536	0.936	0.321
5.2						4.301	1.081	0.368
5.3						5.303	1.249	0.422
5.4						6.661	1.444	0.483
5.5						8.590	1.674	0.553
5.6						11.519	1.944	0.631
5.7						16.446	2.264	0.721
5.8						26.373	2.648	0.823
5.9						56.300	3.113	0.939
6.0							3.683	1.071
6.1							4.394	1.222
6.2							5.298	1.397
6.3							6.480	1.598
6.4							8.077	1.831
6.5							10.341	2.102
6.6							13.770	2.420
6.7							19.532	2.796
6.8							31.127	3.245
6.9							66.055	3.786
7.0								4.447
7.1								5.270
7.2								6.314
7.3								7.675
7.4								9.511
7.5								12.109
7.6								16.039
7.7								22.636
7.8								35.898
7.9								75.827

Appendix 

Equations for Selected Queuing Models

Definition of Symbols

n = number of customers in the system

λ = [lambda] mean arrival rate (e.g., customer arrivals per hour)

μ = [mu] mean service rate per busy server (e.g., service capacity in customers per hour)

ρ = [rho] (λ/μ) mean number of customers in service

N = maximum number of customers allowed in the system

c = number of servers

P_n = probability of exactly n customers in the system

L_s = mean number of customers in the system

L_q = mean number of customers in queue

L_b = mean number of customers in queue for a busy system

W_s = mean time customer spends in the system

W_q = mean time customer spends in the queue

W_b = mean time customer spends in queue for a busy system

I. Standard *M/M/*1 Model ($0 < \rho < 1.0$)

$$P_0 = 1 - \rho \tag{I.1}$$

$$P(n \geq k) = \rho^k \tag{I.2}$$

$$P_n = P_0 \rho^n \tag{I.3}$$

$$L_s = \frac{\lambda}{\mu - \lambda} \tag{I.4}$$

$$L_q = \frac{\rho\lambda}{\mu - \lambda} \tag{I.5}$$

$$L_b = \frac{\lambda}{\mu - \lambda} \tag{I.6}$$

$$W_s = \frac{1}{\mu - \lambda} \tag{I.7}$$

$$W_q = \frac{\rho}{\mu - \lambda} \tag{I.8}$$

$$W_b = \frac{1}{\mu - \lambda} \tag{I.9}$$

II. Standard *M/M/c* Model ($0 < \rho < c$)

$$P_0 = \frac{1}{\left(\sum_{i=0}^{c-1} \frac{\rho^i}{i!}\right) + \frac{\rho^c}{c!(1 - \rho/c)}} \tag{II.1}$$

$$P_n = \begin{cases} \frac{\rho^n}{n!} P_0 & \text{for } 0 \le n \le c \\ \frac{\rho^n}{c!c^{n-c}} P_0 & \text{for } n \ge c \end{cases} \tag{II.2}$$

$$P(n \ge c) = \frac{\rho^c \mu c}{c!(\mu c - \lambda)} p_0 \tag{II.3}$$

$$L_s = \frac{\rho^{c+1}}{(c - 1)!(c - \rho)^2} P_0 + \rho \tag{II.4}$$

$$L_q = L_s - \rho \tag{II.5}$$

$$L_b = \frac{L_q}{P(n \ge c)} \tag{II.6}$$

$$W_s = \frac{L_q}{\lambda} + \frac{1}{\mu} \tag{II.7}$$

$$W_q = \frac{L_q}{\lambda} \tag{II.8}$$

$$W_b = \frac{W_q}{P(n \geq c)} \tag{II.9}$$

III. Standard *M/G/*1 Model (*V*(*t*) = service time variance)

$$L_s = L_q + \rho \tag{III.1}$$

$$L_q = \frac{\rho^2 + \lambda^2 V(t)}{2(1-\rho)} \tag{III.2}$$

$$W_s = \frac{L_s}{\lambda} \tag{III.3}$$

$$W_b = \frac{L_q}{\lambda} \tag{III.4}$$

IV. Self-Service *M/G/*∞ Model (e = 2.718, the base of natural logarithms)

$$P_n = \frac{e^{-\rho}}{n!}\rho^n \text{ for } n \geq 0 \tag{IV.1}$$

$$L_s = \rho \tag{IV.2}$$

$$W_s = \frac{1}{\mu} \tag{IV.3}$$

V. Finite-Queue *M/M/*1 Model

$$P_0 = \begin{cases} \dfrac{1-\rho}{1-\rho^{N+1}} & \text{for } \lambda \neq \mu \\ \dfrac{1}{N+1} & \text{for } \lambda = \mu \end{cases} \tag{V.1}$$

$$P(n > 0) = 1 - P_0 \tag{V.2}$$

$$P_n = P_0\rho^n \text{ for } n \le N \tag{V.3}$$

$$L_s = \begin{cases} \dfrac{\rho}{1-\rho} - \dfrac{(N+1)\rho^{N+1}}{1-\rho^{N+1}} & \text{for } \lambda \ne \mu \\ \dfrac{N}{2} & \text{for } \lambda = \mu \end{cases} \tag{V.4}$$

$$L_q = L_s - (1 - P_0) \tag{V.5}$$

$$L_b = \frac{L_q}{1 - P_0} \tag{V.6}$$

$$W_s = \frac{L_q}{\lambda(1 - P_N)} + \frac{1}{\mu} \tag{V.7}$$

$$W_q = W_s - \frac{1}{\mu} \tag{V.8}$$

$$W_b = \frac{W_q}{1 - P_0} \tag{V.9}$$

VI. Finite-Queue *M/M/c* Model

$$P_0 = \frac{1}{\left(\sum_{i=0}^{c} \frac{\rho^i}{i!}\right) + \left(\frac{1}{c!}\right)\left(\sum_{i=c+1}^{N} \frac{\rho^i}{c^{i-c}}\right)} \tag{VI.1}$$

$$P_n = \begin{cases} \dfrac{\rho^n}{n!}P_0 & \text{for } 0 \le n \le c \\ \dfrac{\rho^n}{c!c^{n-c}}P_0 & \text{for } c \le n \le N \end{cases} \tag{VI.2}$$

$$P(n \ge c) = 1 - P_0 \sum_{i=0}^{c-1} \frac{\rho^i}{i!} \tag{VI.3}$$

$$L_s = \frac{P_0\rho^{c+1}}{(c-1)!(c-\rho)^2}\left[1 - \left(\frac{\rho}{c}\right)^{N-c} - (N-c)\left(\frac{\rho}{c}\right)^{N-c}\left(1 - \frac{\rho}{c}\right)\right] + \rho(1 - P_N) \tag{VI.4}$$

$$L_q = L_s - \rho(1 - P_N) \tag{VI.5}$$

$$L_b = \frac{L_q}{P(n \geq c)} \tag{VI.6}$$

$$W_s = \frac{L_q}{\lambda(1 - P_N)} + \frac{1}{\mu} \tag{VI.7}$$

$$W_q = W_s - \frac{1}{\mu} \tag{VI.8}$$

$$W_b = \frac{W_q}{P(n \geq c)} \tag{VI.9}$$

Name Index

Note: Page numbers followed by *n* indicate source notes and endnotes.

Subject Index

G

H

R

S